T0003831

THE
BASEBALL
MANIAC'S
ALMANAC

6TH EDITION

Also by Bert Randolph Sugar
Bert Sugar's Baseball Hall of Fame
Baseball's 50 Greatest Games
Baseball Picture Quiz Book
The Baseball Trivia Book
The Baseball Trivia Book to End All Baseball Trivia Books, Promise!
The Great Baseball Players from McGraw to Mantle
Rain Delays
Who Was Harry Steinfeldt? & Other Baseball Trivia Questions

THE
BASEBALL MANIAC'S ALMANAC

6TH EDITION

The ABSOLUTELY, POSITIVELY, and WITHOUT QUESTION GREATEST BOOK of FACTS, FIGURES, and ASTONISHING LISTS EVER COMPILED

**Edited by Bert Randolph Sugar
with Ken Samelson**

SPORTS
PUBLISHING

Copyright © 2005, 2010, 2012, 2016, 2019, 2023 by Bert Randolph Sugar
New Material © 2012, 2016, 2019, 2023 by Skyhorse Publishing, Inc.

All Rights Reserved. No part of this book may be reproduced in any manner without the
express written consent of the publisher, except in the case of brief excerpts in critical
reviews or articles. All inquiries should be addressed to Sports Publishing, 307 West 36th
Street, 11th Floor, New York, NY 10018.

Sports Publishing books may be purchased in bulk at special discounts for sales pro-
motion, corporate gifts, fund-raising, or educational purposes. Special editions can also
be created to specifications. For details, contact the Special Sales Department, Sports
Publishing, 307 West 36th Street, 11th Floor, New York, NY 10018 or
sportspubbooks@skyhorsepublishing.com.

Sports Publishing® is a registered trademark of Skyhorse Publishing, Inc.®, a Delaware
corporation.

CONTENTS

Batting Title   23

Home Runs 31

Batting Miscellany   105

2 **Pitching**   113

Wins   113

Cy Young Award   192

Rookie of the Year   194

9 **All-Star Game**   238

10 **Teams**   241

Part 2 **Team-by-Team Histories** 267

American League 269

National League 335

Statistics (or as they are known in their circumcised, smaller version of the word, "stats") have been a part of baseball—indeed, the very mortar of the sport—since the dawn of the game, even if in the beginning their number was so few they could be entered on a postcard with more than enough room left for an oversized one-cent stamp and a generous message. And those few reduced to paper could be called statistics only in the same way raisins could be called fruit—technically and only in a manner of speaking.

Take, for example, one of the very first recorded: that of the number of miles traveled by the first professional baseball team, the Cincinnati Red Stockings, as they criss-crossed the country in 1869, their first year in existence. One of the early recordkeepers estimated that the Red Stockings had covered some 11,877 miles, playing in 57 games—of which they won 56 and tied one. However, one historian, ever Thomas the Doubter, doubling back on the historic breadcrumbs laid down by the Red Stockings, discovered that Harry Wright's team had played at least 80 games in their inaugural season and figured they had many a mile more to go than that originally estimated.

Many of those early records set down by recordkeepers were something of a hit-or-miss proposition—mostly miss. One of those came on the afternoon of Thursday, September 6, 1883, when Cap Anson's Chicago White Stockings set a record by scoring 18 runs in the seventh inning against the Detroit Wolverines. However, when the report of the game was wired to the *Detroit Free Press*, as well as other papers around the country, most of the details of the game were MIA. The sporting editor of the Free Press, taking note of the omissions, apologized to his readers, writing that the paper "would be pleased to submit the full score of this remarkable game to its readers, but the Western Union Telegraph Company, which has no excuse for its poor service, has furnished it bobtailed and in ludicrous deformity . . . the Company was requested to supply the missing links, but the head operator declined to do so."

There were several other instances of reporters or Western Union operatives exhibiting a polite fiction of the non-existence of such relevant statistics, several times omitting the names of batterymates. However, here it must be noted that many's the time in those early days of organized-and-disorganized-baseball, even the pitcher and the catcher didn't know the names of their batterymates. Such was the case in 1897 when the pitcher and the catcher of the Louisville team were as unfamiliar to one another as two shipwrecked survivors coming ashore on a wave-swept beach, neither knowing the name of the other. None of their teammates knew their names either, both having just joined the team—the pitcher the day before; the catcher being signed on a trial basis just before the game. When the pitcher was asked by writers who his catcher was, he answered, "Couldn't tell you, first time I ever saw him." The catcher's answer to the identity of the pitcher was ditto. Still at a loss as to the names of the two, the writers now approached manager Fred Clarke and asked the same question. As lost as Robinson Crusoe without a boat, all Clarke could do was point to the name "Weddel" on the scorecard and say, "This man will pitch." Then, pointing to the tall man putting on his catcher's gear, said, "And that tall fellow over there will catch." Calling over to his catcher, Clarke had him spell out his name for the writers, which he did: "S-c-h-r-e-c-k-e-n-g-o-s-t." Then, asked by the writers if the "Weddel" on the scorecard was the correct spelling, Clarke shrugged his shoulders and responded, "Don't know, you'll have to ask him." They did, discovering it was spelled "Waddell." (Ironically, after their dual Major League debut, Ossee Schreckengost and Rube Waddell's faces would become as recognizable to one another as those seen in the mirror every morning as they became batterymates for six seasons with the Philadelphia A's.)

The shoddy record keeping of the time also resulted in several other records being overlooked, there being no mention of the-then-record 11 RBIs in one game by Baltimore Oriole Wilbert Robinson nor the 27 home runs by Chicago White Stocking Ned Williamson in 1884, both records forgotten by the time they were broken—Robinson's by Jim Bottomley and Williamson's by Babe Ruth.

Ernest Lanigan, baseball's first great historian, noted that the omission of Williamson's season record of 27 home runs was occasioned by the fact that whenever Henry Chadwick—known as "The Father of Baseball," but whom Lanigan called "that human eliminator"—wrote on the subject of home runs, "which variety of hits he detested . . . (he) eliminated them from the guides."

Early records were thus cut and restitched to fit any pattern the recordkeeper wanted, many of their entries unable to stand up to the slightest investigation. In one classic case Wee Willie Keeler was credited by the Baltimore scorekeeper with four hits in a 1897 game versus St. Louis. However, St. Louis sportswriter Frank Houseman, pulling up the game to study its roots, wrote the following rundown of Keeler's run-up of hits: "Down in Baltimore, Keeler sent two flies to (Bud) Larry, who muffed both of them. Then he hit to (Fred) Hartman, who fumbled the ball and threw wild. Then Keeler made a good single. The next morning, four hits appeared to Keeler's credit in the Baltimore papers." Houseman couldn't resist adding, "Talk about stuffing records."

And, as if it wasn't enough that telegraphers or writers "stuffed" a player's performance, sometimes they even "stuffed" the line-up itself. In one of those moments that inspires a reference to A. Lincoln's sonnet about "fooling all the people . . . ," a St. Louis Western Union operative up in the press box named Lou Proctor, in a "Forgive us our Press Passes" moment, inserted his own name in a 1912 St. Louis Browns boxscore, fooling even the Macmillan *Baseball Encyclopedia* editors who included it in their first edition, giving him equal standing with "Moonlight" Graham before discovering the error and dropping Proctor from its later editions.

As sportswriters and fans voyaged, Columbus-like, into the new world of baseball statistics, commissions and omissions weren't the only problems they faced. One of those problems was the determinate criteria for stolen bases, there being no baseline (good word, that!) of agreed-upon standards. At given times over the years, runners were given credit for a stolen base when they scored from third on a fly out, when they took two bases on an infield out, when they were the successful half of a double-steal when the other half was thrown out, or even when they overslid a base and were tagged out.

Other statistics, like strikeouts, runs scored and batted in, and sacrifices, hitherto unaccountable in whole or in part, came late to the table and were incorporated into baseball's growing world of stats—soon to be joined by others.

Still, with annuals like the early day *Reach* and *Spalding Guides* and Balldom as well as *The Sporting Life Base Ball Guide and Handbook* and the while-you-get-your-haircut weeklies serving up heaping platefuls of statistics to satisfy the appetite of ever-increasingly hungry fans for such fare, statistics took on a life of their own, framing the game and providing a basis of comparison of the past and the present.

As baseball archaeologists like the aforementioned Lanigan began spackling the cracks by correcting some of the early statistics that had been recorded with all the innocence of Adam naming the animals on his first day in the Garden by early recordkeepers even they created problems of their own. One such error occurred when the *Reach Guide* of 1903, in a typographical error, credited Nap Lajoie with 43 triples in 1897 when the actual number of triples should have read 23. And so, when Pirate outfielder Owen Wilson, better known as "Chief," began belting the ball all over the lot, hitting seven triples against Chicago and Cincinnati pitching, five against St. Louis and New York, and three each versus Philadelphia and Brooklyn, sports-writers took little note of his feat, figuring his total of 36 still seven shy of Lajoie's "43." It would take some of baseball's best archaeologists to dig back through Lajoie's game-by-game record to exhume his real total and properly acknowledge Wilson's record.

By the 1920s, recordkeeping had approached the foothills of accuracy as statistical cryptographers resurrected and decoded the facts and figures of earlier historians, thus providing a correction to baseball's past. No longer random and haphazard, baseball statistics now had a relativism to earlier-day records and accomplishments, ensuring that no feat would vanish down the hole of history—for baseball records, like everything else, except maybe Eve telling Adam about all the men she could have married, are relative.

It was that thesis of baseball relativity that enabled Lanigan to compare Tip O'Neill's otherworldly .492 batting average in

1887 (later amended to .485) to Babe Ruth's .378 in his great offensive year of 1921 when he hit 59 home runs and drove in 171 runs. Pointing out that in 1887 batters received credit for base hits when they walked, producing helium-like averages, he calculated that Ruth would have an equally lofty .509 in '21 had his then-record of 145 bases on balls counted as hits.

In fact, it was the explosion of the long ball (as personified by The Babe, who held the original copyright) that changed the game. And along with it, its statistics. Suddenly, the trickle of records became a Niagara as statisticians wore a carload of pencils down to their stubs recording them as records lasting about as long as Hollywood bridegrooms.

As the game continued to evolve, so too did the statistics, growing with the game. And nothing proved that the body of statistics was growing at an exponential rate more than a quiz show back in the '50s called *The $64,000 Question*, where one contestant, a Georgian housewife named Myrtle Powers, was asked to name the seven players who "had a lifetime total of 3,000 or more hits." Ms. Powers correctly answered: "Ty Cobb, Honus Wagner, Nap Lajoie, Eddie Collins, Tris Speaker, Cap Anson, and Paul Waner," the number who had climbed that statistical mountain over the past 80- plus years. Now, a half-century later, a total of 29 players, over a fourfold number, have reached that magic mark.

But, even as baseball's "official" recordkeepers continue to collect each and every statistic from the obvious to the most minute, amateur historians who OD on baseball stats continue to find omissions and commissions—such as an extra run batted in by Hack Wilson in his record-setting 190 RBI season of 1930, an extra triple in the lifetime total of Lou Gehrig, and a double-counting of a two-for-three day by Ty Cobb in 1910, which would have cost him the batting title to Nap Lajoie by one point. (Such a finding of an error even occurred in that Holiest of Holy places, the Baseball Hall of Fame, when an eagle-eyed fan standing in front of the Babe Ruth plaque noted that the inscription for his playing days read "1915–1935" and pointed out to the powers-that-be that Ruth had first played for the Red Sox in 1914, not 1915.)

Now I had always considered myself as part of that amateur array of baseballogists, one of a large group of enthusiasts who accumulate lists of stats, especially those with more variations on the theme than even Mussorgsky had imagined.

But it wasn't until I met a fellow traveler in stats named Jack McClain that I realized that my variations were as nothing compared to those Jack had conceived—his lists defying normal categorization, like "Most Pitching Wins by Zodiac Sign," "Most Home Runs by State of Birth," et cetera, etc., etc., etc.—the et ceteras going on for about five pages or more. We decided on the spot to collaborate on a book of what we called "fun stats," a novel approach of combining our efforts into one volume that would be different from anything before.

Unfortunately, Jack passed away before we had finished our book, leaving me to carry on alone. But over the years, I have continued to develop list after list—so many, in fact, they are available at a discount. And now, with the able assistance of many others, including Bill Francis of the Baseball Hall of Fame, Cornell Richardson, the Office of the Baseball Commissioner, Mark Weinstein, Parker Bena, Frances J. Buonarota, Jason Katzman, and a cast of hundreds, if not thousands, it is my pleasure to give you a different perspective (call it a "different view from the same pew," if you will) on America's second most popular pastime: baseball statistics.

—Bert Randolph Sugar

THE
BASEBALL
MANIAC'S
ALMANAC

6TH EDITION

PART 1

Individual Statistics

1

BATTING

Base Hits

Most Hits by Decade

continued on next page

1980–89		
1731	Robin Yount	
1642	Eddie Murray	
1639	Willie Wilson	
1597	Wade Boggs	
1553	Dale Murphy	
1547	Harold Baines	
1539	Andre Dawson	
1507	Rickey Henderson	
1504	Alan Trammell	
1497	Dwight Evans	

1990–99	
1754	Mark Grace
1747	Rafael Palmeiro
1728	Craig Biggio
1713	Tony Gwynn
1678	Roberto Alomar
1622	Ken Griffey Jr.
1589	Cal Ripken Jr.
1584	Dante Bichette
1573	Fred McGriff
1568	Paul Molitor

2000–09	
2030	Ichiro Suzuki
1940	Derek Jeter
1860	Miguel Tejada
1756	Todd Helton
1751	Vladimir Guerrero
1745	Johnny Damon
1740	Alex Rodriguez
1721	Bobby Abreu
1717	Albert Pujols
1674	Carlos Lee

2010–19	
1695	Robinson Cano
1651	Nick Markakis
1647	Adam Jones
1617	Starlin Castro
1595	Elvis Andrus
1595	Miguel Cabrera
1568	Jose Altuve
1540	Andrew McCutchen
1532	Joey Votto
1485	Albert Pujols

2019–22	
467	Trea Turner
452	Freddie Freeman
421	Vladimir Guerrero Jr.
417	Bo Bichette
413	Paul Goldschmidt
407	Jose Abreu
397	Manny Machado
392	Austin Riley
390	Rafael Devers
388	Xander Bogaerts
388	Dansby Swanson

Evolution of Singles Record

American League

1901	Nap Lajoie, Phi. A's	154
1903	Patsy Dougherty, Bos. Red Sox	161
1904	Willie Keeler, N.Y. Yankees	164
1906	Willie Keeler, N.Y. Yankees	166
1911	Ty Cobb, Det. Tigers	169
1920	George Sisler, St.L. Browns	171
1921	Jack Tobin, St.L. Browns	179
1925	Sam Rice, Was. Senators	182
1980	Willie Wilson, K.C. Royals	184
1985	Wade Boggs, Bos. Red Sox	187
2001	Ichiro Suzuki, Sea. Mariners	192
2004	Ichiro Suzuki, Sea. Mariners	225

National League (Post-1900)

1900	Willie Keeler, Brk. Dodgers	179
1901	Jesse Burkett, St.L. Cardinals	180
1927	Lloyd Waner, Pit. Pirates	198

Most Hits, Season

American League

Ichiro Suzuki, Sea. Mariners, 2004	262
George Sisler, St.L. Browns, 1920	257
Al Simmons, Phi. A's, 1925	253
Ty Cobb, Det. Tigers, 1911	248
George Sisler, St.L. Browns, 1922	246
Ichiro Suzuki, Sea. Mariners, 2001	242
Heine Manush, St.L. Browns, 1928	241
Wade Boggs, Bos. Red Sox, 1985	240
Darin Erstad, Ana. Angels, 2000	240

National League (Post-1900)

Lefty O'Doul, Phi. Phillies, 1929	254
Bill Terry, N.Y. Giants, 1930	254
Rogers Hornsby, St.L. Cardinals, 1922	250
Chuck Klein, Phi. Phillies, 1930	250
Babe Herman, Brk. Dodgers, 1930	241

Base Hit Leaders by State of Birth

Alabama	Hank Aaron (Mobile)	3771
Alaska	Josh Phelps (Anchorage)	380
Arizona	Ian Kinsler (Tucson)	1999
Arkansas	Lou Brock (El Dorado)	3023
California	Eddie Murray (Los Angeles)	3255
Colorado	Chase Headley (Fountain)	1337
Connecticut	Jim O'Rourke (Bridgeport)	2639

Delaware	Paul Goldschmidt* (Wilmington)	1750
Florida	Andre Dawson (Miami)	2774
Georgia	Ty Cobb (Narrows)	4189
Hawaii	Kurt Suzuki* (Wailuku)	1421
Idaho	Harmon Killebrew (Payette)	2086
Illinois	Robin Yount (Danville)	3142
Indiana	Sam Rice (Morocco)	2987

continued on next page

Iowa......................Cap Anson (Marshalltown)..........3435
Kansas...................Johnny Damon (Fort Riley)...........2769
Kentucky................Pee Wee Reese (Ekron)................2170
Louisiana................Mel Ott (Gretna).........................2876
Maine....................George Gore (Saccarappa).........1612
Maryland...............Cal Ripken Jr. (Havre de Grace)...3184
Massachusetts.........Rabbit Maranville (Springfield).....2605
Michigan................Charlie Gehringer (Fowlerville).....2839
Minnesota..............Paul Molitor (St. Paul).................3319
Mississippi..............Dave Parker (Grenada)...............2712
Missouri.................Jake Beckley (Hannibal)..............2938
Montana...............John Lowenstein (Wolf Point)..........881
Nebraska...............Wade Boggs (Omaha)................3010
Nevada.................Bryce Harper* (Las Vegas)...........1379
New Hampshire......Arlie Latham (West Lebanon)........1836
New Jersey............Derek Jeter (Pequannock).............3465
New Mexico...........Vern Stephens (McAllister)...........1859
New York...............Carl Yastrzemski (Southampton)....3419
North Carolina.......Luke Appling (High Point)............2749
North Dakota.........Darin Erstad (Jamestown)............1697
Ohio.....................Pete Rose (Cincinnati)................4256
Oklahoma.............Paul Waner (Harrah)..................3152

Oregon.................Dale Murphy (Portland)..............2111
Pennsylvania...........Stan Musial (Donora).................3630
Rhode Island...........Nap Lajoie (Woonsocket)...........3243
South Carolina.......Jim Rice (Anderson)....................2452
South Dakota.........Mark Ellis (Rapid City)...............1343
Tennessee..............Vada Pinson (Memphis)..............2757
Texas....................Tris Speaker (Lake Whitney).........3514
Utah.....................Duke Sims (Salt Lake City)............580
Vermont................Carlton Fisk (Bellows Falls)..........2356
Virginia.................Paul Hines (Norfolk)...................2133
Washington............Ryne Sandberg (Spokane)...........2386
West Virginia.........George Brett (Glen Dale)............3154
Wisconsin..............Al Simmons (Milwaukee)............2927
Wyoming..............Mike Lansing (Rawlings).............1124

American Samoa.....Tony Solaita (Nuuuli).....................336
District of Columbia.Maury Wills..............................2134
Puerto Rico............Roberto Clemente (Carolina)........3000
Virgin Islands.........Horace Clarke (St. Croix)............1230
* Still active.

Players with 200 Hits and 40 Home Runs, Season

American League

	Hits	Home Runs
Babe Ruth, N.Y. Yankees, 1921	204	59
Babe Ruth, N.Y. Yankees, 1923	205	41
Babe Ruth, N.Y. Yankees, 1924	200	46
Lou Gehrig, N.Y. Yankees, 1927	218	47
Lou Gehrig, N.Y. Yankees, 1930	220	41
Lou Gehrig, N.Y. Yankees, 1931	211	46
Jimmie Foxx, Phi. A's, 1932	213	58
Jimmie Foxx, Phi. A's, 1933	204	48
Lou Gehrig, N.Y. Yankees, 1934	210	49
Lou Gehrig, N.Y. Yankees, 1936	205	49
Hal Trosky, Cle. Indians, 1936	216	42
Joe DiMaggio, N.Y. Yankees, 1937	215	46
Hank Greenberg, Det. Tigers, 1937	200	40
Al Rosen, Cle. Indians, 1953	201	43
Jim Rice, Bos. Red Sox, 1978	213	46
Mo Vaughn, Bos. Red Sox, 1996	207	44
Albert Belle, Chi. White Sox, 1998	200	49
Alex Rodriguez, Sea. Mariners, 1998	213	42
Mo Vaughn, Bos. Red Sox, 1998	205	40
Alex Rodriguez, Tex. Rangers, 2001	201	52
Miguel Cabrera, Det. Tigers, 2012	205	44

National League (Post-1900)

	Hits	Home Runs
Rogers Hornsby, St.L. Cardinals, 1922	250	42
Rogers Hornsby, Chi. Cubs, 1929	229	40
Chuck Klein, Phi. Phillies, 1929	219	43
Chuck Klein, Phi. Phillies, 1930	250	40
Hank Aaron, Mil. Braves, 1963	201	44
Billy Williams, Chi. Cubs, 1970	205	42
Ellis Burks, Col. Rockies, 1996	211	40
Mike Piazza, L.A. Dodgers, 1997	201	40
Larry Walker, Col. Rockies, 1997	208	49
Vinny Castilla, Col. Rockies, 1998	206	46
Todd Helton, Col. Rockies, 2000	216	42
Albert Pujols, St.L. Cardinals, 2003	212	43
Adrian Beltre, L.A. Dodgers, 2004	200	44

Players with 200 Base Hits and Fewer Than 40 Extra-Base Hits, Season (Post-1900)

American League	Hits	Extra-Base Hits	National League (Post-1900)	Hits	Extra-Base Hits
Johnny Pesky, Bos. Red Sox, 1947,	207	35	Willie Keeler, Brk. Dodgers, 1900	204	29
Nellie Fox, Chi. White Sox, 1954	201	34	Willie Keeler, Brk. Dodgers, 1901	202	32
Harvey Kuenn, Det. Tigers, 1954	201	393	Milt Stock, St.L. Cardinals, 1920	204	34
Cesar Tovar, Min. Twins, 1971	204	33	Milt Stock, Brk. Dodgers, 1925	202	38
Steve Sax, N.Y. Yankees, 1989	205	34	Lloyd Waner, Pit. Pirates, 1927	223	25
Ichiro Suzuki, Sea. Mariners, 2004	262	37	Chick Fullis, Phi. Phillies, 1933	200	38
Ichiro Suzuki, Sea. Mariners, 2006	224	38	Richie Ashburn, Phi. Phillies, 1953	205	36
Ichiro Suzuki, Sea. Mariners, 2007	238	35	Richie Ashburn, Phi. Phillies, 1958	215	39
Ichiro Suzuki, Sea. Mariners, 2008	213	33	Maury Wills, L.A. Dodgers, 1962	208	28
Ichiro Suzuki, Sea. Mariners, 2010	214	39	Curt Flood, St.L. Cardinals, 1964	211	33
			Matty Alou, Pit. Pirates, 1970	201	30
			Ralph Garr, Atl. Braves, 1971	219	39
			Dave Cash, Phi. Phillies, 1974	206	39
			Rod Carew, Min. Twins, 1974	218	38
			Tony Gwynn, S.D. Padres, 1984	213	36
			Tony Gwynn, S.D. Padres, 1989	203	38
			Juan Pierre, Colo. Rockies, 2001	202	39
			Juan Pierre, Fla. Marlins, 2003	204	36
			Juan Pierre, Fla. Marlins, 2004	221	37
			Dee Strange-Gordon, Mia. Marlins, 2015	205	36
			Dee Strange-Gordon, Mia. Marlins, 2017	201	31

Players with 3000 Hits, Career

	Hits	Date of 3000th Hit	Opposing Pitcher
Pete Rose	4256	May 5, 1978	Steve Rogers, Mon. Expos (NL)
Ty Cobb	4189	Aug. 19, 1921	Elmer Myers, Bos. Red Sox (AL)
Hank Aaron	3771	May 17, 1970	Wayne Simpson, Cin. Reds (NL)
Stan Musial	3630	May 13, 1958	Moe Drabowsky, Chi. Cubs (NL)
Tris Speaker	3514	May 17, 1925	Tom Zachary, Was. Senators (AL)
Derek Jeter	3465	Jul. 9, 2011	David Price, T.B. Rays (AL)
Cap Anson	3435	Jul. 18, 1897	George Blackburn, Bal. Orioles (NL)
Honus Wagner	3420	Jun. 9, 1914	Erskine Mayer, Phi. Phillies (NL)
Carl Yastrzemski	3419	Sep. 12, 1979	Jim Beattie, N.Y. Yankees (AL)
Albert Pujols	3384	May 4, 2018	Mike Leake, Sea. Mariners (AL)
Paul Molitor	3319	Sep. 16, 1996	Jose Rosado, K.C. Royals (AL)
Eddie Collins	3315	Jun. 3, 1925	Rip Collins, Det. Tigers (AL)
Willie Mays	3283	Jul. 18, 1970	Mike Wegener, Mon. Expos (NL)
Eddie Murray	3255	Jun. 30, 1995	Mike Trombley, Min. Twins (AL)
Nap Lajoie	3242	Sep. 27, 1914	Marty McHale, N.Y. Yankees (AL)
Cal Ripken Jr.	3184	Apr. 15, 2000	Hector Carrasco, Min. Twins (AL)
Adrian Beltre	3166	Jul. 30, 2017	Wade Miley, Bal. Orioles (AL)
George Brett	3154	Sep. 30, 1992	Tim Fortugno, Cal. Angels (AL)
Paul Waner	3152	Jun. 19, 1942	Rip Sewell, Pit. Pirates (NL)
Robin Yount	3142	Sep. 9, 1992	Jose Mesa, Cle. Indians (AL)
Tony Gwynn	3141	Aug. 6, 1999	Dan Smith, Mon. Expos (NL)
Alex Rodriguez	3115	Jun. 19, 2015	Justin Verlander, Det. Tigers (AL)
Dave Winfield	3110	Sep. 16, 1993	Dennis Eckersley, Oak. A's (AL)
Ichiro Suzuki	3089	Aug. 16, 2016	Tony Cingrani, Cin. Reds (NL)
Miguel Cabrera	3088	Apr. 23, 2022	Austin Gomber, Col. Rockies (NL)
Craig Biggio	3060	Jun. 28, 2007	Aaron Cook, Col. Rockies (NL)
Rickey Henderson	3055	Oct. 7, 2001	John Thomson, Col. Rockies (NL)
Rod Carew	3053	Aug. 4, 1985	Frank Viola, Min. Twins (AL)

continued on next page

	Hits	Date of 3000th Hit	Opposing Pitcher
Lou Brock	3023	Aug. 13, 1979	Dennis Lamp, Chi. Cubs (NL)
Rafael Palmeiro	3020	Jul. 15, 2005	Joel Piniero, Sea. Mariners (AL)
Wade Boggs	3010	Aug. 7, 1999	Chris Haney, Cle. Indians (AL)
Al Kaline	3007	Sep. 24, 1974	Dave McNally, Bal. Orioles (AL)
Roberto Clemente	3000	Sep. 30, 1972	Jon Matlack, N.Y. Mets (NL)

Most Hits by Position, Season

American League

First Base 257 George Sisler, St.L. Browns, 1920
Second Base 232 Nap Lajoie, Phi. A's, 1901
Third Base 240 Wade Boggs, Bos. Red Sox, 1985
Shortstop 219 Derek Jeter, N.Y. Yankees, 1999
Outfield 262 Ichiro Suzuki, Sea. Mariners, 2004
Catcher 199 Ivan Rodriguez, Tex. Rangers, 1999
Pitcher 52 George Uhle, Cle. Indians, 1923
Designated Hitter 225 Paul Molitor, Min. Twins, 1996

National League (Post-1900)

First Base 254 Bill Terry, N.Y. Giants, 1930
Second Base 250 Rogers Hornsby, St.L. Cardinals, 1922
Third Base 231 Fred Lindstrom, N.Y. Giants, 1928 and 1930
Shortstop 211 Garry Templeton, St.L. Cardinals, 1979
Outfield 254 Lefty O'Doul, Phi. Phillies, 1929
Catcher 201 Mike Piazza, L.A. Dodgers, 1997
Pitcher 47 Red Lucas, Cin. Reds, 1927
Designated Hitter 104 Nelson Cruz, Was. Nationals, 2022

Players Hitting for the Cycle Two or More Times (Post-1900)

Three Times

Babe Herman, Brk. Dodgers (NL), 1931 (2); Chi. Cubs (NL), 1933
Adrian Beltre, Sea. Mariners (AL), 2008; Tex. Rangers (AL), 2012, 2015

Bob Meusel, N.Y. Yankees (AL), 1921, 1922, 1928
Trea Turner, Was. Nationals (NL), 2017, 2019, 2021
Christian Yelich, Mil. Brewers (NL), 2018 (2), 2022

Two Times

Nolan Arenado, Col. Rockies (NL), 2017; St.L. Cardinals (NL), 2022
Ken Boyer, St.L. Cardinals (NL), 1961, 1964
George Brett, K.C. Royals (AL), 1979, 1990
Cesar Cedeno, Hou. Astros (NL), 1972, 1976
Fred Clarke, Pit. Pirates (NL), 1901, 1903
Michael Cuddyer, Min. Twins (AL), 2009; Col. Rockies (NL), 2014
Mickey Cochrane, Phi. A's (AL), 1932, 1933
Joe Cronin, Was. Senators (AL), 1929; Bos. Red Sox (AL), 1940
Joe DiMaggio, N.Y. Yankees (AL), 1937, 1948
Bobby Doerr, Bos. Red Sox (AL), 1944, 1947
Freddie Freeman, Atl. Braves (NL), 2016, 2021
Jim Fregosi, L.A., Cal. Angels (AL), 1964, 1968
Lou Gehrig, N.Y. Yankees (AL), 1934, 1937

Carlos Gomez, Min. Twins (AL), 2008; Tex. Rangers (AL), 2017
Aaron Hill, Ari. D'backs (NL), 2012 (2)
Brock Holt, Bos. Red Sox (AL), 2015, 2018*
Chuck Klein, Phi. Phillies (NL), 1931, 1933
John Olerud, Sea. Mariners (AL) 2001; N.Y. Mets (NL) 1997
George Sisler, St.L. Browns (AL), 1920, 1921
Chris Speier Mon. Expos (NL) 1978; S.F. Giants (NL) 1988
Arky Vaughan, Pit. Pirates (NL), 1933, 1939
Bob Watson, Hou. Astros (NL), 1977; Bos. Red Sox (AL), 1979
Wally Westlake, Pit. Pirates (NL), 1948, 1949
Frank White, K.C. Royals (AL), 1979, 1982
Brad Wilkerson, Mon. Expos (NL), 2003; Was. Nationals (NL), 2005

* Hit for cycle in playoffs.

Most Times at Bat Without a Hit, Season

American League

61	Bill Wight, Chi. White Sox, 1950
46	Karl Drews, St.L. Browns, 1949
41	Ernie Koob, St.L. Browns, 1916
39	Ed Rakow, Det. Tigers, 1964

National League (Post-1900)

70	Bob Buhl, Mil. Braves–Chi. Cubs, 1962
59	Max Scherzer, Was. Nationals–L.A. Dodgers, 2021
47	Ron Herbel, S.F. Giants, 1964
44	Wei-Yin Chen, Mia. Marlins, 2016
41	Randy Tate, N.Y. Mets, 1975
40	Jason Bergmann, Was. Nationals, 2008
40	Joey Hamilton, S.D. Padres, 1994
38	Darryl Kile, Hou. Astros, 1991

Players with 200 Hits in Each of First Three Full Major League Seasons

Willie Keeler, Bal. Orioles (NL) 1894 (219), 1895 (221), and 1896 (214)
Lloyd Waner, Pit. Pirates (NL) 1927 (223), 1928 (221), and 1929 (234)
Johnny Pesky, Bos. Red Sox (AL) 1942 (205), 1946 (208), and 1947 (207)
Ichiro Suzuki, Sea. Mariners (AL) 2001 (242), 2002 (208), and 2003 (212)

Players with 600 Total Hits in First Three Full Major League Seasons

	Seasons: Hits	Total Hits
Lloyd Waner	1927: 223; 1928: 221; 1929: 234	678
Ichiro Suzuki	2001: 242; 2002: 202; 2003: 212	662
Willie Keeler	1894: 219; 1895: 221; 1896: 214	654
Paul Waner	1926: 180; 1927: 237; 1928: 223	640
Al Simmons	1924: 183; 1925: 253; 1926: 199	635
Johnny Pesky*	1942: 205; 1946: 208; 1947: 207	620
Earle Combs	1925: 203; 1926: 181; 1927: 231	615
Joe DiMaggio	1936: 206; 1937: 215; 1938: 194	615

* Was in the military in 1943.

Players with 200-Hit Seasons in Each League

Bill Buckner	Chi. Cubs (NL), 1982	Al Oliver	Tex. Rangers (AL), 1980
	Bos. Red Sox (AL), 1985		Mon. Expos (NL), 1982
Vladimir Guerrero	Mon. Expos (NL), 1998, 2002;	Steve Sax	L.A. Dodgers (NL), 1986
	Ana.–L.A. Angels (AL), 2004, 2006		N.Y. Yankees (AL), 1989
		George Sisler	St.L. Browns (AL), 1920–22,1925, and 1927;
			Bos. Braves (NL), 1929

Players with 200 Hits in Five Consecutive Seasons

	Seasons
Ichiro Suzuki, Sea. Mariners (AL), 2001–10	10
Willie Keeler, Bal. Orioles (NL), 1894–98, and Brk. Dodgers (NL), 1899–1901	8
Wade Boggs, Bos. Red Sox (AL), 1983–89	7
Chuck Klein, Phi. Phillies (NL), 1929–33	5
Al Simmons, Phi. A's (AL), 1929–32, and Chi. White Sox (AL), 1933	5
Charlie Gehringer, Det. Tigers (AL), 1933–37	5
Michael Young, Tex. Rangers (AL), 2003–07	5

Rookies with 200 or More Hits

American League

Ichiro Suzuki, Sea. Mariners, 2001	242
Joe Jackson, Cle. Indians, 1911	233
Tony Oliva, Min. Twins, 1964	217
Dale Alexander, Det. Tigers, 1929	215
Harvey Kuenn, Det. Tigers, 1953	209
Nomar Garciaparra, Bos. Red Sox, 1997	209
Kevin Seitzer, K.C. Royals, 1987	207
Hal Trosky, Cle. Indians, 1934	206
Joe DiMaggio, N.Y. Yankees, 1936	206
Johnny Pesky, Bos. Red Sox, 1942	205
Earle Combs, N.Y. Yankees, 1925	203
Roy Johnson, Det. Tigers, 1929	201
Dick Wakefield, Det. Tigers, 1943	200

National League (Post-1900)

Lloyd Waner, Pit. Pirates, 1927	223
Johnny Frederick, Brk. Dodgers, 1929	209
Frank McCormick, Cin. Reds, 1938	209
Billy Herman, Chi. Cubs, 1932	206
Vada Pinson, Cin. Reds, 1959	205
Dick Allen, Phi. Phillies, 1964	201

Teammates Finishing One-Two in Base Hits

American League

Season	Team	Leader	Hits	Runner-Up	Hits
1908	Det. Tigers	Ty Cobb	188	Sam Crawford	184
1915	Det. Tigers	Ty Cobb	208	Sam Crawford	183
1919	Det. Tigers (Tie)	Bobby Veach	191	Ty Cobb	191
1923	Cle. Indians	Charlie Jamieson	222	Tris Speaker	218

continued on next page

Season	Team	Leader	Hits	Runner-Up	Hits
1927	N.Y. Yankees	Earle Combs	231	Lou Gehrig	218
1929	Det. Tigers (Tie)	Dale Alexander	215	Charlie Gehringer	215
1938	Bos. Red Sox	Joe Vosmik	201	Doc Cramer	198
1956	Det. Tigers	Harvey Kuenn	196	Al Kaline	194
1960	Chi. White Sox	Minnie Minoso	184	Nellie Fox	175
1965	Min. Twins	Tony Oliva	185	Zoilo Versalles	182
1982	Mil. Brewers	Robin Yount	210	Cecil Cooper	205
1993	Tor. Blue Jays	Paul Molitor	211	John Olerud	200
2001	Sea. Mariners	Ichiro Suzuki	242	Bret Boone	206
2011	Bos. Red Sox	Adrian Gonzalez*	213	Jacoby Ellsbury	212
2021	Tor. Blue Jays	Bo Bichette	191	Vladimir Guerrero Jr.	188

* Gonzalez tied for lead with Michael Young of Tex. Rangers.

National League (Post-1900)

Season	Team	Leader	Hits	Runner-Up	Hits
1910	Pit. Pirates (Tie)	Bobby Byrne	178	Honus Wagner	178
1920	St.L. Cardinals	Rogers Hornsby	218	Milt Stock	204
1927	Pit. Pirates	Paul Waner	237	Lloyd Waner	223
1933	Phi. Phillies	Chuck Klein	223	Chick Fullis	200
1952	St.L. Cardinals	Stan Musial	194	Red Schoendienst	188
1957	Mil. Braves	Red Schoendienst	200*	Hank Aaron	198
1965	Cin. Reds	Pete Rose	209	Vada Pinson	204
1979	St.L. Cardinals	Garry Templeton	211	Keith Hernandez	210
2008	N.Y. Mets	Jose Reyes	204	David Wright	189
2022	L.A. Dodgers	Freddie Freeman	199	Trea Turner	194

* Schoendienst had 78 with N.Y. Giants and 122 hits with Mil. Braves in 1957.

Players Getting 1000 Hits Before Their 25th Birthday

Ty Cobb, Det. Tigers (AL), 1911 ... 24 years, 4 months
Mel Ott, N.Y. Giants (NL), 1933 ... 24 years, 5 months
Al Kaline, Det. Tigers (AL), 1959 ... 24 years, 7 months
Freddie Lindstrom, N.Y. Giants (NL), 1930 ... 24 years, 8 months
Buddy Lewis, Was. Senators (AL), 1941 ... 24 years, 9 months
Robin Yount, Mil. Brewers (AL), 1980 ... 24 years, 11 months

Players with 10,000 At-Bats and Fewer Than 3000 Hits, Career

	At-Bats	Hits		At-Bats	Hits
Brooks Robinson (1955–77)	10,654	2848	Rabbit Maranville (1912–33, 1935)	10,078	2605
Omar Vizquel (1989–2011)	10,586	2877	Frank Robinson (1956–76)	10,006	2943
Luis Aparicio (1956–73)	10,230	2677			

Players with 200 Hits, Batting Under .300, Season

	Hits	Batting Average
Jo-Jo Moore, N.Y. Giants (NL), 1935	201	.295
Maury Wills, L.A. Dodgers (NL), 1962	208	.299
Lou Brock, St.L. Cardinals (NL), 1967	206	.299
Matty Alou, Pit. Pirates (NL), 1970	201	.297
Ralph Garr, Atl. Braves (NL), 1973	200	.299
Buddy Bell, Tex. Rangers (AL), 1979	200	.299
Bill Buckner, Bos. Red Sox (AL), 1985	201	.299
Juan Pierre, Chi. Cubs (NL), 2006	204	.292
Jimmy Rollins, Phi. Phillies (NL), 2007	212	.296
Jose Reyes, N.Y. Mets (NL), 2008	204	.297

Players with 2500 Hits and Career .300 Batting Average, Never Winning Batting Title (Post-1900)

	Career Hits	Career Batting Average
Paul Molitor	3319	.306
Eddie Collins	3314	.333
Derek Jeter	3465	.310
Sam Rice	2987	.322
Sam Crawford	2925*	.309
Frankie Frisch	2880	.316
Mel Ott	2876	.304
Roberto Alomar	2724	.300
Robinson Cano	2639	.301
Vladimir Guerrero	2590	.318

* 1899 totals not included.

Former Negro Leaguers with 1500 Major League Hits

3771—Hank Aaron, Mil. Braves (NL), 1954–65; Atl. Braves (NL), 1966–74; Mil. Brewers (AL), 1975–76. (Played in the Negro Leagues with Indianapolis Clowns.)

3283—Willie Mays, N.Y. Giants (NL), 1951–52, 1954–57; S.F. Giants (NL), 1958–71; N.Y. Mets (NL), 1972–73. (Played in the Negro Leagues with Chattanooga Choo-Choos, 1947; Birmingham Black Barons, 1948–50.)

2583—Ernie Banks, Chi. Cubs (NL), 1953–71. (Played in the Negro Leagues with Kansas City Monarchs, 1950–53.)

1963—Minnie Minoso, Cle. Indians (AL), 1949, 1951, 1958–59; Chi. White Sox (AL), 1951–57, 1960–61, 1964, 1976, 1980; St.L. Cardinals (NL), 1962; Was. Senators (AL), 1963. (Played in the Negro Leagues with New York Cubans.)

1889—Jim "Junior" Gilliam, Brk. Dodgers (NL), 1953–57; L.A. Dodgers (NL), 1958–66. (Played in the Negro Leagues with Nashville Black Vols, 1946; Baltimore Elite Giants, 1946–51)

1518—Jackie Robinson, Brk. Dodgers (NL), 1947–56). (Played in the Negro Leagues with Kansas City Monarchs, 1944–45.)

1515—Larry Doby, Cle. Indians (AL), 1947–55; Chi. White Sox (AL), 1956–57, 1959. (Played in the Negro Leagues with Newark Eagles, 1942–43, 1946–47.)

Players with 2500 Career Hits, Never Having a 200-Hit Season

	Career Hits	Most in One Season
Cap Anson (1871–97)	3435	187 (1886)
Carl Yastrzemski (1961–83)	3419	191 (1962)
Eddie Murray (1977–97)	3255	186 (1980)
Dave Winfield (1973–95)	3110	193 (1984)
Rickey Henderson (1979–2003)	3055	179 (1980)
Jake Beckley (1888–1907)	2938	190 (1900)
Barry Bonds (1987–2007)	2935	181 (1993)
Omar Vizquel (1989–2012)	2877	191 (1999)
Mel Ott (1926–47)	2876	191 (1935)
Harold Baines (1980–98)	2866	198 (1985)
Brooks Robinson (1955–77)	2848	194 (1964)
Ivan Rodriguez (1991–2011)	2844	199 (1999)
Ken Griffey Jr. (1989–2010)	2781	185 (1997)
Andre Dawson (1976–96)	2774	189 (1983)
Tony Perez (1964–86)	2732	186 (1970)

continued on next page

	Career Hits	Most in One Season
Chipper Jones (1993, 1995–2012)	2726	189 (2001)
Carlos Beltran (1998–2017)	2725	194 (1999)
Roberto Alomar (1988–2004)	2724	193 (1996)
Rusty Staub (1963–85)	2716	186 (1971)
Gary Sheffield (1988–2009)	2689	190 (2003)
Luis Aparicio (1956–73)	2677	182 (1966)
George Davis (1890–1909)	2665	195 (1893)
Ted Williams (1939–42, 1946–60)	2654	194 (1949)
Jim O' Rourke (1872–93, 1904)	2639	172 (1890)
Rabbit Maranville (1912–33, 1935)	2605	198 (1922)
Tim Raines (1979–2002)	2605	194 (1986)
Reggie Jackson (1967–87)	2584	158 (1973)
Ernie Banks (1953–71)	2583	193 (1958)
Manny Ramirez (1993–2011)	2574	185 (2003)
Willie Davis (1960–76, 1979)	2561	198 (1971)
Steve Finley (1989–2007)	2548	195 (2006)
Joe Morgan (1963–84)	2517	167 (1973)
Jimmy Ryan (1885–1900, 1902–03)	2513	187 (1889)

Latino Players with 2500 Hits

3384	Albert Pujols	2757	Vada Pinson
3166	Adrian Beltre	2732	Tony Perez
3115	Alex Rodriguez	2724	Roberto Alomar
3088	Miguel Cabrera*	2677	Luis Aparicio
3053	Rod Carew	2591	Luis Gonzalez
3020	Rafael Palmeiro	2590	Vladimir Guerrero
3000	Roberto Clemente	2586	Julio Franco
2877	Omar Vizquel	2574	Manny Ramirez
2844	Ivan Rodriguez		

* Still active.

3000 Hits, 500 Home Runs, and a .300 Batting Average, Career

	Hits	Home Runs	Batting Average		Hits	Home Runs	Batting Average
Hank Aaron	3771	755	.305	Willie Mays	3283	660	.302
Miguel Cabrera	3088	507	.308				

Most Hits by Switch-Hitter, Career

4256	Pete Rose (1963–86)	2725	Carlos Beltran (1998–2017)
3255	Eddie Murray (1977–97)	2724	Roberto Alomar (1988–2004)
2880	Frankie Frisch (1919–37)	2665	Max Carey (1910–29)
2877	Omar Vizquel (1989–2012)	2665	George Davis (1890–1909)
2726	Chipper Jones (1993, 1995–2012)	2605	Tim Raines (1979–99, 2001–02)

Most Hits by Catcher, Career*

2844	Ivan Rodriguez (1999–2011)	2150	Yogi Berra (1946–65)
2472	Ted Simmons (1968–88)	2127	Mike Piazza (1992–2007)
2356	Carlton Fisk (1977–97)	2092	Gary Carter (1974–92)
2195	Jason Kendall (1996–2010)	2048	Johnny Bench (1967–83)

* Played more than 50 percent of their games at catcher.

Most Singles, Career

3215.............................Pete Rose (1963–86)	2163.............................Doc Cramer (1929–48)
3053.....................................Ty Cobb (1905–28)	2162.............................Luke Appling (1930–50)
2643.........................Eddie Collins (1906–30)	2161.............................Nellie Fox (1947–65)
2614.............................Cap Anson (1871–97)	2156.............................Eddie Murray (1977–97)
2595.........................Derek Jeter (1995–2014)	2154.........................Roberto Clemente (1955–72)
2514.........................Ichiro Suzuki (2001–18)	2130.............................Jake Beckley (1888–1907)
2513.........................Willie Keeler (1892–1910)	2121.........................George Sisler (1915–22, 1924–30)
2424.........................Honus Wagner (1897–1917)	2119.........................Richie Ashburn (1948–62)
2404.............................Rod Carew (1967–85)	2108.............................Luis Aparicio (1956–73)
2383.............................Tris Speaker (1907–28)	2106.............................Cal Ripken Jr. (1981–98)
2378.............................Tony Gwynn (1982–2001)	2104.............................Zack Wheat (1909–27)
2366.............................Paul Molitor (1978–98)	2097.............................Sam Crawford (1899–1917)
2340.............................Nap Lajoie (1896–1916)	2056.............................Lave Cross (1887–1907)
2294.............................Hank Aaron (1954–1976)	2046.............................Craig Biggio (1988–2007)
2273.............................Jesse Burkett (1890–1905)	2035.............................Al Kaline (1953–74)
2271.............................Sam Rice (1915–34)	2035.............................George Brett (1973–93)
2264.............................Omar Vizquel (1989–2012)	2033.............................Lloyd Waner (1927–45)
2262.............................Carl Yastrzemski (1961–83)	2030.............................Fred Clarke (1894–1911, 1913–15)
2253.........................Stan Musial (1941–44, 1946–63)	2030.............................Brooks Robinson (1955–77)
2253.............................Wade Boggs (1982–98)	2028.............................George Van Haltren (1887–1903)
2247.............................Lou Brock (1961–79)	2020.............................Rabbit Maranville (1912–33, 1935)
2243.............................Paul Waner (1926–45)	2017.............................Max Carey (1910–29)
2182.............................Robin Yount (1974–93)	2017.............................Dave Winfield (1973–95)
2182.............................Rickey Henderson (1979–2003)	2015.............................Adrian Beltre (1998–2018)
2171.............................Frankie Frisch (1919–37)	

Fewest Singles, Season (Min. 140 Games, Min. 300 At-Bats)

American League

Singles		Games	Total Hits
32	Joey Gallo, Tex. Rangers, 2017	145	94
38	Joey Gallo, Tex. Rangers, 2018	148	103
42	Taylor Walls, T.B. Rays, 2022	142	70
45	Chris Young, N.Y. Yankees, 2015	140	80
46	Rougned Odor, Tex. Rangers, 2019	145	107
47	Joey Gallo, Tex. Rangers–N.Y. Yankees, 2021	153	99
49	Carlos Pena, T.B. Rays, 2010	144	95
49	Daniel Vogelbach, Sea. Mariners, 2019	144	96
50	Adam Dunn, Chi. White Sox, 2012	151	110
53	Mickey Stanley, Det. Tigers, 1967	145	70
53	Mark McGwire, Oak. A's, 1991	154	97
53	Mark Reynolds, Bal. Orioles, 2011	155	118
54	Mike Cameron, Chi. White Sox, 1998	141	83
54	Brendan Ryan, Sea. Mariners, 2012	141	79
54	Todd Frazier, Chi. White Sox–N.Y. Yankees, 2017	147	101
55	Reggie Jackson, Oak. A's, 1970	149	101
55	Paul Blair, Bal. Orioles, 1976	145	74
56	Jose Bautista, Tor. Blue Jays, 2011	161	148
56	David Murphy, Tex. Rangers, 2013	142	96
56	Chris Carter, Hou. Astros, 2014	145	115
56	Matthew Joyce, Oak. A's, 2017	141	114
56	Hunter Dozier, K.C. Royals, 2021	144	105

continued on next page

Singles		Games	Total Hits
56	Brett Gardner, N.Y. Yankees, 2021	140	86
57	Jerry Kennedy, N.Y. Yankees, 1970	140	78
57	Mike Napoli, L.A. Angels, 2010	140	108
57	Matthew Joyce, T.B. Rays, 2013	140	97
58	Don Lock, Was. Senators, 1965	143	90
58	Gene Tenace, Oak. A's, 1974	158	102
58	Chris Carter, Hou. Astros, 2013	148	113
58	Brandon Moss, Oak. A's, 2013	145	114
58	Shohei Ohtani, L.A. Angels, 2021	155	138
59	Ray Oyler, Det. Tigers, 1967	148	76
59	Paul Blair, Bal. Orioles, 1968	141	89
59	Pedro Garcia, Mil. Brewers, 1974	141	90
59	Darren Lewis, Chi. White Sox, 1996	141	77
59	Jack Cust, Oak. A's, 2008	148	111
59	Jack Hannahan, Oak. A's, 2008	143	95
59	Nick Swisher, N.Y. Yankees, 2009	150	124
59	Mitch Moreland, Tex. Rangers, 2013	147	107
59	Jackie Bradley Jr., Bos. Red Sox, 2019	147	111
60	Mario Mendoza, Sea, Mariners, 1979	148	74
60	Dick Schofield, Cal. Angels, 1984	140	77
60	Darrell Evans, Det. Tigers, 1988	144	91
60	Fred Manrique, Chi. White Sox, 1988	140	81
60	Carlos Pena, T.B. Rays, 2012	160	98
60	Mike Moustakas, K.C. Royals, 2014	140	97

National League (Post-1900)

Singles		Games	Total Hits
40	Ruben Rivera, S.D. Padres, 1999	147	80
42	Curtis Granderson, N.Y. Mets–L.A. Dodgers, 2017	147	95
42	Hunter Renfroe, S.D. Padres, 2019	140	95
43	Joc Pederson, L.A. Dodgers, 2018	148	98
43	Brad Miller, Phi. Phillies, 2021	140	75
46	Sean Rodriguez, Pit. Pirates, 2016	140	81
46	Eugenio Suarez, Cin. Reds, 2019	145	100
47	Tommie Aaron, Mil. Braves, 1962	141	77
48	Mark Reynolds, Ari. D'backs, 2010	145	99
48	Eric Thames, Mil. Brewers, 2019	149	98
48	Trent Grisham, S.D. Padres, 2022	152	83
49	Barry Bonds, S.F. Giants, 2001	153	156
50	Ian Stewart, Col. Rockies, 2009	147	97
51	Garrett Jones, Pit. Pirates, 2013	144	94
52	Gene Tenace, S.D. Padres, 1978	142	90
52	Mark Reynolds, St.L. Cardinals, 2015	140	88
52	Keon Broxton, Mil. Brewers, 2017	143	91
53	Mike Cameron, N.Y. Mets, 2001	140	114
53	Patt Burrell, Phi. Phillies, 2003	146	109
53	Carlos Pena, Chi. Cubs, 2011	153	111
53	Chris Carter, Mil. Brewers, 2016	160	122
53	Scott Schebler, Cin. Reds, 2017	141	110
54	Jim Hickman, N.Y. Mets, 1965	141	87
54	Greg Dobbs, Phi. Phillies, 2007	142	88
54	Brian Bogusevic, Hou. Astros, 2012	146	72
54	Ike Davis, N.Y. Mets–Pit. Pirates, 2014	143	84
54	Ian Happ, Chi. Cubs, 2018	142	90
54	Mike Yastrzemski, S.F. Giants, 2022	148	104

continued on next page

Singles		Games	Total Hits
55	Chuck Workman, Bos. Braves, 1944	140	87
55	Andruw Jones, Atl. Braves, 1997	153	92
55	Joc Pederson, L.A. Dodgers, 2015	151	101
55	Andrew McCutchen, Phi. Phillies, 2021	144	107
56	Jim Wynn, Atl. Braves, 1976	148	93
56	Steve Jeltz, Phi. Phillies, 1988	148	71
56	Jose Valentin, Mil. Brewers, 1998	151	96
56	Jim Edmonds, St.L. Cardinals, 2005	142	123
56	Garrett Jones, Pit. Pirates, 2011	148	103
56	Travis Snider, Pit. Pirates, 2014	140	85
56	Kyle Schwarber, Phi. Phillies, 2022	155	126
57	Kevin Young, Pit. Pirates, 2001	142	104
57	Adam Dunn, Cin. Reds, 2005	160	134
57	Wilson Betemit, Atl. Braves–L.A. Dodgers, 2006	143	98
57	Mike Jacobs, Fla. Marlins, 2008	141	118
57	Yasmani Grandal, L.A. Dodgers, 2018	140	106
57	Joc Pederson, L.A. Dodgers, 2019	149	112
57	Cody Bellinger, L.A. Dodgers, 2022	144	106
58	Mark McGwire, St.L. Cardinals, 1999	153	145
58	Ian Desmond, Col. Rockies, 2019	140	113
58	Rowdy Tellez, Mil. Brewers, 2022	153	116
59	Gene Tenace, S.D. Padres, 1977	147	102
59	Derrek Lee, Fla. Marlins, 1998	141	106
59	Adam Dunn, Cin. Reds–Ari. D'backs, 2008	158	122
59	Manuel Margot, S.D. Padres, 2019	151	93
59	Ian Happ, Chi. Cubs, 2021	148	105
60	Mark Bellhorn, Chi. Cubs, 2002	146	115
60	Barry Bonds, S.F. Giants, 2004	147	135
60	Carlos Beltran, N.Y. Mets, 2006	140	140
60	Ike Davis, N.Y. Mets, 2012	156	118
60	Adam Duvall, Atl. Braves–Mia. Marlins, 2021	146	117
60	Max Muncy, L.A. Dodgers, 2021	144	124

Most Singles, Season

American League

Singles		Total Hits
225	Ichiro Suzuki, Sea. Mariners, 2004	262
203	Ichiro Suzuki, Sea. Mariners, 2007	238
192	Ichiro Suzuki, Sea. Mariners, 2001	242
187	Wade Boggs, Bos. Red Sox, 1985	240
186	Ichiro Suzuki, Sea. Mariners, 2006	224
184	Willie Wilson, K.C. Royals, 1980	230
182	Sam Rice, Was. Senators, 1925	227
180	Rod Carew, Min. Twins, 1974	218
180	Ichiro Suzuki, Sea. Mariners, 2008	213
179	Jack Tobin, St.L. Browns, 1921	236
179	Ichiro Suzuki, Sea. Mariners, 2009	225
178	George Sisler, St.L. Browns, 1922	246
176	George Sisler, St.L. Browns, 1925	224

continued on next page

National League (Post-1900)

Singles		Total Hits
198	Lloyd Waner, Pit. Pirates, 1927	223
184	Juan Pierre, Fla. Marlins, 2004	221
183	Matty Alou, Pit. Pirates, 1969	231
181	Jesse Burkett, St.L. Cardinals, 1901	226
181	Lefty O'Doul, Phi. Phillies, 1929	254
181	Lloyd Waner, Pit. Pirates, 1929	234
181	Richie Ashburn, Phi. Phillies, 1951	221
181	Pete Rose, Cin. Reds, 1973	230
180	Lloyd Waner, Pit. Pirates, 1928	221
180	Ralph Garr, Atl. Braves, 1971	219
179	Maury Wills, L.A. Dodgers, 1962	208
178	Paul Waner, Pit. Pirates, 1937	219
178	Curt Flood, St.L. Cardinals, 1964	211
177	Bill Terry, N.Y. Giants, 1930	254
177	Tony Gwynn, S.D. Padres, 1984	213
176	Richie Ashburn, Phi. Phillies, 1958	215
175	Willie Keeler, Brk. Dodgers, 1900	204

20 Triple Seasons (Since 1930)

American League

1930	Earle Combs, N.Y. Yankees	22
1935	Joe Vosmik, Cle. Indians	20
1941	Jeff Heath, Cle. Indians	20
1945	Snuffy Stirnweiss, N.Y. Yankees	22
1949	Dale Mitchell, Cle. Indians	23
1979	George Brett, K.C. Royals	20
1985	Willie Wilson, K.C. Royals	21
2000	Cristian Guzman, Min. Twins	20
2007	Curtis Granderson, Det. Tigers	23

National League (Post-1900)

1930	Adam Comorosky, Pit. Pirates	23
1931	Bill Terry, N.Y. Giants	20
1943	Stan Musial, St.L. Cardinals	20
1946	Stan Musial, St.L. Cardinals	20
1957	Willie Mays, N.Y. Giants	20
1996	Lance Johnson, N.Y. Mets	21
2007	Jimmy Rollins, Phi. Phillies	20

Largest Differential Between League Leader in Hits and Runner-Up

American League

Differential	Season	Leader	Hits	Runner-Up	Hits
+46	2004	Ichiro Suzuki, Sea. Mariners	262	Michael Young, Tex. Rangers	216
+42	1901	Nap Lajoie, Phi. A's	232	John Anderson, Mil. Brewers	190
+37	1974	Rod Carew, Min. Twins	218	Tommy Davis, Bal. Orioles	181
+36	2001	Ichiro Suzuki, Sea. Mariners	242	Bret Boone, Sea. Mariners	206
+35	1917	Ty Cobb, Det. Tigers	225	George Sisler, St.L. Browns	190
+35	1922	George Sisler, St.L. Browns	246	Ty Cobb, Det. Tigers	211
+33	1910	Nap Lajoie, Cle. Indians	227	Ty Cobb, Det. Tigers	194
+33	1920	George Sisler, St.L. Browns	257	Eddie Collins, Chi. White Sox	224
+31	1928	Heinie Manush, St.L. Browns	241	Lou Gehrig, N.Y. Yankees	210
+29	1985	Wade Boggs, Bos. Red Sox	240	Don Mattingly, N.Y. Yankees	211
+27	1945	Snuffy Stirnweiss, N.Y. Yankees	195	Wally Moses, Chi. White Sox	168
+27	1977	Rod Carew, Min. Twins	239	Ron LeFlore, Det. Tigers	212
+26	1925	Al Simmons, Phi. A's	253	Sam Rice, Was. Senators	227
+26	2000	Darin Erstad, Ana. Angels	240	Johnny Damon, K.C. Royals	214

continued on next page

National League (Post-1900)

Differential	Season	Leader	Hits	Runner-Up	Hits
+44	1946	Stan Musial, St.L. Cardinals	228	Dixie Walker, Brk. Dodgers	184
+40	1948	Stan Musial, St.L. Cardinals	230	Tommy Holmes, Bos. Braves	190
+35	1922	Rogers Hornsby, St.L. Cardinals	250	Carson Bigbee, Pit. Pirates	215
+34	1987	Tony Gwynn, S.D. Padres	218	Pedro Guerrero, L.A. Dodgers	184
+30	1973	Pete Rose, Cin. Reds	230	Ralph Garr, Atl. Braves	200
+27	1945	Tommy Holmes, Bos. Braves	224	Goody Rosen, Brk. Dodgers	197

Batting Average

Evolution of Batting Average Record

American League	National League (Pre-1900)	National League (Post-1899)
1901 Nap Lajoie, Phi. A's .... .426	1876 Ross Barnes, Chi. Cubs ...... .404	1900 Honus Wagner, Pit. Pirates .... .381
	1879 Cap Anson, Chi. Cubs .... .407	1901 Jesse Burkett, St.L. Cardinals .... .382
	1887 Cap Anson, Chi. Cubs .... .421	1921 Rogers Hornsby, St.L. Cardinals .... .397
	1887 Cap Anson, Chi. Cubs .... .421	1922 Rogers Hornsby, St.L. Cardinals .... .401
	1894 Hugh Duffy, Bos. Beaneaters... .438	1924 Rogers Hornsby, St.L. Cardinals .... .424

Highest Batting Average by Position, Season

American League	National League (Post-1900)
First Base .... .420 ....George Sisler, St.L. Browns, 1922	**First Base** .... .401 ....Bill Terry, N.Y. Giants, 1930
Second Base .... .426 ....Nap Lajoie, Phi. A's, 1901	**Second Base** .... .424 ....Rogers Hornsby, St. L. Cardinals, 1924
Third Base .... .390 ......George Brett, K.C. Royals, 1980	**Third Base** .... .379 .... Fred Lindstrom, N.Y. Giants, 1930
Shortstop .... .388 ....Luke Appling, Chi. White Sox, 1936	**Shortstop** .... .385 ....Arky Vaughan, Pit. Pirates, 1935
Outfield .... .420 .... Ty Cobb, Det. Tigers, 1911	**Outfield** .... .398 ....Lefty O'Doul, Phi. Phillies, 1929
Catcher .... .365 .... Joe Mauer, Min. Twins, 2009	**Catcher** .... .367 ......Babe Phelps, Brk. Dodgers, 1936
Pitcher .... .433 ... Walter Johnson, Was. Senators, 1925	**Pitcher** .... .427 ....Jack Bentley, N.Y. Giants, 1923
Designated Hitter .... .356 ... Edgar Martinez, Sea. Mariners, 1995	**Designated Hitter** ...... .296 .... Bryce Harper, Phi. Phillies, 2022

Highest Batting Average by Decade (Min. 2000 At-Bats)

Pre-1900	1900–09	1910–19
.384 .... Willie Keeler	.352 ....Honus Wagner	.387 .... Ty Cobb
.356 ....Jesse Burkett	.346 ....Nap Lajoie	.354 ....Joe Jackson
.349 .... Billy Hamilton	.338 .... Mike Donlin	.344 ....Tris Speaker
.345 ....Ed Delahanty	.337 .... Ty Cobb	.331 ....George Sisler
.342 ....Dan Brouthers	.312 ....Jesse Burkett	.326 ....Eddie Collins
.342 ....Dave Orr	.312 ....Elmer Flick	.321 ....Nap Lajoie
.341 .... Pete Browning	.311 ....Willie Keeler	.314 ....Edd Roush
.340 ....Joe Kelley	.311 .... Cy Seymour	.313 ....Sam Crawford
.338 ....Jake Stenzel	.310 ....George Stone	.313 ....Benny Kauff
.336 ....John McGraw	.309 ....Ginger Beaumont	.310 ....Home Run Baker
		.310 .... Vin Campbell
		.310 ....Rogers Hornsby

continued on next page

1920–29

.382	Rogers Hornsby
.364	Harry Heilmann
.357	Ty Cobb
.356	Al Simmons
.356	Paul Waner
.355	Babe Ruth
.354	Tris Speaker
.347	George Sisler
.346	Eddie Collins
.342	Fats Fothergill

1930–39

.352	Bill Terry
.346	Johnny Mize
.345	Lefty O'Doul
.343	Lou Gehrig
.341	Joe DiMaggio
.338	Joe Medwick
.336	Jimmie Foxx
.336	Paul Waner
.331	Charlie Gehringer
.331	Babe Ruth

1940–49

.356	Ted Williams
.346	Stan Musial
.325	Joe DiMaggio
.321	Barney McCosky
.316	Johnny Pesky
.312	Enos Slaughter
.311	Luke Appling
.311	Dixie Walker
.308	Taffy Wright
.305	George Kell
.305	Joe Medwick

1950–59

.336	Ted Williams
.330	Stan Musial
.323	Hank Aaron
.317	Willie Mays
.314	Harvey Kuenn
.313	Richie Ashburn
.311	Al Kaline
.311	Mickey Mantle
.311	Jackie Robinson
.308	George Kell
.308	Duke Snider

1960–69

.328	Roberto Clemente
.312	Matty Alou
.309	Pete Rose
.308	Hank Aaron
.308	Tony Oliva
.304	Frank Robinson
.300	Dick Allen
.300	Willie Mays
.297	Curt Flood
.297	Manny Mota

1970–79

.343	Rod Carew
.320	Bill Madlock
.317	Dave Parker
.314	Pete Rose
.311	Lyman Bostock
.310	George Brett
.310	Ken Griffey Sr.
.310	Jim Rice
.307	Ralph Garr
.300	Fred Lynn

1980–89

.352	Wade Boggs
.332	Tony Gwynn
.323	Don Mattingly
.323	Kirby Puckett
.314	Rod Carew
.311	George Brett
.308	Pedro Guerrero
.307	Al Oliver
.305	Robin Yount
.304	Will Clark

1990–99

.344	Tony Gwynn
.328	Mike Piazza
.322	Edgar Martinez
.320	Frank Thomas
.318	Derek Jeter
.313	Paul Molitor
.313	Larry Walker
.312	Kirby Puckett
.310	Mark Grace
.310	Kenny Lofton

2000–09

.334	Albert Pujols
.333	Ichiro Suzuki
.331	Todd Helton
.323	Vladimir Guerrero
.322	Barry Bonds
.317	Derek Jeter
.317	Manny Ramirez
.316	Magglio Ordonez
.311	Miguel Cabrera
.311	Chipper Jones

2010–19

.317	Miguel Cabrera
.315	Jose Altuve
.307	Adrian Beltre
.306	Joey Votto
.305	Mike Trout
.304	Charlie Blackmon
.302	Buster Posey
.302	DJ LeMahieu
.301	Mookie Betts
.301	Daniel Murphy

2020–22*

.317	Freddie Freeman
.316	Trea Turner
.309	Tim Anderson
.308	Luis Arraez
.305	Paul Goldschmidt
.301	Xander Bogaerts
.298	Jeff McNeil
.297	Starling Marte
.296	Aaron Judge
.295	Bo Bichette

* Min. 1000 At-Bats.

Highest Batting Batting Average for a Rookie, Each League (Min. 100 Games)

American League	National League (Post-1900)
.408...............................Joe Jackson, Cle. Indians, 1911	.373.....................George Watkins, St.L. Cardinals, 1930
.350............................Taffy Wright, Was. Senators, 1938	.355.........................Lloyd Waner, Pit. Pirates, 1927
.350.............................Ichiro Suzuki, Sea. Mariners, 2001	.354..............................Kiki Cuyler, Pit. Pirates, 1924
.349............................Wade Boggs, Bos. Red Sox, 1982	.352...........................Hack Miller, Chi. Cubs, 1922
.343............................Dale Alexander, Det. Tigers, 1929	.350.........Cuckoo Christiansen, Cin. Reds, 1926
.343...............................Jeff Heath, Cle. Indians, 1938	.348...........................Carl Taylor, Pit. Pirates, 1969
.342.........................Patsy Dougherty, Bos. Red Sox, 1902	.343..........................Ralph Garr, Atl. Braves, 1971
.342.............................Earle Combs, N.Y. Yankees, 1925	.340............................Hal Morris, Cin. Reds, 1990
.337..............................Ike Boone, Bos. Red Sox, 1924	.339...................Lonnie Smith, Phi. Phillies, 1980
.337................................Al Bumbry, Bal. Orioles, 1973	.336...........................Paul Waner, Pit. Pirates, 1926
.334............................Socks Seybold, Phi. A's, 1901	.333...........Richie Ashburn, Phi. Phillies, 1948
.334...........................Heinie Manush, Det. Tigers, 1923	.330..........................Rico Carty, Mil. Braves, 1964
.334.......................Charlie Keller, N.Y. Yankees, 1939	.329.................Johnny Gooch, Pit. Pirates, 1922
.332...............................Earl Averill, Cle. Indians, 1929	.329......................Dick Cox, Brk. Dodgers, 1925
.331.................Hank Steinbacher, Chi. White Sox, 1938	.329...............Johnny Mize, St.L. Cardinals, 1936
.331.........................Mickey Cochrane, Phi. A's, 1925	.329............Albert Pujols, St.L. Cardinals, 2001
.331...................................Fred Lynn, Bos. Red Sox, 1975	.329..............................Norris Hopper, Cin. Reds, 2007

Lifetime Batting Averages of 20-Year Players (Not Including Pitchers)

.366.................Ty Cobb (24 years)	.297..........Ivan Rodriguez (21 years)	.279................Tony Perez (23 years)
.359.........Rogers Hornsby (23 years)	.296..............Albert Pujols (22 years)	.279...............Rusty Staub (23 years)
.345............Tris Speaker (22 years)	.296..............Ivan Rodriguez (21 years)	.279...........Andre Dawson (21 years)
.342................Babe Ruth (22 years)	.296..............Doc Cramer (20 years)	.279............Carlos Beltran (20 years)
.338.............Nap Lajoie (21 years)	.295.........Alex Rodriguez (22 years)	.278.......Deacon McGuire (26 years)
.338.............Tony Gwynn (20 years)	.295...........George Davis (20 years)	.277.............Harry Davis (22 years)
.334...............Cap Anson (22 years)	.294................Tim Raines (23 years)	.277...........Jason Giambi (20 years)
.334.............Al Simmons (20 years)	.294.........Frank Robinson (21 years)	.276.............Jim Thome (22 years)
.333...........Eddie Collins (25 years)	.293...........Phil Cavarretta (22 years)	.276.............Cal Ripken Jr. (21 years)
.333..............Paul Waner (20 years)	.292.........Gary Sheffield (22 years)	.273............Bob O'Farrell (21 years)
.331..............Stan Musial (22 years)	.292.............Lave Cross (21 years)	.273.........Sandy Alomar (20 years)
.328.........Honus Wagner (21 years)	.290.........Charlie Grimm (20 years)	.272.........Omar Vizquel (24 years)
.325.............Jimmie Foxx (20 years)	.289..........Harold Baines (22 years)	.272.............Bill Dahlen (22 years)
.322.................Sam Rice (20 years)	.289.............Bill Buckner (22 years)	.271..............Joe Morgan (22 years)
.312............Fred Clarke (21 years)	.288.........Rafael Palmeiro (20 years)	.271........Tim McCarver (21 years)
.310.............Luke Appling (20 years)	.287............Eddie Murray (21 years)	.270........Willie McCovey (22 years)
.310.............Derek Jeter (20 years)	.286...........Adrian Beltre (21 years)	.269..............Carlton Fisk (24 years)
.308.............Jake Beckley (20 years)	.286........Johnny Cooney (20 years)	.268.........Bobby Wallace (25 years)
.308.......Miguel Cabrera (20 years)	.286.........Mickey Vernon (20 years)	.267........Brooks Robinson (23 years)
.306.............Paul Molitor (21 years)	.286.............David Ortiz (20 years)	.267........Brian Downing (20 years)
.305...........Hank Aaron (23 years)	.285........Carl Yastrzemski (23 years)	.267.......Jay Johnstone (20 years)
.305............George Brett (21 years)	.285............Ted Simmons (21 years)	.266............Ron Fairly (21 years)
.304....................Mel Ott (22 years)	.285.............Max Carey (20 years)	.263.........Jack O'Connor (21 years)
.304........Manny Mota (20 years)	.285.........Alan Trammell (20 years)	.261.............Kid Gleason (22 years)
.303..................Pete Rose (24 years)	.285..............Robin Yount (20 years)	.259..............Luke Sewell (20 years)
.302.............Willie Mays (22 years)	.284..........Ken Griffey Jr. (22 years)	.258.......Rabbit Maranville (23 years)
.301............Joe Cronin (20 years)	.283.........Dave Winfield (22 years)	.256.......Harmon Killebrew (22 years)
.298...........Julio Franco (23 years)	.282.........Willie Stargell (21 years)	.255.............Gary Gaetti (20 years)
.298..........Barry Bonds (22 years)	.282............Elmer Valo (20 years)	.248............Graig Nettles (22 years)
.298...............Joe Judge (20 years)	.280.........Jimmy Dykes (22 years)	.248............Darrell Evans (21 years)
.297.................Al Kaline (22 years)	.279......Rickey Henderson (25 years)	.233...........Rick Dempsey (24 years)

Players Never Hitting Below .270 in Career (Min. 10 Years)

	Lifetime Batting Average	Lowest Batting Average	Seasons
Cap Anson (1876–97)	.334	.272 (1892)	27
Sam Rice (1915–34)	.322	.293 (1934)	20
Tony Gwynn (1982–2001)	.338	.289 (1982)	20
Rod Carew (1967–85)	.328	.273 (1968)	19
Vladimir Guerrero (1996–2011)	.318	.290 (2011)	16
George Sisler (1915–22, 1924–30)	.340	.285 (1915)	15
Joe Sewell (1920–33)	.312	.272 (1932)	14
Mickey Cochrane (1925–37)	.320	.270 (1936)	13
Bruce Campbell (1930–42)	.290	.275 (1941)	13
Bibb Falk (1920–31)	.314	.285 (1921)	12
Fats Fothergill (1922–33)	.325	.281 (1930)	12
Earle Combs (1924–35)	.325	.282 (1935)	12
Dom DiMaggio (1940–42, 1946–53)	.298	.283 (1941, 1947)	11
Homer Summa (1920, 1922–30)	.302	.272 (1929)	10

* Still active.

Players Batting .300 for 10 or More Consecutive Seasons From Start of Career

17 .... Willie Keeler (1892–1906)	11 .... Al Simmons (1924–34)
17 ....Stan Musial (1941–44, 1946–58)	10 .... Wade Boggs (1982–91)
15 ....Ted Williams (1939–42, 1946–51, 1954–58)	10 .... Ichiro Suzuki (2001–10)
12 ....Paul Waner (1926–37)	10 ....Albert Pujols (2001–10)

.400 Hitters and How Their Team Finished

American League

	Batting Average	Team's Wins–Losses	Place	Games Behind
Nap Lajoie, Phi. A's, 1901	.427	74–62	4	9.5
Ty Cobb, Det. Tigers, 1911	.420	89–65	2	13.5
Joe Jackson, Cle. Indians, 1911	.408	80–73	3	22.0
Ty Cobb, Det. Tigers, 1912	.409	69–84	6	36.5
George Sisler, St.L. Browns, 1920	.407	76–77	4	21.5
George Sisler, St.L. Browns, 1922	.420	93–61	2	1.0
Ty Cobb, Det. Tigers, 1922	.401	79–75	3	15.0
Harry Heilmann, Det. Tigers, 1923	.403	83–71	2	16.0
Ted Williams, Bos. Red Sox, 1941	.406	84–70	2	17.0

National League (Post-1900)

	Batting Average	Team's Wins–Losses	Place	Games Behind
Rogers Hornsby, St.L. Cardinals, 1922	.401	85–69	3	8.0
Rogers Hornsby, St.L. Cardinals, 1924	.424	65–89	6	28.5
Rogers Hornsby, St.L. Cardinals, 1925	.403	77–76	4	18.0
Bill Terry, N.Y. Giants, 1930	.401	87–67	3	5.0

.400 Hitters Versus League Batting Average (Post-1900)

	Batting Average	League Batting Average	Differential
Nap Lajoie, Phi. A's (AL), 1901	.426	.277	+.149
Ty Cobb, Det. Tigers (AL), 1911	.420	.273	+.147

continued on next page

	Batting Average	League Batting Average	Differential
Ty Cobb, Det. Tigers (AL), 1912	.409	.265	+.144
Rogers Hornsby, St.L. Cardinals (NL), 1924	.424	.283	+.141
Ted Williams, Bos. Red Sox (AL), 1941	.406	.266	+.140
George Sisler, St.L. Browns (AL), 1922	.420	.284	+.136
Joe Jackson, Cle. Indians (AL), 1911	.408	.273	+.135
George Sisler, St.L. Browns (AL), 1920	.407	.283	+.124
Harry Heilmann, Det. Tigers (AL), 1923	.403	.282	+.121
Ty Cobb, Det. Tigers (AL), 1922	.401	.284	+.117
Rogers Hornsby, St.L. Cardinals (NL), 1925	.403	.292	+.111
Rogers Hornsby, St.L. Cardinals (NL), 1922	.401	.292	+.109
Bill Terry, N.Y. Giants (NL), 1930	.401	.303	+.098

Players Hitting .370 Since Ted Williams's .406 Season (1941)

American League		National League	
Ted Williams, Bos. Red Sox, 1957	.388	Stan Musial, St.L. Cardinals, 1948	.376
Rod Carew, Min. Twins, 1977	.388	Tony Gwynn, S.D. Padres, 1987	.370
George Brett, K.C. Royals, 1980	.390	Andres Galarraga, Col. Rockies, 1993	.370
Nomar Garciaparra, Bos. Red Sox, 2000	.372	Tony Gwynn, S.D. Padres, 1994	.394
Ichiro Suzuki, Sea. Mariners, 2004	.372	Tony Gwynn, S.D. Padres, 1997	.372
		Larry Walker, Col. Rockies, 1999	.379
		Todd Helton, Col. Rockies, 2000	.372
		Barry Bonds, S.F. Giants, 2002	.370

Players Hitting .300 in Rookie *and* Final Seasons (Post-1900; Min. Five Years)

First Year			Final Year	
Richie Ashburn	Phi. Phillies (NL), 1948	.333	N.Y. Mets (NL), 1962	.306
Wade Boggs	Bos. Red Sox (AL), 1982	.349	T.B. Devil Rays (AL), 1999	.301
Tony Cuccinello	Cin. Reds (NL), 1930	.312	Chi. White Sox (AL), 1945	.308
Fats Fothergill	Det. Tigers (AL), 1923	.315	Bos. Red Sox (AL), 1933	.344
Joe Jackson	Cle. Indians (AL), 1911	.408	Chi. White Sox (AL), 1920	.382
Del Pratt	St.L. Browns (AL), 1912	.302	Det. Tigers (AL), 1924	.303
Ted Williams	Bos. Red Sox (AL), 1939	.327	Bos. Red Sox (AL), 1960	.316
Buster Posey	S.F. Giants (NL), 2010	.305	S.F. Giants (NL), 2021	.304

Players Hitting .300 in Their Only Major League Season (Post-1900; Min. 100 Games, 300 At-Bats)

Irv Waldron, Mil. Brewers–Was. Senators (AL), 1901	.311
Tex Vache, Bos. Red Sox (AL), 1925	.313
Buzz Arlett, Phi. Phillies (NL), 1931	.313

Players Batting .350 with 50 Home Runs

American League	Batting Average	Home Runs	National League	Batting Average	Home Runs
Babe Ruth, N.Y. Yankees, 1920	.356	54	Hack Wilson, Chi. Cubs, 1930	.356	56
Babe Ruth, N.Y. Yankees, 1921	.378	59			
Babe Ruth, N.Y. Yankees, 1927	.356	60			
Jimmie Foxx, Phi. A's, 1932	.364	58			
Mickey Mantle, N.Y. Yankees, 1956	.353	52			

Players 40 or Older* Hitting .300 (Min. 50 Games)

American League

	Age	Batting Average
Ty Cobb, Phi. A's, 1927	40	.357
Sam Rice, Was. Senators, 1930	40	.349
Paul Molitor, Min. Twins, 1996	40	.341
Eddie Collins, Phi. A's, 1927	40	.338
Ted Williams, Bos. Red Sox, 1958	40	.328
Ty Cobb, Phi. A's, 1928	41	.323
Sam Rice, Was. Senators, 1932	42	.323
Bert Campaneris, N.Y. Yankees, 1983	41	.322
Ted Williams, Bos. Red Sox, 1960	41	.316
Rickey Henderson, N.Y. Yankees, 1999	42	.315
David Ortiz, Bos. Red Sox, 2016	40	.315
Luke Appling, Chi. White Sox, 1948	41	.314
Harold Baines, Bal. Orioles–Cle. Indians	40	.312
Sam Rice, Was. Senators, 1931	41	.310
Birdie Tebbetts, Bos. Red Sox, 1950	40	.310
Luke Appling, Chi. White Sox, 1947	40	.306
Paul Molitor, Min. Twins, 1997	41	.305
Bing Miller, Bos. Red Sox, 1935	41	.304
Enos Slaughter, N.Y. Yankees, 1958	42	.304
Nelson Cruz, Min. Twins, 2020	40	.303
Luke Appling, Chi. White Sox, 1949	42	.301
Wade Boggs, T.B. Devil Rays, 1999	40	.301

* As of September of that year.

National League

	Age	Batting Average
Cap Anson, Chi. Colts, 1894	43	.388
Barry Bonds, S.F. Giants, 2004	40	.362
Moises Alou, N.Y. Mets 2007	40	.341
Cap Anson, Chi. Colts, 1895	44	.335
Cap Anson, Chi. Colts, 1896	45	.331
Stan Musial, St.L. Cardinals, 1962	41	.330
Tony Perez, Cin. Reds, 1985	43	.328
Jack Saltzgaver, Pit. Pirates, 1945	40	.325
Pete Rose, Phi. Phillies, 1984	40	.325
Tony Gwynn, S.D. Padres, 2001	41	.324
Johnny Cooney, Bos. Braves, 1941	40	.319
Rickey Henderson, N.Y. Mets, 1999	40	.315
Cap Anson, Chi. Colts, 1893	42	.314
Al Nixon, Phi. Phillies, 1927	41	.312
Paul Waner, Brk. Dodgers, 1943	40	.311
Julio Franco, Atl. Braves, 2004	46	.309
Jim O'Rourke, N.Y. Giants, 1892	40	.304
Andres Galarraga, S.F. Giants, 2003	42	.301
Gabby Hartnett, N.Y. Giants, 1941	40	.300

Players Hitting .325 for Two or More Different Clubs (Post-1945)

Player	Club	Year	Average
Roberto Alomar	Tor. Blue Jays (AL)	1993	.326
	Bal. Orioles (AL)	1996	.328
		1997	.333
	Cle. Indians (AL)	2001	.336
Moises Alou	Mon. Expos (NL)	1994	.339
	Hou. Astros (NL)	2000	.355
		2001	.331
Albert Belle	Cle. Indians (AL)	1994	.357
	Chi. White Sox (AL)	1998	.328
Wade Boggs	Bos. Red Sox (AL)	1982	.349
		1983	.361
		1984	.325
		1985	.368
		1986	.357
		1987	.363
		1988	.366
		1989	.330
		1991	.332
	N.Y. Yankees (AL)	1994	.342
Smoky Burgess	Phi. Phillies (NL)	1954	.368
	Pit. Pirates (NL)	1962	.328
Ellis Burks	Col. Rockies (NL)	1996	.344
	S.F. Giants (NL)	2000	.344
Miguel Cabrera	Fla. Marlins (NL)	2006	.339
	Det. Tigers (AL)	2010	.328
		2011	.344
		2012	.330

continued on next page

		2013	.348
		2015	.338
Rod Carew	Min. Twins (AL)	1969	.332
		1970	.366
		1973	.350
		1974	.364
		1975	.359
		1976	.331
		1977	.388
		1978	.333
	Cal. Angels (AL)	1980	.331
		1983	.339
Will Clark	S.F. Giants (NL)	1989	.333
	Tex. Rangers (AL)	1994	.329
		1997	.326
Jeff Cirillo	Mil. Brewers (NL)	1996	.325
		1999	.326
	Col. Rockies (NL)	2000	.326
Juan Gonzalez	Tex. Rangers (AL)	1999	.326
	Cle. Indians (AL)	2001	.325
Vladimir Guerrero	Mon. Expos (NL)	2000	.345
		2002	.336
		2003	.330
	Ana.–L.A. Angels (AL)	2004	.337
		2006	.329
Johnny Hopp	Bos. Braves (NL)	1946	.333
	N.Y. Yankees (AL)–Pit. Pirates (NL)	1950	.339
Carney Lansford	Bos. Red Sox (AL)	1981	.336
	Oak. A's (AL)	1989	.336
DJ LeMahieu	Col. Rockies (NL)	2016	.348
	N.Y. Yankees (AL)	2019	.327
		2020	.364
Kenny Lofton	Cle. Indians (AL)	1993	.325
		1994	.349
	Atl. Braves (NL)	1997	.333
	Phi. Phillies (NL)	2005	.335
Bill Madlock	Chi. Cubs (NL)	1975	.354
		1976	.339
	Pit. Pirates (NL)	1981	.341
Paul Molitor	Mil. Brewers (AL)	1987	.353
	Tor. Blue Jays (AL)	1993	.332
		1994	.341
	Min. Twins (AL)	1996	.341
John Olerud	Tor. Blue Jays (AL)	1993	.363
	N.Y. Mets (NL)	1998	.354
Mike Piazza	L.A. Dodgers (NL)	1995	.346
		1996	.336
		1997	.362
	L.A. Dodgers (NL)–Fla. Marlins (NL)–N.Y. Mets (NL)	1998	.328
Juan Pierre	Col. Rockies (NL)	2001	.327
	Fla. Marlins (NL)	2004	.326
Hanley Ramirez	Fla. Marlins (NL)	2007	.332
		2009	.342
	L.A. Dodgers (NL)	2013	.345
Manny Ramirez	Cle. Indians (AL)	1997	.328
		1999	.333
		2000	.351
	Bos. Red Sox (AL)	2002	.349
		2003	.325
	Bos. Red Sox (AL)–L.A. Dodgers (NL)	2008	.332
Edgar Renteria	St.L. Cardinals (NL)	2003	.330
	Atl. Braves (NL)	2007	.332
Mickey Rivers	N.Y. Yankees (AL)	1977	.326
	Tex. Rangers (AL)	1980	.333
Ivan Rodriguez	Tex. Rangers (AL)	1999	.332

continued on next page

		2000	.347
Det. Tigers (AL)		2004	.334
Pete Rose	Cin. Reds (NL)	1968	.335
		1969	.348
		1973	.338
	Phi. Phillies (NL)	1979	.331
		1981	.325
Gary Sheffield	S.D. Padres (NL)	1992	.330
	L.A. Dodgers (NL)	2000	.325
	Atl. Braves (NL)	2003	.330
Al Zarilla	St.L. Browns (AL)	1948	.329
	Bos. Red Sox (AL)	1950	.325

Batting Title

Closest Batting Races

American League

Spread	Season		Batting Average
.0001	1945	Snuffy Stirnweiss, N.Y. Yankees	.3085
		Tony Cuccinello, Chi. White Sox	.3084
.0001	1949	George Kell, Det. Tigers	.3429
		Ted Williams, Bos. Red Sox	.3428
.0004	1970	Alex Johnson, Cal. Angels	.3290
		Carl Yastrzemski, Bos. Red Sox	.3286
.0006	1935	Buddy Myer, Was. Senators	.3490
		Joe Vosmik, Cle. Indians	.3484
.0009	1982	Willie Wilson, K.C. Royals	.3316
		Robin Yount, Mil. Brewers	.3307
.0010	1910	Ty Cobb, Det. Tigers	.3851
		Nap Lajoie, Cle. Indians	.3841
.0012	1976	George Brett, K.C. Royals	.3333
		Hal McRae, K.C. Royals	.3321
.0012	2003	Bill Mueller, Bos. Red Sox	.3263
		Manny Ramirez, Bos. Red Sox	.3251
.0016	1953	Mickey Vernon, Was. Senators	.3372
		Al Rosen, Cle. Indians	.3356
.0017	1928	Goose Goslin, Was. Senators	.3794
		Heinie Manush, St.L. Browns	.3777
.0022	1930	Al Simmons, Phi. A's	.3809
		Lou Gehrig, N.Y. Yankees	.3787
.0022	2008	Joe Mauer, Min. Twins	.3284
		Dustin Pedroia, Bos. Red Sox	.3262

National League (Post-1900)

Spread	Season		Batting Average
.0002	2003	Albert Pujols, St.L. Cardinals	.3587
		Todd Helton, Col. Rockies	.3585
.0003	1931	Chick Hafey, St.L. Cardinals	.3489
		Bill Terry, N.Y. Giants	.3486
.0006	2019	Christian Yelich, Mil. Brewers	.3292
		Ketel Marte, Ari. D'backs	.3286

continued on next page

Spread	Season		Batting Average
.0011	1991	Terry Pendleton, Atl. Braves	.3191
		Hal Morris, Cin. Reds	.3180
.0013	1911	Honus Wagner, Pit. Pirates	.3340
		Doc Miller, Bos. Rustlers	.3327
.0013	2016	DJ LeMahieu, Col. Rockies	.3478
		Daniel Murphy, Was. Nationals	.3465
.0013	2022	Jeff McNeil, N.Y. Mets	.3265
		Freddie Freeman, L.A. Dodgers	.3252
.0016	1918	Zack Wheat, Brk. Dodgers	.3349
		Edd Roush, Cin. Reds	.3333
.0022	1976	Bill Madlock, Chi. Cubs	.3385
		Ken Griffey Sr., Cin. Reds	.3363

Teammates Finishing One-Two in Batting Race

American League

Season	Team	Leader	Batting Average	Runner-Up	Batting Average
1907	Det. Tigers	Ty Cobb	.350	Sam Crawford	.323
1908	Det. Tigers	Ty Cobb	.324	Sam Crawford	.311
1919	Det. Tigers	Ty Cobb	.384	Bobby Veach	.355
1921	Det. Tigers	Harry Heilmann	.394	Ty Cobb	.389
1942	Bos. Red Sox	Ted Williams	.356	Johnny Pesky	.331
1958	Bos. Red Sox	Ted Williams	.388	Pete Runnels	.322
1959	Det. Tigers	Harvey Kuenn	.353	Al Kaline	.327
1961	Det. Tigers	Norm Cash	.361	Al Kaline	.324
1976	K.C. Royals	George Brett	.333	Hal McRae	.332
1977	Min. Twins	Rod Carew	.388	Lyman Bostock	.336
1984	N.Y. Yankees	Don Mattingly	.343	Dave Winfield	.340
1993	Tor. Blue Jays	John Olerud	.363	Paul Molitor	.332
2003	Bos. Red Sox	Bill Mueller	.326	Manny Ramirez	.325
2018	Bos. Red Sox	Mookie Betts	.346	J.D. Martinez	.330
2021	Hou. Astros	Yuli Gurriel	.319	Michael Brantley	.311

National League (Post-1900)

Season	Team	Leader	Batting Average	Runner-Up	Batting Average
1903	Pit. Pirates	Honus Wagner	.355	Fred Clarke	.351
1923	St.L. Cardinals	Rogers Hornsby	.384	Jim Bottomley	.371
1925	St.L. Cardinals	Rogers Hornsby	.403	Jim Bottomley	.367
1926	Cin. Reds	Bubbles Hargrave	.353	Cuckoo Christenson	.350
1933	Phi. Phillies	Chuck Klein	.368	Spud Davis	.349
1937	St.L. Cardinals	Joe Medwick	.374	Johnny Mize	.364
1954	N.Y. Giants	Willie Mays	.354	Don Mueller	.342
2014	Pit. Pirates	Josh Harrison	.315	Andrew McCutchen	.313

Switch-Hitting Batting Champions

American League

Mickey Mantle, N.Y. Yankees, 1956	.353	Bernie Williams, N.Y. Yankees, 1998	.339
Willie Wilson, K.C. Royals, 1982	.332	Bill Mueller, Bos. Red Sox, 2003	.326

National League (Post-1900)

Pete Rose, Cin. Reds, 1968	.335	Willie McGee*, St.L. Cardinals, 1990	.335
Pete Rose, Cin. Reds, 1969	.348	Terry Pendleton, Atl. Braves, 1991	.319
Pete Rose, Cin. Reds, 1973	.338	Chipper Jones, Atl. Braves, 2008	.364
Willie McGee, St.L. Cardinals, 1985	.353	Jose Reyes, N.Y. Mets, 2011	.337
Tim Raines, Mon. Expos, 1986	.334	* Also with Oak. A's (AL).	

Catchers Winning Batting Titles

Bubbles Hargrave, Cin. Reds (NL), 1926 .... .353 (326 at bats, 115 hits)
Ernie Lombardi, Cin. Reds (NL), 1938 .... .342 (489 at bats, 167 hits)
Ernie Lombardi, Bos. Braves (NL), 1942 .... .330 (309 at bats, 102 hits)
Joe Mauer, Min. Twins (AL), 2006 .... .347 (521 at bats, 181 hits)
Joe Mauer, Min. Twins (AL), 2008 .... .328 (536 at bats, 176 hits)
Joe Mauer, Min. Twins (AL), 2009 .... .365 (523 at bats, 191 hits)
Buster Posey, S.F. Giants (NL), 2012 .... .336 (530 at bats, 178 hits)

Batting Champions on Last-Place Teams

American League	National League (Post-1900)
Dale Alexander*, Bos. Red Sox, 1932 .... .367	Larry Doyle, N.Y. Giants, 1915 .... .320
Edgar Martinez, Sea. Mariners, 1992 .... .343	Richie Ashburn, Phi. Phillies, 1958 .... .350
Ichiro Suzuki, Sea. Mariners, 2004 .... .373	Tony Gwynn, S.D. Padres, 1987 .... .370
	Willie McGee**, St.L. Cardinals, 1990 .... .335
	Tony Gwynn, S.D. Padres, 1994 .... .394
	Tony Gwynn, S.D. Padres, 1997 .... .372
	Larry Walker, Col. Rockies, 1999 .... .379
	Larry Walker, Col. Rockies, 2001 .... .350
* Also with Det. Tigers (AL)	Michael Cuddyer, Col. Rockies, 2013 .... .331
** Also with Oak. A's (AL)	Juan Soto, Was. Nationals, 2020 .... .351

Batting Title Winners Without a Home Run

Ginger Beaumont, Pit. Pirates (NL), 1902 .... .357
Zack Wheat, Brk. Dodgers (NL), 1918 .... .335
Rod Carew, Min. Twins (AL), 1972 .... .318

Batting Champions Driving in Fewer Than 40 Runs

	Batting Average	RBIs
Richie Ashburn, Phi. Phillies (NL), 1958	.350	33
Pete Runnels, Bos. Red Sox (AL), 1960	.320	35
Matty Alou, Pit. Pirates (NL), 1966	.342	27
DJ LeMahieu, N.Y. Yankees (AL), 2020*	.364	27
Juan Soto, Was. Nationals (NL), 2020*	.351	37
Luis Arraez, Min. Twins (AL), 2022	.315	49

* Covid-shortened season.

Batting Champions with 100 Strikeouts in Year They Led League

Roberto Clemente, Pit. Pirates (NL), 1967	.357	103 strikeouts
Dave Parker, Pit. Pirates (NL), 1977	.338	107 strikeouts
Alex Rodriguez, Sea. Mariners (AL), 1996	.358	104 strikeouts
Larry Walker, Col. Rockies (NL), 2001	.350	103 strikeouts
Derrek Lee, Chi. Cubs (NL), 2005	.335	109 strikeouts
Matt Holliday, Col. Rockies (NL), 2007	.340	126 strikeouts
Hanley Ramirez, Fla. Marlins (NL), 2009	.342	101 strikeouts
Carlos Gonzalez, Col. Rockies (NL), 2010	.336	135 strikeouts
Michael Cuddyer, Col. Rockies (NL), 2013	.331	100 strikeouts
Charlie Blackmon, Col. Rockies (NL), 2017	.331	135 strikeouts
Christian Yelich, Mil. Brewers (NL), 2018	.326	135 strikeouts
Christian Yelich, Mil. Brewers (NL), 2019	.329	118 strikeouts
Tim Anderson, Chi. White Sox (AL), 2019	.335	109 strikeouts
Trea Turner, Was. Nationals–L.A. Dodgers (NL), 2021	.328	110 strikeouts

Lowest Batting Averages to Lead League

American League		National League (Post-1900)	
.301	Carl Yastrzemski, Bos. Red Sox, 1968	.313	Tony Gwynn, S.D. Padres, 1988
.308	Elmer Flick, Cle. Indians, 1905	.319	Terry Pendleton, Atl. Braves, 1991
.309	Snuffy Stirnweiss, N.Y. Yankees, 1945	.319	Justin Morneau, Col. Rockies, 2014
.315	Luis Arraez, Min. Twins, 2022	.320	Larry Doyle, N.Y. Giants, 1915
.316	Frank Robinson, Bal. Orioles, 1966	.321	Edd Roush, Cin. Reds, 1919
.318	Rod Carew, Min. Twins, 1972	.323	Bill Madlock, Pit. Pirates, 1983
.319	Yuli Gurriel, Hou. Astros, 2021	.324	Bill Buckner, Chi. Cubs, 1980
.320	Pete Runnels, Bos. Red Sox, 1960	.325	Dick Groat, Pit. Pirates, 1960
.321	Carl Yastrzemski, Bos. Red Sox, 1963	.326	Tommy Davis, L.A. Dodgers, 1962
.321	Tony Oliva, Min. Twins, 1965	.326	Christian Yelich, Mil. Brewers, 2018
.323	Tony Oliva, Min. Twins, 1964	.326	Jeff McNeil, N.Y. Mets, 2022
.324	Ty Cobb, Det. Tigers, 1908	.328	Hank Aaron, Mil. Braves, 1956
.326	Pete Runnels, Bos. Red Sox, 1962	.328	Trea Turner, Was. Nationals–L.A. Dodgers, 2021
.326	Carl Yastrzemski, Bos. Red Sox, 1967	.329	Jake Daubert, Brk. Dodgers 1914
.326	Bill Mueller, Bos. Red Sox, 2003	.329	Roberto Clemente, Pit. Pirates, 1965
.327	Lou Boudreau, Cle. Indians, 1944	.329	Christian Yelich, Mil. Brewers, 2019
.327	Ferris Fain, Phi. A's, 1952	.330	Ernie Lombardi, Bos. Braves, 1942
		.330	Gary Sheffield, S.D. Padres, 1992

Highest Batting Average *Not* to Win Batting Title

American League

Batting Average	Season		Winner
.408	1911	Joe Jackson	Ty Cobb (.420)
.401	1922	Ty Cobb	George Sisler (.420)
.395	1912	Joe Jackson	Ty Cobb (.409)
.393	1923	Babe Ruth	Harry Heilmann (.403)
.392	1927	Al Simmons	Harry Heilmann (.398)
.389	1921	Ty Cobb	Harry Heilmann (.394)
.389	1925	Tris Speaker	Harry Heilmann (.393)
.388	1920	Tris Speaker	George Sisler (.407)
.387	1925	Al Simmons	Harry Heilmann (.393)
.383	1910	Ty Cobb	Nap Lajoie (.384)
.383	1912	Tris Speaker	Nap Lajoie (.384)
.382	1920	Joe Jackson	George Sisler (.407)
.379	1930	Lou Gehrig	Al Simmons (.381)
.378	1911	Sam Crawford	Ty Cobb (.420)
.378	1921	Babe Ruth	Harry Heilmann (.394)
.378	1922	Tris Speaker	George Sisler (.425)
.378	1925	Ty Cobb	Harry Heilmann (.393)
.378	1928	Heinie Manush	Goose Goslin (.379)
.378	1936	Earl Averill	Luke Appling (.388)
.376	1902	Ed Delahanty	Nap Lajoie (.378)
.376	1920	Babe Ruth	George Sisler (.407)

National League (Post-1900)

Batting Average	Season		Winner
.393	1930	Babe Herman	Billy Terry (.401)
.386	1930	Chuck Klein	Billy Terry (.401)
.383	1930	Lefty O'Doul	Billy Terry (.401)
.381	1929	Babe Herman	Lefty O'Doul (.398)

continued on next page

Batting Average	Season		Winner
.380	1929	Rogers Hornsby	Lefty O'Doul (.398)
.379	1930	Fred Lindstrom	Bill Terry (.401)
.375	1924	Zack Wheat	Rogers Hornsby (.424)
.373	1930	George Watkins	Bill Terry (.401)
.372	1929	Bill Terry	Lefty O'Doul (.398)
.371	1923	Jim Bottomley	Rogers Hornsby (.384)
.370	1928	Paul Waner	Rogers Hornsby (.387)
.368	1930	Paul Waner	Bill Terry (.401)
.368	1994	Jeff Bagwell	Tony Gwynn (.394)
.367	1900	Elmer Flick	Honus Wagner (.381)
.367	1925	Jim Bottomley	Rogers Hornsby (.403)
.367	1936	Babe Phelps	Paul Waner (.373)
.366	1930	Pie Traynor	Bill Terry (.401)

Runners-Up for Batting Titles in Both Leagues

American League

Mike Donlin	Bal. Orioles, 1901	.341
Willie Keeler	N.Y. Yankees, 1904	.343
	N.Y. Yankees, 1905	.302
Al Oliver	Tex. Rangers, 1978	.324
Frank Robinson	Bal. Orioles, 1967	.311
Miguel Cabrera	Det. Tigers, 2010	.328

National League

Cin. Reds, 1903	.351
Cin. Reds–N.Y. Giants, 1904	.329
N.Y. Giants, 1908	.334
Brk. Dodgers, 1901	.355
Brk. Dodgers, 1902	.338
Pit. Pirates, 1974	.321
Cin. Reds, 1962	.342
Fla. Marlins, 2006	.339

Players Winning Batting Title in Season *After* Joining New Club

American League

Nap Lajoie (.426), Phi. A's, 1901	Jumped from Phi. Phillies (NL)
Ed Delahanty (.376), Was. Senators, 1902	Jumped from Phi. Phillies (NL)
Tris Speaker (.386), Cle. Indians, 1916	Traded from Bos. Red Sox
Frank Robinson (.316), Bal. Orioles, 1966	Traded from Cin. Reds (NL)
Alex Johnson (.329), Cal. Angels, 1970	Traded from Cin. Reds (NL)
Carney Lansford (.336), Bos. Red Sox, 1981	Traded from Cal. Angels
Bill Mueller (.326), Bos. Red Sox, 2003	Free agent

National League (Post-1900)

Hal Chase (.339), Cin. Reds, 1916	Jumped from Federal League
Rogers Hornsby (.387), Bos. Braves, 1928	Traded from N.Y. Giants
Lefty O'Doul (.398), Phi. Phillies, 1929	Traded from N.Y. Giants
Debs Garms (.355), Pit. Pirates, 1940	Traded from Bos. Braves
Ernie Lombardi (.330), Bos. Braves, 1942	Traded from Cin. Reds
Matty Alou (.342), Pit. Pirates, 1966	Traded from S.F. Giants
Al Oliver (.331), Mon. Expos, 1982	Traded from Tex. Rangers (AL)
Terry Pendleton (.319), Atl. Braves, 1991	Traded from St.L. Cardinals
Gary Sheffield (.330), S.D. Padres, 1992	Traded from Mil. Brewers (AL)
Andres Galarraga (.370), Col. Rockies, 1993	Free agent
Justin Morneau (.331), Col. Rockies, 2014	Free agent
Dee Strange-Gordon (.333), Mia. Marlins, 2015	Traded from L.A. Dodgers
Christian Yelich (.323), Mil. Brewers, 2018	Traded from Mia. Marlins

Players Changing Team in Season *After* Winning Batting Title

American League

Nap Lajoie (.426), Phi. A's, 1901 .... Sold to Cle. Indians, Jun. 1902

Ferris Fain (.327), Phi. A's, 1952 .... Traded to Chi. White Sox, Jan. 1953

Harvey Kuenn (.353), Det. Tigers, 1959 .... Traded to Cle. Indians in off-season for Rocky Colavito

Pete Runnels (.326), Bos. Red Sox, 1962 .... Traded to Hou. Astros in off-season for Roman Mejias

Rod Carew (.333), Min. Twins, 1978 .... Traded to Cal. Angels in off-season for Ken Landreaux and 3 other players

National League (Post-1900)

Chick Hafey (.349), St.L. Cardinals, 1931 .... Traded to Cin. Reds, Apr. 1932

Chuck Klein (.368), Phi. Phillies, 1933 .... Traded to Chi. Cubs in off-season for 3 players and $65,000

Bill Madlock (.339), Chi. Cubs, 1976 .... Traded to S.F. Giants in off-season for Bobby Murcer and 2 other players

Willie McGee (.335), St.L. Cardinals, 1990 .... Traded to Oak. A's (AL), end-of-season, 1990

Gary Sheffield (.330), S.D. Padres, 1992 .... Traded to Fla. Marlins, midseason, 1993

Jose Reyes (.337), N.Y. Mets, 2011 .... Signed as a free agent in off-season with Mia. Marlins

Largest Margin Between Batting Champion and Runner-Up

American League

Margin	Season	Winner	Batting Average	Runner-Up	Batting Average
+.086	1901	Nap Lajoie, Phi. A's	.426	Mike Donlin, Bal. Orioles	.340
+.052	1977	Rod Carew, Min. Twins	.388	Lyman Bostock, Min. Twins	.336
+.052	2020	DJ LeMahieu, N.Y. Yankees	.364	Tim Anderson, Chi. White Sox	.322
+.048	1974	Rod Carew, Min. Twins	.364	Jorge Orta, Chi. White Sox	.316
+.047	1941	Ted Williams, Bos. Red Sox	.406	Cecil Travis, Was. Senators	.359
+.044	1973	Rod Carew, Min. Twins	.350	George Scott, Mil. Brewers	.306
+.038	1904	Nap Lajoie, Cle. Indians	.381	Willie Keeler, N.Y. Yankees	.343
+.038	1980	George Brett, K.C. Royals	.390	Cecil Cooper, Mil. Brewers	.352
+.037	1915	Ty Cobb, Det. Tigers	.369	Eddie Collins, Chi. White Sox	.332
+.037	1961	Norm Cash, Det. Tigers	.361	Al Kaline, Det. Tigers	.324
+.033	1904	Nap Lajoie, Cle. Indians	.376	Willie Keeler, N.Y. Yankees	.343
+.033	1985	Wade Boggs, Bos. Red Sox	.368	George Brett, K.C. Royals	.335
+.032	2004	Ichiro Suzuki, Sea. Mariners	.372	Melvin Mora, Bal. Orioles	.340
+.031	2010	Josh Hamilton, Tex. Rangers	.359	Miguel Cabrera, Det. Tigers	.328
+.031	1993	John Olerud, Tor. Blue Jays	.363	Paul Molitor, Tor. Blue Jays	.332
+.030	1909	Ty Cobb, Det. Tigers	.377	Eddie Collins, Phi. A's	.347
+.030	1917	Ty Cobb, Det. Tigers	.383	George Sisler, St.L. Browns	.353
+.030	1918	Ty Cobb, Det. Tigers	.382	George Burns, Phi. A's	.352

National League (Post-1900)

Margin	Season	Winner	Batting Average	Runner-Up	Batting Average
+.049	1924	Rogers Hornsby, St.L. Cardinals	.424	Zack Wheat, Brk. Dodgers	.375
+.047	1922	Rogers Hornsby, St.L. Cardinals	.401	Ray Grimes, Chi. Cubs	.354
+.046	1947	Harry Walker, St.L. Cardinals– Phi. Phillies	.363	Bob Elliott, Bos. Braves	.317
+.045	1921	Rogers Hornsby, St.L. Cardinals	.397	Edd Roush, Cin. Reds	.352
+.043	1948	Stan Musial, St.L. Cardinals	.376	Richie Ashburn, Phi. Phillies	.333
+.043	1999	Larry Walker, Col. Rockies	.379	Luis Gonzalez, Ari. D'backs	.336

continued on next page

Margin	Season	Winner	Batting Average	Runner-Up	Batting Average
+.041	1970	Rico Carty, Atl. Braves	.366	Joe Torre, St.L. Cardinals	.325
+.036	1925	Rogers Hornsby, St.L. Cardinals	.403	Jim Bottomley, St.L. Cardinals	.367
+.036	1940	Debs Garms, Pit. Pirates	.355	Ernie Lombardi, Cin. Reds	.319
+.033	1985	Willie McGee, St.L. Cardinals	.353	Pedro Guerrero, L.A. Dodgers	.320
+.032	1935	Arky Vaughan, Pit. Pirates	.385	Joe Medwick, St.L. Cardinals	.353
+.032	1946	Stan Musial, St.L. Cardinals	.365	Tommy Holmes, Bos. Braves	.333
+.032	1974	Ralph Garr, Atl. Braves	.353	Al Oliver, Pit. Pirates	.321
+.032	1987	Tony Gwynn, S.D. Padres	.370	Pedro Guerrero, L.A. Dodgers	.338
+.032	2002	Barry Bonds, S.F. Giants	.370	Larry Walker, Col. Rockies	.338

Champions Whose Next Season's Batting Average Declined the Most

American League

	Season (Batting Average)	Change
Norm Cash, Det. Tigers	1961 (.361), 1962 (.243)	–.118
George Sisler, St.L. Browns*	1922 (.420), 1924 (.305)	–.115
Julio Franco, Tex. Rangers	1991 (.341), 1992 (.234)	–.107
Goose Goslin, Was. Senators	1928 (.379), 1929 (.288)	–.091
Lew Fonseca, Cle. Indians	1929 (.369), 1930 (.279)	–.090
Babe Ruth, N.Y. Yankees	1924 (.378), 1925 (.290)	–.088
Mickey Vernon, Was. Senators	1946 (.353), 1947 (.265)	–.088
Dale Alexander, Det. Tigers–Bos. Red Sox	1932 (.367), 1933 (.281)	–.086

National League (Post-1900)

	Season (Batting Average)	Change
Chipper Jones, Atl. Braves	2008 (.364), 2009 (.264)	–.100
Willie McGee, St.L. Cardinals	1985 (.353), 1986 (.256)	–.097
Cy Seymour, Cin. Reds (N.Y. Giants)	1905 (.377), 1906 (.286)	–.091
Debs Garms, Pit. Pirates	1940 (.355), 1941 (.264)	–.091
Rico Carty, Atl. Braves*	1970 (.366), 1972 (.277)	–.089
Rogers Hornsby, St.L. Cardinals	1925 (.403), 1926 (.317)	–.086
Richie Ashburn, Phi. Phillies	1958 (.350), 1959 (.266)	–.084
Lefty O'Doul, Brk. Dodgers (N.Y. Giants)	1932 (.368), 1933 (.284)	–.084

* Missed season after winning batting championship.

Lowest Lifetime Batting Averages for Players Who Led League

.268	Snuffy Stirnweiss (1943–52)	Led AL with .309 in 1945
.270	Terry Pendleton (1984–98)	Led NL with .319 in 1991
.271	Norm Cash (1958–74)	Led AL with .361 in 1961
.277	Michael Cuddyer (2001–15)	Led NL with .331 in 2013
.281	Bobby Avila (1949–59)	Led AL with .341 in 1954
.281	Derrek Lee (1997–2011)	Led NL with .335 in 2005
.281	Justin Morneau (2003–16)	Led NL with .319 in 2014
.283	Jose Reyes (2003–18)	Led NL with .337 in 2011
.284	Fred Lynn (1974–89)	Led AL with .333 in 1979
.284	Yuli Gurriel (2016–)	Led AL with .319 in 2021
.285	Carl Yastrzemski (1961–83)	Led AL with .321 in 1963

continued on next page

.285...........Carlos Gonzalez (2008–19) ....Led NL with .336 in 2010
.286...........Mickey Vernon (1939–43, 1946–60)...Led AL with .353 in 1946
Led AL with .337 in 1953
.286...........Dick Groat (1952, 1955–67)...Led NL with .325 in 1960
Led AL with .326 in 1967
Led AL with .301 in 1968
.286...........Dee Strange-Gordon (2011–)...Led NL with .333 in 2015
.287...........Christian Yelich (2013–) ....Led NL with .326 in 2018
Led NL with .329 in 2019
.288...........Alex Johnson (1964–76) ....Led AL with .329 in 1970
.288...........Paul O'Neill (1985–2001)..Led AL with .359 in 1994
.288...........Tim Anderson (2016–)...Led AL with .335 in 2019
.289...........Bill Buckner (1969–90) ....Led NL with .324 in 1980

Two-Time Batting Champions with Lifetime Batting Averages Below .300

Barry Bonds (1986–2007)......................................	.298	Won NL batting titles in 2002 and 2004
Willie McGee (1982–99)......................................	.295	Won NL batting titles in 1985 and 1990
Tommy Davis (1959–76)	.294	Won NL batting titles in 1962 and 1963
Ferris Fain (1947–55)...	.290	Won AL batting titles in 1951 and 1952
Dave Parker (1973–91)	.290	Won NL batting titles in 1977 and 1978
Pete Runnels (1951–64)	.291	Won AL batting titles in 1960 and 1962
Mickey Vernon (1939–43, 1946–60)......................	.286	Won AL batting titles in 1946 and 1953
Carl Yastrzemski (1961–83).................................	.285	Won AL batting titles in 1963, 1967, and 1968
Christian Yelich (2013–)......................................	.287	Won NL batting titles in 2018 and 2019

Years in Which Right-Handed Batters Won Batting Titles in Both Leagues

Season	American League	National League
1903	Nap Lajoie, Cle. Indians	Honus Wagner, Pit. Pirates
1904	Nap Lajoie, Cle. Indians	Honus Wagner, Pit. Pirates
1921	Harry Heilmann, Det. Tigers.............................	Rogers Hornsby, St.L. Cardinals
1923	Harry Heilmann, Det. Tigers.............................	Rogers Hornsby, St.L. Cardinals
1925	Harry Heilmann, Det. Tigers.............................	Rogers Hornsby, St.L. Cardinals
1931	Al Simmons, Phi. A's	Chick Hafey, St.L. Cardinals
1938	Jimmie Foxx, Bos. Red Sox..............................	Ernie Lombardi, Cin. Reds
1949	George Kell, Det. Tigers	Jackie Robinson, Brk. Dodgers
1954	Bobby Avila, Cle. Indians	Willie Mays, N.Y. Yankees
1959	Harvey Kuenn, Det. Tigers	Hank Aaron, Mil. Braves
1970	Alex Johnson, Cal. Angels	Rico Carty, Atl. Braves
1981	Carney Lansford, Bos. Red Sox........................	Bill Madlock, Pit. Pirates
1992	Edgar Martinez, Sea. Mariners	Gary Sheffield, S.D. Padres
2005	Michael Young, Tex. Rangers	Derrek Lee, Chi. Cubs
2007	Magglio Ordonez, Chi. White Sox	Matt Holliday, Col. Rockies
2012	Miguel Cabrera, Det. Tigers.............................	Buster Posey, S.F. Giants
2013	Miguel Cabrera, Det. Tigers.............................	Michael Cuddyer, Col. Rockies
2016	Jose Altuve, Hou. Astros	DJ LeMahieu, Col. Rockies
2021	Yuli Gurriel, Hou. Astros...................................	Trea Turner, Was. Nationals–L.A. Dodgers

Fewest Strikeouts For Batting Champions

American League		National League	
Strikeouts	Batting Average	Strikeouts	Batting Average
9...... Nap Lajoie, Phi. A's, 1901...........................	.426	6 ..... Debs Garms, Pit. Pirates, 1940	.355
13 ..... George Kell, Det. Tigers, 1949	.343	12 ..... Ernie Lombardi, Bos. Braves, 1942	.330

continued on next page

Strikeouts	Batting Average	Strikeouts	Batting Average
14 ..... George Sisler, St.L. Browns, 1922	.420	14 .....Paul Waner, Pit. Pirates, 1927	.380
16 ..... Harry Heilmann, Det. Tigers, 1927	.398	14 ....Ernie Lombardi, Cin. Reds, 1938	.342
19 ..... Nap Lajoie, Cle. Indians, 1904	.376	15 ....Tony Gwynn, S.D. Padres, 1995	.368
19 ..... George Sisler, St.L. Browns, 1920	.407	17 ....Honus Wagner, Pit. Pirates, 1903	.355
19 ..... Goose Goslin, Was. Senators, 1928	.379	17 ....Zack Wheat, Brk. Dodgers, 1918	.335
20 ..... Tris Speaker, Cle. Indians, 1916	.386	17 ....Bubbles Hargrove, Cin. Reds, 1926	.353
20 ..... Joe DiMaggio, N.Y. Yankees, 1939	.381	18 ....Arky Vaughan, Pit. Pirates, 1935	.385
20 ..... Ferris Fain, Phi. A's, 1951	.344	18 ....Stan Musial, St. L. Cardinals, 1943	.357
		18 ....Bill Buckner, Chi. Cubs, 1980	.324
		19 .....Edd Roush, Cin. Reds, 1919	.321
		19 ....Lefty O'Doul, Phi. A's, 1926	.398
		19 ....Tony Gwynn, S.D. Padres, 1994	.394
		20 .....Lefty O'Doul, Brk. Dodgers, 1932	.368

Home Runs

Evolution of Home Run Record

American League

1901	Nap Lajoie, Phi. A's	14	1921	Babe Ruth, N.Y. Yankees	59
1902	Socks Seybold, Phi. A's	16	1927	Babe Ruth, N.Y. Yankees	60
1919	Babe Ruth, Bos. Red Sox	29	1961	Roger Maris, N.Y. Yankees	61
1920	Babe Ruth, N.Y. Yankees	54	2022	Aaron Judge, N.Y. Yankees	62

National League (Pre-1900)

1876	George Hall, Phi. A's	5	1883	Buck Ewing, N.Y. Gothams	10
1879	Charley Jones, Bos. Red Stockings	9	1884	Ned Williamson, Chi. Colts	27

National League (Post-1900)

1900	Herman Long, Bos. Beaneaters	12	1929	Chuck Klein, Phi. Phillies	43
1901	Sam Crawford, Cin. Reds	16	1930	Hack Wilson, Chi. Cubs	56
1911	Frank Schulte, Chi. Cubs	21	1998	Mark McGwire, St.L. Cardinals	70
1915	Gavvy Cravath, Phi. Phillies	24	2001	Barry Bonds, S.F. Giants	73
1922	Rogers Hornsby, St.L. Cardinals	42			

Most Home Runs by Decade

Pre-1900		1900–09		1910–19	
138	Roger Connor	67	Harry Davis	116	Gavvy Cravath
126	Sam Thompson	58	Charlie Hickman	83	Fred Luderus
122	Harry Stovey	57	Sam Crawford	76	Home Run Baker
106	Mike Tiernan	54	Buck Freeman	75	Frank Schulte
106	Dan Brouthers	51	Socks Seybold	64	Larry Doyle
102	Hugh Duffy	51	Honus Wagner	61	Sherry Magee
100	Jimmy Ryan	47	Nap Lajoie	58	Heinie Zimmerman
97	Cap Anson	43	Cy Seymour	57	Fred Merkle
94	Fred Pfeffer	40	Jimmy Williams	55	Vic Saier
80	Ed Delahanty	40	Hobe Ferris	52	Owen Wilson

1920–29		1930–39		1940–49	
467	Babe Ruth	415	Jimmie Foxx	234	Ted Williams
250	Rogers Hornsby	347	Lou Gehrig	217	Johnny Mize
202	Cy Williams	308	Mel Ott	211	Bill Nicholson
190	Ken Williams	241	Wally Berger	189	Rudy York
146	Jim Bottomley	238	Chuck Klein	181	Joe Gordon
146	Lou Gehrig	218	Earl Averill	180	Joe DiMaggio
146	Bob Meusel	206	Hank Greenberg	177	Vern Stephens
142	Harry Heilmann	198	Babe Ruth	173	Charlie Keller
137	Hack Wilson	190	Al Simmons	168	Ralph Kiner
134	George Kelly	186	Bob Johnson	164	Bobby Doerr

continued on next page

1950–59

326	Duke Snider
310	Gil Hodges
299	Eddie Mathews
280	Mickey Mantle
266	Stan Musial
256	Yogi Berra
250	Willie Mays
239	Ted Kluszewski
232	Gus Zernial
228	Ernie Banks

1960–69

393	Harmon Killebrew
375	Hank Aaron
350	Willie Mays
316	Frank Robinson
300	Willie McCovey
288	Frank Howard
278	Norm Cash
269	Ernie Banks
256	Mickey Mantle
254	Orlando Cepeda

1970–79

296	Willie Stargell
292	Reggie Jackson
290	Johnny Bench
280	Bobby Bonds
270	Lee May
252	Dave Kingman
252	Graig Nettles
235	Mike Schmidt
226	Tony Perez
225	Reggie Smith

1980–89

313	Mike Schmidt
308	Dale Murphy
274	Eddie Murray
256	Dwight Evans
250	Andre Dawson
230	Darrell Evans
225	Tony Armas
225	Lance Parrish
223	Dave Winfield
216	Jack Clark

1990–99

405	Mark McGwire
382	Ken Griffey Jr.
361	Barry Bonds
351	Albert Belle
339	Juan Gonzalez
332	Sammy Sosa
328	Rafael Palmeiro
303	Jose Canseco
301	Frank Thomas
300	Fred McGriff
300	Matt Williams

2000–09

435	Alex Rodriguez
368	Jim Thome
366	Albert Pujols
348	Manny Ramirez
324	Carlos Delgado
317	Barry Bonds
316	Adam Dunn
315	Vladimir Guerrero
309	Lance Berkman
308	Andruw Jones

2010–19

346	Nelson Cruz
335	Edwin Encarnacion
308	Giancarlo Stanton
290	Albert Pujols
285	Jose Bautista
285	Mike Trout
269	Jay Bruce
268	Miguel Cabrera
257	Chris Davis
255	Justin Upton

2020–22

110	Aaron Judge
93	Pete Alonso
89	Vladimir Guerrero Jr.
89	Kyle Schwarber
87	Matt Olson
87	Shohei Ohtani
82	Jose Ramirez
82	Salvador Perez
79	Austin Riley
78	Marcus Semien

Career Home Run Leaders by Zodiac Sign

Aquarius (Jan. 20–Feb. 18)	Hank Aaron	755
Pisces (Feb. 19–Mar. 20)	Mel Ott	511
Aries (Mar. 21–Apr. 19)	Miguel Cabrera*	507
Taurus (Apr. 20–May 20)	Willie Mays	660
Gemini (May 21–Jun. 21)	Manny Ramirez	555
Cancer (Jun. 22–Jul. 22)	Harmon Killebrew	573
Leo (Jul. 23–Aug. 22)	Barry Bonds	762
Virgo (Aug. 23–Sep. 22)	Jim Thome	612
Libra (Sep. 23–Oct. 23)	Mark McGwire	583
Scorpio (Oct. 24–Nov. 21)	Ken Griffey Jr.	630
Sagittarius (Nov. 22–Dec. 21)	Dave Kingman	442
Capricorn (Dec. 22–Jan. 19)	Albert Pujols	703

* Still active.

All-Time Home Run Leaders by First Letter of Last Name

A	Hank Aaron (1954–76)	755	N	Graig Nettles (1967–88)	390
B	Barry Bonds (1986–2007)	762	O	David Ortiz (1997–2016)	541
C	Miguel Cabrera* (2003–)	507	P	Albert Pujols (2001–22)	703
D	Carlos Delgado (1993–2009)	473	Q	Carlos Quentin (2006–14)	154
E	Edwin Encarnacion (2005–20)	424	R	Babe Ruth (1914–35)	714
F	Jimmie Foxx (1925–42, 1944–45)	534	S	Sammy Sosa (1989–2007)	609
G	Ken Griffey Jr. (1989–2010)	630	T	Jim Thome (1991–2012)	612
H	Frank Howard (1958–73)	382	U	Justin Upton* (2007–)	325
	Ryan Howard (2004–16)	382	V	Greg Vaughn (1989–2003)	355
I	Raul Ibanez (1996–2014)	305	W	Ted Williams (1939–42, 1946–60)	521
J	Reggie Jackson (1967–87)	563	X	[No player]	
K	Harmon Killebrew (1954–75)	573	Y	Carl Yastrzemski (1961–83)	452
L	Carlos Lee (1999–2012)	358	Z	Ryan Zimmerman (2005–21)	284
M	Willie Mays (1951–52, 1954–73)	660			

* Still active.

Home Run Leaders by State of Birth

Alabama	Hank Aaron (Mobile)	755
Alaska	Josh Phelps (Anchorage)	64
Arizona	Ian Kinsler (Tucson)	257
Arkansas	Torii Hunter (Pine Bluff)	353
California	Barry Bonds (Riverside)	762
Colorado	Chase Headley (Fountain)	130
Connecticut	Mo Vaughn (Norwalk)	328
Delaware	Paul Goldschmidt* (Wilmington)	315
Florida	Gary Sheffield (Tampa)	509
Georgia	Frank Thomas (Columbus)	521
Hawaii	Kurt Suzuki* (Wailuku)	143
Idaho	Harmon Killebrew (Payette)	573
Illinois	Jim Thome (Peoria)	612
Indiana	Gil Hodges (Princeton)	370
Iowa	Hal Trosky (Norway)	228
Kansas	Tony Clark (Newton)	251
Kentucky	Jay Buhner (Louisville)	310
Louisiana	Mel Ott (Gretna)	511
Maine	Del Bissonette (Winthrop)	66
Maryland	Babe Ruth (Baltimore)	714
Massachusetts	Jeff Bagwell (Boston)	449
Michigan	John Mayberry (Detroit) and Kirk Gibson (Pontiac)	255
Minnesota	Dave Winfield (St. Paul)	465
Mississippi	Ellis Burks (Vicksburg)	352
Missouri	Ryan Howard (St. Louis)	382
Montana	John Lowenstein (Wolf Point)	116
Nebraska	Alex Gordon (Lincoln)	190
Nevada	Bryce Harper* (Las Vegas)	285
New Hampshire	Phil Plantier (Manchester)	91
New Jersey	Mike Trout* (Vineland)	350
New Mexico	Ralph Kiner (Santa Rita)	369
New York	Alex Rodriguez (Manhattan)	696
North Carolina	Ryan Zimmerman (Washington)	284

continued on next page

North Dakota..Travis Hafner (Jamestown) 213
Ohio .... Mike Schmidt (Dayton) 548
Oklahoma...Mickey Mantle (Spavinaw) 536
Oregon.. Dave Kingman (Pendleton) 442
Pennsylvania...Ken Griffey Jr. (Donora) 630
Rhode Island...Paul Konerko (Providence) 439
South Carolina ....Jim Rice (Anderson) 382
South Dakota ....Jason Kubel (Belle Fourche) 140
Tennessee..Todd Helton (Knoxville) 369
Texas .... Frank Robinson (Beaumont) 586
Utah ....Duke Sims (Salt Lake City) 100
Vermont ....Carlton Fisk (Bellows Falls) 376
Virginia .... Willie Horton (Arno) and Justin Upton* (Norfolk) 325
Washington...Ron Santo (Seattle) 342
West Virginia...George Brett (Glen Dale) 317
Wisconsin ....Al Simmons (Milwaukee) 307
Wyoming .... John Buck (Kemmerer) 134

American Samoa..Tony Solaita (Nuuuli) 50
District of Columbia ....Don Money 176
Puerto Rico...Carlos Delgado (Aguadilla) 473
Virgin Islands..................................... Elrod Hendricks (St. Thomas) 62
* Still active.

500th Home Run of 500 Home Run Hitters

Hitter	Career Home Runs	Date of 500th Home Run	Pitcher
Barry Bonds	762	Apr. 17, 2004	Terry Adams, L.A. Dodgers
Hank Aaron	755	Jul. 14, 1968	Mike McCormick, S.F. Giants
Babe Ruth	714	Aug. 11, 1929	Willis Hudlin, Cle. Indians
Albert Pujols	703	Apr. 22, 2014	Taylor Jordan, Was. Nationals
Alex Rodriguez	696	Aug. 4, 2007	Kyle Davies, K.C. Royals
Willie Mays	660	Sep. 13, 1965	Don Nottebart, Atl. Braves
Ken Griffey Jr.	630	Jun. 6, 2004	Matt Morris, St.L. Cardinals
Jim Thome	612	Sep. 16, 2007	Dustin Mosley, L.A. Dodgers
Sammy Sosa	609	Apr. 4, 2004	Scott Sullivan, Cin. Reds
Frank Robinson	586	Sep. 13, 1971	Fred Scherman, Det. Tigers
Mark McGwire	583	Aug. 5, 1999	Andy Ashby S.D. Padres
Harmon Killebrew	573	Aug. 10, 1971	Mike Cuellar, Bal. Orioles
Rafael Palmeiro	569	May 11, 2003	Dave Elder, Cle. Indians
Reggie Jackson	563	Sep. 17, 1984	Bud Black, K.C. Royals
Manny Ramirez	555	May 31, 2008	Chad Bradford, Bal. Orioles
Mike Schmidt	548	Apr. 18, 1987	Don Robinson, Pit. Pirates
David Ortiz	541	Sep. 12, 2015	Matt Moore, T.B. Rays
Mickey Mantle	536	May 14, 1967	Stu Miller, Bal. Orioles
Jimmie Foxx	534	Sep. 24, 1940	George Caster, Phi. A's
Ted Williams	521	Jun. 17, 1960	Wynn Hawkins, Cle. Indians
Willie McCovey	521	Jun. 30, 1978	Jamie Easterly, Atl. Braves
Frank Thomas	521	Jun. 28, 2007	Carlos Silva, Min. Twins
Eddie Mathews	512	Jul. 14, 1967	Juan Marichal, S.F. Giants
Ernie Banks	512	May 12, 1970	Pat Jarvis, Atl. Braves
Mel Ott	511	Aug. 1, 1945	John Hutchings, Bos. Braves
Gary Sheffield	509	Apr. 17, 2009	Mitch Stetter, Mil. Brewers

continued on next page

Hitter	Career Home Runs	Date of 500th Home Run	Pitcher
Miguel Cabrera*	507	Aug. 22, 2021	Steven Matz, Tor. Blue Jays
Eddie Murray	504	Sep. 6, 1996	Felipe Lira, Det. Tigers

* Still active.

Most Home Runs in First Three Seasons in Majors

114	Ralph Kiner, Pit. Pirates (NL)	1946 (23), 1947 (51), and 1948 (40)
114	Albert Pujols, St.L. Cardinals (NL)	2001 (37), 2002 (34), and 2003 (43)
111	Cody Bellinger, L.A. Dodgers (NL)	2017 (39), 2018 (25), 2019 (47)
112	Eddie Mathews, Bos.–Mil. Braves (NL)	1952 (25), 1953 (47), and 1954 (40)
107	Joe DiMaggio, N.Y. Yankees (AL)	1936 (29), 1937 (46), and 1938 (32)
107	Mark Teixeira, Tex. Rangers (AL)	2003 (26), 2004 (38), and 2005 (43)
106	Pete Alonso, N.Y. Mets	2019 (53), 2020 (16), 2021 (37)
103	Ryan Braun, Mil. Brewers	2007 (34), 2008 (37), 2009 (32)

Most Home Runs for One Club

733	Hank Aaron	Mil.–Atl. Braves* (NL) (1954–74)
659	Babe Ruth	N.Y. Yankees (AL) (1920–34)
646	Willie Mays	N.Y.–S.F. Giants* (NL) (1951–52, 1954–72)
586	Barry Bonds	S.F. Giants (NL) (1993–2007)
559	Harmon Killebrew	Was. Senators–Min. Twins* (AL) (1954–74)
548	Mike Schmidt	Phi. Phillies (NL) (1972–89)
545	Sammy Sosa	Chi. Cubs (NL) (1992–2004)
536	Mickey Mantle	N.Y. Yankees (AL) (1951–68)
521	Ted Williams	Bos. Red Sox (AL) (1939–42, 1946–60)
512	Ernie Banks	Chi. Cubs (NL) (1953–71)
511	Mel Ott	N.Y. Giants (NL) (1926–47)
493	Lou Gehrig	N.Y. Yankees (AL) (1923–39)
493	Eddie Mathews	Bos.–Mil.–Atl. Braves* (NL) (1952–66)
483	David Ortiz	Bos. Red Sox (AL) (2003–16)
475	Stan Musial	St.L. Cardinals (NL) (1941–44, 1946–63)
475	Willie Stargell	Pit. Pirates (NL) (1962–82)
469	Willie McCovey	S.F. Giants (NL) (1959–80)
469	Albert Pujols	St.L. Cardinals (NL) (2001–11, 2022)
468	Chipper Jones	Atl. Braves (NL) (1993, 1995–2012)
452	Carl Yastrzemski	Bos. Red Sox (AL) (1939–42, 1946–60)
449	Jeff Bagwell	Hou. Astros (NL) (1991–2005)
448	Frank Thomas	Chi. White Sox (AL) (1990–2005)
432	Paul Konerko	Chi. White Sox (AL) (1999–2014)
431	Cal Ripken Jr.	Bal. Orioles (AL) (1981–2001)
417	Ken Griffey Jr.	Sea. Mariners (AL) (1989–99, 2009–10)

* Franchises that moved.

Most Home Runs by Position*, Career

First Base	566	Mark McGwire
Second Base	351	Jeff Kent
Third Base	509	Mike Schmidt
Shortstop	345	Cal Ripken Jr.
Outfield	748	Barry Bonds
Catcher	396	Mike Piazza
Pitcher	36	Wes Ferrell
Designated Hitter	447	David Ortiz

* While in lineup at position indicated.

Most Home Runs *Not* Leading League, Season

American League

Home Runs	Season		Winner
54	1961	Mickey Mantle, N.Y. Yankees	Roger Maris (61), N.Y. Yankees
52	2002	Jim Thome, Cle. Indians	Alex Rodriguez (57), Tex. Rangers
50	1938	Jimmie Foxx, Bos. Red Sox	Hank Greenberg (58), Det. Tigers
50	1996	Brady Anderson, Bal. Orioles	Mark McGwire (52), Oak. A's
49	1996	Ken Griffey Jr., Sea. Mariners	Mark McGwire (52), Oak. A's
49	1998	Albert Belle, Chi. White Sox	Ken Griffey Jr. (56), Sea. Mariners
49	2001	Jim Thome, Cle. Indians	Alex Rodriguez (52), Tex. Rangers
48	1969	Frank Howard, Was. Senators II	Harmon Killebrew (49), Min. Twins
48	1996	Albert Belle, Cle. Indians	Mark McGwire (52), Oak. A's
47	1927	Lou Gehrig, N.Y. Yankees	Babe Ruth (60), N.Y. Yankees
47	1969	Reggie Jackson, Oak. A's	Harmon Killebrew (49), Min. Twins
47	1987	George Bell, Tor. Blue Jays	Mark McGwire (49), Oak. A's
47	1996	Juan Gonzalez, Tex. Rangers	Mark McGwire (52), Oak. A's
47	1999	Rafael Palmeiro, Tex. Rangers	Ken Griffey Jr. (48), Sea. Mariners
47	2001	Rafael Palmeiro, Tex. Rangers	Alex Rodriguez (52), Tex. Rangers
47	2005	David Oritz, Bos. Red Sox	Alex Rodriguez (48), N.Y. Yankees
46	1961	Jim Gentile, Bal. Orioles	Roger Maris (61), N.Y. Yankees
46	1961	Harmon Killebrew, Min. Twins	Roger Maris (61), N.Y. Yankees
46	1998	Jose Canseco, Tor. Blue Jays	Ken Griffey Jr. (56), Sea. Mariners
46	2007	Carlos Pena, T.B. Rays	Alex Rodriguez (54), N.Y. Yankees
46	2021	Shohei Ohtani, L.A. Angels	Salvador Perez (48), K.C. Royals; Vladimir Guerrero Jr. (48), Tor. Blue Jays

National League

66	1998	Sammy Sosa, Chi. Cubs	Mark McGwire (70), St.L. Cardinals
64	2001	Sammy Sosa, Chi. Cubs	Barry Bonds (73), S.F. Giants
63	1999	Sammy Sosa, Chi. Cubs	Mark McGwire (65), St.L. Cardinals
57	2001	Luis Gonzalez, Ari. D'backs	Barry Bonds (73), S.F. Giants
50	1998	Greg Vaughn, S.D. Padres	Mark McGwire (70), St.L. Cardinals
49	1971	Hank Aaron, Atl. Braves	Willie Stargell (48), Pit. Pirates
49	2000	Barry Bonds, S.F. Giants	Sammy Sosa (50), Chi. Cubs
49	2001	Shawn Green, L.A. Dodgers	Barry Bonds (73), S.F. Giants
49	2001	Todd Helton, Col. Rockies	Barry Bonds (73), S.F. Giants
49	2006	Albert Pujols, St.L. Cardinals	Ryan Howard (58), Phi. Phillies
49	2019	Eugenio Suarez, Cin. Reds	Pete Alonso (53), N.Y. Mets
47	1955	Ted Kluszewski, Cin. Reds	Willie Mays (51), N.Y. Giants
47	2000	Jeff Bagwell, Hou. Astros	Sammy Sosa (50), Chi. Cubs
47	2007	Ryan Howard, Phi. Phillies	Prince Fielder (50), Mil. Brewers
46	1998	Vinny Castilla, Col. Rockies	Mark McGwire (70), St.L. Cardinals
46	2002	Barry Bonds, S.F. Giants	Sammy Sosa (49), Chi. Cubs
46	2005	Derrek Lee, Chi. Cubs	Andruw Jones (51), Atl. Braves
46	2006	Alfonso Soriano, Was. Nationals	Albert Pujols (49), St.L. Cardinals
46	2009	Prince Fielder, Mil. Brewers	Albert Pujols (47), St.L. Cardinals

Most Home Runs, Never Leading League, Career

569	Rafael Palmeiro (1986–2005)	473	Carlos Delgado (1993–2009)
521	Frank Thomas (1990–2008)	468	Chipper Jones (1993, 1995–2012)
509	Gary Sheffield (1988–2009)	465	Dave Winfield (1973–95)
475	Stan Musial (1941–44, 1946–63)	462	Adam Dunn (2001–14)

continued on next page

449...Jeff Bagwell (1991–2005)	427.. Mike Piazza (1992–2007)
449............................... Vladimir Guerrero (1996–2011)	426.. Billy Williams (1959–76)
440.................................... Jason Giambi (1995–2014)	424...................................Edwin Encarnacion (2005–20)
439.................................... Paul Konerko (1997–2011)	412................................... Alfonso Soriano (1999–2014)
435....................................Carlos Beltran (1998–2017)	399.. Al Kaline (1953–74)
431.................................... Cal Ripken Jr. (1981–2001)	

Most Inside-the-Park Home Runs, Career (Post-1898)

51 .... Sam Crawford (1899–1917)	29 .... Chief Wilson (1908–16)
48 ....Tommy Leach (1898–1918)	28 .... Ed Konetchy (1907–21)
46 ....Ty Cobb (1905–28)	27 .... Ginger Beaumont (1988–1910)
38 .... Tris Speaker (1907–28)	27 ....Max Carey (1910–29)
33 .... Rogers Hornsby (1915–37)	27 ....Mike Donlin (1899–1914)
31 ....Edd Roush (1913–29, 1931)	27 .... Hobe Ferris (1901–09)
30 ....Jake Daubert (1910–24)	22 ....Rabbit Maranville (1912–35)

Players with 10 or More Letters in Last Name, Hitting 40 or More Home Runs in Season

	Season	Home Runs
Roy Campanella, Brk. Dodgers (NL)........................	1953	41
Edwin Encarnacion, Tor. Blue Jays (AL)....................	2012	42
	2016	42
Curtis Granderson, N.Y. Yankees (AL)	2011	41
	2012	43
Ted Kluszewski, Cin. Reds (NL)...............................	1953	40
	1954	49
	1955	47
Rico Petrocelli, Bos. Red Sox (AL)	1969	40
Carl Yastrzemski, Bos. Red Sox (AL).......................	1967	44
	1969	40
	1970	40

Most Home Runs by Visiting Player by Stadium

Stadium	Team	Years Open	Player	Home Runs
Sportsman's Park (Busch Stadium)	St.L. (NL)	1875–77 (Brown Stockings).........	Babe Ruth	58
		1882–93 (Brown Stockings)		
		1902–53 (Browns)		
		1920–66 (Cardinals)		
Baker Bowl	Phi. (NL)	1887–1938	Mel Ott	40
League Park	Cle. (AL)	1891–99, 1901–32, 1934–46	Babe Ruth	46
Polo Grounds	N.Y. (NL)	1891–1957 (Giants)	Stan Musial	49
		1913–22 (Yankees)		
		1962–63 (Mets)		
Shibe Park	Phi. (AL)	1909–54 (A's)	Babe Ruth	68
		1938–70 (Phillies)		
Forbes Field	Pit. (NL)	1909–70	Eddie Mathews	38
Comiskey Park I	Chi. (AL)	1910–90	Babe Ruth	45
Griffith Stadium	Was. (AL)	1911–60 (Senators I)	Babe Ruth	34
		1961 (Senators II)		

continued on next page

Stadium	Team	Years Open	Player	Home Runs
Crosley Field	Cin. (NL)	1912–70	Eddie Mathews	50
Tiger Stadium	Det. (AL)	1912–99	Babe Ruth	60
Fenway Park	Bos. (AL)	1912–present (Red Sox) 1914–15 (Braves)	Mickey Mantle/Babe Ruth	38
Ebbets Field	Brk. (NL)	1913–57	Stan Musial	37
Braves Field	Bos. (NL)	1915–52	Bill Nicholson	20
Wrigley Field	Chi. (NL)	1916–present	Willie Mays	54
Yankee Stadium	N.Y. (AL)	1923–73, 1976–2008	Goose Goslin	32
Cleveland Stadium	Cle. (AL)	1932–33, 1936–93	Mickey Mantle	36
Milwaukee County Stadium	Mil. (NL) (Braves–Brewers)	1953–65, 1970–2000	Frank Robinson	35
Memorial Stadium	Bal. (AL)	1954–91	Harmon Killebrew	30
Municipal Stadium	K.C. (AL) (A's–Royals)	1955–67, 1969–72	Harmon Killebrew	33
Los Angeles Memorial Coliseum	L.A. (NL)	1958–61	Ken Boyer/Frank Thomas	17
Candlestick Park	S.F. (NL)	1960–99	Dale Murphy/Willie Stargell	25
Metropolitan Stadium	Min. (AL)	1961–81	Reggie Jackson	20
Robert F. Kennedy Memorial Stadium	Was. (AL/NL)	1962–71 (Senators II) 2005–07 (Nationals)	Harmon Killebrew	25
Dodger Stadium	L.A. (NL)	1962–present (Dodgers) 1962–65 (Angels)	Barry Bonds	29
Shea Stadium	N.Y. (NL)	1964–2008 (Mets) 1974–75 (Yankees)	Willie Stargell/Mike Schmidt	26
Astrodome	Hou. (NL)	1965–99	Tony Perez	19
Atlanta-Fulton County Stadium	Atl. (NL)	1966–96	Johnny Bench/Willie McCovey	32
Busch Memorial Stadium (Busch Stadium II)	St.L. (NL)	1966–2005	Mike Schmidt	27
Angel Stadium of Anaheim	L.A. (AL)	1966–present	Alex Rodriguez	38
Oakland-Alameda County Stadium	Oak. (AL)	1968–present	Alex Rodriguez	21
Jarry Park Stadium	Mon. (NL)	1969–76	Willie Stargell	17
Qualcomm Stadium	S.D. (NL)	1969–2003	Barry Bonds	39
Three Rivers Stadium	Pit. (NL)	1970–2000	Mike Schmidt	25
Cinergy Field	Cin. (NL)	1970–2002	Barry Bonds	31
Veterans Stadium	Phi. (NL)	1971–2003	Barry Bonds	27
Arlington Stadium	Tex. (AL)	1972–93	Reggie Jackson	23
Kauffman Stadium	K.C. (AL)	1973–present	Juan Gonzalez	22
Exhibition Stadium	Tor. (AL)	1977–89	Jim Rice	18
Kingdome	Sea. (AL)	1977–99	Brian Downing	19
Olympic Stadium	Mon. (NL)	1977–2004	Barry Bonds	30
Hubert H. Humphrey Metrodome	Min. (AL)	1982–2009	Jim Thome	28
Rogers Centre	Tor. (AL)	1989–present	David Ortiz	41
Guaranteed Rate Field	Chi. (AL)	1991–present	Miguel Cabrera	25
Camden Yards	Bal. (AL)	1992–present	Alex Rodriguez	34
Sun Life Stadium	Fla. (NL)	1993–2011	Chipper Jones	16
Progressive Field	Cle. (AL)	1994–present	Miguel Cabrera	26
Globe Life Park in Arlington	Tex. (AL)	1994–present	Jason Giambi	20
Coors Field	Col. (NL)	1995–present	Barry Bonds	26

continued on next page

Stadium	Team	Years Open	Player	Home Runs
Turner Field	Atl. (NL)	1997–2016	Ryan Howard	23
Chase Field	Ari. (NL)	1998–present	Adrian Gonzalez	21
Tropicana Field	T.B. (AL)	1998–present	David Ortiz	35
Safeco Field	Sea. (AL)	1999–present	Mike Trout	33
Comerica Park	Det. (AL	2000–present	David Ortiz	23
Minute Maid Park	Hou. (NL–AL)	2000–present	Albert Pujols	33
AT&T Park	S.F. (NL)	2000–present	Paul Goldschmidt	13
Miller Park	Mil. (AL–NL)	2001–present	Andrew McCutchen	23
PNC Park	Pit. (NL)	2001–present	Albert Pujols	35
Great American Ball Park	Cin. (NL)	2003–present	Ryan Braun	28
Citizens Bank Park	Phi. (NL)	2004–present	David Wright	22
Petco Park	S.D. (NL)	2004–present	Nolan Arenado	15
Busch Stadium (Busch Stadium III)	St.L. (NL)	2006–present	Joey Votto	16
Nationals Park	Was. (NL)	2008–present	Giancarlo Stanton	22
Yankee Stadium	N.Y. (AL)	2009–present	Jose Bautista	19
Citi Field	N.Y. (NL)	2009–present	Giancarlo Stanton	23
Target Field	Min. (AL)	2010–present	Salvador Perez	20
Marlins Park	Mia. (NL)	2012–present	Freddie Freeman	16
Truist Park	Atl. (NL)	2017–present	Bryce Harper	12

Most Home Runs, Month by Month

American League

Mar.	3	Matt Davidson, Chi. White Sox, 2018
Apr.	14	Alex Rodriguez, N.Y. Yankees, 2007
May	16	Mickey Mantle, N.Y. Yankees, 1956
	16	Edwin Encarnacion, Tor. Blue Jays, 2014
Jun.	15	Babe Ruth, N.Y. Yankees, 1930
		Bob Johnson, Phi. A's, 1934
		Roger Maris, N.Y. Yankees, 1961
Jul.	16	Albert Belle, Chi. White Sox, 1998
Aug.	18	Rudy York, Det. Tigers, 1937
Sep.	17	Babe Ruth, N.Y. Yankees, 1927
		Albert Belle, Cle. Indians, 1995
Oct.	4	Gus Zernial, Chi. White Sox, 1950
		George Brett, K.C. Royals, 1985
		Ron Kittle, Chi. White Sox, 1985
		Wally Joyner, Cal. Angels, 1987
		Jose Cruz Jr., Tor. Blue Jays, 2001

National League

4	Cody Bellinger, L.A. Dodgers, 2019
	Christian Yelich, Mil. Brewers, 2019
14	Albert Pujols, St.L. Cardinals, 2006
17	Barry Bonds, S.F. Giants, 2001
20	Sammy Sosa, Chi. Cubs, 1998
16	Mark McGwire, St.L. Cardinals, 1999
18	Giancarlo Stanton, Mia. Marlins, 2017
16	Ralph Kiner, Pit. Pirates, 1949
5	Richie Sexson, Mil. Brewers, 2001
	Sammy Sosa, Chi. Cubs, 2001

Most Home Runs by Position, Season*

American League

First Base 58 Hank Greenberg, Det. Tigers, 1938

Second Base 39 Alfonso Soriano, N.Y. Yankees, 2002

National League

First Base 69 Mark McGwire, St.L. Cardinals, 1998

Second Base 42 Rogers Hornsby, St.L. Cardinals, 1922

42 Davey Johnson, Atl. Braves, 1973

continued on next page

American League	
Third Base	52....... Alex Rodriguez, N.Y. Yankees, 2007
Shortstop	57........ Alex Rodriguez, Tex. Rangers, 2002
Outfield	61............Roger Maris, N.Y. Yankees, 1961
Catcher	35........Ivan Rodriguez, Tex. Rangers, 1999
Pitcher	9 .... Wes Ferrell, Cle. Indians, 1931
Designated Hitter	47............David Ortiz, Bos. Red Sox, 2006

National League	
Third Base	48...........Mike Schmidt, Phi. Phillies, 1980
	48..........Adrian Beltre, L.A. Dodgers, 2004
Shortstop	47...............Ernie Banks, Chi. Cubs, 1958
Outfield	71.............Barry Bonds, S.F. Giants, 2001
Catcher	42................Javy Lopez, Atl. Braves, 2003
Pitcher	7.......Don Newcombe, Brk. Dodgers, 1955
	7...........Don Drysdale, L.A. Dodgers, 1958
	L.A. Dodgers, 1965
	Mike Hampton, Col. Rockies, 2001
Designated Hitter	17...........Bryce Harper, Phi. Phillies, 2022
	Daniel Vogelbach, N.Y. Mets, 2022

* While in lineup at position indicated.

Players Leading League in Home Runs for Different Teams

Tony Armas	Oak. A's (AL)	1981	22
	Bos. Red Sox (AL)	1984	43
Sam Crawford	Cin. Reds (NL)	1901	16
	Det. Tigers (AL)	1908	7
		1914	8
Jimmie Foxx	Phi. A's (AL)	1932	58
		1933	48
		1935	36
	Bos. Red Sox (AL)	1939	35
Buck Freeman	Was. Senators (NL)	1899	25
	Bos. Americans (AL)	1903	13
Reggie Jackson	Oak. A's (AL)	1973	32
		1975	36
	N.Y. Yankees (AL)	1980	41
	Cal. Angels (AL)	1982	39
Harmon Killebrew	Was. Senators (AL)	1959	42
	Min. Twins (AL)	1962	48
		1963	45
		1964	49
		1967	44
		1969	49
Dave Kingman	Chi. Cubs (NL)	1979	48
	N.Y. Mets (NL)	1982	37
Fred McGriff	Tor. Blue Jays (AL)	1989	36
	S.D. Padres (NL)	1992	35
Mark McGwire	Oak. A's (AL)	1987	49
		1996	52
	St.L. Cardinals (NL)	1998	70
		1999	65
Johnny Mize	St.L. Cardinals (NL)	1939	28
		1940	43
	N.Y. Giants (NL)	1947	51 (Tie)
		1948	40 (Tie)
Alex Rodriguez	Tex. Rangers (AL)	2001	52
		2002	57
		2003	47
	N.Y. Yankees (AL)	2005	48
		2007	54
Babe Ruth	Bos. Red Sox (AL)	1918	11
		1919	29
	N.Y. Yankees (AL)	1920	54
		1921	59
		1923	41
		1924	46
		1926	47
		1927	60
		1928	54
		1929	46
		1930	49
		1931	46 (Tie)
Cy Williams	Chi. Cubs (NL)	1916	12
	Phi. Phillies (NL)	1920	15
		1923	41

Players with 40 Home Run Seasons in Each League

Adam Dunn	Cin. Reds (NL)	2004	46
		2005	40
		2006	40
		2007	40
	Cin. Reds–Ari. D'backs (NL)	2008	40
	Chi. White Sox (AL)	2012	41
Darrell Evans	Atl. Braves (NL)	1973	41
	Det. Tigers (AL)	1985	40
Shawn Green	Tor. Blue Jays (AL)	1999	42
	L.A. Dodgers (NL)	2001	49
		2002	42
Ken Griffey Jr.	Sea. Mariners (AL)	1993	45
		1994	40
		1996	49
		1997	56
		1998	56
		1999	48
	Cin. Reds (NL)	2000	40
David Justice	Atl. Braves (NL)	1993	40
	Cle. Indians (AL)–N.Y. Yankees (AL)	2000	41*
Mark McGwire	Oak. A's (AL)	1987	49
		1992	42
		1996	52
	St.L. Cardinals (NL)	1998	70
		1999	65
Albert Pujols	St.L. Cardinals (NL)	2003	43
		2004	46
		2005	41
		2006	49
		2009	47
		2010	42
	L.A. Angels (AL)	2015	40
Jim Thome	Cle. Indians (AL)	1997	40
		2001	49
		2002	52
	Phi. Philles (NL)	2003	47
		2004	42
	Chi. White Sox (AL)	2006	42

* 21 with Cle. Indians (AL) and 20 with N.Y. Yankees (AL).

Players Hitting a Total of 100 Home Runs in Two Consecutive Seasons

	Total Home Runs
Mark McGwire, St.L. Cardinals (NL), 1998 (70) and 1999 (65)	135
Sammy Sosa, Chi. Cubs (NL), 1998 (66) and 1999 (63)	129
Mark McGwire, St.L. Cardinals (NL), 1997 (58*) and 1998 (70)	128
Barry Bonds, S.F. Giants (NL), 2000 (49) and 2001 (73)	122
Barry Bonds, S.F. Giants (NL), 2001 (73) and 2002 (46)	119
Babe Ruth, N.Y. Yankees (AL), 1927 (60) and 1928 (54)	114
Sammy Sosa, Chi. Cubs (NL), 2000 (50) and 2001 (64)	114
Babe Ruth, N.Y. Yankees (AL), 1920 (54) and 1921 (59)	113
Sammy Sosa, Chi. Cubs (NL), 1999 (63) and 2000 (50)	113
Sammy Sosa, Chi. Cubs (NL), 2001 (64) and 2002 (49)	113
Ken Griffey Jr., Sea. Mariners (AL), 1997 (56) and 1998 (56)	112
Mark McGwire, Oak. A's (AL), 1996 (52) and 1997 (58*)	110
Alex Rodriguez, Tex. Rangers (AL), 2001 (52) and 2002 (57)	109
Babe Ruth, N.Y. Yankees (AL), 1926 (47) and 1927 (60)	107
Jimmie Foxx, Phi. A's (AL), 1932 (58) and 1933 (48)	106
Ken Griffey Jr., Sea. Mariners (AL), 1996 (49) and 1997 (56)	105
Ryan Howard, Phi. Phillies (NL) 2006 (58) and 2007 (47)	105
Ken Griffey Jr., Sea. Mariners (AL), 1998 (56) and 1999 (48)	104

continued on next page

	Total Home Runs
Alex Rodriguez, Tex. Rangers (AL), 2002 (57) and 2003 (47)	104
Ralph Kiner, Pit. Pirates (NL), 1949 (54) and 1950 (47)	101
David Ortiz, Bos. Red Sox (AL) 2005 (47) and 2006 (54)	101
Aaron Judge, N.Y. Yankees (AL), 2021 (39) and 2022 (62)	
Roger Maris, N.Y. Yankees (AL), 1960 (39) and 1961 (61)	100

* 34 with Oak. A's (AL) and 24 with St.L. Cardinals (NL).

Players with First 20-Home Run Season After 35th Birthday

	Season	Home Runs	35th Birthday
Cy Williams, Phi. Phillies (NL)	1922	26	Dec. 21, 1921
Charlie Gehringer, Det. Tigers (AL)	1938	20	May 11, 1938
Luke Easter, Cle. Indians (AL)	1950	28	Aug. 4, 1949
Mickey Vernon, Was. Senators (AL)	1954	20	Apr. 22, 1953
George Crowe, Cin. Reds (NL)	1957	31	Mar. 22, 1956
John Lowenstein, Bal. Orioles (AL)	1982	24	Jan. 27, 1982
Frank White, K.C. Royals (AL)	1985	20	Sep. 4, 1985
Buddy Bell, Cin. Reds (NL)	1986	20	Aug. 27, 1986
Ken Griffey Sr., N.Y. Yankees (AL)–Atl. Braves (NL)	1986	21	Apr. 10, 1985
Julio Franco, Chi. White Sox (AL)	1994	20	Aug. 23, 1993
Tony Phillips, Cal. Angels (AL)	1995	27	Apr. 25, 1994
Mike Bordick, Bal. Orioles (AL)–N.Y. Mets (NL)	2000	20	Jul. 21, 2000
Bengie Molina, S.F. Giants (NL)	2009	20	Jul. 20, 2009
A.J. Pierzynski, Chi. White Sox (AL)	2012	27	Dec. 30, 2011
Yuli Gurriel, Hou. Astros (AL)	2019	31	Jun. 9, 1984

Shortstops with at Least Seven Consecutive 20-Home Run Seasons

		Season	Home Runs
Cal Ripken Jr., Bal. Orioles (AL) (10 seasons)		1982	28
		1983	27
		1984	27
		1985	26
		1986	25
		1987	27
		1988	23
		1989	21
		1990	21
		1991	34
Alex Rodriguez, Tex. Rangers (AL) (8 seasons)		1996	36
		1997	23
		1998	44
		1999	42
		2000	41
		2001	52
		2002	57
		2003	47
Miguel Tejada (8 seasons)	Oak. A's (AL) (5 seasons)	1999	21
		2000	30
		2001	31
		2002	34
		2003	27
	Bal. Orioles (AL) (3 seasons)	2004	34
		2005	26
		2006	24

continued on next page

	Season	Home Runs
Ernie Banks, Chi. Cubs (NL) (7 seasons)	1955	44
	1956	28
	1957	43*
	1958	47
	1959	45
	1960	41
	1961	29**

* Played 58 games at third base.
** Played 28 games in outfield, 76 at first base.

Players Hitting Four Home Runs in One Game

American League

Batter	Date	Opposing Pitcher(s)
Lou Gehrig, N.Y. Yankees	Jun. 3, 1932	George Earnshaw (3 home runs) and Roy Mahaffey (1 home run), Phi. A's
Pat Seerey, Chi. White Sox	Jul. 18, 1948	Carl Scheib (2 home runs), Bob Savage (1 home run), and Lou Brissie (1 home run), Phi. A's
Rocky Colavito, Cle. Indians	Jun. 10, 1959	Jerry Walker (2 home runs), Arnold Portocarrero (1 home run), and Ernie Johnson (1 home run), Bal. Orioles
Mike Cameron, Sea. Mariners	May 2, 2002	Jon Rauch (1 home run) and Jim Parque (3 home runs), Chi. White Sox
Carlos Delgado, Tor. Blue Jays	Sep. 25, 2003	Jorge Sosa (2 home runs), Joe Kennedy (1 home run), and Lance Carter (1 home run), T.B. Devil Rays
Josh Hamilton, Tex Rangers	May 8, 2012	Jake Arietta (2 home runs), Zach Phillips (1 home run), Darren O'Day (1 home run), Bal. Orioles

National League

Batter	Date	Opposing Pitcher(s)
Bobby Lowe, Bos. Beaneaters	May 30, 1894	Icebox Chamberlain (4 home runs), Cin. Reds
Ed Delahanty, Phi. Phillies	Jul. 13, 1896	Adonis Bill Terry (4 home runs), Chi. Cubs
Chuck Klein, Phi. Phillies	Jul. 10, 1936	Jim Weaver (1 home run), Mace Brown (2 home runs), and Bill Swift (1 home run), Pit. Pirates
Gil Hodges, Brk. Dodgers	Aug. 31, 1950	Warren Spahn (1 home run), Normie Roy (1 home run), Bob Hall (1 home run), and Johnny Antonelli (1 home run), Bos. Braves
Joe Adcock, Mil. Braves	Jul. 31, 1954	Don Newcombe (1 home run), Erv Palica (1 home run), Pete Wojey (1 home run), and Johnny Podres (1 home run), Brk. Dodgers
Willie Mays, S.F. Giants	Apr. 30, 1961	Lew Burdette (2 home runs), Seth Morehead (1 home run), and Don McMahon (1 home run), Mil. Braves
Mike Schmidt, Phi. Phillies	Apr. 17, 1976	Rick Reuschel (2 home runs), Mike Garman (1 home run), and Paul Reuschel (1 home run), Chi. Cubs
Bob Horner, Atl. Braves	Jul. 6, 1986	Andy McGaffigan (3 home runs) and Jeff Reardon (1 home run), Mon. Expos
Mark Whiten, St.L. Cardinals	Sep. 7, 1993	Larry Luebbers (1 home run), Mike Anderson (2 home runs), and Rob Dibble (1 home run), Cin. Reds
Shawn Green, L.A. Dodgers	May 23, 2002	Glendon Rusch (1 home run), Brian Mallette (2 home runs), and Jose Cabrera (1 home run), Mil. Brewers
Scooter Gennett, Cin. Reds	Jun. 6, 2017	Adam Wainwright (1 home run), John Gant (2 home runs), and John Brebbia (1 home run), St.L. Cardinals
J.D. Martinez, Ari. D'backs	Sep. 4, 2017	Rich Hill (1 home run), Pedro Baez (1 home run), Josh Fields (1 home run), and Wilmer Font (1 home run), Chi. Cubs

Career Home Runs by Players Hitting Four Home Runs in One Game

American League

Batter	Date	Result	Career Home Runs
Lou Gehrig, N.Y. Yankees	Jun. 3, 1932	N.Y. Yankees 20, Phi. A's 13	493
Pat Seerey, Chi. White Sox	Jul. 18, 1948	Chi. White Sox 12, Phi. A's 11	86
Rocky Colavito, Cle. Indians	Jun. 10, 1959	Cle. Indians 11, Bal. Orioles 8	374
Mike Cameron, Sea. Mariners	May 2, 2002	Sea. Mariners 15, Chi. White Sox 4	278
Carlos Delgado, Tor. Blue Jays	Sep. 25, 2003	Tor. Blue Jays 10, T.B. Devil Rays 8	473
Josh Hamilton, Tex. Rangers	May 8, 2012	Tex. Rangers 10, Bal. Orioles 3	200

National League

Batter	Date	Result	Career Home Runs
Bobby Lowe, Bos. Beaneaters	May 30, 1894	Bos. Beaneaters 20, Cin. Reds 11	71
Ed Delahanty, Phi. Phillies	Jul. 13, 1896	Chi. Cubs 9, Phi. Phillies 8	101
Chuck Klein, Phi. Phillies	Jul. 10, 1936	Phi. Phillies 9, Pit. Pirates 6	300
Gil Hodges, Brk. Dodgers	Aug. 31, 1950	Blyn. Dodgers 19, Bos. Braves 3	370
Joe Adcock, Mil. Brewers	Jul. 31, 1954	Mil. Brewers 15, Brk. Dodgers 7	336
Willie Mays, S.F. Giants	Apr. 30, 1961	S.F. Giants 14, Mil. Brewers 4	660
Mike Schmidt, Phi. Phillies	Apr. 17, 1976	Phi. Phillies 18, Chi. Cubs 16	548
Bob Horner, Atl. Braves	Jul. 6, 1986	Mon. Expos 11, Atl. Braves 8	218
Mark Whiten, St.L. Cardinals	Sep. 7, 1993	St.L. Cardinals 15, Cin. Reds 2	105
Shawn Green, L.A. Dodgers	May 23, 2002	L.A. Dodgers 16, Mil. Brewers 3	328
Scooter Gennett, Cin. Reds	Jun. 6, 2017	Cin. Reds 13, St.L. Cardinals 1	87
J.D. Martinez*, Ari. D'backs	Sep. 4, 2017	Ari. D'backs 13, L.A. Dodgers 0	282

* Still active.

Players with Three Home Runs in One Game, Fewer Than 10 in Season

American League

	Home Runs
Mickey Cochrane, Phi. A's, 1925	6
Merv Connors, Chi. White Sox, 1938	6
Billy Glynn, Cle. Indians, 1954	5
Preston Ward, K.C. A's, 1958	6
Don Leppert, Was. Senators II, 1963	6
Joe Lahoud, Bos. Red Sox, 1969	9
Fred Patek, Cal. Angels, 1980	5
Juan Beniquez, Bal. Orioles, 1986	6
Dan Johnson, Chi. White Sox, 2012	3
Seby Zavala, Chi. White Sox, 2021	5

National League (Post-1900)

	Home Runs
Hal Lee, Bos. Braves, 1934	8
Babe Ruth, Bos. Braves, 1935	6
Clyde McCullough, Chi. Cubs, 1942	5
Jim Tobin, Bos. Braves, 1942	6
Tommy Brown, Brk. Dodgers, 1950	8
Del Wilber, Phi. Phillies, 1951	8
Jim Pendleton, Mil. Braves, 1953	7
Bob Thurman, Cin. Reds, 1956	8
Roman Mejias, Pit. Pirates, 1958	5
Gene Oliver, Atl. Braves, 1966	8
Mike Lum, Atl. Braves, 1970	7
George Mitterwald, Chi. Cubs, 1974	7
Pete Rose, Cin. Reds, 1978	7
Karl Rhodes, Chi. Cubs, 1994	8
Cory Snyder, L.A. Dodgers, 1994	6
Bobby Estalella, Phi. Phillies, 1999	4
Todd Hollandsworth, Col. Rockies, 2001	6
Damion Easley, Ari. D'backs, 2006	9
Kirk Nieuwenhuis, N.Y. Mets, 2015	4
Jarrett Parker, S.F. Giants, 2015	6
Michael Perez, Pit. Pirates, 2022	6
Josh Rojas, Ari. D'backs, 2022	9

Rookies Hitting 30 or More Home Runs

Pete Alonso, N.Y. Mets (NL), 2019	53	Jose Canseco, Oak. A's (AL), 1986	33
Aaron Judge, N.Y. Yankees (AL), 2017	52	Ryan Mountcastle, Bal. Orioles (AL), 2021	33
Mark McGwire, Oak. A's (AL), 1987	49	Tony Oliva, Min. Twins (AL), 1964	32
Cody Bellinger, L.A. Dodgers (NL), 2017	39	Matt Nokes, Det. Tigers (AL), 1987	32
Wally Berger, Bos. Braves (NL), 1930	38	Chris Young, Ari. D'backs (NL), 2007	32
Frank Robinson, Cin. Reds (NL), 1956	38	Ted Williams, Bos. Red Sox (AL), 1939	31
Al Rosen, Cle. Indians (AL), 1950	37	Jim Hart, S.F. Giants (NL), 1964	31
Albert Pujols, St.L. Cardinals (NL), 2001	37	Tim Salmon, Cal. Angels (AL), 1993	31
Jose Abreu, Chi. White Sox (AL), 2014	36	Eloy Jimenez, Chi. White Sox (AL), 2019	31
Hal Trosky, Cle. Indians (AL), 1934	35	Adolis Garcia, Tex. Rangers (AL), 2021	31
Rudy York, Det. Tigers (AL), 1937	35	Bob Allison, Was. Senators (AL), 1959	30
Ron Kittle, Chi. White Sox (AL), 1983	35	Willie Montanez, Phi. Phillies (NL), 1971	30
Mike Piazza, L.A. Dodgers (NL), 1993	35	Pete Incaviglia, Tex. Rangers (AL), 1986	30
Walt Dropo, Bos. Red Sox (AL), 1950	34	Nomar Garciaparra, Bos. Red Sox (AL), 1997	30
Ryan Braun, Mil. Brewers (NL), 2007	34	Mike Trout, L.A. Angels (AL), 2012	30
Jimmie Hall, Min. Twins (AL), 1963	33		
Earl Williams, Atl. Braves (NL), 1971	33		

Former Negro Leaguers Who Led Major Leagues in Home Runs

Hank Aaron	Mil. Braves (NL)	1957	44
	Mil. Braves (NL)	1963	44
	Atl. Braves (NL)	1966	44
	Atl. Braves (NL)	1967	39
	(Played in Negro Leagues with Indianapolis Clowns, 1952.)		
Willie Mays	N.Y. Giants (NL)	1955	51
	S.F. Giants (NL)	1962	49
	S.F. Giants (NL)	1964	47
	S.F. Giants (NL)	1965	52
	(Played in Negro Leagues with Chattanooga Choo-Choos, 1947; Birmingham Black Barons, 1948–50.)		
Ernie Banks	Chi. Cubs (NL)	1958	47
	Chi. Cubs (NL)	1960	41
	(Played in Negro Leagues with Kansas City Monarchs, 1950–53.)		
Larry Doby	Cle. Indians (AL)	1952	32
	Cle. Indians (AL)	1954	32
	(Played in Negro Leagues with Newark Eagles, 1942–43, 1946–47.)		

Players with 50 Home Runs, Batting Under .300, Season

	Home Runs	Batting Average
Mark McGwire, St.L. Cardinals (NL), 1998	70	.299
Brady Anderson, Bal. Orioles (AL), 1996	50	.297
Sammy Sosa, Chi. Cubs (NL), 1999	63	.288
Prince Fielder, Mil. Brewers (NL), 2007	50	.288
David Ortiz, Bos. Red Sox (AL), 2006	54	.287
Chris Davis, Bal. Orioles (AL), 2013	53	.286
Ken Griffey Jr., Sea. Mariners (AL), 1998	56	.284
Aaron Judge, N.Y. Yankees (AL), 2017	52	.284
Giancarlo Stanton, Mia. Marlins (NL), 2017	59	.281
Mark McGwire, St.L. Cardinals (NL), 1999	65	.278
Cecil Fielder, Det. Tigers (AL), 1990	51	.277
Mark McGwire, Oak. A's (AL)–St.L. Cardinals (NL), 1997	58	.274
Greg Vaughn, S.D. Padres (NL), 1998	50	.272
Roger Maris, N.Y. Yankees (AL), 1961	61	.269
Andruw Jones, Atl. Braves (NL), 2005	51	.263
Jose Bautista, Tor. Blue Jays (AL) 2010	54	.260
Pete Alonso, N.Y. Mets (NL), 2019	53	.260

Players Hitting 49 Home Runs in Season, Never Hitting 50

American League	National League
Lou Gehrig, N.Y. Yankees, 1934 and 1936	Ted Kluszewski, Cin. Reds, 1954
Harmon Killebrew, Min. Twins, 1964 and 1969	Andre Dawson, Chi. Cubs, 1987
Frank Robinson, Bal. Orioles, 1966	Larry Walker, Col. Rockies, 1997
	Shawn Green, L.A. Dodgers, 2001
	Todd Helton, Col. Rockies, 2001
	Albert Pujols, St.L. Cardinals, 2006
	Eugenio Suarez, Cin. Reds, 2019

Players Hitting 40 or More Home Runs in Season, Never Hitting 30 or More in Any Other Season, Career

	40+ HR Season	Next Highest HR Season
Rico Petrocelli	1969 (40)	1970 (29)
Davey Johnson	1973 (43)	1971 (18)
Jesse Barfield	1986 (40)	1987 (28)
Ken Caminiti	1996 (40)	1998 (29)
Brady Anderson	1996 (50)	1999 (24)
Richard Hidalgo	2000 (44)	2003 (28)
Ronald Acuna*	2019 (41)	2018 (26)
Jorge Soler*	2019 (48)	2021 (27)
Fernando Tatis Jr.*	2021 (42)	2019 (22)

* Active.

Most Multi-Home Run Games, Career

72	Babe Ruth (1914–35)
71	Barry Bonds (1986–2007)
69	Sammy Sosa (1989–2007)
67	Mark McGwire (1914–35)
65	Albert Pujols (2001–22)
63	Willie Mays (1951–52, 1954–73)
62	Hank Aaron (1954–76)
62	Alex Rodriguez (1994–2013, 2015–16)
55	Jimmie Foxx (1925–42, 1944–45)
55	Ken Griffey Jr. (1989–2010)
54	Frank Robinson (1956–76)
54	Manny Ramirez (1993–2011)
51	David Ortiz (1997–2016)

Most Grand Slams, Career

25	Alex Rodriguez (1994–2013, 2015–16)	17	Carlos Lee (1999–2012)
23	Lou Gehrig (1923–39)	16	Dave Kingman (1971–86)
21	Manny Ramirez (1993–2011)	16	Babe Ruth (1914–35)
19	Eddie Murray (1977–97)	16	Hank Aaron (1954–76)
18	Willie McCovey (1959–80)	16	Albert Pujols (2001–22)
18	Robin Ventura (1989–2004)	15	Ken Griffey Jr. (1989–2010)
17	Jimmie Foxx (1925–42, 1944–45)	15	Richie Sexson (1997–2008)
17	Ted Williams (1939–42, 1946–60)	15	Ryan Howard (2004–16)

Players Hitting Two Grand Slams, Same Game

American League	National League
Tony Lazzeri, N.Y. Yankees, May 24, 1936	Tony Cloninger, Atl. Braves, Jul. 3, 1966
Jim Tabor, Bos. Red Sox, Jul. 4, 1939	Fernando Tatis, St.L. Cardinals, Apr. 23, 1999*
Rudy York, Bos. Red Sox, Jul. 27, 1946	Josh Willingham, Was. Nationals, Jul. 17, 2009
Jim Gentile, Bal. Orioles, May 9, 1961	* Same inning.
Jim Northrup, Det. Tigers, Jun. 24, 1968	
Frank Robinson, Bal. Orioles, Jun. 26, 1970	
Robin Ventura, Chi. White Sox, Sep. 4, 1995	
Chris Hoiles, Bal. Orioles, Aug. 14, 1998	
Nomar Garciaparra, Bos. Red Sox, May 10, 1999	
Bill Mueller, Bos. Red Sox, Jul. 29, 2003	

Most Home Runs by Age

Teens

24	Tony Conigliaro
22	Bryce Harper
22	Juan Soto
19	Mel Ott
18	Phil Cavarretta
16	Ken Griffey Jr.
13	Mickey Mantle
12	Ed Kranepool
11	Robin Yount

Twenties

424	Alex Rodriguez
382	Ken Griffey Jr.
376	Jimmie Foxx
370	Eddie Mathews
366	Albert Pujols
361	Mickey Mantle
342	Hank Aaron
339	Juan Gonzalez
337	Andruw Jones
324	Frank Robinson

Thirties

444	Barry Bonds
424	Babe Ruth
396	Rafael Palmeiro
371	Hank Aaron
356	Jim Thome
354	Mark McGwire
349	Willie Mays
340	Nelson Cruz
336	Sammy Sosa
326	David Ortiz

Forties

72	Carlton Fisk
67	Darrell Evans
59	Dave Winfield
59	Barry Bonds
53	Raul Ibanez
48	Carl Yastrzemski
47	Albert Pujols
46	Stan Musial
42	Nelson Cruz
42	Hank Aaron

Teenagers Hitting Grand Slams

Scott Stratton, Lou. Colonels (AA), May 27, 1889	19 years, 7 months
George S. Davis, Cle. Spiders (NL), May 30, 1890	19 years, 9 months
Eddie Onslow, Det. Tigers (AL), Aug. 22, 1912	19 years, 6 months
Phil Cavarretta, Chi. Cubs (NL), May 16, 1936	19 years, 10 months
Al Kaline, Det. Tigers (AL), Jun. 11, 1954	19 years, 6 months
Harmon Killebrew, Was. Senators (AL), Jun. 11, 1954	19 years, 11 months
Vada Pinson, Cin. Reds (NL), Apr. 18, 1958	19 years, 8 months
Tony Conigliaro, Bos. Red Sox (AL), Jun. 3, 1964	19 years, 5 months

Oldest Players to Hit Grand Slams

American League

Henry Blanco, Sea. Mariners, Aug. 1, 2013	41 years, 11 months
Henry Blanco, Sea. Mariners, Jun. 15, 2013	41 years, 9 months
Minnie Minoso, Was. Senators II, Jul. 24, 1963	41 years, 5 months
Raul Ibanez, Sea. Mariners, May 15, 2013	40 years, 11 months
Rafael Palmeiro, Bal. Orioles, Jun. 4, 2005	40 years, 9 months
Nelson Cruz, Min. Twins, Apr. 5, 2021	40 years, 9 months
Albert Pujols, L.A. Angels, Aug. 2, 2020	40 years, 7 months
Darrell Evans, Det. Tigers, Sep. 5, 1987	40 years, 3 months
Matt Stairs, Tor. Blue Jays, May 14, 2008	40 years, 3 months
Raul Ibanez, N.Y. Yankees, Jul. 16, 2012	40 years, 1 month
Mickey Vernon, Cle. Indians, Apr. 25, 1958	40 years, 0 months
Alex Rodriguez, N.Y. Yankees, Aug. 18, 2015	40 years, 0 months

National League

Julio Franco, Atl. Braves, Jun. 25, 2005	46 years, 10 months
Julio Franco, Atl. Braves, Jun. 3, 2004	45 years, 10 months
Albert Pujols, St.L. Cardinals, Aug. 18, 2022	42 years, 8 months
Cap Anson, Chi. Cubs, Aug. 1, 1894	42 years, 3 months
Craig Biggio, Hou. Astros, Jul. 29, 2007	41 years, 8 months
Matt Stairs, Phi. Phillies, Sep. 10, 2009	41 years, 7 months
Honus Wagner, Pit. Pirates, Jul. 29, 1915	41 years, 5 months

continued on next page

Craig Biggio, Hou. Astros, Apr. 20, 2007..41 years, 5 months
Stan Musial, St.L. Cardinals, Jun. 23, 1961...40 years, 7 months
Hank Aaron, Atl. Braves, Jun. 4, 1974 ....40 years, 3 months
Hank Aaron, Atl. Braves, Apr. 26, 1974 ....40 years, 2 months

Oldest Home Run Champions*

American League

	Age	Home Runs
Darrell Evans, Det. Tigers, 1985	38 years, 5 months	40
Babe Ruth, N.Y. Yankees, 1931	36 years, 8 months	46
Reggie Jackson, Cal. Angels, 1982	36 years, 5 months	39
Hank Greenberg, Det. Tigers, 1946	35 years, 9 months	44
Babe Ruth, N.Y. Yankees, 1930	35 years, 8 months	49

National League (Post-1900)

	Age	Home Runs
Cy Williams, Phi. Phillies, 1927	39 years, 10 months	30
Gavvy Cravath, Phi. Phillies, 1919	38 years, 7 months	12
Gavvy Cravath, Phi. Phillies, 1918	37 years, 7 months	8
Barry Bonds, S.F. Giants, 2001	37 years, 3 months	73
Mike Schmidt, Phi. Phillies, 1986	37 years, 1 month	37
Gavvy Cravath, Phi. Phillies, 1917	36 years, 7 months	12
Mark McGwire, St.L. Cardinals, 1999	36 years, 0 months	65
Cy Williams, Phi. Phillies, 1923	35 years, 10 months	41
Johnny Mize, N.Y. Giants, 1948	35 years, 9 months	40
Sam Thompson, Phi. Phillies, 1895	35 years, 7 months	18
Hank Sauer, Chi. Cubs, 1952	35 years, 7 months	37
Andres Galarraga, Col. Rockies, 1996	35 years, 4 months	47
Jack Fournier, Brk. Dodgers, 1924	35 years, 1 month	27
Mike Schmidt, Phi. Phillies, 1984	35 years, 1 month	35
Mark McGwire, St.L. Cardinals, 1998	35 years, 0 months	70

* As of October that year.

Most Career Home Runs by Players Hitting Home Run on First Pitch in Majors

360.............Gary Gaetti, Min. Twins (AL), Sep. 20, 1981
284.................Will Clark, S.F. Giants (NL), Apr. 8, 1986
260.............Tim Wallach, Mon. Expos (NL), Sep. 6, 1980
238.............Earl Averill, Cle. Indians (AL), Apr. 16, 1929
202.................Bill White, N.Y. Giants (NL), May 7, 1956
195.................Jay Bell, Cle. Indians (AL), Sep. 29, 1986
182............Terry Steinbach, Oak. A's (AL), Sep. 12, 1986
142........Wally Moon, St.L. Cardinals (NL), Apr. 13, 1954
125...........Bob Nieman, St.L. Browns (AL), Sep. 13, 1951
115.......Marcus Thames, N.Y. Yankees (AL), Jun. 10, 2002
114..........Whitey Lockman, N.Y. Giants (NL), Jul. 5, 1945
87......Kevin Kouzmanoff, Cle. Indians (AL), Sep. 2, 2006
85...........Starling Marte*, Pit. Pirates (NL), Jul. 26, 2012
80...........J.P. Arencibia, Tor. Blue Jays (AL), Aug. 7, 2010
79..............Bert Campaneris, K.C. A's (AL), Jul. 23, 1964

74.............Eddie Rosario*, Min. Twins (AL), May 6, 2015
69...............Clyde Vollmer, Cin. Reds (NL), May 31, 1942
55.............Junior Felix, Tor. Blue Jays (AL), May 14, 1989
43........Willson Contreras*, Chi. Cubs (NL), Jun. 19, 2016
38.........Brant Alyea, Was. Senators II (AL), Sep. 12, 1965
35.................Al Woods, Tor. Blue Jays (AL), Apr. 7, 1977
34..........Chris Richard, St.L. Cardinals (NL), Jul. 17, 2000
32.................Kazuo Matsui, N.Y. Mets (NL), Apr. 6, 2004
29.............Daniel Nava, Bos. Red Sox (AL), Jun. 12, 2010
21.............Chuck Tanner, Mil. Braves (NL), Apr. 12, 1955
15.................Akil Baddoo, Det. Tigers (AL), Apr. 4, 2021
14.......Andy Phillips, N.Y. Yankees (AL), Sep. 26, 2004
12................George Vico, Det. Tigers (AL), Apr. 20, 1948
10....Adam Wainwright*, St.L. Cardinals (NL), May 24, 2006
8....................Jim Bullinger, Chi. Cubs (NL), Jun. 8, 1992

continued on next page

3............ Clise Dudley, Brk. Dodgers (NL), Apr. 27, 1929
3............... ..Jay Gainer, Col. Rockies (NL), May 14, 1993
2............... Frank Ernaga, Chi. Cubs (NL), May 24, 1957
1.................... Don Rose, Cal. Angels (AL), May 24, 1972
1.......... Eddie Morgan, St.L. Cardinals (NL), Apr. 14, 1936

1...................... Esteban Yan, T.B. Devil Rays, Jun. 4, 2000
1.......... Gene Stechschulte, St.L. Cardinals, Apr. 27, 2001
1............... Mark Saccomanno, Hou. Astros, Sep. 8, 2008
1.............. Tommy Milone*, Was. Nationals, Sep. 3, 2011

* Still active.

Players Hitting Home Run in First Time At-Bat, Never Hitting Another

American League

Luke Stuart, St.L. Browns, Aug. 8, 1921 (Career: 1921)
Bill Lefebvre, Bos. Red Sox, Jun. 10, 1938
  (Career: 1938–39, 1943–44)
Hack Miller, Det. Tigers, Apr. 23, 1944 (Career: 1944–45)
Bill Roman, Det. Tigers, Sep. 30, 1964 (Career: 1964–65)
Don Rose, Cal. Angels, May 24, 1972
  (Career: 1971–72, 1974)

Dave Machemer, Cal. Angels, Jun. 21, 1978
  (Career: 1978–79)
Andre David, Min. Twins, Jun. 29, 1984
  (Career: 1984, 1986)
Esteban Yan, T.B. Devil Rays, Jun. 4, 2000
  (Career: 1996–2006)

National League (Post-1900)

Eddie Morgan, St.L. Cardinals, Apr. 14, 1936
  (Career: 1936–37)
Dan Bankhead, Brk. Dodgers, Aug. 26, 1947
  (Career: 1947, 1950–51)
Hoyt Wilhelm, N.Y. Giants, Apr. 23, 1952
  (Career: 1952–72)
Cuno Barragan, Chi. Cubs, Sep. 1, 1961 (Career: 1961–63)
Jose Sosa, Hou. Astros, Jul. 30, 1975 (Career: 1975–76)

Dave Eiland, S.D. Padres, Apr. 10, 1992
  (Career: 1988–93, 1995, 1998–2000)
Mitch Lyden, Fla. Marlins, Jun. 6, 1993 (Career: 1993)
Gene Stechschulte, St.L. Cardinals, Apr. 17, 2001
  (Career: 2000–02)
David Matranga, Hou. Astros, Jun. 27, 2003 (Career: 2003)
Mark Worrell, St.L. Cardinals, Jun. 5, 2008 (Career: 2008–11)
Mark Saccomanno, Hou. Astros, Sep. 8, 2008 (Career: 2008)
Tommy Milone, Was. Nationals, Sep. 3, 2011 (Career: 2011–)
Eddy Rodriguez, S.D. Padres, Aug. 2, 2012 (Career: 2012)

Most At-Bats, No Home Runs, Career (Post-1900)

2736...Jack McCarthy (1900–07)
1931............................... Tom Oliver (1930–33)
1904...Irv Hall (1943–46)
1426.......................................Roxy Walters (1915–25)
1354........................... Don Sutton (1966–89)

1287... Waite Hoyt (1918–38)
1271..Gil Torres (1940–46)
1269...Tim Johnson (1973–79)
1251... Luis Gomez (1974–81)
1212... Joe Sugden (1901–12)

Most Consecutive At-Bats Without a Home Run

3347.................................... Tommy Thevenow...Sep. 22, 1926–end of career, 1938
3278.................................... Eddie Foster..Apr. 20, 1916–end of career, 1923
3246.................................... Al Bridwell.................................Start of career, 1905–Apr. 30, 1913
3186.................................... Terry Turner................................Jul. 16, 1906–Jun. 30, 1914
3104.................................... Sparky Adams................................Jul. 26, 1925–Jun. 30, 1931
3021.................................... Jack McCarthy.................................Jun. 28, 1899–end of career, 1907
2701.................................... Lee Tannehill................................. Sep. 2, 1903–Jul. 31, 1910
2663.................................... Doc Cramer................................. Sep. 8, 1935–May 21, 1940
2617.................................... Donie Bush.................................Aug. 29, 1915–Aug. 21, 1920
2568.................................... Mike Tresh................................May 19, 1940–Apr. 20, 1948
2480.................................... Bill Bergen................................Jun. 3, 1901–Sep. 6, 1909
2426.................................... Joe Sugden................................. May 31, 1895–end of career, 1912
2423.................................... Emil Verban ....Start of career, 1944–Sep. 6, 1948
2401.................................... Everett Scott...Aug. 1, 1914–Apr. 26, 1920

Lowest Batting Average for Home Run Leaders, Season (Post-1900)

Batting Average   **Home Runs**

.204	Dave Kingman, N.Y. Mets (NL), 1982	37
.218	Kyle Schwarber, Phi. Phillies (NL), 2022	46
.222	Chris Carter, Mil. Brewers (NL), 2016	41
.227	Carlos Pena, T.B. Rays (AL), 2009	39
.232	Gavvy Cravath, Phi. Phillies (NL), 1918	8
.233	Pedro Alvarez, Pit. Pirates (NL), 2013	36
.241	Fred Odwell, Cin. Reds (NL), 1905	9
.242	Harmon Killebrew, Min. Twins (AL), 1959	42
.243	Harmon Killebrew, Min. Twins (AL), 1962	48
.244	Wally Pipp, N.Y. Yankees (AL), 1917	9
.244	Ralph Kiner, Pit. Pirates (NL), 1952	37
.244	Gorman Thomas, Mil. Brewers (AL), 1979	45
.245	Gorman Thomas, Mil. Brewers (AL), 1982	39
.247	Tim Jordan, Brk. Dodgers (NL), 1908	12
.247	Ralph Kiner, Pit. Pirates (NL), 1946	23
.247	Khris Davis, Oak. A's (AL), 2018	48
.248	Darrell Evans, Det. Tigers (AL), 1985	40
.249	Mike Schmidt, Phi. Phillies (NL), 1975	38

Players Hitting 30 or More Home Runs in First Three Seasons

Jose Canseco, Oak. A's (AL)	1986 (33), 1987 (31), and 1988 (42*)
Mark McGwire, Oak. A's (AL)	1987 (49*), 1988 (32), and 1989 (33)
Albert Pujols, St.L. Cardinals (NL)	2001 (37), 2002 (34), and 2003 (43)
Ryan Braun, Mil. Brewers (NL)	2007 (34), 2008 (37), and 2009 (32)

* Led the league.

Reverse 30–30 Club: Players with 30 Home Runs and 30 Errors, Season

American League (Post-1900)

	Home Runs	Errors
Harmon Killebrew, Wash Senators, 1959	42	30
Mark Reynolds, Bal. Orioles, 2011	37	31
Troy Glaus, Ana. Angels, 2000	47	33

National League (Post-1900)

	Home Runs	Errors
Rogers Hornsby, St.L. Cardinals, 1922	42	30
Davey Johnson, Atl. Braves, 1973	43	30
Pedro Guerrero, L.A. Dodgers, 1983	32	30
Howard Johnson, N.Y. Mets, 1991	38	31
Ernie Banks, Chi. Cubs, 1958	47	32
Tony Perez, Cin. Reds, 1969	37	32
Rogers Hornsby, St.L. Cardinals, 1924	39	34
Tony Perez, Cin. Reds, 1970	40	35

Players Increasing Their Home Run Production in Seven Consecutive Seasons

Darrin Fletcher	Phi. Phillies (NL), 1990	0
	Phi. Phillies (NL), 1991	1
	Mon. Expos (NL), 1992	2
	Mon. Expos (NL), 1993	9
	Mon. Expos (NL), 1994	10
	Mon. Expos (NL), 1995	11
	Mon. Expos (NL), 1996	12
	Mon. Expos (NL), 1997	17

continued on next page

Tim McCarver	St.L. Cardinals (NL), 1960	0
	St.L. Cardinals (NL), 1961	1
	St.L. Cardinals (NL), 1963	4
	St.L. Cardinals (NL), 1964	9
	St.L. Cardinals (NL), 1965	11
	St.L. Cardinals (NL), 1966	12
	St.L. Cardinals (NL), 1967	14
David Ortiz	Min. Twins (AL), 1999	0
	Min. Twins (AL), 2000	10
	Min. Twins (AL), 2001	18
	Min. Twins (AL), 2002	20
	Bos. Red Sox (AL), 2003	31
	Bos. Red Sox (AL), 2004	41
	Bos. Red Sox (AL), 2005	47
	Bos. Red Sox (AL), 2006	54
Salvador Perez	K.C. Royals (AL), 2011	3
	K.C. Royals (AL), 2012	11
	K.C. Royals (AL), 2013	13
	K.C. Royals (AL), 2014	17
	K.C. Royals (AL), 2015	21
	K.C. Royals (AL), 2016	22
	K.C. Royals (AL), 2017	27
Jimmy Piersall	Bos. Red Sox (AL), 1950	0
	Bos. Red Sox (AL), 1952	1
	Bos. Red Sox (AL), 1953	3
	Bos. Red Sox (AL), 1954	8
	Bos. Red Sox (AL), 1955	13
	Bos. Red Sox (AL), 1956	14
	Bos. Red Sox (AL), 1957	19
Eddie Robinson	Cle. Indians (AL), 1942	0
	Cle. Indians (AL), 1946	3
	Cle. Indians (AL), 1947	14
	Cle. Indians (AL), 1948	16
	Was. Senators (AL), 1949	18
	Was. Senators (AL)–Chi. White Sox (AL), 1950	21
	Chi. White Sox (AL), 1951	29
John Shelby	Bal. Orioles (AL), 1981	0
	Bal. Orioles (AL), 1982	1
	Bal. Orioles (AL), 1983	5
	Bal. Orioles (AL), 1984	6
	Bal. Orioles (AL), 1985	7
	Bal. Orioles (AL), 1986	11
	L.A. Dodgers (NL), 1987	22
Jim Thome	Cle. Indians (AL), 1991	1
	Cle. Indians (AL), 1991	1
	Cle. Indians (AL), 1991	1
	Cle. Indians (AL), 1991	1
	Cle. Indians (AL), 1991	1
	Cle. Indians (AL), 1991	1
	Cle. Indians (AL), 1991	1
Cy Williams	Chi. Cubs (NL), 1917	5
	Phi. Phillies (NL), 1918	6
	Phi. Phillies (NL), 1919	9
	Phi. Phillies (NL), 1920	15
	Phi. Phillies (NL), 1921	18
	Phi. Phillies (NL), 1922	26
	Phi. Phillies (NL), 1923	41

Most Home Runs by Switch-Hitters, Career

536	Mickey Mantle (1951–68)
504	Eddie Murray (1977–97)
468	Chipper Jones (1993, 1995–2012)
435	Carlos Beltran (1998–2017)
409	Mark Teixeira (2003–16)

Most Home Runs by Catcher, Season*

42	Javy Lopez, Atl. Braves (NL), 2003
41	Todd Hundley, N.Y. Mets (NL), 1996
40	Roy Campanella, Brk. Dodgers (NL), 1953
40	Mike Piazza, L.A. Dodgers (NL), 1997
40	Mike Piazza, N.Y. Mets (NL), 1999
38	Johnny Bench, Cin. Reds (NL), 1970
36	Gabby Hartnett, Chi. Cubs (NL), 1930
36	Mike Piazza, L.A. Dodgers (NL), 1996

* While in lineup as catcher.

Most Home Runs by Catcher, Career*

396	Mike Piazza (1992–2007)
351	Carlton Fisk (1969, 1971–93)
327	Johnny Bench (1967–83)
306	Yogi Berra (1946–65)
304	Ivan Rodriguez (1991–2011)
299	Lance Parrish (1977–95)
298	Gary Carter (1974–92)

* While in lineup as catcher.

300 Career Home Runs with 100 Home Runs, Both Leagues

	American League	National League	Total
Adrian Beltre	330	147	477
Carlos Beltran	200	235	435
Bobby Bonds	135	197	332
Ellis Burks	177	175	352
Miguel Cabrera*	369	138	507
Chili Davis	249	101	350
Adam Dunn	108	354	462
Carlos Delgado	336	137	473
Jim Edmonds	121	272	393
Darrell Evans	141	273	414
Curtis Granderson	228	116	344
Shawn Green	119	209	328
Ken Griffey Jr.	420	210	630
Vladimir Guerrero	215	234	449
Frank Howard	259	123	382
David Justice	145	160	305
Carlos Lee	161	197	358
Lee May	126	228	354
Fred McGriff	224	269	493
Mark McGwire	363	220	583
Eddie Murray	396	108	504
Albert Pujols	222	481	703
Frank Robinson	262	324	586
Richie Sexson	164	142	306
Gary Sheffield	141	368	509
Reggie Smith	149	165	314
Alfonso Soriano	185	227	412
Giancarlo Stanton*	111	267	378
Jim Thome	511	101	612
Justin Upton*	135	190	325
Greg Vaughn	229	126	355

* Still active.

Most Home Runs Hit in One Ballpark, Career

323	Mel Ott	Polo Grounds
293	Sammy Sosa	Wrigley Field
290	Ernie Banks	Wrigley Field
266	Mickey Mantle	Yankee Stadium
265	Mike Schmidt	Veterans Stadium
263	Frank Thomas	U.S. Cellular Field
259	Babe Ruth	Yankee Stadium
259	Paul Konerko	U.S. Cellular Field
252	Stan Musial	Sportsman's Park

continued on next page

251	Lou Gehrig	Yankee Stadium
248	Ted Williams	Fenway Park
246	Harmon Killebrew	Metropolitan Stadium
237	Carl Yastrzemski	Fenway Park
236	Willie McCovey	Candlestick Park
231	Billy Williams	Wrigley Field
227	Todd Helton	Coors Field
226	Al Kaline	Tiger Stadium
226	Chipper Jones	Turner Field

Players Whose Home Run in "Cycle" Was Grand Slam

American League

Nap Lajoie, Phi. A's, Jul. 30, 1901
Tony Lazzeri, N.Y. Yankees, Jun. 3, 1932
Jimmie Foxx, Phi. A's, Aug. 14, 1933
Jay Buhner, Sea. Mariners, Jul. 23, 1993
Miguel Tejada, Oak. A's, Sep. 29, 2001
Jason Kubel, Min. Twins, Apr. 17, 2009
Bengie Molina, Tex. Rangers, Jul. 16, 2010

National League

Bill Terry, N.Y. Giants, May 29, 1928

Players with the Highest Percentage of Team's Total Home Runs, Season

American League

88%	Babe Ruth, Bos. Red Sox, 1919	29 of team's 33
73%	Babe Ruth, Bos. Red Sox, 1918	11 of team's 15
56%	Smoky Joe Wood, Cle. Indians, 1918	5 of team's 9
55%	Goose Goslin, Was. Senators, 1924	12 of team's 22
55%	Stan Spence, Was. Senators, 1944	18 of team's 33
51%	Jimmie Foxx, Bos. Red Sox, 1938	50 of team's 98
50%	Erve Beck, Cle. Blues, 1901	6 of team's 12
50%	Tilly Walker, Phi. A's, 1918	11 of team's 22
50%	Joe Judge, Was. Senators, 1917	2 of team's 4
50%	Sam Chapman, Phi. A's, 1946	20 of team's 40

National League (Post-1900)

60%	Shad Barry, Phi. Phillies, 1902	3 of team's 5
60%	Jimmy Seckard, Brk. Dodgers, 1903	9 of team's 15
60%	Harry Lumley, Brk. Dodgers, 1904	9 of team's 15
58%	Wally Berger, Bos. Braves, 1930	38 of team's 66
56%	Wally Berger, Bos. Braves, 1931	19 of team's 34
56%	Bill Nicholson, Chi. Cubs, 1943	29 of team's 52
53%	Ed Konetchy, St.L. Cardinals, 1913	8 of team's 15
53%	Cy Williams, Phi. Phillies, 1927	30 of team's 57
52%	Dick Hoblitzel, Cin. Reds, 1911	11 of team's 21
50%	Homer Smoot, St.L. Cardinals, 1903	4 of team's 8
50%	Sherry Magee, Phi. Phillies, 1906	6 of team's 12
50%	Harry Lumley, Brk. Dodgers, 1907	9 of team's 18
50%	Wally Berger, Bos. Braves, 1933	27 of team's 54

Shortstops Leading League in Home Runs

American League

Vern Stephens, St.L. Browns, 1945 ... 24
Alex Rodriguez, Tex. Rangers, 2001 ... 52
Alex Rodriguez, Tex. Rangers, 2002 ... 57
Alex Rodriguez, Tex. Rangers, 2003 ... 47

National League

Ernie Banks, Chi. Cubs, 1958 ... 47
Ernie Banks, Chi. Cubs, 1959 ... 45
Fernando Tatis Jr., S.D. Padres, 2021 ... 42

Most Home Runs by Left-Handed Hitting Shortstops

Home Runs		Games at Short
139	Brandon Crawford* (2011–)	1525
137	Corey Seager* (2015–)	750
134	Didi Gregorius* (2012–)	1049
123	Stephen Drew (2006–17)	1007
87	Arky Vaughan (1932–43, 1947–48)	1067
78	Dick McAuliffe (1960–75)	1485
49	Tony Kubek (1957–65)	882
38	Craig Reynolds (1975–89)	1240
33	Solly Hemus (1949–59)	471

* Still active.

Players Hitting Home Runs in 20 Consecutive Seasons Played

Rickey Henderson (1979–2003)	25		Ron Fairly (1958–78)	21
Ty Cobb (1905–28)	24		Reggie Jackson (1967–87)	21
Hank Aaron (1954–76)	23		Graig Nettles (1968–88)	21
Carl Yastrzemski (1961–83)	23		Eddie Murray (1977–97)	21
Rusty Staub (1963–85)	23		Harold Baines (1980–2000)	21
Carlton Fisk (1971–93)	23		Tim Raines (1981–99, 2001–02)	21
Stan Musial (1941–44, 1946–63)	22		Cal Ripken Jr. (1981–2001)	21
Willie Mays (1951–52, 1954–73)	22		Ken Griffey Jr. (1989–2009)	21
Al Kaline (1953–74)	22		Ivan Rodriguez (1991–2011)	21
Brooks Robinson (1956–77)	22		Adrian Beltre (1998–2018)	21
Willie McCovey (1959–80)	22		Mel Ott (1927–46)	20
Tony Perez (1965–86)	22		Dwight Evans (1972–91)	20
Dave Winfield (1973–88, 1990–95)	22		Brian Downing (1973–92)	20
Barry Bonds (1986–2007)	22		George Brett (1974–93)	20
Gary Sheffield (1988–2009)	22		Robin Yount (1974–93)	20
Jim Thome (1991–2012)	22		Andre Dawson (1977–96)	20
Alex Rodriguez (1995–2013, 2015–16)	22		Tony Gwynn (1982–2001)	20
Albert Pujols (2001–22)	22		Rafael Palmiero (1986–2005)	20
Babe Ruth (1915–35)	21		Jason Giambi (1995–2014)	20
Frank Robinson (1956–76)	21		Miguel Cabrera (2003–22)	20

Players with 100 Home Runs, Three Different Teams

Adrian Beltre	L.A. Dodgers (NL), 1998–2004	147
	Sea. Mariners (AL), 2005–09	103
	Tex Rangers (AL), 2011–2018	199
Darrell Evans	Atl. Braves (NL), 1969–76, 1989	131
	S.F. Giants (NL), 1976–83	142
	Det. Tigers (AL), 1984–88	141
Reggie Jackson	K.C.–Oak. A's (AL), 1967–75, 1987	269
	N.Y. Yankees (AL), 1977–81	144
	Cal. Angels (AL), 1982–86	123
Jim Thome	Cle. Indians (AL), 1991–2002, 2011	337
	Phi. Phillies (NL), 2003–2005, 2012	101
	Chi. White Sox (AL), 2006–09	134
Alex Rodriguez	Sea. Mariners (AL), 1994–2000	189
	Tex. Rangers (AL), 2001–03	156
	N.Y. Yankees (AL), 2004–13, 2015–16	351

Players with 40-Home Run Seasons Before 25th Birthday

		Home Runs	Age
Hank Aaron	Mil. Braves (NL), 1957	44	23
Ronald Acuna Jr.	Atl. Braves (NL), 2019	41	21

continued on next page

		Home Runs	Age
Dick Allen	Phi. Phillies (NL), 1966	40	24
Pete Alonso	N.Y. Mets (NL), 2019	53	24
Nolan Arenado	Col. Rockies (NL), 2015	42	24
Ernie Banks	Chi. Cubs (NL), 1955	44	24
Cody Bellinger	L.A. Dodgers (NL), 2019	47	23
Johnny Bench	Cin. Reds (NL), 1970	45	22
	Cin. Reds (NL), 1972	40	24
Jose Canseco	Oak. A's (AL), 1988	42	23
Orlando Cepeda	S.F. Giants (NL), 1961	46	23
Rocky Colavito	Cle. Indians (AL), 1958	41	24
Joe DiMaggio	N.Y. Yankees (AL), 1937	46	22
Adam Dunn	Cin. Reds (NL), 2004	46	24
Prince Fielder	Mil. Brewers (NL), 2007	50	23
Jimmie Foxx	Phi. A's (AL), 1932	58	24*
Joey Gallo	Tex. Rangers (AL), 2017	41	23
	Tex. Rangers (AL), 2018	40	24
Lou Gehrig	N.Y. Yankees (AL), 1927	47	24
Troy Glaus	Ana. Angels (AL), 2000	47	23
	Ana. Angels (AL), 2001	41	24
Juan Gonzalez	Tex. Rangers (AL), 1992	43	22
	Tex. Rangers (AL), 1993	46	23
Ken Griffey Jr.	Sea. Mariners (AL), 1993	45	23
	Sea. Mariners (AL), 1994	40	24
Vladimir Guerrero	Mon. Expos (NL), 1999	42	24
Vladimir Guerrero Jr.	Tor. Blue Jays (AL), 2021	48	22
Bryce Harper	Was. Nationals (NL), 2015	42	22
Reggie Jackson	Oak. A's (AL), 1969	47	23
Harmon Killebrew	Was. Senators (AL), 1959	42	23
Ralph Kiner	Pit. Pirates (NL), 1947	51	24*
Chuck Klein	Phi. Phillies (NL), 1929	43	24*
Mickey Mantle	N.Y. Yankees (AL), 1956	52	24*
Eddie Mathews	Mil. Braves (NL), 1953	47	21
	Mil. Braves (NL), 1954	40	22
	Mil. Braves (NL), 1955	41	23
Willie Mays	N.Y. Giants (NL), 1954	41	23
	N.Y. Giants (NL), 1955	51	24
Mark McGwire	Oak. A's (AL), 1987	49	23
Mel Ott	N.Y. Giants (NL), 1929	42	20
Albert Pujols	St.L. Cardinals (NL), 2003	43	23
	St.L. Cardinals (NL), 2004	46	24
Alex Rodriguez	Sea. Mariners (AL), 1998	42	23
	Sea. Mariners (AL), 1999	42	24
	Sea. Mariners (AL), 2000	41	25
Fernando Tatis Jr.	S.D. Padres (NL), 2021	42	22
Hal Trosky	Cle. Indians (AL), 1936	42	23
Mike Trout	L.A. Angels (AL), 2015	41	23

* Turned 25 during season.

Players with More Home Runs Than Strikeouts, Season (Min. 10 Home Runs)

American League

	Home Runs	Strikeouts	Differential
Lou Gehrig, N.Y. Yankees, 1934	49	31	+18
Joe DiMaggio, N.Y. Yankees, 1941	30	13	+17
Yogi Berra, N.Y. Yankees, 1950	28	12	+16
Ken Williams, St.L. Browns, 1925	25	14	+11
Joe DiMaggio, N.Y. Yankees, 1938	32	21	+11
Joe DiMaggio, N.Y. Yankees, 1939	30	20	+10
Ted Williams, Bos. Red Sox, 1941	37	27	+10
Joe DiMaggio, N.Y. Yankees, 1937	46	37	+9

continued on next page

	Home Runs	Strikeouts	Differential
Joe DiMaggio, N.Y. Yankees, 1948	39	30	+9
Lou Boudreau, Cle. Indians, 1948	18	9	+9
Ken Williams, St.L. Browns, 1922	39	31	+8
Joe Sewell, N.Y. Yankees, 1932	11	3	+8
Bill Dickey, N.Y. Yankees, 1937	29	22	+7
Ted Williams, Bos. Red Sox, 1950	28	21	+7
Yogi Berra, N.Y. Yankees, 1951	27	20	+7
Yogi Berra, N.Y. Yankees, 1955	27	20	+7
Bill Dickey, N.Y. Yankees, 1936	22	16	+6
Yogi Berra, N.Y. Yankees, 1952	30	24	+6
Mickey Cochrane, Phi. A's, 1927	12	7	+5
Bill Dickey, N.Y. Yankees, 1938	27	22	+5
Ted Williams, Bos. Red Sox, 1955	28	24	+4
Charlie Gehringer, Det. Tigers, 1935	19	16	+3
Bill Dickey, N.Y. Yankees, 1935	14	11	+3
Lou Gehrig, N.Y. Yankees, 1936	49	46	+3
Ted Williams, Bos. Red Sox, 1953	13	10	+3
Lou Skizas, K.C. A's, 1957	18	15	+3
Tris Speaker, Cle. Indians, 1923	17	15	+2
Al Simmons, Phi. A's, 1930	36	34	+2
Bill Dickey, N.Y. Yankees, 1932	15	13	+2
Charlie Gehringer, Det. Tigers, 1936	15	13	+2
Vic Power, K.C. A's–Cle. Indians, 1958	16	14	+2
George Brett, K.C. Royals, 1980	24	22	+2
Ken Williams, St.L. Browns, 1924	18	17	+1
Mickey Cochrane, Phi. A's, 1932	23	22	+1
Joe DiMaggio, N.Y. Yankees, 1940	31	30	+1
Joe DiMaggio, N.Y. Yankees, 1946	25	24	+1
Johnny Mize, N.Y. Yankees, 1950	25	24	+1
Yogi Berra, N.Y. Yankees, 1956	30	29	+1

National League

	Home Runs	Strikeouts	Differential
Tommy Holmes, Bos. Braves, 1945	28	9	+19
Ted Kluszewski, Cin. Reds, 1954	49	35	+14
Lefty O'Doul, Phi. Phillies, 1929	32	19	+13
Johnny Mize, N.Y. Giants, 1947	51	42	+9
Cap Anson, Chi. Colts, 1884	21	13	+8
Ernie Lombardi, N.Y. Giants, 1945	19	11	+8
Sam Thompson, Phi. Phillies, 1895	18	11	+7
Ted Kluszewski, Cin. Reds, 1955	47	40	+7
Jack Clements, Phi. Phillies, 1895	13	7	+6
Billy Southworth, St.L. Cardinals, 1926	16	10	+6
Ernie Lombardi, Cin. Reds, 1935	12	6	+6
Willard Marshall, N.Y. Giants, 1947	36	30	+6
Ted Kluszewski, Cin. Reds, 1953	40	34	+6
Bill Terry, N.Y. Giants, 1932	28	23	+5
Ernie Lombardi, Cin. Reds, 1938	19	14	+5
Stan Musial, St.L. Cardinals, 1948	39	34	+5
Mel Ott, N.Y. Giants, 1929	42	38	+4
Frank McCormick, Cin. Reds, 1941	17	13	+4
Andy Pafko, Chi. Cubs, 1950	36	32	+4
Ted Kluszewski, Cin. Reds, 1956	35	31	+4
Barry Bonds, S.F. Giants, 2004	45	41	+4
Dan Brouthers, Det. Wolverines, 1887	12	9	+3
Hugh Duffy, Bos. Beaneaters, 1894	18	15	+3
Irish Meusel, N.Y. Giants, 1923	19	16	+3
Frank McCormick, Cin. Reds, 1944	20	17	+3

continued on next page

	Home Runs	Strikeouts	Differential
Johnny Mize, N.Y. Giants, 1948	40	37	+3
Don Mueller, N.Y. Giants, 1951	16	13	+3
Billy O'Brien, Was. Statesmen, 1887	19	17	+2
Irish Meusel, N.Y. Giants, 1925	21	19	+2
Frank McCormick, Cin. Reds, 1939	18	16	+2
Tommy Holmes, Bos. Braves, 1944	13	11	+2
Lefty O'Doul, Phi. Phillies, 1930	22	21	+1
Lefty O'Doul, Brk. Dodgers, 1932	21	20	+1
Arky Vaughan, Pit. Pirates, 1935	19	18	+1
Ernie Lombardi, Cin. Reds, 1939	20	19	+1

Players with the Most Career Home Runs, Never Striking Out 100 Times in a Season

	Career HRs	Most HR in Season	Most K in Season
Hank Aaron	755	47 (1971)	97 (1967)
Babe Ruth	714	60 (1927)	93 (1923)
Albert Pujols	703	49 (2006)	93 (2001*, 2017)
Ted Williams	521	43 (1949)	64 (1939*)
Mel Ott	511	42 (1929)	69 (1937)
Gary Sheffield	509	43 (2000)	83 (2004, 2008)
Lou Gehrig	493	49 (1934, 1936)	84 (1927)
Stan Musial	475	39 (1948)	46 (1962)
Chipper Jones	468	45 (1999)	99 (1995*)
Carl Yastrzemski	452	44 (1967)	96 (1961*)
Vladimir Guerrero	449	44 (2000)	95 (1998)
Cal Ripken Jr.	431	34 (1991)	97 (1983)
Mike Piazza	427	40 (1997, 1999)	93 (1996)
Billy Williams	426	42 (1970)	84 (1964)

* Rookie season.

Largest Differential Between Leader in Home Runs and Runner-Up

American League

Differential	Season	Leader	Home Runs	Runner-Up	Home Runs
+35	1920	Babe Ruth, N.Y. Yankees	54	George Sisler, St.L. Browns	19
+35	1921	Babe Ruth, N.Y. Yankees	59	Ken Williams, St.L. Browns; and Bob Meusel, N.Y. Yankees	24
+28	1926	Babe Ruth, N.Y. Yankees	47	Al Simmons, Phi. A's	19
+27	1928	Babe Ruth, N.Y. Yankees	54	Lou Gehrig, N.Y. Yankees	27
+22	2022	Aaron Judge, N.Y. Yankees	62	Mike Trout, L.A. Angels	40
+20	1956	Mickey Mantle, N.Y. Yankees	52	Vic Wertz, Cle. Indians	32
+19	1919	Babe Ruth, Bos. Red Sox	29	Home Run Baker, N.Y. Yankees; George Sisler, St.L. Browns; and Tilly Walker, Phi. A's	10
+19	1924	Babe Ruth, N.Y. Yankees	46	Joe Hauser, Phi. A's	27
+17	1932	Jimmie Foxx, Phi. A's	58	Babe Ruth, N.Y. Yankees	41
+15	2010	Jose Bautista, Tor. Blue Jays	54	Paul Konerko, Chi. White Sox	39
+14	1933	Jimmie Foxx, Phi. A's	48	Babe Ruth, N.Y. Yankees	34
+13	1927	Babe Ruth, N.Y. Yankees	60	Lou Gehrig, N.Y. Yankees	47
+12	1923	Babe Ruth, N.Y. Yankees	41	Ken Williams, St.L. Browns	29
+12	1978	Jim Rice, Bos. Red Sox	46	Don Baylor, Cal. Angels; and Larry Hisle, Mil. Brewers	34
+12	1990	Cecil Fielder, Det. Tigers	51	Mark McGwire, Oak. A's	39
+12	1997	Ken Griffey Jr., Sea. Mariners	56	Tino Martinez, N.Y. Yankees	44
+11	1929	Babe Ruth, N.Y. Yankees	46	Lou Gehrig, N.Y. Yankees	35

continued on next page

National League

Differential	Season	Leader	Home Runs	Runner-Up	Home Runs
+20	1917	Giancarlo Stanton, Mia. Marlins	59	Cody Bellinger, L.A. Dodgers	39
+19	1923	Cy Williams, Phi. Phillies	41	Jake Fournier, Brk. Dodgers	22
+18	1940	Johnny Mize, St.L. Cardinals	43	Bill Nicholson, Chi. Cubs	25
+18	1949	Ralph Kiner, Pit. Pirates	54	Stan Musial, St.L. Cardinals	36
+16	1922	Rogers Hornsby, St.L. Cardinals	42	Cy Williams, Phi. Phillies	26
+16	1930	Hack Wilson, Chi. Cubs	56	Chuck Klein, Phi. Phillies	40
+15	1925	Rogers Hornsby, St.L. Cardinals	39	Gabby Hartnett, Chi. Cubs	24
+14	1964	Willie Mays, S.F. Giants	47	Billy Williams, Chi. Cubs	33
+13	1899	Buck Freeman, Was. Senators	25	Bobby Wallace, St.L. Cardinals	12
+13	1965	Willie Mays, S.F. Giants	52	Willie McCovey, S.F. Giants	39
+13	1980	Mike Schmidt, Phi. Phillies	48	Bob Horner, Atl. Braves	35
+12	1958	Ernie Banks, Chi. Cubs	47	Frank Thomas, Pit. Pirates	35
+11	1915	Gavvy Cravath, Phi. Phillies	24	Cy Williams, Chi. Cubs	13
+11	1943	Bill Nicholson, Chi. Cubs	29	Mel Ott, N.Y. Giants	18
+11	1950	Ralph Kiner, Pit. Pirates	47	Andy Pafko, Chi. Cubs	36
+11	1977	George Foster, Cin. Reds	52	Jeff Burroughs, Atl. Braves	41
+11	1989	Kevin Mitchell, S.F. Giants	47	Howard Johnson, N.Y. Mets	36

Most Home Runs, Last Season in Majors

38	David Ortiz, Bos. Red Sox (AL), 2016
35	Dave Kingman, Oak. A's (AL), 1986
29	Ted Williams, Bos. Red Sox (AL), 1960
29	Mark McGwire, St.L. Cardinals (NL), 2001
28	Barry Bonds, S.F. Giants (NL), 2007
27	Jermaine Dye, Chi. White Sox (AL), 2009
25	Hank Greenberg, Pit. Pirates (NL), 1947
25	Ryan Howard, Phi. Phillies (NL), 2016
24	Roy Cullenbine, Det. Tigers (AL), 1947
24	Jack Graham, St.L. Browns (AL), 1949
24	Albert Pujols, St.L. Cardinals (NL), 2022
23	Kirby Puckett, Min. Twins (AL), 1995
23	Albert Belle, Bal. Orioles (AL), 2000
22	Phil Nevin, Tex. Rangers (AL)–Chi. Cubs (NL)–Min. Twins (AL), 2006
22	Adam Dunn, Chi. White Sox (AL)–Oak. A's (AL), 2014
22	Torii Hunter, Min. Twins (AL), 2015
22	Brandon Moss, K.C. Royals (AL), 2017
21	Dave Nilsson, Mil. Brewers (NL), 1999
21	Will Clark, Bal. Orioles (AL)–St.L. Cardinals (NL), 2000
21	Paul O'Neill, N.Y. Yankees (AL), 2001
21	Sammy Sosa, Tex. Rangers (AL), 2007
21	Dayan Viciedo, Chi. White Sox (AL), 2014
20	Melvin Upton, S.D. Padres (NL)–Tor. Blue Jays (AL), 2016

Fewest Career Home Runs for League Leader (Post-1920)

American League

89	Nick Etten (N.Y. Yankees), led league in 1944 with 22
104	Vladimir Guerrero Jr.* (Tor. Blue Jays), led league in 2021 with 48
134	Jorge Soler* (K.C. Royals), led league in 2019 with 48
156	Bob Meusel (N.Y. Yankees), led league in 1925 with 33
160	Bill Melton (Chi. White Sox), led league in 1971 with 33
166	Tony Conigliaro (Bos. Red Sox), led league in 1965 with 32
192	Al Rosen (Cle. Indians), led league in 1950 with 37 and in 1953 with 43
196	Ken Williams (St.L. Browns), led league in 1922 with 39
218	Mark Trumbo (Bal. Orioles), led leagues in 2016 with 47
220	Aaron Judge* (N.Y. Yankees), led league in 2017 with 52 and 2022 with 62
221	Khris Davis (Oak. A's), led league in 2018 with 48
223	Salvador Perez* (K.C. Royals), led league in 2021 with 48
224	Bobby Grich (Cal. Angels), led league in 1981 with 22
235	Ben Oglivie (Mil. Brewers), led league in 1980 with 41
237	Gus Zernial (Phi. A's), led league in 1951 with 33
241	Jesse Barfield (Tor. Blue Jays), led league in 1986 with 40
247	Vern Stephens (St.L. Browns), led league in 1945 with 24

National League

88	Tommy Holmes (Bos. Braves), led league in 1945 with 28
135	Ripper Collins (St.L. Cardinals), led league in 1934 with 35

continued on next page

136..Jack Fournier (Brk. Dodgers), led league in 1924 with 27
146..Pete Alonso* (N.Y. Mets), led league in 2019 with 53
148...George Kelly (N.Y. Giants), led league in 1921 with 23
158..Chris Carter (Mil. Brewers), led league in 2016 with 41
199...Kyle Schwarber* (Phi. Phillies), led league in 2022 with 46
205...Joe Medwick (St.L. Cardinals), led league in 1937 with 31
219..Jim Bottomley (St.L. Cardinals), led league in 1928 with 31
228...Howard Johnson (N.Y. Mets), led league in 1991 with 38
234..Kevin Mitchell (S.F. Giants), led league in 1989 with 47
235.......................................Bill Nicholson (Chi. Cubs), led league in 1943 with 29 and in 1944 with 33
239...Dolph Camilli (Brk. Dodgers), led league in 1941 with 34
242...Wally Berger (Bos. Braves), led league in 1935 with 34
244.........Hack Wilson (Chi. Cubs), led league in 1926 with 21, in 1927 with 30, in 1928 with 31, and in 1930 with 56
* Still active.

Highest Percentage of Home Runs to Hits

% of Hits Being HRs		Home Runs	Hits
46.79	Barry Bonds, S.F. Giants, 2001	73	156
46.05	Mark McGwire, St.L. Cardinals, 1998	70	152
45.83	Mike Zunino, T.B. Rays, 2021	33	72
44.83	Mark McGwire, Oak. A's, 1995	39	87
44.83	Mark McGwire, St.L. Cardinals, 1999	65	145
44.44	Mark McGwire, St.L. Cardinals, 2000	32	72
43.62	Joey Gallo, Tex. Rangers, 2017	41	94
39.39	Mark McGwire, Oak. A's, 1996	52	132
39.19	Mark McGwire, Oak. A's–St.L. Cardinals, 1997	58	148
38.83	Joey Gallo, Tex. Rangers, 2018	40	103
38.38	Joey Gallo, N.Y. Yankees–Tex. Rangers, 2021	38	99
38.36	Roger Maris, N.Y. Yankees, 1961	61	159
37.27	Adam Dunn, Chi. White Sox, 2012	41	110
36.96	Gary Sanchez, N.Y. Yankees, 2019	34	92
36.90	Giancarlo Stanton, N.Y. Yankees, 2022	31	84
36.56	Barry Bonds, S.F. Giants, 1999	34	93
36.49	Jose Bautista, Tor. Blue Jays, 2010	54	148
36.47	Mitch Garver, Min. Twins, 2019	31	85
36.45	Carlos Pena, T.B. Rays, 2009	39	107
36.17	Miguel Sano, Min. Twins, 2019	34	94
36.13	Matt Williams, S.F. Giants, 1994	43	119

Runs Batted In

Evolution of RBI Record

American League

1901	Nap Lajoie, Phi. A's	125
1911	Ty Cobb, Det. Tigers	127
1912	Home Run Baker, Phi. A's	130
1920	Babe Ruth, N.Y. Yankees	137
1921	Babe Ruth, N.Y. Yankees	170
1927	Lou Gehrig, N.Y. Yankees	175
1931	Lou Gehrig, N.Y. Yankees	184

National League (Pre-1900)

1876	Deacon White, Chi. White Stockings	60
1879	Charley Jones, Bos. Red Stockings	62
	John O'Rourke, Bos. Red Stockings	62
1880	Cap Anson, Chi. White Stockings	74
1881	Cap Anson, Chi. White Stockings	82
1882	Cap Anson, Chi. White Stockings	83
1883	Dan Brouthers, Buf. Bisons	97
1884	Cap Anson, Chi. White Stockings	102
1885	Cap Anson, Chi. White Stockings	108

continued on next page

| 1886 | Cap Anson, Chi. White Stockings | 147 |
| 1887 | Sam Thompson, Det. Wolverines | 166 |

National League (Post-1899)

1900	Elmer Flick, Phi. Phillies	110
1901	Honus Wagner, Pit. Pirates	126
1910	Sherry Magee, Phi. Phillies	123
1913	Gavvy Cravath, Phi. Phillies	128
1922	Rogers Hornsby, St.L. Cardinals	152
1929	Hack Wilson, Chi. Cubs	159
1930	Hack Wilson, Chi. Cubs	191

Most RBIs by Decade

Pre-1900		1900–09		1910–19	
1880	Cap Anson	956	Honus Wagner	828	Ty Cobb
1323	Roger Connor	808	Sam Crawford	793	Home Run Baker
1302	Sam Thompson	793	Nap Lajoie	765	Heinie Zimmerman
1296	Dan Brouthers	688	Harry Davis	746	Sherry Magee
1218	Hugh Duffy	685	Cy Seymour	718	Tris Speaker
1135	Ed Delahanty	680	Jimmy Williams	718	Duffy Lewis
1124	Ed McKean	638	Bobby Wallace	697	Sam Crawford
1080	Jake Beckley	610	Harry Steinfeldt	687	Ed Konetchy
1072	Bid McPhee	597	Bill Dahlen	682	Eddie Collins
1021	Fred Pfeffer	590	Charlie Hickman	665	Gavvy Cravath

1920–29		1930–39		1940–49	
1331	Babe Ruth	1403	Jimmie Foxx	903	Bob Elliott
1153	Rogers Hornsby	1358	Lou Gehrig	893	Ted Williams
1133	Harry Heilmann	1135	Mel Ott	887	Bobby Doerr
1005	Bob Meusel	1081	Al Simmons	854	Rudy York
923	George Kelly	1046	Earl Averill	835	Bill Nicholson
885	Jim Bottomley	1036	Joe Cronin	824	Vern Stephens
860	Ken Williams	1003	Charlie Gehringer	786	Joe DiMaggio
827	George Sisler	979	Chuck Klein	759	Dixie Walker
821	Goose Goslin	937	Bill Dickey	744	Johnny Mize
821	Joe Sewell	893	Wally Berger	710	Joe Gordon

1950–59		1960–69		1970–79	
1031	Duke Snider	1107	Hank Aaron	1013	Johnny Bench
1001	Gil Hodges	1013	Harmon Killebrew	954	Tony Perez
997	Yogi Berra	1011	Frank Robinson	936	Lee May
972	Stan Musial	1003	Willie Mays	922	Reggie Jackson
925	Del Ennis	937	Ron Santo	906	Willie Stargell
863	Jackie Jensen	925	Ernie Banks	860	Rusty Staub
841	Mickey Mantle	896	Orlando Cepeda	856	Bobby Bonds
823	Ted Kluszewski	862	Roberto Clemente	846	Carl Yastrzemski
817	Gus Bell	853	Billy Williams	840	Bobby Murcer
816	Larry Doby	836	Brooks Robinson	832	Bob Watson

1980–89		1990–99		2000–09	
996	Eddie Murray	1099	Albert Belle	1243	Alex Rodriguez
929	Dale Murphy	1091	Ken Griffey Jr.	1112	Albert Pujols
929	Mike Schmidt	1076	Barry Bonds	1106	Manny Ramirez
900	Dwight Evans	1068	Juan Gonzalez	1046	Miguel Tejada
899	Dave Winfield	1068	Rafael Palmeiro	1045	Carlos Delgado
895	Andre Dawson	1040	Frank Thomas	1037	Vladimir Guerrero
868	Jim Rice	979	Dante Bichette	1026	Lance Berkman
851	George Brett	975	Fred McGriff	1019	Carlos Lee
835	Harold Baines	961	Jeff Bagwell	1016	David Ortiz
821	Robin Yount	960	Matt Williams	993	Bobby Abreu

continued on next page

2010–19		2020–22	
963	Albert Pujols	275	Jose Ramirez
961	Nelson Cruz	260	Pete Alonso
956	Edwin Encarnacion	256	Matt Olson
941	Miguel Cabrera	255	Manny Machado
878	Robinson Cano	252	Jose Abreu
824	Jay Bruce	251	Aaron Judge
817	Evan Longoria	244	Rafael Devers
811	Ryan Braun	241	Vladimir Guerrero Jr.
807	Paul Goldschmidt	241	Kyle Tucker
806	Adam Jones	236	Freddie Freeman

Career RBI Leaders by First Letter of Last Name

A	Hank Aaron (1954–76)	2297	N	Graig Nettles (1967–88)	1314
B	Barry Bonds (1986–2007)	1996	O	Mel Ott (1926–47)	1860
C	Ty Cobb (1905–28)	1938	P	Albert Pujols (2001–22)	2218
D	Andre Dawson (1976–96)	1591	Q	Joe Quinn (1884–86, 1888–1901)	800
E	Dwight Evans (1972–91)	1384	R	Babe Ruth (1914–35)	2214
F	Jimmie Foxx (1925–42, 1944–45)	1922	S	Al Simmons (1924–41, 1943–44)	1828
G	Lou Gehrig (1923–39)	1995	T	Frank Thomas (1990–2008)	1704
H	Rogers Hornsby (1915–37)	1584	U	Chase Utley (2003–18)	1025
I	Raul Ibanez (1996–2014)	1207	V	Mickey Vernon (1939–43, 1946–60)	1311
J	Reggie Jackson (1967–87)	1702	W	Ted Williams (1939–42, 1946–60)	1839
K	Harmon Killebrew (1954–75)	1584	X	[No player]	
L	Nap Lajoie (1896–1916)	1599	Y	Carl Yastrzemski (1961–83)	1844
M	Stan Musial (1941–44, 1946–63)	1951	Z	Todd Zeile (1989–2004)	1110

* Still active.

Teammates Finishing One-Two in RBIs

American League

Season	Team	Leader	RBIs	Runner-Up	RBIs
1902	Bos. Americans	Buck Freeman	121	Charlie Hickman*	110
1905	Phi. A's	Harry Davis	83	Lave Cross	77
1908	Det. Tigers	Ty Cobb	108	Sam Crawford	80
1909	Det. Tigers	Ty Cobb	107	Sam Crawford	97
1910	Det. Tigers	Sam Crawford	120	Ty Cobb	91
1913	Phi. A's	Home Run Baker	126	Stuffy McInnis	90
1915	Det. Tigers	Bobby Veach	112 (Tie)	Sam Crawford	112
1917	Det. Tigers	Bobby Veach	103	Ty Cobb	102
1926	N.Y. Yankees	Babe Ruth	146	Tony Lazzeri	114 (Tie)
1927	N.Y. Yankees	Lou Gehrig	175	Babe Ruth	164
1928	N.Y. Yankees	Lou Gehrig	142 (Tie)	Babe Ruth	142
1931	N.Y. Yankees	Lou Gehrig	184	Babe Ruth	163
1932	Phi. A's	Jimmie Foxx	169	Al Simmons	151
1940	Det. Tigers	Hank Greenberg	150	Rudy York	134
1949	Bos. Red Sox	Vern Stephens	159 (Tie)	Ted Williams	159
1950	Bos. Red Sox	Vern Stephens	144 (Tie)	Walt Dropo	144
1952	Cle. Indians	Al Rosen	105	Larry Doby	104 (Tie)
1980	Mil. Brewers	Cecil Cooper	122	Ben Oglivie	118
1984	Bos. Red Sox	Tony Armas	123	Jim Rice	122
2011	N.Y. Yankees	Curtis Granderson	119	Robinson Cano	118

* 32 with Bos. Americans and 161 with Cle. Bronchos.

National League (Post-1900)

Season	Team	Leader	RBIs	Runner-Up	RBIs
1900	Phi. Phillies	Elmer Flick	110	Ed Delahanty	109
1902	Pit. Pirates	Honus Wagner	91	Tommy Leach	85
1904	N.Y. Giants	Bill Dahlen	80	Sam Mertes	78
1914	Phi. Phillies	Sherry Magee	103	Gavvy Cravath	100

continued on next page

Season	Team	Leader	RBIs	Runner-Up	RBIs
1932	Phi. Phillies	Don Hurst	143	Chuck Klein	137
1960	Mil. Braves	Hank Aaron	126	Eddie Mathews	124
1965	Cin. Reds	Deron Johnson	130	Frank Robinson	113
1970	Cin. Reds	Johnny Bench	148	Tony Perez	129
1976	Cin. Reds	George Foster	121	Joe Morgan	111
1996	Col. Rockies	Andres Galarraga	150	Dante Bichette	141
2020	Atl. Braves	Marcell Ozuna	56	Freddie Freeman	53
2021	Atl. Braves	Adam Duvall*	113	Austin Riley	107

* 68 with Mia. Marlins and 45 with Atl. Braves.

Largest Differential Between League Leader in RBIs and Runner-Up

American League

Differential	Season	Leader	RBIs	Runner-Up	RBIs
+51	1935	Hank Greenberg, Det. Tigers	170	Lou Gehrig, N.Y. Yankees	119
+36	1913	Home Run Baker, Phi. A's	126	Stuffy McInnis, Phi. A's; and Duffy Lewis, Bos. Red Sox	90
+32	1921	Babe Ruth, N.Y. Yankees	171	Harry Heilmann, Det. Tigers	139
+31	1926	Babe Ruth, N.Y. Yankees	145	George H. Bums, Cle. Indians; and Tony Lazzeri, N.Y. Yankees	114
+30	1953	Al Rosen, Cle. Indians	145	Mickey Vernon, Was. Senators	115
+29	1910	Sam Crawford, Det. Tigers	120	Ty Cobb, Det. Tigers	91
+29	1911	Ty Cobb, Det. Tigers	144	Sam Crawford, Det. Tigers; and Home Run Baker, Phila A's	115
+29	1922	Ken Williams,. St.L. Browns	155	Bobby Veach, Det. Tigers	126
+29	1938	Jimmie Foxx, Bos. Red Sox	175	Hank Greenberg, Det. Tigers	146
+28	1908	Ty Cobb, Det. Tigers	108	Sam Crawford, Det. Tigers	80

National League (Post-1900)

Differential	Season	Leader	RBIs	Runner-Up	RBIs
+39	1937	Joe Medwick, St.L. Cardinals	154	Frank Demaree, Chi. Cubs	115
+35	1910	Sherry Magee, Phi. Phillies	123	Mike Mitchell, Cin. Reds	88
+33	1913	Gavvy Cravath, Phi. Phillies	128	Heinie Zimmerman, Chi. Cubs	95
+28	1915	Gavvy Cravath, Phi. Phillies	115	Sherry Magee, Bos. Braves	87
+27	1943	Bill Nicholson, Chi. Cubs	128	Bob Elliott, Pit. Pirates	101
+27	1957	Hank Aaron, Mil. Braves	132	Del Ennis, St.L. Cardinals	105

Career RBI Totals, Players Hitting 500 Home Runs

	HRs	RBIs		HRs	RBIs		HRs	RBIs
Barry Bonds	762	1996	Mark McGwire	583	1414	Frank Thomas	521	1704
Hank Aaron	755	2297	Harmon Killebrew	573	1584	Willie McCovey	521	1555
Babe Ruth	714	2213	Rafael Palmeiro	569	1835	Ernie Banks	512	1636
Albert Pujols	703	2218	Reggie Jackson	563	1702	Eddie Mathews	512	1453
Alex Rodriguez	687	2055	Manny Ramirez	555	1831	Mel Ott	511	1860
Willie Mays	660	1903	Mike Schmidt	548	1595	Gary Sheffield	509	1676
Ken Griffey Jr.	630	1836	David Ortiz	541	1768	Miguel Cabrera*	507	1847
Jim Thome	612	1699	Mickey Mantle	536	1509	Eddie Murray	504	1917
Sammy Sosa	609	1667	Jimmie Foxx	534	1922	* Still active.		
Frank Robinson	586	1812	Ted Williams	521	1839			

Players Driving in 100 Runs in First Two Seasons in Majors

American League

Al Simmons, Phi. A's	1924 (102) and 1925 (129)
Tony Lazzeri, N.Y. Yankees	1926 (114) and 1927 (102)
Dale Alexander, Det. Tigers	1929 (137) and 1930 (135)

continued on next page

Hal Trosky, Cle. Indians.. 1934 (142) and 1935 (113)
Joe DiMaggio, N.Y. Yankees.. 1936 (125) and 1937 (167)
Rudy York, Det. Tigers... 1937 (103) and 1938 (127)
Ted Williams, Bos. Red Sox .... 1939 (145) and 1940 (113)
Jose Canseco, Oak. A's.. 1986 (117) and 1987 (113)
Wally Joyner, Cal. Angels .... 1986 (100) and 1987 (117)
Frank Thomas, Chi. White Sox .... 1991 (109) and 1992 (115)
Hideki Matsui, N.Y. Yankees .... 2003 (106) and 2004 (108)
Jose Abreu, Chi. White Sox... 2014 (107) and 2015 (101)

National League (Post-1900)

Glenn Wright, Pit. Pirates .... 1924 (111) and 1925 (121)
Pinky Whitney, Phi. Phillies .... 1928 (103) and 1929 (115)
Ray Jablonski, St.L. Cardinals.. 1953 (112) and 1954 (104)
Albert Pujols, St.L. Cardinals .... 2001 (130) and 2002 (127)

Players Driving in 500 Runs in First Four Full Years of Career

558 ....Joe DiMaggio, 1936–39, N.Y. Yankees (AL)
545 ....Hal Troksy, 1934–37, Cle. Indians (AL)
515 ....Ted Williams, 1939–42, Bos. Red Sox (AL)
504 ....Albert Pujols, 2001–04, St.L. Cardinals (NL)

Most RBIs by a Player in a Single Game

	Date	RBIs
Jim Bottomley, St.L. Cardinals	Sep. 16, 1924 (vs. Brk. Dodgers)	12
Mark Whiten**, St.L. Cardinals	Jul. 9, 1993 (vs. Cin. Reds)	12
Tony Lazzeri, N.Y. Yankees	May 24, 1936 (vs. Phi. A's)	11
Phil Weintraub*, N.Y. Giants	April 30, 1944 (vs. Brk. Dodgers)	11
Rudy York, Bos. Red So	Jul. 27, 1946 (vs. St.L. Browns)	10
Walker Cooper, Cin. Reds	Jul. 6, 1949 (vs. Chi. Cubs)	10
Norm Zauchin, Bos. Red Sox	May 27, 1955 (vs. Was. Senators)	10
Reggie Jackson, Oak. A's	Jun. 14, 1969 (vs. Bos. Red Sox)	10
Fred Lynn, Bos. Red Sox	Jun. 18, 1975 (vs. Det. Tigers)	10
Nomar Garciaparra, Bos. Red Sox	May 10, 1999 (vs. Sea. Mariners)	10
Alex Rodriguez, N.Y. Yankees	April 26, 2005 (vs. L.A. Angels)	10
Garret Anderson, L.A. Angels	Aug. 21, 2007 (vs. N.Y. Yankees)	10
Anthony Rendon, Was. Nationals	April 30, 2017 (vs. N.Y. Mets)	10
Scooter Gennett, Cin. Reds	Jun. 6, 2017 (vs. St.L. Cardinals)	10
Mark Reynolds, Was. Nationals	Jul. 7, 2018 (vs. Mia. Marlins)	10

* Game one of a doubleheader.
** Game two of a doubleheader.

Catchers with 100 RBIs and 100 Runs Scored, Season

American League

	RBIs	Runs
Mickey Cochrane, Phi. A's, 1932	112	118
Yogi Berra, N.Y. Yankees, 1950	124	116
Carlton Fisk, Bos. Red Sox, 1977	102	106
Darrell Porter, K.C. Royals, 1979	112	101
Ivan Rodriguez, Tex. Rangers, 1999	113	116

National League (Post-1900)

	RBIs	Runs
Roy Campanella, Brk. Dodgers, 1953	142	103
Johnny Bench, Cin. Reds, 1974	129	108
Mike Piazza, L.A. Dodgers, 1997	124	104
Mike Piazza, N.Y. Mets, 1999	124	100

Catchers Hitting .300 with 30 Home Runs and 100 RBIs, Season

American League

	Home Runs	RBIs	Batting Average
Rudy York*, Det. Tigers, 1937	35	103	.307
Ivan Rodriguez, Tex. Rangers, 1999	35	113	.332

National League (Post-1900)

	Home Runs	RBIs	Batting Average
Gabby Hartnett, Chi.Cubs, 1930	37	122	.339
Walker Cooper, N.Y. Giants, 1947	35	122	.305
Roy Campanella, Brk. Dodgers, 1951	33	108	.325
Roy Campanella, Brk. Dodgers, 1953	41	142	.312
Roy Campanella, Brk. Dodgers, 1955	32	107	.318
Joe Torre,** Atl. Braves, 1966	36	101	.315
Mike Piazza, L.A. Dodgers, 1993	35	112	.318
Mike Piazza, L.A. Dodgers, 1996	36	105	.336
Mike Piazza, L.A. Dodgers, 1997	40	124	.362
Mike Piazza, L.A. Dodgers– Fla. Marlins–N.Y. Mets, 1998	32	111	.328
Mike Piazza, N.Y. Mets, 1999	40	124	.303
Mike Piazza, N.Y. Mets, 2000	38	113	.324
Javy Lopez, Atl. Braves, 2003	43	109	.328

* 54 at catcher, 43 at other positions.
** 114 at catcher, 36 at other positions.

Players with 40 or More Home Runs and Fewer Than 100 RBIs, Season

American League

	Home Runs	RBIs
Mickey Mantle, N.Y. Yankees, 1958	42	97
Mickey Mantle, N.Y. Yankees, 1960	40	94
Harmon Killebrew, Min. Twins, 1963	45	96
Rico Petrocelli, Bos. Red Sox, 1969	40	97
Darrell Evans, Det. Tigers, 1985	40	94
Ken Griffey Jr., Sea. Mariners, 1994	40	90
Adam Dunn, Chi. White Sox, 2012	41	96
Nelson Cruz, Sea. Mariners, 2015	44	93
Albert Pujols, L.A. Angels, 2015	40	95
Mike Trout, L.A. Angels, 2015	41	90
Todd Frazier, Chi. White Sox, 2016	40	98
Brian Dozier, Min. Twins, 2016	42	99
Joey Gallo, Tex. Rangers, 2017	41	80
Joey Gallo, Tex. Rangers, 2018	40	92
Mike Trout, L.A. Angels, 2022	40	80

National League (Post-1900)

	Home Runs	RBIs
Duke Snider, Brk. Dodgers, 1957	40	92
Hank Aaron, Atl. Braves, 1969	44	97
Hank Aaron, Atl. Braves, 1973	40	96
Davey Johnson, Atl. Braves, 1973	43	99
Matt Williams, S.F. Giants, 1994	43	96
Barry Bonds, S.F. Giants, 2003	45	90
Adam Dunn, Cin. Reds, 2006	40	92
Alfonso Soriano, Was. Nationals, 2006	46	95
Adrian Gonzalez, S.D. Padres, 2009	40	99
Carlos Gonzalez, Col. Rockies, 2015	40	97
Bryce Harper, Was. Nationals, 2015	42	99
Chris Carter, Mil. Brewers, 2016	41	94
Christian Yelich, Mil. Brewers, 2019	44	97
Fernando Tatis Jr., S.D. Padres, 2021	42	97
Kyle Schwarber, Phi. Phillies, 2022	46	94

Players with More Than 100 RBIs and Fewest Home Runs, Season

American League

	RBIs	Home Runs
Lave Cross, Phi. A's, 1902	108	0
Larry Gardner, Cle. Indians, 1920	118	3
Larry Gardner, Cle. Indians, 1921	115	3
Stuffy McInnis, Phi. A's, 1912	101	3
Joe Sewell, Cle. Indians, 1923	109	3
Joe Sheely, Chi. White Sox, 1924	103	3
Bobby Veach, Det. Tigers, 1915	112	3

National League (Post-1900)

	RBIs	Home Runs
Ross Youngs, N.Y. Giants, 1921	102	3
Pie Traynor, Pit. Pirates, 1928	124	3
Pie Traynor, Pit. Pirates, 1931	103	2

Players with Most Career RBIs, Never Leading League

Willie Mays (1951–52, 1954–73)	1903	Tony Perez (1964–86)	1652
Rafael Palmeiro (1986–2005)	1835	Harold Baines (1980–2000)	1628
Adrian Beltre (1998–2018)	1707	Chipper Jones (1993, 1995–2012)	1623
Frank Thomas (1990–2008)	1704	George Brett (1973–93)	1595
Jim Thome (1991–2012)	1699	Carlos Beltran (1998–2017)	1587
Cal Ripken Jr. (1981–2001)	1695	Al Kaline (1953–74)	1583
Gary Sheffield (1988–2009)	1676	Jake Beckley (1888–1907)	1575

Players with 1000 Career RBIs, Never Driving in 100 in One Season

Pete Rose (1963–86)	1314	Brian Downing (1973–92)	1073
Julio Franco (1982–94, 1996–97, 1999, 2001–07)	1194	Jimmy Dykes (1918–39)	1069
Craig Biggio (1988–2007)	1175	Willie Davis (1960–79)	1053
Steve Finley (1989–2007)	1167	Ron Fairly (1958–78)	1044
Mark Grace (1988–2003)	1146	Bobby Murcer (1965–83)	1043
Johnny Damon (1995–2012)	1139	Joe Judge (1915–34)	1034
Tommy Corcoran (1890–1907)	1135	Yadier Molina (2004–22)	1022
Rickey Henderson (1979–2003)	1115	Brian McCann (2005–19)	1018
Lou Whitaker (1977–95)	1084	Wade Boggs (1982–99)	1014
Charlie Grimm (1916, 1918–36)	1077	Dusty Baker (1968–86)	1013
Sam Rice (1915–34)	1077	Amos Otis (1967–84)	1007
Jose Cruz (1970–88)	1077	Andrew McCutchen (2009–)	1002

Batters Driving in 100 Runs with Three Different Teams

Bobby Abreu	Phi. Phillies (NL)	2001	110
		2003	101
		2004	105
		2005	102
	N.Y. Yankees (AL)	2007	101
		2008	100
	L.A. Angels (AL)	2009	103
Dick Allen	Phi. Phillies (NL)	1966	110
	St.L. Cardinals (NL)	1970	101
	Chi. White Sox (AL)	1972	113
Moises Alou	Fla. Marlins (NL)	1997	115
	Hou. Astros (NL)	1998	124
		2000	114
		2001	108
	Chi. Cubs (NL)	2004	106
Albert Belle	Cle. Indians (AL)	1992	112
		1993	129
		1994	101
		1995	126
		1996	148

continued on next page

	Chi. White Sox (AL)	1997	116
		1998	152
	Bal. Orioles (AL)	1999	117
		2000	103
Adrian Beltre	L.A. Dodgers (NL)	2004	121
	Bos. Red Sox (AL)	2010	102
	Tex. Rangers (AL)	2011	105
		2012	102
		2016	104
Dan Brouthers	Det. Wolverines (NL)	1887	101
	Bos. Beaneaters (NL)	1889	118
	Brk. Grooms (NL)	1892	124
		1894	128
Joe Carter	Cle. Indians (AL)	1986	121
		1987	106
		1989	105
	S.D. Padres (NL)	1990	115
	Tor. Blue Jays (AL)	1991	108
		1992	119
		1993	121
		1994	103
		1996	107
		1997	102
Orlando Cepeda	S.F. Giants (NL)	1959	105
		1961	142
		1962	114
	St.L. Cardinals (NL)	1967	111
	Atl. Braves (NL)	1970	111
Rocky Colavito	Cle. Indians (AL)	1958	113
		1959	111
		1965	108
	Det. Tigers (AL)	1961	140
		1962	112
Nelson Cruz	Bal. Orioles (AL)	2014	108
	Sea. Mariners (AL)	2016	105
		2017	119
	Min. Twins (AL)	2019	108
Carlos Delgado	Tor. Blue Jays (AL)	1998	115
		1999	134
		2000	137
		2001	102
		2002	108
		2003	145
	Fla. Marlins (NL)	2005	115
	N.Y. Mets (NL)	2006	114
		2008	115
Adrian Gonzalez	S.D. Padres (NL)	2007	100
		2008	119
		2010	101
	Bos. Red Sox (AL)	2011	117
	Bos. Red Sox (AL)–L.A. Dodgers (NL)	2012	108
	L.A. Dodgers (NL)	2013	100
		2014	116
Goose Goslin	Was. Senators (AL)	1924	129
		1925	113
		1926	109
		1927	120
		1928	102
	Was. Senators (AL)–St.L. Browns (AL)	1930	138
	St.L. Browns (AL)	1931	105
		1932	104
	Det. Tigers (AL)	1934	100
		1935	111
		1936	125
Vladimir Guerrero	Mon. Expos (NL)	1998	109
		1999	131
		2000	123
		2004	108
	L.A. Angels (AL)	2009	126
		2005	108

continued on next page

		2006	116
		2007	125
	Tex. Rangers (AL)	2010	115
Rogers Hornsby	St.L. Cardinals (NL)	1921	126
		1922	152
		1925	143
	N.Y. Giants (NL)	1927	125
	Chi. Cubs (NL)	1929	149
Reggie Jackson	Oak. A's (AL)	1969	118
		1973	117
		1975	104
	N.Y. Yankees (AL)	1977	110
		1980	111
	Cal. Angels (AL)	1982	101
Jeff Kent	S.F. Giants (NL)	1997	121
		1998	128
		1999	101
		2000	125
		2001	106
		2002	108
	Hou. Astros (NL)	2004	107
	L.A. Dodgers (NL)	2005	105
Nap Lajoie	Phi. Phillies (NL)	1897	127
		1898	127
	Phi. A's (AL)	1901	125
	Cle. Naps (AL)	1904	102
Carlos Lee	Chi. White Sox (AL)	2003	113
	Mil. Brewers (NL)	2005	114
	Mil. Brewers (NL)–Tex. Rangers (AL)	2006	116
	Hou. Astros (NL)	2007	119
		2008	100
		2009	102
Lee May	Cin. Reds (NL)	1969	110
	Hou. Astros (NL)	1973	105
	Bal. Orioles (AL)	1976	109
Fred McGriff	S.D. Padres (NL)	1991	106
		1992	104
	S.D. Padres (NL)–Atl. Braves (NL)	1993	101
	Atl. Braves (NL)	1996	107
	T.B. Devil Rays (AL)	1999	104
		2000	106
	T.B. Devil Rays (AL)–Chi. Cubs (NL)	2001	102
	Chi. Cubs (NL)	2002	103
John Olerud	Tor. Blue Jays (AL)	1993	107
	N.Y. Mets (NL)	1997	102
	Sea. Mariners (AL)	2000	103
		2002	102
Dean Palmer	Tex. Rangers (AL)	1996	107
	K.C. Royals (AL)	1998	119
	Det. Tigers (AL)	1999	100
		2000	102
Del Pratt	St.L. Browns (AL)	1916	103
	N.Y. Yankees (AL)	1920	108
	Bos. Red Sox (AL)	1921	102
Aramis Ramirez	Pit. Pirates (NL)	2001	112
	Pit. Pirates (NL)–Chi. Cubs (NL)	2003	106
	Chi. Cubs (NL)	2004	103
		2006	119
		2007	101
		2008	111
	Mil. Brewers (NL)	2012	105
Alex Rodriguez	Sea. Mariners (AL)	1996	123
		1998	124
		1999	111
		2000	132
	Tex. Rangers (AL)	2001	135
		2002	142
		2003	118
	N.Y. Yankees (AL)	2004	106

continued on next page

		2005	130
		2006	121
		2007	156
		2008	103
		2009	100
		2010	125
Richie Sexson	Cle. Indians (AL)	1999	116
	Mil. Brewers (NL)	2001	125
		2002	102
		2003	124
	Sea. Mariners (AL)	2005	121
		2006	107
	K.C. A's (AL)	1964	102
Gary Sheffield	S.D. Padres (NL)	1992	100
	Fla. Marlins (NL)	1996	120
	L.A. Dodgers (NL)	1999	116
		2000	100
		2001	101
	Atl. Braves (NL)	2003	132
	N.Y. Yankees (AL)	2004	121
		2005	123
Alfonso Soriano	N.Y. Yankees (AL)	2002	102
	Tex. Rangers (AL)	2005	104
	Chi. Cubs. (NL)	2012	108
	Chi Cubs (NL)–N.Y. Yankees (AL)	2013	101
Danny Tartabull	K.C. Royals (AL)	1987	101
		1988	102
		1991	100
	N.Y. Yankees (AL)	1993	102
	Chi. White Sox (AL)	1996	101
Mark Teixeira	Tex. Rangers (AL)	2004	112
		2005	144
		2006	110
	Tex. Rangers (AL)–Atl. Braves (NL)	2007	105
	Atl. Braves (NL)–L.A. Angels (AL)	2008	121
	N.Y. Yankees (AL)	2009	122
		2010	108
		2011	111
Jim Thome	Cle. Indians (AL)	1996	116
		1997	102
		1999	108
		2000	106
		2001	124
		2002	118
	Phi. Phillies (NL)	2003	131
		2004	105
	Chi. White Sox (AL)	2006	109
Vic Wertz	Det. Tigers (AL)	1949	133
		1950	123
	Cle. Indians (AL)	1956	106
		1957	105
	Bos. Red Sox (AL)	1960	103
Matt Williams	S.F. Giants (NL)	1990	122
		1993	110
	Cle. Indians (AL)	1997	105
	Ari. D'backs (NL)	1999	142
Dave Winfield	S.D. Padres (NL)	1979	118
	N.Y. Yankees (AL)	1982	106
		1983	116
		1984	100
		1985	114
		1985	104
		1988	107
	Tor. Blue Jays (AL)	1992	108

Players Driving in 130 Teammates During Season

American League

	Teammates	Home Runs	RBIs
Hank Greenberg, Det. Tigers, 1937	144	40	184
Lou Gehrig, N.Y. Yankees, 1935	139	46	185
Ty Cobb, Det. Tigers, 1911	136	8	144
Lou Gehrig, N.Y. Yankees, 1930	132	41	173
Hank Greenberg, Det. Tigers, 1935	132	36	168

National League (Post-1900)

	Teammates	Home Runs	RBIs
Hack Wilson, Chi. Cubs, 1930	135	56	191
Chuck Klein, Phi. Phillies, 1930	130	40	170

Players Driving in 100 Runs, Season, in Each League

Player	League	Team, Year	
Bobby Abreu	National League	Phi. Phillies, 2001	110
		Phi. Phillies, 2003	101
		Phi. Phillies, 2004	105
		Phi. Phillies, 2005	102
	American League	N.Y. Yankees, 2007	101
		N.Y. Yankees, 2008	100
		L.A. Angels, 2009	103
Dick Allen	National League	Phi. Phillies, 1966	110
		St.L. Cardinals, 1970	101
	American League	Chi. White Sox, 1972	113
Jason Bay	National League	Pit. Pirates, 2005	101
		Pit. Pirates, 2006	104
	American League	Bos. Red Sox, 2009	119
Carlos Beltran	American League	K.C. Royals, 1999	108
		K.C. Royals, 2001	101
		K.C. Royals, 2002	105
		K.C. Royals, 2003	100
	National League	N.Y. Mets, 2006	116
		N.Y. Mets, 2007	112
		N.Y. Mets, 2008	112
Adrian Beltre	National League	L.A. Dodgers, 2004	121
	American League	Bos. Red Sox, 2010	102
		Tex Rangers, 2011	105
		Tex Rangers, 2012	102
		Tex Rangers, 2016	104
Bobby Bonds	National League	S.F. Giants, 1971	102
	American League	Cal. Angels, 1977	115
Bill Buckner	National League	Chi. Cubs, 1982	105
	American League	Bos. Red Sox, 1985	110
		Bos. Red Sox, 1986	102
Jeff Burroughs	American League	Tex. Rangers, 1974	118
	National League	Atl. Braves, 1977	114
Miguel Cabrera	National League	Fla. Marlins, 2004	112
		Fla. Marlins, 2005	116
		Fla. Marlins, 2006	114
		Fla. Marlins, 2007	119
	American League	Det. Tigers, 2008	127
		Det. Tigers, 2009	103
		Det. Tigers, 2010	126

continued on next page

continued on next page

continued on next page

		St.L. Cardinals, 2004	123
		St.L. Cardinals, 2005	117
		St.L. Cardinals, 2006	137
		St.L. Cardinals, 2007	103
		St.L. Cardinals, 2008	116
		St.L. Cardinals, 2009	135
		St.L. Cardinals, 2010	118
	American League	L.A. Angels, 2012	105
		L.A. Angels, 2014	105
		L.A. Angels, 2016	119
		L.A. Angels, 2017	101
Hanley Ramirez	National League	Fla. Marlins, 2009	106
	American League	Bos. Red Sox, 2016	111
Frank Robinson	National League	Cin. Reds, 1959	125
		Cin. Reds, 1961	124
		Cin. Reds, 1962	136
		Cin. Reds, 1965	113
	American League	Bal. Orioles, 1966	122
		Bal. Orioles, 1969	100
Richie Sexson	American League	Cle. Indians, 1999	116
		Sea. Mariners, 2005	121
		Sea. Mariners, 2006	107
	National League	Mil. Brewers, 2001	125
		Mil. Brewers, 2002	102
		Mil. Brewers, 2003	124
Gary Sheffield	National League	S.D. Padres, 1992	100
		Fla. Marlins, 1996	120
		L.A. Dodgers, 1999	101
		L.A. Dodgers, 2000	109
		L.A. Dodgers, 2001	100
		Atl. Braves, 2003	132
	American League	N.Y. Yankees, 2004	121
		N.Y. Yankees, 2005	123
Ken Singleton	National League	Mon. Expos, 1973	103
	American League	Bal. Orioles, 1979	111
		Bal. Orioles, 1980	104
Alfonso Soriano	American League	N.Y. Yankees, 2002	102
		Tex. Rangers, 2005	104
	National League	Chi. Cubs, 2012	108
Giancarlo Stanton	National League	Mia. Marlins, 2014	105
		Mia. Marlins, 2017	132
	American League	N.Y. Yankees, 2018	100
Rusty Staub	National League	N.Y. Mets, 1975	105
	American League	Det. Tigers, 1977	101
		Det. Tigers, 1978	121
Dick Stuart	National League	Pit. Pirates, 1961	117
	American League	Bos. Red Sox, 1963	118
		Bos. Red Sox, 1964	114
Jim Thome	American League	Cle. Indians, 1996	116
		Cle. Indians, 1997	102
		Cle. Indians, 1999	108
		Cle. Indians, 2000	106
		Cle. Indians, 2001	124
		Cle. Indians, 2002	118
		Chi. White Sox, 2006	109
	National League	Phi. Phillies, 2003	131
		Phi. Phillies, 2004	105

continued on next page

Justin Upton	National League	Atl. Braves, 2014	102
	American League	Det. Tigers–L.A. Angels, 2017	109
Matt Williams	National League	S.F. Giants, 1990	122
		S.F. Giants, 1993	110
		Ari. D'backs, 1999	142
	American League	Cle. Indians, 1997	105
Richie Zisk	National League	Pit. Pirates, 1974	100
	American League	Chi. White Sox, 1977	101

Players with More RBIs Than Games Played, Season (Min. 100 Games)

American League

	RBIs	Games	Differential
Lou Gehrig, N.Y. Yankees, 1931	184	155	+29
Hank Greenberg, Det. Tigers, 1937	183	154	+29
Al Simmons, Phi. A's, 1930	165	138	+27
Jimmie Foxx, Bos. Red Sox, 1938	175	149	+26
Lou Gehrig, N.Y. Yankees, 1927	175	155	+20
Lou Gehrig, N.Y. Yankees, 1930	174	154	+20
Babe Ruth, N.Y. Yankees, 1921	171	152	+19
Babe Ruth, N.Y. Yankees, 1929	154	135	+19
Babe Ruth, N.Y. Yankees, 1931	163	145	+18
Hank Greenberg, Det. Tigers, 1935	170	152	+18
Manny Ramirez, Cle. Indians, 1999	165	147	+18
Joe DiMaggio, N.Y. Yankees, 1937	167	151	+16
Jimmie Foxx, Phi. A's, 1932	169	154	+15
Al Simmons, Phi. A's, 1929	157	143	+14
Jimmie Foxx, Phi. A's, 1933	163	149	+14
Babe Ruth, N.Y. Yankees, 1927	164	151	+13
Lou Gehrig, N.Y. Yankees, 1934	165	154	+11
Hal Trosky, Cle. Indians, 1936	162	151	+11
Juan Gonzalez, Tex. Rangers, 1996	144	134	+10
Babe Ruth, N.Y. Yankees, 1930	153	145	+8
Walt Dropo, Bos. Red Sox, 1950	144	136	+8
Joe DiMaggio, N.Y. Yankees, 1939	126	120	+6
Babe Ruth, N.Y. Yankees, 1932	137	133	+4
Vern Stephens, Bos. Red Sox, 1949	159	155	+4
Ted Williams, Bos. Red Sox, 1949	159	155	+4
Kirby Puckett, Min. Twins, 1994	112	108	+4
Manny Ramirez, Cle. Indians, 2000	122	118	+4
Ken Williams, St.L. Browns, 1925	105	102	+3
Jimmie Foxx, Phi. A's, 1930	156	153	+3
Juan Gonzalez, Tex. Rangers, 1998	157	154	+3
Ken Williams, St.L. Browns, 1922	155	153	+2
Al Simmons, Phi. A's, 1927	108	106	+2
Lou Gehrig, N.Y. Yankees, 1937	159	157	+2
Hank Greenberg, Det. Tigers, 1940	150	148	+2
Joe DiMaggio, N.Y. Yankees, 1948	155	153	+2
Joe DiMaggio, N.Y. Yankees, 1940	133	132	+1
George Brett, K.C. Royals, 1980	118	117	+1

National League (Post-1900)

	RBIs	Games	Differential
Hack Wilson, Chi. Cubs, 1930	190	155	+35
Chuck Klein, Phi. Phillies, 1930	170	156	+14
Hack Wilson, Chi. Cubs, 1929	159	150	+9

continued on next page

	RBIs	Games	Differential
Jeff Bagwell, Hou. Astros, 1994	116	110	+6
Rogers Hornsby, St.L. Cardinals, 1925	143	138	+5
Mel Ott, N.Y. Giants, 1929	151	150	+1

Players Driving in 20 Percent of Their Team's Runs, Season

Nate Colbert, S.D. Padres (NL), 1972	111 of 488	22.75%
Wally Berger, Bos. Braves (NL), 1935	130 of 575	22.61%
Ernie Banks, Chi. Cubs (NL), 1959	143 of 673	21.25%
Sammy Sosa, Chi. Cubs (NL), 2001	160 of 777	20.59%
Jim Gentile, Bal. Orioles (AL), 1961	141 of 691	20.40%
Bill Buckner, Chi. Cubs (NL), 1981	75 of 370	20.27%
Bill Nicholson, Chi. Cubs (NL), 1943	128 of 632	20.25%
Frank Howard, Was. Senators II (AL), 1968	106 of 524	20.23%
Babe Ruth, Bos. Red Sox (AL), 1919	114 of 565	20.18%
Frank Howard, Was. Senators II (AL), 1970	126 of 626	20.13%

Players with Lowest Batting Average for 100-RBI Season

	RBIs	Batting Average
Kyle Seager, Sea. Mariners (AL), 2021	101	.212
Tony Armas, Bos. Red Sox (AL), 1983	107	.218
Carlos Pena, T.B. Rays (AL), 2009	100	.227
Adam Duvall, Atl. Braves (NL)–Mia. Marlins (NL), 2021	113	.228
Roy Sievers, Was. Senators (AL), 1954	102	.232
Joe Carter, S.D. Padres (NL), 1990	115	.232
Curtis Granderson, N.Y. Yankees (AL), 2012	106	.232
Ruben Sierra, Oak. A's (AL), 1993	101	.233
Pedro Alvarez, Pit. Pirates (NL), 2013	100	.233
Joe Carter, Tor. Blue Jays (AL) ,1997	102	.234
Mark Trumbo, L.A. Angels (AL), 2013	100	.234
Austin Meadows, T.B. Rays (AL), 2021	106	.234
Mark McGwire, Oak. A's (AL), 1990	108	.235
Adam Dunn, Cin. Reds (NL)–Ari. D'backs (NL), 2008	100	.236
Jose Canseco, Tor. Blue Jays (AL), 1998	107	.237
Carlton Fisk, Chi. White Sox (AL), 1985	107	.238
Jeff King, K.C. Royals (AL), 1997	112	.238
Gorman Thomas, Mil. Brewers (AL), 1980	105	.239
Mike Napoli, Cle. Indians (AL), 2016	101	.239
Jose Canseco, Oak. A's (AL), 1986	117	.240
Phil Plantier, S.D. Padres (NL), 1993	100	.240
Matt Olson, Atl. Braves (NL), 2022	103	.240
Ron Cey, L.A. Dodgers (NL), 1977	110	.241
Tony Batista. Mon. Expos (NL), 2004	110	.241
Adam Duvall, Cin. Reds (NL), 2016	103	.241
Albert Pujols, L.A. Angels (AL), 2017	101	.241
Harmon Killebrew, Min. Twins (AL), 1959	105	.242

Players on Last-Place Teams Leading League in RBIs, Season

	RBIs		RBIs
Alex Rodriguez, Tex. Rangers (AL), 2002	142	Nolan Arenado, Col. Rockies (NL), 2015	130
Andre Dawson, Chi. Cubs (NL), 1987	137	Frank Howard, Was. Senators II (AL), 1970	126
Wally Berger, Bos. Braves (NL), 1935	130	Roy Sievers, Was. Senators (AL), 1957	114

Players Driving in 95 or More Runs in Season Three Times, Never 100

Donn Clendenon (1961–72)	1965	96
	1966	98
	1970	97
Kevin McReynolds (1983–94)	1986	96
	1987	95
	1988	99
Arky Vaughan (1932–43, 1947–48)	1933	97
	1935	99
	1940	95

Runs Scored

Evolution of Runs Scored Record

American League

1901 Nap Lajoie, Phi. A's	145	1920 Babe Ruth, N.Y. Yankees 158
1911 Ty Cobb, Det. Tigers	147	1921 Babe Ruth, N.Y. Yankees 177

National League (Pre-1900)

1876 Ross Barnes, Chi. White Stockings	126	1894 Billy Hamilton, Phi. Phillies 198
1886 King Kelly, Chi. White Stockings	155	

National League (Post-1899)

1900 Roy Thomas, Phi. Phillies	132	1929 Rogers Hornsby, Chi. Cubs 156
1901 Jesse Burkett, St.L. Cardinals	142	1930 Chuck Klein, Phi. Phillies 158
1925 Kiki Cuyler, Pit. Pirates	144	

Most Runs Scored by Decade

Pre-1900

1722	Cap Anson
1684	Bid McPhee
1620	Roger Connor
1523	Dan Brouthers
1523	Tom Brown
1523	Billy Hamilton
1492	Harry Stovey
1480	Arlie Latham
1470	Hugh Duffy
1445	Jim O'Rourke

1900–09

1014	Honus Wagner
885	Fred Clarke
862	Roy Thomas
835	Ginger Beaumont
828	Tommy Leach
813	Sam Crawford
807	Jimmy Sheckard
806	Nap Lajoie
799	Fielder Jones
797	Willie Keeler

1910–19

1051	Ty Cobb
991	Eddie Collins
967	Tris Speaker
958	Donie Bush
868	Harry Hooper
765	Joe Jackson
758	Clyde Milan
745	Larry Doyle
733	Home Run Baker
727	Max Carey
727	Jake Daubert

1920–29

1365	Babe Ruth
1195	Rogers Hornsby
1001	Sam Rice
992	Frankie Frisch
962	Harry Heilmann
896	Lu Blue
894	George Sisler
868	Charlie Jamieson
830	Ty Cobb
830	Tris Speaker

1930–39

1257	Lou Gehrig
1244	Jimmie Foxx
1179	Charlie Gehringer
1102	Earl Averill
1095	Mel Ott
1009	Ben Chapman
973	Paul Waner
955	Chuck Klein
930	Al Simmons
885	Joe Cronin

1940–49

951	Ted Williams
815	Stan Musial
803	Bob Elliott
764	Bobby Doerr
758	Lou Boudreau
743	Bill Nicholson
721	Dom DiMaggio
708	Vern Stephens
704	Dixie Walker
684	Joe DiMaggio

continued on next page

1950-59	1960-69	1970-79
994....................Mickey Mantle	1091 .... Hank Aaron	1068 ....Pete Rose
970......................... Duke Snider	1050 .... Willie Mays	1020 ....Bobby Bonds
952....................... Richie Ashburn	1013 ....Frank Robinson	1005 .... Joe Morgan
948............................Stan Musial	916 .... Roberto Clemente	861 ....Amos Otis
902............................Nellie Fox	885..............................Vada Pinson	845.......................Carl Yastrzemski
898............................Minnie Minoso	874..........................Maury Wills	843..............................Lou Brock
898............................Eddie Yost	864..........................Harmon Killebrew	837.............................. Rod Carew
890............................Gil Hodges	861 ....Billy Williams	833..........................Reggie Jackson
860............................Alvin Dark	816..............................Ron Santo	816..........................Bobby Murcer
848............................Yogi Berra	811 ....Al Kaline	792..........................Johnny Bench

1980-89	1990-99	2000-09
1122.......................Keith Hernandez	1091 .... Barry Bonds	1190 ....Alex Rodriguez
957............................Robin Yount	1042 .... Craig Biggio	1115 ....Johnny Damon
956........................ Dwight Evans	1002 .... Ken Griffey Jr.	1088 ....Derek Jeter
938............................Dale Murphy	968 ....Frank Thomas	1071 ....Albert Pujols
866............................ Tim Raines	965 ....Rafael Palmeiro	1061 ....Bobby Abreu
858............................Eddie Murray	951 ....Roberto Alomar	1017 .... Todd Helton
845............................Willie Wilson	950 ....Chuck Knoblauch	973 ....Ichiro Suzuki
832............................Mike Schmidt	946 ....Tony Phillips	961 ....Carlos Beltran
828............................ Paul Molitor	932 ....Rickey Henderson	960 ....Miguel Tejada
823............................ Wade Boggs	921 ....Jeff Bagwell	959 ....Lance Berkman

2010-19	2020-22	
903.............................Mike Trout	288 ....Freddie Freeman	
879............................Ian Kinsler	257 .... Mookie Betts	
868................... Andrew McCutchen	254 ....Trea Turner	
847............................Joey Votto	252 ....Jose Altuve	
836............................Justin Upton	247 ....Vladimir Guerrero Jr.	
828............................Robinson Cano	246 ....Jose Ramirez	
819....................... Edwin Encarnacion	245 .... Aaron Judge	
810............................. Elvis Andrus	244 ....Marcus Semien	
810............................. Brett Gardner	243 ....Juan Soto	
806............................Paul Goldschmidt	239 ....Paul Goldschmidt	

Players with More Runs Scored Than Games Played, Season (Min. 100 Games)

American League

	Runs	Games	Differential
Babe Ruth, N.Y. Yankees, 1921 ....177............................ 152 ....+25	177	152	+25
Babe Ruth, N.Y. Yankees, 1920 ....158............................ 142 ....+16	158	142	+16
Nap Lajoie, Phi. A's, 1901 ....145............................ 131 ....+14	145	131	+14
Al Simmons, Phi. A's, 1930 ....152............................ 138 ....+14	152	138	+14
Lou Gehrig, N.Y. Yankees, 1936 ....167............................ 155 ....+12	167	155	+12
Babe Ruth, N.Y. Yankees, 1928 ....163............................ 154 ....+9	163	154	+9
Lou Gehrig, N.Y. Yankees, 1932 ....163............................ 155 ....+8	163	155	+8
Babe Ruth, N.Y. Yankees, 1927 ....158............................ 151 ....+7	158	151	+7
Jimmie Foxx, Bos. Red Sox, 1939.................130............................ 124 ....+6	130	124	+6
Babe Ruth, N.Y. Yankees, 1930 ....150............................ 145 ....+5	150	145	+5
Babe Ruth, N.Y. Yankees, 1931 ....149............................ 145 ....+4	149	145	+4
Rickey Henderson, N.Y. Yankees, 1985..........146............................ 143 ....+3	146	143	+3
Ty Cobb, Det. Tigers, 1911 :.......................147............................ 146 ....+1	147	146	+1

National League (Post-1900)

	Runs	Games	Differential
Chuck Klein, Phi. Phillies, 1930 ....158............................ 156 ....+2	158	156	+2

Players Scoring 1000 Runs in Career, Never 100 in One Season

	Career Runs	Most in One Season
Luis Aparicio (1956–73)	1335	98 (1959)
Harold Baines (1980–2001)	1299	89 (1982)
Torii Hunter (1997–2015)	1296	94 (2007)
Chili Davis (1981–99)	1240	87 (1984)
Willie Randolph (1975–92)	1239	99 (1980)
Brooks Robinson (1955–77)	1232	91 (1966)
Paul Hines (1872–91)	1217	94 (1883, 1884)
Graig Nettles (1967–88)	1193	99 (1977)
Rusty Staub (1963–85)	1189	98 (1970)
Al Oliver (1968–85)	1189	96 (1974)
Bert Campaneris (1964–81, 1983)	1181	97 (1970)
Paul Konerko (1997–2014)	1162	98 (2005)
Buddy Bell (1972–89)	1151	89 (1979, 1988)
Steve Garvey (1969–87)	1143	95 (1974)
Deacon White (1871–90)	1140	82 (1884)
Gary Gaetti (1981–2000)	1130	95 (1987)
Jack Clark (1975–92)	1118	93 (1987)
Jimmy Dykes (1918–39)	1108	93 (1925)
Edd Roush (1913–29, 1931)	1099	95 (1926)
Aramis Ramirez (1998–2015)	1098	99 (2004)
Garret Anderson (1994–2010)	1084	93 (2002)
Nelson Cruz (2005–)	1081	96 (2016)
Bill Buckner (1969–90)	1077	93 (1982)
Ted Simmons (1968–88)	1074	84 (1980)
Mike Cameron (1995–2011)	1064	99 (2001)
Bob Elliott (1939–53)	1064	99 (1948)
Bobby Wallace (1894–1918)	1057	99 (1897)
Tony Fernandez (1983–2000)	1057	91 (1986)
Paul O'Neill (1985–2001)	1041	95 (1998)
Reggie Sanders (1991–2007)	1037	92 (1999)
Jose Cruz (1970–88)	1036	96 (1984)
Bobby Grich (1970–86)	1033	93 (1976)
Gary Carter (1974–92)	1025	91 (1982)
Kid Gleason (1888–1908, 1912)	1022	95 (1905)
Joe Mauer (2004–18)	1018	98 (2008)
Tino Martinez (1990–2005)	1009	96 (1997)
Robin Ventura (1989–2004)	1006	96 (1996)
Harry Davis (1895–1917)	1001	94 (1906)

Most Runs Scored by Position, Season

American League

First Base	167	Lou Gehrig, N.Y. Yankees, 1936
Second Base	145	Nap Lajoie, Phi. A's, 1901
Third Base	141	Harlond Clift, St.L. Browns, 1936
Shortstop	141	Alex Rodriguez, Sea. Mariners, 1996
Outfield	177	Babe Ruth, N.Y. Yankees, 1921
Catcher	118	Mickey Cochrane, Phi. A's, 1932
Pitcher	31	Jack Coombs, Phi. A's, 1911
Designated Hitter	133	Paul Molitor, Mil. Brewers, 1991

National League

First Base	152	Jeff Bagwell, Hou. Astros, 2000
Second Base	156	Rogers Hornsby, Chi. Cubs, 1929
Third Base	130	Pete Rose, Cin. Reds, 1976
Shortstop	139	Jimmy Rollins, Phi. Phillies, 2008
Outfield	158	Chuck Klein, Phi. Phillies, 1930
Catcher	112	Jason Kendall, Pit. Pirates, 2000
Pitcher	25	Claude Hendrix, Pit. Pirates, 1912
Designated Hitter	55	Bryce Harper, Phi. Phillies, 2022

Walks

Evolution of Batters' Walks Record

American League

1901	Dummy Hoy, Chi. White Sox	86
1902	Topsy Hartsel, Phi. A's	87
1905	Topsy Hartsel, Phi. A's	121
1920	Babe Ruth, N.Y. Yankees	150
1923	Babe Ruth, N.Y. Yankees	170

National League (Pre-1900)

1876	Ross Barnes, Chi. Cubs	20
1879	Charley Jones, Bos. Red Stockings	29
1881	John Clapp, Cle. Spiders	35
1883	Tom York, Cle. Spiders	37
1884	George Gore, Chi. Cubs	61
1885	Ned Williamson, Chi. Cubs	75
1886	George Gore, Chi. Cubs	102
1890	Cap Anson, Chi. Cubs	113
1892	John Crooks, St.L. Cardinals	136

National League (Post-1900)

1900	Roy Thomas, Phi. Phillies	115
1910	Miller Huggins, St.L. Cardinals	116
1911	Jimmy Sheckard, Chi. Cubs	147
1945	Eddie Stanky, Brk. Dodgers	148
1996	Barry Bonds, S.F. Giants	151
1998	Mark McGwire, St.L. Cardinals	162
2001	Barry Bonds, S.F. Giants	177
2002	Barry Bonds, S.F. Giants	198
2004	Barry Bonds, S.F. Giants	232

Players with 1000 Walks, 2000 Hits, and 300 Home Runs, Career

	Walks	Hits	Home Runs
Hank Aaron (1954–76)	1402	3771	755
Jeff Bagwell (1991–2005)	1401	2314	449
Harold Baines (1980–2000)	1054	2855	384
Carlos Beltran (1998–2017)	1084	2725	435
Barry Bonds (1986–2007)	2558	2935	762
George Brett (1973–93)	1096	3154	317
Miguel Cabrera* (2003–)	1227	3088	507
Chili Davis (1981–99)	1194	2380	350
Carlos Delgado (1993–2009)	1109	2038	473
Darrell Evans (1969–89)	1605	2223	414
Dwight Evans (1972–91)	1391	2446	385
Jimmie Foxx (1925–42, 1944–45)	1452	2646	534
Lou Gehrig (1923–39)	1508	2721	493
Jason Giambi (1995–2014)	1366	2010	440
Luis Gonzalez (1990–2008)	1155	2591	354
Ken Griffey Jr. (1989–2010)	1312	2781	630
Todd Helton (1997–2013)	1335	2519	369
Rogers Hornsby (1915–37)	1038	2930	301
Reggie Jackson (1967–87)	1375	2584	563
Chipper Jones (1993, 1995–2012)	1512	2726	468
Al Kaline (1953–74)	1277	3007	399
Harmon Killebrew (1954–75)	1559	2086	573

continued on next page

	Walks	Hits	Home Runs
Mickey Mantle (1951–68)	1733	2415	536
Edgar Martinez (1987–2004)	1283	2247	309
Eddie Mathews (1952–68)	1444	2315	512
Willie Mays (1951–52, 1954–73)	1464	3283	660
Willie McCovey (1959–80)	1345	2211	521
Fred McGriff (1986–2004)	1305	2484	493
Eddie Murray (1977–97)	1333	3255	504
Stan Musial (1941–44, 1946–63)	1599	3630	475
Graig Nettles (1967–88)	1088	2225	390
David Ortiz (1997–2016)	1319	2472	541
Mel Ott (1926–47)	1708	2876	511
Rafael Palmeiro (1986–2005)	1353	3020	569
Albert Pujols (2001–22)	1373	3384	703
Manny Ramirez (1993–2011)	1329	2574	555
Cal Ripken Jr. (1981–2001)	1129	3164	431
Frank Robinson (1956–76)	1420	2943	586
Alex Rodriguez (1994–2013, 2015–16)	1338	3115	696
Babe Ruth (1914–35)	2062	2873	714
Ron Santo (1960–74)	1108	2254	342
Mike Schmidt (1972–89)	1507	2234	548
Gary Sheffield (1988–2009)	1475	2689	509
Frank Thomas (1990–2008)	1667	2468	521
Jim Thome (1991–2012)	1747	2328	612
Joey Votto* (2007–)	1338	2093	342
Billy Williams (1959–76)	1045	2711	426
Ted Williams (1939–42, 1946–60)	2021	2654	521
Dave Winfield (1973–95)	1216	3110	465
Carl Yastrzemski (1961–83)	1845	3419	452

* Still active.

Players Leading League in Base Hits and Walks, Season

American League

	Hits	Walks
Carl Yastrzemski, Bos. Red Sox, 1963	183	95

National League (Post-1900)

	Hits	Walks
Rogers Hornsby, St.L. Cardinals, 1924	227	89
Richie Ashburn, Phi. Phillies, 1958	215	97
Lenny Dykstra, Phi. Phillies, 1993	194	129

Players with 200 Base Hits and 100 Walks, Season

American League

	Hits	Walks
Ty Cobb, Det. Tigers, 1915	208	118
Babe Ruth, N.Y. Yankees, 1921	204	145
Babe Ruth, N.Y. Yankees, 1923	205	170
Babe Ruth, N.Y. Yankees, 1924	200	142
Lou Gehrig, N.Y. Yankees, 1927	218	109
Lou Gehrig, N.Y. Yankees, 1930	220	101
Lou Gehrig, N.Y. Yankees, 1931	211	117
Jimmie Foxx, Phi. A's, 1932	213	116
Lou Gehrig, N.Y. Yankees, 1932	208	138
Lou Gehrig, N.Y. Yankees, 1934	210	109
Lou Gehrig, N.Y. Yankees, 1936	205	130
Lou Gehrig, N.Y. Yankees, 1937	200	127
Hank Greenberg, Det. Tigers, 1937	200	102
Wade Boggs, Bos. Red Sox, 1986	207	105
Wade Boggs, Bos. Red Sox, 1987	200	105

National League (Post-1900)

	Hits	Walks
Woody English, Chi. Cubs, 1930	214	100
Hack Wilson, Chi. Cubs, 1930	208	105
Stan Musial, St.L. Cardinals, 1949	207	107
Stan Musial, St.L. Cardinals, 1953	200	105
Todd Helton, Col. Rockies, 2000	216	103
Todd Helton, Col. Rockies, 2003	209	111

continued on next page

American League

	Hits	Walks
Wade Boggs, Bos. Red Sox, 1988	214	125
Wade Boggs, Bos. Red Sox, 1989	205	107
John Olerud, Tor. Blue Jays, 1993	200	114
Bernie Williams, N.Y. Yankees, 1999	202	100

Players with More Walks Than Hits, Season (Min. 100 Walks)

American League

	Walks	Hits	Differential
Roy Cullenbine, Det. Tigers, 1947	137	104	+33
Eddie Yost, Was. Senators, 1956	151	119	+32
Max Bishop, Phi. A's, 1929	128	110	+18
Max Bishop, Phi. A's, 1930	128	111	+17
Joey Gallo, Tex. Rangers–N.Y. Yankees, 2021	111	99	+12
Eddie Joost, Phi. A's, 1949	149	138	+11
Max Bishop, Phi. A's, 1926	116	106	+10
Gene Tenace, Oak. A's, 1974	110	102	+8
Mickey Tettleton, Bal. Orioles, 1990	106	99	+7
Max Bishop, Phi. A's, 1932	110	104	+6
Toby Harrah, Tex. Rangers, 1985	113	107	+6
Mickey Tettleton, Tex. Rangers, 1995	107	102	+5
Jack Cust, Oak. A's, 2007	105	101	+4
Eddie Joost, Phi. A's, 1947	114	111	+3
Ted Williams, Bos. Red Sox, 1954	136	133	+3
Mickey Mantle, N.Y. Yankees, 1968	106	103	+3
Max Bishop, Phi. A's, 1927	105	103	+2
Mickey Mantle, N.Y. Yankees, 1962	122	121	+1

National League (Post-1900)

	Walks	Hits	Differential
Barry Bonds, S.F. Giants, 2004	232	135	+97
Barry Bonds, S.F. Giants, 2002	198	149	+49
Barry Bonds, S.F. Giants, 2007	132	94	+38
Jim Wynn, Atl. Braves, 1976	127	93	+34
Wes Westrum, N.Y. Giants, 1951	104	79	+25
Gene Tenace, S.D. Padres, 1977	125	102	+23
Jack Clark, S.D. Padres, 1989	132	110	+22
Barry Bonds, S.F. Giants, 2001	177	156	+21
Jack Clark, St.L. Cardinals, 1987	136	120	+16
Barry Bonds, S.F. Giants, 2006	115	99	+16
Jim Wynn, Hou. Astros, 1969	148	133	+15
Jack Clark, S.D. Padres, 1990	104	89	+15
Barry Bonds, S.F. Giants, 2003	148	133	+15
Rickey Henderson, S.D. Padres, 1996	125	112	+13
Gene Tenace, S.D. Padres, 1978	101	90	+11
Gary Sheffield, Fla. Marlins, 1997	121	111	+10
Mark McGwire, St.L. Cardinals, 1998	162	152	+10
Morgan Ensberg, Hou. Astros, 2006	101	91	+10
Jim Wynn, L.A. Dodgers, 1975	110	102	+8
Juan Soto, Was. Nationals–S.D. Padres, 2022	135	127	+8
Eddie Stanky, Brk. Dodgers, 1945	148	143	+5
Eddie Stanky, Brk. Dodgers, 1946	137	132	+5
Hank Greenberg, Pit. Pirates, 1947	104	100	+4
Willie McCovey, S.F. Giants, 1973	105	102	+3

Players Hitting 40 or More Home Runs, with More Home Runs Than Walks, Season

American League

	Home Runs	Walks	Differential
Tony Armas, Bos. Red Sox, 1984	43	32	+11
Juan Gonzalez, Tex. Rangers, 1993	46	37	+9
Juan Gonzalez, Tex. Rangers, 1997	42	33	+9
George Bell, Tor. Blue Jays, 1987	47	39	+8
Juan Gonzalez, Tex. Rangers, 1992	43	35	+8
Hal Trosky, Cle. Indians, 1936	42	36	+6
Tony Batista, Tor. Blue Jays, 2000	41	35	+6
Juan Gonzalez, Tex. Rangers, 1996	47	45	+2

National League (Post-1900)

	Home Runs	Walks	Differential
Salvador Perez, K.C. Royals, 2021	48	28	+20
Dante Bichette, Col. Rockies, 1995	40	22	+18
Andre Dawson, Chi. Cubs, 1987	49	32	+17
Matt Williams, S.F. Giants, 1994	43	33	+10
Javy Lopez, Atl. Braves, 2003	43	33	+10
Nolan Arenado, Col. Rockies, 2015	42	34	+8
Orlando Cepeda, S.F. Giants, 1961	46	39	+7
Andres Galarraga, Col. Rockies, 1996	47	40	+7
Sammy Sosa, Chi. Cubs, 1996	40	34	+6
Vinny Castilla, Col. Rockies, 1998	46	40	+6
Vinny Castilla, Col. Rockies, 1996	40	35	+5
Dave Kingman, Chi. Cubs, 1979	48	45	+3

Players with 90 Walks in Each of First Two Seasons

Jack Crooks, Col. Solons (AA)	1890 (96) and 1891 (103)
Alvin Davis, Sea. Mariners (AL)	1984 (97) and 1985 (90)
Ferris Fain, Phi. A's (AL)	1947 (95) and 1948 (113)
Roy Thomas, Phi. Phillies (NL)	1899 (115) and 1900 (115)
Ted Williams, Bos. Red Sox (AL)	1939 (107) and 1940 (96)

Strikeouts

Average League Strikeouts (Minimum 300 At-Bats)

Year	American League	National League	Year	American League	National League
1920	33.60	31.46	1930	37.05	36.58
1921	33.13	30.15	1931	36.60	35.29
1922	32.55	28.84	1932	36.54	35.73
1923	33.02	30.38	1933	38.09	34.02
1924	29.56	30.66	1934	40.48	39.09
1925	30.10	30.22	1935	38.35	39.12
1926	31.07	30.34	1936	39.06	38.30
1927	30.07	30.89	1937	41.33	41.99
1928	31.82	31.90	1938	42.37	38.83
1929	33.00	32.90	1939	40.66	36.75

continued on next page

Year	American League	National League
1940	47.16	39.62
1941	41.51	41.22
1942	39.42	38.44
1943	46.07	39.12
1944	39.96	37.21
1945	38.37	35.49
1946	47.78	39.88
1947	43.24	41.42
1948	40.77	43.00
1949	40.89	40.89

Year	American League	National League
1950	45.26	48.34
1951	42.62	44.52
1952	49.27	48.36
1953	45.62	52.03
1954	45.41	50.20
1955	50.55	53.11
1956	54.39	55.95
1957	51.72	55.94
1958	55.22	54.52
1959	56.26	61.05

Year	American League	National League
1960	57.06	61.45
1961	61.39	61.70
1962	64.78	66.66
1963	69.78	71.98
1964	76.85	66.01
1965	69.07	74.35
1966	68.88	70.32
1967	75.01	70.17
1968	72.15	69.47
1969	65.50	71.72

Year	American League	National League
1970	68.46	70.73
1971	61.85	63.47
1972	62.36	64.41
1973	65.44	66.24
1974	64.74	63.97
1975	64.87	61.75
1976	63.92	59.36
1977	67.27	68.14
1978	61.68	65.56
1979	59.67	64.96

Year	American League	National League
1980	59.34	60.70
1981	47.86	45.74
1982	65.72	66.62
1983	63.98	69.04
1984	66.55	70.71
1985	70.93	69.68
1986	79.48	71.08
1987	79.52	75.32
1988	72.75	71.71
1989	69.89	72.58

Year	American League	National League
1990	71.08	72.16
1991	76.57	72.90
1992	71.30	68.75
1993	75.80	74.32
1994	61.84	63.60
1995	74.02	72.60
1996	84.62	83.22
1997	86.56	84.03
1998	86.35	84.44
1999	82.43	83.12

Year	American League	National League
2000	84.10	82.20
2001	86.40	86.72
2002	82.26	85.04
2003	79.83	80.02
2004	85.37	83.33
2005	81.67	77.85
2006	84.74	84.54
2007	85.79	85.13
2008	83.22	87.85
2009	89.57	89.84

Year	American League	National League
2010	87.95	95.03
2011	89.10	90.08
2012	101.60	94.51
2013	98.87	92.71
2014	98.36	98.78
2015	97.94	96.64
2016	106.66	102.97
2017	107.62	103.21
2018	108.01	105.60
2019	108.63	107.51
2020*	50.12	48.49
2021	116.38	103.74
2022	102.19	108.55

* Min. 175 At-Bats (COVID-shortened season).

Players with 250 More Career Strikeouts Than Hits (Min. 400 Strikeouts)

	Strikeouts	Hits	Differential
Adam Dunn (2001–14)	2379	1631	+748
Chris Davis (2008–20)	2379	1631	+692
Mark Reynolds (2007–19)	1927	1283	+644
Joey Gallo* (2015–)	1048	471	+577
Rob Deer (1984–96)	1409	853	+556
Mike Zunino* (2013–)	1027	535	+492
Miguel Sano* (2015–)	1042	585	+457
Russell Branyan (1998–2011)	1118	682	+436
Carlos Pena (2001–14)	1577	1146	+431
Chris Carter (2010–17)	951	536	+415
Ryan Howard (2004–16)	1843	1475	+368
Alex Avila (2009–21)	1068	714	+354
Jeff Mathis (2005–21)	872	526	+346
Mike Napoli (2006–17)	1468	1125	+343
Jarrod Saltalamacchia (2007–18)	984	662	+322
Giancarlo Stanton* (2010–)	1696	1383	+313
Jack Cust (2001–11)	819	510	+309
Melvin Upton (2004, 2006–16)	1561	1260	+301
Danny Espinosa (2010–17)	943	644	+299
Jason Castro* (2010–)	970	678	+292
Gorman Thomas (1973–86)	1339	1051	+288
Drew Stubbs (2009–17)	972	687	+285
Dave Nicholson (1960–67)	573	301	+272
Tyler Flowers (2009–20)	852	582	+270
Kyle Schwarber* (2015–)	918	648	+270
Kelly Shoppach (2005–13)	624	361	+263
Jonny Gomes (2003–15)	1088	835	+253

* Still active.

Players with Most Strikeouts, Season

223 .... Mark Reynolds, Ari. D'backs, 2009
222 .... Adam Dunn, Chi. White Sox, 2012
219 .... Chris Davis, Bal. Orioles, 2016
217 .... Yoan Moncada, Chi. White Sox, 2018
213 .... Joey Gallo, Tex. Rangers–N.Y. Yankees, 2021
212 .... Chris Carter, Hou. Astros, 2013
211 .... Mark Reynolds, Ari. D'backs, 2010
211 .... Giancarlo Stanton, N.Y. Yankees, 2018
208 .... Chris Davis, Bal. Orioles, 2015
208 .... Aaron Judge, N.Y. Yankees, 2017
207 .... Joey Gallo, Tex. Rangers, 2018
206 .... Chris Carter, Mil. Brewers, 2016
205 .... Drew Stubbs, Cin. Reds, 2011
204 .... Mark Reynolds, Ari. D'backs, 2008
202 .... Matt Chapman, Oak. A's, 2021
200 .... Kyle Schwarber, Phi. Phillies, 2022

Players with 500 At-Bats and Fewer Than 10 Strikeouts, Season

American League (Post-1913)*

	At-Bats	Strikeouts
Sam Rice, Was. Senators, 1929	616	9
Joe Sewell, Cle. Indians, 1925	608	4
Joe Sewell, Cle. Indians, 1928	588	9
Stuffy McInnis, Bos. Red Sox, 1921	584	9
Homer Summa, Cle. Indians, 1926	581	9
Joe Sewell, Cle. Indians, 1926	578	7
Joe Sewell, Cle. Indians, 1929	578	4
Joe Sewell, Cle. Indians, 1927	569	7
Lou Boudreau, Cle. Indians, 1948	560	9
Stuffy McInnis, Cle. Indians, 1922	537	5
Joe Sewell, N.Y. Yankees, 1933	524	4
Tris Speaker, Was. Senators, 1927	523	8
Mickey Cochrane, Phi. A's, 1929	514	8
Dale Mitchell, Cle. Indians, 1952	511	9
Eddie Collins, Chi. White Sox, 1923	505	8
Joe Sewell, N.Y. Yankees, 1932	503	3

National League (Post-1910)*

	At-Bats	Strikeouts
Tommy Holmes, Bos. Braves, 1945	636	9
Charlie Hollocher, Chi. Cubs, 1922	592	5
Stuffy McInnis, Bos. Braves, 1924	581	6
Emil Verban, Phi. Phillies, 1947	540	8
Pie Traynor, Pit. Pirates, 1929	540	7
Freddy Leach, N.Y. Giants, 1931	515	9
Lloyd Waner, Pit. Pirates, 1933	500	8

* Official strikeouts first recorded by American League in 1913 and National League in 1910.

Players with 200 Hits and 100 Strikeouts, Season

American League

	Hits	Strikeouts
Hank Greenberg, Det. Tigers, 1937	200	101
Ron LeFlore, Det. Tigers, 1977	212	121
Jim Rice, Bos. Red Sox, 1977	206	120
Jim Rice, Bos. Red Sox, 1978	213	126
Alex Rodriguez, Sea. Mariners, 1996	215	104
Mo Vaughn, Bos. Red Sox, 1996	207	154
Derek Jeter, N.Y. Yankees, 1998	203	119
Alex Rodriguez, Sea. Mariners, 1998	213	121
Mo Vaughn, Bos. Red Sox, 1998	205	144
Derek Jeter, N.Y. Yankees, 1999	219	116
Alex Rodriguez, Tex. Rangers, 2001	201	131
Bret Boone, Sea. Mariners, 2001	206	110
Alfonso Soriano, N.Y. Yankees, 2002	209	157
Michael Young, Tex. Rangers, 2003	204	103
Derek Jeter, N.Y. Yankees, 2005	202	117

continued on next page

	Hits	Strikeouts
Derek Jeter, N.Y. Yankees, 2006	214	102
Derek Jeter, N.Y. Yankees, 2007	206	100
Michael Young, Tex. Rangers, 2007	201	107
Adrian Gonzalez, Bos. Red Sox, 2011	213	119
Rafael Devers, Bos. Red Sox, 2019	201	119
Whit Merrifield, K.C. Royals, 2019	206	126

National League (Post-1900)

	Hits	Strikeouts
Bill White, St.L. Cardinals, 1963	200	100
Dick Allen, Phi. Phillies, 1964	201	138
Lou Brock, Chi. Cubs–St.L. Cardinals, 1964	200	127
Roberto Clemente, Pit. Pirates, 1966	202	109
Lou Brock, St.L. Cardinals, 1967	206	109
Roberto Clemente, Pit. Pirates, 1967	209	103
Bobby Bonds, S.F. Giants, 1970	200	189
Lou Brock, St.L. Cardinals, 1971	200	107
Dave Parker, Pit. Pirates, 1977	215	107
Ryne Sandberg, Chi. Cubs, 1984	200	101
Ellis Burks, Col. Rockies, 1996	211	114
Craig Biggio, Hou. Astros, 1998	210	113
Chase Utley, Phi. Phillies, 2006	203	132
Matt Holliday, Col. Rockies, 2007	216	126
Ryan Braun, Mil. Brewers, 2009	203	121
Jean Segura, Ari. D'backs, 2016	203	101
Charlie Blackmon, Col. Rockies, 2017	213	135

Players with 40 or More Home Runs and 50 or Fewer Strikeouts, Season

American League

	Home Runs	Strikeouts
Lou Gehrig, N.Y. Yankees, 1934	49	31
Lou Gehrig, N.Y. Yankees, 1936	49	46
Joe DiMaggio, N.Y. Yankees, 1937	46	37
Ted Williams, Bos. Red Sox, 1949	43	48
Al Rosen, Cle. Indians, 1953	43	48

National League

	Home Runs	Strikeouts
Rogers Hornsby, St.L. Cardinals, 1922	42	50
Mel Ott, N.Y. Giants, 1929	42	38
Chuck Klein, Phi. Phillies, 1930	40	50
Johnny Mize, St.L. Cardinals, 1940	43	49
Johnny Mize, N.Y. Giants, 1947	51	42
Johnny Mize, N.Y. Giants, 1948	40	37
Ted Kluszewski, Cin. Reds, 1953	40	34
Ted Kluszewski, Cin. Reds, 1954	49	35
Ted Kluszewski, Cin. Reds, 1955	47	40
Hank Aaron, Atl. Braves, 1969	44	47
Barry Bonds, S.F. Giants, 2002	46	47
Barry Bonds, S.F. Giants, 2004	45	41
Albert Pujols, St.L. Cardinals, 2006	49	50

Players with 100 More Strikeouts Than RBIs, Season

American League

	Strikeouts	RBIs	Differential
Yoan Moncada, Chi. White Sox, 2018	217	61	+156
Chris Davis, Bal. Orioles, 2018	192	49	+143
Austin Jackson, Det. Tigers, 2011	181	45	+136
Joey Gallo, Tex. Rangers–N.Y. Yankees, 2021	213	77	+136

continued on next page

	Strikeouts	RBIs	Differential
Adam Dunn, Chi. White Sox, 2011	177	42	+135
Chris Davis, Bal. Orioles, 2016	219	84	+135
Chris Davis, Bal. Orioles, 2017	195	61	+134
Chris Carter, Hou. Astros, 2013	212	82	+130
Matt Chapman, Oak. A's, 2021	202	72	+130
Austin Jackson, Det. Tigers, 2010	170	41	+129
Adam Dunn, Chi. White Sox, 2012	222	96	+126
Carlos Pena, T.B. Rays, 2012	182	61	+121
Jack Cust, Oak. A's, 2008	197	77	+120
Anthony Gose, Det. Tigers, 2015	145	26	+119
Joey Gallo, Tex. Rangers, 2017	196	80	+116
Rob Deer, Det. Tigers–Bos. Red Sox, 1993	169	55	+114
Jack Cust, Oak. A's, 2009	185	70	+115
Joey Gallo, Tex. Rangers, 2018	207	92	+115
Miguel Sano, Min. Twins, 2016	178	66	+112
Rob Deer, Det. Tigers, 1991	175	64	+111
Giancarlo Stanton, N.Y. Yankees, 2018	211	100	+111
Mark Reynolds, Bal. Orioles, 2011	196	86	+110
Steven Souza, T.B. Rays, 2016	159	49	+110
Mickey Tettleton, Bal. Orioles, 1990	160	51	+109
Tyler Flowers, Chi. White Sox, 2014	159	50	+109
Eugenio Suarez, Sea. Mariners, 2022	196	87	+109
Alex Gordon, K.C. Royals, 2016	148	40	+108
JaCoby Jones, Det. Tigers, 2018	142	34	+108
Miguel Sano, Min. Twins, 2021	183	75	+108
Gary Pettis, Cal. Angels, 1987	124	17	+107
Rob Deer, Mil. Brewers, 1987	186	80	+106
Curtis Granderson, Det. Tigers, 2006	174	68	+106
Tim Anderson, Chi. White Sox, 2017	162	56	+106
Jeimer Candelario, Det. Tigers, 2018	160	54	+106
Teoscar Hernandez, Tor. Blue Jays, 2018	163	57	+106
Mike Zunino, Sea. Mariners, 2018	150	44	+106
Dave Nicholson, Chi. White Sox, 1963	175	70	+105
Bo Jackson, K.C. Royals, 1987	158	53	+105
Jose Bautista, Tor. Blue Jays, 2017	170	65	+105
Tim Beckham, T.B. Rays–Bal. Orioles, 2017	167	62	+105
Kelly Johnson, Tor. Blue Jays, 2012	159	55	+104
Alex Avila, Det. Tigers, 2014	151	47	+104
Steven Souza, T.B. Rays, 2015	144	40	+104
Mike Zunino, Sea. Mariners, 2015	132	28	+104
Shin-Soo Choo, Tex. Rangers, 2019	165	61	+104
Mallex Smith, Sea. Mariners, 2019	141	37	+104
Adolis Garcia, Tex. Rangers, 2021	194	90	+104
Adam Dunn, Chi. White Sox, 2013	189	86	+103
Matt Davidson, Chi. White Sox, 2018	165	62	+103
Chris Davis, Bal. Orioles, 2019	139	36	+103
Jonathan Villar, Bal. Orioles, 2019	176	73	+103
Ron LeFlore, Det. Tigers, 1975	139	37	+102
Melvin Upton, T.B. Rays, 2010	164	62	+102
Leonys Martin, Sea. Mariners, 2016	149	47	+102
Benji Gil, Tex. Rangers, 1995	147	46	+101
Chris Davis, Bal. Orioles, 2014	173	72	+101
Steven Souza, T.B. Rays, 2017	179	78	+101
Willy Adames, T.B. Rays, 2019	153	52	+101
Randy Arozarena, T.B. Rays, 2021	170	69	+101
Michael Saunders, Tor. Blue Jays, 2016	157	57	+100
Adam Engel, Chi. White Sox, 2018	129	29	+100
Hunter Dozier, K.C. Royals, 2021	154	54	+100

continued on next page

National League

	Strikeouts	RBIs	Differential
Drew Stubbs, Cin. Reds, 2011	205	44	+161
Melvin Upton, Atl. Braves, 2014	173	35	+138
Danny Espinosa, Was. Nationals, 2012	189	56	+133
Mark Reynolds, Ari. D'backs, 2010	211	85	+126
Drew Stubbs, Cin. Reds, 2012	166	40	+126
Keon Broxton, Mil. Brewers, 2017	175	49	+126
Ian Desmond, Was. Nationals, 2015	187	62	+125
Melvin Upton, Atl. Braves, 2013	151	26	+125
Ian Happ, Chi. Cubs, 2018	167	44	+123
Mark Reynolds, Ari. D'backs, 2009	223	102	+121
Jose Hernandez, Col. Rockies–Chi. Cubs–Pit. Pirates, 2003	177	57	+120
Chris Taylor, L.A. Dodgers, 2022	160	43	+117
Patrick Wisdom, Chi. Cubs, 2022	183	66	+117
Dan Uggla, Atl. Braves, 2013	171	55	+116
Joc Pederson, L.A. Dodgers, 2015	170	54	+116
Jose Hernandez, Mil. Brewers, 2002	188	73	+115
Chris Taylor, L.A. Dodgers, 2018	178	63	+115
Wil Myers, S.D. Padres, 2019	168	53	+115
Chris Carter, Mil. Brewers, 2016	206	94	+112
Bobby Bonds, S.F. Giants, 1970	189	78	+111
Jonathan Villar, Mil. Brewers, 2016	174	63	+111
Mark Reynolds, Ari. D'backs, 2011	196	86	+110
Luke Voit, S.D. Padres–Was. Nationals, 2022	179	69	+110
Trevor Story, Col. Rockies, 2017	191	82	+109
Dexter Fowler, Chi. Cubs, 2015	154	46	+108
Mark Reynolds, Ari. D'backs, 2008	204	97	+107
Jose Hernandez, Mil. Brewers, 2001	185	78	+107
Rickie Weeks, Mil. Brewers, 2012	169	63	+106
Wil Myers, S.D. Padres, 2017	180	74	+106
Kyle Schwarber, Phi. Phillies, 2022	200	94	+106
Michael Bourn, Hou. Astros, 2009	140	35	+105
Christian Yelich, Mil. Brewers, 2022	162	57	+105
Starling Marte, Pit. Pirates, 2013	138	35	+103
Jackie Bradley Jr., Mil. Brewers, 2021	132	29	+103
Billy Hamilton, Cin. Reds, 2018	132	29	+103
Brad Wilkerson, Mon. Expos, 2002	161	59	+102
Adam Dunn, Cin. Reds, 2006	194	92	+102
Jayson Werth, Was. Nationals, 2011	160	58	+102
Danny Espinosa, Was. Nationals, 2016	174	72	+102
Rickie Weeks, Mil. Brewers, 2010	184	83	+101
Chris Johnson, Atl. Braves, 2014	159	58	+101
Chris Owings, Ari. D'backs, 2015	144	43	+101
Jorge Alfaro, Phi. Phillies, 2018	138	37	+101
Austin Jackson, S.F. Giants–N.Y. Mets, 2018	133	32	+101
Delino DeShields, Mon. Expos, 1991	151	51	+100
Ron Gant, St.L. Cardinals, 1997	162	62	+100
Danny Espinosa, Was. Nationals, 2011	166	66	+100
Kris Bryant, Chi. Cubs, 2015	199	99	+100
Marlon Byrd, Phi. Phillies, 2014	185	85	+100
Eric Thames, Mil. Brewers, 2017	163	63	+100

National/American League

	Strikeouts	RBIs	Differential
Joey Gallo, N.Y. Yankees (AL)–L.A. Dodgers (NL), 2022	163 (106–57)	47 (24–23)	+116
Franmil Reyes, Cle. Indians (AL)–Chi. Cubs (NL), 2022	157 (104–53)	47 (28–19)	+110
Brandon Marsh, L.A. Angels (AL)–Phi. Phillies (NL), 2022	158 (117–41)	52 (37–15)	+106
Kelly Johnson, Ari. D'backs (NL)–Tor. Blue Jays (AL), 2011	163 (132–31)	58 (49–9)	+105
Tommy Pham, Cin. Reds (NL)–Bos. Red Sox (AL), 2022	167 (100–67)	63 (39–24)	+104

Toughest Batters to Strike Out, Career*

	At-Bats	Strikeouts
Joe Sewell (1920–33)	7132	113 (1 every 63 at bats)
Lloyd Waner (1927–45)	7772	173 (1 every 45 at bats)
Nellie Fox (1947–65)	9232	216 (1 every 43 at bats)
Tommy Holmes (1942–52)	4992	122 (1 every 41 at bats)
Tris Speaker (1913–28)	7899	220 (1 every 36 at bats)
Stuffy McInnis (1913–27)	6667	189 (1 every 35 at bats)
Frankie Frisch (1919–37)	9112	272 (1 every 34 at bats)
Homer Summa (1920–30)	3001	88 (1 every 34 at bats)
Andy High (1922–34)	4440	130 (1 every 34 at bats)
Dale Mitchell (1946–56)	3984	119 (1 every 34 at bats)
Sam Rice (1915–34)	9269	276 (1 every 33 at bats)
Johnny Cooney (1921–44)	3372	107 (1 every 32 at bats)
Jimmy Brown (1937–46)	3512	110 (1 every 32 at bats)

* Batter strikeouts not recorded until 1913 in American League and 1910 in National League.

Teams with 1000+ Strikeouts, Winning World Series

Strikeouts	Team	Record
1453	Atl. Braves, 2021	88–73
1339	Chi. Cubs, 2016	103–58
1308	Bos. Red Sox, 2013	97–65
1308	Was. Nationals, 2019	93–69
1253	Bos. Red Sox, 2018	108–54
1245	S.F. Giants, 2014	88–74
1189	Bos. Red Sox, 2004	98–64
1179	Hou. Astros, 2022	106–56
1117	Phi. Phillies, 2008	92–70
1099	S.F. Giants, 2010	92–70
1097	S.F. Giants, 2012	94–68
1089	N.Y. Mets, 1969	100–62
1087	Hou. Astros, 2017	101–61
1074	Fla. Marlins, 1997	92–70
1052	Ari. D'backs, 2001	92–70
1042	Bos. Red Sox, 2007	96–66
1025	N.Y. Yankees, 1998	114–48
1014	N.Y. Yankees, 2009	103–59
1007	N.Y. Yankees, 2000	87–74
1002	Chi. White Sox, 2005	99–63

Pinch Hits

Highest Batting Average for Pinch Hitter, Season (Min. 25 At-Bats)

American League

.467	Smead Jolley, Chi. White Sox, 1931	14-for-30
.457	Rick Miller, Bos. Red Sox, 1983	16-for-35
.452	Elmer Valo, K.C. A's, 1955	14-for-31
.450	Gates Brown, Det. Tigers, 1968	18-for-40
.433	Ted Easterly, Cle. Indians–Chi. White Sox, 1912	13-for-30
.433	Randy Bush, Min. Twins, 1986	13-for-30
.429	Joe Cronin, Bos. Red Sox, 1943	18-for-42
.429	Don Dillard, Cle. Indians, 1961	15-for-35
.419	Dick Williams, Bal. Orioles, 1962	13-for-31
.414	Jose Offerman, Min. Twins, 2004	12-for-29
.412	Bob Hansen, Mil. Brewers, 1974	14-for-34

National League (Post-1900)

.486	Ed Kranepool, N.Y. Mets, 1974	17-for-35
.472	Seth Smith, Col. Rockies, 2009	17-for-36
.465	Frenchy Bordagaray, St.L. Cardinals, 1938	20-for-43
.462	Jose Martinez, St.L. Cardinals, 2017	12-for-26
.455	Bill Spiers, Hou. Astros, 1997	15-for-33

continued on next page

.455	Jorge Piedra, Col. Rockies, 2005	15-for-33
.452	Jose Pagan, Pit. Pirates, 1969	19-for-42
.452	Mark Johnson, Pit. Pirates, 1996	19-for-31
.433	Milt Thompson, Atl. Braves, 1985	13-for-30
.419	Bob Bowman, Phi. Phillies, 1958	13-for-31
.425	Candy Maldonado, S.F. Giants, 1986	17-for-40
.423	Colin Moran, Pit. Pirates, 2018	11-for-26
.419	Reed Johnson, Chi. Cubs–Atl. Braves, 2012	18-for-43
.419	Richie Ashburn, N.Y. Mets, 1962	13-for-31
.415	Merritt Ranew, Chi. Cubs, 1963	17-for-41

Extra-Base Hits

Evolution of Total Bases Record

American League

1901	Nap Lajoie, Phi. A's	350
1911	Ty Cobb, Det. Tigers	367
1920	George Sisler, St.L. Browns	399
1921	Babe Ruth, N.Y. Yankees	457

National League (Pre-1900)

1876	Ross Barnes, Chi. White Stockings	190
1879	Paul Hines, Pro. Grays	197
1883	Dan Brouthers, Buff. Bisons	243
1884	Abner Dalrymple, Chi. Cubs	263
1886	Dan Brouthers, Det. Wolverines	284
1887	Sam Thompson, Det. Wolverines	308
1893	Ed Delahanty, Phi. Phillies	347
1894	Hugh Duffy, Bos. Beaneaters	374

National League (Post-1900)

1921	Rogers Hornsby, St.L. Cardinals	378
1922	Rogers Hornsby, St.L. Cardinals	450

Players with 100 Extra-Base Hits, Season

	Doubles	Triples	Home Runs	Total
Babe Ruth, N.Y. Yankees (AL), 1921	44	16	59	119
Lou Gehrig, N.Y. Yankees (AL), 1927	52	18	47	117
Chuck Klein, Phi. Phillies (NL), 1930	59	8	40	107
Barry Bonds, S.F. Giants (NL), 2001	32	2	73	107
Todd Helton, Col. Rockies (NL), 2001	54	2	49	105
Chuck Klein, Phi. Phillies (NL), 1932	50	15	38	103
Hank Greenberg, Det. Tigers (AL), 1937	49	14	40	103
Stan Musial, St.L. Cardinals (NL), 1948	46	18	39	103
Albert Belle, Cle. Indians (AL), 1995	52	1	50	103
Todd Helton, Col. Rockies (NL), 2000	59	2	42	103
Sammy Sosa, Chi. Cubs (NL), 2001	34	5	64	103
Rogers Hornsby, St.L. Cardinals (NL), 1922	46	14	42	102
Lou Gehrig, N.Y. Yankees (AL), 1930	42	17	41	100
Jimmie Foxx, Phi. A's (AL), 1932	33	9	58	100
Luis Gonzalez, Ari. D'backs (NL), 2001	36	7	57	100

Players with 400 Total Bases, Season

American League

Babe Ruth, N.Y. Yankees, 1921 457
Lou Gehrig, N.Y. Yankees, 1927 447
Jimmie Foxx, Phi. A's, 1932 438
Lou Gehrig, N.Y. Yankees, 1930 419
Joe DiMaggio, N.Y. Yankees, 1937 418
Babe Ruth, N.Y. Yankees, 1927 417
Lou Gehrig, N.Y. Yankees, 1931 410
Lou Gehrig, N.Y. Yankees, 1934 409
Jim Rice, Bos. Red Sox, 1978 406
Hal Trosky, Cle. Indians, 1936 405
Jimmie Foxx, Phi. A's, 1933 403
Lou Gehrig, N.Y. Yankees, 1936 403

National League (Post-1900)

Rogers Hornsby, St.L. Cardinals, 1922 450
Chuck Klein, Phi. Phillies, 1930 445
Stan Musial, St.L. Cardinals, 1948 429
Sammy Sosa, Chi. Cubs, 2001 425
Hack Wilson, Chi. Cubs, 1930 423
Chuck Klein, Phi. Phillies, 1932 420
Luis Gonzalez, Ari. D'backs, 2001 419
Babe Herman, Brk. Dodgers, 1930 416
Sammy Sosa, Chi. Cubs, 1998 416
Barry Bonds, S.F. Giants, 2001 411
Rogers Hornsby, Chi. Cubs, 1929 409
Larry Walker, Col. Rockies, 1997 409
Joe Medwick, St.L. Cardinals, 1937 406
Chuck Klein, Phi. Phillies, 1929 405
Todd Helton, Col. Rockies, 2000 405
Todd Helton, Col. Rockies, 2001 402
Hank Aaron, Mil. Braves, 1959 400

Evolution of Doubles Record

American League

Year	Player	Total
1901	Nap Lajoie, Phi. A's	48
1904	Nap Lajoie, Cle. Blues	49
1910	Nap Lajoie, Cle. Naps	51
1912	Tris Speaker, Bos. Red Sox	53
1923	Tris Speaker, Cle. Indians	59
1926	George H. Burns, Cle. Indians	64
1931	Earl Webb, Bos. Red Sox	67

National League (Pre-1900)

Year	Player	Total
1876	Ross Barnes, Chi. White Stockings	21
	Dick Higham, Har. Dark Blues	21
	Paul Hines, Chi. White Stockings	21
1878	Dick Higham, Pro. Grays	22
1879	Charlie Eden, Cle. Spiders	31
1882	King Kelly, Chi. White Stockings	37
1883	Ned Williamson, Chi. White Stockings	49
1894	Hugh Duffy, Bos. Beaneaters	51
1899	Ed Delahanty, Phi. Phillies	55

National League (Post-1899)

Year	Player	Total
1900	Honus Wagner, Pit. Pirates	45
1922	Rogers Hornsby, St.L. Cardinals	46
1928	Paul Waner, Pit. Pirates	50
1929	Johnny Frederick, Brk. Dodgers	52
1930	Chuck Klein, Pit. Pirates	59
1932	Paul Waner, Pit. Pirates	62
1936	Joe Medwick, St.L. Cardinals	64

Players Hitting 40 Home Runs and 40 Doubles, Season

American League

	Home Runs	Doubles
Babe Ruth, N.Y. Yankees, 1921	59	44
Babe Ruth, N.Y. Yankees, 1923	41	45
Lou Gehrig, N.Y. Yankees, 1927	47	52
Lou Gehrig, N.Y. Yankees, 1930	41	42
Lou Gehrig, N.Y. Yankees 1934	49	40
Hal Trosky, Cle. Indians, 1936	42	45
Hank Greenberg, Det. Tigers, 1937	40	49
Hank Greenberg, Det. Tigers, 1940	41	50
Albert Belle, Cle. Indians, 1995	50	52
Albert Belle, Chi. White Sox, 1998	49	48
Juan Gonzalez, Tex. Rangers, 1998	45	50
Shawn Green, Tor. Blue Jays, 1999	42	45
Frank Thomas, Chi. White Sox, 2000	43	44
Carlos Delgado, Tor. Blue Jays, 2000	41	57
Manny Ramirez, Bos. Red Sox, 2004	43	44
David Ortiz, Bos. Red Sox, 2004	41	47
David Ortiz, Bos. Red Sox, 2005	47	40
Mark Teixeira, Tex. Rangers, 2005	43	41
Miguel Cabrera, Det. Tigers, 2012	44	40
Chris Davis, Bal. Orioles, 2013	53	42
Josh Donaldson, Tor. Blue Jays, 2015	41	41

National League (Post-1900)

	Home Runs	Doubles
Rogers Hornsby, St.L. Cardinals, 1922	42	46
Chuck Klein, Phi. Phillies, 1929	43	45
Chuck Klein, Phi. Phillies, 1930	40	59
Willie Stargell, Pit. Pirates, 1973	44	43
Ellis Burks, Col. Rockies, 1996	40	45
Larry Walker, Col. Rockies, 1997	49	46
Jeff Bagwell, Hou. Astros, 1997	43	40
Chipper Jones, Atl. Braves, 1999	45	41
Todd Helton, Col. Rockies, 2000	42	59
Richard Hidalgo, Hou. Astros, 2000	44	42
Todd Helton, Col. Rockies, 2001	49	54
Albert Pujols, St.L. Cardinals, 2003	43	51
Albert Pujols, St.L. Cardinals, 2004	46	51
Derrek Lee, Chi. Cubs, 2005	46	50
Alfonso Soriano, Was. Nationals, 2006	46	41
Albert Pujols, St.L. Cardinals, 2009	47	45
Nolan Arenado, Col. Rockies, 2015	42	43

Evolution of Triples Record

American League

1901	Jimmy Williams, Bal. Orioles	21
1903	Sam Crawford, Det. Tigers	25
1912	Joe Jackson, Cle. Indians	26

continued on next page

National League (Pre-1900)

1876	Ross Barnes, Chi. White Stockings	14
1882	Roger Connor, Tro. Haymakers	18
1884	Buck Ewing, N.Y. Gothams	20
1887	Sam Thompson, Det. Wolverines	23
1890	Long John Reilly, Cin. Reds	26
1893	Perry Werden, St.L. Cardinals	29
1894	Heinie Reitz, Bal. Orioles	31

National League (Post-1899)

1900	Honus Wagner, Pit. Pirates	22
1911	Larry Doyle, N.Y. Giants	25
1912	Owen Wilson, Pit. Pirates	36

Leaders in Doubles and Triples, Season

American League

	Doubles	Triples
Ty Cobb, Det. Tigers, 1908	36	20
Ty Cobb, Det. Tigers, 1911	47	24
Ty Cobb, Det. Tigers, 1917	44	23
Bobby Veach, Det. Tigers, 1919	45	17
Charlie Gehringer, Det. Tigers, 1929	45	19
Joe Vosmik, Cle. Indians, 1935	47	20
Zoilo Versalles, Min. Twins, 1964	45	12
Cesar Tovar, Min. Twins, 1970	36	13

National League (Post-1900)

	Doubles	Triples
Honus Wagner, Pit. Pirates, 1900	45	22
Honus Wagner, Pit. Pirates, 1908	39	19
Rogers Hornsby, St.L. Cardinals, 1921	44	18
Stan Musial, St.L. Cardinals, 1943	48	20
Stan Musial, St.L. Cardinals, 1946	50	20
Stan Musial, St.L. Cardinals, 1948	46	18
Stan Musial, St.L. Cardinals, 1949	41	13
Lou Brock, St.L. Cardinals, 1968	46	14

Leaders in Doubles and Home Runs, Season

American League

	Doubles	Home Runs
Nap Lajoie, Phi. A's, 1901	48	14
Tris Speaker, Bos. Red Sox, 1912	53	10 (Tie)
Hank Greenberg, Det. Tigers, 1940	50	41
Ted Williams, Bos. Red Sox, 1949	39	43
Albert Belle, Cle. Indians, 1995	52	50

continued on next page

National League (Post-1900)

	Doubles	Home Runs
Heinie Zimmerman, Chi. Cubs, 1912	41	14
Rogers Hornsby, St.L. Cardinals, 1922	46	42
Chuck Klein, Phi. Phillies, 1933	44	28
Joe Medwick, St.L. Cardinals, 1937	56	31 (Tie)
Willie Stargell, Pit. Pirates, 1973	43	44

Leaders in Triples and Home Runs, Season

American League

	Triples	Home Runs
Mickey Mantle, N.Y. Yankees, 1955	11 (Tie)	37
Jim Rice, Bos. Red Sox, 1978	15	46

National League (Post-1900)

	Triples	Home Runs
Tommy Leach, Pit. Pirates, 1902	22	6
Harry Lumley, Brk. Dodgers, 1904	18	9
Jim Bottomley, St.L. Cardinals, 1928	20	31 (Tie)
Willie Mays, N.Y. Giants, 1955	15 (Tie)	51

Players Hitting 20 Home Runs, 20 Triples, and 20 Doubles, Season

American League

	Doubles	Triples	Home Runs
Jeff Heath, Cle. Indians, 1941	32	20	24
George Brett, K.C. Royals, 1979	42	20	23
Curtis Granderson, Det. Tigers, 2007	38	23	23

National League (Post-1900)

	Doubles	Triples	Home Runs
Frank Schulte, Chi. Cubs, 1911	30	21	21
Jim Bottomley, St.L. Cardinals, 1928	42	20	31
Willie Mays, N.Y. Giants, 1957	26	20	35
Jimmy Rollins, Phi. Phillies, 2007	38	20	30

Players Leading League in Doubles, Triples, and Home Runs During Career (Post-1900)

Jim Bottomley
Doubles: 1925 (44) and 1926 (40)
Triples: 1928 (20)
Home Runs: 1928 (31)

Ty Cobb
Doubles: 1908 (36), 1911 (47), and 1917 (44)
Triples: 1908 (20), 1911 (24), 1917 (24), and 1918 (14)
Home Runs: 1909 (9)

Sam Crawford
Doubles: 1909 (35)
Triples: 1902 (23), 1903 (25), 1910 (19), 1913 (23), 1914 (26), and 1915 (19)
Home Runs: 1908 (7)

Lou Gehrig
Doubles: 1927 (52)
Triples: 1926 (20)
Home Runs: 1931 (46), 1934 (49), and 1936 (49)

Rogers Hornsby
Doubles: 1920 (44), 1921 (44), and 1922 (46)
Triples: 1917 (17) and 1921 (18)
Home Runs: 1922 (42) and 1925 (39)

continued on next page

Johnny Mize...Doubles: 1941 (39)
Triples: 1938 (16)
Home Runs: 1939 (28), 1940 (43), 1947 (51, Tie), and 1948 (40, Tie)

Players Since World War II with 100 Doubles, Triples, Home Runs, and Stolen Bases, Career

	Doubles	Triples	Home Runs	Stolen Bases
George Brett (1973–93)	665	137	317	201
Lou Brock (1961–79)	486	141	149	938
Carl Crawford (2002–16)	309	123	136	480
Johnny Damon (1995–2012)	307	122	136	480
Willie Davis (1960–79)	395	138	182	398
Steve Finley (1989–2007)	449	124	304	320
Kenny Lofton (1991–2007)	383	116	130	622
Willie Mays (1951–73)	523	140	660	338
Paul Molitor (1978–98)	605	114	234	504
Vada Pinson (1958–75)	485	127	256	305
Tim Raines (1979–2002)	430	113	170	808
Jose Reyes (2003–18)	387	131	145	517
Jimmy Rollins (2000–16)	511	115	231	470
Pete Rose (1963–86)	746	135	160	198
Juan Samuel (1983–98)	287	102	161	396
Mickey Vernon (1939–60)	490	120	172	137
Robin Yount (1974–93)	583	126	251	271

Players with 200 Hits and Fewer than 40 Extra-Base Hits, Season

American League

	Hits	Extra-Base Hits
Cesar Tovar, Min. Twins, 1971	204	33
Ichiro Suzuki, Sea. Mariners, 2008	213	33
Nellie Fox, Chi. White Sox, 1954	201	34
Steve Sax, N.Y. Yankees, 1989	205	34
Johnny Pesky, Bos. Red Sox, 1947	207	35
Ichiro Suzuki, Sea. Mariners, 2007	238	35
Ichiro Suzuki, Sea. Mariners, 2004	262	37
Rod Carew, Min. Twins, 1974	218	38
Ichiro Suzuki, Sea. Mariners, 2006	224	38
Harvey Kuenn, Det. Tigers, 1954	201	39
Ichiro Suzuki, Sea. Mariners, 2010	214	39

National League (Post-1900)

	Hits	Extra-Base Hits
Lloyd Waner, Pit. Pirates, 1927	223	25
Maury Wills, L.A. Dodgers, 1962	208	29
Matty Alou, Pit. Pirates, 1970	201	30
Dee Strange-Gordon, Mia. Marlins, 2017	201	31
Willie Keeler, Brk. Dodgers, 1901	202	33
Curt Flood, St.L. Cardinals, 1964	211	33
Milt Stock, St.L. Cardinals, 1920	204	34
Richie Ashburn, Phi. Phillies, 1953	205	36
Tony Gwynn, S.D. Padres, 1984	213	36
Juan Pierre, Fla. Marlins, 2003	204	36
Dee Strange-Gordon, Mia. Marlins, 2015	205	36
Juan Pierre, Fla. Marlins, 2004	221	37
Milt Stock, Brk. Dodgers, 1925	202	38
Chick Fullis, Phi. Phillies, 1933	200	38
Tony Gwynn, S.D. Padres, 1989	203	38
Richie Ashburn, Phi. Phillies, 1958	215	39
Ralph Garr, Atl. Braves, 1971	219	39
Dave Cash, Phi. Phillies, 1974	213	39
Juan Pierre, Col. Rockies, 2001	202	39

Most Doubles by Position, Season

American League

First Base.......64...... George H. Burns, Cle. Indians, 1926
Second Base ..60.......Charlie Gehringer, Det. Tigers, 1936
Third Base .....56...............George Kell, Det. Tigers, 1950
Shortstop......56.......Nomar Garciaparra, Bos. Red Sox, 2002
Outfield.........67.............Earl Webb, Bos. Red Sox, 1931
Catcher.........47........ Ivan Rodriguez, Tex. Rangers, 1996
Pitcher...........13.... Smoky Joe Wood, Bos. Red Sox, 1912
                13............ Red Ruffing, Bos. Red Sox, 1928
Designated
   Hitter ....52.....Edgar Martinez, Sea. Mariners, 1995
                52..... Edgar Martinez, Sea. Mariners, 1996
                52............David Ortiz, Bos. Red Sox, 2007

National League (Post-1900)

First Base.........59........... Todd Helton, Col. Rockies, 2000
Second Base ...57...Billy Herman, Chi. Cubs, 1935 and 1936
Third Base.....53...............Jeff Cirillo, Col. Rockies, 2000
              53........Freddie Sanchez, Pit. Pirates, 2006
Shortstop .....54..Mark Grudzielanek, Mon. Expos, 1997
Outfield ....64.......Joe Medwick, St.L. Cardinals, 1936
Catcher ....46......Jonathan Lucroy, Mil. Brewers, 2014
Pitcher ....11..................Red Lucas, Cin. Reds, 1932
Designated
   Hitter..........24........... Bryce Harper, Phi. Phillies, 2022

Most Triples by Position, Season

American League

First Base.......20............Lou Gehrig, N.Y. Yankees, 1926
Second Base ..22.....Snuffy Stirnweiss, N.Y. Yankees, 1945
Third Base .....22............. Bill Bradley, Cle. Indians, 1903
Shortstop.......21.................Bill Keister, Bal. Orioles, 1901
Outfield.........26...............Joe Jackson, Cle. Indians, 1912
              26............ Sam Crawford, Det. Tigers, 1914
Catcher..........12............Mickey Cochrane, Phi. A's, 1928
              12...........Eddie Ainsmith, Det. Tigers, 1919
Pitcher...........6.......Jesse Tannehill, N.Y. Yankees, 1904
              6....... Walter Johnson, Was. Senators, 1913
Designated
   Hitter ....13.............Paul Molitor, Mil. Brewers, 1991

National League (Post-1900)

First Base ....22.............Jake Daubert, Cin. Reds, 1922
Second Base ...25............. Larry Doyle, N.Y. Giants, 1911
Third Base......22............. Tommy Leach, Pit. Pirates, 1902
Shortstop ....20.......... Honus Wagner, Pit. Pirates, 1912
              20........... Jimmy Rollins, Phi. Phillies, 2007
Outfield   36............Owen Wilson, Pit. Pirates, 1912
Catcher ....13.............Johnny Kling, Chi. Cubs, 1903
              13....Tim McCarver, St.L. Cardinals, 1966
Pitcher ....6...........Claude Hendrix, Pit. Pirates, 1912
Designated
   Hitter..........5......Charlie Blackmon, Col. Rockies, 2022

Most Total Bases by Position, Season

American League

First Base.......447...........Lou Gehrig, N.Y. Yankees, 1927
Second Base ..381....Alfonso Soriano, N.Y. Yankees, 2002
Third Base .....376.....Alex Rodriguez, N.Y. Yankees, 2007
Shortstop......393......Alex Rodriguez, Tex. Rangers, 2001
Outfield.........457............ Babe Ruth, N.Y. Yankees, 1921
Catcher.........335......Ivan Rodriguez, Tex. Rangers, 1999

Pitcher............ 80............ Wes Ferrell, Cle. Indians, 1931
Designated
   Hitter..........363 .... David Ortiz, Bos. Red Sox, 2005

National League (Post-1900)

First Base ....405......... Todd Helton, Col. Rockies, 2000
Second Base ...450. Rogers Hornsby, St.L. Cardinals, 1922
Third Base......380.......Vinny Castilla, Col. Rockies, 1998
Shortstop ....380.........Jimmy Rollins, Phi. Phillies, 2007
Outfield ....445...........Chuck Klein, Phi. Phillies, 1930
Catcher ....355.......Mike Piazza, L.A. Dodgers, 1997
              355........Johnny Bench, Cin. Reds, 1970
Pitcher .... 74...Don Newcombe, Brk. Dodgers, 1955
Designated
   Hitter.............178........... Bryce Harper, Phi. Phillies, 2022

Stolen Bases

Evolution of Stolen Base Record

American League

1901............................Frank Isbell, Chi. White Sox 52
1907........................Ty Cobb, Det. Tigers 53
1909...........................Ty Cobb, Det. Tigers 76

continued on next page

1910.....................Eddie Collins, Phi. A's...81
1911.....................Ty Cobb, Det. Tigers..83
1912.....................Clyde Milan, Was. Senators..88
1915.....................Ty Cobb, Det. Tigers..96
1980.....................Rickey Henderson, Oak. A's..100
1982.....................Rickey Henderson, Oak. A's..130

National League (Pre-1900)

1886.....................Ed Andrews, Phi. Phillies..56
1887.....................Monte Ward, N.Y. Gothams..111

National League (Post-1899)

1900.....................George Van Haltren, N.Y. Giants..45
                Patsy Donovan, St.L. Cardinals
1901.....................Honus Wagner, Pit. Pirates...49
1903.....................Jimmy Sheckard, Brk. Dodgers..67
                Frank Chance, Chi. Cubs..67
1910.....................Bob Bescher, Cin. Reds...70
1911.....................Bob Bescher, Cin. Reds...81
1962.....................Maury Wills, L.A. Dodgers...104
1974.....................Lou Brock, St.L. Cardinals...118

Most Stolen Bases by Position, Season

American League

First Base.......52.........Frank Isbell, Chi. White Sox, 1901
Second Base ..81..................Eddie Collins, Phi. A's, 1910
Third Base .....74............Fritz Maisel, N.Y. Yankees, 1914
Shortstop......62...........Bert Campaneris, Oak. A's, 1968
Outfield........130........Rickey Henderson, Oak. A's, 1982
Catcher.........36............John Wathan, K.C. Royals, 1982
Pitcher...........10... Nixey Callahan, Chi. White Sox, 1901
Designated
  Hitter .... 22................. Hal McRae, K.C. Royals, 1976
           22 ....Paul Molitor, Tor. Blue Jays, 1993
           22 ....Gary Sheffield, Det. Tigers, 2007

National League (Post-1900)

First Base ....67...........Frank Chance, Chi. Cubs, 1903
Second Base ...77..........Davey Lopes, L.A. Dodgers, 1975
Third Base ......59...............Art Devlin, N.Y. Giants, 1905
Shortstop ....104.........Maury Wills, L.A. Dodgers, 1962
Outfield ....118....Lou Brock, St.L. Cardinals, 1974
Catcher ....26.........Jason Kendall, Pit. Pirates, 1998
Pitcher ....8........ Bill Dinneen, Bos. Beaneaters, 1901
Designated
  Hitter ....9 ....Bryce Harper, Phi. Phillies, 2022

Most Stolen Bases by Decade

Pre-1900

862....................Billy Hamilton
741.........................Arlie Latham
657............................Tom Brown
568...........................Bid McPhee
558.........................Dummy Hoy
548............................Hugh Duffy
540.........................Monte Ward
509........................Harry Stovey
494.............George Van Haltren
473........................ Mike Griffin

1900–09

487 ....Honus Wagner
359.............................Frank Chance
305.............................Sam Mertes
295..........................Jimmy Sheckard
275 .... Elmer Flick
252 ....Jimmy Slagle
250 ....Frank Isbell
239 ....Fred Clarke
239 ....Wid Conroy
239 ....Fielder Jones

1910–19

576 .... Ty Cobb
489 ....Eddie Collins
434 ....Clyde Milan
392 ....Max Carey
364 ....Bob Bescher
340 ....Tris Speaker
324 ....Donie Bush
293 ....George J. Burns
286 ....Buck Herzog
285 ....Burt Shotton

1920–29

346...........................Max Carey
310.........................Frankie Frisch
254.............................Sam Rice
214.........................George Sisler

1930–39

269 ....Ben Chapman
176 ....Bill Werber
158 ....Lyn Lary
158 ....Gee Walker

1940–49

285 ....George Case
130 ....Snuffy Stirnweiss
126 ....Wally Moses
117 ....Johnny Hopp

continued on next page

1920–29

210	Kiki Cuyler
180	Eddie Collins
175	Johnny Mostil
167	Bucky Harris
145	Cliff Heathcote
144	Jack Smith

1930–39

136	Pepper Martin
118	Kiki Cuyler
115	Roy Johnson
101	Charlie Gehringer
100	Pete Fox
100	Stan Hack

1940–49

108	Pee Wee Reese
108	Mickey Vernon
93	Joe Kuhel
91	Luke Appling
90	Bob Dillinger
88	Jackie Robinson

1950–59

179	Willie Mays
167	Minnie Minoso
158	Richie Ashburn
150	Jim Rivera
134	Luis Aparicio
134	Jackie Jensen
132	Jim Gilliam
124	Pee Wee Reese
121	Billy Bruton
109	Jackie Robinson

1960–69

535	Maury Wills
387	Lou Brock
342	Luis Aparicio
292	Bert Campaneris
240	Willie Davis
208	Tommy Harper
204	Hank Aaron
202	Vada Pinson
161	Don Buford
157	Tony Taylor

1970–79

551	Lou Brock
488	Joe Morgan
427	Cesar Cedeno
380	Bobby Bonds
375	Davey Lopes
344	Fred Patek
336	Bert Campaneris
324	Billy North
294	Ron LeFlore
294	Amos Otis

1980–89

838	Rickey Henderson
583	Tim Raines
472	Vince Coleman
451	Willie Wilson
364	Ozzie Smith
333	Steve Sax
331	Lonnie Smith
307	Brett Butler
293	Mookie Wilson
284	Dave Collins

1990–99

478	Otis Nixon
463	Rickey Henderson
433	Kenny Lofton
393	Delino DeShields
381	Marquis Grissom
343	Barry Bonds
335	Chuck Knoblauch
319	Craig Biggio
311	Roberto Alomar
297	Lance Johnson

2000–09

459	Juan Pierre
362	Carl Crawford
341	Ichiro Suzuki
326	Jimmy Rollins
301	Jose Reyes
295	Bobby Abreu
280	Chone Figgins
276	Luis Castillo
271	Rafael Furcal
266	Scott Podsednik

2010–19

330	Dee Strange-Gordon
322	Rajai Davis
299	Billy Hamilton
269	Elvis Andrus
254	Jose Altuve
250	Jarrod Dyson
239	Starling Marte
228	Brett Gardner
220	Michael Bourn
216	Jose Reyes

2020–22

75	Starling Marte
71	Cedric Mullins
71	Trea Turner
68	Whit Merrifield
64	Tommy Edman
58	Jon Berti
57	Jose Ramirez
57	Myles Straw
56	Randy Arozarena
54	Ronald Acuna
54	Dylan Moore

Teammates Combining for 125 Stolen Bases, Season

American League

Rickey Henderson (130) and Davey Lopes (28), Oak. A's, 1982	158
Rickey Henderson (108) and Mike Davis (33), Oak. A's, 1983	141
Clyde Milan (75) and Danny Moeller (62), Was. Senators, 1913	137
Ty Cobb (96) and Donie Bush (35), Det. Tigers, 1915	131
Ty Cobb (76) and Donie Bush (53), Det. Tigers, 1909	129
Bill North (75) and Bert Campaneris (54), Oak. A's, 1976	129
Rickey Henderson (100) and Dwayne Murphy (26), Oak. A's, 1980	126

National League (Post-1900)

Vince Coleman (110) and Willie McGee (56), St.L. Cardinals, 1985	166
Ron LeFlore (96) and Rodney Scott (63), Mon. Expos, 1980	159
Vince Coleman (109) and Ozzie Smith (43), St.L. Cardinals, 1987	152
Lou Brock (118) and Bake McBride (30), St.L. Cardinals, 1974	148
Vince Coleman (107) and Ozzie Smith (31), St.L. Cardinals, 1986	138
Vince Coleman (81) and Ozzie Smith (57), St.L. Cardinals, 1988	138
Maury Wills (104) and Willie Davis (32), L.A. Dodgers, 1962	136

Players Stealing 30 Bases for 10 Consecutive Seasons

	Seasons
Rickey Henderson, 1979–93	15
Lou Brock, 1964–77	14
Ty Cobb, 1907–18	12
Tim Raines, 1981–92	12
Honus Wagner, 1899–1909	11
Willie Wilson, 1978–88	11
Brett Butler, 1983–93	11
Bert Campaneris, 1965–74	10
Otis Nixon, 1988–97	10
Juan Pierre, 2001–10	10

Players Leading League in Stolen Bases and Total Bases, Season

American League

	Stolen Bases	Total Bases
Ty Cobb, Det. Tigers, 1907	49	286
Ty Cobb, Det. Tigers, 1909	76	296
Ty Cobb, Det. Tigers, 1911	83	367
Ty Cobb, Det. Tigers, 1915	96	274
Ty Cobb, Det. Tigers, 1917	55	336
Snuffy Stirnweiss, N.Y. Yankees, 1945	33	301

National League (Post-1900)

	Stolen Bases	Total Bases
Honus Wagner, Pit. Pirates, 1904	53	255
Honus Wagner, Pit. Pirates, 1907	61	264
Honus Wagner, Pit. Pirates, 1908	53	308
Chuck Klein, Phi. Phillies, 1932	20	420

Players with 200 Home Runs and 200 Stolen Bases, Career

	Home Runs	Stolen Bases
Hank Aaron (1954–76)	755	240
Bobby Abreu (1996–2014)	288	400
Roberto Alomar (1988–2004)	210	474
Brady Anderson (1988–2002)	210	315
Jeff Bagwell (1991–2005)	449	202
Don Baylor (1970–88)	338	285
Carlos Beltran (1998–2017)	435	312
Craig Biggio (1988–2007)	291	414
Barry Bonds (1986–2007)	762	514
Bobby Bonds (1968–81)	332	461
Ryan Braun (2007–20)	352	216
George Brett (1973–93)	317	201
Mike Cameron (1995–2011)	278	297
Jose Canseco (1985–2001)	462	200
Joe Carter (1983–98)	396	231
Johnny Damon (1995–2012)	235	408
Eric Davis (1984–94, 1996–2001)	282	349
Andre Dawson (1976–96)	438	314
Steve Finley (1989–2007)	304	320
Ron Gant (1987–2003)	321	243
Kirk Gibson (1979–95)	255	284
Marquis Grissom (1989–2005)	227	429
Rickey Henderson (1979–2003)	297	1406
Reggie Jackson (1967–87)	563	228

continued on next page

	Home Runs	Stolen Bases
Derek Jeter (1996–2014)	260	358
Howard Johnson (1982–95)	228	231
Ian Kinsler (2006–19)	257	231
Ray Lankford (1990–2002, 2004)	238	258
Willie Mays (1951–52, 1954–73)	660	338
Andrew McCutchen* (2009–)	287	205
Paul Molitor (1978–98)	234	504
Raul Mondesi (1993–2005)	271	229
Joe Morgan (1963–84)	268	689
Vada Pinson (1958–75)	256	305
Brandon Phillips (2002–18)	211	209
Hanley Ramirez (2005–19)	271	281
Frank Robinson (1956–76)	586	204
Alex Rodriguez (1994–2013, 2015–16)	696	329
Jimmy Rollins (2000–16)	231	470
Ryne Sandberg (1981–97)	282	344
Reggie Sanders (1991–2007)	305	304
Gary Sheffield (1988–2009)	509	253
Alfonso Soriano (1999–2014)	412	289
Sammy Sosa (1989–2005, 2007)	609	234
Darryl Strawberry (1983–99)	335	221
Mike Trout* (2011–)	350	204
Larry Walker (1989–2005)	383	230
Devon White (1985–2001)	208	346
Dave Winfield (1973–88, 1990–95)	465	223
Jimmy Wynn (1963–77)	291	225
Robin Yount (1974–93)	251	271

* Still active.

Players with 400 Home Runs and 10 Steals of Home, Career

	Home Runs	Steals of Home
Lou Gehrig	493	15
Babe Ruth	714	10

Players with 200 Hits, 20 Home Runs, and 20 Stolen Bases, Season

American League

	Hits	Home Runs	Stolen Bases
Joe Carter, Cle. Indians, 1986	200	29	29
Kirby Puckett, Min. Twins, 1986	223	31	20
Alan Trammell, Det. Tigers, 1987	205	28	21
Paul Molitor, Tor. Blue Jays, 1993	211	22	22
Nomar Garciaparra, Bos. Red Sox, 1997	209	30	22
Alex Rodriguez, Sea. Mariners, 1998	213	42	46
Darin Erstad, Ana. Angels, 2000	240	25	28
Alfonso Soriano, N.Y. Yankees, 2002	209	39	41
Jacoby Ellsbury, Bos. Red Sox, 2011	212	32	39
Michael Brantley, Cle. Indians, 2014	200	20	23
Jose Altuve, Hou. Astros, 2016	216	24	30
Mookie Betts, Bos. Red Sox, 2016	214	31	26
Jose Altuve, Hou. Astros, 2017	204	24	32

continued on next page

National League

	Hits	Home Runs	Stolen Bases
Babe Herman, Brk. Dodgers, 1929	217	21	21
Chuck Klein, Phi. Phillies, 1932	226	38	20
Willie Mays, S.F. Giants, 1958	208	29	31
Vada Pinson, Cin. Reds, 1959	205	20	21
Hank Aaron, Mil. Braves, 1963	201	44	31
Vada Pinson, Cin. Reds, 1963	204	22	27
Vada Pinson, Cin. Reds, 1965	205	22	21
Lou Brock, St.L. Cardinals, 1967	206	21	52
Bobby Bonds, S.F. Giants, 1970	200	26	48
Marquis Grissom, Atl. Braves, 1996	207	23	28
Ellis Burks, Col. Rockies, 1996	211	40	32
Larry Walker, Col. Rockies, 1997	208	49	33
Craig Biggio, Hou. Astros, 1998	210	20	50
Vladimir Guerrero, Mon. Expos, 2002	206	39	40
Hanley Ramirez, Fla. Marlins, 2007	212	29	51
Jimmy Rollins, Phi. Phillies, 2007	212	30	41
Ryan Braun, Mil. Brewers, 2009	203	32	20
Jean Segura, Ari. D'backs, 2016	203	20	33

Players with 10 Doubles, Triples, Home Runs, and Steals in Each of First Three Seasons in Majors

		Doubles	Triples	Home Runs	Steals
Ben Chapman	N.Y. Yankees (AL), 1930	31	10	10	14
	N.Y. Yankees (AL), 1931	28	11	17	61
	N.Y. Yankees (AL), 1932	41	15	10	38
Juan Samuel	Phi. Phillies (NL), 1984	36	19	15	72
	Phi. Phillies (NL), 1985	31	13	19	53
	Phi. Phillies (NL), 1986	36	12	16	42
	Phi. Phillies (NL), 1987	37	15	28	35

Players Who Have Stolen Second, Third, and Home in Same Inning

American League

Dave Fultz, Phi. A's, Sep. 4, 1902
Wild Bill Donovan, Det. Tigers, May 7, 1906
Bill Coughlin, Det. Tigers, Jun. 4, 1906
Ty Cobb, Det. Tigers, Jul. 22, 1909
Ty Cobb, Det. Tigers, Jul. 12, 1911
Ty Cobb, Det. Tigers, Jul. 4, 1912
Joe Jackson, Cle. Indians, Aug. 11, 1912
Eddie Collins, Phi. A's, Sep. 22, 1912
Eddie Ainsmith, Was. Senators, Jun. 26, 1913
Red Faber, Chi. White Sox, Jul. 14, 1915
Don Moeller, Was. Senators, Jul. 19, 1915
Fritz Maisel, N.Y. Yankees, Aug. 17, 1915
Buck Weaver, Chi. White Sox, Sep. 6, 1919
Bobby Roth, Was. Senators, May 31, 1920
Bob Meusel, N.Y. Yankees, May 16, 1927

National League (Post-1900)

Honus Wagner, Pit. Pirates, Sep. 25, 1907
Hans Lobert, Cin. Reds, Sep. 27, 1908
Honus Wagner, Pit. Pirates, May 2, 1909
Dode Paskert, Cin. Reds, May 23, 1910
Wilbur Good, Chi. Cubs, Aug. 18, 1915
Jim Johnstone, Brk. Dodgers, Sep. 22, 1916
Greasy Neale, Cin. Reds, Aug. 15, 1919
Max Carey, Pit. Pirates, Aug. 13, 1923
Max Carey, Pit. Pirates, May 26, 1925
Harvey Hendrick, Brk. Dodgers, Jun. 12, 1928
Pete Rose, Phi. Phillies, May 11, 1980
Dusty Baker, S.F. Giants, Jun. 27, 1984
Eric Young, Col. Rockies, Jun. 30, 1996
Jayson Werth, Phi. Phillies, May 12, 2009
Dee Strange-Gordon, L.A. Dodgers, Jul. 1, 2011

continued on next page

American League

Jack Tavener, Det. Tigers, Jul. 10, 1927
Jack Tavener, Det. Tigers, Jul. 25, 1928
Don Kolloway, Chi. White Sox, Jun. 28, 1941
Rod Carew, Min. Twins, May 18, 1969
Dave Nelson, Tex. Rangers, Aug. 30, 1974
Paul Molitor, Mil. Brewers, Jul. 26, 1987
Devon White, Cal. Angels, Sep. 9, 1989
Chris Stynes, K.C. Royals, May 12, 1996
Kevin Pillar, Tor. Blue Jays, Mar. 31, 2018
Mallex Smith, Sea. Mariners, May 27, 2019

National League (Post-1900)

Wil Myers, S.D. Padres, Aug. 16, 2017
Jon Berti, Mia. Marlins, Aug. 25, 2020

Most Stolen Bases by Catcher, Season

36 ....John Wathan, K.C. Royals (AL), 1982
30 .... Ray Schalk, Chi. White Sox (AL), 1916
28 .... John Wathan, K.C. Royals (AL), 1983*
26 .... Jason Kendall, Pit. Pirates (NL), 1998
25 .... Johnny Kling Chi. Cubs (NL), 1902
25 .... Roger Bresnahan, N.Y. Giants (NL), 1906*
25 ....John Stearns, N.Y. Mets (NL), 1978
25 ....Ivan Rodriguez, Tex. Rangers (AL), 1999
25 ....Craig Biggio, Hou. Astros (NL), 1990
24 ....Ray Schalk, Chi. White Sox (AL), 1914

23 ....Johnny Kling, Chi. Cubs (NL), 1903
22 ....Jason Kendall, Pit. Pirates (NL), 1999
22 ....Jason Kendall, Pit. Pirates (NL), 2000
21 .... Benito Santiago, S.D. Padres (NL), 1987
21 ...........................B.J. Surhoff, Mil. Brewers (AL), 1988
21 .... Craig Biggio, Hou. Astros (NL), 1989
21 .... Russell Martin, L.A. Dodgers (NL), 2007
21 ........................J.T. Realmuto, Phi. Phillies (NL), 2022
20 .... Red Dooin, Phi. Phillies (NL), 1908

* Caught in majority of games played during season.

Most Stolen Bases by Catcher, Career

212.....................................Roger Bresnahan* (1900–15)
189...Jason Kendall (1996–2010)
177....................................... Ray Schalk (1912–29)
133.....................................Red Dooin (1902–16)
128....................................Carlton Fisk (1969–93)
127.................................... Ivan Rodriguez (1991–2011)
124....................................Johnny Kling (1900–13)
121.................................. Wally Schang (1913–31)
105............................... John Wathan* (1976–85)

102 ....Brad Ausmus (1993–2010)
101 ....Russell Martin (2006–19)
92 .... Billy Sullivan (1899–14)
91 ....Benito Santiago (1986–2005)
91 .... John Stearns (1975–84)
87 .... Ivy Wingo (1911–29)
86 .... Eddie Ainsmith (1910–24)
86 ....Jimmie Wilson (1923–40)
80 ....Tony Pena (1980–1997)

* Caught in majority of games played during career.

Players with 50 Stolen Bases and 100 RBIs, Season (Post-1900)

	Stolen Bases	RBIs
Sam Mertes, N.Y. Giants (NL), 1905	52	108
Honus Wagner, Pit. Pirates (NL), 1905	57	101
Ty Cobb, Det. Tigers (AL), 1908	53	119
Honus Wagner, Pit. Pirates (NL), 1908	53	109
Ty Cobb, Det. Tigers (AL), 1909	76	107
Ty Cobb, Det. Tigers (AL), 1911	83	127
Ty Cobb, Det. Tigers (AL), 1917	55	102
George Sisler, St.L. Browns (AL), 1922	51	105
Ben Chapman, N.Y. Yankees (AL), 1931	61	122
Cesar Cedeno, Hou. Astros (NL), 1974	57	102
Joe Morgan, Cin. Reds (NL), 1976	60	111
Eric Davis, Cin. Reds (NL), 1987	50	100
Barry Bonds, S.F. Giants (NL), 1990	52	114

Most Stolen Bases by Home Run Champion, Season

American League

76	Ty Cobb, Det. Tigers, 1909 (9 home runs)
52	Tris Speaker, Bos. Red Sox, 1912 (10 home runs) (Tie)
40	Home Run Baker, Phi. A's, 1912 (10 home runs) (Tie)
40	Jose Canseco, Oak. A's, 1988 (42 home runs)
38	Home Run Baker, Phi. A's, 1911 (11 home runs)
37	Ken Williams, St.L. Browns, 1922 (39 home runs)
36	Harry Davis, Phi. A's, 1905 (8 home runs)
34	Home Run Baker, Phi. A's, 1913 (12 home runs)
27	Nap Lajoie, Phi. A's, 1901 (14 home runs)
26	Jose Canseco, Oak. A's, 1991 (44 home runs)

National League (Post-1900)

67	Jimmy Sheckard, Brk. Dodgers, 1903 (9 home runs)
48	Red Murray, N.Y. Giants, 1909 (7 home runs)
40	Matt Kemp L.A. Dodgers, 2011 (39 home runs)
33	Larry Walker, Col. Rockies, 1997 (49 home runs)
31	Hank Aaron, Atl. Braves, 1963 (44 home runs)
30	Harry Lumley, Brk. Dodgers, 1904 (9 home runs)
30	Howard Johnson, N.Y. Mets, 1991 (38 home runs)
30	Ryan Braun, Mil. Brewers, 2012 (41 home runs)
29	Mike Schmidt, Phi. Phillies, 1975 (38 home runs)
29	Darryl Strawberry, N.Y. Mets, 1988 (39 home runs)
29	Barry Bonds, S.F. Giants, 1993 (46 home runs)
25	Tommy Leach, Pit. Pirates, 1902 (6 home runs)
25	Ryne Sandberg, Chi. Cubs, 1990 (40 home runs)
25	Fernando Tatis Jr., S.D. Padres, 2021 (42 home runs)

Players Stealing Bases in Four Decades

	Decades	Total
Rickey Henderson (1979–2003)	1970s (33), 1980s (838), 1990s (463), 2000s (72)	1406
Tim Raines (1979–99, 2001–02)	1970s (2), 1980s (583), 1990s (222), 2000s (1)	808
Omar Vizquel (1989–2012)	1980s (1) 1990s (237), 2000s (151), 2010s (15)	404
Ted Williams (1939–42, 1946–60)	1930s (2), 1940s (14), 1950s (7), 1960s (1)	24

Best On-Base Percentage (OBP) by Decade

Pre-1900		1900–09		1910–19	
.461	John McGraw	.417	Honus Wagner	.457	Ty Cobb
.459	Billy Hamilton	.411	Roy Thomas	.428	Tris Speaker
.435	Bill Joyce	.397	Frank Chance	.424	Eddie Collins
.433	Jesse Burkett	.391	Mike Donlin	.422	Joe Jackson
.432	Joe Kelley	.389	Roger Bresnahan	.402	Miller Huggins
.430	Willie Keeler	.388	Nap Lajoie	.399	Johnny Bates
.428	Cupid Childs	.388	Jesse Burkett	.395	Jimmy Sheckard
.424	Dan Brouthers	.386	Topsy Hartsel	.389	Benny Kauff
.410	Ed Delahanty	.383	Elmer Flick	.384	Wally Schang
.408	Jake Stenzel	.380	Fred Clarke	.382	Johnny Evers
		.380	Ty Cobb		

continued on next page

1920–29

.488	Babe Ruth
.460	Rogers Hornsby
.441	Tris Speaker
.436	Eddie Collins
.436	Lou Gehrig
.433	Harry Heilmann
.431	Paul Waner
.431	Ty Cobb
.420	Max Bishop
.420	Johnny Bassler

1930–39

.472	Babe Ruth
.453	Lou Gehrig
.440	Jimmie Foxx
.434	Mickey Cochrane
.427	Max Bishop
.425	Johnny Mize
.420	Mel Ott
.420	Arky Vaughan
.415	Hank Greenberg
.414	Charlie Gehringer

1940–49

.496	Ted Williams
.428	Stan Musial
.414	Augie Galan
.411	Roy Cullenbine
.406	Charlie Keller
.404	Joe DiMaggio
.404	Elbie Fletcher
.403	Luke Appling
.403	Eddie Stanky
.403	Mel Ott

1950–59

.476	Ted Williams
.431	Ferris Fain
.425	Mickey Mantle
.421	Stan Musial
.416	Jackie Robinson
.406	Eddie Yost
.403	Elmer Valo
.400	Minnie Minoso
.399	Richie Ashburn
.398	Ralph Kiner

1960–69

.415	Mickey Mantle
.402	Frank Robinson
.387	Harmon Killebrew
.383	Carl Yastrzemski
.381	Al Kaline
.380	Dick Allen
.380	Norm Cash
.379	Joe Morgan
.379	Albie Pearson
.378	Willie McCovey

1970–79

.408	Rod Carew
.404	Joe Morgan
.400	Mike Hargrove
.398	Ken Singleton
.390	Ron Hunt
.389	Pete Rose
.388	Bernie Carbo
.386	Gene Tenace
.384	Carl Yastrzemski
.383	Fred Lynn

1980–89

.443	Wade Boggs
.403	Rickey Henderson
.392	George Brett
.392	Alvin Davis
.391	Tim Raines
.391	Mike Hargrove
.390	Keith Hernandez
.389	Jack Clark
.389	Tony Gwynn
.388	Rod Carew

1990–99

.440	Frank Thomas
.434	Barry Bonds
.430	Edgar Martinez
.416	Jeff Bagwell
.412	Rickey Henderson
.412	Jim Thome
.411	Mark McGwire
.406	John Olerud
.402	John Kruk
.401	Gary Sheffield

2000–09

.517	Barry Bonds
.436	Todd Helton
.427	Albert Pujols
.421	Larry Walker
.419	Manny Ramirez
.418	Jason Giambi
.413	Lance Berkman
.413	Chipper Jones
.408	Joe Mauer
.402	Bobby Abreu
.402	Nick Johnson

2010–19

.428	Joey Votto
.419	Mike Trout
.399	Miguel Cabrera
.391	Paul Goldschmidt
.385	Bryce Harper
.385	Kris Bryant
.384	Alex Bregman
.383	David Ortiz
.383	Christian Yelich
.383	Prince Fielder

2020–22*

.440	Juan Soto
.410	Freddie Freeman
.405	Bryce Harper
.395	Aaron Judge
.391	Mike Trout
.389	Paul Doldschmidt
.384	Brandon Nimmo
.383	Yandy Diaz
.375	Ronald Acuna
.375	Yordan Alvarez

* Min. 150 games played.

Best On-Base Plus Slugging (OPS) by Decade

Pre-1900

.943	Dan Brouthers
.925	Joe Kelley
.915	Ed Delahanty
.912	Willie Keeler
.902	Jesse Burkett
.902	Bill Joyce
.900	Billy Hamilton
.891	Sam Thompson
.887	Jake Stenzel
.883	Roger Connor

1900–09

.925	Honus Wagner
.876	Nap Lajoie
.865	Mike Donlin
.839	Ty Cobb
.829	Elmer Flick
.802	Sam Crawford
.799	Jesse Burkett
.797	Fred Clarke
.795	Frank Chance
.785	Buck Freeman

1910–19

.998	Ty Cobb
.933	Joe Jackson
.913	Tris Speaker
.871	Gavvy Cravath
.844	Eddie Collins
.839	Benny Kauff
.831	Sam Crawford
.819	George Sisler
.811	Rogers Hornsby
.810	Home Run Baker

1920–29

1.228	Babe Ruth
1.096	Rogers Hornsby
1.058	Lou Gehrig
.991	Harry Heilmann
.976	Tris Speaker
.970	Paul Waner
.966	Al Simmons
.954	Hack Wilson
.945	Ken Williams
.938	Jim Bottomley

1930–39

1.116	Babe Ruth
1.091	Jimmie Foxx
1.091	Lou Gehrig
1.032	Hank Greenberg
1.030	Johnny Mize
1.019	Joe DiMaggio
.980	Mel Ott
.939	Hal Trosky
.938	Bob Johnson
.937	Lefty O'Doul

1940–49

1.143	Ted Williams
1.005	Stan Musial
.989	Hank Greenberg
.972	Joe DiMaggio
.966	Ralph Kiner
.954	Johnny Mize
.926	Charlie Keller
.879	Mel Ott
.876	Enos Slaughter
.871	Jeff Heath
.871	Tommy Henrich

1950–59

1.098	Ted Williams
.994	Mickey Mantle
.989	Stan Musial
.981	Willie Mays
.959	Duke Snider
.931	Hank Aaron
.931	Eddie Mathews
.931	Ralph Kiner
.917	Frank Robinson
.913	Ernie Banks

1960–69

.962	Frank Robinson
.957	Mickey Mantle
.941	Hank Aaron
.935	Willie Mays
.933	Dick Allen
.933	Harmon Killebrew
.923	Willie McCovey
.878	Norm Cash
.875	Roberto Clemente
.875	Al Kaline

1970–79

.928	Willie Stargell
.910	Jim Rice
.909	Fred Lynn
.899	Hank Aaron
.891	Dave Parker
.889	Dick Allen
.885	Mike Schmidt
.881	Reggie Smith
.870	Reggie Jackson
.869	George Foster

1980–89

.925	Mike Schmidt
.922	Wade Boggs
.913	George Brett
.905	Will Clark
.879	Eric Davis
.889	Don Mattingly
.888	Pedro Guerrero
.882	Dwight Evans
.880	Ken Phelps
.878	Darryl Strawberry

1990–99

1.036	Barry Bonds
1.025	Mark McGwire
1.013	Frank Thomas
.975	Manny Ramirez
.966	Mike Piazza
.965	Ken Griffey Jr.
.962	Edgar Martinez
.961	Jeff Bagwell
.961	Larry Walker
.959	Jim Thome

2000–09

1.241	Barry Bonds
1.055	Albert Pujols
1.018	Manny Ramirez
1.006	Todd Helton
.988	Alex Rodriguez
.983	Larry Walker
.972	Lance Berkman
.962	Jim Thome
.961	Jason Giambi
.961	Ryan Howard

2010–19

1.000	Mike Trout
.945	David Ortiz
.944	Joey Votto
.943	Miguel Cabrera
.916	Paul Goldschmidt
.911	Alex Bregman
.905	Giancarlo Stanton
.901	Kris Bryant
.897	Nolan Arenado
.897	Bryce Harper

2020–22*

1.013	Mike Trout
1.006	Aaron Judge
.971	Bryce Harper
.963	Fernando Tatis Jr.
.959	Juan Soto
.944	Yordan Alvarez
.937	Freddie Freeman
.923	Paul Goldschmidt
.899	Jose Ramirez

* Min. 150 games played.

Batting Miscellany

Best Wins Above Replacement (WAR) by Decade (Hitters Only)

Pre-1900		1900–09		1910–19	
94.2	Cap Anson	85.8	Honus Wagner	84.3	Ty Cobb
84.3	Roger Connor	69.5	Nap Lajoie	76.5	Tris Speaker
79.9	Dan Brouthers	49.7	Bobby Wallace	73.3	Eddie Collins
62.0	Jack Glasscock	44.9	Sam Crawford	55.2	Shoeless Joe Jackson
56.7	Billy Hamilton	44.0	Elmer Flick	53.3	Home Run Baker
52.2	Bid McPhee	41.8	George Davis	41.8	Art Fletcher
52.1	Ed Delahanty	41.3	Fred Clarke	37.6	Larry Gardner
51.5	Jim O'Rourke	40.6	Frank Chance	36.1	Larry Doyle
47.7	Buck Ewing	38.0	Bill Bradley	34.3	Honus Wagner
45.2	Deacon White	37.0	Bill Dahlen	34.0	Heinie Groh
				34.0	Heinie Zimmerman

1920–29		1930–39		1940–49	
102.4	Babe Ruth	73.1	Lou Gehrig	65.8	Ted Williams
93.1	Rogers Hornsby	72.8	Jimmie Foxx	59.9	Lou Boudreau
56.8	Harry Heilmann	68.7	Mel Ott	57.6	Stan Musial
54.1	Frankie Frisch	61.1	Charlie Gehringer	45.6	Joe Gordon
51.4	Tris Speaker	53.2	Arky Vaughan	43.6	Joe DiMaggio
44.1	Joe Sewell	50.4	Joe Cronin	41.7	Bobby Doerr
41.1	Ty Cobb	44.5	Earl Averill	41.1	Johnny Mize
41.0	Ken Williams	44.1	Paul Waner	40.8	Luke Appling
39.8	Goose Goslin	42.6	Bill Dickey	39.7	Bob Elliott
39.4	Eddie Collins	41.9	Wally Berger	39.2	Bill Nicholson

1950–59		1960–69		1970–79	
68.1	Mickey Mantle	84.2	Willie Mays	67.0	Joe Morgan
61.2	Stan Musial	81.0	Hank Aaron	58.9	Johnny Bench
58.8	Willie Mays	66.4	Roberto Clemente	56.3	Rod Carew
55.6	Duke Snider	64.6	Frank Robinson	54.5	Graig Nettles
53.7	Eddie Mathews	57.6	Ron Santo	51.3	Reggie Jackson
50.9	Richie Ashburn	53.9	Brooks Robinson	50.6	Pete Rose
47.5	Ted Williams	53.3	Carl Yastrzemski	50.3	Mike Schmidt
47.6	Minnie Minoso	48.7	Al Kaline	49.2	Bobby Bonds
47.1	Yogi Berra	45.8	Harmon Killebrew	49.0	Sal Bando
43.3	Jackie Robinson	44.5	Willie McCovey	46.9	Bobby Grich

1980–89		1990–99		2000–09	
71.1	Rickey Henderson	80.2	Barry Bonds	77.7	Alex Rodriguez
60.2	Wade Boggs	67.5	Ken Griffey Jr.	73.8	Albert Pujols
56.6	Mike Schmidt	56.9	Jeff Bagwell	59.1	Barry Bonds
55.3	Robin Yount	53.2	Craig Biggio	53.1	Todd Helton
52.7	Alan Trammell	52.8	Frank Thomas	51.4	Carlos Beltran
52.9	Ozzie Smith	52.6	Barry Larkin	51.1	Ichiro Suzuki
50.2	Cal Ripken Jr.	51.7	Edgar Martinez	50.6	Chipper Jones
47.7	George Brett	49.7	Rafael Palmeiro	48.4	Scott Rolen
47.3	Andre Dawson	47.8	Larry Walker	46.3	Lance Berkman
47.1	Dale Murphy	47.5	Kenny Lofton	44.8	Bobby Abreu

2010–2019		2020–22*	
72.5	Mike Trout	17.8	Aaron Judge
53.1	Robinson Cano	16.0	Paul Goldschmidt
52.9	Joey Votto	15.2	Jose Ramirez
48.9	Adrian Beltre	15.1	Juan Soto
43.2	Evan Longoria	15.0	Manny Machado
43.1	Miguel Cabrera	14.3	Carlos Correa
42.5	Paul Goldschmidt	14.2	Mookie Betts
42.3	Andrew McCutchen	14.2	Trea Turner
42.2	Mookie Betts	13.9	Freddie Freeman
41.5	Buster Posey	13.5	Nolan Arenado

* Min. 150 games played.

Most Times Leading League in Offensive Category

American League

Seasons

Base Hits	8	Ty Cobb, 1907–09, 1911–12, 1915, 1917, and 1919
Singles	10	Ichiro Suzuki, 2001–10
Doubles	8	Tris Speaker, 1912, 1914, 1916, 1918, and 1920–23
Triples	5	Sam Crawford, 1903, 1910, and 1913–15
Home Runs	12	Babe Ruth, 1918–21, 1923–24, and 1926–31
Total Bases	6	Ty Cobb, 1907–09, 1911, 1915, and 1917
	6	Babe Ruth, 1919, 1921, 1923–24, 1926, and 1928
	6	Ted Williams, 1939, 1942, 1946–47, 1949, and 1951
Slugging Percentage	13	Babe Ruth, 1918–24 and 1926–31
Batting Average	12	Ty Cobb, 1907–15 and 1917–19
Runs	8	Babe Ruth, 1919–21, 1923–24, and 1926–28
RBIs	6	Babe Ruth, 1919–21, 1923, 1926, and 1928
Walks	12	Barry Bonds, 1992, 1994–97, 2000–04, 2006–07
Strikeouts	7	Jimmie Foxx, 1929–31, 1933, 1935–36, and 1941
Stolen Bases	12	Rickey Henderson, 1980–86, 1988–91, 1998

National League (Post-1900)

Seasons

Base Hits	7	Pete Rose, 1965, 1968, 1970, 1972–73, 1976, and 1981
Singles	4	Ginger Beaumont, 1902–04 and 1907
	4	Lloyd Waner, 1927–29 and 1931
	4	Richie Ashburn, 1951, 1953, and 1957–58
	4	Maury Wills, 1961–62, 1965, and 1967
Doubles	8	Stan Musial, 1943–44, 1946, 1948–49, and 1952–54
Triples	5	Stan Musial, 1943, 1946, 1948–49, and 1951
Home Runs	8	Mike Schmidt, 1974–76, 1980–81, 1983–84, and 1986
Total Bases	8	Hank Aaron, 1956–57, 1959–61, 1963, 1967, and 1969
Slugging Percentage	11	Rogers Hornsby, 1917–25 and 1928–29
Batting Average	8	Honus Wagner, 1900, 1903–04, 1906–09, and 1911
		Tony Gwynn, 1984, 1987–89, and 1994–97
Runs	5	Rogers Hornsby, 1921–22, 1924, 1927, and 1929
	5	Stan Musial, 1946, 1948, 1951–52, and 1954
RBIs	4	Honus Wagner, 1901–02 and 1908–09
	4	Rogers Hornsby, 1920–22 and 1925
	4	Hank Aaron, 1957, 1960, 1963, and 1966
	4	Mike Schmidt, 1980–81, 1984, and 1986
Walks	12	Barry Bonds, 1992, 1994–97, 2000–2004, 2006–07
Strikeouts	6	Vince DiMaggio, 1937–38 and 1942–45
Stolen Bases	10	Max Carey, 1913, 1915–18, 1920, and 1922–25

Most Consecutive Seasons Leading League in Offensive Category

American League

Seasons

Batting Average	9	Ty Cobb, 1907–15
Slugging Percentage	7	Babe Ruth, 1918–24
Runs	3	Ty Cobb, 1909–11
	3	Eddie Collins, 1912–14
	3	Babe Ruth, 1919–21 and 1926–28
	3	Ted Williams, 1940–42
	3	Mickey Mantle, 1956–58
	3	Mike Trout, 2012–14
Base Hits	5	Ichiro Suzuki, 2006–10
Singles	10	Ichiro Suzuki, 2001–10

National League (Post-1900)

Seasons

6	Rogers Hornsby, 1920–25
6	Rogers Hornsby, 1920–25
3	Chuck Klein, 1930–32
3	Duke Snider, 1953–55
3	Pete Rose, 1974–76
3	Albert Pujols, 2003–05
3	Freddie Freeman, 2020–22
3	Ginger Beaumont, 1902–04
3	Rogers Hornsby, 1920–22
3	Frank McCormick, 1938–40
3	Ginger Beaumont, 1902–04
3	Lloyd Waner, 1927–29
3	Ryan Theriot, 2008–10

continued on next page

	American League	National League (Post-1900)
	Seasons	**Seasons**

	American League		National League (Post-1900)	
Doubles	4	Tris Speaker, 1920–23	4	Honus Wagner, 1906–09
Triples	3	Elmer Flick, 1905–07	3	Garry Templeton, 1977–79
	3	Sam Crawford, 1913–15		
	3	Zoilo Versalles, 1963–65		
	3	Carl Crawford, 2004–06		
Home Runs	6	Babe Ruth, 1926–31	7	Ralph Kiner, 1946–52
Total Bases	3	Ty Cobb, 1907–09	4	Honus Wagner, 1906–09
	3	Jim Rice, 1977–79	4	Chuck Klein, 1930–33
RBIs	3	Ty Cobb, 1907–09	3	Rogers Hornsby, 1920–22
	3	Babe Ruth, 1919–21	3	Joe Medwick, 1936–38
			3	George Foster, 1976–78
Walks	4	Babe Ruth, 1930–33	5	Barry Bonds, 2000–2004
	4	Ted Williams, 1946–49		
Strikeouts	4	Vince DiMaggio, 1942–45	4	Hack Wilson, 1927–30
	4	Reggie Jackson, 1968–71		
Stolen Bases	9	Luis Aparicio, 1956–64	6	Maury Wills, 1960–65

Players Leading in All Triple Crown Categories, But Not in Same Year*

Hank Aaron — Batting: 1956 (.328) and 1959 (.355)
Home Runs: 1957 (44), 1963 (44 Tie), 1966 (44), and 1967 (39)
RBIs: 1957 (132), 1960 (126), 1963 (130), and 1966 (127)

Barry Bonds — Batting: 2002 (.370) and 2004 (.363)
Home Runs: 1993 (46) and 2001 (73)
RBIs: 1993 (123)

Dan Brouthers — Batting: 1882 (.368), 1883 (.374), 1889 (.373), 1891 (.350), and 1892 (.335)
Home Runs: 1881 (8) and 1886 (11)
RBIs: 1892 (97)

Ed Delahanty — Batting: 1899 (.410) and 1902 (.376)
Home Runs: 1893 (19) and 1896 (13)
RBIs: 1893 (146), 1896 (126), and 1899 (137)

Joe DiMaggio — Batting: 1939 (.381) and 1940 (.352)
Home Runs: 1937 (46) and 1948 (39)
RBIs: 1941 (125) and 1948 (155)

Andres Galarraga — Batting: 1993 (.370)
Home Runs: 1996 (47)
RBIs: 1996 (150) and 1997 (140)

Johnny Mize — Batting: 1939 (.349)
Home Runs: 1939 (28), 1940 (43), 1947 (51 Tie), and 1948 (40 Tie)
RBIs: 1940 (137), 1942 (110), and 1947 (138)

Manny Ramirez — Batting: 2002 (.349)
Home Runs: 2004 (43)
RBIs: 1999 (155)

Albert Pujols — Batting: 2003 (.348)
Home Runs: 2009 (41) and 2010 (42)
RBIs: 2010 (118)

Alex Rodriguez — Batting: 1996 (.358)
Home Runs: 2001 (52), 2002 (57), 2003 (47), 2005 (48), and 2007 (54)
RBIs: 2002 (142) and 2007 (156)

Babe Ruth — Batting: 1924 (.378)
Home Runs: 1918 (11), 1919 (29), 1920 (54), 1921 (59), 1923 (41), 1924 (46), 1926 (47),
1927 (60), 1928 (54), 1929 (46), 1930 (49), and 1931 (46 Tie)
RBIs: 1919 (114), 1920 (137), 1921 (171), 1923 (131), 1926 (146), and 1928 (142 Tie)

Tris Speaker — Batting: 1916 (.386)
Home Runs: 1912 (10)
RBIs: 1923 (130)

Sam Thompson — Batting: 1887 (.372)
Home Runs: 1889 (20) and 1895 (18)
RBIs: 1887 (166), 1894 (149), and 1895 (165)

* Includes only players who *never* won triple crown.

Highest Offensive Career Totals by Players Who Never Led League

American League			National League (Post-1900)		
Base Hits	3315	Eddie Collins	**Base Hits**	3060	Craig Biggio
Singles	2262	Carl Yastrzemski	**Singles**	2424	Honus Wagner
Doubles	544	Derek Jeter	**Doubles**	601	Barry Bonds
Triples	222	Tris Speaker	**Triples**	177	Rabbit Maranville
Home Runs	544	Rafael Palmeiro	**Home Runs**	475	Stan Musial
Total Bases	4984	Rafael Palmeiro	**Total Bases**	5752	Pete Rose
Batting Avg.	.356	Joe Jackson	**Batting Avg.**	.336	Riggs Stephenson
Slugging %	.556	Carlos Delgado	**Slugging %**	.588	Vladimir Guerrero
Runs	1882	Tris Speaker	**Runs**	1619	Chipper Jones
RBIs	1740	Rafael Palmeiro	**RBIs**	1903	Willie Mays
Walks	1476	Bobby Abreu	**Walks**	1566	Pete Rose
Strikeouts	2287	Alex Rodriguez	**Strikeouts**	1753	Craig Biggio
Stolen Bases	504	Paul Molitor	**Stolen Bases**	681	Joe Morgan

Highest Ratio of Three True Outcomes, Season (Home Run, Strikeout, Walk)

American League

Percent		Home Runs	Strikeouts	Walks
63.3%	Joey Gallo, Tex. Rangers, 2019	22	114	52
58.8%	Joey Gallo, Tex. Rangers–N.Y. Yankees, 2021	38	213	111
58.6%	Joey Gallo, Tex. Rangers, 2017	41	196	75
58.2%	Jack Cust, Oak. A's, 2007	26	164	105
58.0%	Joey Gallo, N.Y. Yankees–L.A. Dodgers, 2022	19	163	56
57.1%	Aaron Judge, N.Y. Yankees, 2017	52	208	127
57.0%	Jack Cust, Oak. A's, 2008	33	197	111
57.0%	Keon Broxton, N.Y. Mets–Bal. Orioles–Sea. Mariners, 2019	6	104	20
56.7%	Adam Dunn, Chi. White Sox, 2012	41	105	222
56.5%	Miguel Sano, Min. Twins, 2019	34	159	55
55.6%	Joey Gallo, Tex. Rangers, 2018	40	207	74
54.5%	Brett Phillips, T.B. Rays, 2021	13	113	33
54.0%	Chris Davis, Bal. Orioles, 2019	12	139	39
53.6%	Jim Thome, Cle. Indians, 2001	49	185	111
53.1%	Mike Zunino, T.B. Rays, 2021	33	132	34
51.9%	Aaron Judge, N.Y. Yankees, 2019	27	141	64
51.8%	Shohei Ohtani, L.A. Angels, 2021	46	189	96
51.2%	Aaron Judge, N.Y. Yankees, 2018	27	152	76
51.2%	Yasmani Grandal, Chi. White Sox, 2021	23	82	87
51.1%	Miguel Sano, Min. Twins, 2021	30	183	59
50.0%	Aaron Judge, N.Y. Yankees, 2022	62	175	111

National League

Percent		Home Runs	Strikeouts	Walks
57.9%	Mark McGwire, St.L. Cardinals, 2000	32	78	76
56.8%	Mark McGwire, St.L. Cardinals, 1998	70	162	162
56.8%	Patrick Wisdom, Chi. Cubs, 2021	28	153	32
55.6%	Keston Hiura, Mil. Brewers, 2022	14	111	23
55.5%	Jack Clark, St.L. Cardinals, 1987	35	136	136
55.5%	Mark McGwire, St.L. Cardinals, 2001	29	118	56
54.5%	Ian Happ, Chi. Cubs, 2018	15	167	70
54.5%	Ryan Howard, Phi. Phillies, 2007	47	199	107
51.7%	Barry Bonds, S.F. Giants, 2001	73	93	177
51.5%	Barry Bonds, S.F. Giants, 2004	45	41	232

continued on next page

Percent		Home Runs	Strikeouts	Walks
51.2% ....Joey Bart, S.F. Giants, 2022		11	112................	26
50.9% ....Max Muncy, L.A. Dodgers		35	131	79

Career Offensive Leaders by Players Under Six Feet Tall

Games Played	3562	Pete Rose (5'11")
At-Bats	14,053	Pete Rose (5'11")
Base Hits	4256	Pete Rose (5'11")
Singles	3115	Pete Rose (5'11")
Doubles	793	Tris Speaker (5'11½")
Triples	252	Honus Wagner (5'11")
Home Runs	660	Willie Mays (5'10½")
Extra-Base Hits	1323	Willie Mays (5'10½")
Total Bases	6066	Willie Mays (5'10½")
Runs	2295..	Rickey Henderson (5'10")
RBIs	1903	Willie Mays (5'10½")
Walks	2190	Rickey Henderson (5'10")
Strikeouts	1753	Craig Biggio (5'11")
Batting Average	.358	Rogers Hornsby (5'11")
Slugging Percentage	.577	Rogers Hornsby (5'11")
Stolen Bases	1406	Rickey Henderson (5'10")

Largest Margin Between League Leaders and Runners-Up

American League

	Margin	Season	Leader		Runner-Up	
Batting Average	.086	1901	Nap Lajoie, Phi. A's	.426	Mike Donlin, Bal. Orioles	.340
Hits	46	2004	Ichiro Suzuki, Sea. Mariners	262	Michael Young, Tex. Rangers	216
Doubles	15	1910	Nap Lajoie, Cle. Indians	51	Ty Cobb, Det. Tigers	36
Triples	10	1949	Dale Mitchell, Cle. Indians	23	Bob Dillinger, St.L. Browns	13
Home Runs	35	1920	Babe Ruth, N.Y. Yankees	54	George Sisler, St.L. Browns	19
Runs Scored	45	1921	Babe Ruth, N.Y. Yankees	177	Jack Tobin, St.L. Browns	132
RBIs	51	1935	Hank Greenberg, Det. Tigers	170	Lou Gehrig, N.Y. Yankees	119
Total Bases	92	1921	Babe Ruth, N.Y. Yankees	457	Harry Heilmann, Det. Tigers	365
Slugging Percentage	.240	1921	Babe Ruth, N.Y. Yankees	.846	Harry Heilmann, Det. Tigers	.606
Stolen Bases	76	1982	Rickey Henderson, Oak. A's	130	Damaso Garcia, Tor. Blue Jays	54
Walks	72	1923	Babe Ruth, N.Y. Yankees	170	Joe Sewell, Cle. Indians	98

National League

	Margin	Season	Leader		Runner-Up	
Batting Average	.049	1924	Rogers Hornsby, St.L. Cardinals	.424	Zack Wheat, Brk. Dodgers	.375
Hits	44	1946	Stan Musial, St.L. Cardinals	228	Dixie Walker, Brk. Dodgers	184
Doubles	16	1904	Honus Wagner, Pit. Pirates	44	Sam Mertes, N.Y. Giants	28
Triples	16	1912	Owen Wilson, Pit. Pirates	36	Honus Wagner, Pit. Pirates	20
Home Runs	19	1923	Cy Williams, Phi. Phillies	41	Jack Fournier, Brk. Dodgers	22
Runs Scored	29	1909	Tommy Leach, Pit. Pirates	126	Fred Charles, Pit. Pirates	97
RBIs	39	1937	Joe Medwick, St.L. Cardinals	154	Frank Demaree, Chi. Cubs	115
Total Bases	136	1922	Rogers Hornsby, St.L. Cardinals	450	Irish Meusel, N.Y. Giants	314
Slugging Percentage	.177	2002	Barry Bonds, S.F. Giants	.799	Brian Giles, Pit. Pirates	.622
Stolen Bases	72	1962	Maury Wills, L.A. Dodgers	104	Willie Davis, L.A. Dodgers	32
Walks	105	2004	Barry Bonds, S.F. Giants	232	Bobby Abreu, Phi. Phillies	127
					Lance Berkman, Hou. Astros	127
					Todd Helton, Col. Rockies	127

Evolution of Slugging Percentage Record

American League

1901	Nap Lajoie, Phi. A's		.643
1919	Babe Ruth, Bos. Red Sox		.657
1920	Babe Ruth, N.Y. Yankees		.847

National League (Pre-1900)

1876	Ross Barnes, Chi. White Stockings		.590
1894	Sam Thompson, Phi. Phillies		.696

National League (Post-1899)

1922	Rogers Hornsby, St.L. Cardinals		.722
1925	Rogers Hornsby, St.L. Cardinals		.756
2001	Barry Bonds, S.F. Giants		.863

Players Hitting Safely in at Least 135 Games, Season

American League

Wade Boggs, Bos. Red Sox, 1985 (240 hits in 161 games, .368 batting average)

Derek Jeter, N.Y. Yankees, 1999 (219 hits in 158 games, .349 batting average)

Ichiro Suzuki, Sea. Mariners, 2001 (242 hits in 157 games, .350 batting average)

National League (Post-1900)

Rogers Hornsby, St.L. Cardinals, 1922 (250 hits in 154 games, .401 batting average)

Chuck Klein, Phi. Phillies, 1930 (250 hits in 156 games, .386 batting average)

Players Hitting for the Cycle in Natural Order (Single, Double, Triple, Home Run)

American League

Fats Fothergill, Det. Tigers, Sep. 26, 1926
Tony Lazzeri, N.Y. Yankees, Jun. 3, 1932
Charlie Gehringer, Det. Tigers, May 27, 1939
Leon Culberson, Bos. Red Sox, Jul. 3, 1943
Bob Watson, Bos. Red Sox, Sep. 15, 1979
Jose Valentin, Chi. White Sox, Apr. 27, 2000
Gary Matthews Jr., Tex. Rangers, Sep. 13, 2006

National League (Post-1900)

Bill Collins, Bos. Doves, Oct. 6, 1910
Jim Hickman, N.Y. Mets, Aug. 7, 1963
Ken Boyer, St.L. Cardinals, Jun. 16, 1964
Billy Williams, Chi. Cubs, Jul. 17, 1966
Tim Foli, Mon. Expos, Apr. 22, 1976
John Mabry, St.L. Cardinals, May 18, 1996
Brad Wilkerson, Mon. Expos, Jun. 24, 2003

Highest Slugging Percentage by Position, Season

American League

Position	SLG	Player
First Base	.765	Lou Gehrig, N.Y. Yankees, 1927
Second Base	.643	Nap Lajoie, Phi. A's, 1901
Third Base	.664	George Brett, K.C. Royals, 1980
Shortstop	.631	Alex Rodriguez, Sea. Mariners, 1996
Outfield	.847	Babe Ruth, N.Y. Yankees, 1920
Catcher	.617	Bill Dickey, N.Y. Yankees, 1936
Pitcher	.621	Wes Ferrell, Cle. Indians, 1931
Designated Hitter	.659	Travis Hafner, Cle. Indians, 2006

National League (Post-1900)

Position	SLG	Player
First Base	.752	Mark McGwire, St.L. Cardinals, 1998
Second Base	.756	Rogers Hornsby, St.L. Cardinals, 1925
Third Base	.644	Mike Schmidt, Phi. Phillies, 1981
Shortstop	.614	Ernie Banks, Chi. Cubs, 1958
Outfield	.863	Barry Bonds, S.F. Giants, 2001
Catcher	.687	Javy Lopez, Atl. Braves, 2003
Pitcher	.632	Don Newcombe, Brk. Dodgers, 1955
Designated Hitter	.522	Bryce Harper, Phi. Phillies, 2022

Most Times Awarded First Base on Catcher's Interference or Obstruction

31 .... Jacoby Ellsbury (2007–17)
29 ....Pete Rose (1963–86)
19 .... Josh Reddick (2009–21)
18 ....Julian Javier (1960–72)
18 ....Dale Berra (1977–87)
17 ....Roberto Kelly (1988–2000)
17 .... Andy Van Slyke (1983–95)
17 ....Carl Crawford (2002–16)
16 .... Bob Stinson (1969–80)
16 ....Tommy LaStella (2014–)
15 .... Nick Senzel (2019–)
14 ....Paul Goldschmidt (2011–)
14 ....Jesus Aguilar (2014–)
14 ....\.....Jose Soler (2014–)
13 ....Darin Erstad (1996–2009)
13 ....Ryan Ludwick (2002–05, 2007–14)
13 .... George Springer (2014–)
12 ....Hector Torres (1968–77)
12 .... Craig Counsell (1995–2011)
12 .... Edwin Encarnacion (2005–20)

Winners of Two "Legs" of Triple Crown Since Last Winner*

American League

Chris Davis, Bal. Orioles, 2013 .... 53 home runs, 138 RBIs (batting avg. .286, twenty-first behind Miguel Cabrera's .348)

National League

Paul Goldschmidt, Ari. D'backs, 2013.....36 home runs, 125 RBIs (batting avg. .302, eleventh behind Michael Cuddyer's .331)
Nolan Arenado, Col. Rockies, 2015 .... 42 home runs, 130 RBIs (batting avg. .287, twentieth behind Dee Strange-Gordon's .333)
Nolan Arenado, Col. Rockies, 2016........... 41 home runs (tie), 133 RBIs (batting avg. .294, seventeenth behind DJ LeMahieu's .348)
Giancarlo Stanton, Mia. Marlins, 2017 ...... 59 home runs, 132 RBIs (batting avg. .281, twenty-fifth behind Charlie Blackmon's .331)
* Miguel Cabrera, 2012

2

PITCHING

Wins

Most Victories by Decade

Pre-1900		1900–09		1910–19	
365	Pud Galvin	236	Christy Mathewson	265	Walter Johnson
342	Tim Keefe	230	Cy Young	208	Pete Alexander
328	John Clarkson	218	Joe McGinnity	162	Eddie Cicotte
309	Old Hoss Radbourn	192	Jack Chesbro	156	Hippo Vaughn
307	Mickey Welch	188	Vic Willis	149	Slim Sallee
297	Kid Nichols	186	Eddie Plank	144	Rube Marquard
284	Tony Mullane	183	Rube Waddell	140	Eddie Plank
267	Cy Young	166	Sam Leever	137	Christy Mathewson
265	Jim McCormick	160	Jack Powell	135	Claude Hendrix
258	Gus Weyhing	157	George Mullin	126	Hooks Dauss

1920–29		1930–39		1940–49	
190	Burleigh Grimes	199	Lefty Grove	170	Hal Newhouser
166	Eppa Rixley	188	Carl Hubbell	137	Bob Feller
165	Pete Alexander	175	Red Ruffing	133	Rip Sewell
163	Herb Pennock	170	Wes Ferrell	129	Dizzy Trout
161	Waite Hoyt	165	Lefty Gomez	122	Dutch Leonard
156	Urban Shocker	158	Mel Harder	122	Bucky Walters
154	Eddie Rommel	156	Larry French	114	Mort Cooper
153	Jesse Haines	150	Tommy Bridges	111	Claude Passeau
152	George Uhle	148	Paul Derringer	105	Kirby Higbe
149	Red Faber	147	Dizzy Dean	105	Bobo Newsom
				105	Harry Brecheen

1950–59		1960–69		1970–79	
202	Warren Spahn	191	Juan Marichal	186	Jim Palmer
199	Robin Roberts	164	Bob Gibson	184	Gaylord Perry
188	Early Wynn	158	Don Drysdale	178	Steve Carlton
155	Billy Pierce	150	Jim Bunning	178	Ferguson Jenkins
150	Bob Lemon	142	Jim Kaat	178	Tom Seaver
128	Mike Garcia	141	Larry Jackson	169	Catfish Hunter
126	Lew Burdette	137	Sandy Koufax	166	Don Sutton
126	Don Newcombe	134	Jim Maloney	164	Phil Niekro
121	Whitey Ford	131	Milt Pappas	155	Vida Blue
116	Johnny Antonelli	127	Camilo Pascual	155	Nolan Ryan

113

continued on next page

1980–89

162	Jack Morris
140	Dave Steib
137	Bob Welch
128	Charlie Hough
128	Fernando Valenzuela
123	Bert Blyleven
122	Nolan Ryan
119	Jim Clancy
117	Frank Viola
116	Rick Sutcliffe

1990–99

176	Greg Maddux
164	Tom Glavine
152	Roger Clemens
150	Randy Johnson
143	Kevin Brown
143	John Smoltz
141	David Cone
136	Mike Mussina
135	Chuck Finley
130	Scott Erickson

2000–09

148	Andy Pettitte
143	Randy Johnson
140	Jamie Moyer
139	Roy Halladay
137	Tim Hudson
137	Roy Oswalt
136	CC Sabathia
135	Mark Buehrle
134	Greg Maddux
134	Mike Mussina

2010–19

161	Max Scherzer
160	Justin Verlander
156	Clayton Kershaw
155	Zach Greinke
148	Jon Lester
140	David Price
135	Rick Porcello
123	Gio Gonzalez
119	Madison Bumgarner
116	Adam Wainwright

2020–22

40	Julio Urias
36	Gerrit Cole
35	Max Fried
33	Framber Valdez
33	Adam Wainwright
32	Chris Bassitt
32	Dylan Cease
32	Yu Darvish
31	Max Scherzer
30	Zack Wheeler

Pitchers with the Most Career Wins by First Letter of Last Name

A	Pete Alexander	373	N	Kid Nichols	361
B	Bert Blyleven	287	O	Al Orth	204
C	Roger Clemens	354	P	Eddie Plank	326
D	Hooks Dauss, Paul Derringer	223	Q	Jack Quinn	247
E	Dennis Eckersley	197	R	Nolan Ryan	324
F	Bob Feller	266	S	Warren Spahn	363
G	Pud Galvin	365	T	Frank Tanana	240
H	Carl Hubbell	253	U	George Uhle	200
I	Hisashi Iwakuma	63	V	Justin Verlander	244
J	Walter Johnson	417	W	Mickey Welch	307
K	Tim Keefe	342	X	[No pitcher]	
L	Ted Lyons	260	Y	Cy Young	511
M	Christy Mathewson	373	Z	Tom Zachary	186

Pitchers with the Most Career Victories by Zodiac Sign

Aquarius (Jan. 20–Feb. 18)	Nolan Ryan	324
Pisces (Feb. 19–Mar. 20)	Pete Alexander	373
Aries (Mar. 21–Apr. 19)	Cy Young	511
Taurus (Apr. 20–May 20)	Warren Spahn	363
Gemini (May 21–Jun. 21)	Tommy John	288
Cancer (Jun. 22–Jul. 22)	John Clarkson	328
Leo (Jul. 23–Aug. 22)	Christy Mathewson	373
Virgo (Aug. 23–Sep. 22)	Kid Nichols	361
Libra (Sep. 23–Oct. 23)	Robin Roberts	286
Scorpio (Oct. 24–Nov. 21)	Walter Johnson	417
Sagittarius (Nov. 22–Dec. 21)	Old Hoss Radbourn	309
Capricorn (Dec. 22–Jan. 19)	Pud Galvin	365

Pitchers with the Most Victories by State of Birth

Alabama	Don Sutton (Clio)	324	Delaware	Sadie McMahon (Wilmington)	177
Alaska	Curt Schilling (Anchorage)	216	Florida	Steve Carlton (Miami)	329
Arizona	John Denny (Prescott)	123	Georgia	Tim Hudson (Columbus)	222
Arkansas	Lon Warneke (Mount Ida)	192	Hawaii	Charlie Hough (Honolulu)	216
California	Tom Seaver (Fresno)	311	Idaho	Larry Jackson (Nampa)	194
Colorado	Roy Halladay (Denver)	203	Illinois	Robin Roberts (Springfield)	286
Connecticut	Bill Hutchison (New Haven)	182	Indiana	Tommy John (Terre Haute)	288

continued on next page

Iowa	Bob Feller (Van Meter)	266	Ohio	Cy Young (Gilmore)	511
Kansas	Walter Johnson (Humboldt)	417	Oklahoma	Allie Reynolds (Bethany)	182
Kentucky	Gus Weyhing (Louisville)	264	Oregon	Mickey Lolich (Portland)	217
Louisiana	Ted Lyons (Sulphur)	260	Pennsylvania	Christy Mathewson (Factoryville)	373
Maine	Bob Stanley (Portland)	115	Rhode Island	Tom Lovett (Providence)	88
Maryland	Lefty Grove (Lonaconing)	300	South Carolina	Bobo Newsom (Hartsville)	211
Massachusetts	Tim Keefe (Cambridge)	342	South Dakota	Floyd Bannister (Pierre)	134
Michigan	Jim Kaat (Zeeland)	283	Tennessee	Bob Caruthers (Memphis)	218
Minnesota	Jack Morris (St.Paul)	254	Texas	Greg Maddux (San Angelo)	355
Mississippi	Guy Bush (Aberdeen)	176	Utah	Bruce Hurst (St. George)	145
Missouri	Pud Galvin (St. Louis)	365	Vermont	Ray Fisher (Middlebury)	100
Montana	Dave McNally (Billings)	184	Virginia	Eppa Rixey (Culpepper)	266
Nebraska	Pete Alexander (Elba)	373	Washington	Jon Lester (Tacoma)	200
Nevada	Barry Zito (Las Vegas)	165	West Virginia	Wilbur Cooper (Bearsville)	216
New Hampshire	Mike Flanagan (Manchester)	167	Wisconsin	Kid Nichols (Madison)	361
New Jersey	Al Leiter (Toms River)	162	Wyoming	Tom Browning (Casper)	123
New Mexico	Wade Blasingame (Deming)	46			
New York	Warren Spahn (Buffalo)	363	District of Columbia	Doc White	189
North Carolina	Gaylord Perry (Williamston)	314	Puerto Rico	Javier Vazquez (Ponce)	165
North Dakota	Rick Helling (Devils Lake)	93	Virgin Islands	Al McBean (Charlotte Amalie)	67

Pitchers with Five or More Consecutive 20-Win Seasons (Post-1900)

	Seasons
Christy Mathewson, N.Y. Giants (NL), 1903–14	12
Walter Johnson, Was. Senators (AL), 1910–19	10
Lefty Grove, Phi. A's (AL), 1927–33	7
Mordecai Brown, Chi. Cubs (NL), 1906–11	6
Robin Roberts, Phi. Phillies (NL), 1950–55	6
Warren Spahn, Mil. Braves (NL), 1956–61	6
Ferguson Jenkins, Chi. Cubs (NL), 1967–72	6
Pete Alexander, Phi. Phillies (NL), 1913–17	5
Carl Hubbell, N.Y. Giants (NL), 1933–37	5
Catfish Hunter, Oak. A's (AL), 1971–74; and N.Y. Yankees (AL), 1975	5

100-Game Winners, Both Leagues

	American League	National League	Total Wins
Cy Young	221 (1901–11)	290 (1890–1900, 1911)	511
Nolan Ryan	189 (1972–79, 1989–93)	135 (1966–71, 1980–88)	324
Gaylord Perry	139 (1972–77, 1980, 1982–83)	175 (1962–71, 1978–79, 1981)	314
Randy Johnson	164 (1989–98, 2005–06)	139 (1988–89, 1998–2004, 2007–09)	303
Ferguson Jenkins	115 (1974–81)	169 (1965–73, 1982–83)	284
Dennis Martinez	141 (1976–86, 1994–98)	104 (1986–93)	245
Jim Bunning	118 (1955–63)	106 (1964–71)	224
Pedro Martinez	117 (1998–2004)	102 (1992–97, 2005–09)	219
Kevin Brown	102 (1986–95, 2004–05)	109 (1996–2003)	211
Al Orth	104 (1902–09)	100 (1895–1901)	204

Pitchers with 500 Major League Decisions

	Wins–Losses	Total
Cy Young (1890–1911)	511–316	827
Walter Johnson (1907–27)	417–279	696
Pud Galvin (1879–92)	365–310	675
Nolan Ryan (1966–93)	324–292	616
Warren Spahn (1942, 1946–65)	363–245	608
Phil Niekro (1964–87)	318–274	592
Greg Maddux (1986–2008)	355–277	582
Pete Alexander (1911–30)	373–208	581
Don Sutton (1966–88)	324–256	580
Gaylord Perry (1962–83)	314–265	579
Steve Carlton (1965–88)	329–244	573
Kid Nichols (1890–1901, 1904–06)	361–208	569
Tim Keefe (1880–93)	342–225	567
Christy Mathewson (1900–16)	373–188	561
Early Wynn (1939, 1941–44, 1946–63)	300–244	544
Roger Clemens (1984–2007)	354–184	538
Bert Blyleven (1970–92)	287–250	537
Robin Roberts (1948–66)	286–245	531
Jim Kaat (1959–83)	283–237	520
Eddie Plank (1901–17)	326–194	520
Tommy John (1963–74, 1976–89)	288–231	519
Mickey Welch (1880–92)	307–210	517
Eppa Rixey (1912–17, 1919–33)	266–251	517
Tom Seaver (1967–86)	311–205	516
Ferguson Jenkins (1965–83)	284–226	510
Tom Glavine (1987–2008)	305–203	508
John Clarkson (1882, 1884–94)	328–178	506
Tony Mullane (1881–94)	284–220	504
Old Hoss Radbourn (1880–91)	309–194	503

Most Wins, Major and Minor Leagues Combined

Total		Majors	Minors
526	Cy Young	511	15
481	Joe McGinnity	246	235
445	Kid Nichols	361	84
418	Pete Alexander	373	45
417	Walter Johnson	417	0
415	Warren Spahn	363	52
412	Lefty Grove	300	112
398	Christy Mathewson	373	25
391	Greg Maddux	355	36
369	Gaylord Perry	314	55
366	Early Wynn	300	66
365	Pud Galvin	365	0
364	Roger Clemens	354	10
361	Phil Niekro	318	43
360	Tony Freitas	25	335
355	Joe Martina	6	349
353	Steve Carlton	329	24
350	Bobo Newsom	211	139
348	Stan Coveleski	215	133
348	Don Sutton	324	24

continued on next page

Total		Majors	Minors
348	Bill Thomas	0	348
347	Jack Quinn	247	100
345	Nolan Ryan	324	21
342	Burleigh Grimes	270	72
341	Tim Keefe	341	0
338	Gus Weyhing	264	74
334	Tom Glavine	305	29
332	Red Faber	254	78
332	Dazzy Vance	197	135
331	Randy Johnson	303	28
331	Alex McColl	4	327

Most Wins For One Team

American League

417 .... Walter Johnson, Was. Senators (1907–27)
284 .... Eddie Plank, Phi. A's (1900–14)
268 ....Jim Palmer, Bal. Orioles (1965–84)
266 .... Bob Feller, Cle. Indians (1936–41, 1945–56)
260 .... Ted Lyons, Chi. White Sox (1923–42, 1946)
254 .... Red Faber, Chi. White Sox (1914–33)
236 .... Whitey Ford, N.Y. Yankees (1950, 1953–67)
231 .... Red Ruffing, N.Y. Yankees (1930–42, 1945–46)
223 .... Mel Harder, Cle. Indians (1928–47)
222 .... Hooks Dauss, Det. Tigers (1912–26)
219 ...Andy Pettitte, N.Y. Yankees (1995–2003, 2007–10, 2012–13)
209 ....George Mullin, Det. Tigers (1902–13)
207 .... Bob Lemon, Cle. Indians (1946–58)
207 .... Mickey Lolich, Det. Tigers (1963–75)
200 ....Hal Newhouser, Det. Tigers (1939–53)

National League

372 ....Christy Mathewson, N.Y. Giants (1900–16)
356 .. Warren Spahn, Bos.–Mil. Braves (1942, 1946–64)
329 .... Kid Nichols, Bos. Beaneaters (1899–1901)
266 ....Phil Niekro, Atl. Braves (1966–83)
253 .... Carl Hubbell, N.Y. Giants (1928–43)
251 ....Bob Gibson, St.L. Cardinals (1959–75)
244 .... Tom Glavine, Atl. Braves (1987–2002, 2008)
241 .... Steve Carlton, Phi. Phillies (1972–86)
241 ....Cy Young, Cle. Spiders (1890–98)
238 ....Juan Marichal, S.F. Giants (1960–73)
238 .... Mickey Welch, N.Y. Giants (1885–92)
234 .... Robin Roberts, Phi. Phillies (1948–61)
233 ....Amos Rusie, N.Y. Giants (1890–95, 1897–98)
233 .... Don Sutton, L.A. Dodgers (1966–80, 1988)
218 ....Pud Galvin, Buff. Bisons (1879–85)
210 ....John Smoltz, Atl. Braves (1988–99, 2001–08)
210 ....Jesse Haines, St.L. Cardinals (1920–37)
202 .... Wilbur Cooper, Pit. Pirates (1912–24)
201 .... Charlie Root, Chi. Cubs (1926–41)

Pitchers with 100 More Wins Than Losses, Career

	Wins	Losses	Differential
Cy Young (1890–1911)	511	315	+196
Christy Mathewson (1900–16)	373	188	+185
Roger Clemens (1984–2007)	354	184	+170
Pete Alexander (1911–30)	373	208	+165
Lefty Grove (1925–41)	300	141	+159
Kid Nichols (1890–1901, 1904–06)	361	208	+153
John Clarkson (1882, 1884–94)	328	178	+150
Walter Johnson (1907–27)	417	279	+138
Randy Johnson (1988–2009)	303	166	+137
Eddie Plank (1901–17)	326	194	+132
Whitey Ford (1950, 1953–67)	236	106	+130
Greg Maddux (1986–2008)	355	227	+128
Bob Caruthers (1884–92)	218	97	+121
Pedro Martinez (1992–2009)	219	100	+119
Tim Keefe (1880–93)	341	223	+118

continued on next page

	Wins	Losses	Differential
Warren Spahn (1942, 1946–65)	363	245	+118
Mike Mussina (1991–2008)	270	153	+117
Jim Palmer (1965–84)	268	152	+116
Old Hoss Radbourn (1880–91)	309	194	+115
Justin Verlander* (2005–)	244	133	+111
Clayton Kershaw* (2008–)	197	87	+110
Mordecai Brown (1903–16)	239	130	+109
Tom Seaver (1967–86)	311	205	+106
Joe McGinnity (1899–1908)	246	142	+104
Bob Feller (1936–41, 1945–56)	266	162	+104
Andy Pettitte (1995–2010, 2012–13)	256	153	+103
Tom Glavine (1987–2008)	305	203	+102
Juan Marichal (1960–75)	243	142	+101

* Still active.

Pitchers with Most Career Wins, Never Leading League in One Season

Pud Galvin (1879–92)	365	Tony Mullane (1881–84, 1886–94)	284
Eddie Plank (1901–17)	326	Jamie Moyer (1986–91, 1993–2010, 2012)	269
Nolan Ryan (1966–88)	324	Gus Weyhing (1887–1901)	264
Don Sutton (1966–88)	324	Red Faber (1914–33)	254
Mickey Welch (1880–92)	307	Vic Willis (1898–1910)	249
Tommy John (1963–74, 1976–89)	288	Jack Quinn (1909–15, 1918–33)	247
Bert Blyleven (1970–92)	287	Jack Powell (1897–1912)	246

200-Game Winners, Never Winning 20 Games in Season

	Career Wins	Most in One Season
Dennis Martinez (1976–98)	245	16 (1978, 1982, 1989, and 1992)
Frank Tanana (1973–93)	240	19 (1976)
Jerry Reuss (1969–90)	220	18 (1975, 1980)
Kenny Rogers (1989–2008)	219	18 (2004)
Charlie Hough (1970–94)	216	18 (1987)
Mark Buehrle (2000–15)	214	19 (2002)
Milt Pappas (1957–73)	209	17 (1971, 1972)
Chuck Finley (1986–2002)	200	18 (1990, 1991)
Jon Lester (2006–21)	200	19 (2010)
Tim Wakefield (1991–93, 1995–2011)	200	17 (1998)

Pitchers with 100 Wins and 500 Hits, Career

	Wins	Hits
Charlie Buffinton (1882–93)	231	543
Bob Caruthers (1884–96)	218	694
Dave Foutz (1884–96)	147	1254
Pud Galvin (1875, 1879–92)	365	552
Kid Gleason (1888–1908, 1912)	134	1944
Guy Hecker (1882–90)	177	822
Walter Johnson (1907–27)	417	549
Bobby Mathews (1871–87)	298	505
Win Mercer (1894–1902)	131	502
Tony Mullane (1881–84, 1886–94)	285	661
Old Hoss Radbourn (1880–91)	309	585

continued on next page

	Wins	Hits
Red Ruffing (1924–42, 1945–47)	273	521
Jack Stivetts (1889–99)	207	592
Adonis Terry (1884–97)	197	594
Monte Ward (1878–84)	161	2123
Jim Whitney (1881–90)	192	559
Smoky Joe Wood (1908–15, 1917–22)	116	553
Cy Young (1890–1911)	511	623

Victories in Most Consecutive Seasons

Seasons		Seasons	
26	Nolan Ryan, 1968–93	21	Walter Johnson, 1907–27
24	Don Sutton, 1966–1988	21	Eppa Rixey, 1912–17, 1919–33
24	Roger Clemens, 1984–2007	21	Red Ruffing, 1925–42, 1945–47*
23	Jim Kaat, 1960–82	21	Joe Niekro, 1967–87
23	Phil Niekro, 1965–87	21	Jerry Reuss, 1969–89
23	Dennis Martinez, 1976–98	21	Bert Blyleven, 1970–90
23	Greg Maddux, 1986–2008	21	Frank Tanana, 1973–93
22	Cy Young, 1890–1911	21	David Wells, 1987–2007
22	Early Wynn, 1941–44, 1946–63*	21	Bartolo Colon, 1997–2018
22	Gaylord Perry, 1962–83	20	Red Faber, 1914–33
22	Steve Carlton, 1966–87	20	Warren Spahn, 1946–65
22	Charlie Hough, 1973–94	20	Lindy McDaniel, 1956–75
22	Tom Glavine, 1987–2008	20	Tom Seaver, 1967–86
22	Randy Johnson, 1989–2009	20	Kenny Rogers, 1989–2008

* Missing years were spent in military service.

Most Wins in a Season Without a Complete Game

American League		National League	
21	Max Scherzer, Det. Tigers, 2013	21	Kyle Wright, Atl. Braves, 2022
21	Blake Snell, T.B. Rays, 2018	20	Julio Urias, L.A. Dodgers, 2021
20	Roger Clemens, N.Y. Yankees, 2001	19	Roy Oswalt, Hou. Astros, 2002
20	Mike Mussina, N.Y. Yankees, 2008	19	Jake Peavy, S.D. Padres, 2007
20	J.A. Happ, Tor. Blue Jays, 2016	19	Gerrit Cole, Pit. Pirates, 2015
20	Gerrit Cole, N.Y. Yankees, 2019	18	Roy Face, Pit. Pirates, 1959
19	Collin McHugh, Hou. Astros, 2015	18	Kent Bottenfield, St.L. Cardinals, 1999
19	Eduardo Rodriguez, Bos. Red Sox, 2019	18	Woody Williams, St.L. Cardinals, 2003
18	Roger Clemens, N.Y. Yankees, 2004	18	Chris Capuano, Mil. Brewers, 2005
18	Bartolo Colon, Cle. Indians, 2004	18	Lance Lynn, St.L. Cardinals, 2013
18	Daisuke Matsuzaka, Bos. Red Sox, 2008	18	Jon Lester, Chi. Cubs, 2018
18	Phil Hughes, N.Y. Yankees, 2010	18	Stephen Strasburg, Was. Nationals, 2019
18	Domingo German, N.Y. Yankees, 2019	17	Andy Pettitte, Hou. Astros, 2005
18	Justin Verlander, Hou. Astros, 2022	17	Ted Lilly, Chi. Cubs, 2008
17	John Hiller, Det. Tigers, 1974	17	Edison Volquez, Cin. Reds, 2008
17	Bill Campbell, Min. Twins, 1976	17	Wily Peralta, Mil. Brewers, 2014
17	Milt Wilcox, Det. Tigers, 1984	17	Zack Greinke, L.A. Dodgers, 2014
17	CC Sabathia, Cle. Indians, 2001	17	Michael Wacha, St.L. Cardinals, 2015
17	Kenny Rogers, Det. Tigers, 2006	17	Zach Davies, Mil. Brewers, 2017
17	Tim Wakefield, Bos. Red Sox, 2007	17	Aaron Nola, Phi. Phillies, 2018
17	Scott Feldman, Tex. Rangers, 2009	17	Julio Urias, L.A. Dodgers, 2022
17	C.J. Wilson, L.A. Angels, 2013		
17	Drew Pomeranz, Bos. Red Sox, 2017		
17	Trevor Bauer, Cle. Indians, 2017		

Most Career Wins by Pitchers Six and a Half Feet Tall or Taller

Wins		Height	Wins		Height
303	Randy Johnson (1988–2009)	6'10"	177	John Candelaria (1975–93)	6'7"
251	CC Sabathia (2001–19)	6'7"	176	Derek Lowe (1997–2013)	6'6"
203	Roy Halladay (1998–2013)	6'6"	171	Rick Sutcliffe (1976, 1978–94)	6'7"
200	Chuck Finley (1986–2002)	6'6"	155	Andy Benes (1989–2002)	6'6"
195	Adam Wainwright* (2005–10, 2012–)	6'7"	150	Jered Weaver (2006–17)	6'7"
188	John Lackey (2002–11, 2013–17)	6'6"			

* Still active.

Most Career Wins by Pitchers Under Six Feet Tall

Wins		Height	Wins		Height
365	Pud Galvin (1875, 1879–92)	5'8"	297	Bobby Mathews (1871–87)	5'5"
361	Kid Nichols (1890–1901, 1904–06)	5'10½"	284	Tony Mullane (1881–84, 1886–94)	5'10½"
342	Tim Keefe (1880–93)	5'10½"	270	Burleigh Grimes (1916–34)	5'10"
328	John Clarkson (1882, 1884–94)	5'10"	265	Jim McCormick (1878–87)	5'10½"
326	Eddie Plank (1901–17)	5'11½"	264	Gus Weyhing (1887–96, 1899–1901)	5'10"
309	Old Hoss Radbourn (1881–91)	5'9"	260	Ted Lyons (1923–42, 1946)	5'11"
307	Mickey Welch (1880–92)	5'8"			

Pitchers Winning 20 Games in Season Split Between Two Teams (Post-1900)

Joe McGinnity, 21–18 .... 1902 .... Bal. Orioles (AL), 13–10 .... N.Y. Giants (NL), 8–8
Bob Wicker, 20–9 .... 1903 .... St.L. Cardinals (NL), 0–0 .... Chi. Cubs (NL), 20–9
Patsy Flaherty, 20–11 .... 1904 .... Chi. White Sox (AL), 1–2 .... Pit. Pirates (NL), 19–9
John Taylor, 20–12 .... 1906 .... St.L. Cardinals (NL), 8–9 .... Chi. Cubs (NL), 12–3
Bobo Newsom, 20–11 .... 1939 .... St.L. Browns (AL), 3–1 .... Det. Tigers (AL), 17–10
Red Barrett, 23–12 .... 1945 .... Bos. Braves (NL), 2–3 .... St.L. Cardinals (NL), 21–9
Hank Borowy, 21–7 .... 1945 .... N.Y. Yankees (AL), 10–5 .... Chi. Cubs (NL), 11–2
Virgil Trucks, 20–10 .... 1953 .... St.L. Browns (AL), 5–4 .... Chi. White Sox (AL), 15–6
Tom Seaver, 21–6 .... 1977 .... N.Y. Mets (NL), 7–3 .... Cin. Reds (NL), 14–3
Rick Sutcliffe, 20–6 .... 1984 .... Cle. Indians (AL), 4–5 .... Chi. Cubs (NL), 16–1
Bartolo Colon, 20–8 .... 2002 .... Cle. Indians (AL), 10–4 .... Mon. Expos (NL), 10–4

Pitchers Winning 20 Games with 3 Different Teams

Pete Alexander	Phi. Phillies	1911, 1913–17
	Chi. Cubs	1920, 1923
	St.L. Cardinals	1927
Roger Clemens	Bos. Red Sox	1986, 1987, 1990
	Tor. Blue Jays	1997, 1998
	N.Y. Yankees	2001
Carl Mays	Bos. Red Sox	1917, 1918
	N.Y. Yankees	1920, 1921
	Cin. Reds	1924
Joe McGinnity	Bal. Orioles (NL)	1899
	Brk. Dodgers	1900
	Bal. Orioles (AL)	1901
	N.Y. Giants	1903–06
Gaylord Perry	S.F. Giants	1966, 1970
	Cle. Indians	1972, 1974
	S.D. Padres	1978
Jack Powell	Cle. Spiders	1898
	St.L. Perfectos	1899

continued on next page

	St.L. Browns	1902
	N.Y. Yankees	1904
Cy Young	Cle. Spiders	1891–98
	St.L. Cardinals	1899
	Bos. Red Sox	1901–04, 1907

Oldest Pitchers to Win 20 Games for First Time

American League

	Age	Wins–Losses
Mike Mussina, N.Y. Yankees, 2008	39	20–9
Jamie Moyer, Sea. Mariners, 2001	38	20–6
Allie Reynolds, N.Y. Yankees, 1952	37	20–8
David Wells, Tor. Blue Jays, 2000	37	20–8
Spud Chandler, N.Y. Yankees, 1943	36	20–4
Thornton Lee, Chi. White Sox, 1941	35	22–11
Dick Donovan, Cle. Indians, 1962	35	20–10
Earl Whitehill, Was. Senators, 1933	34	22–8
Roger Wolff, Was. Senators, 1945	34	20–10
Rube Walberg, Phi. A's, 1931	34	20–12

National League (Post-1899)

	Age	Wins–Losses
R.A. Dickey, N.Y. Mets, 2012	37	20–6
Curt Davis, St.L. Cardinals, 1939	36	22–16
Rip Sewell, Pit. Pirates, 1943	36	21–9
Preacher Roe, Brk. Dodgers, 1951	36	22–3
Murry Dickson, Pit. Pirates, 1951	35	20–16
Slim Sallee, Cin. Reds, 1919	34	21–7
Jim Turner, Bos. Braves, 1937	34	20–11
Whit Wyatt, Brk. Dodgers, 1941	34	22–10
Sal Maglie, N.Y. Giants, 1951	34	23–6
Sal Maglie, N.Y. Giants, 1951	34	23–6
Sam Jones, S.F. Giants, 1959	34	21–15
Tommy John, L.A. Dodgers, 1977	34	20–7
Joe Niekro, Hou. Astros, 1979	34	21–11
Mike Krukow, S.F. Giants, 1986	34	20–9
Curt Schilling, Ari. D'backs, 2001	34	22–6

Youngest Pitchers to Win 20 Games

American League

	Age	Wins–Losses
Bob Feller, Cle. Indians, 1939	20 years, 10 months	24–9
Bret Saberhagen, K.C. Royals, 1985	21 years, 5 months	20–6
Babe Ruth, Bos. Red Sox, 1916	21 years, 7 months	23–12
Wes Ferrell, Cle. Indians, 1929	21 years, 8 months	21–10
Bob Feller, Cle. Indians, 1940	21 years, 10 months	27–11

National League (Post-1900)

	Age	Wins–Losses
Christy Mathewson, N. Y. Giants, 1901	20 years, 1 month	20–17
Dwight Gooden, N.Y. Mets, 1985	20 years, 10 months	24–4
Al Mamaux, Pit. Pirates, 1915	21 years, 4 months	21–8
Ralph Branca, Brk. Dodgers, 1947	21 years, 9 months	21–12
Nick Maddox, Pit. Pirates, 1908	21 years, 10 months	23–8

Rookies Winning 20 Games

American League

Roscoe Miller, Det. Tigers, 1901	23–13
Roy Patterson, Chi. White Sox, 1901	20–16
Ed Summers, Det. Tigers, 1908	24–12
Russ Ford, N.Y. Yankees, 1910	26–6
Vean Gregg, Cle. Indians, 1911	23–7
Reb Russell, Chi. White Sox, 1913	21–17
Scott Perry, Phi. A's, 1918	21–19

National League (Post-1900)

Christy Mathewson, N.Y. Giants, 1901	20–17
Henry Schmidt, Brk. Bridegrooms, 1903	21–13
Jake Weimer, Chi. Cubs, 1903	21–9
Irv Young, Bos. Beaneaters, 1905	20–21
George McQuillan, Phi. Phillies, 1908	23–17
King Cole, Chi. Cubs, 1910	20–4
Pete Alexander, Phi. Phillies, 1911	28–13

continued on next page

American League		National League (Post-1900)	
Wes Ferrell, Cle. Indians, 1929	21–10	Larry Cheney, Chi. Cubs, 1912	26–10
Monte Weaver, Was. Senators, 1932	22–10	Jeff Pfeffer, Brk. Dodgers, 1914	23–12
Dave Ferriss, Bos. Red Sox, 1945	21–10	Lou Fette, Bos. Braves, 1937	20–10
Gene Bearden, Cle. Indians, 1948	20–7	Cliff Melton, N.Y. Giants, 1937	20–9
Alex Kellner, Phi. A's, 1949	20–12	Jim Turner, Bos. Braves, 1937	20–11
Bob Grim, N.Y. Yankees, 1954	20–6	Johnny Beazley, St.L. Cardinals, 1942	21–6
		Bill Voiselle, N.Y. Giants, 1944	21–16
		Larry Jansen, N.Y. Giants, 1947	21–5
		Harvey Haddix, St.L. Cardinals, 1953	20–9
		Tom Browning, Cin. Reds, 1985	20–9

Most Seasons Logged Before First 20-Win Season

Seasons		20-Win Season
18	Mike Mussina (1991–2008)	20–9 in 2008
14	Tommy John (1963–74, 1976–89)	20–7 in 1977
14	Jamie Moyer (1986–91, 1993–10, 2012)	20–6 in 2001
14	Curt Schilling (1988–2007)	22–6 in 2001
13	Red Ruffing (1924–42, 1945–47)	20–12 in 1936
13	David Wells (1987–2007)	20–8 in 2000
12	Slim Sallee (1908–21)	21–7 in 1919
12	Lee Meadows (1915–29)	20–9 in 1926
12	Whit Wyatt (1929–45)	22–10 in 1941
11	Wee Willie Sherdel (1918–32)	21–10 in 1928
11	Earl Whitehill (1923–39)	22–8 in 1933
11	Early Wynn (1939, 1941–44, 1946–63)	20–13 in 1951
11	Allie Reynolds (1942–54)	20–8 in 1952
10	Mike Krukow (1976–89)	20–9 in 1986
9	Rube Walberg (1923–37)	20–12 in 1931
9	Preacher Roe (1938, 1944–54)	22–3 in 1951
	CC Sabathia (2001–19)	21–9 in 2010
9	R.A. Dickey (2001, 2003–06, 2008–17)	20–6 in 2012
9	J.A. Happ (2007–21)	20–4 in 2016

Rookie Pitchers with 20 Wins and 200 Strikeouts

	Wins–Losses	Strikeouts
Christy Mathewson, N.Y. Giants (NL), 1901	20–17	221
Russ Ford, N.Y. Yankees (AL), 1910	26–6	209
Pete Alexander, Phi. Phillies (NL), 1911	28–13	227

Pitchers Winning 20 Games in Rookie Year, Fewer Than 20 Balance of Career

	Rookie Year	Career
Roscoe Miller, Det. Tigers (AL) (1901–04)	23–13 (1901)	39–46
Henry Schmidt, Brk. Bridegrooms (NL) (1903)	21–13 (1903)	21–13
Johnny Beazley, St.L. Cardinals (NL) (1941–42, 1946–49)	21–6 (1942)	31–12

20-Game Winners Who Didn't Win 20 More Games in Career (Post-1900)

Sandy Koufax, Brk.–L.A. Dodgers (NL) (1955–66)* ... 27 wins (1966) ... 0 rest of career

Steve Stone, S.F. Giants (NL) (1971–72), Chi. White Sox (AL) (1973, 1977–78), Chi. Cubs (NL) (1974–76),
Bal. Orioles (AL) (1978–80) ... 25 wins (1980) ... 4 rest of career

Denny McLain, Det. Tigers (AL) (1963–70), Was. Senators II (AL) (1971), Oak. A's (AL) (1972),
Atl. Braves (NL) (1972) ... 24 wins (1969) ... 17 rest of career

continued on next page

Ron Bryant, S.F. Giants (NL) (1967, 1969–75).............................24 wins (1973)................................ 3 rest of career
Roscoe Miller, Det. Tigers (AL) (1901–04)...23 wins (1901)............................ 16 rest of career
Lefty Williams, Det. Tigers (AL) (1913–14),
                Chi. White Sox (AL) (1916–20)*........ 22 wins (1920) ....0 rest of career
Eddie Cicotte, Det. Tigers (AL) (1905), Bos. Red Sox (AL) (1908–12),
                Chi. White Sox (AL) (1912–1920)** 21 wins (1920)................................ 0 rest of career
Henry Schmidt, Brk. Bridegrooms (NL) (1903)............................21 wins (1903)................................ 0 rest of career
Buck O'Brien, Bos. Red Sox (AL) (1911–13) ....20 wins (1912)................................ 9 rest of career
Bill James, Bos. Braves (NL) (1913–15, 1919) ....26 wins (1914)............................ 11 rest of career
Brandon Webb, Ari. D'backs (NL) (2003–09) ....22 wins (2008)................................ 0 rest of career
George McConnell, Chi. Whales (FL) (1909, 1912–16).............25 wins (1915)............................ 16 rest of career
Jack Morris, Det. Tigers (AL) (1977–90), Min. Twins (AL) (1991), Tor. Blue Jays (AL) (1992–93),
                Cle. Indians (AL) (1994) ....21 wins (1992)............................ 17 rest of career
Joaquin Andujar, Hou. Astros (NL) (1976–81, 1988), St.L. Cardinals (NL) (1981–85),
                Oak. A's (AL) (1986–87) ....21 wins (1985)............................ 17 rest of career
Johnny Beazley, St.L. Cardinals (NL) (1941–42, 1946–49) ....21 wins (1942)............................ 10 rest of career
Mike Mussina, Bal. Orioles (AL) (1991–2000),
                N.Y. Yankees (AL) (2001–08)* ....20 wins (2008)................................ 0 rest of career

* Retired after season.
** Banned from baseball for gambling after season.

Pitchers Winning 20 Games in Last Season in Majors

Henry Schmidt, Brk. Dodgers (NL), 1903.............. 21–13   Sandy Koufax, L.A. Dodgers (NL), 1966.................. 27–9
Eddie Cicotte, Chi. White Sox (AL), 1920 21–10   Mike Mussina, N.Y. Yankees (AL), 2008.................. 20–9
Lefty Williams, Chi. White Sox (AL), 1920............. 22–14

Earliest 20-Game Winner During Season

American League

		Final Record
Jul. 25, 1931	Lefty Grove, Phi. A's	31–4
Jul. 27, 1968	Denny McLain, Det. Tigers	31–6

National League

		Final Record
Jul. 19, 1912	Rube Marquard, N.Y. Giants	26–11

Most Wins After Turning 40

Wins After 40		Total Career Wins	Wins After 40		Total Career Wins
121	Phil Niekro	318	72	Bartolo Colon	247
105	Jamie Moyer	269	71	Nolan Ryan	324
96	Jack Quinn	247	67	Charlie Hough	216
75	Cy Young	511	61	Roger Clemens	354
75	Warren Spahn	363	54	David Wells	239
73	Randy Johnson	303	54	Hoyt Wilhelm	143

Pitchers on Losing Teams, Leading League in Wins

American League

Pitcher	Wins–Losses	Team Record
Walter Johnson, Was. Senators, 1916	25–20	76–77
Eddie Rommel, Phi. A's, 1922	27–13	65–89
Ted Lyons, Chi. White Sox, 1927	22–14	70–83
Bob Feller, Cle. Indians, 1941	25–13	75–79
Bob Feller, Cle. Indians, 1946	26–15	68–86
Jim Perry, Cle. Indians, 1960	18–10	76–78
Gaylord Perry, Cle. Indians, 1972	24–16	72–84

continued on next page

Pitcher	Wins–Losses	Team Record
Wilbur Wood, Chi. White Sox, 1973	24–20	77–85
Roger Clemens, Bos. Red Sox, 1987	20–9	78–84
Kevin Brown, Tex. Rangers, 1992	21–11	77–85
Roger Clemens, Tor. Blue Jays, 1997	21–7	76–86
Jason Vargas, K.C. Royals, 2017	18–11	80–82

National League (Post-1900)

Pitcher	Wins–Losses	Team Record
Pete Alexander, Phi. Phillies, 1914	27–15	74–80
Pete Alexander, Chi. Cubs, 1920	27–14	75–79
Dazzy Vance, Brk. Dodgers, 1925	22–9	68–85
Jumbo Elliott, Phi. Phillies, 1931	19–14 (Tie)	66–88
Heine Meine, Pit. Pirates, 1931	19–13 (Tie)	75–79
Ewell Blackwell, Cin. Reds, 1947	22–8	73–81
Warren Spahn, Bos. Braves, 1949	21–14	75–79
Robin Roberts, Phi. Phillies, 1954	23–15	75–79
Larry Jackson, Chi. Cubs, 1964	24–11	76–86
Bob Gibson, St.L. Cardinals, 1970	23–7	76–86
Steve Carlton, Phi. Phillies, 1972	27–10	59–97
Randy Jones, S.D. Padres, 1976	22–14	73–89
Phil Niekro, Atl. Braves, 1979	21–20	66–94
Fernando Valenzuela, L.A. Dodgers, 1986	21–11	73–89
Rick Sutcliffe, Chi. Cubs, 1987	18–10	76–85
Greg Maddux, Chi. Cubs, 1992	20–11	78–84
Brandon Webb, Ari. D'backs, 2006	16–8	76–86

20-Game Winners on Last-Place Teams

American League

Pitcher	Wins–Losses	Team Record
Scott Perry, Phi. A's, 1918	20–19	52–76
Howard Ehmke, Bos. Red Sox, 1923	20–17	61–91
Sloppy Thurston, Chi. White Sox, 1924	20–14	66–87
Ned Garver, St.L. Browns, 1951	20–12	52–102
Nolan Ryan, Cal. Angels, 1974	22–16	68–94
Roger Clemens, Tor. Blue Jays, 1997	21–7	76–86

National League (Post-1900)

Pitcher	Wins–Losses	Team Record
Noodles Hahn, Cin. Reds, 1901	22–19	52–87
Steve Carlton, Phi. Phillies, 1972	27–10	59–97
Phil Niekro, Atl. Braves, 1979	21–20	66–94

20-Game Winners with Worst Lifetime Winning Percentage (Post-1900)

	Percentage	Lifetime	20-Win Season(s)
Scott Perry	.376	41–68	1918
Irv Young	.397	62–94	1905
Pete Schneider	.399	57–86	1917
Ben Cantwell	.413	76–108	1933
Joe Oeschger	.417	83–116	1921
Tom Hughes	.427	128–172	1903
Willie Sudhoff	.430	102–135	1903

continued on next page

	Percentage	Lifetime	20-Win Season(s)
Roger Wolff	.430	52–69	1945
Frank Allen	.431	50–66	1915
Otto Hess	.434	69–90	1906
Bob Harmon	.436	103–133	1911
Al Schulz	.440	48–61	1915
Vem Kennedy	.441	104–132	1936
Patsy Flaherty	.443	66–83	1904
Bob Groom	.446	121–150	1912
Oscar Jones	.446	45–56	1903
Randy Jones	.448	100–123	1975, 1976
Ned Garver	.451	129–157	1951
George McConnell	.452	42–51	1915
Chick Fraser	.454	176–212	1901

"Pure" 20-Game Winners (Pitchers with 20 or More Wins Than Losses)

American League

Cy Young, Bos. Americans, 1901	33–10
Cy Young, Bos. Americans, 1902	32–11
Jack Chesbro, N.Y. Highlanders, 1904	41–12
Ed Walsh, Chi. White Sox, 1908	40–15
George Mullin, Det. Tigers, 1909	29–8
Jack Coombs, Phi. A's, 1910	31–9
Russ Ford, N.Y. Highlanders, 1910	26–6
Smoky Joe Wood, Bos. Red Sox, 1912	34–5
Walter Johnson, Was. Senators, 1912	32–12
Eddie Plank, Phi. A's, 1912	26–6
Walter Johnson, Was. Senators, 1913	36–7
Eddie Cicotte, Chi. White Sox, 1919	29–7
Lefty Grove, Phi. A's, 1930	28–5
Lefty Grove, Phi. A's, 1931	31–4
Lefty Gomez, N.Y. Yankees, 1934	26–5
Hal Newhouser, Det. Tigers, 1944	29–9
Whitey Ford, N.Y. Yankees, 1961	25–4
Denny McLain, Det. Tigers, 1968	31–6
Ron Guidry, N.Y. Yankees, 1978	25–3
Roger Clemens, Bos. Red Sox, 1986	24–4

National League (Post-1900)

Joe McGinnity, Brk. Bridegrooms, 1900	29–9
Jack Chesbro, Pit. Pirates, 1902	28–6
Joe McGinnity, N.Y. Giants, 1904	35–8
Christy Mathewson, N.Y. Giants, 1904	33–12
Christy Mathewson, N.Y. Giants, 1905	31–8
Mordecai Brown, Chi. Cubs, 1906	26–6
Mordecai Brown, Chi. Cubs, 1908	29–9
Christy Mathewson, N.Y. Giants, 1908	37–11
Pete Alexander, Phi. Phillies, 1914	31–10
Pete Alexander, Phi. Phillies, 1916	33–12
Dazzy Vance, Brk. Dodgers, 1923	28–6
Dizzy Dean, St.L. Cardinals, 1934	30–7
Carl Hubbell, N.Y. Giants, 1935	26–6
Robin Roberts, Phi. Phillies, 1951	28–7
Don Newcombe, Brk. Dodgers, 1955	27–7
Sandy Koufax, L.A. Dodgers, 1962	25–5
Dwight Gooden, N.Y. Mets, 1985	24–4

Lefties Winning 20 Games Twice Since World War II

American League

Vida Blue	Oak. A's	1971	24
	Oak. A's	1973	20
	Oak. A's	1975	22
Mike Cuellar	Bal. Orioles	1969	23
	Bal. Orioles	1970	24
	Bal. Orioles	1974	22
Whitey Ford	N.Y. Yankees	1961	25
	N.Y. Yankees	1963	24
Ron Guidry	N.Y. Yankees	1978	25
	N.Y. Yankees	1983	21
	N.Y. Yankees	1985	22
Tommy John*	N.Y. Yankees	1979	21

continued on next page

	N.Y. Yankees	1980	22
Jim Kaat	Min. Twins	1966	25
	Chi. White Sox	1974	21
	Chi. White Sox	1975	20
Mickey Lolich	Det. Tigers	1971	25
	Det. Tigers	1972	22
Dave McNally	Bal. Orioles	1968	22
	Bal. Orioles	1969	20
	Bal. Orioles	1970	24
	Bal. Orioles	1971	21
Jamie Moyer	Sea. Mariners	2001	21
	Sea. Mariners	2003	21
Hal Newhouser	Det. Tigers	1946	26
	Det. Tigers	1948	21
Mel Parnell	Bos. Red Sox	1949	25
	Bos. Red Sox	1953	21
Andy Pettitte	N.Y. Yankees	1996	21
	N.Y. Yankees	2003	21
Billy Pierce	Chi. White Sox	1956	20
	Chi. White Sox	1957	20
Frank Viola**	Min. Twins	1988	24
Wilbur Wood	Chi. White Sox	1971	22
	Chi. White Sox	1972	24
	Chi. White Sox	1973	24
	Chi. White Sox	1974	20

National League

Johnny Antonelli	N.Y. Giants	1954	21
	N.Y. Giants	1956	20
Steve Carlton	St.L. Cardinals	1971	20
	Phi. Phillies	1972	27
	Phi. Phillies	1976	20
	Phi. Phillies	1977	23
	Phi. Phillies	1980	24
	Phi. Phillies	1982	23
Tom Glavine	Atl. Braves	1991	20
	Atl. Braves	1992	20
	Atl. Braves	1993	22
	Atl. Braves	1998	20
	Atl. Braves	2000	21
Randy Johnson***	Ari. D'backs	2001	21
	Ari. D'backs	2002	24
Randy Jones	S.D. Padres	1975	20
	S.D. Padres	1976	22
Clayton Kershaw	L.A. Dodgers	2011	21
	L.A. Dodgers	2014	21
Jerry Koosman	N.Y. Mets	1976	21
Sandy Koufax	L.A. Dodgers	1963	25
	L.A. Dodgers	1965	26
	L.A. Dodgers	1966	27
Claude Osteen	L.A. Dodgers	1969	20
	L.A. Dodgers	1972	20
Howie Pollet	St.L. Cardinals	1946	21
	St.L. Cardinals	1949	20

continued on next page

Warren Spahn	Bos. Braves	1947	21
	Bos. Braves	1949	21
	Bos. Braves	1950	21
	Bos. Braves	1951	22
	Mil. Braves	1953	23
	Mil. Braves	1954	21
	Mil. Braves	1956	20
	Mil. Braves	1957	21
	Mil. Braves	1958	22
	Mil. Braves	1959	21
	Mil. Braves	1960	21
	Mil. Braves	1961	21
	Mil. Braves	1963	23

* Also won 20 games in 1977 with the L.A. Dodgers.
** Also won 20 games in 1990 with the N.Y. Mets.
*** Also won 20 games in 1997 with the Sea. Mariners.
**** Also won 20 games in 1979 with the Min. Twins.

Pitchers with 20-Win Seasons After Age 40

		Age	Season	Wins–Losses
Pete Alexander	St.L. Cardinals (NL)	40	1927	21–10
Jamie Moyer	Sea. Mariners (AL)	40	2003	21–7
Phil Niekro	Atl. Braves (NL)	40	1979	21–20
Gaylord Perry	S.D. Padres (NL)	40	1978	21–6
Eddie Plank	St.L. Terriers (FL)	40	1915	21–11
Warren Spahn	Mil. Braves (NL)	40	1961	21–13
	Mil. Braves (NL)	42	1963	23–7
Cy Young	Bos. Americans (AL)	40	1907	21–15
	Bos. Americans (AL)	41	1908	21–11

Pitchers Leading Both Leagues in Wins, Season

American League			National League	
Jack Chesbro	N.Y. Highlanders, 1904	41–13	Pit. Pirates, 1902	28–6
Roy Halladay	Tor. Blue Jays, 2003	22–7	Phi. Phillies, 2010	21–10
Ferguson Jenkins	Tex. Rangers, 1974	25–12 (Tie)	Chi. Cubs, 1971	24–13
Gaylord Perry	Cle. Indians, 1972	24–16 (Tie)	S.F. Giants, 1970	23–13 (Tie)
			S.D. Padres, 1978	21–6
Max Scherzer	Det. Tigers, 2013	21–3	Was. Nationals, 2016	20–7
	Det. Tigers, 2014	18–5 (Tie)	Was. Nationals, 2018	18–7 (Tie)
Curt Schilling	Bos. Red Sox, 2004	21–6	Ari. D'backs, 2001	22–6
Cy Young	Bos. Americans, 1901	33–10	Cle. Spiders, 1892	36–12 (Tie)
	Bos. Americans, 1902	32–11	Cle. Spiders, 1895	35–10
	Bos. Americans, 1903	28–9		

20-Game Winners One Season, 20-Game Losers the Next

American League

George Mullin, Det. Tigers	21–18 (1906)	20–20 (1907)
Al Orth, N.Y. Highlanders	27–17 (1906)	27–21 (1907)
Russ Ford, N.Y. Highlanders	22–11 (1911)	13–21 (1912)
Walter Johnson, Was. Senators	27–13 (1915)	25–20 (1916)
Hooks Dauss, Det. Tigers	21–9 (1919)	13–21 (1920)
Bobo Newsom, Det. Tigers	21–5 (1940)	12–20 (1941)
Alex Kellner, Phi. A's	20–12 (1949)	8–20 (1950)

continued on next page

Mel Stottlemyre, N.Y. Yankees..................................20–9 (1965) 12–20 (1966)

Luis Tiant, Cle. Indians ....21–9 (1968) 9–20 (1969)

Stan Bahnsen, Chi. White Sox ....21–16 (1972) 18–21 (1973)

Wilbur Wood, Chi. White Sox ....24–17 (1972) 24–20 (1973)

Wilbur Wood, Chi. White Sox ....20–19 (1974) 16–20 (1975)

National League (Post-1900)

Joe McGinnity, Brk. Bridegrooms (NL), Bal. Orioles (AL) ....28–8 (1900) 26–20 (1901)

Vic Willis, Bos. Beaneaters ....20–17 (1901) 27–20 (1902)

Togie Pittinger, Bos. Beaneaters ....27–16 (1902) 18–22 (1903)

Jack Taylor, St.L. Cardinals ....20–19 (1904) 15–21 (1905)

Irv Young, Bos. Beaneaters ....20–21 (1905) 16–25 (1906)

Nap Rucker, Brk. Dodgers ....22–18 (1911) 18–21 (1912)

Rube Marquard, N.Y. Giants.................................23–10 (1913) 12–22 (1914)

Eppa Rixey, Phi. Phillies ....22–10 (1916) 16–21 (1917)

Joe Oeschger, Bos. Braves ....20–14 (1921) 6–21 (1922)

Murry Dickson, Pit. Pirates ....20–16 (1951) 14–21 (1952)

Larry Jackson, Chi. Cubs.......................................24–11 (1964) 14–21 (1965)

Steve Carlton, Phi. Phillies ....27–10 (1972) 13–20 (1973)

Jerry Koosman, N.Y. Mets ....21–10 (1976) 8–20 (1977)

20-Game Winners and Losers, Same Season

American League

Joe McGinnity, Bal. Orioles, 1901............................26–20

Bill Dinneen, Bos. Americans, 1902........................21–21

George Mullin, Det. Tigers, 1905.............................21–21

George Mullin, Det. Tigers, 1907 20–20

Jim Scott, Chi. White Sox, 1913 20–20

Walter Johnson, Was. Senators, 1916 25–20

Wilbur Wood, Chi. White Sox, 1973 24–20

National League (Post-1900)

Vic Willis, Bos. Beaneaters, 1902...........................27–20

Joe McGinnity, N.Y. Giants, 1903 31–20

Irv Young, Bos. Beaneaters, 1905 20–21

Phil Niekro, Atl. Braves, 1979.................................21–20

Pitchers Who Led League in Wins in Successive Seasons

American League

Seasons

4 .... Walter Johnson, Wash, Senators, 1913–16

3 .... Cy Young, Bos. Americans, 1901–03

3 ....Bob Feller, Cle. Indians, 1939–41

3 ....Hal Newhouser, Det. Tigers, 1944–46

3 ....Jim Palmer, Bal. Orioles, 1975–77

2 ....Jack Coombs, Phila A's, 1910–11

2 .... Lefty Grove, Phila A's, 1930–31

2 ....General Crowder, Was. Senators, 1932–33

2 ....Bob Feller, Cle. Indians, 1946–47

2 .... Bob Lemon, Cle. Indians, 1954–55

2 ....Denny McLain, Det. Tigers, 1968–69

2 ....Wilbur Wood, Chi. White Sox, 1972–73

2 .... Catfish Hunter, Oak. A's, 1974–75

2 .... LaMarr Hoyt, Chi. White Sox, 1982–83

2 .... Roger Clemens, Bos. Red Sox, 1986–87

National League

Seasons

5 ....Warren Spahn, Mil. Braves, 1957–61

4 .... Pete Alexander, Phi. Phillies, 1914–17

4 ....Robin Roberts, Phi. Phillies, 1952–55

3 .... Bill Hutchison, Chi. Colts, 1890–92

3 .... Kid Nichols, Bos. Beaneaters, 1896–98

3 .... Tom Glavine, Atl. Braves, 1991–93

2 ....Tommy Bond, Bos. Red Caps, 1877–78

2 .... Old Hoss Radbourn, Pro. Grays, 1883–84

2 ....Joe McGinnity, Bal. Orioles, 1899–1900

2 ....Joe McGinnity, N.Y. Giants, 1903–04

2 .... Christy Mathewson, N.Y. Giants, 1907–08

2 .... Dazzy Vance, Brk. Dodgers, 1924–25

2 .... Pat Malone, Chi. Cubs, 1929–30

2 .... Dizzy Dean, St.L. Cardinals, 1934–35

2 ....Carl Hubbell, N.Y. Giants, 1936–37

continued on next page

Seasons

2 ....Roger Clemens, Tor. Blue Jays, 1997–98
2 ....CC Sabathia, N.Y. Yankees, 2009–10
2 ....Max Scherzer, Det. Tigers, 2013–14

Seasons

2 ....Bucky Walters, Cin. Reds, 1939–40
2 ....Mort Cooper, St.L. Cardinals, 1942–43
2 .... Warren Spahn, Bos. Braves, 1949–50
2 .... Sandy Koufax, L.A. Dodgers, 1965–66
2 .... Greg Maddux, Atl. Braves, 1994–95

Most Pitching Wins for One Season

Pitcher	Wins	Year	Team
Old Hoss Radbourn	59	1884	Pro. Grays (NL)
John Clarkson	53	1885	Chi. White Stockings (NL)
Guy Hecker	52	1884	Lou. Colonels (AA)
John Clarkson	49	1889	Bos. Beaneaters (NL)
Old Hoss Radbourn	48	1883	Pro. Grays (NL)
Charlie Buffinton	48	1884	Bos. Beaneaters (NL)
Al Spalding	47	1876	Chi. White Stockings (NL)
Monte Ward	47	1879	Pro. Grays (NL)
Pud Galvin	46	1883	Buff. Bisons (NL)
Pud Galvin	46	1884	Buff. Bisons (NL)
Matt Kilroy	46	1887	Bal. Orioles (AA)
George Bradley	45	1876	St.L. Brown Stockings (NL)
Jim McCormick	45	1880	Cle. Blues (NL)
Silver King	45	1888	St.L. Browns (AA)
Mickey Welch	44	1885	N.Y. Giants (NL)
Bill Hutchison	44	1891	Chi. Colts (NL)
Will White	43	1879	Cin. Reds (NL)
Larry Corcoran	43	1880	Chi. White Stockings (NL)
Will White	43	1883	Cin. Red Stockings (AA)
Billy Taylor	43	1884	Phi. A's (AA)– St.L. Maroons (UA)
Tommy Bond	43	1897	Bos. Red Caps (NL)
Lady Baldwin	42	1886	Det. Wolverines (NL)
Tim Keefe	42	1886	N.Y. Giants (NL)
Bill Hutchison	42	1890	Chi. Colts (NL)
Tim Keefe	41	1883	N.Y. Metropolitans (AA)
Charlie Sweeney	41	1884	Pro. Grays (NL)– St.L. Maroons (UA)
Dave Foutz	41	1886	St.L. Browns (AA)
Ed Morris	41	1886	Pit. Alleghenys (AA)
Jack Chesbro	41	1904	N.Y. Highlanders (AL)
Tommy Bond	40	1877	Bos. Red Caps (NL)
Tommy Bond	40	1878	Bos. Red Caps (NL)
Will White	40	1882	Cin. Red Stockings (AA)
Jim McCormick	40	1884	Cle. Blues (NL)– Cin. Outlaw Reds (UA)
Bill Sweeney	40	1884	Bal. Monumentals (UA)
Bob Caruthers	40	1885	St.L. Browns (AA)
Bob Caruthers	40	1889	Brk. Bridegrooms (AA)
Ed Walsh	40	1908	Chi. White Sox (AL)

Most Total Wins, Two Pitchers on Same Staff, Career Together as Teammates

American League

440	Eddie Plank (247) and Chief Bender (193), Phi. A's (1903–14)
408	Lefty Grove (257) and Rube Walberg (151), Phi. A's (1925–33) and Bos. Red Sox (1934–37)
408	Red Ruffing (219) and Lefty Gomez (189), N.Y. Yankees (1930–42)
361	Hal Newhouser (200) and Dizzy Trout (161), Det. Tigers (1939–52)
355	Bob Lemon (201) and Bob Feller (154), Cle. Indians (1946–56)
349	Early Wynn (177) and Bob Lemon (172), Cle. Indians (1949–58)
332	Ed Walsh (190) and Doc White (142), Chi. White Sox (1904–13)
331	Bob Lemon (192) and Mike Garcia (139), Cle. Indians (1948–58)

National League

443	Warren Spahn (264) and Lew Burdette (179), Bos.–Mil. Braves (1951–63)
433	Christy Mathewson (297) and Hooks Wiltse (136), N.Y. Giants (1904–14)
408	Tom Glavine (242) and John Smoltz (166), Atl. Braves (1988–2002, 2008)
358	Carl Hubbell (204) and Hal Schumacher (154), N.Y. Giants (1931–42)
347	Greg Maddux (178) and Tom Glavine (169), Atl. Braves (1993–2002)
342	Christy Mathewson (191) and Joe McGinnity (151), N.Y. Giants (1902–08)
340	Sam Leever (172) and Deacon Phillippe (168), Pit. Pirates (1900–10)
340	Don Drysdale (177) and Sandy Koufax (163), Brk.–L.A. Dodgers (1956–66)
336	Juan Marichal (202) and Gaylord Perry (134), S.F. Giants (1962–71)
326	Robin Roberts (212) and Curt Simmons (114), Phi. Phillies (1948–50, 1952–60)
318	Mordecai Brown (182) and Ed Reulbach (136), Chi. Cubs (1905–13)
317	Bob Friend (176) and Vern Law (141), Pit. Pirates (1951, 1954–65)

Most Wins, Right-Hander and Left-Hander on Same Staff, Season

American League

58	Ed Walsh (RH, 40) and Doc White (LH, 18), Chi. White Sox, 1908
56	Hal Newhouser (LH, 29) and Dizzy Trout (RH, 27), Det. Tigers, 1944
53	Walter Johnson (RH, 36) and Joe Boehling (LH, 17), Was. Senators, 1913
52	Eddie Cicotte (RH, 29) and Lefty Williams (LH, 23), Chi. White Sox, 1919
52	Lefty Grove (LH, 31) and George Earnshaw (RH, 21), Phi. A's, 1931
51	Doc White (LH, 27) and Ed Walsh (RH, 24), Chi. White Sox, 1907
51	Jack Coombs (RH, 28) and Eddie Plank (LH, 23), Phi. A's, 1911
50	Ed Killian (LH, 25) and Bill Donovan (RH, 25), Det. Tigers, 1907
50	Lefty Grove (LH, 28) and George Earnshaw (RH, 22), Phi. A's, 1930
48	Mel Parnell (LH, 25) and Ellis Kinder (RH, 23), Bos. Red Sox, 1949
48	Denny McLain (RH, 31) and Mickey Lolich (LH, 17), Det. Tigers, 1968
47	Cy Young (RH, 26) and Jesse Tannehill (LH, 21), Bos. Red Sox, 1904
47	Jack Coombs (RH, 31) and Eddie Plank (LH, 16), Phi. A's, 1910
47	Smoky Joe Wood (RH, 34) and Ray Collins, (LH, 13), Bos. Red Sox, 1912
47	Eddie Plank (LH, 26) and Jack Coombs (RH, 21), Phi. A's, 1912
46	Hooks Dauss (RH, 24) and Harry Coveleski (LH, 22), Det. Tigers, 1915
46	Babe Ruth (LH, 24) and Carl Mays (RH, 22), Bos. Red Sox, 1917
46	General Crowder (RH, 24) and Earl Whitehill (LH, 22), Was. Senators, 1933

National League (Post-1900)

60	Christy Mathewson (RH, 37) and Hooks Wiltse (LH, 23), N.Y. Giants, 1908
55	Pete Alexander (RH, 33) and Eppa Rixey (LH, 22), Phi. Phillies, 1916

continued on next page

50	Christy Mathewson (RH, 26) and Rube Marquard (LH, 24), N.Y. Giants, 1911
49	Rube Marquard (LH, 26) and Christy Mathewson (RH, 23), N.Y. Giants, 1912
49	Sandy Koufax (LH, 26) and Don Drysdale (RH, 23), L.A. Dodgers, 1965
48	Jack Chesbro (RH, 28) and Jesse Tannehill (LH, 20), Pit. Pirates, 1902
48	Joe McGinnity (RH, 35) and Hooks Wiltse (LH, 13), N.Y. Giants, 1904
48	Christy Mathewson (RH, 25) and Rube Marquard (LH, 23), N.Y. Giants, 1913
47	Dolf Luque (RH, 27) and Eppa Rixey (LH, 20), Cin. Reds, 1923
47	Randy Johnson (LH, 24) and Curt Schilling (RH, 23), Ari. D'backs, 2002
46	Christy Mathewson (RH, 31) and Hooks Wiltse (LH, 15), N.Y. Giants, 1905
46	Mordecai Brown (RH, 26) and Jack Pfiester (LH, 20), Chi. Cubs, 1906
46	Pete Alexander (RH, 30) and Eppa Rixey (LH, 16), Phi. Phillies, 1917
46	Pete Alexander (RH, 27) and Hippo Vaughn (LH, 19), Chi. Cubs, 1920

Largest Differential Between League Leader in Wins and Runner-Up

American League

Differential		Leader	Runner(s)-Up
+16	1908	Ed Walsh, Chi. White Sox (40)	Addie Joss, Cle. Indians (24)
			Ed Summers, Det. Tigers (24)
+15	1904	Jack Chesbro, N.Y. Yankees (41)	Eddie Plank, Phi. A's (26)
			Cy Young, Bos. Americans (26)
+13	1913	Walter Johnson, Was. Senators (36)	Cy Falkenberg, Cle. Indians (23)
+9	1931	Lefty Grove, Phi. A's (31)	Wes Ferrell, Cle. Indians (22)
+9	1968	Denny McLain, Det. Tigers (31)	Dave McNally, Bal. Orioles (22)
+8	1902	Cy Young, Bos. Americans (32)	Rube Waddell, Phi. A's (24)

National League (Post-1900)

Differential		Leader	Runner(s)-Up
+10	1952	Robin Roberts, Phi. Phillies (28)	Sal Maglie, N.Y. Giants (18)
+9	1915	Pete Alexander, Phi. Phillies (31)	Dick Rudolph, Bos. Braves (22)
+8	1900	Joe McGinnity, Brk. Bridegrooms (28)	Bill Dinneen, Bos. Beaneaters (20)
			Brickyard Kennedy, Brk. Dodgers (20)
			Deacon Phillippe, Pit. Pirates (20)
			Jesse Tannehill, Pit. Pirates (20)
+8	1905	Christy Mathewson, N.Y. Giants (31)	Togie Pittinger, Phi. Phillies (23)
+8	1908	Christy Mathewson, N.Y. Giants (37)	Mordecai Brown, Chi. Cubs (29)
+8	1916	Pete Alexander, Phi. Phillies (33)	Jeff Pfeffer, Brk. Dodgers (25)

Highest Percentage of Team's Total Wins for Season

American League

45.6%	Jack Chesbro (N.Y. Highlanders, 1904)	41 of team's 92 wins
45.5%	Ed Walsh (Chi. White Sox, 1908)	40 of team's 88 wins
41.8%	Cy Young (Bos. Americans, 1901)	33 of team's 79 wins
41.7%	Joe Bush (Phi. A's, 1916)	15 of team's 36 wins
41.6%	Cy Young (Bos. Red Sox, 1902)	32 of team's 77 wins
41.5%	Eddie Rommel (Phi. A's, 1922)	27 of team's 65 wins
40.3%	Red Faber (Chi. White Sox, 1921)	25 of team's 62 wins
40.0%	Walter Johnson (Was. Senators, 1913)	36 of team's 90 wins
39.1%	Walter Johnson (Was. Senators, 1911)	25 of team's 64 wins
38.9%	Elmer Myers (Phi. A's, 1916)	14 of team's 36 wins

continued on next page

38.5%..Ned Garver (St.L. Browns, 1951)	....	20 of team's 52 wins
38.5%...Scott Perry (Phi. A's, 1918)	....	20 of team's 52 wins
38.2%..................................Joe McGinnity, (Bal. Orioles, 1901)	....	26 of team's 68 wins
38.2%.................................Bob Feller (Cle. Indians, 1946)	....	26 of team's 68 wins
37.9%...........................Walter Johnson (Was. Senators, 1910)	....	25 of team's 66 wins

National League (Post-1900)

45.8%.............................Steve Carlton (Phi. Phillies, 1972)	....	27 of team's 59 wins
42.3%...............................Noodles Hahn (Cin. Reds, 1901)	....	22 of team's 52 wins
39.2%................................Irv Young (Bos. Beaneaters, 1905)	....	20 of team's 51 wins
38.5%................Christy Mathewson (N.Y. Giants, 1901)	....	20 of team's 52 wins
37.8%................Christy Mathewson (N.Y. Giants, 1908)	....	37 of team's 98 wins
37.3%......................Slim Sallee (St.L. Cardinals, 1913)	....	19 of team's 51 wins
37.0%.......................Togie Pittinger (Bos. Beaneaters, 1902)	....	27 of team's 73 wins
37.0%.............................Vic Willis (Bos. Beaneaters, 1902)	....	27 of team's 73 wins
36.9%.............................Joe McGinnity (N.Y. Giants, 1903)	....	31 of team's 84 wins

Pitchers Winning 300 Games, Never Striking Out 200 Batters, Season

Pitcher	Wins	Most Strikeouts (Season)
Tom Glavine	305	192 (1991)
Warren Spahn	363	191 (1950)
Early Wynn	300	184 (1957)

Won-Loss Percentage of 300-Game Winners

Won-Loss Percentage	Player	Years	Record
.680	Lefty Grove	(1925–41)	300–141
.665	Christy Mathewson	(1900–16)	373–188
.658	Roger Clemens	(1984–2007)	354–184
.648	John Clarkson	(1882–94)	328–178
.646	Randy Johnson	(1988–2009)	303–166
.642	Pete Alexander	(1911–30)	373–208
.634	Kid Nichols	(1890–1906)	361–208
.627	Eddie Plank	(1901–17)	326–194
.619	Cy Young	(1890–1911)	511–316
.614	Old Hoss Radbourn	(1880–91)	309–194
.610	Greg Maddux	(1986–2008)	355–227
.603	Tim Keefe	(1880–93)	341–225
.603	Tom Seaver	(1967–86)	311–205
.600	Tom Glavine	(1987–2008)	305–203
.599	Walter Johnson	(1907–27)	417–279
.597	Warren Spahn	(1946–65)	363–245
.594	Mickey Welch	(1880–92)	307–210
.574	Steve Carlton	(1965–88)	329–244
.559	Don Sutton	(1966–88)	324–256
.551	Early Wynn	(1939, 1941–44, 1946–63)	300–244
.542	Gaylord Perry	(1962–83)	314–265
.540	Pud Galvin	(1879–92)	365–310
.537	Phil Niekro	(1964–87)	318–274
.526	Nolan Ryan	(1966, 1968–93)	324–292

Shutouts

Evolution of Shutout Record

American League

1901	Clark Griffith, Chi. White Sox	5
	Cy Young, Bos. Americans	5
1903	Cy Young, Bos. Americans	7
1904	Cy Young, Bos. Americans	10
1908	Ed Walsh, Chi. White Sox	11
1910	Jack Coombs, Phi. A's	13

National League (Pre-1900)

| 1876 | George Bradley, St.L. Brown Stockings | 16 |

National League (Post-1899)

1900	Clark Griffith, Chi. Cubs	4
	Noodles Hahn, Cin. Reds	4
	Kid Nichols, Bos. Beaneaters	4
	Cy Young, St.L. Cardinals	4
1901	Jack Chesbro, Pit. Pirates	6
	Al Orth, Phi. Phillies	6
	Vic Willis, Bos. Beaneaters	6
1902	Jack Chesbro, Pit. Pirates	8
	Christy Mathewson, N.Y. Giants	8
	Jack Taylor, Chi. Cubs	8
1904	Joe McGinnity, N.Y. Giants	9
1908	Christy Mathewson, N.Y. Giants	11
1915	Pete Alexander, Phi. Phillies	12
1916	Pete Alexander, Phi. Phillies	16

20-Game Winners with No Complete Game Shutouts

American League

Wins	Losses		
26	7	Joe Bush, N.Y. Yankees, 1922
24	15	General Crowder, Was. Senators, 1933
23	5	Barry Zito, Oak. A's, 2002
22	4	Rick Porcello, Bos. Red Sox, 2016
22	11	Earl Wilson, Det. Tigers, 1967
22	14	Lefty Williams, Chi. White Sox, 1920
21	3	Max Scherzer, Det. Tigers, 2013
21	5	Blake Snell, T.B. Rays, 2018
21	6	Curt Schilling, Bos. Red Sox, 2004
21	7	Jamie Moyer, Sea. Mariners, 2003
21	7	CC Sabathia, N.Y. Yankees, 2010
21	8	Andy Pettitte, N.Y. Yankees, 1996
21	8	Andy Pettitte, N.Y. Yankees, 2003
21	8	Bartolo Colon, L.A. Angels, 2005
21	9	Dave Stewart, Oak. A's, 1989
21	9	Esteban Loaiza, Chi. White Sox, 2003
20	9	Hugh Bedient, Bos. Red Sox, 1912
20	9	Bill Gullickson, Det. Tigers, 1991
20	9	Mike Mussina, N.Y. Yankees, 2008
20	12	Alex Kellner, Phi. A's, 1949
20	12	Dave Boswell, Min. Twins, 1969
20	13	Luis Tiant, Bos. Red Sox, 1973
20	16	Bobo Newsom, St.L. Browns, 1938
20	3	Roger Clemens, N.Y. Yankees, 2001
20	4	Pedro Martinez, Bos. Red Sox, 2002
20	4	J.A. Happ, Tor. Blue Jays, 2016
20	6	Jamie Moyer, Sea. Mariners, 2001
20	5	Gerrit Cole, Hou. Astros, 2019
20	7	David Cone, N.Y. Yankees, 1998
20	7	Josh Beckett, Bos. Red Sox, 2007

National League (Post-1900)

Wins	Losses		
24	12	Ron Bryant, S.F. Giants, 1973
23	12	Christy Mathewson, N.Y. Giants, 1912
21	10	Willie Sherdel, St.L. Cardinals, 1928
21	10	Jose Lima, Hou. Astros, 1999
21	12	Mordecai Brown, Chi. Cubs, 1911
21	5	Kyle Wright, Atl. Braves, 2022
20	7	Max Scherzer, Was. Nationals, 2016
20	3	Julio Urias, L.A. Dodgers, 2021
20	19	Pete Schneider, Cin. Reds, 1917

Pitchers Leading League in Wins, No Complete Game Shutouts

American League

Wins	Losses	
24	15	General Crowder, Was. Senators, 1933
23	5	Barry Zito, Oak. A's, 2002
22	4	Rick Porcello, Bos. Red Sox, 2016
22	6	Tex Hughson, Bos. Red Sox, 1942
22	11	Earl Wilson, Det. Tigers, 1967
21	3	Max Scherzer, Det. Tigers, 2013
21	5	Blake Snell, T.B. Rays, 2018
21	6	Curt Schilling, Bos. Red Sox, 2004
21	7	CC Sabathia, N.Y. Yankees, 2010
21	8	Andy Pettitte, N.Y. Yankees, 1996
21	8	Bartolo Colon, L.A. Angels, 2005
20	7	David Cone, N.Y. Yankees, 1998
20	7	Josh Beckett, Bos. Red Sox, 2007
20	9	Bill Gullickson, Det. Tigers, 1991
19	6	Johan Santana, Min. Twins, 2006
18	4	Justin Verlander, Hou. Astros, 2022
18	6	Carlos Carrasco, Cle. Indians, 2017
18	9	Jered Weaver, L.A. Angels, 2014
18	10	Bob Lemon, Cle. Indians, 1955

National League (Post-1900)

Wins	Losses	
24	12	Ron Bryant, S.F. Giants, 1973
20	7	Max Scherzer, Was. Nationals, 2016
20	3	Julio Urias, L.A. Dodgers, 2021
19	6	Jake Peavy, S.D. Padres, 2007
19	8	Adam Wainwright, St.L. Cardinals, 2009
18	4	Clayton Kershaw, L.A. Dodgers, 2017
18	6	Stephen Strasburg, Was. Nationals, 2019
16	7	Carlos Zambrano, Chi. Cubs, 2006
16	8	Derek Lowe, L.A. Dodgers, 2006
16	9	Brad Penny, L.A. Dodgers, 2006
8	3	Yu Darvish, Chi. Cubs, 2020

Most Shutouts by a Rookie

American League

8	Russ Ford, 1910 N.Y. Yankees
	Reb Russell, 1913 Chi. White Sox
7	Harry Krause, 1909 Phi. A's
6	Fred Glade, 1904 St.L. Browns
	Gene Bearden, 1948 Cle. Indians

National League

8	Fernando Valenzuela, 1981 L.A. Dodgers
7	Irv Young, 1905 Bos. Beaneaters
	George McQuillan, 1908 Phi. Phillies
	Pete Alexander, 1911 Phi. Phillies
	Jerry Koosman, 1968 N.Y. Mets
6	Harvey Haddix, 1953 St.L. Cardinals
	Ewell Blackwell, 1946 Cin. Reds

Most Career Starts, No Shutouts

Starts		Overall Record
256	Mike Pelfrey (2006–17)	68–103
241	Jorge De La Rosa (2004–18)	104–87
237	Jake Odorizzi* (2012–)	74–69
228	Kevin Gausman* (2013–)	76–82
221	Chris Young (2004–12, 2014–17)	79–67
204	Danny Duffy* (2011–)	68–68
203	Jason Bere (1993–2003)	71–65
201	Adam Eaton (2000–09)	71–68
194	Marco Estrada (2008–19)	55–52
190	Alex Wood* (2013–)	71–60
188	Bud Norris (2009–18)	64–84
187	Nate Robertson (2002–10)	57–77
183	Chase Anderson* (2014–)	58–50
182	Zach Davies* (2015–)	58–53
180	Michael Pineda* (2011, 2014–17, 2019–)	64–21
170	Wei-Yin Chen (2012–19)	59–50
170	Eduardo Rodriguez* (2015–19, 2021–)	69–44
167	Tony Armas (1999–2008)	53–65
167	Shaun Marcum (2005–08, 2010–13, 2015)	61–48
160	Josh Johnson (2005–13)	58–45
153	Paul Wilson (1996–2005)	40–58

* Still active.

Most Career Shutouts, Never Led League

Starts		Overall Record
50	Rube Waddell (1897, 1899–1910)	191–145
49	Ferguson Jenkins (1965–83)	284–226
46	Doc White (1901–13)	190–157
45	Phil Niekro (1964–87)	318–274
42	Catfish Hunter (1965–79)	224–166
41	Chief Bender (1903–17, 1925)	210–127
40	Mickey Welch (1880–92)	311–207
40	Ed Reulbach (1905–17)	181–105
40	Claude Osteen (1957, 1959–75)	196–195
40	Mel Stottlemyre (1964–74)	164–139

Pitchers with Shutouts in First Two Major League Starts

American League

	Season Record	Shutouts
Joe Doyle, N.Y. Highlanders, 1906	2–2	2
Johnny Marcum, Phi. A's, 1933	3–2	2
Hal White, Det. Tigers, 1941	12–12	4
Dave Ferriss, Bos. Red Sox, 1945	21–10	5
Tom Phoebus, Bal. Orioles, 1966	2–1	2

National League (Post-1900)

	Season Record	Shutouts
Al Worthington, N.Y. Giants, 1953	4–8	2
Karl Spooner, Brk. Dodgers, 1954	2–0	2

Most Hits Allowed by Pitcher Throwing Shutout

American League

15 .... Walter Johnson, Was. Senators, Jul. 3, 1913
14 .... Ernie Koob, St.L. Browns, Jul. 14, 1916
           Milt Gaston, Was. Senators, Jul. 10, 1928
13 .... Mudcat Grant, Min. Twins, Jul. 15, 1964
12 .... Bob Shawkey, N.Y. Yankees, Jun. 13, 1920
           Duster Mails, Cle. Indians, Jul. 10, 1926
           Stan Bahnsen, Chi. White Sox, Jun. 21, 1973

National League (Post-1900)

14 .... Larry Cheney, Chi. Cubs, Sep. 14, 1913
13 .... Dizzy Dean, St.L. Cardinals, Apr. 20, 1937
           Bill Lee, Chi. Cubs, Sep. 17, 1938
12 .... Pol Perritt, N.Y. Giants, Sep. 14, 1917
           Rube Benton, N.Y. Giants, Aug. 28, 1920
           Leon Cadore, Brk. Dodgers, Sep. 4, 1920
           George Smith, Phi. Phillies, Aug. 12, 1921
           Hal Schumacher, N.Y. Giants, Jul. 19, 1934
           Tom Zachary, Brk. Dodgers, May 16, 1935
           Fritz Ostermueller, Pit. Pirates, May 17, 1947
           Lew Burdette, Mil. Braves, May 26, 1959
           Bob Friend, Pit. Pirates, Sep. 24, 1959
           Rick Reuschel , Chi. Cubs, Jun. 20, 1974
           Dennis Martinez, Mon. Expos, Jun. 2, 1998

Players with Highest Percentage of Shutouts to Games Started, Career

	Games Started	Shutouts	Percentage
Ed Walsh (1904–17)	315	57	18.10
Smoky Joe Wood (1908–15, 1917–20)	158	28	17.72
Addie Joss (1902–10)	260	46	17.69
Mordecai Brown (1903–16)	332	57	17.17
Walter Johnson (1907–27)	666	110	16.52
Pete Alexander (1911–30)	598	90	15.05
Lefty Leifield (1905–13, 1918–20)	217	32	14.75
Rube Waddell (1897, 1899–1910)	340	50	14.71
Christy Mathewson (1900–16)	552	80	14.49
Spud Chandler (1937–47)	184	26	14.13

continued on next page

	Games Started	Shutouts	Percentage
Nap Rucker (1907–16)	273	38	13.92
Mort Cooper (1938–47, 1949)	239	33	13.81
Ed Reulbach (1905–17)	299	40	13.38
Babe Adams (1906–07, 1909–26)	355	47	13.24
Eddie Plank (1901–17)	527	69	13.09
Sam Leever (1898–1910)	299	39	13.04

Losses

Most Losses by Decade

Pre-1900

310	Pud Galvin
225	Gus Weyhing
225	Tim Keefe
220	Tony Mullane
214	Jim McCormick
210	Mickey Welch
204	Jim Whitney
194	Adonis Terry
194	Old Hoss Radbourn
178	John Clarkson

1900–09

172	Vic Willis
163	Jack Powell
146	Cy Young
143	Al Orth
141	Bill Dinneen
139	Rube Waddell
138	Harry Howell
135	Long Tom Hughes
134	Chick Fraser
134	George Mullin

1910–19

143	Walter Johnson
124	Bob Groom
122	Bob Harmon
120	Eddie Cicotte
117	Red Ames
114	Slim Sallee
110	Hippo Vaughn
104	Claude Hendrix
104	Ray Caldwell
103	Rube Marquard
103	Pet Ragan

1920–29

146	Dolf Luque
142	Eppa Rixey
137	Howard Ehmke
135	Slim Harriss
130	Burleigh Grimes
128	Jimmy Ring
124	George Uhle
122	Tom Zachary
119	Jesse Haines
118	Sad Sam Jones

1930–39

137	Paul Derringer
134	Larry French
123	Mel Harder
119	Bump Hadley
115	Wes Ferrell
115	Ted Lyons
112	Ed Brandt
111	Danny MacFayden
107	Earl Whitehill
106	Willis Hudlin

1940–49

123	Dutch Leonard
120	Bobo Newsom
119	Dizzy Trout
118	Hal Newhouser
100	Sid Hudson
92	Johnny Vander Meer
92	Early Wynn
90	Bucky Walters
89	Ken Raffensberger
88	Jim Tobin

1950–59

149	Robin Roberts
131	Warren Spahn
127	Bob Friend
124	Murry Dickson
123	Bob Rush
121	Billy Pierce
119	Early Wynn
117	Ned Garver
113	Chuck Stobbs
100	Alex Kellner

1960–69

133	Jack Fisher
132	Dick Ellsworth
132	Larry Jackson
126	Don Drysdale
121	Claude Osteen
119	Jim Kaat
118	Jim Bunning
111	Don Cardwell
105	Bob Gibson
105	Ken Johnson

1970–79

151	Phil Niekro
146	Nolan Ryan
133	Gaylord Perry
130	Ferguson Jenkins
128	Bert Blyleven
127	Jerry Koosman
126	Steve Carlton
123	Wilbur Wood
117	Mickey Lolich
117	Rick Wise

1980–89

126	Jim Clancy
122	Frank Tanana
119	Jack Morris
118	Bob Knepper
114	Charlie Hough
109	Floyd Bannister
109	Rich Dotson
109	Dave Steib
107	Mike Moore
104	Nolan Ryan

1990–99

116	Andy Benes
115	Tim Belcher
113	Bobby Witt
112	Jaime Navarro
110	Tom Candiotti
108	Scott Erickson
108	Chuck Finley
101	John Burkett
101	Mike Morgan
100	Terry Mulholland

2000–09

124	Livan Hernandez
116	Javier Vasquez
110	Jeff Suppan
106	Jeff Weaver
106	Barry Zito
103	Kevin Millwood
102	Jon Garland
101	Greg Maddux
101	Jarrod Washburn
99	Derek Lowe

continued on next page

2010–19		2020–22	
109	Rick Porcello	42	Patrick Corbin
103	James Shields	30	Jordan Lyles
101	Jeff Samardzija	30	German Marquez
99	Ian Kennedy	30	Mike Minor
98	Mike Leake	29	Madison Bumgarner
95	Felix Hernandez	29	Cole Irvin
94	Edwin Jackson	29	Brad Keller
92	Madison Baumgartner	28	JT Brubaker
92	Jon Lester	28	Luis Castillo
92	Francisco Liriano	27	Aaron Nola

Evolution of Pitchers' Losses Record

American League

1901	Pete Dowling, Mil. Brewers–Cle. Blues	25
1904	Happy Townsend, Was. Senators	25

National League (Pre-1900)

1876	Jim Devlin, Lou. Colonels	35
1879	George Bradley, Tro. Trojans	40
	Jim McCormick, Cle. Spiders	40
1880	Will White, Cin. Reds	42
1883	John Coleman, Phi. Quakers	48

National League (Post-1899)

1900	Bill Carrick, N.Y. Giants	22
1901	Dummy Taylor, N.Y. Giants	27
1905	Vic Willis, Bos. Beaneaters	29

Pitchers with Seven or More Consecutive Losing Seasons

Seasons

10 .... Bill Bailey, St.L. Browns (AL), 1908–12; Bal. (FL), 1913; Bal.–Chi. (FL), 1914; Det. Tigers (AL), 1918; and St.L. Cardinals (NL), 1921–22

10 .... Ron Kline, Pit. Pirates (NL), 1952, 1955–59; St.L. Cardinals (NL), 1960; L.A. Angels–Det. Tigers (AL), 1961; Det. Tigers (AL), 1962; and Was. Senators II (AL), 1963

9 .... Milt Gaston, St.L. Browns (AL), 1926–27; Was. Senators (AL), 1928; Bos. Red Sox (AL), 1929–31; and Chi. White Sox (AL), 1932–34

8 .... Bill Hart, Phi. A's (AA), 1886–87; Brk. Trolley Dodgers (NL), 1892; Pit. Pirates (NL), 1895; St.L. Cardinals (NL), 1896–97; Pit. Pirates (NL), 1898; and Cle. Blues (AL), 1901

8 .... Charlie Robertson, Chi. White Sox (AL), 1919 and 1922–25; St.L. Browns (AL), 1926; and Bos. Braves (NL), 1927–28

8 .... Jamey Wright, Mil. Brewers (NL), 2000–02; St.L. Cardinals (NL), 2002; K.C. Royals (AL), 2003; Col. Rockies(NL), 2004–05; S.F. Giants (NL), 2006; Tex. Rangers (AL), 2007

8 .... Jack Fisher, Bal. Orioles (AL), 1961–62; S.F. Giants (NL), 1963; N.Y. Mets (NL), 1964–67; and Chi. White Sox (AL), 1968

8 .... Ken Raffensberger, Cin. Reds (NL), 1940–41; Phi. Phillies (NL), 1943–46; Phi. Phillies–Cin. Reds (NL), 1947; and Cin. Reds (NL), 1948

8 .... Pete Broberg, Was. Senators II (AL), 1971; Tex. Rangers (AL), 1972–74; Mil. Brewers (NL), 1975–76; Chi. Cubs (NL), 1977; and Oak. A's (AL), 1978

8 .... Socks Seibold, Phi. A's (AL), 1916–17 and 1919; and Bos. Braves (NL), 1929–33

7 .... Bert Cunningham, Brk. Bridegrooms (AA), 1887; Bal. Orioles (AA), 1888–89; Phi. Quakers–Buf. Bisons (PL), 1890; Bal. Orioles (AA), 1891; and Lou. Colonels (NL), 1895–96

7 .... Bill Dietrich, Phi. A's (AL), 1933–35; Phi. A's–Was. Senators–Chi. White Sox (AL), 1936; and Chi. White Sox (AL), 1937–39

7 .... Bob Weiland, Chi. White Sox (AL), 1929–31; Bos. Red Sox (AL), 1932–33; Bos. Red Sox–Cle. Indians (AL), 1934; and St.L. Browns (AL), 1935

7 .... Boom Boom Beck, St.L. Browns (AL), 1928; Brk. Dodgers (NL), 1933–34; and Phi. Phillies (NL), 1939–42

7 .... Buck Ross, Phi. A's (AL), 1936–40; Phi. A's–Chi. White Sox (AL), 1941; and Chi. White Sox (AL), 1942

7 .... Carlton Willey, Mil. Braves (NL), 1959–62; and N.Y. Mets (NL), 1963–65

continued on next page

Seasons

7 ....Dick Littlefield, Det. Tigers–St.L. Browns (AL), 1952; St.L. Browns (AL), 1953; Bal. Orioles (AL)–Pit. Pirates (NL), 1954; Pit. Pirates (NL), 1955; Pit. Pirates–St.L. Cardinals–N.Y. Giants (NL), 1956; Chi. Cubs (NL), 1957; and Mil. Braves (NL), 1958

7 ....Eric Rasmussen, St.L. Cardinals (NL), 1976–77; St.L. Cardinals–S.D. Padres (NL), 1978; S.D. Padres (NL), 1979–80; St.L. Cardinals (NL), 1982; and St.L. Cardinals (NL)–K.C. Royals (AL), 1983

7 ....Herm Wehmeier, Cin. Reds (NL), 1949–53; Cin. Reds–Phi. Phillies (NL), 1954; and Phi. Phillies (NL), 1955

7 ....Howie Judson, Chi. White Sox (AL), 1948–52; and Cin. Reds (NL), 1953–54

7 ....Jack Russell, Bos. Red Sox (AL), 1926–31; and Bos. Red Sox–Cle. Indians (AL), 1932

7 ....Jeff Francis, Col. Rockies (NL), 2008, 2010; K.C. Royals (AL), 2011; Col. Rockies (NL), 2012–13; Cin. Reds (NL)–Oak. A's–N.Y. Yankees (AL), 2014; and Tor. Blue Jays (AL), 2015

7 ....Jesse Jefferson, Bal. Orioles–Chi. White Sox (AL), 1975; Chi. White Sox (AL), 1976; Tor. Blue Jays (AL), 1977–79; Tor. Blue Jays (AL)–Pit. Pirates (NL), 1980; and Cal. Angels (AL), 1981

7 ....Kevin Gregg, L.A. Angels (AL), 2005–06; Fla. Marlins (NL), 2007–08; Chi. Cubs (NL), 2009; Tor. Blue Jays (AL), 2010; and Bal. Orioles (AL), 2011

7 ....Kip Wells, Chi. White Sox , AL, 1999–2001; Pit. Pirates (NL), 2002–05; Pit. Pirates (NL)–Tex Rangers (AL), 2006; St.L. Cardinals (NL), 2007, Col. Rockies(NL)–K.C. Royals (AL), 2008; Was. Nationals–Cin. Reds, 2009; and S.D. Padres, 2012

7 ....Roberto Hernandez, Cle. Indians (AL), 2009–12; T.B. Rays (AL), 2013; Phi. Phillies–L.A. Dodgers (NL), 2014; and Hou. Astros (AL), 2015

7 ....Skip Lockwood, Sea. Pilots (AL), 1969; Mil. Brewers (AL), 1970–73; Cal. Angels (AL), 1974; and N.Y. Mets (NL), 1975

7 ....Tim Redding, Hou. Astros (NL), 2002–04; S.D. Padres(NL)–N.Y. Yankees (AL), 2005; Was. Nationals (NL), 2007–08; and N.Y. Mets (NL), 2009

7 ....Jacob Turner, Det. Tigers (AL), 2011–12; Det Tigers (AL)–Mia. Marlins (NL), 2012; Mia. Marlins (NL) 2013; Mia. Marlins (NL)–Chi. Cubs (NL), 2014; Chi. White Sox (AL), 2016; Was. Nationals (NL), 2017; and Mia. Marlins (NL)–Det. Tigers (AL), 2018

7 ....Trevor Rosenthal, St.L. Cardinals (NL). 2012–17; and Was. Nationals (NL)–Det. Tigers (AL), 2019

Pitchers with 150 Wins with More Losses Than Wins, Career

	Career Record	Winning Percentage
Jack Powell (1897–1912)	245–254	.491
Bobo Newsom (1929–30, 1932, 1934–48, 1952–53)	211–222	.487
Bob Friend (1951–66)	197–230	.461
Jim Whitney (1881–90)	191–204	.484
Tom Zachary (1918–36)	186–191	.493
Chick Fraser (1896–1909)	175–212	.452
Murry Dickson (1939–40, 1942–43, 1946–59)	172–181	.487
Danny Darwin (1978–98)	171–182	.484
Bill Dinneen (1898–1909)	170–177	.490
Pink Hawley (1892–1901)	167–179	.483
Red Donahue (1893, 1895–1906)	164–175	.484
Mike Moore (1982–95)	161–176	.478
Bump Hadley (1926–41)	161–165	.494
Ted Breitenstein (1891–1901)	160–170	.485
Mark Baldwin (1887–93)	154–165	.483
Rudy May (1965–83)	152–156	.494
Tom Candiotti (1983–99)	151–164	.479
Jim Slaton (1971–86)	151–158	.489

Pitchers on Winning Teams, Leading League in Losses, Season

American League

Pitcher	Wins–Losses	Team Wins–Losses
Bill Dinneen, Bos. Americans, 1902	21–21	77–60
Herman Pillette, Det. Tigers, 1923	14–19 (Tie)	83–71
Hal Newhouser, Det. Tigers, 1947	17–17	85–69
Brian Kingman, Oak. A's, 1980	8–20	83–79
Bert Blyleven, Min. Twins, 1988	10–17	91–71
Corey Kluber, Cle. Indians, 2015	9–16	81–80
Rick Porcello, Bos. Red Sox, 2017	11–17	93–69
Cole Irvin, Oak. A's,2021	10–15	86–76
Marco Gonzalez. Sea. Mariners, 2022	10–15	90–72

continued on next page

National League (Post-1900)

Pitcher	Wins–Losses	Team Wins–Losses
Dick Rudolph, Bos. Braves, 1915	22–19 (Tie)	83–69
Dolf Luque, Cin. Reds, 1922	13–23	86–68
Wilbur Cooper, Pit. Pirates, 1923	17–19	87–67
Charlie Root, Chi. Cubs, 1926	18–17 (Tie)	82–72
Rip Sewell, Pit. Pirates, 1941	14–17	81–73
Ron Kline, Pit. Pirates, 1958	13–16	84–70
Bob Friend, Pit. Pirates, 1959	8–19	78–76
Phil Niekro, Atl. Braves, 1980	15–18	81–80
Ken Hill, St.L. Cardinals, 1989	7–15	86–76
Doug Drabek, Hou. Astros, 1993	9–18	85–7
Livan Hernandez, S.F. Giants, 2002	12–16	95–66
Jason Marquis, St.L. Cardinals, 2006	14–16	83–78
Derek Lowe, Atl. Braves, 2011	9–17	89–73
Tim Lincecum, S.F. Giants, 2012	10–15	94–68
Tanner Roark, Was. Nationals, 2018	9–15, 2018	82–80
Merrill Kelly, Ari. D'backs, 2019	13–14	85–77
Luis Castillo, Cin. Reds, 2021	8–16	83–79
Miles Mikolas, St.L. Cardinals, 2021	9–14	91–71

Pitchers Winning 20 Games in Rookie Year, Losing 20 in Second Year

Roscoe Miller, Det. Tigers (AL), 1901 (23–13), 1902 (7–20)   Alex Kellner, Phi. A's (AL), 1949 (20–12), 1950 (8–20)

300-Game Winners with Fewer Than 200 Losses

Differential		Wins	Losses
+185	Christy Mathewson (1900–16)	373	188
+170	Roger Clemens (1984–2007)	354	184
+154	Lefty Grove (1925–41)	300	141
+150	John Clarkson (1882, 1884–94)	328	178
+137	Randy Johnson (1988–2009)	303	166
+132	Eddie Plank (1901–17)	326	194
+115	Old Hoss Radbourn (1880–91)	309	194

Earned Run Average

Best ERA by Decade (Min. 1000 Innings)

Pre-1900		1900–09		1910–19	
1.89	Jim Devlin	1.63	Mordecai Brown	1.59	Walter Johnson
2.10	Monte Ward	1.68	Ed Walsh	1.97	Smoky Joe Wood
2.25	Tommy Bond	1.72	Ed Reulbach	1.98	Ed Walsh
2.28	Will White	1.87	Addie Joss	2.09	Pete Alexander
2.36	Larry Corcoran	1.98	Christy Mathewson	2.15	Carl Mays
2.43	Terry Larkin	2.11	Rube Waddell	2.19	Babe Ruth
2.43	Jim McCormick	2.12	Cy Young	2.20	Jeff Pfeffer
2.50	George Bradley	2.13	Orval Overall	2.22	Dutch Leonard
2.62	Tim Keefe	2.19	Frank Smith	2.25	Eddie Plank
2.67	Charlie Ferguson	2.20	Lefty Leifield	2.28	Fred Toney
		2.20	Doc White		

1920–29		1930–39		1940–49	
3.04	Pete Alexander	2.71	Carl Hubbell	2.67	Spud Chandler
3.09	Lefty Grove	2.91	Lefty Grove	2.68	Max Lanier
3.09	Dolf Luque	2.96	Dizzy Dean	2.74	Harry Brecheen
3.10	Dazzy Vance	3.21	Bill Lee	2.84	Hal Newhouser

continued on next page

1920–29

3.20	Stan Coveleski
3.24	Eppa Rixey
3.24	Tommy Thomas
3.33	Urban Shocker
3.33	Walter Johnson
3.34	Red Faber
3.36	Wilbur Cooper

1930–39

3.23	Lon Warneke
3.24	Lefty Gomez
3.38	Hal Schumacher
3.42	Larry French
3.42	Van Lingle Mungo
3.50	Curt Davis
3.50	Paul Derringer
3.50	Charlie Root

1940–49

2.90	Bob Feller
2.93	Mort Cooper
2.94	Tex Hughson
2.94	Claude Passeau
2.97	Bucky Walters
2.99	Howie Pollet

1950–59

2.66	Whitey Ford
2.79	Hoyt Wilhelm
2.92	Warren Spahn
3.06	Billy Pierce
3.07	Allie Reynolds
3.12	Eddie Lopat
3.14	Bob Buhl
3.18	Johnny Antonelli
3.19	Sal Maglie
3.28	Early Wynn

1960–69

2.16	Hoyt Wilhelm
2.36	Sandy Koufax
2.57	Juan Marichal
2.74	Bob Gibson
2.76	Mike Cuellar
2.77	Dean Chance
2.81	Tommy John
2.83	Don Drysdale
2.83	Whitey Ford
2.83	Joe Horlen
2.83	Bob Veale

1970–79

2.58	Jim Palmer
2.61	Tom Seaver
2.88	Bert Blyleven
2.89	Rollie Fingers
2.92	Gaylord Perry
2.93	Andy Messersmith
2.93	Frank Tanana
2.97	Jon Matlack
2.98	Mike Marshall
3.01	Don Wilson

1980–89

2.64	Dwight Gooden
2.69	Orel Hershiser
3.06	Roger Clemens
3.08	Dave Righetti
3.13	Dave Dravecky
3.13	John Tudor
3.14	Nolan Ryan
3.19	Fernando Valenzuela
3.21	Bob Welch
3.22	Sid Fernandez

1990–99

2.54	Greg Maddux
2.74	Jose Rijo
2.83	Pedro Martinez
3.02	Roger Clemens
3.14	Randy Johnson
3.21	David Cone
3.21	Tom Glavine
3.25	Kevin Brown
3.31	Curt Schilling
3.32	John Smoltz

2000–09

3.01	Pedro Martinez
3.12	Johan Santana
3.23	Roy Oswalt
3.26	Jake Peavy
3.27	Brandon Webb
3.28	John Smoltz
3.34	Roger Clemens
3.34	Randy Johnson
3.40	Roy Halladay
3.50	Tim Hudson

2010–19

2.31	Clayton Kershaw
2.62	Jacob deGrom
3.03	Chris Sale
3.06	Johnny Cueto
3.10	Juston Verlander
3.12	Max Scherzer
3.14	Madison Bumgarner
3.16	Corey Kluber
3.17	Stephen Strasburg
3.18	Zach Greinke

2020–22

2.62	Max Scherzer
2.62	Corbin Burnes
2.66	Julio Urias
2.68	Max Fried
2.74	Sandy Alcantara
2.82	Zack Wheeler
2.84	Brandon Woodruff
3.05	Framber Valdez
3.13	Chris Bassitt
3.13	Joe Musgrove

Teammates Finishing One-Two in ERA, Season

American League

Season	Team	Leader	ERA	Runner-Up	ERA
1914	Bos. Red Sox	Dutch Leonard	1.01	Rube Foster	1.65
1924	Was. Senators	Walter Johnson	2.72	Tom Zachary	2.75
1927	N.Y. Yankees	Wilcy Moore	2.28	Waite Hoyt	2.63
1933	Cle. Indians	Monte Pearson	2.33	Mel Harder	2.95
1943	N.Y. Yankees	Spud Chandler	1.64	Tiny Bonham	2.27
1944	Det. Tigers	Dizzy Trout	2.12	Hal Newhouser	2.22
1945	Det. Tigers	Hal Newhouser	1.81	Al Benton	2.02
1948	Cle. Indians	Gene Bearden	2.43	Bob Lemon	2.82 (Tie)
1957	N.Y. Yankees	Bobby Shantz	2.45	Tom Sturdivant	2.54
1963	Chi. White Sox	Gary Peters	2.33	Juan Pizarro	2.39
1966	Chi. White Sox	Gary Peters	1.98	Joe Horlen	2.43

continued on next page

Season	Team	Leader	ERA	Runner-Up	ERA
1967	Chi. White Sox	Joe Horlen	2.06	Gary Peters	2.28
1968	Cle. Indians	Luis Tiant	1.60	Sam McDowell	1.81
1979	N.Y. Yankees	Ron Guidry	2.78	Tommy John	2.97
1996	Tor. Blue Jays	Juan Guzman	2.93	Pat Hentgen	3.22
2002	Bos. Red Sox	Pedro Martinez	2.26	Derek Lowe	2.58

National League

Season	Team	Leader	ERA	Runner-Up	ERA
1901	Pit. Pirates	Jesse Tannehill	2.18	Deacon Phillippe	2.22
1906	Chi. Cubs	Mordecai Brown	1.04	Jack Pfiester	1.56
1907	Chi. Cubs	Jack Pfiester	1.15	Carl Lundgren	1.17
1912	N.Y. Giants	Jeff Tesreau	1.96	Christy Mathewson	2.12
1918	Chi. Cubs	Hippo Vaughn	1.74	Lefty Tyler	2.00
1919	Chi. Cubs	Pete Alexander	1.72	Hippo Vaughn	1.79
1923	Cin. Reds	Dolf Luque	1.93	Eppa Rixey	2.80
1925	Cin. Reds	Dolf Luque	2.63	Eppa Rixey	2.88
1931	N.Y. Giants	Bill Walker	2.26	Carl Hubbell	2.66
1935	Pit. Pirates	Cy Blanton	2.58	Bill Swift	2.70
1942	St.L. Cardinals	Mort Cooper	1.78	Johnny Beazley	2.13
1943	St.L. Cardinals	Howie Pollet	1.75	Max Lanier	1.90
1944	Cin. Reds	Ed Heusser	2.38	Bucky Walters	2.40
1945	Chi. Cubs	Hank Borowy*	2.13	Ray Prim	2.40
1956	Mil. Braves	Lew Burdette	2.70	Warren Spahn	2.78
1957	Brk. Dodgers	Johnny Podres	2.66	Don Drysdale	2.69
1959	S.F. Giants	Sam Jones	2.83	Stu Miller	2.84
1964	L.A. Dodgers	Sandy Koufax	1.74	Don Drysdale	2.18
1974	Atl. Braves	Buzz Capra	2.28	Phil Niekro	2.38
1981	Hou. Astros	Nolan Ryan	1.69	Bob Knepper	2.18
2001	Ari. D'backs	Randy Johnson	2.49	Curt Schilling	2.98
2005	Hou. Astros	Roger Clemens	1.87	Andy Pettitte	2.39
2016	Chi. Cubs	Kyle Hendricks	2.13	Jon Lester	2.44

* Also with N.Y. Yankees (3.13 ERA).

Pitchers with 3000 Innings Pitched and an ERA Lower Than 3.00 (Post-1900)

	Innings	ERA
Mordecai Brown (1903–16)	3172	2.06
Christy Mathewson (1901–16)	4755	2.11
Cy Young (1901–11)	3312	2.12
Walter Johnson (1907–27)	5914	2.17
Eddie Plank (1905–17)	4496	2.35
Eddie Cicotte (1905–20)	3226	2.38
Doc White (1901–13)	3041	2.39
Chief Bender (1903–25)	3017	2.46
Vic Willis (1901–10)	3106	2.50
Pete Alexander (1911–30)	5190	2.56
Red Ames (1905–19)	3069	2.65
Whitey Ford (1950, 1953–67)	3170	2.75
Jack Powell (1901–12)	3161	2.75
George Mullin (1902–13)	3687	2.82
Jim Palmer (1965–84)	3948	2.86
Tom Seaver (1967–86)	4782	2.86
Juan Marichal (1960–75)	3507	2.89
Stanley Coveleski (1912, 1916–28)	3082	2.89
Wilbur Cooper (1912–26)	3480	2.89
Bob Gibson (1959–75)	3884	2.91

continued on next page

	Innings	ERA
Carl Mays (1915–29)	3020	2.92
Don Drysdale (1956–69)	3432	2.95
Carl Hubbell (1928–43)	3589	2.97

Pitchers Leading League in ERA After Their 40th Birthday

	Age	ERA
Ted Lyons, Chi. White Sox (AL), 1942	42	2.10
Spud Chandler, N.Y. Yankees (AL), 1947	40	2.46
Nolan Ryan, Hou. Astros (NL), 1987	40	2.76

ERA Under 2.00, Season (Since 1920, Min. 162 Innings)

American League

1.60	Luis Tiant, Cle. Indians, 1968
1.63	Shane Bieber, Cle. Indians, 2020**
1.64	Spud Chandler, N.Y. Yankees, 1943
1.65	Dean Chance, L.A. Angels, 1964
1.74	Ron Guidry, N.Y. Yankees, 1978
1.74	Pedro Martinez, Bos. Red Sox, 2000
1.81	Sam McDowell, Cle. Indians, 1968
1.81	Hal Newhouser, Det. Tigers, 1945
1.82	Vida Blue, Oak. A's, 1971
1.88	Joe Horlen, Chi. White Sox, 1964
1.89	Blake Snell, T.B. Rays, 2018
1.91	Luis Tiant, Bos. Red Sox, 1972
1.91	Wilbur Wood, Chi. White Sox, 1971
1.92	Gaylord Perry, Cle. Indians, 1972
1.93	Roger Clemens, Bos. Red Sox, 1990
1.94	Hal Newhouser, Det. Tigers, 1946
1.95	Dave McNally, Bal. Orioles, 1968
1.96	Denny McLain, Det. Tigers, 1968
1.97	Billy Pierce, Chi. White Sox, 1955
1.98	Tommy John, Chi. White Sox, 1968
1.98	Gary Peters, Chi. White Sox, 1966
1.99	Dallas Keuchel, Chi. White Sox, 2020**

* Strike-shortened season.

** COVID-shortened season.

National League

1.12	Bob Gibson, St.L. Cardinals, 1968
1.53	Dwight Gooden, N.Y. Mets, 1986
1.56	Greg Maddux, Atl. Braves, 1994
1.63	Greg Maddux, Atl. Braves, 1995
1.66	Carl Hubbell, N.Y. Giants, 1933
1.66	Zack Greinke, L.A. Dodgers, 2015
1.69	Nolan Ryan, Hou. Astros, 1981*
1.70	Jacob deGrom, N.Y. Mets, 2018
1.73	Sandy Koufax, L.A. Dodgers, 1966
1.73	Trevor Bauer, Cin. Reds, 2020**
1.74	Sandy Koufax, L.A. Dodgers, 1964
1.76	Tom Seaver, N.Y. Mets, 1971
1.77	Clayton Kershaw, L.A. Dodgers, 2014
1.77	Jake Arietta, Chi. Cubs, 2015
1.78	Mort Cooper, St.L. Cardinals, 1942
1.83	Clayton Kershaw, L.A. Dodgers, 2013
1.87	Roger Clemens, Hou. Astros, 2005
1.87	Phil Niekro, Atl. Braves, 1967
1.88	Sandy Koufax, L.A. Dodgers, 1963
1.89	Kevin Brown, Fla. Marlins, 1996
1.90	Pedro Martinez, Mon. Expos, 1997
1.90	Max Lanier, St.L. Cardinals, 1943
1.91	Pete Alexander, Chi. Cubs, 1920
1.93	John Tudor, St.L. Cardinals, 1985
1.93	Dolph Luque, Cin. Reds, 1923
1.97	Steve Carlton, Phi. Phillies, 1972
1.99	Gary Nolan, Cin. Reds, 1972
1.99	Bobby Bolin, S.F. Giants, 1968

Pitchers with Losing Record, Leading League in ERA

American League

	ERA	Wins–Losses
Ed Siever, Det. Tigers, 1902	1.91	8–11
Ed Walsh, Chi. White Sox, 1910	1.27	18–20
Stan Coveleski, Cle. Indians, 1923	2.76	13–14
Kevin Millwood, Cle. Indians, 2005	2.86	9–11

National League (Post-1900)

	ERA	Wins–Losses
Rube Waddell, Pit. Pirates, 1900	2.37	8–13
Dolf Luque, Cin. Reds, 1925	2.63	16–18
Dave Koslo, N.Y. Giants, 1949	2.50	11–14
Stu Miller, S.F. Giants, 1958	2.47	6–9

continued on next page

	ERA	Wins–Losses
Nolan Ryan, Hou. Astros, 1987	2.76	8–16
Joe Magrane, St.L. Cardinals, 1988	2.18	5–9

20-Game Winners with 4.00 ERA, Season

American League

	ERA	Wins–Losses
Bobo Newsom, St.L. Browns, 1938	5.08	20–16
Vern Kennedy, Chi. White Sox, 1936	4.63	21–9
George Earnshaw, Phi. A's, 1930	4.44	22–13
Rick Helling, Tex. Rangers, 1998	4.41	20–7
Lefty Gomez, N.Y. Yankees, 1932	4.21	24–7
Wes Ferrell, Bos. Red Sox, 1936	4.19	20–15
Tim Hudson, Oak. A's, 2000	4.14	20–6
David Wells, Tor. Blue Jays, 2000	4.11	20–8
Monte Weaver, Was. Senators, 1932	4.08	22–10
George Uhle, Cle. Indians, 1922	4.07	22–16
Billy Hoeft, Det. Tigers, 1956	4.06	20–14
Jack Morris, Tor. Blue Jays, 1992	4.04	21–6
Andy Pettitte, N.Y. Yankees, 2003	4.02	21–8
Vic Raschi, N.Y. Yankees, 1950	4.00	21–8

National League (Post-1899)

	ERA	Wins–Losses
Ray Kremer, Pit. Pirates, 1930	5.02	20–12
Jim Merritt, Cin. Reds, 1970	4.08	20–12
Lew Burdette, Mil. Braves, 1959	4.07	21–15
Murry Dickson, Pit. Pirates, 1951	4.02	20–16

20-Game Losers with ERA Below 2.00

American League

	ERA	Wins–Losses
Ed Walsh, Chi. White Sox, 1910	1.27	18–20
Walter Johnson, Was. Senators, 1916	1.90	25–20
Jim Scott, Chi. White Sox, 1913	1.90	20–20
Harry Howell, St.L. Browns, 1905	1.98	15–22

National League

	ERA	Wins–Losses
Kaiser Wilhelm, Brk. Dodgers, 1908	1.87	16–22

ERA Leaders with Fewer Than 10 Wins

American League

Wins		ERA
6	Steve Ontiveros, Oak. A's, 1994*	2.65
8	Ed Siever, Det. Tigers, 1902	1.91
8	Shane Bieber, Cle. Indians, 2020**	
9	Kevin Millwood, Cle. Indians, 2005	2.86

National League

Wins		ERA
5	Joe Magrane, St.L. Cardinals, 1988	2.18
5	Trevor Bauer, Cin. Reds, 2020**	
6	Stu Miller, S.F. Giants, 1958	2.47
8	Rube Waddell, Pit. Pirates, 1900	2.37
	Fred Anderson, N.Y. Giants, 1917	1.44
	Nolan Ryan, Hou. Astros, 1987	2.76
9	Craig Swan, N.Y. Mets, 1978	2.43

* Strike-shortened season.
** COVID-shortened season.

Pitchers with Lowest ERA in Both Leagues

Roger Clemens	1986 Bos. Red Sox (AL)	2.48
	1990 Bos. Red Sox (AL)	1.93
	1991 Bos. Red Sox (AL)	2.62
	1992 Bos. Red Sox (AL)	2.41
	1997 Tor. Blue Jays (AL)	2.05
	1998 Tor. Blue Jays (AL)	2.65
	2005 Hou. Astros (NL)	1.87
Zack Greinke	2009 K.C. Royals (AL)	2.16
	2015 L.A. Dodgers (NL)	1.66
Randy Johnson	1995 Sea. Mariners (AL)	2.48
	1999 Ari. D'backs (NL)	2.49
	2001 Ari. D'backs (NL)	2.49
	2002 Ari. D'backs (NL)	2.32
Pedro Martinez	1997 Mon. Expos (NL)	1.90
	1999 Bos. Red Sox (AL)	2.07
	2000 Bos. Red Sox (AL)	1.74
	2002 Bos. Red Sox (AL)	2.26
	2003 Bos. Red Sox (AL)	2.22
Johan Santana	2004 Min. Twins (AL)	2.61
	2006 Min. Twins (AL)	2.77
	2008 N.Y. Mets (NL)	2.53
Rube Waddell	1900 Pit. Pirates (NL)	2.37
	1905 Phi. A's (AL)	1.48
Hoyt Wilhelm	1952 N.Y. Giants (NL)	2.43
	1959 Bal. Orioles (AL)	2.19
Cy Young	1892 Cle. Spiders (NL)	1.93
	1901 Bos. Red Sox (AL)	1.62

ERA Leaders with 25 or More Wins, Season

American League

	ERA	Wins
Cy Young, Bos. Americans, 1901	1.62	33
Rube Waddell, Phi. A's, 1905	1.48	26
Walter Johnson, Was. Senators, 1912	1.39	32
Walter Johnson, Was. Senators, 1913	1.14	36
Eddie Cicotte, Chi. White Sox, 1917	1.53	28
Red Faber, Chi. White Sox, 1921	2.48	25
Lefty Grove, Phi. A's, 1930	2.54	28
Lefty Grove, Phi. A's, 1931	2.06	31
Lefty Grove, Phi. A's, 1932	2.84	25
Lefty Gomez, N.Y. Yankees, 1934	2.33	26
Bob Feller, Cle. Indians, 1940	2.61	27
Dizzy Trout, Det. Tigers, 1944	2.12	27
Hal Newhouser, Det. Tigers, 1945	1.81	25
Hal Newhouser, Det. Tigers, 1946	1.94	26
Mel Parnell, Bos. Red Sox, 1949	2.77	25
Catfish Hunter, Oak. A's, 1974	2.49	25
Ron Guidry, N.Y. Yankees, 1978	1.74	25

National League (Post-1900)

	ERA	Wins
Sam Leever, Pit. Pirates, 1903	2.06	25
Joe McGinnity, N.Y. Giants, 1904	1.61	35
Christy Mathewson, N.Y. Giants, 1905	1.28	31
Mordecai Brown, Chi. Cubs, 1906	1.04	26
Christy Mathewson, N.Y. Giants, 1908	1.43	37

continued on next page

	ERA	Wins
Christy Mathewson, N.Y. Giants, 1909	1.14	25
Christy Mathewson, N.Y. Giants, 1911	1.99	26
Christy Mathewson, N.Y. Giants, 1913	2.06	25
Pete Alexander, Phi. Phillies, 1915	1.22	31
Pete Alexander, Phi. Phillies, 1916	1.55	33
Pete Alexander, Chi. Cubs, 1920	1.91	27
Dolf Luque, Cin. Reds, 1923	1.93	27
Dazzy Vance, Brk. Dodgers, 1924	2.16	28
Carl Hubbell, N.Y. Giants, 1936	2.31	26
Bucky Walters, Cin. Reds, 1939	2.29	27
Sandy Koufax, L.A. Dodgers, 1963	1.88	25
Sandy Koufax, L.A. Dodgers, 1965	2.04	26
Sandy Koufax, L.A. Dodgers, 1966	1.73	27
Steve Carlton, Phi. Phillies, 1972	1.97	27

ERAs of 300-Game Winners

	ERA	Wins
Christy Mathewson (1900–16)	2.13	373
Walter Johnson (1907–27)	2.17	417
Eddie Plank (1901–17)	2.35	326
Pete Alexander (1911–30)	2.56	373
Cy Young (1890–1911)	2.63	511
Tim Keefe (1880–93)	2.63	342
Old Hoss Radbourn (1880–91)	2.68	309
Mickey Welch (1880–92)	2.71	307
John Clarkson (1882, 1884–94)	2.81	328
Tom Seaver (1967–86)	2.86	311
Pud Galvin (1879–92)	2.87	365
Kid Nichols (1890–1901, 1904–06)	2.96	361
Lefty Grove (1925–41)	3.06	300
Warren Spahn (1942, 1946–65)	3.09	363
Gaylord Perry (1962–83)	3.11	314
Roger Clemens (1984–2007)	3.12	354
Greg Maddux (1986–2008)	3.16	355
Nolan Ryan (1966, 1968–93)	3.19	324
Steve Carlton (1965–88)	3.22	329
Don Sutton (1966–88)	3.26	324
Randy Johnson (1988–2009)	3.29	303
Phil Niekro (1967–87)	3.35	318
Tom Glavine (1987–2008)	3.54	305
Early Wynn (1939, 1941–44, 1946–63)	3.54	300

Strikeouts

Evolution of Strikeout Record

American League

1901	Cy Young, Bos. Americans	158
1902	Rube Waddell, Phi. A's	210
1903	Rube Waddell, Phi. A's	302
1904	Rube Waddell, Phi. A's	349
1973	Nolan Ryan, Cal. Angels	383

continued on next page

National League (Pre-1900)

1876...................Jim Devlin, Lou. Grays...122
1877...................Tommy Bond, Bos. Red Caps...170
1878...................Tommy Bond, Bos. Red Caps...182
1879...................Monte Ward, Pro. Grays..239
1880...................Larry Corcoran, Chi. White Stockings 268
1883...................Jim Whitney, Bos. Red Caps..345
1884...................Old Hoss Radbourn, Pro. Grays 441

National League (Post-1899)

1900...................Noodles Hahn, Cin. Reds..132
1901...................Noodles Hahn, Cin. Reds..239
1903...................Christy Mathewson, N.Y. Giants 267
1961...................Sandy Koufax, L.A. Dodgers 269
1963...................Sandy Koufax, L.A. Dodgers 306
1965...................Sandy Koufax, L.A. Dodgers 382

Most Strikeouts by Decade

Pre-1900		1900–09		1910–19	
2564	Tim Keefe	2251	Rube Waddell	2219	Walter Johnson
1978	John Clarkson	1799	Christy Mathewson	1539	Pete Alexander
1944	Amos Rusie	1565	Cy Young	1253	Hippo Vaughn
1850	Mickey Welch	1342	Eddie Plank	1141	Rube Marquard
1830	Old Hoss Radbourn	1304	Vic Willis	1104	Eddie Cicotte
1803	Tony Mullane	1293	Wild Bill Donovan	1028	Bob Groom
1799	Pud Galvin	1237	Jack Chesbro	1020	Claude Hendrix
1704	Jim McCormick	1209	Jack Powell	938	Lefty Tyler
1700	Charlie Buffinton	1115	Long Tom Hughes	926	Larry Cheney
1650	Gus Weyhing	1105	Doc White	913	Willie Mitchell

1920–29		1930–39		1940–49	
1464	Dazzy Vance	1337	Lefty Gomez	1579	Hal Newhouser
1018	Burleigh Grimes	1313	Lefty Grove	1396	Bob Feller
904	Dolf Luque	1281	Carl Hubbell	1070	Bobo Newsom
895	Walter Johnson	1260	Red Ruffing	972	Johnny Vander Meer
837	Lefty Grove	1207	Tommy Bridges	930	Dizzy Trout
824	Howard Ehmke	1144	Dizzy Dean	853	Kirby Higbe
808	George Uhle	1022	Van Lingle Mungo	791	Allie Reynolds
804	Red Faber	1018	Paul Derringer	779	Dutch Leonard
788	Bob Shawkey	1006	Bump Hadley	772	Mort Cooper
753	Urban Shocker	963	Bobo Newsom	760	Virgil Trucks

1950–59		1960–69		1970–79	
1544	Early Wynn	2071	Bob Gibson	2678	Nolan Ryan
1516	Robin Roberts	2019	Jim Bunning	2304	Tom Seaver
1487	Billy Pierce	1910	Don Drysdale	2097	Steve Carlton
1464	Warren Spahn	1910	Sandy Koufax	2082	Bert Blyleven
1093	Harvey Haddix	1840	Juan Marichal	1907	Gaylord Perry
1072	Bob Rush	1663	Sam McDowell	1866	Phil Niekro
1026	Johnny Antonelli	1585	Jim Maloney	1841	Ferguson Jenkins
1000	Mike Garcia	1435	Jim Kaat	1767	Don Sutton
994	Sam Jones	1428	Bob Veale	1600	Vida Blue
983	Bob Turley	1391	Camilo Pascual	1587	Jerry Koosman

1980–89		1990–99		2000–09	
2167	Nolan Ryan	2538	Randy Johnson	2182	Randy Johnson
1644	Fernando Valenzuela	2101	Roger Clemens	2001	Javier Vazquez
1629	Jack Morris	1928	David Cone	1733	Johan Santana
1480	Bert Blyleven	1893	John Smoltz	1620	Pedro Martinez
1457	Bob Welch	1784	Chuck Finley	1590	CC Sabathia
1453	Steve Carlton	1764	Greg Maddux	1545	Curt Schilling
1380	Dave Stieb	1655	Andy Benes	1501	Barry Zito

continued on next page

1980–89	
1363	Charlie Hough
1360	Mario Soto
1356	Floyd Bannister

1990–99	
1581	Kevin Brown
1561	Curt Schilling
1534	Pedro Martinez

2000–09	
1488	Mike Mussina
1473	Roy Oswalt
1441	Andy Pettitte

2010–19	
2452	Max Scherzer
2260	Justin Verlander
2179	Clayton Kershaw
2007	Chris Sale
1872	Zach Greinke
1872	Cole Hamels
1868	Jon Lester
1867	David Price
1784	Madison Bumgarner
1714	Felix Hernandez

2020–22	
594	Gerrit Cole
565	Corbin Burnes
554	Aaron Nola
528	Robbie Ray
511	Kevin Gausman
501	Max Scherzer
497	Dylan Cease
492	Brandon Woodruff
489	Yu Darvish
475	Lucas Giolito

Members of Same Pitching Staff Finishing One-Two in Strikeouts, Season

American League

Season	Team	Leader	Strikeouts	Runner-Up	Strikeouts
1905	Phi. A's	Rube Waddell	287	Eddie Plank	210
1918	Was. Senators	Walter Johnson	162	Jim Shaw	129
1919	Was. Senators	Walter Johnson	147	Jim Shaw	128
1927	Phi. A's	Lefty Grove	174	Rube Walberg	136
1929	Phi. A's	Lefty Grove	170	George Earnshaw	149
1930	Phi. A's	Lefty Grove	209	George Earnshaw	193
1931	Phi. A's	Lefty Grove	175	George Earnshaw	152
1935	Det. Tigers	Tommy Bridges	163	Schoolboy Rowe	140
1944	Det. Tigers	Hal Newhouser	187	Dizzy Trout	144
1948	Cle. Indians	Bob Feller	164	Bob Lemon	147
1949	Det. Tigers	Virgil Trucks	153	Hal Newhouser	144
1953	Chi. White Sox	Billy Pierce	186	Virgil Trucks	149*
1976	Cal. Angels	Nolan Ryan	327	Frank Tanana	261
1990	Tex. Rangers	Nolan Ryan	232	Bobby Witt	221
2012	Det. Tigers	Justin Verlander	239	Max Scherzer	231
2018	Hou. Astros	Justin Verlander	290	Gerrit Cole	276
2019	Hou. Astros	Gerrit Cole	326	Justin Verlander	300

National League (Post-1900)

Season	Team	Leader	Strikeouts	Runner-Up	Strikeouts
1903	N.Y. Giants	Christy Mathewson	267	Joe McGinnity	171
1905	N.Y. Giants	Christy Mathewson	206	Red Ames	198
1920	Chi. Cubs	Pete Alexander	173	Hippo Vaughn	131 (Tie)
1924	Brk. Dodgers	Dazzy Vance	262	Burleigh Grimes	135
1960	L.A. Dodgers	Don Drysdale	246	Sandy Koufax	197
1961	L.A. Dodgers	Sandy Koufax	269	Stan Williams	205
1962	L.A. Dodgers	Don Drysdale	232	Sandy Koufax	216
1987	Hou. Astros	Nolan Ryan	270	Mike Scott	233
1990	N.Y. Mets	David Cone	233	Dwight Gooden	223
2001	Ari. D'backs	Randy Johnson	372	Curt Schilling	293
2002	Ari. D'backs	Randy Johnson	334	Curt Schilling	316
2003	Chi. Cubs	Kerry Wood	266	Mark Prior	245

* Trucks also pitched 16 games with St.L. Browns, striking out 47; 102 strikeouts with Chi. White Sox.

Pitchers Leading League with 100 More Strikeouts Than Runner-Up

American League

Season	Leader	Strikeouts	Runner-Up	Strikeouts
1903	Rube Waddell, Phi. A's	302	Wild Bill Donovan, Det. Tigers	187
1904	Rube Waddell, Phi. A's	349	Jack Chesbro, N.Y. Highlanders	239
1973	Nolan Ryan, Cal. Angels	383	Bert Blyleven, Min. Twins	258
1974	Nolan Ryan, Cal. Angels	367	Bert Blyleven, Min. Twins	249
1993	Randy Johnson, Sea. Mariners	308	Mark Langston, Cal. Angels	196
1999	Pedro Martinez, Bos. Red Sox	313	Chuck Finley, Ana. Angels	200

National League (Post-1900)

Season	Leader	Strikeouts	Runner-Up	Strikeouts
1924	Dazzy Vance, Brk. Dodgers	262	Burleigh Grimes, Brk. Dodgers	135
1965	Sandy Koufax, L.A. Dodgers	382	Bob Veale, Pit. Pirates	276
1979	J.R. Richard, Hou. Astros	313	Steve Carlton, Phi. Phillies	213
1999	Randy Johnson, Ari. D'backs	364	Kevin Brown, L.A. Dodgers	221
2000	Randy Johnson, Ari. D'backs	347	Chan Ho Park, L.A. Dodgers	217

Pitchers with 3000 Strikeouts, Never Leading League

Don Sutton (1966–88) 3574
Gaylord Perry (1962–83) 3534
Greg Maddux (1986–2008) 3371

Pitchers Striking Out 1000 Batters Before Their 24th Birthday

	Number of Strikeouts on 24th Birthday	Date of Birth
Bob Feller (1936–41)	1233	Nov. 3, 1918
Bert Blyleven (1970–74)	1094	Apr. 6, 1951
Dwight Gooden (1984–88)	1067	Nov. 16, 1964

Most Times Striking Out 10 or More Batters in a Game, Season

23 .... Nolan Ryan, Cal. Angels (AL), 1973
23 .... Randy Johnson, Ari. D'backs (NL), 1999
23 .... Randy Johnson, Ari. D'backs (NL), 2000
23 .... Randy Johnson, Ari. D'backs (NL), 23
21 .... Sandy Koufax, L.A. Dodgers (NL), 1965
21 .... Gerrit Cole, Hou. Astros (AL), 2019
20 .... Nolan Ryan, Cal. Angels (AL), 1977
20 .... Randy Johnson, Sea. Mariners (AL)–Hou. Astros (NL), 1998
19 .... Pedro Martinez, Bos. Red Sox (AL), 1999
18 .... Nolan Ryan, Tex. Rangers (AL), 1989
18 .... Pedro Martinez, Bos. Red Sox (AL), 1997
18 .... Chris Sale, Bos. Red Sox (AL), 2017
18 .... Max Scherzer, Was. Nationals (NL), 2018

Most Times Striking Out 10 or More Batters in a Game, Career

215.....Nolan Ryan	97 ......Sandy Koufax	74 ......Sam McDowell
212.....Randy Johnson	93 ......Curt Schilling	74 ......Bob Gibson
110.....Roger Clemens	84 ......Steve Carlton	72 ......Justin Verlander
110.....Max Scherzer	82 ...... Max Scherzer	70 ......Tom Seaver
108.....Pedro Martinez	78 ......Chris Sale	70 ......Rube Waddell

Pitchers Averaging 10 Strikeouts per Nine Innings, Season (Min. 165 Innings)

American League

	Average	Strikeouts	Innings
Gerrit Cole, Hou. Astros, 2019	13.82	326	212
Pedro Martinez, Bos. Red Sox, 1999	13.20	313	213
Chris Sale, Bos. Red Sox, 2017	12.93	308	214
Gerrit Cole, Hou. Astros, 2018	12.40	276	200
Dylan Cease, Chi. White Sox, 2021	12.28	226	166
Randy Johnson, Sea. Mariners, 1995	12.35	294	214
Randy Johnson, Sea. Mariners, 1997	12.30	291	213
Justin Verlander, Hou. Astros, 2018	12.20	290	214
Justin Verlander, Hou. Astros, 2019	12.11	300	223
Gerrit Cole, N.Y. Yankees, 2021	12.06	243	181
Yu Darvish, Tex. Rangers, 2013	11.89	277	210
Shohei Ohtani, L.A. Angels, 2022	11.87	219	166
Chris Sale, Chi. White Sox, 2015	11.82	274	209
Pedro Martinez, Bos. Red Sox, 2000	11.78	284	217
Corey Kluber, Cle. Indians, 2017	11.71	265	203
Lucas Giolito, Chi. White Sox, 2019	11.62	228	177
Matthew Boyd, Det. Tigers, 2019	11.56	238	185
Robbie Ray, Tor. Blue Jays, 2021	11.54	248	193
Gerrit Cole, N.Y. Yankees, 2022	11.53	257	201
Trevor Bauer, Cle. Indians, 2018	11.34	221	175
Nolan Ryan, Tex. Rangers, 1989	11.32	301	239
Chris Archer, T.B. Rays, 2017	11.15	249	201
Charlie Morton, T.B. Rays, 2019	11.10	240	195
Dylan Cease, Chi. White Sox, 2022	11.10	227	184
Max Scherzer, Det. Tigers, 2012	11.08	240	214
Blake Snell, T.B. Rays, 2018	11.01	221	180
Shane Bieber, Cle. Indians, 2019	10.88	259	214

National League

	Average	Strikeouts	Innings
Randy Johnson, Ari. D'backs, 2001	13.41	372	249
Max Scherzer, Was. Nationals, 2019	12.69	243	172
Corbin Burnes, Mil. Brewers, 2021	12.61	234	167
Kerry Wood, Chi. Cubs, 1998	12.58	233	166
Randy Johnson, Ari. D'backs, 2000	12.56	347	248
Jose Fernandex, Mia. Marlins, 2016	12.49	253	182
Max Scherzer, Was. Nationals, 2018	12.24	300	220
Robbie Ray, Ari. D'backs, 2019	12.13	235	174
Randy Johnson, Ari. D'backs, 1999	12.06	364	271
Max Scherzer, Was. Nationals, 2017	12.02	268	200
Carlos Rodon, S.F. Giants, 2022	11.98	237	178
Max Scherzer, Was. Nationals-L.A. Dodgers, 2021	11.84	236	179
Clayton Kershaw, L.A. Dodgers, 2015	11.64	301	233
Randy Johnson, Ari. D'backs, 2002	11.56	334	260
Yu Darvish, Chi. Cubs, 2019	11.54	229	179
Nolan Ryan, Hou. Astros, 1987	11.48	270	211
Dwight Gooden, N.Y. Mets, 1984	11.39	276	218
Pedro Martinez, Mon. Expos, 1997	11.37	305	241
Kerry Wood, Chi. Cubs, 2003	11.35	266	211
Curt Schilling, Phi. Phillies, 1997	11.29	319	254
Robbie Ray, Ari. D'backs, 2016	11.25	218	174
Jacob deGrom, N.Y. Mets, 2019	11.25	255	204
Kerry Wood, Chi. Cubs, 2001	11.20	217	174
Max Scherzer, Was. Nationals, 2016	11.19	284	228
Jacob deGrom, N.Y. Mets, 2018	11.16	269	217
Aaron Nola, Phi. Phillies, 2021	11.11	223	181
Hideo Nomo, L.A. Dodgers, 1995	11.10	236	191
Patrick Corbin, Ari. D'backs, 2018	11.07	246	200

Pitchers with Combined Total of 500 Strikeouts and Walks, Season

American League

	Strikeouts	Walks	Total
Bob Feller, Cle. Indians, 1946	348	153	501
Nolan Ryan, Cal. Angels, 1973	383	162	545
Nolan Ryan, Cal. Angels, 1974	367	202	569
	Strikeouts	Walks	Total
Nolan Ryan, Cal. Angels, 1976	327	183	510
Nolan Ryan, Cal. Angels, 1977	341	204	545

National League

[None]

Pitchers Striking Out the Side on Nine Pitches

American League

Rube Waddell, Phi. A's, Jul. 1, 1902 (3rd inning)
Sloppy Thurston, Chi. White Sox, Aug. 22, 1923 (12th inning)
Lefty Grove, Phi. A's, Aug. 23, 1928 (2nd inning)
Lefty Grove, Phi. A's, Sep. 27, 1928 (7th inning)
Billy Hoeft, Det. Tigers, Sep. 7, 1953 (7th inning, 2nd game)
Jim Bunning, Det. Tigers, Aug. 2, 1959 (9th inning)
Al Downing, N.Y. Yankees, Aug. 11, 1967 (2nd inning, 1st game)
Nolan Ryan, Cal. Angels, Jul. 9, 1972 (2nd inning)
Ron Guidry, N.Y. Yankees, Aug. 7, 1984 (9th inning, 2nd game)
Jeff Montgomery, K.C. Royals, Apr. 29, 1990 (8th inning)
Stan Belinda, K.C. Royals, Aug. 6, 1994 (9th inning)
Roger Clemens, Tor. Blue Jays. Sep. 18, 1997 (1st inning)
Doug Jones, Mil. Brewers, Sep. 23, 1997 (9th inning)
Jimmy Key, Bal. Orioles, Apr. 14, 1998 (4th inning)
Mike Mussina, Bal. Orioles, May 9, 1998 (9th inning)
B.J. Ryan, Bal. Orioles, Sep. 5, 1999 (6th inning)
Pedro Martinez, Bos. Red Sox, May 18, 2002 (1st inning)
Rich Harden, Oak. A's, Jun. 8, 2008 (1st inning)
Felix Hernandez, Sea. Mariners, Jun. 17, 2008 (4th inning)
A. J. Burnett, N. Y. Yankees, Jun. 20, 2009 (3rd inning)
Rafael Soriano, T. B Rays, Aug. 23, 2010 (9th inning)
Clay Buchholz, Bos. Red Sox, Aug. 16, 2012 (6th inning)
Ivan Nova, N.Y. Yankees, May 29, 2013 (8th inning)
Steve Delabar, Tor. Blue Jays, Jul. 30, 2013 (8th inning)
Brad Boxberger, T.B. Rays, May 8, 2014 (6th inning)
Justin Masterson, Cle. Indians, Jun. 2, 2014 (4th inning)
Garrett Richards, L.A. Angels, Jun. 4, 2014 (2nd inning)
Brandon McCarthy, N.Y. Yankees, Sep. 17, 2014 (7th inning)
Craig Kimbrel, Bos. Red Sox, May 11, 2017 (9th inning)
Carlos Carrasco, Cle. Indians, Jul. 7, 2017 (5th inning)
Dellin Betances, N.Y. Yankees, Aug. 2, 2017 (8th inning)
Jose Alvarado, T.B. Rays, Aug. 4, 2017 (9th inning)
Rick Porcello, Bos. Red Sox, Aug. 9, 2017 (5th inning)

National League (Post-1900)

Pat Ragan, Brk. Dodgers, Oct. 5, 1914
   (8th inning, 2nd game)
Hod Eller, Cin. Reds, Aug. 21, 1917 (9th inning)
Joe Oeschger, Bos. Braves, Sep. 8, 1921
   (4th inning, 1st game)
Dazzy Vance, Brk. Dodgers, Sep. 14, 1924 (3rd inning)
Warren Spahn, Bos. Braves, Jul. 2, 1949 (2nd inning)
Robin Roberts, Phi. Phillies, Aug. 17, 1956 (2nd inning)
Sandy Koufax, L.A. Dodgers, Jun. 30, 1962 (1st inning)
Tony Cloninger, Mil. Braves, Jun. 15, 1963 (8th inning)
Sandy Koufax, L.A. Dodgers, Apr. 18, 1964 (3rd inning)
Bob Bruce, Hou. Astros, Apr. 19, 1964 (8th inning)
Nolan Ryan, N.Y. Mets, Apr. 19, 1968 (3rd inning)
Bob Gibson, St.L. Cardinals, May 12, 1969 (7th inning)
Billy Wilson, Phi. Phillies, Jul. 6, 1971 (6th inning)
John Strohmayer, Mon. Expos, Jul. 10, 1971 (5th inning)
Milt Pappas, Chi. Cubs, Sep. 24, 1971 (4th inning)
Bruce Sutter, Chi. Cubs, Sep. 8, 1977 (9th inning)
Pedro Borbon, Cin. Reds, Jun. 23, 1979 (9th inning)
Lynn McGlothen, Chi. Cubs, Aug. 25, 1979 (3rd inning)
Joey McLaughlin, Atl. Braves, Sep. 11, 1979 (7th inning)
Jeff Robinson, Pit. Pirates, Sep. 7, 1987 (8th inning)
Rob Dibble, Cin. Reds, Jun. 4, 1989 (8th inning)
Andy Ashby, Phi. Phillies, Jun. 15, 1991 (4th inning)
David Cone, N.Y. Mets, Aug. 30, 1991 (5th inning)
Pete Harnisch, Hou. Astros, Sep. 6, 1991 (7th inning)
Trevor Wilson, S.F. Giants, Jun. 7, 1992 (9th inning)
Mel Rojas, Mon. Expos, May 11, 1994 (9th inning)
Todd Worrell, L.A. Dodgers, Aug. 13, 1995 (9th inning)
Mike Magnante, Hou. Astros, Aug. 22, 1997 (9th inning)
Orel Hershiser, S.F. Giants, Jun. 16, 1998 (4th inning)
Randy Johnson, Hou. Astros, Sep. 2, 1998 (6th inning)
Jesus Sanchez, Fla. Marlins, Sep. 13, 1998 (3rd inning)
Shane Reynolds, Hou. Astros, Jun. 15, 1999 (1st inning)

continued on next page

American League

Thomas Pannone, Tor. Blue Jays, Apr. 14, 2019 (5th inning)
Chris Sale, Bos. Red Sox, May 8, 2019 (7th inning)
Chris Sale, Bos. Red Sox, Jun. 5, 2010 (8th inning)
Will Harris, Hou. Astros, Sep. 27, 2019 (8th inning)
Zach Plesac, Cle. Indians, Sep. 18, 2020 (2nd inning)
Michael King, N.Y. Yankees, Jun. 4, 2021 (4th inning)
Chad Green, N.Y. Yankees, Jul. 4, 2021 (7th inning)
Chris Sale, Bos. Red Sox, Aug. 26, 2021 (3rd inning)
Nestor Cortes, N.Y. Yankees, Apr. 17, 2022 (4th inning)
Luis Garcia, Hou. Astros, Jun. 15, 2022 (2nd inning)
Phil Maton, Hou. Astros, Jun. 15, 2022 (7th inning)
Reid Detmers, L.A. Angels, Jul. 31, 2022 (2nd inning)
Enyel De Los Santos, Cle. Guardians, Sep. 27, 2022
    (7th inning)

National League (Post-1900)

Ugueth Urbina, Mon. Expos, Apr. 4, 2000 (9th inning)
Randy Johnson, Ari. D'backs, Aug. 23, 2001 (6th inning)
Jason Isringhausen, St.L. Cardinals, Apr. 13, 2002 (9th inning)
Byung-Hyun Kim, Ari. D'backs, May 11, 2002 (8th inning)
Brian Lawrence, S.D. Padres, Jun. 12, 2002 (3rd inning)
Brandon Backe, Hou. Astros, Apr. 15, 2004 (8th inning)
Ben Sheets, Mil. Brewers, Jun. 13, 2004 (3rd inning)
LaTroy Hawkins, Chi. Cubs, Sep. 11, 2004 (9th inning)
Rick Helling, Mil. Brewers, Jun. 20, 2006 (1st inning)
Buddy Carlyle, Atl. Braves, Jul. 6, 2007 (4th inning)
Ross Ohlendorf, Pit. Pirates, Sep. 5, 2009 (7th inning)
Jordan Zimmermann, Was. Nationals, May 6, 2011 (2nd inning)
Juan Perez, Phi. Phillies, Jul. 8, 2011 (10th inning)
Wade Miley, Ari. D'backs, Oct. 1, 2012 (3rd inning)
Cole Hamels, Phi. Phillies, May 17, 2014 (3rd inning)
Rex Brothers, Col. Rockies, Jun. 14, 2014 (8th inning)
Carlos Contreras, Cin. Reds, Jul. 11, 2014 (7th inning)
Mike Fiers, Mil. Brewers, May 7, 2015 (4th inning)
Santiago Casilla, S.F. Giants, May 17, 2015 (9th inning)
Juan Nicasio, Pit. Pirates, Jul. 4, 2016 (8th inning)
Drew Storen, Cin. Reds, Apr. 18, 2017 (9th inning)
Max Scherzer, Was. Nationals, May 14, 2017 (5th inning)
Kenley Jansen, L.A. Dodgers, May 18, 2017 (9th inning)
Max Scherzer, Was. Nationals, Jun. 5, 2018 (6th inning)
German Marquez, Col. Rockies, Aug. 8, 2018 (4th inning)
Zac Rosscup, L.A. Dodgers, Aug. 19, 2018 (9th inning)
Josh Hader, Mil. Brewers, Mar. 30, 2019 (9th inning)
Stephen Strasburg, Was. Nationals, Jul. 3, 2019 (4th inning)
Kevin Gausman, Cin. Reds, Aug. 18, 2019 (9th inning)
Chris Martin, Atl. Braves, Sep. 11, 2019 (7th inning)
Kyle Finnegan, Was. Nationals, May 5, 2021 (6th inning)
Max Scherzer, L.A. Dodgers, Sep. 12, 2021 (2nd inning)
Ryan Helsley, St.L. Cardinals, Sep. 16, 2022 (9th inning)
Hayden Wesneski, Chi. Cubs, Sep. 22, 2022 (5th inning)

Pitchers with 200 Strikeouts and Fewer Than 50 Walks, Season

American League

	Strikeouts	Walks
Cy Young, Bos. Americans, 1904	200	29
Cy Young, Bos. Americans, 1905	210	30
Walter Johnson, Was. Senators, 1913	243	38
Jim Kaat, Min. Twins, 1967	211	42
Ferguson Jenkins, Tex. Rangers, 1974	225	45
Pedro Martinez, Bos. Red Sox, 1999	313	37
Pedro Martinez, Bos. Red Sox, 2000	284	32
Mike Mussina, Bal. Orioles, 2000	210	46
Mike Mussina, N.Y. Yankees, 2001	214	42
Pedro Martinez, Bos. Red Sox, 2002	239	40
Pedro Martinez, Bos. Red Sox, 2003	206	47
Roy Halladay, Tor. Blue Jays, 2003	204	32
Curt Schilling, Bos. Red Sox, 2004	203	35
Randy Johnson, N.Y. Yankees, 2005	211	47

continued on next page

	Strikeouts	Walks
Johan Santana, Min. Twins, 2005	238	45
Johan Santana, Min. Twins, 2006	245	47
CC Sabathia, Cle. Indians, 2007	209	37
Ervin Santana, L.A. Angels, 2008	214	47
Roy Halladay, Tor. Blue Jays, 2008	206	39
Roy Halladay, Tor. Blue Jays, 2009	208	35
Chris Sale, Chi. White Sox, 2013	226	46
Felix Hernandez, Sea. Mariners, 2013	216	46
David Price, T.B. Rays–Det. Tigers, 2014	271	38
Felix Hernandez, Sea. Mariners, 2014	248	46
Jon Lester, Bos. Red Sox–Oak. A's, 2014	220	48
Chris Sale, Chi. White Sox, 2015	274	42
Corey Kluber, Cle. Indians, 2015	245	45
David Price, Det. Tigers–Tor. Blue Jays, 2015	225	47
Carlos Carrasco, Cle. Indians, 2015	216	43
Chris Sale, Chi. White Sox, 2016	533	45
Carlos Carrasco, Cle. Indians, 2017	226	46
Corey Kluber, Cle. Indians, 2017	265	36
Chris Sale, Bos. Red Sox, 2017	308	43
Carlos Carrasco, Cle. Indians, 2018	231	43
Corey Kluber, Cle. Indians, 2018	222	34
James Paxton, Sea. Mariners, 2018	208	42
Chris Sale, Bos. Red Sox, 2018	237	34
Luis Severino, N.Y. Yankees, 2018	220	46
Justin Verlander, Hou. Astros, 2018	290	37
Shane Bieber, Cle. Indians, 2019	259	40
Gerrit Cole, Hou. Astros, 2019	326	48
Chris Sale, Bos. Red Sox, 2019	218	37
Justin Verlander, Hou. Astros, 2019	300	42
Jose Berrios, Min. Twins–Tor. Blue Jays, 2021	204	45
Gerrit Cole, N.Y. Yankees, 2021	243	41
Shohei Ohtani, L.A. Angels, 2022	219	44
Kevin Gausman, Tor. Blue Jays, 2022	205	28

National League (Post-1900)

	Strikeouts	Walks
Christy Mathewson, N.Y. Giants, 1908	259	42
Jim Bunning, Phi. Phillies, 1964	219	46
Juan Marichal, S.F. Giants, 1965	240	46
Juan Marichal, S.F. Giants, 1966	222	36
Gaylord Perry, S.F. Giants, 1966	201	40
Juan Marichal, S.F. Giants, 1968	218	46
Tom Seaver, N.Y. Mets, 1968	205	48
Ferguson Jenkins, Chi. Cubs, 1971	263	37
Shane Reynolds, Hou. Astros, 1996	204	44
Greg Maddux, Atl. Braves, 1998	204	45
Kevin Brown, S.D. Padres, 1998	257	49
Kevin Brown, L.A. Dodgers, 2000	216	47
Curt Schilling, Ari. D'backs, 2001	293	39
Javier Vazquez, Mon. Expos, 2001	208	44
Curt Schilling, Ari. D'backs, 2002	316	33
Jason Schmidt, S.F. Giants, 2003	208	46
Randy Johnson, Ari. D'backs, 2004	290	44
Ben Sheets, Mil. Brewers, 2004	264	32
Pedro Martinez, N.Y. Mets, 2005	208	47
Dan Haren, Ari. D'backs, 2008	206	40
Javier Vazquez, Atl. Braves, 2008	238	44
Dan Haren, Ari. D'backs, 2009	223	38
Roy Halladay, Phi. Phillies, 2010	219	30
Zack Greinke, Mil. Brewers, 2011	201	45

continued on next page

	Strikeouts	Walks
Roy Halladay, Phi. Phillies, 2011	220	35
Cliff Lee, Phi. Phillies, 2011	238	42
Cliff Lee, Phi. Phillies, 2012	238	42
Cliff Lee, Phi. Phillies, 2013	222	32
Adam Wainwright, St.L. Cardinals, 2013	219	35
Stephen Strasburg, Was. Nationals, 2014	242	43
Clayton Kershaw, L.A. Dodgers, 2014	239	31
Madison Bumgarner, S.F. Giants, 2014	219	43
Zack Greinke, L.A. Dodgers, 2014	207	43
Clayton Kershaw, L.A. Dodgers, 2015	301	42
Max Scherzer, Was. Nationals, 2015	276	34
Jake Arietta, Chi. Cubs, 2015	236	48
Madison Bumgarner, S.F. Giants, 2015	234	39
Jon Lester, Chi. Cubs, 2015	207	47
Jacob deGrom, N.Y. Mets, 2015	205	38
Gerrit Cole, Pit. Pirates, 2015	202	44
Zack Greinke, L.A. Dodgers, 2015	200	40
Noah Syndergaard, N.Y. Mets, 2016	218	43
Stephen Strasburg, Was. Nationals, 2017	204	47
Clayton Kershaw, L.A. Dodgers, 2017	202	30
Jeff Samardzija, S.F. Giants, 2017	205	32
Zack Greinke, Ari. D'backs, 2017	215	45
Patrick Corbin, Ari. D'backs, 2018	246	48
Jacob deGrom, N.Y. Mets, 2018	269	46
Madison Bumgarner, S.F. Giants, 2019	203	43
Walker Buehler, L.A. Dodgers, 2019	215	37
Jacob deGrom, N.Y. Mets, 2019	255	44
Max Scherzer, Was. Nationals, 2019	243	33
Corbin Burnes, Mil. Brewers, 2021	234	34
Aaron Nola, Phi. Phillies, 2021	223	39
Max Scherzer, Was. Nationals–L.A. Dodgers, 2021	236	36
Zach Wheeler. Phi. Phillies, 2021	247	46
Brandon Woodruff, Mil. Brewers, 2021	211	43
Aaron Nola, Phi. Phillies, 2022	235	29
Spencer Strider, Atl. Braves, 2022	202	45

Rookie Pitchers Striking Out 200 Batters

American League

Herb Score, Cle. Indians, 1955	245
Yu Darvish, Tex. Rangers, 2012	221
Russ Ford, N.Y. Highlanders, 1910	209
Bob Johnson, K.C. Royals, 1970	206
Mark Langston, Sea. Mariners, 1984	204
Daisuke Matsuzaka, Bos. Red Sox, 2007	201

National League (Post-1900)

Dwight Gooden, N.Y. Mets, 1984	276
Hideo Nomo, L.A. Dodgers, 1995	236
Kerry Wood, Chi. Cubs, 1998	233
Pete Alexander, Phi. Phillies, 1911	227
Tom Hughes, Chi. Cubs, 1901	225
Christy Mathewson, N.Y. Giants, 1901	221
John Montefusco, S.F. Giants, 1975	215
Don Sutton, L.A. Dodgers, 1966	209
Gary Nolan, Cin. Reds, 1967	206
Spencer Strider, Atl. Braves, 2022	202
Tom Griffin, Hou. Astros, 1969	200

Rookies Leading League in Strikeouts

<table>
<tr><td>

American League

Lefty Grove, Phi. A's, 1925	116
Allie Reynolds, Cle. Indians, 1943	151
Herb Score, Cle. Indians, 1955	245
Mark Langston, Sea. Mariners, 1984	204

</td><td>

National League (Post-1900)

Dazzy Vance, Brk. Dodgers, 1922	134
Dizzy Dean, St.L. Cardinals, 1932	191
Bill Voiselle, N.Y. Giants, 1944	161
Sam Jones, Chi. Cubs, 1955	198
Jack Sanford, Phi. Phillies, 1957	188
Fernando Valenzuela, L.A. Dodgers, 1981	180
Dwight Gooden, N.Y. Mets, 1984	276
Hideo Nomo, L.A. Dodgers, 1995	236

</td></tr>
</table>

Pitchers Leading League in Strikeouts, 10 or More Years Apart

Steve Carlton	Phi. Phillies (NL), 1972	Phi. Phillies (NL), 1982 and 1983
Roger Clemens	Bos. Red Sox (AL), 1988	Tor. Blue Jays (AL), 1998
Bob Feller	Cle. Indians (AL), 1938	Cle. Indians (AL), 1948
Randy Johnson	Sea. Mariners (AL), 1992	Ari. D'backs (NL), 2002 and 2004
Walter Johnson	Was. Senators (AL), 1910	Was. Senators (AL), 1924
Nolan Ryan	Cal. Angels (AL), 1972	Hou. Astros (NL), 1987 and 1988

Oldest Pitchers to Lead League in Strikeouts

<table>
<tr><td>

American League

Age		Strikeouts
43	Nolan Ryan, Tex. Rangers, 1990	232
42	Nolan Ryan, Tex. Rangers, 1989	301
38	Early Wynn, Chi. White Sox, 1958	184
37	Early Wynn, Chi. White Sox, 1957	154
36	Walter Johnson, Was. Senators, 1924	158
36	Roger Clemens, Tor. Blue Jays, 1998	271
35	Walter Johnson, Was. Senators, 1923	130
35	Allie Reynolds, N.Y. Yankees, 1952	160
35	Roger Clemens, Tor. Blue Jays, 1997	257

</td><td>

National League

Age		Strikeouts
41	Nolan Ryan, Hou. Astros, 1988	228
41	Randy Johnson, Ari. D'backs, 2004	290
40	Nolan Ryan, Hou. Astros, 1987	270
39	Randy Johnson, Ari. D'backs, 2002	334
38	Phil Niekro, Atl. Braves, 1977	262
38	Steve Carlton, Phi. Phillies, 1983	275
38	Randy Johnson, Ari. D'backs, 2001	372
37	Dazzy Vance, Brk. Dodgers, 1928	200
37	Steve Carlton, Phi. Phillies, 1982	286
37	Randy Johnson, Ari. D'backs, 2000	347
37	R.A. Dickey, N.Y. Mets, 2012	230
36	Dazzy Vance, Brk. Dodgers, 1927	184
36	Randy Johnson, Ari. D'backs, 1999	364
35	Dazzy Vance, Brk. Dodgers, 1926	140
35	Jim Bunning, Phi. Phillies, 1967	253
35	Steve Carlton, Phi. Phillies, 1980	286
35	Justin Verlander, Hou. Astros, 2018	290

</td></tr>
</table>

Strikeout Leaders on Last-Place Teams

<table>
<tr><td>

American League

Sam McDowell, 1969 Cle. Indians	279
Nolan Ryan, 1974 Cal. Angels	367
Frank Tanana, 1975 Cal. Angels	269
Scott Kazmir, 2007 T.B. Devil Rays	239

</td><td>

National League

Kirby Higbe, 1940 Phi. Phillies	134
Sam Jones, 1956 Chi. Cubs	176
Steve Carlton, 1972 Phi. Phillies	310
Phil Niekro, 1977 Atl. Braves	262
Randy Johnson, 2004 Ari. D'backs	290

</td></tr>
</table>

Highest Single-Season Strikeout Rate (Min. 50 Innings)

K Rate		IP	Strikeouts
52.5	Aroldis Chapman, Cin. Reds (NL), 2014	54.0	106
50.2	Craig Kimbrel*, Atl. Braves (NL), 2012	62.2	116
50.2	Edwin Diaz, N.Y. Mets (NL), 2022	62.0	118
49.6	Craig Kimbrel*, Bos. Red Sox (AL), 2017	69.0	126
47.8	Josh Hader*, Mil. Brewers (NL), 2019	75.2	138

continued on next page

K Rate		IP	Strikeouts
46.7	Josh Hader*, Mil. Brewers (NL), 2018	81.1	143
45.5	Josh Hader*, Mil. Brewers (NL), 2021	58.2	102
45.1	Jacob deGrom, N.Y. Mets (NL), 2021	92.0	146
44.8	Eric Gagne*, L.A. Dodgers (NL), 2003	82.1	137
44.7	Andrew Miller, N.Y. Yankees (AL)–Cle. Indians (AL), 2016	74.1	123
44.3	Edwin Diaz*, Sea. Mariners (AL), 2018	73.1	124
44.2	Aroldis Chapman, Cin. Reds (NL), 2012	71.2	122
44.0	Kenley Jansen, L.A. Dodgers (NL), 2011	53.2	96

* Won league Relief Award.

Highest Single-Season Strikeout Rate (Min. 200 Innings)

K Rate		IP	Strikeouts
39.9	Gerrit Cole, Hou. Astros (AL), 2019	212.1	326**
37.5	Pedro Martinez*, Bos. Red Sox (AL), 1999	213.1	313**
37.4	Randy Johnson*, Ari. D'backs (NL), 2001	249.2	372**
36.2	Chris Sale, Bos. Red Sox (NL), 2017	214.1**	308**
35.4	Justin Verlander*, Hou. Astros (AL), 2019	223.0**	300
34.8	Justin Verlander, Hou. Astros (AL), 2018	214.0	290**
34.8	Pedro Martinez*, Bos. Red Sox (AL), 2000	217.0	284**
34.7	Randy Johnson*, Ari. D'backs (NL), 2000	248.2	347**
34.6	Max Scherzer, Was. Nationals (NL), 2018	220.2**	300**
34.5	Gerrit Cole, Hou. Astros (AL), 2018	200.1	276
34.4	Max Scherzer*, Was. Nationals (NL), 2017	200.2	268**
34.2	Randy Johnson, Sea. Mariners (AL), 1997	213.0	291
34.1	Corey Kluber*, Cle. Indians (AL), 2017	203.2	265

* Won Cy Young Award.
** Led league.

Walks

Pitchers Walking 20 or Fewer Batters, Season (Min. 200 Innings, Post–1900)

	Walks	Pitcher's Record
Slim Sallee, Cin. Reds (NL), 1919	20 (in 227⅔ innings)	21–7
LaMarr Hoyt, S.D. Padres (NL), 1985	20 (in 210⅓ innings)	16–8
Bob Tewksbury, St.L. Cardinals (NL), 1992	20 (in 233 innings)	16–5
Bob Tewksbury, St.L. Cardinals (NL), 1993	20 (in 213⅔ innings)	17–10
Greg Maddux, Atl. Braves (NL), 1997	20 (in 232⅔ innings)	19–4
David Wells, N.Y. Yankees (AL), 2003	20 (in 213 innings)	15–7
Babe Adams, Pit. Pirates (NL), 1920	18 (in 263 innings)	17–13
Red Lucas, Cin. Reds (NL), 1933	18 (in 219⅔ innings)	10–16
Cliff Lee, Sea. Mariners (AL)–Tex. Rangers (AL), 2010	18 (in 212⅓ innings)	12–9
Phil Hughes, Min. Twins (AL), 2014	16 (in 209⅔ innings)	16–10

Fewest Walks, Season (Min. One Inning Pitched Each Team Game)

American League	Innings	National League	Innings
9 Carlos Silva, Min. Twins, 2005	188⅓	13 Bret Saberhagen, N.Y. Mets, 1994	177⅓
16 Phil Hughes, Min. Twins, 2014	209⅔	15 Babe Adams, Pit. Pirates, 1922	171⅓
18 Jon Lieber, N.Y. Yankees, 2004	176⅔	18 Babe Adams, Pit. Pirates, 1920	263
18 Cliff Lee, Sea. Mariners–Tex. Rangers, 2010	212⅓	18 Red Lucas, Cin. Reds, 1933	219⅔
		18 Bill Burns, Pit. Pirates, 1908	165
		18 Babe Adams, Pit. Pirates, 1921	160
		19 Dennis Eckersley, Chi. Cubs, 1985	169⅓

Pitchers Walking Fewer Than One Batter Every Nine Innings, Season (Min. 160 Innings)

American League

	Walks	Innings
Cy Young, Bos. Americans, 1901	37	371
Cy Young, Bos. Americans, 1903	37	342
Cy Young, Bos. Americans, 1904	29	380
Cy Young, Bos. Americans, 1905	30	321
Cy Young, Bos. Americans, 1906	25	288
Addie Joss, Cle. Indians, 1908	30	325
Bill Burns, Was. Senators, 1908	18	164
Walter Johnson, Was. Senators, 1913	38	346
Tiny Bonham, N.Y. Yankees, 1942	24	226
David Wells, N.Y. Yankees, 2003	20	213
Jon Lieber, N.Y. Yankees, 2004	18	177
Carlos Silva, Min. Twins, 2005	9	188
Cliff Lee, Sea. Mariners–Tex. Rangers, 2010	18	212
Phil Hughes, Min. Twins, 2014	16	210

National League (Post-1900)

	Walks	Innings
Deacon Phillippe, Pit. Pirates, 1902	26	272
Jesse Tannehill, Pit. Pirates, 1902	25	231
Deacon Phillippe, Pit. Pirates, 1903	29	289
Christy Mathewson, N.Y. Giants, 1908	42	390
Christy Mathewson, N.Y. Giants, 1912	34	310
Christy Mathewson, N.Y. Giants, 1913	21	306
Christy Mathewson, N.Y. Giants, 1914	23	312
Christy Mathewson, N.Y. Giants, 1915	20	186
Babe Adams, Pit. Pirates, 1919	23	263
Slim Sallee, Cin. Reds, 1919	20	228
Babe Adams, Pit. Pirates, 1920	18	263
Babe Adams, Pit. Pirates, 1922	15	171
Pete Alexander, Chi. Cubs, 1923	30	305
Red Lucas, Cin. Reds, 1933	18	220
LaMarr Hoyt, S.D. Padres, 1985	20	210
Bob Tewksbury, St.L. Cardinals, 1992	20	233
Bob Tewksbury, St.L. Cardinals, 1993	20	213
Bret Saberhagen, N.Y. Mets, 1994	13	177
Greg Maddux, Atl. Braves, 1995	23	210
Greg Maddux, Atl. Braves, 1997	20	232
David Wells, S.D. Padres, 2004	20	196

Highest Percentage of Walks to Innings Pitched, Season

American League

	Walks	Innings	Percentage
Tommy Byrne, N.Y. Yankees–St.L. Browns, 1951	150	143⅔	1.044
Bobby Witt, Tex. Rangers, 1987	140	143	.979
Mickey McDermott, Bos. Red Sox, 1950	124	130	.954
Tommy Byrne, N.Y. Yankees, 1949	179	196	.913
Bob Wiesler, Was. Senators, 1956	112	123	.911
Bobby Witt, Tex. Rangers, 1986	143	157⅔	.907
Eric Plunk, Oak. A's, 1986	102	120⅓	.848
Emmett O'Neill, Bost, Red Sox, 1945	117	141⅔	.826
Bill Kennedy, Cle. Indians–St.L Browns, 1948	117	143⅓	.816
Hal Newhouser, Det. Tigers, 1941	137	173	.792
Tommy Byrne, N.Y. Yankees, 1950	160	203⅓	.787
Lefty Mills, St.L. Browns, 1939	113	144⅓	.783

continued on next page

	Walks	Innings	Percentage
Bob Turley, N.Y. Yankees, 1956	103	132	.780
Jason Bere, Chi. White Sox, 1995	106	137⅔	.770
Tommy Byrne, N.Y. Yankees, 1948	101	133⅓	.756
Randy Johnson, Sea. Mariners, 1991	152	201⅓	.755
Tex Shirley, St.L. Browns, 1946	105	139⅔	.754
Ken Chase, Was. Senators, 1938	113	150	.753
Bob Feller, Cle. Indians, 1938	208	277⅔	.749
Bob Turley, Bal. Orioles, 1954	181	247⅓	.732
Joe Krakauskas, Was. Senators, 1938	88	121⅓	.725
Bill Burbach, N.Y. Yankees, 1969	102	140⅔	.725
Gene Bearden, Cle. Indians, 1949	92	127	.724
Tracy Stallings, Bos. Red Sox, 1961	96	132⅔	.724
Bob Turley, N.Y. Yankees, 1955	177	246⅔	.718
Vic Albury, Min. Twins, 1975	97	135	.718
Mark Langston, Sea. Mariners, 1985	91	126⅔	.718
Herb Score, Cle. Indians, 1959	115	160⅔	.716
Bob Feller, Cle. Indians, 1937	106	148⅔	.713
Sam McDowell, Cle. Indians, 1971	153	214⅔	.713
Dean Stone, Was. Senators, 1956	93	132	.705
Daniel Cabrera, Bal. Orioles, 2006	104	148	.703
Brian Williams, Det. Tigers, 1996	85	121	.702
Herb Hash, Bos. Red Sox, 1940	84	120	.700

National League (Post-1900)

	Walks	Innings	Percentage
Roy Golden, St.L. Cardinals, 1911	129	148	.868
Sam Jones, Chi. Cubs, 1955	185	241	.766
Nolan Ryan, N.Y. Mets, 1971	116	152	.763
Nolan Ryan, N.Y. Mets, 1970	97	131⅔	.737
Johnny Vander Meer, Cin. Reds, 1939	95	129	.736
Victor Zambrano, T.B Devil Rays–N.Y. Mets, 2004	102	142	.718
Les Sweetland, Phi. Phillies, 1928	97	135⅓	.717
Turk Lown, Chi. Cubs, 1951	90	127	.709
Jose de Jesus, Phi. Phillies, 1991	128	181	.705

Low-Hit Games

Pitchers with a No-Hitter in First Major League Start

Ted Breitenstein, St.L. Browns (vs. Lou. Colonels) (AA), Oct. 4, 1891 (final score: 8–0)

Bumpus Jones, Cin. Reds (vs. Pit. Pirates) (NL), Oct. 15, 1892 (final score: 7–1)

Bobo Holloman, St.L. Browns (vs. Phi. A's) (AL), May 6, 1953 (final score: 6–0)

Tyler Gilbert, Ari. Diamondbacks (vs. S.D. Padres) (NL), Aug. 14, 2021 (final score: 7–0)

Pitchers with a One-Hitter in First Major League Game

Addie Joss, Cle. Indians (AL), Apr. 26, 1902

Ed Albrecht, St.L. Browns (AL), Oct. 2, 1949

Mike Fornieles, Was. Senators (AL), Sep. 2, 1952

Juan Marichal, S.F. Giants (NL), Jul. 19, 1960

Bill Rohr, Bos. Red Sox (AL), Apr. 14, 1967

Jimmy Jones, S.D. Padres (NL), Sep. 21, 1986

Last Outs in Perfect Games*

Lee Richmond, Worc. Brown Stockings (NL)

(vs. Cle. Spiders, NL), Jun. 12, 1880 (final: 1–0) ....Last out: second baseman George Creamer

John M. Ward, Pro. Grays (NL) (vs. Buff. Bisons, NL),

Jun. 17, 1880 (final: 5–0) ....Last out: pitcher Pud Galvin

continued on next page

Cy Young, Bos. Red Sox (AL) (vs. Phi. A's, AL), May 5, 1904
(final: 3–0) ....Last out: pitcher Rube Waddell (fly out to center)
Addie Joss, Cle. Indians (AL) (vs. Chi. White Sox, AL),
Oct. 2, 1908 (final: 1–0) ....Last out: pinch hitter John Anderson (ground out to third)
Charley Robertson, Chi. White Sox (AL) (vs. Det. Tigers, AL),
Apr. 30, 1922 (final: 2–0) ....Last out: pinch hitter John Bassler (fly out to left)
Don Larsen, N.Y. Yankees (AL) (vs. Brk. Dodgers, NL)
(World Series), Oct. 8, 1956 (final: 2–0) ....Last out: pinch hitter Dale Mitchell (strikeout)
Jim Bunning, Phi. Phillies (NL) (vs. N.Y. Mets, NL),
Jun. 21, 1964 (final: 6–0)...Last out: pinch hitter John Stephenson (strikeout)
Sandy Koufax, L.A. Dodgers (NL) (vs. Chi. Cubs, NL),
Sep. 9, 1965 (final: 1–0) ....Last out: pinch hitter Harvey Kuenn (strikeout)
Catfish Hunter, Oak. A's (AL) (vs. Min. Twins, AL),
May 8, 1968 (final: 4–0) ....Last out: pinch hitter Rich Reese (strikeout)
Len Barker, Cle. Indians (AL) (vs. Tor. Blue Jays, AL),
May 15, 1981 (final: 3–0) ....Last out: pinch hitter Ernie Whitt (fly out to center)
Mike Witt, Cal. Angels (AL) (vs. Tex. Rangers, AL),
Sep. 30, 1984 (final: 1–0) ....Last out: pinch hitter Marv Foley (ground out to second)
Tom Browning, Cin. Reds (NL) (vs. L.A. Dodgers, NL),
Sep. 16, 1988 (final: 1–0) ....Last out: pinch hitter Tracy Woodson (strikeout)
Dennis Martinez, Mon. Expos (NL) (vs. L.A. Dodgers, NL),
Jul. 28, 1991 (final: 2–0) ....Last out: pinch hitter Chris Gwynn (fly out to center)
Kenny Rogers, Tex. Rangers (AL) (vs. Cal. Angels, AL),
Jul. 28, 1994 (final: 4–0) ....Last out: shortstop Gary DiSarcina (fly out to center)
David Wells, N.Y. Yankees (AL) (vs. Min. Twins, AL),
May 17, 1998 (final: 4–0) ....Last out: shortstop Pat Meares (fly out to center)
David Cone, N.Y. Yankees (AL) (vs. Mon. Expos, NL),
Jul. 18, 1999 (final: 5–0)...Last out: shortstop Orlando Cabrera (foul pop to third)
Randy Johnson, Ari. D'backs (NL) (vs. Atl. Braves, NL),
May 18, 2004 (final: 2–0) ....Last out: pinch hitter Eddie Perez (strikeout)
Mark Buehrle, Chi. White Sox (AL) (vs. T.B. Rays, AL),
Jul. 23, 2009 (final: 5–0) ....Last out: shortstop Jason Bartlett (ground out to shortstop)
Dallas Braden, Oak. A's (AL) (vs. T.B. Rays, AL),
May 9, 2010 (final: 4–0)...Last out: right fielder Gabe Kapler (ground out to shortstop)
Roy Halladay, Phi. Phillies (NL) (vs Fla. Marlins, NL),
May 29, 2010 (final: 1–0) ....Last out: pinch hitter Ronny Paulino (ground out to third)
Philip Humber, Chi. White Sox (AL) (vs. Sea. Mariners, AL),
Apr. 21, 2012 (final: 4–0) ....Last out: pinch hitter Brendan Ryan (strikeout)
Matt Cain, S.F. Giants (NL) (vs. Hou. Astros, NL),
Jun. 13, 2012 (final: 10–0) ....Last out: pinch hitter Jason Castro (ground out to third)
Felix Hernandez, Sea. Mariners (AL) (vs. T.B. Rays, AL),
Aug. 15, 2012 (final: 1–0) ....Last out: third baseman Sean Rodriguez (strikeout)

* 27 batters up, 27 out.

Perfect Game Pitchers, Career Wins

Cy Young (1890–1911) 511
Randy Johnson (1988–2009) 303
Dennis Martinez (1976–98) 245
David Wells (1988–2007) 239
Jim Bunning (1955–71) 224
Catfish Hunter (1965–79) 224
Kenny Rogers (1989–2008) 219
Mark Buehrle (2000–15) 214
Roy Halladay (1998–2013) 203
David Cone (1986–2001, 2003) 194
Felix Hernandez (2005–19) 169
Sandy Koufax (1955–66) 165

continued on next page

26-Batter Perfect Games (Spoiled by 27th Batter)

Spoiler

Hooks Wiltse, N.Y. Giants (vs. Phi. Phillies) (NL), Jul. 4, 1908...George McQuillan, hit by pitch
Tommy Bridges, Det. Tigers (vs. Was. Senators) (AL), Aug. 5, 1932 ....Dave Harris, singled
Billy Pierce, Chi. White Sox (vs. Was. Senators) (AL), Jun. 28, 1958...................................Ed FitzGerald, doubled
Milt Pappas, Chi. Cubs (vs. S.D. Padres) (NL), Sep. 2, 1972 ....Larry Stahl, walked
Milt Wilcox, Det. Tigers (vs. Chi. White Sox) (AL), Apr. 15, 1983 ....Jerry Hairston, singled
Ron Robinson, Cin. Reds (vs. Mon. Expos) (NL), May 2, 1988 ....Wallace Johnson, singled
Dave Stieb, Tor. Blue Jays (vs. N.Y. Yankees) (AL), Aug. 4, 1989 ....Roberto Kelly, doubled
Brian Holman, Sea. Mariners (vs. Oak. A's) (AL), Apr. 20, 1990 ....Ken Phelps, home run
Mike Mussina, N.Y. Yankees (vs. Bos. Red Sox) (AL), Sep. 2, 2001 ....Carl Everett, singled
Armando Gallaraga, Det. Tigers (vs. Cle. Indians) (AL), Jun. 2 2010...................................Jason Donald, infield hit
Yu Darvish, Tex. Rangers (vs. Hou. Astros) (AL), Apr. 2, 2013 ....Marwin Gonzalez, singled
Yusmeiro Petit, S.F. Giants (vs. Ari. D'backs) (NL), Sep. 6, 2013...Eric Chavez, singled
Max Scherzer, Was. Nationals (vs. Pit. Pirates) (NL), Jun. 20, 2015....................................Jose Tabata, hit by pitch

Most Walks Given Up by No-Hit Pitchers, Game

11 .... Blue Moon Odom (9 in 5 innings) and Francisco Barrios (2 in 4 innings), Chi. White Sox (vs. Oak. A's) (AL),
                Jul. 28, 1976, won 6–0
10 .... Jim Maloney, Cin. Reds (vs. Chi. Cubs) (NL), Aug. 19, 1965, won 1–0
10 .... Steve Barber (10 in 8⅔ innings) and Stu Miller (0 in ⅓ inning), Bal. Orioles (vs. Det. Tigers) (AL),
                Apr. 30, 1967, lost 1–2
9 .... John Klippstein (7 in 7 innings), Hersh Freeman (0 in 1 inning), and Joe Black (2 in 1 inning), Cin. Reds
                (vs. Mil. Braves) (NL), May 26, 1956, lost 1–2
9 .... A.J. Burnett, Fla. Marlins (vs.S.D. Padres) (NL), May 12, 2001, won 3–0
8 .... Amos Rusie, N.Y. Giants (vs. Brk. Bridegrooms) (NL), Jul. 31, 1891, won 6–0
8 .... Johnny Vander Meer, Cin. Reds (vs. Brk. Dodgers) (NL), Jun. 15, 1938, won 6–0
8 .... Cliff Chambers, Pit. Pirates (vs. Bos. Braves) (NL), May 6, 1951, won 3–0
8 .... Dock Ellis, Pit. Pirates (vs. S.D. Padres) (NL), Jun. 12, 1970, won 2–0
8 .... Nolan Ryan, Cal. Angels (vs. Min. Twins) (AL), Sep. 28, 1974, won 4–0
8 .... Edwin Jackson, Ari. D'backs (vs.T.B. Rays) (AL), Jun. 25, 2010, won 1–0
7 .... Bobo Newsom, St.L. Browns (vs. Bos. Red Sox) (AL), Sep. 18, 1934, lost 1–2
7 .... Sam Jones, Chi. Cubs (vs. Pit. Pirates) (NL), May 12, 1955, won 4–0
7 .... Burt Hooton, Chi. Cubs (vs. Phi. Phillies) (NL), Apr. 16, 1972, won 4–0
7 .... Bill Stoneman, Mon. Expos (vs. N.Y. Mets) (NL), Oct. 2, 1972, won 7–0
7 .... Joe Cowley, Chi. White Sox (vs. Cal. Angels) (AL), Sep. 19, 1986, won 7–1
7 .... Tommy Greene, Phi. Phillies (vs. Mon. Expos) (NL), May 23, 1991, won 2–0
7 .... Matt Young, Bos. Red Sox (vs. Cle. Indians) (AL), Apr. 12, 1992, lost 1–2

Pitchers Throwing No-Hitters in 20-Loss Season

	Wins	Losses
Nap Rucker, Brk. Dodgers (vs. Bos. Doves), Sep. 5, 1908	18	20
Joe Bush, Phi. A's (vs. Cle. Indians), Aug. 26, 1916	15	22
Bobo Newsom, St.L. Browns (vs. Bos. Red Sox), Sep. 18, 1934	16	20
Sam Jones, Chi. Cubs (vs. Pit. Pirates), May 12, 1955	14	20

Pitchers Hitting Home Runs in No-Hit Games

	Opposing Pitcher(s)
Wes Ferrell, Cle. Indians (vs. St.L. Cardinals) (NL), Apr. 29, 1931	Sam Gray
Jim Tobin, Bos. Braves (vs. Brk. Dodgers) (NL), Apr. 27, 1944	Fritz Ostermueller
Earl Wilson, Bos. Red Sox (vs. L.A. Angels) (AL), Jun. 26, 1962	Bo Belinsky
Rick Wise, Phi. Phillies (vs. Cin. Reds) (NL), Jun. 23, 1971	Ross Grimsley and Clay Carroll (2)

Pitchers Throwing No-Hitters in Consecutive Seasons

4	Sandy Koufax, L.A. Dodgers	1962–65
3	Nolan Ryan, Cal. Angels	1973–75
2	Warren Spahn, Mil. Braves	1960–61
2	Steve Busby, K.C. Royals	1973–74
2	Homer Bailey, Cin. Reds	2012–13
2	Tim Lincecum, S.F. Giants	2013–14
2	Jake Arrieta, Chi. Cubs	2015–16

No-Hitters Pitched Against Pennant-Winning Teams

American League

Ernie Koob, St.L. Browns (vs. Chi. White Sox), May 5, 1917
Bob Groom, St.L. Browns (vs. Chi. White Sox), May 6, 1917
Virgil Trucks, Det. Tigers (vs. N.Y. Yankees), Aug. 25, 1952
Hoyt Wilhelm, Bal. Orioles (vs. N.Y. Yankees), Sep. 20, 1958
Jim Bibby, Tex. Rangers (vs. Oak. A's), Jul. 30, 1973
Dick Bosman, Cle. Indians (vs. Oak. A's), Jul. 19, 1974
Nolan Ryan, Tex. Rangers (vs. Oak. A's), Jun. 11, 1990
Sean Manaea, Oak. A's (vs. Bos. Red Sox), Apr. 21, 2018

National League (Post-1900)

Tex Carleton, Brk. Dodgers (vs. Cin. Reds), Apr. 30, 1940
Bob Moose, Pit. Pirates (vs. N.Y. Mets), Sep. 20, 1969
Bob Gibson, St.L. Cardinals (vs. Pit. Pirates), Aug. 14, 1971
Nolan Ryan, Hou. Astros (vs. L.A. Dodgers), Sep. 26, 1981
Tom Browning, Cin. Reds (vs. L.A. Dodgers), Sep. 16, 1988 (perfect game)
Roy Oswalt, Pete Munro, Kirk Saarloos, Brad Lidge, Octavio Dotel, and Billy Wagner, Hou. Astros (vs. N.Y. Yankees), Jun. 11, 2003
Chris Heston, S.F. Giants (vs. N.Y. Mets), Jun. 9, 2015
Max Scherzer, Was. Nationals (vs. N.Y. Mets), Oct. 3, 2015
Tylor Megill, Drew Smith, Joely Rodriguez, Seth Lugo, Edwin Diaz, New York Mets (vs. Phi. Phillies), April 29, 2022

No-Hit Starters Going Winless the Next Season After Pitching No-Hitter

American League

Weldon Henley, Phi. A's (vs. St.L. Browns), Jul. 22, 1905
Tom Hughes, N.Y. Highlanders (vs. Cle. Indians), Aug. 30 1910
Addie Joss, Cle. Indians (vs. Chi. White Sox), Apr. 20, 1910*
Ernie Koob, St.L. Browns (vs. Chi. White Sox), May 5, 1917
Ernie Shore, Bos. Red Sox (vs. Was. Senators), Jun. 23, 1917
Bobo Holloman, St.L. Browns (vs. Phi. A's), May 6, 1953**
Mel Parnell, Bos. Red Sox (vs. Chi. White Sox), Jul. 14, 1956*
Bob Keegan, Chi. White Sox (vs. Was. Senators), Aug. 20, 1957
Joe Cowley, Chi. White Sox (vs. Cal. Angels), Sep. 19, 1986
Mike Witt, Cal. Angels (vs. Sea. Mariners), Apr. 11, 1990***
Mike Flanagan, Bal. Orioles (vs. Oak. A's), Jul. 13, 1991***
Philip Humber, Chi. White Sox (vs. Sea. Mariners), Apr. 21, 2012
Kevin Milwood, Sea. Mariners (vs. L.A. Dodgers), Jun. 8, 2012*, ***
John Means, Bal. Orioles (vs. Sea. Mariners), May 5, 2021
Aaron Sanchez, Hou. Astros (vs. Sea. Mariners), Aug. 3, 2019***
Spencer Turnbull, Det. Tigers (vs. Sea. Mariners), May 18, 2021

* Last Major League season.
** Only Major League season.
*** Pitched no-hitter in tandem with other pitcher(s).

National League (Post-1900)

Mal Eason, Brk. Dodgers (vs. St.L. Cardinals), Jul. 20, 1906*
Jeff Pfeffer, Bos. Doves (vs. Cin. Reds), May 8, 1907
Tex Carleton, Brk. Dodgers (vs. Cin. Reds), Apr. 30, 1940*
Clyde Shoun, Cin. Reds (vs. Bos. Braves), May 15, 1944
Ed Head, Brk. Dodgers (vs. Bos. Braves), Apr. 23, 1946*
Jim Maloney, Cin. Reds (vs. Hou. Astros), Apr. 30, 1969
Fernando Valenzuela, L.A. Dodgers (vs. St.L. Cardinals), Jun. 29, 1990
Johan Santana, N.Y. Mets (vs. St.L. Cardinals), Jun. 1, 2012*
Edinson Volquez, Mia. Marlins (vs. Ari. D'backs), Jun. 3, 2017
Tyler Gilbert, Ari. D'Backs (vs. S.D. Padres), Aug. 14, 2021

Back-to-Back One-Hit Games (Post-1900)

Rube Marquard, N.Y. Giants (NL)...Aug. 28 and Sep. 1, 1911
Lon Warneke, Chi. Cubs (NL)...Apr. 17 and Apr. 22, 1934
Mort Cooper, St.L. Cardinals (NL)..May 31 and Jun. 4, 1943
Whitey Ford, N.Y. Yankees (AL)..Sep. 2 and Sep. 7, 1955
Sam McDowell, Cle. Indians (AL)...Apr. 25 and May 1, 1966
Dave Steib, Tor. Blue Jays (AL) ....Sep. 24 and Sep. 30, 1988
R.A. Dickey, N.Y. Mets (NL) ....Jun. 13 and Jun. 18, 2012

Oldest Pitcher to Throw a No-Hitter

	Age	Score
Nolan Ryan, Tex. Rangers (vs. Tor. Blue Jays), May 1, 1991	44 Years 90 Days	3–0
Nolan Ryan, Tex. Rangers(vs. Oak. A's), Jun. 11, 1990	43 Years 131 Days	5–0
Randy Johnson, Ari. D-backs*(vs. Atl. Braves), May 18, 2004	40 Years 251 Days	2–0
Warren Spahn, Mil. Braves(vs. SF Giants), Apr. 28, 1961	40 Years 5 Days	1–0
Sal Maglie, Brk. Dodgers(vs. Phi. Phillies), Sep. 25, 1956	39 Years 152 Days	5–0
Warren Spahn, Mil. Braves(vs. Phi. Phillies), Sep. 16,1990	39 Years 146 Days	4–0

* Perfect game.

Youngest Pitcher to Throw a No-Hitter

	Age	Score
Vida Blue, Oak. A's (vs. Min. Twins), Sep. 21, 1970	21 Years 55 Days	6–0
Wilson Alvarez, Chi. White Sox (vs. Bal. Orioles), Aug. 11, 1991	21 Years 140 Days	7–0
Bob Feller, Cle. Indians (vs. Chi. White Sox), Apr. 16, 1940	21 Years 165 Days	1–0
Bud Smith, St.L. Cardinals (vs. S.D. Padres), Sep. 3, 2001	21 Years 315 Days	4–0
Bob Moose, Pit. Pirates (vs. N.Y. Mets), Sep. 20, 1969	21 Years 346 Days	4–0

Rookies Throwing No-Hitters

American League

Pitcher	Date	Result
Charlie Robertson*	Apr. 30, 1922	Chi. White Sox vs. Cle. Indians, 2–0
Vern Kennedy	Aug. 31, 1935	Chi. White Sox vs. Cle. Indians, 5–0
Bill McCahan	Sep. 3, 1947	Phi. A's vs. Was. Senators, 3–0
Bobo Holloman**	May 6, 1953	St.L. Browns vs. Phi. A's, 6–0
Bo Belinsky	May 5, 1962	L.A. Angels vs. Bal. Orioles, 2–0
Vida Blue	Sep. 21, 1970	Oak. A's vs. Min. Twins, 6–0
Steve Busby	Apr. 27, 1973	K.C. Royals at Det. Tigers, 3–0
Jim Bibby	Jul. 30, 1973	Tex. Rangers at Oak. A's, 6–0
Mike Warren	Sep. 29, 1983	Oak. A's vs. Chi. White Sox, 3–0
Wilson Alvarez***	Aug. 11, 1991	Chi. White Sox at Bal. Orioles, 7–0
Clay Buchholz***	Sep. 1, 2007	Bos. Red Sox vs. Bal. Orioles, 10–0
Reid Detmers	May 10, 2022	L.A. Angels vs. T.B. Rays, 12–0

* Perfect game.
** First Major League start.
*** Second Major League start.

National League

Pitcher	Date	Result
Christy Mathewson	Jul. 15, 1901	N.Y. Giants vs. St.L. Cardinals, 5–0
Nick Maddox	Sep. 20, 1907	Pit. Pirates vs. Brk. Dodgers, 2–1
Jeff Tesreau	Sep. 6, 1912	N.Y. Giants at Phi. Phillies, 3–0
Paul Dean	Sep. 21, 1934	St.L. Cardinals vs. Brk. Dodgers, 3–0
Sam Jones	May 12, 1955	Chi. Cubs vs. Pit. Pirates, 4–0
Don Wilson	Jun. 18, 1967	Hou. Astros vs. Atl. Braves, 2–0
Burt Hooton	Apr. 16, 1972	Chi. Cubs vs. Phi. Phillies, 4–0
Jose Jimenez	Jun. 25, 1999	St.L. Cardinals vs. Ari. D'backs, 1–0
Bud Smith	Sep. 3, 2001	St.L. Cardinals at S.D. Padres, 4–0
Anibal Sanchez	Sep. 6, 2006	Fla. Marlins vs. Ari. D'backs, 2–0
Chris Heston	Jun. 9, 2015	S.F. Giants at N.Y. Mets, 6–0
Tyler Gilbert*	Aug. 14, 2021	Ari. D'backs vs. S.D. Padres, 7–0

* First Major League start.

Longest Stretch by Pitcher Between No-Hitters

Stretch	Pitcher	Date	Date
13 Years, 11 Months, 2 Weeks	Randy Johnson	Jun. 6, 1990	May 18, 2004*
9 Years, 1 Month, 2 Weeks, 1 Day	Nolan Ryan	Sep. 26, 1981	Jun. 11, 1990
7 Years, 2 Weeks	Ted Breitenstein	Oct. 4, 1891	Apr. 22, 1898
6 Years, 9 Months, 1 Week, 6 Days	Nolan Ryan	Jun. 1, 1975	Sep. 26, 1981
6 Years, 8 Months, 6 Days	Cy Young	Sep. 18, 1897	May 5, 1904*
5 Years, 11 Months, 1 Day	Jim Bunning	Jul. 20, 1958	Jun. 21, 1964*

* Perfect game.

Shortest Stretch by Pitcher Between No-Hitters

Stretch	Pitcher	Date	Date
4 Days	Johnny Vander Meer	Jun. 11, 1938	Jun. 15, 1938
2 Months, 5 Days	Nolan Ryan	May 15, 1973	Jul. 15, 1973
2 Months, 2 Weeks, 4 Days	Virgil Trucks	May 15, 1952	Aug. 25, 1952
2 Months, 3 Weeks, 1 Day	Allie Reynolds	Jul. 12, 1951	Sep. 28, 1951
3 Months, 3 Weeks	Max Scherzer	Jun. 20, 2015	Oct. 3, 2015
3 Months, 3 Weeks, 2 Days	Roy Halladay	May 29, 2010*	Oct. 6, 2010

* Perfect game.

Saves/Relief Pitchers
Saves by Decade

Pre-1900
16	Kid Nichols
15	Tony Mullane
14	Harry Wright
13	Al Spalding
12	Jack Manning
9	Brickyard Kennedy
9	Jack Taylor
8	Win Mercer
8	Cy Young
6	Frank Dwyer
6	George Hemming
6	Silver King
6	Adonis Terry
6	Kid Gleason

1900–09
22	Joe McGinnity
19	Mordecai Brown
19	Hooks Wiltse
16	Christy Mathewson
15	Ed Walsh
14	Jack Powell
11	Orval Overall
9	Tom Hughes
9	Cy Young
8	Frank Arellanes
8	Chief Bender
8	Cecil Ferguson
8	Sam Leever
8	Tully Sparks

1910–19
32	Slim Sallee
30	Mordecai Brown
29	Red Ames
26	Chief Bender
22	Eddie Plank
21	Jim Bagby
20	Walter Johnson
20	Ed Walsh
19	Larry Cheney
19	Eddie Cicotte
19	Doc Crandall
19	Hugh Bedient

1920–29
72	Firpo Marberry
30	Waite Hoyt
26	Hooks Dauss
25	Sarge Connally
25	Wilcy Moore
25	Eddie Rommel
25	Allen Russell
24	Bill Sherdel
23	Lefty Grove
23	Sad Sam Jones
23	Herb Pennock

1930–39
54	Johnny Murphy
49	Clint Brown
38	Jack Russell
35	Joe Heving
33	Dick Coffman
33	Chief Hogsett
32	Bob Smith
31	Dizzy Dean
31	Lefty Grove
30	Carl Hubbell
30	Syl Johnson
30	Charlie Root

1940–49
63	Joe Page
53	Hugh Casey
53	Johnny Murphy
50	Al Benton
49	Ace Adams
45	Harry Gumbert
41	Tom Ferrick
39	George Caster
35	Russ Christopher
33	Ed Klieman
33	Gordon Maltzberger

1950–59
98	Ellis Kinder
80	Clem Labine
67	Jim Konstanty
58	Ray Narleski
58	Hoyt Wilhelm
57	Marv Grissom
54	Al Brazle
51	Turk Lown
49	Roy Face
45	Tom Morgan
45	Fritz Dorish

1960–69*
153	Hoyt Wilhelm
142	Roy Face
137	Ron Perranoski
137	Stu Miller
120	Dick Radatz
113	Lindy McDaniel
107	Ted Abernathy
103	Ron Kline
103	John Wyatt
98	Al Worthington

1970–79** ***
209	Rollie Fingers
190	Sparky Lyle
177	Mike Marshall
140	Dave Giusti
132	Tug McGraw
122	Dave LaRoche
115	John Hiller
110	Gene Garber
106	Clay Carroll
105	Bruce Sutter

continued on next page

1980–89		1990–99		2000–09	
264	Jeff Reardon	295	John Wetteland	397	Mariano Rivera
239	Dan Quisenberry	293	Dennis Eckersley	363	Trevor Hoffman
234	Lee Smith	291	Randy Myers	284	Jason Isringhausen
206	Goose Gossage	285	Jeff Montgomery	284	Billy Wagner
195	Bruce Sutter	282	Rick Aguilera	250	Francisco Cordero
188	Dave Righetti	268	John Franco	246	Joe Nathan
176	Dave Smith	260	Rod Beck	243	Francisco Rodriguez
161	Steve Bedrosian	244	Lee Smith	230	Armando Benitez
148	John Franco	234	Roberto Hernandez	219	Troy Percival
146	Greg Minton	228	Trevor Hoffman	195	Brad Lidge
				193	Bob Wickman

2010–19		2020–22	
346	Craig Kimbrel	90	Kenley Jansen
301	Kenley Jansen	89	Liam Hendriks
273	Aroldis Chapman	83	Josh Hader
257	Fernando Rodney	71	Ryan Pressly
217	Jonathan Papelbon	70	Edwin Diaz
206	Greg Holland	68	Mark Melancon
195	Huston Street	66	Emmanuel Clase
194	Mark Melancon	61	Jordan Romano
194	Francisco Rodriguez	60	Daniel Bard
167	Jim Johnson	59	Raisel Iglesias

* For games played before 1969, saves have been figured retroactively using the 1969 definition, which states that "a relief pitcher earned a save when he entered the game with his team in the lead and held the lead for the remainder of the game, provided that he was not credited with the victory."

** Before the 1974 season, the save rule was modified and simplified. Under this new rule, a relief pitcher earned a save under one of the following two conditions:
  1. Pitcher had to enter the game with either the potential tying or winning run either on base or at the plate and preserve the lead.
  2. Pitcher had to pitch at least three or more effective innings and preserve the lead.

*** Beginning the 1975 season, the save rule was modified a final time, stating that a relief pitcher will be awarded a save when they met all of the three following conditions:
  1. Pitcher must finish the game won by his club.
  2. Pitcher is not the winning pitcher.
  3. Pitcher qualifies under one of the following three conditions:
     a. Pitcher enters the game with a lead of no more than three runs and pitches for at least one inning.
     b. Pitcher enters the game, regardless of the score, with the potential tying run either on base, at bat, or on deck.
     c. Pitcher throws for at least three innings, regardless of the score.

Evolution of Saves Record

American League

1901	Bill Hoffer, Cle. Indians	3
1908	Ed Walsh, Chi. White Sox	6
1909	Frank Arellanes, Bos. Americans	8
1912	Ed Walsh, Chi. White Sox	10
1913	Chief Bender, Phi. A's	13
1924	Firpo Marberry, Was. Senators	15
1926	Firpo Marberry, Was. Senators	22
1949	Joe Page, N.Y. Yankees	27
1961	Luis Arroyo, N.Y. Yankees	29
1966	Jack Aker, K.C. A's	32
1970	Ron Perranoski, Min. Twins	34
1972	Sparky Lyle, N.Y. Yankees	35
1973	John Hiller, Det. Tigers	38
1983	Dan Quisenberry, K.C. Royals	45
1986	Dave Righetti, N.Y. Yankees	46
1990	Bobby Thigpen, Chi. White Sox	57
2008	Francisco Rodriguez, L.A. Angels	62

continued on next page

National League (Post-1899)

1900	Frank Kitson, Brk. Dodgers	4
1904	Joe McGinnity, N.Y. Giants	5
1905	Claude Elliott, Bos. Beaneaters	6
1906	Cecil Ferguson, N.Y. Giants	7
1911	Mordecai Brown, Chi. Cubs	13
1931	Jack Quinn, Phi. Phillies	15
1947	Hugh Casey, Brk. Dodgers	18
1950	Jim Konstanty, Phi. Phillies	22
1954	Jim Hughes, Brk. Dodgers	24
1960	Lindy McDaniel, St.L. Cardinals	26
1962	Roy Face, Pit. Pirates	28
1965	Ted Abernathy, Chi. Cubs	31
1970	Wayne Granger, Cin. Reds	35
1972	Clay Carroll, Cin. Reds	37
1984	Bruce Sutter, St.L. Cardinals	45
1991	Lee Smith, St.L. Cardinals	47
1993	Randy Myers, Chi. Cubs	53
2002	John Smoltz, Atl. Braves	55

Pitchers with 100 Wins and 100 Saves, Career

	Wins	Saves
Dennis Eckersley (1975–98)	197	390
Roy Face (1953, 1955–69)	104	193
Rollie Fingers (1968–85)	114	341
Dave Giusti (1962, 1964–77)	100	145
Tom Gordon (1988–2009)	138	158
Goose Gossage (1972–94)	124	310
Ellis Kinder (1946–57)	102	102
Ron Kline (1952, 1955–70)	114	108
Lindy McDaniel (1955–75)	141	172
Stu Miller (1952–54, 1956–68)	105	154
Ron Reed (1966–84)	146	103
John Smoltz (1998–2009)	213	154
Bob Stanley (1977–89)	115	132
Hoyt Wilhelm (1952–72)	143	227

Relief Pitchers with the Most Wins, Season

American League

John Hiller, Det. Tigers, 1974	17–14
Bill Campbell, Min. Twins, 1976	17–5
Tom Johnson, Min. Twins, 1977	16–7
Dick Radatz, Bos. Red Sox, 1964	16–9
Luis Arroyo, N.Y. Yankees, 1961	15–5
Dick Radatz, Bos. Red Sox, 1963	15–6
Eddie Fisher, Chi. White Sox, 1965	15–7

* Started two games, no decisions.

National League (Post-1900)

Roy Face, Pit. Pirates, 1959	18–1
Jim Konstanty, Phi. Phillies, 1950	16–7
Ron Perranoski, L.A. Dodgers, 1963	16–3
Mace Brown, Pit. Pirates, 1938	15–9*
Hoyt Wilhelm, N.Y. Giants, 1952	15–3
Mike Marshall, L.A. Dodgers, 1974	15–12
Dale Murray, Mon. Expos, 1975	15–8

Most Games Won by Relief Pitcher, Career

Hoyt Wilhelm (1952–72)	124
Lindy McDaniel (1955–75)	119
Goose Gossage (1972–94)	115
Rollie Fingers (1968–85)	107
Sparky Lyle (1967–82)	99

continued on next page

Roy Face (1953–69) 96
Gene Garber (1969–87) 94
Kent Tekulve (1974–89) 94
Mike Marshall (1967–81) 92

Teams with Two Pitchers with 20 Saves, Season

Year	Team	Pitcher, Saves	Pitcher, Saves
1965	Chi. White Sox (AL)	Eddie Fisher, 24	Hoyt Wilhelm, 20
1983	S.F. Giants (NL)	Greg Minton, 22	Gary Lavelle, 20
1986	N.Y. Mets (NL)	Roger McDowell, 22	Jesse Orosco, 21
1991	Tor. Blue Jays (AL)	Tom Henke, 32	Duane Ward, 23
1992	Cin. Reds (NL)	Norm Charlton, 26	Rob Dibble, 25
2010	Hou. Astros (NL)	Matt Lindstrom, 23	Brandon Lyon, 20
2017	S.D. Padres (NL)	Brad Hand, 21	Brandon Maurer, 20

Pitchers Having 20-Win Seasons and 20-Save Seasons, Career

		Wins	Saves
Dennis Eckersley	Bos. Red Sox (AL), 1978	20	
	Oak. A's (AL), 1988		45
	Oak. A's (AL), 1989		33
	Oak. A's (AL), 1990		48
	Oak. A's (AL), 1991		43
	Oak. A's (AL), 1992		51
	Oak. A's (AL), 1993		36
	Oak. A's (AL), 1995		29
	St.L. Cardinals (NL), 1996		30
	St.L. Cardinals (NL), 1997		36
Mudcat Grant	Min. Twins (AL), 1965	21	
	Oak. A's (AL)–Pit. Pirates (NL), 1970		24
Ellis Kinder	Bos. Red Sox (AL), 1949	23	
	Bos. Red Sox (AL), 1953		27
Derek Lowe	Bos. Red Sox (AL), 2001		24
	Bos. Red Sox (AL), 2002	21	
Johnny Sain	Bos. Braves (NL), 1946	20	
	Bos. Braves (NL), 1947	21	
	Bos. Braves (NL), 1948	24	
	Bos. Braves (NL), 1950	20	
	N.Y. Yankees (AL), 1954		22
John Smoltz	Atl. Braves (NL), 1996	24	
	Atl. Braves (NL), 2002		55
	Atl. Braves (NL), 2003		45
	Atl. Braves (NL), 2004		45
Wilbur Wood	Chi. White Sox (AL), 1970		21
	Chi. White Sox (AL), 1971	22	
	Chi. White Sox (AL), 1972	24	
	Chi. White Sox (AL), 1973	24	
	Chi. White Sox (AL), 1974	20	

Pitchers with 15 Saves and 15 Wins in Relief, Same Season

American League

	Wins	Saves
Luis Arroyo, N.Y. Yankees, 1961	15	29
Dick Radatz, Bos. Red Sox, 1963	15	25
Dick Radatz, Bos. Red Sox, 1964	16	29
Eddie Fisher, Chi. White Sox, 1965	15	24

continued on next page

	Wins	Saves
Bill Campbell, Min. Twins, 1976	17	20
Tom Johnson, Min. Twins, 1977	16	15

National League (Post-1900)

	Wins	Saves
Jim Konstanty, Phi. Phillies, 1950	16	22
Joe Black, Brk. Dodgers, 1952	15	15
Ron Perranoski, L.A. Dodgers, 1963	16	21
Mike Marshall, L.A. Dodgers, 1974	15	21

Pitching Miscellany

Best Wins Above Replacement (WAR) by Decade (Pitchers Only)

Pre–1900		1900–09		1910–19	
98.1	Kid Nichols	77.4	Cy Young	108.5	Walter Johnson
89.9	Cy Young	68.6	Christy Mathewson	69.0	Pete Alexander
88.8	Tim Keefe	58.9	Rube Waddell	48.1	Eddie Cicotte
85.8	John Clarkson	56.9	Eddie Plank	43.3	Hippo Vaughn
83.3	Pud Galvin	52.4	Vic Willis	34.7	Ed Walsh
76.0	Jim McCormick	51.7	Joe McGinnity	33.9	Slim Sallee
73.1	Old Hoss Radbourn	44.1	Addie Joss	32.9	Babe Adams
68.9	Amos Rusie	41.5	Jack Chesbro	32.4	Russ Ford
63.6	Mickey Welch	40.8	Mordecai Brown	31.3	Eddie Plank
62.4	Bobby Mathews	37.8	Noodles Hahn	30.5	Dutch Leonard

1920–29		1930–39		1940–49	
50.1	Dazzy Vance	80.7	Lefty Grove	54.9	Hal Newhouser
48.6	Pete Alexander	56.5	Carl Hubbell	38.7	Bob Feller
46.8	Red Faber	45.5	Mel Harder	37.6	Dizzy Trout
45.5	Eddie Rommel	43.8	Dizzy Dean	32.7	Harry Brecheen
45.1	Urban Shocker	43.5	Lefty Gomez	31.8	Dutch Leonard
39.6	Herb Pennock	43.1	Wes Ferrell	28.6	Mort Cooper
39.5	Eppa Rixey	38.0	Red Ruffing	28.6	Bucky Walters
38.4	Burleigh Grimes	35.7	Tommy Bridges	27.9	Claude Passeau
38.3	Stan Coveleski	35.5	Larry French	25.6	Tex Hughson
37.2	Dolf Luque	32.2	Ted Lyons	25.1	Rip Sewell

1950–59		1960–69		1970–79	
60.5	Robin Roberts	55.3	Juan Marichal	67.3	Tom Seaver
57.2	Warren Spahn	54.3	Bob Gibson	64.6	Phil Niekro
43.7	Billy Pierce	48.0	Sandy Koufax	59.3	Gaylord Perry
37.4	Early Wynn	46.4	Jim Bunning	58.2	Bert Blyleven
33.0	Bob Rush	44.8	Don Drysdale	54.5	Jim Palmer
31.5	Sal Maglie	36.0	Larry Jackson	52.8	Ferguson Jenkins
31.1	Johnny Antonelli	35.3	Jim Maloney	44.8	Steve Carlton
28.2	Ned Garver	33.7	Dean Chance	43.5	Wilbur Wood
26.3	Whitey Ford	30.3	Sam McDowell	41.8	Nolan Ryan
26.4	Mike Garcia	28.8	Chris Short	40.9	Rick Reuschel

1980–89		1990–99		2000–09	
48.4	Dave Stieb	68.3	Roger Clemens	51.3	Randy Johnson
38.4	Bert Blyleven	65.4	Greg Maddux	46.2	Curt Schilling
35.7	Roger Clemens	53.0	David Cone	46.2	Johan Santana
35.3	Bob Welch	52.2	Randy Johnson	45.7	Pedro Martinez

continued on next page

1980–89
33.3 .... Fernando Valenzuela
33.0 .... Orel Hershiser
32.1 .... Bret Saberhagen
31.3 .... John Tudor
30.7 .... Dwight Gooden
30.6 .... Nolan Ryan

1990–99
48.2 .... Kevin Brown
47.7 .... Kevin Appier
45.1 .... Tom Glavine
44.7 .... Chuck Finley
42.1 .... Mike Mussina
40.5 .... Pedro Martinez

2000–09
45.5 .... Roy Halladay
43.2 .... Roy Oswalt
42.4 .... Javier Vazquez
41.4 .... Mark Buehrle
40.8 .... Mike Mussina
40.3 ....Tim Hudson

2010–19
59.3 .... Clayton Kershaw
56.8 .... Justin Verlander
54.8 .... Max Scherzer
45.5 .... Cole Hamels
44.6 .... Chris Sale
43.9 .... Zach Greinke
37.6 .... David Price
32.6 .... Madison Bumgarner
32.6 .... Jacob deGrom
32.5 .... Corey Kluber

2020–22
15.4 .... Zack Wheeler
13.3 .... Max Scherzer
13.2 ....Max Fried
12.9 .... Sandy Alantara
11.8 .... Corbin Burnes
10.6 .... Aaron Nola
10.5 ....Julio Urias
10.4 .... Brandon Woodruff
10.2 .... Gerrit Cole
10.2 .... Carlos Rodon

Best Winning Percentage by Decade (Min. 100 Decisions)

Pre-1900
.701 .... Bill Hoffer
.690 .... Dave Foutz
.688 .... Bob Caruthers
.665 .... Larry Corcoran
.663 .... Kid Nichols
.650 .... Ted Lewis
.648 .... John Clarkson
.640 .... Lady Baldwin
.639 .... Cy Young
.630 .... Nig Cuppy

1900–09
.713 .... Ed Reulbach
.697 .... Sam Leever
.689 .... Mordecai Brown
.678 .... Christy Mathewson
.636 ....Ed Walsh
.634 ....Hooks Wiltse
.634 .... Jack Pfiester
.634 .... Joe McGinnity
.633 .... Jesse Tannehill
.631 .... Deacon Phillippe

1910–19
.682 .... Smoky Joe Wood
.675 .... Pete Alexander
.663 .... Chief Bender
.659 .... Babe Ruth
.657 ....Eddie Plank
.656 .... Doc Crandall
.650 .... Walter Johnson
.643 .... Christy Mathewson
.621 ....Jack Coombs
.615 .... Jeff Tesreau

1920–29
.660 .... Ray Kremer
.638 .... Carl Mays
.627 .... Urban Shocker
.626 .... Freddie Fitzsimmons
.626 .... Lefty Grove
.620 ....Dazzy Vance
.615 .... Art Nehf
.612 .... Waite Hoyt
.611 .... Pete Alexander
.599 .... Stan Coveleski

1930–39
.724 .... Lefty Grove
.706 .... Johnny Allen
.686 ....Firpo Murberry
.650 ....Lefty Gomez
.648 ....Dizzy Dean
.644 .... Carl Hubbell
.641 .... Red Ruffing
.634 .... Monte Pearson
.629 ....Lon Warneke
.602 .... Bill Lee

1940–49
.714 .... Spud Chandler
.640 .... Tex Hughson
.640 .... Harry Brecheen
.629 ....Howie Pollet
.626 .... Mort Cooper
.626 .... Bob Feller
.621 .... Max Lanier
.619 .... Schoolboy Rowe
.613 ....Warren Spahn
.605 .... Rip Sewell

1950–59
.708 ....Whitey Ford
.669 .... Allie Reynolds
.667 ....Eddie Lopat
.663 .... Sal Maglie
.643 .... Vic Raschi
.633 .... Don Newcombe
.618 ....Bob Buhl

1960–69
.695 ....Sandy Koufax
.685 .... Juan Marichal
.673 ....Whitey Ford
.667 .... Denny McLain
.626 .... Jim Maloney
.621 .... Dave McNally
.610 .... Bob Gibson

1970–79
.686 .... Don Gullett
.648 .... John Candelaria
.647 .... Pedro Borbon
.644 .... Jim Palmer
.638 .... Tom Seaver
.624 .... Catfish Hunter
.613 .... Tommy John

continued on next page

1950–59

.615	Bob Lemon
.612	Early Wynn
.607	Warren Spahn

1960–69

.596	Ray Culp
.593	Bob Purkey
.582	Dick Hall

1970–79

.612	Gary Nolan
.610	Clay Carroll
.607	Luis Tiant

1980–89

.719	Dwight Gooden
.679	Roger Clemens
.639	Ted Higuera
.613	Ron Darling
.612	John Tudor
.607	Ron Guidry
.605	Sid Fernandez
.605	Orel Hershiser
.605	Dennis Rasmussen
.602	Jimmy Key

1990–99

.682	Pedro Martinez
.673	Mike Mussina
.667	Randy Johnson
.667	Greg Maddux
.653	Tom Glavine
.642	Kirk Rueter
.638	Andy Pettitte
.631	Roger Clemens
.626	Jose Rijo
.624	David Cone

2000–09

.691	Pedro Martinez
.682	Roger Clemens
.670	Johan Santana
.668	Roy Halladay
.662	Roy Oswalt
.650	Curt Schilling
.647	Randy Johnson
.643	Tim Hudson
.641	Chris Carpenter
.634	Cliff Lee

2010–19

.719	Clayton Kershaw
.689	Zach Greinke
.685	Max Scherzer
.659	Stephen Strasburg
.657	David Price
.650	Juston Verlander
.644	Gerrit Cole
.636	Masahiro Tanaka
.631	Johnny Cueto
.628	Corey Kluber

2020–22 (Min. 30 Decisions)

.800	Julio Urias
.767	Walker Buehler
.758	Cal Quantrill
.735	Alek Manoah
.714	Max Fried
.705	Max Scherzer
.697	Kyle Wright
.688	Framber Valdez
.683	Shane Bieber
.683	Clayton Kershaw

Best WHIP (Walks and Hits Per Inning Pitched) by Decade (Min. 1000 Innings)

Pre-1900

1.043	Monte Ward
1.067	Charlie Sweeney
1.087	Jim Devlin
1.090	George Bradley
1.091	Tommy Bond
1.105	Larry Corcoran
1.108	Ed Morris
1.111	Will White
1.117	Terry Larkin
1.117	Charlie Ferguson

1900–09

0.963	Addie Joss
0.967	Ed Walsh
0.984	Mordecai Brown
1.000	Cy Young
1.035	Christy Mathewson
1.048	Ed Reulbach
1.079	Chief Bender
1.085	Frank Smith
1.089	Doc White
1.089	Barney Pelty

1910–19

0.953	Walter Johnson
1.04	Ed Walsh
1.052	Pete Alexander
1.053	Babe Adams
1.08	Reb Russell
1.088	Smoky Joe Wood
1.095	Carl Mays
1.096	Christy Mathewson
1.113	Jeff Pfeffer
1.121	Fred Toney

1920–29

1.191	Pete Alexander
1.205	Dazzy Vance
1.258	Tommy Thomas
1.260	Ray Kremer
1.264	Dolf Luque
1.267	Eppa Rixey
1.268	Walter Johnson
1.275	Urban Shocker
1.281	Jesse Petty
1.283	Carl Mays

1930–39

1.118	Carl Hubbell
1.193	Dizzy Dean
1.226	Bill Swift
1.243	Lefty Grove
1.257	Syl Johnson
1.261	Lon Warneke
1.268	Red Lucas
1.277	Charlie Root
1.28	Ben Cantwell
1.29	Curt Davis

1940–49

1.153	Tiny Bonham
1.166	Whit Wyatt
1.167	Harry Brecheen
1.177	Spud Chandler
1.185	Mort Cooper
1.194	Tex Hughson
1.232	Curt Davis
1.236	Paul Derringer
1.245	Preacher Roe
1.246	Dutch Leonard

continued on next page

1950–59

1.129	Robin Roberts
1.180	Warren Spahn
1.192	Don Newcombe
1.214	Harvey Haddix
1.224	Warren Hacker
1.232	Steve Gromek
1.237	Billy Pierce
1.243	Hoyt Wilhelm
1.244	Dick Donovan
1.245	Eddie Lopat

1960–69

0.993	Hoyt Wilhelm
1.005	Sandy Koufax
1.045	Juan Marichal
1.085	Ferguson Jenkins
1.094	Denny McLain
1.118	Don Drysdale
1.125	Sonny Siebert
1.125	Eddie Fisher
1.129	Ralph Terry
1.142	Jim Bunning

1970–79

1.073	Tom Seaver
1.106	Catfish Hunter
1.108	Don Sutton
1.118	Ferguson Jenkins
1.141	Rollie Fingers
1.142	Gaylord Perry
1.142	Jim Palmer
1.144	Frank Tanana
1.149	Gary Nolan
1.160	Andy Messersmith

1980–89

1.109	Dwight Gooden
1.127	Bret Saberhagen
1.136	Roger Clemens
1.149	Orel Hershiser
1.150	Sid Fernandez
1.163	Mario Soto
1.172	Teddy Higuera
1.177	Don Sutton
1.179	Bryn Smith
1.179	Dennis Eckersley

1990–99

1.055	Greg Maddux
1.074	Pedro Martinez
1.134	Curt Schilling
1.154	Bret Saberhagen
1.157	Jose Rijo
1.174	Mike Mussina
1.176	Roger Clemens
1.180	John Smoltz
1.193	Dennis Martinez
1.197	Randy Johnson

2000–09

1.036	Pedro Martinez
1.113	Johan Santana
1.114	Randy Johnson
1.129	Curt Schilling
1.151	John Smoltz
1.171	Roy Halladay
1.172	Greg Maddux
1.178	Dan Haren
1.182	Jake Peavy
1.201	Roger Clemens
1.201	Ben Sheets

2010–19

0.962	Clayton Kershaw
1.035	Chris Sale
1.053	Jacob deGrom
1.068	Max Scherzer
1.077	Justin Verlander
1.086	Stephen Strasburg
1.086	Corey Kluber
1.109	Zach Greinke
1.111	Madison Bumgarner
1.128	Masahiro Tanaka

2020–22 (Min. 200 Innings)

0.731	Jacob deGrom
0.953	Clayton Kershaw
0.963	Corbin Burnes
0.969	Max Scherzer
0.980	Tony Gonsolin
1.007	Yu Darvish
1.009	Brandon Woodruff
1.010	Julio Urias
1.012	Carlos Rodon
1.012	Alek Manoah

Most Seasons Leading League in Pitching Category

American League

	Seasons	
Games Pitched	6	Firpo Marberry, 1924–26, 1928–29, and 1932
Complete Games	6	Walter Johnson, 1910–11 and 1913–16
Innings Pitched	5	Walter Johnson, 1910 and 1913–16
	5	Bob Feller, 1939–41 and 1946–47
Games Won	6	Walter Johnson, 1913–16, 1918, and 1924
Games Lost	4	Bobo Newsom, 1934–35, 1941, and 1945
	4	Pedro Ramos, 1958–61
Won–Lost Percentage	5	Lefty Grove, 1929–31, 1933, and 1939
ERA	9	Lefty Grove, 1926, 1929–32, 1935–36, and 1938–39
Strikeouts	12	Walter Johnson, 1910, 1912–19, 1921, and 1923–24
Shutouts	7	Walter Johnson, 1911, 1913–15, 1918–19, and 1924
Saves	6	Firpo Marberry, 1924–26, 1928–29, and 1932

National League (Post-1900)

	Seasons	
Games Pitched	6	Joe McGinnity, 1900 and 1903–07
Complete Games	9	Warren Spahn, 1949, 1951, and 1957–63
Innings Pitched	7	Pete Alexander, 1911–12, 1914–17, and 1920
Games Won	8	Warren Spahn, 1949–50, 1953, and 1957–61
Games Lost	4	Phil Niekro, 1977–80

continued on next page

Seasons

Won–Lost Percentage	3	Sam Leever, 1901, 1903, and 1905
ERA	5	Christy Mathewson, 1905, 1908–09, 1911, and 1913
	5	Pete Alexander, 1915–17 and 1919–20
	5	Sandy Koufax, 1962–66
	5	Clayton Kershaw, 2011–2014 and 2017
Strikeouts	7	Dazzy Vance, 1922–28
Shutouts	7	Pete Alexander, 1911, 1913, 1915–17, 1919, and 1921
Saves	5	Bruce Sutter, 1979–82 and 1984

Most Consecutive Seasons Leading League in Pitching Category

American League

Seasons

Winning Percentage	3	Lefty Grove, 1929–31
ERA	4	Lefty Grove, 1929–32
Shutouts	3	Walter Johnson, 1913–15
Strikeouts	8	Walter Johnson, 1912–19
Saves	4	Dan Quisenberry, 1982–85

National League (Post-1900)

Seasons

Winning Percentage	3	Ed Reulbach, 1906–08
ERA	5	Sandy Koufax, 1962–66
Shutouts	3	Pete Alexander, 1915–17
Strikeouts	7	Dazzy Vance, 1922–28
Saves	4	Mordecai Brown, 1908–11
	4	Bruce Sutter, 1979–82
	4	Craig Kimbrel, 2011–14

Most Consecutive Scoreless Innings Pitched

American League		National League	
Innings		**Innings**	
55⅔	Walter Johnson, 1913 Was. Senators	59	Orel Hershiser, 1988 L.A. Dodgers
53	Jack Coombs, 1910 Phi. A's	58⅔	Don Drysdale, 1968 L.A. Dodgers
45	Doc White, 1904 Chi. White Sox	47	Bob Gibson, 1968 St.L. Cardinals
45	Cy Young, 1904 Bos. Red Sox	45⅔	Zack Greinke, 2015 L.A. Dodgers
43⅔	Rube Waddell, 1905 Phi. A's	45⅓	Carl Hubbell, 1933 N.Y. Giants
42	Rube Foster, 1914 Bos. Red Sox	45	Sal Maglie, 1950 N.Y. Giants

Highest Career Pitching Totals by Pitchers Who Never Led League

American League		National League	
Games Pitched			
1178	Mariano Rivera	1119	John Franco
Complete Games			
289	Early Wynn	290	Eppa Rixey
Innings Pitched			
4344	Red Ruffing	4413	Tom Glavine
Games Won			
305	Eddie Plank	257	Don Sutton

continued on next page

Games Lost

279 .... Walter Johnson   245 ....Warren Spahn

Winning Percentage (Min. 100 Wins)

.630 ....Allie Reynolds   .653 ....Kevin Brown

ERA (Min. 100 Wins)

2.24 .... Frank Smith   2.26 ....Orval Overall

Strikeouts

3093 ....CC Sabathia   3371 .... Greg Maddux

Shutouts

47 ....Rube Waddell   43 .... Phil Niekro

Saves

377 ....Joe Nathan   422 .... Billy Wagner

Career Pitching Leaders Under Six Feet Tall

Games Pitched	1119	John Franco (5'10")
Games Won	365	Pud Galvin (5'8")
Games Lost	310	Pud Galvin (5'8")
Winning Percentage (Min. 150 Wins)	.690	Whitey Ford (5'10")
ERA (Min. 100 Wins)	2.03	Smoky Joe Wood (5'11")
Complete Games	646	Pud Galvin (5'8")
Innings Pitched	6003	Pud Galvin (5'8")
Games Started	688	Pud Galvin (5'8")
Strikeouts	3154	Pedro Martinez (5'11")
Shutouts	69	Eddie Plank (5'11")
Walks	1570	Gus Weyhing (5'10")
Saves	424	John Franco (5'10")

Pitching's Triple Crown Winners (Led League in Wins, ERA, and Strikeouts, Same Season)

American League

	Wins	ERA	Strikeouts
Cy Young, Bos. Americans, 1901	33	1.62	158
Rube Waddell, Phi. A's, 1905	26	1.48	287
Walter Johnson, Was. Senators, 1913	36	1.09	243
Walter Johnson, Was. Senators, 1918	23	1.27	162
Walter Johnson, Was. Senators, 1924	23	2.72	158
Lefty Grove, Phi. A's, 1930	28	2.54	209
Lefty Grove, Phi. A's, 1931	31	2.06	175
Lefty Gomez, N.Y. Yankees, 1934	26	2.33	158
Lefty Gomez, N.Y. Yankees, 1937	21	2.33	194
Bob Feller, Cle. Indians, 1940	27	2.61	261
Hal Newhouser, Det. Tigers, 1945	25	1.81	212
Roger Clemens, Tor. Blue Jays, 1997	21	2.05	292
Roger Clemens, Tor. Blue Jays, 1998	20	2.65	271
Pedro Martinez, Bos. Red Sox, 1999	23	2.07	313
Johan Santana, Min. Twins, 2006	19	2.77	245
Justin Verlander, Det. Tigers, 2011	24	2.40	250
Shane Bieber*, Cle. Indians, 2020	8	1.63	122

* COVID-shortened season.

continued on next page

National League (Post-1900)

	Wins	ERA	Strikeouts
Christy Mathewson, N.Y. Giants, 1905	31	1.27	206
Christy Mathewson, N.Y. Giants, 1908	37	1.43	259
Pete Alexander, Phi. Phillies, 1915	31	1.22	241
Pete Alexander, Phi. Phillies, 1916	33	1.55	167
Pete Alexander, Phi. Phillies, 1917	30	1.86	201
Hippo Vaughn, Chi. Cubs, 1918	22	1.74	148
Pete Alexander, Chi. Cubs, 1920	27	1.91	173
Dazzy Vance, Brk. Dodgers, 1924	28	2.16	262
Bucky Walters, Cin. Reds, 1939	27	2.29	137
Sandy Koufax, L.A. Dodgers, 1963	25	1.88	306
Sandy Koufax, L.A. Dodgers, 1965	26	2.04	382
Sandy Koufax, L.A. Dodgers, 1966	27	1.73	317
Steve Carlton, Phi. Phillies, 1972	27	1.97	310
Dwight Gooden, N.Y. Giants, 1985	24	1.53	268
Randy Johnson, Ari. D'backs, 2002	24	2.32	334
Jake Peavy, S.D. Padres, 2007	19	2.54	240
Clayton Kershaw, L.A. Dodgers, 2011	21	2.28	248

Most Home Runs Given Up, Season

American League

50	Bert Blyleven, Min. Twins, 1986 (in 271 innings)
46	Bert Blyleven, Min. Twins, 1987 (in 267 innings)
44	Jamie Moyer, Sea. Mariners, 2004 (in 202 innings)
43	Pedro Ramos, Was. Senators, 1957 (in 231 innings)
42	Denny McLain, Det. Tigers, 1966 (in 264 innings)
41	Rick Helling, Tex. Rangers, 1999 (in 219 innings)
41	Dylan Bundy, Bal. Orioles, 2018 (in 171 innings)
40	Ralph Terry, N.Y. Yankees, 1962 (in 298 innings)
40	Orlando Pena, K.C. A's, 1964 (in 219 innings)
40	Ferguson Jenkins, Tex. Rangers, 1979 (in 259 innings)
40	Jack Morris, Det. Tigers, 1986 (in 267 innings)
40	Shawn Boskie, Cal. Angels, 1996 (in 189 innings)
40	Brad Radke, Min. Twins, 1996 (in 232 innings)
40	Ramon Ortiz, Ana. Angels, 2002 (in 217 innings)
40	James Shields, Chi. White Sox, 2016 (in 181 innings)*

National League (Post-1900)

48	Jose Lima, Hou. Astros, 2000 (in 196 innings)
46	Robin Roberts, Phi. Phillies, 1956 (in 297 innings)
46	Bronson Arroyo, Cin. Reds, 2011 (in 199 innings)
43	Eric Milton, Phi. Phillies, 2004 (in 201 innings)
41	Robin Roberts, Phi. Phillies, 1955 (in 305 innings)
41	Phil Niekro, Atl. Braves, 1979 (in 229 innings)
40	Robin Roberts, Phi. Phillies, 1957 (in 249 innings)
40	Phil Niekro, Atl. Braves, 1979 (in 342 innings)
40	Eric Milton, Cin. Reds, 2005 (in 186 innings)

* Pitched for both the S.D. Padres (NL) and Chi. White Sox (AL), giving up 9 HRs with the Padres and 31 HRs with the White Sox.

Most Home Runs Given Up, Career

522	Jamie Moyer (1986–91, 1993–2012)
505	Robin Roberts (1948–66)
484	Ferguson Jenkins (1965–83)
482	Phil Niekro (1964–87)
472	Don Sutton (1966–88)
448	Frank Tanana (1973–93)
439	Bartolo Colon (1997–2018)
434	Warren Spahn (1942, 1946–65)
430	Bert Blyleven (1970–92)
418	Tim Wakefield (1992–93, 1995–2011)
414	Steve Carlton (1965–88)
411	Randy Johnson (1988–2009)
407	David Wells (1987–2007)

Pitchers Giving Up Most Grand Slams, Season

American League	National League
4 .... Ray Narleski, Det. Tigers, 1959	4 ...... Tug McGraw, Phi. Phillies, 1979
Mike Schooler, Sea. Mariners, 1992	Chan Ho Park, L.A. Dodgers, 1999
J.A. Happ, Tor. Blue Jays–N.Y. Yankees, 2018	Matt Clement, S.D. Padres, 2000

Pitchers with 2000 Innings Pitched, Allowing No Grand Slams

Old Hoss Radbourn (1880–91)	4535	Harvey Haddix (1952–65)	2235
Eddie Plank (1901–17)	4505	Joaquin Andujar (1976–88)	2153
Jim McCormick (1878–87)	4275	Bob Smith (1925–36)	2197
Jim Palmer (1965–84)	3948	Freddy Garcia (1993–2013)	2193
Bobo Newsome (1934–53)	3746	Mike Krukow (1977–89)	2186
Herb Pennock (1912–17, 1919–34)	3558	Mike Boddicker (1982–93)	2110
Freddie Fitzsimmons (1925–43)	3218	Matt Cain (2005–17)	2085
Danny MacFayden (1927–43)	2690	Gary Peters (1959–72)	2081
Hal Schumacher (1931–46)	2479	Jack Russell (1926–40)	2047
Red Lucas (1926–38)	2325		

20-Game Winners Batting .300, Same Season

American League

	Wins	Batting Average
Clark Griffith, Chi. White Sox, 1901	24	.303
Cy Young, Bos. Americans, 1903	28	.321
Ed Killian, Det. Tigers, 1907	25	.320
Jack Coombs, Phi. A's, 1911	29	.319
Babe Ruth, Bos. Red Sox, 1917	24	.325
Carl Mays, N.Y. Yankees, 1921	27	.343
Joe Bush, N.Y. Yankees, 1922	26	.326
George Uhle, Cle. Indians, 1923	26	.361
Joe Shaute, Cle. Indians, 1924	20	.318
Walter Johnson, Was. Senators, 1925	20	.433
Ted Lyons, Chi. White Sox, 1930	22	.311
Wes Ferrell, Cle. Indians, 1931	22	.319
Schoolboy Rowe, Det. Tigers, 1934	24	.303
Wes Ferrell, Bos. Red Sox, 1935	25	.347
Red Ruffing, N.Y. Yankees, 1939	21	.307
Ned Garver, St.L. Browns, 1951	20	.305
Catfish Hunter, Oak. A's, 1971	21	.350
Catfish Hunter, Oak. A's, 1973	21	1.000

National League (Post-1900)

	Wins	Batting Average
Brickyard Kennedy, Brk. Bridegrooms, 1900	20	.301
Jesse Tannehill, Pit. Pirates, 1900	20	.336
Claude Hendrix, Pit. Pirates, 1912	24	.322
Burleigh Grimes, Brk. Dodgers, 1920	23	.306
Wilbur Cooper, Pit. Pirates, 1924	20	.346
Pete Donahue, Cin. Reds, 1926	20	.311
Burleigh Grimes, Pit. Pirates, 1928	25	.321
Curt Davis, St.L. Cardinals, 1939	22	.381
Bucky Walters, Cin. Reds, 1939	27	.325
Johnny Sain, Bos. Braves, 1947	21	.346
Don Newcombe, Brk. Dodgers, 1955	20	.359
Warren Spahn, Mil. Braves, 1958	22	.333
Don Drysdale, L.A. Dodgers, 1965	23	.300
Bob Gibson, St.L. Cardinals, 1970	23	.303
Mike Hampton, Hou. Astros, 1999	22	.311

Complete Games by Decade

Pre-1900

646	Pud Galvin
554	Tim Keefe
525	Mickey Welch
525	Bobby Mathews
488	Old Hoss Radbourn
485	John Clarkson
468	Tony Mullane
466	Jim McCormick
448	Gus Weyhing
443	Kid Nichols
418	Cy Young

1900–09

337	Cy Young
312	Vic Willis
282	Christy Mathewson
277	Jack Powell
276	Joe McGinnity
263	Eddie Plank
258	George Mullin
254	Bill Dinneen
251	Rube Waddell
246	Bill Donovan

1910–19

327	Walter Johnson
242	Gover C. Alexander
193	Eddie Cicotte
183	Hippo Vaughn
172	Claude Hendrix
167	Dick Rudolph
163	Slim Sallee
160	Ray Caldwell
159	Lefty Tyler
156	Hooks Dauss

1920–29

234	Burleigh Grimes
194	Pete Alexander
185	Eppa Rixey
182	George Uhle
181	Red Faber
181	Herb Pennock
172	Dazzy Vance
169	Jesse Haines
168	Dolf Luque
168	Urban Shocker

1930–39

207	Wes Ferrell
201	Red Ruffing
197	Lefty Grove
197	Carl Hubbell
168	Ted Lyons
163	Paul Derringer
163	Lefty Gomez
161	Larry French
156	Tommy Bridges
151	Dizzy Dean

1940–49

181	Hal Newhouser
155	Bob Feller
153	Bucky Walters
139	Dutch Leonard
132	Rip Sewell
132	Dizzy Trout
130	Claude Passeau
127	Jim Tobin
120	Mort Cooper
115	Bobo Newsom

1950–59

237	Robin Roberts
215	Warren Spahn
162	Billy Pierce
162	Early Wynn
139	Bob Lemon
125	Ned Garver
116	Don Newcombe
105	Bob Rush
104	Lew Burdette
103	Mike Garcia

1960–69

197	Juan Marichal
164	Bob Gibson
135	Don Drysdale
122	Sandy Koufax
116	Larry Jackson
108	Jim Bunning
102	Jim Kaat
95	Warren Spahn
93	Denny McLain
93	Camilo Pascual

1970–79

197	Gaylord Perry
184	Ferguson Jenkins
175	Jim Palmer
165	Steve Carlton
164	Nolan Ryan
160	Phil Niekro
147	Tom Seaver
145	Bert Blyleven
140	Catfish Hunter
133	Mickey Lolich

1980–89

133	Jack Morris
102	Fernando Valenzuela
94	Bert Blyleven
93	Charlie Hough
92	Dave Stieb
70	Mike Witt
70	Mario Soto
64	Bruce Hurst
62	Mike Moore
62	Scott McGregor

1990–99

75	Greg Maddux
65	Randy Johnson
61	Jack McDowell
58	Kevin Brown
57	Roger Clemens
57	Curt Schilling
47	Scott Erickson
46	Chuck Finley
42	John Smoltz
41	Terry Mulholland
41	Doug Drabek

2000–09

47	Roy Halladay
36	Livan Hernandez
32	Randy Johnson
28	CC Sabathia
26	Curt Schilling
25	Mark Mulder
24	Mark Buehrle
23	Bartolo Colon
23	Sidney Ponson
23	Javier Vazquez

continued on next page

2010–19		2020–22	
25	Clayton Kershaw	7	Sandy Alcantara
20	Justin Verlander	6	Adam Wainwright
19	Adam Wainwright	5	Aaron Nola
18	Felix Hernandez	4	Gerrit Cole
18	James Shields	4	Framber Valdez
18	Roy Halladay	3	Trevor Bauer
17	Johnny Cueto	3	German Marquez
17	Corey Kluber	3	Zack Wheeler
17	David Price		
16	Ervin Santana		
16	Cliff Lee		
16	Chris Sale		

Evolution of Complete Games Record

American League

1901 Joe McGinnity, Bal. Orioles 39   1904 Jack Chesbro, N.Y. Yankees 48
1902 Cy Young, Bos. Red Sox 41

National League (Pre-1900)

1876 Jim Devlin, Lou. Colonels.............. 66   1879 Will White, Cin. Reds 75

National League (Post-1899)

1900 Pink Hawley, N.Y. Giants 34   1902 Vic Willis, Bos. Beaneaters 45
1901 Noodles Hahn, Cin. Reds.............. 41

Most Games Started By a Pitcher, Career

Starts		Starts	
815	Cy Young (1890–1911)	682	Tom Glavine (1987–2008)
773	Nolan Ryan (1968–93)	666	Walter Johnson (1907–27)
756	Don Sutton (1966–88)	665	Warren Spahn (1942, 1946–65)
740	Greg Maddux (1986–2008)	647	Tom Seaver (1967–86)
716	Phil Niekro (1964–87)	638	Jamie Moyer (1986–91, 1993–2010, 2012)
709	Steve Carlton (1965–88)	625	Jim Kaat (1959–83)
707	Roger Clemens (1984–2007)	616	Frank Tanana (1973–93)
700	Tommy John (1963–74, 1976–89)	612	Early Wynn (1939, 1941–44, 1946–63)
690	Gaylord Perry (1962–83)	609	Robin Roberts (1948–66)
688	Pud Galvin (1875, 1879–92)	603	Randy Johnson (1988–2009)
685	Bert Blyleven (1970–92)	600	Pete Alexander (1911–30)

Highest Percentage of Complete Games to Games Started

		Games Started	Complete Games
.898	Cy Young (1900–11*)	404	363
.825	George Mullin (1902–15)	428	353
.820	Vic Willis (1900–10*)	395	324
.797	Walter Johnson (1907–27)	666	531
.793	Jack Powell (1900–12*)	406	322

continued on next page

		Games Started	Complete Games
.788	Christy Mathewson (1900–16)	529	435
.775	Eddie Plank (1900–17*)	529	410
.736	Ted Lyons (1923–42, 1946)	484	356
.728	Pete Alexander (1911–30)	600	437
.652	Lefty Grove (1925–41)	457	298
.632	Burleigh Grimes (1916–34)	497	314
.623	Red Ruffing (1924–42, 1945–47)	538	335
.574	Warren Spahn (1942, 1946–65)	665	382

* Record only from 1900.

Pitchers Starting 20 Games in 20 Consecutive Seasons

	Seasons	Teams
Nolan Ryan, 1971–92	22	N.Y. Mets (NL), 1971; Cal. Angels (AL), 1972–79; Hou. Astros (NL), 1980–88; Tex. Rangers (AL), 1989–92
Don Sutton, 1966–87	22	L.A. Dodgers (NL), 1966–80, 1988; Hou. Astros (NL), 1980–82; Mil. Brewers (AL), 1982–85; Oak. A's (AL), 1985; Cal. Angels (AL), 1986–88
Greg Maddux, 1987–2008	22	Chi. Cubs (NL), 1987–92; Atl. Braves (NL), 1993–2003; Chi. Cubs (NL), 2004–06; L.A. Dodgers (NL), 2006; S.D. Padres (NL), 2007–08; L.A. Dodgers (NL), 2008
Phil Niekro, 1965–87	21	Atl. Braves (NL), 1967–83; N.Y. Yankees (AL), 1984–85; Cle. Indians (AL), 1986–87
Cy Young, 1891–1910	20	Cle. Spiders (NL), 1891–98; St.L. Cardinals (NL), 1899–1900; Bos. Americans (AL), 1901–08; Cle. Naps (AL), 1909–11; Bos. Rustlers (NL), 1911
Tom Seaver, 1967–86	20	N.Y. Mets (NL), 1967–77, 1983; Cin. Reds (NL), 1977–82; Chi. White Sox (AL), 1984–86; Bos. Red Sox (AL), 1986
Roger Clemens, 1986–2005	20	Bos. Red Sox (AL), 1986–96; Tor. Blue Jays (AL), 1997–98; N.Y. Yankees (AL), 1999–2003; Hou. Astros (NL), 2004–05
Tom Glavine, 1988–2007	20	Atl. Braves (NL), 1988–2002; N.Y. Mets (NL), 2003–07

Evolution of Record for Most Games Pitched in a Season

American League

1901	Joe McGinnity, Bal. Orioles	48
1904	Jack Chesbro, N.Y. Yankees	55
1907	Ed Walsh, Chi. White Sox	56
1908	Ed Walsh, Chi. White Sox	66
1953	Ellis Kinder, Bos. Red Sox	69
1960	Mike Fornieles, Bos. Red Sox	70
1963	Stu Miller, Bal. Orioles	71
1964	John Wyatt, K.C. A's	81
1965	Eddie Fisher, Chi. White Sox	82
1968	Wilbur Wood, Chi. White Sox	88
1979	Mike Marshall, Min. Twins	90

National League (Pre-1900)

1876	Jim Devlin, Lou. Colonels	68
1879	Will White, Cin. Reds	76

National League (Post-1899)

1900	Bill Carrick, N.Y. Giants	45
1902	Vic Willis, Bos. Beaneaters	51
1903	Joe McGinnity, N.Y. Giants	55
1908	Christy Mathewson, N.Y. Giants	56
1942	Ace Adams, N.Y. Giants	61
1943	Ace Adams, N.Y. Giants	70
1950	Jim Konstanty, Phi. Phillies	74
1965	Ted Abernathy, Chi. Cubs	84
1969	Wayne Granger, Cin. Reds	90
1973	Mike Marshall, Mon. Expos	92
1974	Mike Marshall, L.A. Dodgers	106

Evolution of Innings Pitched Record

American League

Year	Player	IP
1901	Joe McGinnity, Bal. Orioles	382
1902	Cy Young, Bos. Americans	385
1904	Jack Chesbro, N.Y. Highlanders	455
1908	Ed Walsh, Chi. White Sox	464

National League (Pre-1900)

Year	Player	IP
1876	Jim Devlin, Lou. Colonels	622
1879	Will White, Cin. Reds	680
1900	Joe McGinnity, Brk. Bridegrooms	343
1901	Noodles Hahn, Cin. Reds	375
1902	Vic Willis, Bos. Beaneaters	410
1903	Joe McGinnity, N.Y. Giants	434

Most Quality Starts, Season

American League

39	Ed Walsh, Chi. White Sox, 1908
34	Denny McLain, Det. Tigers, 1968
34	Gaylord Perry, Cle. Indians, 1972
33	Frank Smith, Chi. White Sox, 1909
33	Wilbur Wood, Chi. White Sox, 1971
32	Walter Johnson, Was. Senators, 1910 and 1912
32	Bob Feller, Cle. Indians, 1946
31	Walter Johnson, Was. Senators, 1914
31	Dave McNally, Bal. Orioles, 1968
31	Wilbur Wood, Chi. White Sox, 1972

National League

37	Christy Mathewson, N.Y. Giants, 1908
35	Pete Alexander, Phi. Phillies, 1916
35	Sandy Koufax, L.A. Dodgers, 1966
34	Pete Alexander, Phi. Phillies, 1917
33	George McQuillan, Phi. Phillies, 1908
33	Pete Alexander, Phi. Phillies, 1915
33	Sandy Koufax, L.A. Dodgers, 1965
32	Dwight Gooden, N.Y. Mets, 1985
32	Mike Scott, Hou. Astros, 1986
31	Sandy Koufax, L.A. Dodgers, 1963
31	Claude Osteen, L.A. Dodgers, 1965
31	Tom Seaver, N.Y. Mets, 1971
31	Steve Carlton, Phi. Phillies, 1972

Most Quality Starts, Career

513	Walter Johnson (1907–27)
483	Don Sutton (1966–88)
481	Nolan Ryan (1966, 1968–93)
480	Greg Maddux (1986–2008)
465	Roger Clemens (1984–2007)
456	Gaylord Perry (1962–83)
454	Tom Seaver (1967–86)
447	Steve Carlton (1965–88)

442	Phil Niekro (1964–87)
436	Tom Glavine (1987–2008)
435	Pete Alexander (1911–30)
431	Tommy John (1963–74, 1976–89)
429	Bert Blyleven (1970–90, 1992)
426	Warren Spahn (1942, 1946–65)
404	Randy Johnson (1988–2009)

Most Wild Pitches, Season (Since 1900)

American League

26	Juan Guzman, 1993 Tor. Blue Jays
25	A.J. Burnett, 2011 N.Y. Yankees
24	Jack Morris, 1987 Det. Tigers
23	Tim Leary, 1990 N.Y. Yankees

National League

30	Red Ames, 1905 N.Y. Giants
27	Tony Cloninger, 1966 Atl. Braves
26	Larry Cheney, 1914 Chi. Cubs
23	Christy Mathewson, 1901 N.Y. Giants
23	Matt Clement, 2000 S.D. Padres

Last Legal Spitball Pitchers

American League

Doc Ayers .... (1913–21)
Ray Caldwell .... (1910–21)
Stan Coveleski .... (1912–28)
Urban Faber .... (1914–33)
Hub Leonard* .... (1913–25)
Jack Quinn .... (1909–33)
Allan Russell .... (1915–25)
Urban Shocker .... (1916–28)
Allan Sothoron .... (1914–26)
* Left-hander.

National League

Bill Doak .... (1912–29)
Phil Douglas .... (1912–22)
Dana Fillingim .... (1915–25)
Ray Fisher .... (1910–20)
Marvin Goodwin .... (1916–25)
Burleigh Grimes .... (1916–34)
Claude Hendrix .... (1911–20)
Clarence Mitchell* .... (1911–32)
Dick Rudolph .... (1910–27)

Left-Handed Pitchers Appearing in More Than 700 Games, Career

Jesse Orosco (1979, 1981–2003) 1252
Mike Stanton (1989–2007) 1158
John Franco (1984–2005) 1119
Dan Plesac (1986–2003) 1064
Eddie Guardado (1993–2009) 908
Arthur Rhodes (1991–2011) 900
Sparky Lyle (1967–82) 899
Jim Kaat (1959–83) 898
Paul Assenmacher (1986–99) 884
Mike Myers (1995–2007) 883
Alan Embree (1992–2009) 882
Billy Wagner (1995–2010) 853
Javier Lopez (2003–16) 839
Tug McGraw (1965–84) 824
Rick Honeycutt (1977–97) 797
Steve Kline (1997–2007) 796
Buddy Groom (1992–2005) 786

Jeremy Affeldt (2002–15) 774
Darren Oliver (1993–2004, 2006–13) 766
Darold Knowles (1965–80) 765
Mark Guthrie (1989–2003) 765
Kenny Rogers (1989–2008) 762
Tommy John (1963–74, 1976–89) 760
Warren Spahn (1942, 1946–65) 750
Matt Thornton (2004–16) 748
Tom Burgmeier (1968–84) 745
Gary Lavelle (1974–87) 745
Willie Hernandez (1977–89) 744
Steve Carlton (1965–88) 741
Ron Perranoski (1961–73) 737
Randy Myers (1985–98) 728
Jeff Fassero (1991–2006) 720
Dave Righetti (1979–95) 718
Ron Villone (1995–2009) 717
Oliver Perez (2002–10, 2012–22) 703

Pitchers Who Have Stolen Home

American League

Frank Owen, Chi. White Sox (vs. Was. Senators), Aug. 2, 1904
Bill Donovan, Det. Tigers (vs. Cle. Indians), May 7, 1906
Frank Owen, Chi. White Sox (vs. St.L. Browns), Apr. 27, 1908
Ed Walsh, Chi. White Sox (vs. N.Y. Yankees), Jun. 13, 1908
Ed Walsh, Chi. White Sox (vs. St.L. Browns), Jun. 2, 1909
Eddie Plank, Phi. A's (vs. Chi. White Sox), Aug. 30, 1909
Jack Warhop, N.Y. Yankees (vs. Chi. White Sox), Aug. 27, 1910
Jack Warhop, N.Y. Yankees (vs. St.L. Browns), Jul. 12, 1912
Red Faber, Chi. White Sox (vs. Phi. A's), Jul. 14, 1915
Reb Russell, Chi. White Sox (vs. Bos. Red Sox), Aug. 7, 1916
Babe Ruth, Bos. Red Sox (vs. St.L. Browns), Aug. 24, 1918
Dickie Kerr, Chi. White Sox (vs. N.Y. Yankees), Jul. 8, 1921
Red Faber, Chi. White Sox (vs. St.L. Browns), Apr. 23, 1923
George Mogridge, Was. Senators (vs. Chi. White Sox),
    Aug. 15, 1923
Joe Haynes, Chi. White Sox (vs. St.L. Browns), Sep. 17, 1944
Fred Hutchinson, Det. Tigers (vs. St.L. Browns), Aug. 29, 1947
Harry Dorish, St.L. Browns (vs. Was. Senators), Jun. 2, 1950

National League (Post-1900)

John Menafee, Chi. Cubs (vs. Brk. Dodgers), Jul. 15, 1902
Joe McGinnity, N.Y. Giants (vs. Brk. Dodgers), Aug. 8, 1903
Joe McGinnity, N.Y. Giants (vs. Bos. Beaneaters), Apr. 29, 1904
Christy Mathewson, N.Y. Giants (vs. Bos. Rustlers), Sep. 12, 1911
Leon Ames, N.Y. Giants (vs. Brk. Dodgers), May 22, 1912
Christy Mathewson, N.Y. Giants (vs. Bos. Braves), Jun. 28, 1912
Slim Sallee, N.Y. Giants (vs. St.L. Cardinals), Jul. 22, 1913
Sherry Smith, Brk. Dodgers (vs. N.Y. Giants), Apr. 16, 1916
Tom Seaton, Chi. Cubs (vs. Cin. Reds), Jun. 23, 1916
Bob Steele, N.Y. Giants (vs. St.L. Cardinals), Jul. 26, 1918
Hippo Vaughn, Chi. Cubs (vs. N.Y. Giants), Aug. 9, 1919
Dutch Reuther, Cin. Reds (vs. Chi. Cubs), Sep. 3, 1919
Jesse Barnes, N.Y. Giants (vs. St.L. Cardinals), Jul. 27, 1920
Dutch Reuther, Brk. Dodgers (vs. N.Y. Giants), May 4, 1921
Johnny Vander Meer, Cin. Reds (vs. N.Y. Giants), Sep. 23, 1943
Bucky Walters, Cin. Reds (vs. Pit. Pirates), Apr. 20, 1946
Don Newcombe, Brk. Dodgers (vs. Pit. Pirates), May 26, 1955
Curt Simmons, St.L. Cardinals (vs. Phi. Phillies), Sep. 1, 1963
Pascual Perez, Atl. Braves (vs. S.F. Giants). Sep. 7, 1984
Rick Sutcliffe, Chi. Cubs (vs. Phi. Phillies), Jul. 29, 1988
Kevin Ritz, Col. Rockies (vs. S.D. Padres), Jun. 5, 1997
Darren Dreifort, L.A. Dodgers (vs. Tex. Rangers), Jun. 12, 2001

3

First Players Elected to Hall of Fame from Each Position

First Base...Cap Anson, 1939
George Sisler, 1939
Second Base ....Nap Lajoie, 1937
Third Base ....Jimmy Collins, 1945
Shortstop...Honus Wagner, 1936
Left Field ....Fred Clarke, 1945
Center Field .... Ty Cobb, 1936
Right Field ....Babe Ruth, 1936
Catcher ....Roger Bresnahan, 1945
King Kelly, 1945
Right-Handed Pitcher ....Walter Johnson, 1936
Christy Mathewson, 1936
Left-Handed Pitcher ....Eddie Plank, 1946
Rube Waddell, 1946
Relief Pitcher ....Hoyt Wilhelm, 1985
Designated Hitter ....Paul Molitor, 2004

Highest Lifetime Batting Average for Hall of Fame Pitchers

	At-Bats	Hits	Average
Red Ruffing (1924–42, 1945–47)	1937	521	.269
Burleigh Grimes (1916–34)	1535	380	.248
Amos Rusie (1889–98, 1901)	1730	428	.247
Walter Johnson (1907–27)	2324	547	.235
Old Hoss Radbourn (1880–91)	2487	585	.235
Ted Lyons (1923–42, 1946)	1563	364	.233
Bob Lemon (1941–42, 1946–58)	1183	274	.232
Catfish Hunter (1965–79)	658	149	.226
Kid Nichols (1890–1901, 1904–06)	2086	471	.226
Dizzy Dean (1930, 1932–41, 1947)	717	161	.225

Hall of Famers with Lifetime Batting Averages Below .265 (Excluding Pitchers)

Joe Tinker, shortstop (1902–16)	.262	Elected 1946
Luis Aparicio, shortstop (1956–73)	.262	Elected 1984
Reggie Jackson, outfield (1967–87)	.262	Elected 1993
Ozzie Smith, shortstop (1978–96)	.262	Elected 2002
Gary Carter, catcher (1974–92)	.262	Elected 2003
Bill Mazeroski, second base (1956–72)	.260	Elected 2001
Rabbit Maranville, shortstop and second base (1912–35)	.258	Elected 1954
Harmon Killebrew, first base and third base (1954–75)	.256	Elected 1984
Ray Schalk, catcher (1912–29)	.253	Elected 1955

Hall of Famers with Lowest Marks in Offensive Categories*

Games	Ross Youngs (1917–26)	1211
At-Bats	Roy Campanella (1948–57)	4205
Hits	Roy Campanella (1948–57)	1161
Batting Average	Ray Schalk (1912–29)	.253
On-Base Percentage	Bill Mazeroski (1956–72)	.299
Slugging Percentage	Ray Schalk (1912–29)	.316
On-Base Plus Slugging	Luis Aparicio (1956–73)	.653
Doubles	Roy Campanella (1948–57)	178
Triples	Mike Piazza (1992–2007)	8
Home Runs	Ray Schalk (1912–29)	11
Runs Scored	Ray Schalk (1912–29)	579
Runs Batted In	Roger Bresnahan (1897–1915)	530
Stolen Bases	Ernie Lombardi (1931–47)	8

* Position players with at least 10 years.

Teams Fielding Most Future Hall of Fame Players

8 .........N.Y. Giants (NL), 1923.........Dave Bancroft (shortstop), Frankie Frisch (second base), Travis Jackson (infield), George Kelly (first base), Casey Stengel (outfield), Bill Terry (first base), Hack Wilson (outfield), and Ross Youngs (outfield)

8 .........N.Y. Yankees (AL), 1930.......Earle Combs (outfield), Bill Dickey (catcher), Lou Gehrig (first base), Lefty Gomez (pitcher), Waite Hoyt (pitcher), Herb Pennock (pitcher), Red Ruffing (pitcher), and Babe Ruth (outfield)

8 .........N.Y. Yankees (AL), 1931.......Earle Combs (outfield), Bill Dickey (catcher), Lou Gehrig (first base), Lefty Gomez (pitcher), Herb Pennock (pitcher), Red Ruffing (pitcher), Babe Ruth (outfield), and Joe Sewell (third base)

8 .........N.Y. Yankees (AL), 1933.......Earle Combs (outfield), Bill Dickey (catcher), Lou Gehrig (first base), Lefty Gomez (pitcher), Herb Pennock (pitcher), Red Ruffing (pitcher), Babe Ruth (outfield), and Joe Sewell (third base)

Infields Fielding Four Future Hall of Famers

N.Y. Giants (NL), 1925......................First Base: Bill Terry
Second Base: George Kelly
Third Base: Fred Lindstrom
Shortstop: Travis Jackson

N.Y. Giants (NL), 1926.................First Base: George Kelly
Second Base: Frankie Frisch
Third Base: Fred Lindstrom
Shortstop: Travis Jackson

N.Y. Giants (NL), 1927......................First Base: Bill Terry
Second Base: Rogers Hornsby
Third Base: Fred Lindstrom
Shortstop: Travis Jackson

Hall of Fame Pitchers Who Batted Right and Threw Left

Carl Hubbell (1928–43)   Eppa Rixey (1912–33)   Rube Waddell (1897, 1899–1910)
Randy Johnson (1988–2009)

Switch-Hitting Pitchers in Hall of Fame

Mordecai Brown (1903–16)   Ted Lyons (1923–42, 1946)   Kid Nichols (1890–1901, 1904–06)
Red Faber (1914–24, 1926–33)*   Rube Marquard (1908–24)**   Robin Roberts (1948–66)
Herb Pennock (1912–17, 1919–34)   Early Wynn (1946–63)***

* Batted right-handed in 1925.
** Batted left-handed in 1925.
*** Batted right-handed 1939–44.

Hall of Fame Pitchers Who Played Most Games at Other Positions

	Games
John Clarkson (outfield: 27; third base: 4; first base: 2)	33
Bob Lemon (outfield: 14; third base: 2)	16
Walter Johnson (outfield)	15

Hall of Fame Position Players Who Also Pitched

	Appearances	
Cap Anson	3	1883 (2) and 1884 (1)
Jake Beckley	1	1902
Wade Boggs	2	1997 (1) and 1999 (1)
Roger Bresnahan	9	1897 (6), 1901 (2), and 1901 (1)
Dan Brouthers	4	1897 (3) and 1883 (1)
Jesse Burkett	23	1890 (21), 1894 (1), and 1902 (1)
Ty Cobb	3	1918 (2) and 1925 (1)
George Davis	3	1891
Buck Ewing	9	1882 (1), 1884 (1), 1885 (1), 1888 (2), 1889 (3), and 1890 (1)
Jimmie Foxx	10	1939 (1) and 1945 (9)
Harry Hooper	1	1913
George Kelly	1	1917
King Kelly	12	1880 (1), 1883 (1), 1884 (2), 1888 (3), 1890 (1), 1891 (3), and 1892 (1)
Tommy McCarthy	13	1884 (7), 1886 (1), 1888 (2), 1889 (1), 1891 (1), and 1894 (1)
Stan Musial	1	1952
Jim O'Rourke	6	1883 (2) and 1884 (4)
Sam Rice	9	1915 (4) and 1916 (5)
Babe Ruth	163	1914 (4), 1915 (32), 1916 (44), 1917 (41), and 1918 (20), 1919 (17), 1920 (1), 1921 (2), 1930 (1), and 1933 (1)
George Sisler	23	1915 (15), 1916 (3), and 1918 (2)
Tris Speaker	1	1914 (1)
Honus Wagner	2	1900 (1) and 1902 (1)
Bobby Wallace	57	1894 (4), 1895 (30), 1896 (22), and 1902 (1)
Ted Williams	1	1940

Hall of Fame Pitchers with Losing Records

	Wins–Losses
Rollie Fingers (1968–82, 1984–85)	114–118
Bruce Sutter (1976–86, 1988)	68–71
Satchel Paige (1948–49, 1951–53, 1965)	28–31
Trevor Hoffman (1993–2010)	61–75

Leading Career Pitching Marks by Those Not In Hall of Fame

Most Games Pitched	Jesse Orosco (1979–2003)	1252
Most Games Started	Roger Clemens (1984–2007)	707
Most Complete Games	Bobby Mathews (1871–1887)	525
Most Innings Pitched	Bobby Mathews (1871–1887)	4956
Most Walks Allowed	Bobo Newsom (1929–30, 1932, 1934–48, 1952–53)	1732
Most Strikeouts	Roger Clemens (1984–2007)	4672
Most Shutouts	Luis Tiant (1964–82)	49
Most Games Won	Roger Clemens (1984–2007)	354
Most Games Lost	Jack Powell (1897–1912)	254
Most	Francisco Rodriguez (2002–17)	437
Lowest ERA	Smoky Joe Wood (1908–20)	2.03
Winning Percentage	Spud Chandler (1937–47)	.717

Leading Career Batting Marks by Players Not In Hall of Fame

Most Games Played	Pete Rose (1963–86)	3562
Most At-Bats	Pete Rose (1963–86)	14,053
Most Base Hits	Pete Rose (1963–86)	4256
Most Singles	Pete Rose (1963–86)	2264
Most Doubles	Barry Bonds (1986–2007)	746
Most Triples	Ed Konetchy (1907–21)	182

continued on next page

Most Home Runs ....Barry Bonds (1986–2007)......................................762
Most Runs Scored ....Barry Bonds (1986–2007).....................................2227
Most RBIs ....Alex Rodriguez (1994–2013, 2015–16) 2086
Most Walks ....Barry Bonds (1986–2007).....................................2558
Most Strikeouts ....Adam Dunn (2001–14)..2379
Most Stolen Bases..............................Vince Coleman (1985–97) 752
Highest Lifetime Batting Average.......Joe Jackson (1908–20) .... .356
Highest Lifetime Slugging Percentage........Barry Bonds (1986–2007)..............................607
Highest Lifetime On-Base Percentage ....John McGraw* (1891–1906) .... .466

* Elected to Hall of Fame in 1937 as a manager.

Most Career Hits by Players Not in Hall of Fame

4256............................... Pete Rose (1963–86)	2716.................................... Rusty Staub (1963–85)
3166................... Adrian Beltre (1998–2018)**	2715.................................... Bill Buckner (1969–90)
3384...............Albert Pujols***** (2001–22)	2712.................................... Dave Parker (1973–91)
3166.....................Adrian Beltre*** (1998–2018)	2705.................................... Doc Cramer (1929–48)
3115.....Alex Rodriguez (1994–2013, 2015–16)	2689.................................... Gary Sheffield (1988–2009)
3089.............................Ichiro Suzuki**** (2001–19)	2651.................................... Lave Cross (1887–1907)
3088........................ Miguel Cabrera* (2003–)	2639....................................Robinson Cano* (2005–)
3020....................... Rafael Palmeiro (1986–2005)	2599.................................... Steve Garvey (1969–87)
2935............................. Barry Bonds (1986–2007)	2591.................................... Luis Gonzalez (1990–2008)
2877............................. Omar Vizquel (1989–2012)	2586.....Julio Franco (1982–94, 1996–97, 1999, 2001–07)
2866........................... Harold Baines (1980–2001)	2574.................................... Manny Ramirez (1993–2011)
2769............................. Johnny Damon (1995–2012)	2561.................................... Willie Davis (1960–79)
2757............................. Vada Pinson (1958–75)	2548....................................Steve Finley (1989–2007)
2743............................. Al Oliver (1968–85)	2544.................... George Van Haltren (1887–1903)
2725............................. Carlos Beltran** (1998–2017)	

* Active.
** Will be eligible for Hall of Fame in 2023.
*** Will be eligible for Hall of Fame in 2024.
**** Will be eligible for Hall of Fame in 2025.
***** Will be eligible for Hall of Fame in 2028.

Most Career Wins by Pitchers Not In Hall of Fame

354................................ Roger Clemens (1984–2007)	265.................................... Jim McCormick (1878–1887)
297................................ Bobby Mathews (1871–1887)	264.................................... Gus Weyhing (1887–1901)
288................................ Tommy John (1963–89)	256.................................... Andy Pettitte (1995–2013)
284................................ Tony Mullane (1881–94)	252.................................... Al Spalding (1871–87)
283................................ Jim Kaat (1959–83)	251....................................CC Sabathia** (2001–19)
270................................ Mike Mussina (1991–2008)	247.................................... Jack Quinn (1909–33)
269................................ Jamie Moyer (1986–2012)	247....................Bartolo Colon* (1997–2009, 2011–18)

* Will be eligible for Hall of Fame in 2024.
** Will be eligible for Hall of Fame in 2025.

Most Career Home Runs by Players Not In Hall of Fame

762........................... Barry Bonds (1986–2007)	462.................................... Adam Dunn (2001–14)
703...........................Albert Pujols***** (2001–22)	442.................................... Dave Kingman (1971–86)
696................... Alex Rodriguez (1994–2013, 2015–16)	440.................................... Jason Giambi (1995–2014)
609............................. Sammy Sosa (1989–2007)	439.................................... Paul Konerko* (1997–2014)
583............................. Mark McGwire (1986–2001)	435.................................... Carlos Beltran** (1998–2017)
569............................. Rafael Palmeiro (1986–2005)	434.................................... Juan Gonzalez (1989–2005)
555............................. Manny Ramirez (1993–2011)	434.................................... Andruw Jones (1996–2012)
509............................. Gary Sheffield (1988–2009)	424.................... Edwin Encarnacion**** (2005–20)
507............................. Miguel Cabrera* (2003–)	414.................................... Darrell Evans (1969–89)
477...........................Adrian Beltre*** (1998–2018)	412.................................... Alfonso Soriano (1999–2014)
473............................. Carlos Delgado (1993–2009)	409.................................... Mark Teixeira (2003–16)
462............................. Jose Canseco (1986–2001)	

* Active.
** Will be eligible for Hall of Fame in 2023.
*** Will be eligible for Hall of Fame in 2024.
**** Will be eligible for Hall of Fame in 2026.
***** Will be eligible for Hall of Fame in 2028.

Hall of Fame Inductees Receiving 90 Percent of Vote

Mariano Rivera, 2019 (425 ballots cast)..................100.0
Derek Jeter, 2020 (397 ballots cast) 99.7
Ken Griffey Jr., 2016 (440 ballots cast).....................99.3
Tom Seaver, 1992 (425 ballots cast)..........................98.8
Nolan Ryan, 1999 (491 ballots cast)...........................98.8
Cal Ripken Jr., 2007 (532 ballots cast) 98.5
Ty Cobb, 1936 (226 ballots cast)...............................98.2
Hank Aaron, 1982 (415 ballots cast)..........................97.8
Tony Gwynn, 2007 (532 ballots cast) 97.6
Randy Johnson, 2015 (549 ballots cast)....................97.3
Greg Maddux, 2014 (571 ballots cast)........................97.2
Chipper Jones, 2018 (410 ballots cast) 97.2
Johnny Bench, 1989 (431 ballots cast)........................96.4
Babe Ruth, 1936 (226 ballots cast) 95.1
Honus Wagner, 1936 (226 ballots cast)......................95.1
Rickey Henderson, 2009 (539 ballots cast)................94.8

Carl Yastrzemski, 1989 (423 ballots cast).................94.6
Willie Mays, 1979 (432 ballots cast).........................94.6
Bob Feller, 1962 (160 ballots cast)............................93.8
Reggie Jackson, 1993 (396 ballots cast) 93.6
Ted Williams, 1966 (302 ballots cast).......................93.4
Stan Musial, 1969 (340 ballots cast).........................93.2
Vladimir Guerrero, 2018 (392 ballots cast) 92.9
Roberto Clemente, 1973 (424 ballots cast)...............92.7
Jim Palmer, 1990 (444 ballots cast)..........................92.5
Brooks Robinson, 1983 (374 ballots cast).................92.0
Tom Glavine, 2014 (571 ballots cast) 91.9
Wade Boggs, 2005 (516 ballots cast)........................91.9
Pedro Martinez, 2015 (549 ballots cast)...................91.1
Christy Mathewson, 1936 (226 ballots cast).............90.7
Rod Carew, 1991 (401 ballots cast)..........................90.5
Roberto Alomar, 2011 (523 ballots cast)..................90.0

Won–Lost Percentage of Hall of Famers Elected as Players Who Managed in Majors

		Teams Managed	Career Wins–Losses
.593	Frank Chance	Chi. Cubs (NL), 1905–12	932–640
		N.Y. Yankees (AL), 1913–14	
		Bos. Red Sox (AL), 1923	
.582	Mickey Cochrane	Det. Tigers (AL), 1934–38	413–297
.576	Fred Clarke	Lou. Colonels (NL), 1897–99	1602–1179
		Pit. Pirates (NL), 1900–15	
.575	Cap Anson	Chi. White Stockings–Colts (NL), 1879–97	1297–957
		N.Y. Giants (NL), 1898	
.562	Monte Ward	N.Y. Gothams (NL), 1884	394–307
		Brk. Wonders (PL), 1890	
		Brk. Bridegrooms (NL), 1891–92	
		N.Y. Giants (NL), 1893–94	
.555	Bill Terry	N.Y. Giants (NL), 1932–41	823–661
.553	Buck Ewing	N.Y. Giants (PL), 1890	489–395
		Cin. Reds (NL), 1895–99	
		N.Y. Giants (NL), 1900	
.551	Walter Johnson	Was. Senators (AL), 1929–32	530–432
		Cle. Indians (AL), 1933–35	
.546	Nap Lajoie	Cle. Naps (AL), 1905–09	397–330
.544	Jimmy Collins	Bos. Americans (AL), 1901–06	464–389
.543	Bill Dickey	N.Y. Yankees (AL), 1946	57–48
.542	Tris Speaker	Cle. Indians (AL), 1919–26	616–520
.541	King Kelly	Bos. Reds (PL), 1890	124–105
		Cin. Reds–Mil. Brewers (AA), 1891	
.540	Joe Cronin	Was. Senators (AL), 1933–34	1236–1055
		Bos. Red Sox (AL), 1935–47	
.538	Hughie Jennings	Det. Tigers (AL), 1907–20	1131–972
.536	Gabby Hartnett	Chi. Cubs (NL), 1938–40	203–176
.530	Pie Traynor	Pit. Pirates (NL), 1934–39	457–406
.522	Yogi Berra	N.Y. Yankees (AL), 1964, 1984–85	484–444
		N.Y. Mets (NL), 1972–75	
.521	Eddie Collins	Chi. White Sox (AL), 1925–26	160–147

continued on next page

	Teams Managed	Career Wins-Losses
.521 ....Red Schoendienst	St.L. Cardinals (NL), 1965–76 and 1980	1028–944
.519 ....Ty Cobb..............	Det. Tigers (AL), 1921–26	479–444
.519 ....Bob Lemon	K.C. Royals (AL), 1970–72..............	432–401
	Chi. White Sox (AL), 1977–78	
	N.Y. Yankees (AL), 1978–79 and 1981–82	
.513 ....Frankie Frisch	St.L. Cardinals (NL), 1933–38	1137–1078
	Pit. Pirates (NL), 1940–46	
	Chi. Cubs (NL), 1949–51	
.500 ....Deacon White	Cin. Reds (NL), 1879	9–9
.512 ....Joe Kelley..............	Cin. Reds (NL), 1902–05	337–321
	Bos. Doves (NL), 1908	
.498 ....Joe Gordon	Cle. Indians (AL), 1958–60	305–308
	Det.Tigers (AL), 1960	
	K.C. A's (AL), 1961	
	K.C. Royals (AL), 1969	
.497 ....Joe Tinker..............	Cin. Reds (NL), 1913	304–308
	Chi. Whales (FL), 1914–15	
	Chi. Cubs (NL), 1916	
.488 ....Jim O'Rourke	Buff. Bisons (NL), 1881–84	246–258
	Was. Senators (NL), 1893	
.487 ....Lou Boudreau..............	Cle. Indians (AL), 1942–50	1162–1224
	Bos. Red Sox (AL), 1952–54	
	K.C. A's (AL), 1955–57	
	Chi. Cubs (NL), 1960	
.485 ....Johnny Evers..............	Chi. Cubs (NL), 1913 and 1921	196–208
	Chi. White Sox (AL), 1924	
.482 ....Christy Mathewson	Cin. Reds (NL), 1916–18	164–176
.481 ....Eddie Mathews	Atl. Braves (NL), 1972–74	149–161
.476 ....Max Carey..............	Brk. Dodgers (NL), 1932–33	146–161
.475 ....George Sisler	St.L. Browns (AL), 1924–26	218–241
.475 ....Frank Robinson	Cle. Indians (AL), 1975–77	1065–1176
	S.F. Giants (NL), 1981–84	
	Bal. Orioles (AL), 1988–91	
	Mon. Expos (NL), 2002–04	
	Was. Nationals (NL), 2005–06	
.467..............Mel Ott..............	N.Y. Giants (NL), 1942–48	464–530
.467..............Gil Hodges..............	Was. Senators (AL), 1963–67..............	660–753
	N.Y. Mets (NL), 1968–71	
.460..............Rogers Hornsby..............	St.L. Cardinals (NL), 1925–26	680–798
	Bos. Braves (NL), 1928	
	Chi. Cubs (NL), 1930–32	
	St.L. Browns (AL), 1933–37 and 1952	
	Cin. Reds (NL), 1952–53	
.444..............Hugh Duffy..............	Mil. Brewers (AL), 1901	535–671
	Phi. Phillies (NL), 1904–06	
	Chi. White Sox (AL), 1910–11	
	Bos. Red Sox (AL), 1921–22	
.442..............Mordecai Brown	St.L. Terriers (FL), 1914	50–63
.434..............Rabbit Maranville..............	Chi. Cubs (NL), 1925	23–30

continued on next page

	Teams Managed	Career Wins–Losses
.432 .... Roger Bresnahan	St.L. Cardinals (NL), 1909–12	328–432
	Chi. Cubs (NL), 1915	
.432 .... Burleigh Grimes	Brk. Dodgers (NL), 1937–38	130–171
.430 .... Ted Lyons	Chi. White Sox (AL), 1946–48	185–245
.429 .... Cy Young	Bos. Americans (AL), 1907	3–4
.429 .... Ted Williams	Was. Senators II (AL), 1969–71	273–364
	Tex. Rangers (AL), 1972	
.428 .... Ryne Sandberg	Phi. Phillies (NL), 2013–15	119–159
.425 .... Larry Doby	Chi. White Sox (AL), 1978	37–50
.408 .... Billy Herman	Pit. Pirates (NL), 1947	189–274
	Bos. Red Sox (AL), 1964–66	
.407 .... Dave Bancroft	Bos. Braves (NL), 1924–27	249–363
.389 .... Bid McPhee	Cin. Reds (NL), 1901–02	79–124
.287 .... Bobby Wallace	St.L. Browns (AL), 1911–12	62–154
	Cin. Reds (NL), 1937	
.267 .... Pud Galvin	Buff. Bisons (NL), 1885	8–22
.266 .... Jim Bottomley	St.L. Browns (AL), 1937	21–58
.250 .... Luke Appling	K.C. A's (AL), 1967	10–30
.200 .... Honus Wagner	Pit. Pirates (NL), 1917	1–4

Hall of Famers Making Last Out in World Series

1903 ......Honus Wagner (Pit. Pirates, NL)....... strikeout
1926 ......Babe Ruth (N.Y. Yankees, AL)....... caught stealing
1938 ......Billy Herman (Chi. Cubs, NL) .... ground out
1940 ......Earl Averill (Det. Tigers, AL) .... ground out
1949 ......Gil Hodges (Brk. Dodgers, NL) .... strikeout
1952 ......Pee Wee Reese (Brk. Dodgers, NL) .... fly out
1958 ......Red Schoendienst (Mil. Braves, NL) .... fly out
1959 ......Luis Aparicio (Chi. White Sox, AL) .... line out
1962 ......Willie McCovey (S.F. Giants, NL) .... line out
1975 ......Carl Yazstremski (Bos. Red Sox, AL) .... fly out
1984 ......Tony Gwynn (S.D. Padres, NL) .... fly out
2000 ......Mike Piazza (N.Y. Mets, NL) .... fly out

Hall of Famers Who Played for the Harlem Globetrotters

Ernie Banks   Ferguson Jenkins
Lou Brock   Satchel Paige
Bob Gibson

Hall of Famers Who Died on Their Birthday

Stanley "Bucky" Harris, born Nov. 8, 1896, and died Nov. 8, 1977
Charles "Gabby" Hartnett, born Dec. 20, 1900, and died Dec. 20, 1972
Joe Tinker, born Jul. 27, 1880, and died Jul. 27, 1948

4

AWARDS

Most Valuable Player

Unanimous Choice for MVP

American League

Ty Cobb, outfield, Det. Tigers, 1911
Babe Ruth, outfield, N.Y. Yankees, 1923
Hank Greenberg, first base, Det. Tigers, 1935
Al Rosen, third base, Cle. Indians, 1953
Mickey Mantle, outfield, N.Y. Yankees, 1956
Frank Robinson, outfield, Bal. Orioles, 1966
Denny McLain, pitcher, Det. Tigers, 1968
Reggie Jackson, outfield, Oak. A's, 1973
Jose Canseco, outfield, Oak. A's, 1988
Frank Thomas, first base, Chi. White Sox, 1993
Ken Griffey Jr., outfield, Sea. Mariners, 1997
Mike Trout, outfield, L.A. Angels, 2014
Shohei Ohtani, L.A. Angels, 2021

National League

Carl Hubbell, pitcher, N.Y. Giants, 1936
Orlando Cepeda, first base, St.L. Cardinals, 1967
Mike Schmidt, third base, Phi. Phillies, 1980
Jeff Bagwell, first base, Hou. Astros, 1994
Ken Caminiti, third base, S.D. Padres, 1996
Barry Bonds, outfield, S.F. Giants, 2002
Albert Pujols, first base, St.L. Cardinals, 2009
Bryce Harper, outfield, Was. Nationals, 2015

Closest Winning Margins in MVP Voting

American League

Margin	Season	MVP	Votes	Runner-Up	Votes
+1	1947	Joe DiMaggio, N.Y. Yankees	202	Ted Williams, Bos. Red Sox	201
+2	1928	Mickey Cochrane, Phi. A's	53	Heinie Manush, St.L. Browns	51
+2	1934	Mickey Cochrane, Det. Tigers	67	Charlie Gehringer, Det. Tigers	65
+3	1960	Roger Maris, N.Y. Yankees	225	Mickey Mantle, N.Y. Yankees	222
+3	1996	Juan Gonzalez, Tex. Rangers	290	Alex Rodriguez, Sea. Mariners	287
+4	1925	Roger Peckinpaugh, Was. Senators	45	Al Simmons, Phi. A's	41
+4	1937	Charlie Gehringer, Det. Tigers	78	Joe DiMaggio, N.Y. Yankees	74
+4	1944	Hal Newhouser, Det. Tigers	236	Dizzy Trout, Det. Tigers	232
+4	1961	Roger Maris, N.Y. Yankees	202	Mickey Mantle, N.Y. Yankees	198

National League

Margin	Season	MVP	Votes	Runner-Up	Votes
0 (Tie)	1979	Keith Hernandez, St.L. Cardinals	216	Willie Stargell, Pit. Pirates	216
+1	1944	Marty Marion, St.L. Cardinals	190	Bill Nicholson, Chi. Cubs	189
+2	1937	Joe Medwick, St.L. Cardinals	70	Gabby Hartnett, Chi. Cubs	68
+2	2017	Giancarlo Stanton, Mia. Marlins	302	Joey Votto, Cin. Reds	300
+4	1911	Frank Schulte, Chi. Cubs	29	Christy Mathewson, N.Y. Giants	25
+5	1912	Larry Doyle, N.Y. Giants	48	Honus Wagner, Pit. Pirates	43
+5	1955	Roy Campanella, Brk. Dodgers	226	Duke Snider, Brk. Dodgers	221

Widest Winning Margins in MVP Voting

American League

Margin	Season	MVP	Votes	Runner-Up	Votes
+191	2014	Mike Trout, L.A. Angels	420	Victor Martinez, Det. Tigers	229
+183	1993	Frank Thomas, Chi. White Sox	392	Paul Molitor, Tor. Blue Jays	209
+169	1953	Al Rosen, Cle. Indians	336	Yogi Berra, N.Y. Yankees	167
+169	1975	Fred Lynn, Bos. Red Sox	326	John Mayberry, K.C. Royals	157
+164	1973	Reggie Jackson, Oak. A's	336	Jim Palmer, Bal. Orioles	172
+157	1972	Dick Allen, Chi. White Sox	321	Joe Rudi, Oak. A's	164
+157	1982	Robin Yount, Mil. Brewers	385	Eddie Murray, Bal. Orioles	228
+151	2021	Shohei Ohtani, L.A. Angels	420	Vladimir Guerrero Jr., Tor. Blue Jays	269
+150	1956	Mickey Mantle, N.Y. Yankees	336	Yogi Berra, N.Y. Yankees	186
+150	1988	Jose Canseco, Oak. A's	392	Mike Greenwell, Bos. Red Sox	242

National League

Margin	Season	MVP	Votes	Runner-Up	Votes
+215	2009	Albert Pujols, St.L. Cardinals	448	Hanley Ramirez, Fla. Marlins	233
+191	1994	Jeff Bagwell, Hou. Astros	392	Matt Williams, S.F. Giants	201
+186	2015	Bryce Harper, Was. Nationals	420	Paul Goldscmidt, Ari. D'backs	234
+172	2002	Barry Bonds, S.F. Giants	448	Albert Pujols, St.L. Cardinals	276
+170	2016	Kris Bryant, Chi. Cubs	415	Daniel Murphy, Was. Nationals	245
+167	2013	Andrew McCutchen, Pit. Pirates	409	Paul Goldschmidt, Ari. D'backs	242
+166	1998	Sammy Sosa, Chi. Cubs	438	Mark McGwire, St.L. Cardinals	272
+164	2010	Joey Votto, Cin. Reds	443	Albert Pujols, St.L. Cardinals	279
+160	2001	Barry Bonds, S.F. Giants	438	Sammy Sosa, Chi. Cubs	278
+156	1999	Chipper Jones, Atl. Braves	432	Jeff Bagwell, Hou. Astros	276
+155	1996	Ken Caminiti, S.D. Padres	392	Mike Piazza, L.A. Dodgers	237

Won MVP Award in Consecutive Years, by Position

First Base .... Jimmie Foxx, Phi. A's (AL), 1932–33
Frank Thomas, Chi. White Sox (AL), 1993–94
Albert Pujols, St.L. Cardinals (NL), 2008–09
Second Base .... Joe Morgan, Cin. Reds (NL), 1975–76
Third Base .... Mike Schmidt, Phi. Phillies (NL), 1980–81
Miguel Cabrera, Det. Tigers (AL), 2012–13
Shortstop .... Ernie Banks, Chi. Cubs (NL), 1959–60
Outfield .... Mickey Mantle, N.Y. Yankees (AL), 1956–57
Roger Maris, N.Y. Yankees (AL), 1960–61
Dale Murphy, Atl. Braves (NL), 1982–83
Barry Bonds, Pit. Pirates (NL), 1992; S.F. Giants (NL), 1993
Barry Bonds, S.F. Giants (NL), 2001–04
Catcher .... Yogi Berra, N.Y. Yankees (AL), 1954–55
Pitcher .... Hal Newhouser, Det. Tigers (AL), 1944–45

Teammates Finishing One-Two in MVP Balloting

American League

Season	Team	Leader	Position	Runner-Up	Position
1934	Det. Tigers	Mickey Cochrane	Catcher	Charlie Gehringer	Second base
1944	Det. Tigers	Hal Newhouser	Pitcher	Dizzy Trout	Pitcher
1945	Det. Tigers	Hal Newhouser	Pitcher	Eddie Mayo	Second base
1956	N.Y. Yankees	Mickey Mantle	Outfield	Yogi Berra	Catcher
1959	Chi. White Sox*	Nellie Fox	Second base	Luis Aparicio	Shortstop
1960	N.Y. Yankees	Roger Maris	Outfield	Mickey Mantle	Outfield

continued on next page

Season	Team	Leader	Position	Runner-Up	Position
1961	N.Y. Yankees	Roger Maris	Outfield	Mickey Mantle	Outfield
1962	N.Y. Yankees	Mickey Mantle	Outfield	Bobby Richardson	Second base
1965	Min. Twins	Zoilo Versalles	Shortstop	Tony Oliva	Outfield
1966	Bal. Orioles*	Frank Robinson	Outfield	Brooks Robinson	Third base
1968	Det. Tigers	Denny McLain	Pitcher	Bill Freehan	Catcher
1971	Oak. A's	Vida Blue	Pitcher	Sal Bando	Third base
1983	Bal. Orioles	Cal Ripken Jr.	Shortstop	Eddie Murray	First base

National League

Season	Team	Leader	Position	Runner-Up	Position
1914	Bos. Braves*	Johnny Evers	Second base	Rabbit Maranville	Shortstop
1941	Brk. Dodgers*	Dolph Camilli	First base	Pete Reiser	Outfield
1942	St.L. Cardinals	Mort Cooper	Pitcher	Enos Slaughter	Outfield
1943	St.L. Cardinals	Stan Musial	Outfield	Mort Cooper	Pitcher
1955	Brk. Dodgers	Roy Campanella	Catcher	Duke Snider	Outfield
1956	Brk. Dodgers	Don Newcombe	Pitcher	Sal Maglie	Pitcher
1960	Pit. Pirates	Dick Groat	Shortstop	Don Hoak	Third base
1967	St.L. Cardinals	Orlando Cepeda	First base	Tim McCarver	Catcher
1976	Cin. Reds	Joe Morgan	Second base	George Foster	Outfield
1989	S.F. Giants	Kevin Mitchell	Outfield	Will Clark	First base
1990	Pit. Pirates	Barry Bonds	Outfield	Bobby Bonilla	Outfield
2000	S.F. Giants	Jeff Kent	Second base	Barry Bonds	Outfield

* Teammates finished one-two-three in voting (AL 1959: Early Wynn, pitcher; AL 1966: Boog Powell, first base; NL 1914: Bill James, pitcher; and NL 1941: Whit Wyatt, pitcher).

Triple Crown Winners *Not* Winning MVP

American League

Season	Triple Crown Winner	MVP Winner
1934	Lou Gehrig, N.Y. Yankees	Mickey Cochrane, Det. Tigers
1942	Ted Williams, Bos. Red Sox	Joe Gordon, N.Y. Yankees
1947	Ted Williams, Bos. Red Sox	Joe DiMaggio, N.Y. Yankees

National League

Season	Triple Crown Winner	MVP Winner
1912	Heinie Zimmerman, Chi. Cubs	Larry Doyle, N.Y. Giants
1933	Chuck Klein, Phi. Phillies	Carl Hubbell, N.Y. Giants

MVPs on Nonwinning Teams

American League

Team	Wins–Losses
Robin Yount, Mil. Brewers, 1989	81–81
Alex Rodriguez, Tex. Rangers, 2003	71–91
Mike Trout, L.A. Angels, 2016	74–88
Mike Trout, L.A. Angels, 2019	72–90
Shohei Ohtani, L.A. Angels, 2021	77–85

National League

Team	Wins–Losses
Hank Sauer, Chi. Cubs, 1952	77–77
Ernie Banks, Chi. Cubs, 1958	72–82
Ernie Banks, Chi. Cubs, 1959	74–80
Andre Dawson, Chi. Cubs, 1987	76–85
Giancarlo Stanton, Mia. Marlins, 2017	77–85

MVPs *Not* Batting .300, Hitting 30 Home Runs, or Driving in 100 Runs (Not Including Pitchers)*

American League

	Batting Average	Home Runs	RBIs
Roger Peckinpaugh, Was. Senators, 1925	.294	4	64
Mickey Cochrane, Phi. A's, 1928	.293	10	57
Yogi Berra, N.Y. Yankees, 1951	.294	27	88
Elston Howard, N.Y. Yankees, 1963	.287	28	85
Zoilo Versalles, Min. Twins, 1965	.273	19	77

National League

	Batting Average	Home Runs	RBIs
Johnny Evers, Bos. Braves, 1914	.279	1	40
Bob O'Farrell, St.L Cardinals, 1926	.293	7	68
Marty Marion, St.L. Cardinals, 1944	.267	6	63
Maury Wills, L.A. Dodgers, 1962	.299	6	48
Kirk Gibson, L.A. Dodgers, 1988	.273	25	76

* Excluding 2020.

Pitchers Winning MVP Award

American League

Walter Johnson, Was. Senators, 1912*
Walter Johnson, Was. Senators, 1924**
Lefty Grove, Phi. A's, 1931
Spud Chandler, N.Y. Yankees, 1943
Hal Newhouser, Det. Tigers, 1944
Hal Newhouser, Det. Tigers, 1945
Bobby Shantz, Phi. A's, 1952
Denny McLain, Det. Tigers, 1968
Vida Blue, Oak. A's, 1971
Rollie Fingers, Mil. Brewers, 1981
Willie Hernandez, Det. Tigers, 1984
Roger Clemens, Bos. Red Sox, 1986
Dennis Eckersley, Oak. A's, 1992
Justin Verlander, Det. Tigers, 2011
Shohei Ohtani, L.A. Angels 2021***
* Chalmers Award.
** League Award.
*** Two-way player.

National League

Dazzy Vance, Brk. Dodgers, 1924*
Carl Hubbell, N.Y. Giants, 1933
Dizzy Dean, St.L. Cardinals, 1934
Carl Hubbell, N.Y. Giants, 1936
Bucky Walters, Cin. Reds, 1939
Mort Cooper, St.L. Cardinals, 1942
Jim Konstanty, Phi. Phillies, 1950
Don Newcombe, Brk. Dodgers, 1956
Sandy Koufax, L.A. Dodgers, 1963
Bob Gibson, St.L. Cardinals, 1968
Clayton Kershaw, L.A. Dodgers, 2014

Players Winning MVP Award First Season in League

American League

Frank Robinson, Bal. Orioles, 1966
Dick Allen, Chi. White Sox, 1972
Fred Lynn, Bos. Red Sox, 1975
Willie Hernandez, Det. Tigers, 1984
Ichiro Suzuki, Sea. Mariners, 2001
Vladimir Guerrero, Ana. Angels, 2004

National League

Kirk Gibson, L.A. Dodgers, 1988

MVPs Receiving Fewer First-Place Votes Than Runner-Up

American League

1944   Hal Newhouser (Det. Tigers, pitcher) winner over Dizzy Trout (Det. Tigers, pitcher), 236–232
1960   Roger Maris (N.Y. Yankees, outfield) winner over Mickey Mantle (N.Y. Yankees, outfield), 225–222
1991   Ivan Rodriguez (Tex. Rangers, catcher) winner over Pedro Martinez (Bos. Red Sox, pitcher), 252–239

National League

1966   Roberto Clemente (Pit. Pirates, outfield) winner over Sandy Koufax (L.A. Dodgers, pitcher), 218–205

Teams with Most Consecutive MVP Awards

5	S.F. Giants (NL), 2000–04	Jeff Kent, second base, 2000
		Barry Bonds, outfield, 2001–04
4	N.Y. Yankees (AL), 1954–57	Yogi Berra, catcher, 1954 and 1955
		Mickey Mantle, outfield, 1956 and 1957
4	N.Y. Yankees (AL), 1960–63	Roger Maris, outfield, 1960 and 1961
		Mickey Mantle, outfield, 1962
		Elston Howard, catcher, 1963

Players Winning MVP Award with Two Different Teams

		MVP Seasons
Barry Bonds	Pit. Pirates (NL)	1990 and 1992
	S.F. Giants (NL)	1993 and 2001–04
Mickey Cochrane	Phi. A's (AL)	1928
	Det. Tigers (AL)	1934
Jimmie Foxx	Phi. A's (AL)	1932–33
	Bos. Red Sox (AL)	1938
Rogers Hornsby	St.L. Cardinals (NL)	1925
	Chi. Cubs (NL)	1929
Frank Robinson	Cin. Reds (NL)	1961
	Bal. Orioles (AL)	1966
Alex Rodriguez	Tex. Rangers (AL)	2003
	N.Y. Yankees (AL)	2005 and 2007

MVPs with Fewest Hits

119 — Willie Stargell, 1979, Pit. Pirates (NL)
124 — Roger Peckinpaugh, 1925, Was. Senators I (AL)
133 — Barry Bonds, 2003, S.F. Giants (NL)
135 — Marty Marion, 1944, St.L. Cardinals (NL)
135 — Barry Bonds, 2004, S.F. Giants (NL)

Switch-Hitting MVPs

American League

Mickey Mantle, N.Y. Yankees, 1956
Mickey Mantle, N.Y. Yankees, 1957
Mickey Mantle, N.Y. Yankees, 1962
Vida Blue, Oak. A's, 1971

National League

Frankie Frisch, St.L. Cardinals, 1931
Maury Wills, L.A. Dodgers, 1962
Pete Rose, Cin. Reds, 1973
Willie McGee, St.L. Cardinals, 1985
Terry Pendleton, Atl. Braves, 1991
Ken Caminiti, S.D. Padres, 1996
Chipper Jones, Atl. Braves, 1999
Jimmy Rollins, Phi. Phillies, 2007

Cy Young Award

Pitchers Winning 25 Games, Not Winning Cy Young Award

American League

		Wins–Losses	Cy Young Award Winner	Wins–Losses
1966	Jim Kaat, Min. Twins	25–13	Sandy Koufax, L.A. Dodgers	27–9*
1971	Mickey Lolich, Det. Tigers	25–14	Vida Blue, Oak. A's	24–8
1974	Ferguson Jenkins, Tex. Rangers	25–12	Catfish Hunter, Oak. A's	25–12

National League

		Wins–Losses	Cy Young Award Winner	Wins–Losses
1963	Juan Marichal, S.F. Giants	25–8	Sandy Koufax, L.A. Dodgers	25–5*
1966	Juan Marichal, S.F. Giants	25–6	Sandy Koufax, L.A. Dodgers	27–9*
1968	Juan Marichal, S.F. Giants	26–9	Bob Gibson, St.L. Cardinals	22–9

* One winner, both leagues, 1956–67.

Pitchers Winning 20 Games Only Once and Cy Young Award Same Season

American League

	Wins
Jim Lonborg, Bos. Red Sox, 1967	22
Mike Flanagan, Bal. Orioles, 1979	23
Steve Stone, Bal. Orioles, 1980	25
Bob Welch, Oak. A's, 1990	27
Pat Hentgen, Tor. Blue Jays, 1996	20
Barry Zito, Oak. A's, 2002	23
Johan Santana, Min. Twins, 2004	20
Cliff Lee, Cle. Indians, 2008	22
Justin Verlander*, Det. Tigers, 2011	24
David Price, T.B. Rays, 2012	20
Dallas Keuchel*, Hou. Astros, 2015	20
Rick Porcello, Bos. Red Sox, 2016	22
Blake Snell*, T.B. Rays, 2018	21

* Still active.

National League

	Wins
Vern Law, Pit. Pirates, 1960	20
Mike McCormick, S.F. Giants, 1967	22
Doug Drabek, Pit. Pirates, 1990	22
John Smoltz, Atl. Braves, 1996	24
Chris Carpenter, St.L. Cardinals, 2005	21
R.A. Dickey, N.Y. Mets, 2012	20
Jake Arrieta, Chi. Cubs, 2015	22

Cy Young Winners *Not* in Top 10 in League in ERA, Season

American League

	ERA	Place in League
Jim Lonborg, Bos. Red Sox, 1967	3.16	18th
LaMarr Hoyt, Chi. White Sox, 1983	3.66	17th

National League

	ERA	Place in League
Mike McCormick, S.F. Giants, 1967	2.85	16th

Cy Young Winners with Lowest Run Support

American League

		Run Support
Gaylord Perry, Cle. Indians, 1972	24–16 (1 SV), 1.92 ERA, 234 SO	2.87
Dean Chance, L.A. Angels, 1964	20–9 (4 SV), 1.65 ERA, 207 SO	2.94
Felix Hernandez, Sea. Mariners, 2010	13–12, 2.27 ERA, 232 SO	3.07
Zack Greinke, K.C. Royals, 2009	16–8, 2.16 ERA, 242 SO	3.78
Vida Blue, Oak. A's, 1971	24–8, 1.82 ERA, 301 SO	3.95

continued on next page

National League

		Run Support
Bob Gibson, St.L. Cardinals, 1968	22–9, 1.12 ERA, 268 SO	3.03
Jacob deGrom, N.Y. Mets, 2018	10–9, 1.70 ERA, 269 SO	3.50
Fernando Valenzuela, L.A. Dodgers, 1981	13.7, 2.48 ERA, 180 SO	3.59
Pedro Martinez, Mon. Expos, 1997	17–8, 1.90 ERA, 305 SO	3.67
Tom Seaver, N.Y. Mets, 1973	19–10, 2.08 ERA, 251 SO	3.73
Greg Maddux, Chi. Cubs, 1992	20–11, 2.18 ERA, 199 SO	3.76
Steve Carlton, Phi. Phillies, 1972	27–10, 1.97 ERA, 310 SO	3.83
Clayton Kershaw, L.A. Dodgers, 2013	16–9, 1.83 ERA, 232 SO	3.85
Mike Scott, Hou. Astros, 1986	18–10, 2.22 ERA, 306 SO	3.98

Relief Pitchers Winning Cy Young Award

American League	National League
Sparky Lyle, N.Y. Yankees, 1977	Mike Marshall, L.A. Dodgers, 1974
Rollie Fingers, Mil. Brewers, 1981	Bruce Sutter, Chi. Cubs, 1979
Willie Hernandez, Det. Tigers, 1984	Steve Bedrosian, Phi. Phillies, 1987
Dennis Eckersley, Oak. A's, 1992	Mark Davis, S.D. Padres, 1989
	Eric Gagne, L.A. Dodgers, 2003

Cy Young Winners Increasing Their Number of Victories the Following Season

American League

	Award-Winning Season	Following Season
Mike Cuellar, Bal. Orioles, 1969	23–11	24–8
David Cone, K.C. Royals, 1994	16–5	18–8
Felix Hernandez, Sea. Mariners, 2010	13–12	14–14
Corey Kluber, Cle. Indians, 2017	18–4	20–7

National League

	Award-Winning Season	Following Season
Warren Spahn, Mil. Braves, 1957	21–11	22–11
Sandy Koufax, L.A. Dodgers, 1965	26–8	27–9*
Steve Bedrosian, Phi. Phillies, 1987	5–3	6–6
Greg Maddux, Atl. Braves, 1994	16–6	19–2*
Pedro Martinez, Mon. Expos, 1997	17–8	19–7
Randy Johnson, Ari. D'backs, 1999	17–9	19–7*
Randy Johnson, Ari. D'backs, 2000	19–7	21–6*
Randy Johnson, Ari. D'backs, 2001	21–6	24–5*
Eric Gagne, L.A. Dodgers, 2003	2–3	7–3
Brandon Webb, Ari. D'backs, 2007	16–8	18–10
Tim Lincecum, S.F. Giants, 2009	15–7	16–10
Clayton Kershaw, L.A. Dodgers, 2013	16–9	21–3*
Max Scherzer, Was. Nationals, 2017	16–6	18–7
Jacob deGrom, N.Y. Mets, 2018	10–9	11–9*
Corbin Burnes, Mil. Brewers, 2021	11–5	12–8

* Won Cy Young Award.

Won Cy Young in Both Leagues

Gaylord Perry	S.F. Giants (NL), 1972	Pedro Martinez	Mon. Expos (NL), 1997
	S.D. Padres (AL), 1978		Bos. Red Sox (AL), 1999–2000
Roger Clemens	Bos. Red Sox (AL), 1986–87, 1991	Randy Johnson	Sea. Mariners (AL), 1995
	Tor. Blue Jays (AL), 1997–98		Ari. D'backs (NL), 1999–2002
	N.Y. Yankees (AL), 2000	Max Scherzer	Det. Tigers (AL), 2013
	Hou. Astros (NL), 2004		Was. Nationals (NL), 2016–17

Won Both Cy Young and MVP Same Season

American League	National League
1968..Denny McLain, Det. Tigers	1956 .... Don Newcombe, Brk. Dodgers
1971...Vida Blue, Oak. A's	1963 .... Sandy Koufax, L.A. Dodgers
1981.................................... Rollie Fingers, Mil. Brewers	1968 .... Bob Gibson, St.L. Cardinals
1984................................Willie Hernandez, Det. Tigers	2014 ....Clayton Kershaw, L.A. Dodgers
1986................................ Roger Clemens, Bos. Red Sox	
1992....................................... Dennis Eckersley, Oak. A's	
2011.....................................Justin Verlander, Det. Tigers	

Cy Young Winners with Higher Batting Averages Than That Year's Home Run Leader

American League

Cy Young Winner	Home Run Leader
1959...........................Early Wynn, Chi. White Sox, .244 ....Harmon Killebrew, Min. Twins, .242 (Tie)

National League (Post-1900)

Cy Young Winner	Home Run Leader
1970...........................Bob Gibson, St.L. Cardinals, .303 ....Johnny Bench, Cin. Reds, .293
1982...........................Steve Carlton, Phi. Phillies, .218 ....Dave Kingman, N.Y. Mets, .204

Rookie of the Year

Rookie of the Year Winners on Team Other Than the One First Played On

	Team First Played On
Tommie Agee, Chi. White Sox (AL), 1966 .... First came up for 5 games with Cle. Indians (AL), 1962
Sandy Alomar Jr., Cle. Indians (AL), 1990.............................. First came up for 1 game with S.D. Padres (NL), 1988
Jason Bay, Pit. Pirates (NL), 2004... First came up for 3 games with S.D. Padres (NL), 2003
Alfredo Griffin, Tor. Blue Jays (AL), 1979 (co-winner) .... First came up for 12 games with Cle. Indians (AL), 1976
Lou Piniella, K.C. Royals (AL), 1969 .... First came up for 4 games with Bal. Orioles (AL), 1964
Hanley Ramirez, Fla. Marlins (NL), 2006 .... First came up for 4 games with Bos. Red Sox (AL), 2005
Randy Arozarena, T.B. Rays (AL), 2021 .... First came up for 19 games with St.L. Cardinals (NL), 2019

Relief Pitchers Winning Rookie of the Year

American League	National League
Kazuhiro Sasaki, Sea. Mariners, 2000	Joe Black, Brk. Dodgers, 1952
Huston Street, Oak. A's, 2005	Butch Metzger, S.D. Padres, 1976 (Tie)
Andrew Bailey, Oak. A's, 2009	Steve Howe, L.A. Dodgers, 1980
Neftali Feliz, Tex. Rangers, 2010	Todd Worrell, St.L. Cardinals, 1986
	Scott Williamson, Cin. Reds, 1999
	Craig Kimbrel, Atl. Braves, 2011
	Devin Williams, Mil. Brewers, 2020

Rookie of the Year on Pennant-Winning Teams

American League	National League
Gil McDougald, second base and third base, N.Y. Yankees, 1951	Jackie Robinson, first base, Brk. Dodgers, 1947
Tony Kubek, outfield and shortstop, N.Y. Yankees, 1957	Alvin Dark, shortstop, Bos. Braves, 1948
Tom Tresh, shortstop, N.Y. Yankees, 1962	Don Newcombe, pitcher, Brk. Dodgers, 1949
Fred Lynn, outfield, Bos. Red Sox, 1975	Willie Mays, outfield, N.Y. Giants, 1951
Dave Righetti, pitcher, N.Y. Yankees, 1981	Joe Black, pitcher, Brk. Dodgers, 1952
Walt Weiss, shortstop, Oak. A's, 1988	Junior Gilliam, second base, Brk. Dodgers, 1953
Chuck Knoblauch, second base, Min. Twins, 1991	Jim Lefebvre, second base, L.A. Dodgers, 1965
Derek Jeter, shortstop, N.Y. Yankees, 1996	Pat Zachry, pitcher, Cin. Reds, 1976
Dustin Pedroia, shortstop, Bos. Red Sox, 2007	Fernando Valenzuela, pitcher, L.A. Dodgers, 1981
Evan Longoria, third base, T.B. Rays, 2008	Vince Coleman, outfield, St.L. Cardinals, 1985
Neftali Feliz, pitcher, Tex. Rangers, 2010	Buster Posey, catcher, S.F. Giants, 2010
Yordan Alvarez, designated hitter and outfield, Hou. Astros, 2019	Corey Seager, shortstop, L.A. Dodgers, 2016
	Cody Bellinger, first base and outfield, L.A. Dodgers, 2017

Rookies of the Year Elected to Hall of Fame

	Rookie of the Year	HOF		Rookie of the Year	HOF
1947	Jackie Robinson	1962	1968	Johnny Bench	1989
1951	Willie Mays	1979	1972	Carlton Fisk	2000
1956	Frank Robinson	1982	1977	Eddie Murray	2003
1956	Luis Aparicio	1984	1977	Andre Dawson	2010
1958	Orlando Cepeda	1999	1982	Cal Ripken Jr.	2007
1959	Willie McCovey	1986	1989	Ken Griffey Jr.	2016
1961	Billy Williams	1978	1991	Jeff Bagwell	2017
1964	Tony Oliva	2022	1993	Mike Piazza	2016
1967	Tom Seaver	1992	1996	Derek Jeter	2020
1967	Rod Carew	2003	1997	Scott Rolen	2023

Gold Gloves

Most Gold Gloves, by Position

American League

First Base ....9........ Don Mattingly (1985–89, 1991–94)
Second Base ...10.....Roberto Alomar (1991–96, 1998–2001)
Third Base......16...................,, Brooks Robinson (1960 75)
Shortstop..........9..... Luis Aparicio (1958–62, 1964, 1966, 1968, 1970)
 9...................Omar Vizquel (1993–2001)
Outfield ....10...............Al Kaline (1957–59, 1961–67)
 10.......................Ken Griffey Jr. (1990–99)
 10........................Ichiro Suzuki (2001–10)
Catcher..........13........ Ivan Rodriguez (1992–2001, 2004, 2006–07)
Pitcher...........14...............................Jim Kaat (1962–75)

National League

First Base...........11 .... Keith Hernandez (1978–88)
Second Base........9 .... Ryne Sandberg (1983–91)
Third Base.........10 ....Mike Schmidt (1976–84, 1986)
Shortstop ....13 .... Ozzie Smith (1980–92)
Outfield............12 ....Roberto Clemente (1961–72)
 12 ....Willie Mays (1957–68)
Catcher............10 ....Johnny Bench (1968–77)
Pitcher ....18 .... Greg Maddux (1990–2002, 2004–08)

5

MANAGERS

Winningest Managers by First Letter of Last Name

			Percentage
A	Sparky Anderson (1970–95)	2194–1834	.545
B	Dusty Baker* (1993–2006, 2008–13, 2006–17, 2020–)	2093–1790	.539
C	Bobby Cox (1978–2010)	2504–2001	.521
D	Leo Durocher (1939–46, 1948–55, 1966–73)	2008–1709	.540
E	Buck Ewing (1890, 1895–1900)	489–395	.553
F	Terry Francona* (1997–2000, 2004–11, 2013–)	1874–1586	.542
G	Clark Griffith (1901–20)	1491–1367	.522
H	Bucky Harris (1924–43, 1947–48, 1950–56)	2158–2219	.493
I	Arthur Irwin (1889, 1891–92, 1894–96, 1898–99)	416–427	.493
J	Davey Johnson (1984–90, 1993–97, 1999–2000, 2011–13)	1372–1071	.562
K	Tom Kelly (1986–2001)	1140–1244	.478
L	Tony La Russa (1979–2011, 2021–22)	2900–2514	.536
M	Connie Mack (1894–96, 1901–50)	3731–3948	.486
N	Jerry Narron (2001–07)	291–341	.460
O	Steve O'Neill (1935–37, 1943–48, 1950–54)	1040–821	.559
P	Lou Piniella (1986–88, 1990–2010)	1835–1713	.517
Q	Frank Quilici (1972–75)	280–267	.494
R	Wilbert Robinson (1902, 1914–31)	1399–1398	.503
S	Casey Stengel (1934–36, 1938–43, 1949–60, 1962–65)	1905–1842	.508
T	Joe Torre (1977–84, 1990–2010)	2326–1997	.540
U	Bob Unglaub (1907)	9–20	.310
V	Bobby Valentine (1985–92, 1996–2002, 2012)	1186–1165	.504
W	Dick Williams (1967–69, 1971–88)	1571–1451	.520
X	[No manager]		
Y	Ned Yost (2003–08, 2010–19)	1203–1341	.473
Z	Don Zimmer (1972–73, 1976–82, 1988–91, 1999)	885–858	.508

* Still active.

Winningest Managers by Zodiac Sign

Aquarius (Jan. 20–Feb. 18)	Davey Johnson	1372
Pisces (Feb. 19–Mar. 20)	Sparky Anderson	2194
Aries (Mar. 21–Apr. 19)	John McGraw	2763
Taurus (Apr. 20–May 20)	Joe McCarthy	2125
Gemini (May 21–Jun. 21)	Bobby Cox	2504
Cancer (Jun. 22–Jul. 22)	Joe Torre	2326
Leo (Jul. 23–Aug. 22)	Leo Durocher	2008

continued on next page

Virgo (Aug. 23–Sep. 22)..................................Lou Piniella.. 1835
Libra (Sep. 23–Oct. 23)..................................Tony La Russa.................................... 2900
Scorpio (Oct. 24–Nov. 21)..............................Bucky Harris...................................... 2158
Sagittarius (Nov. 22–Dec. 21)..........................Walter Alston..................................... 2040
Capricorn (Dec. 22–Jan. 19) ....Connie Mack...................................... 3731

Managers During Most Presidential Administrations

10 .... Connie Mack........................ Cleveland, McKinley, T. Roosevelt, Taft, Wilson, Harding, Hoover, F. Roosevelt, Truman
7 .... Tony La Russa .... Carter, Reagan, G. Bush, Clinton, G.W. Bush, Obama
7 .... Gene Mauch .... Eisenhower, Kennedy, L. Johnson, Nixon, Ford, Carter, Reagan
7 .... John McGraw........................ McKinley, T. Roosevelt, Taft, Wilson, Harding, Coolidge, Hoover
7 .... Harry Wright........................ Grant, Hayes, Garfield, Arthur, Cleveland, B. Harrison, Cleveland
6 .... Dusty Baker.......................... G. Bush, Clinton, G.W. Bush, Obama, Trump, Biden
6 .... Bobby Cox........................... Carter, Reagan, G. Bush, Clinton, G. Bush, G.W. Bush, Obama, Biden
6 .... Ralph Houk .... Kennedy, L. Johnson, Nixon, Ford, Carter, Reagan
6 .... Bill McKechnie..................... Wilson, Harding, Coolidge, Hoover, F. Roosevelt, Truman
6 .... John McNamara .... Nixon, Ford, Carter, Reagan, G. Bush, Clinton
6 .... Joe Torre............................. Carter, Reagan, G. Bush, Clinton, G.W. Bush, Obama

Managers Winning 1000 Games with One Franchise

Connie Mack, Phi. A's (AL), 1901–50... 3637
John McGraw, N.Y. Giants (NL), 1902–32 2658
Bobby Cox, Atl. Braves (NL), 1978–81 and 1990–2010................................ 2149
Walter Alston, Brk.–L.A. Dodgers (NL), 1954–76... 2040
Tommy Lasorda, L.A. Dodgers (NL), 1976–96 1599
Earl Weaver, Bal. Orioles (AL), 1968–82 and 1985–86.................................. 1480
Joe McCarthy, N.Y. Yankees (AL), 1931–46... 1460
Fred Clarke, Pit. Pirates (NL), 1900–1915... 1422
Mike Scioscia, Ana.–L.A. Angels (AL), 2000–18.. 1650
Tony La Russa, St.L. Cardinals (NL) 1996–2011 1408
Wilbert Robinson, Brk. Robins (NL), 1914–31 1375
Bucky Harris, Was. Senators (AL), 1924–28, 1935–42, and 1950–54 1336
Sparky Anderson, Det. Tigers (AL) 1979–95... 1331
Cap Anson, Chi. Colts–Cubs (NL), 1879–97... 1288
Joe Torre, N.Y. Yankees (AL), 1996–2007 1173
Casey Stengel, N.Y. Yankees (AL), 1949–60... 1149
Tom Kelly, Min. Twins (AL), 1986–2001 1140
Hughie Jennings, Det. Tigers (AL), 1907–20.. 1131
Danny Murtaugh, Pit. Pirates (NL), 1957–64, 1967, 1970–71, and 1973–76 1115
Joe Cronin, Bos. Red Sox (AL), 1935–47... 1071
Ron Gardenhire, Min. Twins (AL), 2002–14.. 1068
Miller Huggins, N.Y. Yankees (AL), 1918–29 1067
Red Schoendienst, St.L. Cardinals (NL), 1965–76 and 1980............................ 1028
Frank Selee, Bos. Beaneaters (NL), 1890–1901 1004

Managers with Over 1000 Career Wins and sub-.500 Winning Percentage

	Record	Percentage	
Ned Yost	1203–1341	.473	Mil. Brewers (NL), 2003–08
			K.C. Royals (AL), 2010–19
Frank Robinson	1065–1176	.475	Cle. Indians (AL), 1975–77
			S.F. Giants (NL), 1981–84
			Bal. Orioles (AL), 1988–91
			Mon. Expos (NL), 2002–04
			Was. Nationals (NL), 2005–06
Jimmy Dykes	1406–1541	.477	Chi. White Sox (AL), 1934–46
			Phi. A's (AL), 1951–53
			Bal. Orioles (AL), 1954
			Cin. Reds (NL), 1958
			Det. Tigers (AL), 1959–60
			Cle. Indians (AL), 1960–61
Tom Kelly	1140–1244	.478	Min. Twins (AL), 1986–2001
Bud Black	1006–1166	.478	S.D. Padres (NL), 2007–15
			Col. Rockies (NL), 2017–
Gene Mauch	1902–2037	.483	Phi. Phillies (NL), 1960–68
			Mon. Expos (NL), 1969–75
			Min. Twins (AL), 1976–80
			Cal. Angels (AL), 1981–87
Jim Fregosi	1028–1094	.484	Cal. Angels (AL), 1978–81
			Chi. White Sox (AL), 1986–88
			Phi. Phillies (NL), 1991–96
			Tor. Blue Jays (AL), 1999–2000
Bill Rigney	1239–1321	.484	N.Y. Giants (NL), 1956–57
			S.F. Giants (NL), 1958–60
			L.A. Angels (AL), 1961–64
			Cal. Angels (AL), 1965–69
			Min. Twins (AL), 1970–72
Ron Gardenhire	1200–1280	.484	Min. Twins (AL), 2002–14
			Det. Tigers (AL), 2018–20
John McNamara	1160–1233	.485	Oak A's (AL), 1969–70
			S.D. Padres (NL), 1974–77
			Cin. Reds (NL), 1979–82
			Cal. Angels (AL), 1983–84, 1996
			Bos. Red Sox (AL), 1985–88
			Cle. Indians (AL), 1900–91
Clint Hurdle	1269–1345	.485	Col. Rockies (NL), 2002–09
			Pit. Pirates (NL), 2011–19
Connie Mack	3731–3948	.486	Pit. Pirates (NL), 1894–96
			Phi. A's (AL), 1901–50
Lou Boudreau	1162–1224	.487	Cle. Indians (AL), 1942–50
			Bos. Red Sox (AL), 1942–50
			K.C. A's (AL), 1955–57
			Chi. Cubs (NL), 1960
Bucky Harris	2158–2218	.493	Was. Senators (AL), 1924–28, 1935–42, 1950–54
			Det. Tigers (AL), 1929–33, 1955–56
			Bos. Red Sox (AL), 1934
			Phi. Phillies (NL), 1943
			N.Y. Yankees (AL), 1947–48
Chuck Tanner	1352–1381	.495	Chi. White Sox (AL), 1970–75
			Oak. A's (AL), 1976
			Pit. Pirates (NL), 1977–85
			Atl. Braves (NL), 1986–88
Bruce Bochy	2003–2029	.497	S.D. Padres (NL), 1995–2006
			S.F. Giants (NL), 2007–19
Art Howe	1129–1137	.498	Hou. Astros (NL), 1989–93
			Oak. A's (AL), 1996–2002
			N.Y. Mets (NL), 2003–04

Managers with Most Career Victories for Each Franchise

American League

Bal. Orioles	Earl Weaver, 1968–82 and 1985–86	1480–1060	.583
Bos. Red Sox	Joe Cronin, 1935–47	1071–916	.539
Chi. White Sox	Jimmy Dykes, 1934–46	899–938	.489
Cle. Guardians	Terry Francona**, 2013–	845–671	.557
Det. Tigers	Sparky Anderson, 1979–95	1331–1248	.516
Hou. Astros*	Bill Virdon, 1975–82	544–522	.510
K.C. A's	Harry Craft, 1957–59	162–196	.452
K.C. Royals	Ned Yost, 2010–19	746–839	.471
Ana.–L.A. Angels	Mike Scioscia, 2000–18	1650–1428	.536
Min. Twins	Tom Kelly, 1986–2001	1140–1244	.478
N.Y. Yankees	Joe McCarthy, 1931–46	1460–867	.627
Oak. A's	Bob Melvin, 2011–21	853–764	.528
Phi. A's	Connie Mack, 1901–50	3627–3891	.482
Sea. Mariners	Lou Piniella, 1993–2002	840–711	.542
Sea. Pilots	Joe Schultz, 1969	64–98	.395
St.L. Browns	Jimmy McAleer, 1902–09	551–632	.466
T.B. Rays	Joe Maddon, 2006–14	754–705	.517
Tex. Rangers	Ron Washington, 2007–14	664–611	.521
Tor. Blue Jays	Cito Gaston, 1989–97 and 2008–10	894–837	.516
Was. Senators	Bucky Harris, 1924–28, 1935–42, and 1950–54	1336–1416	.485
Was. Senators II	Gil Hodges, 1963–67	321–445	.419

National League (Post-1900)

Ari. D'backs	Torey Lovullo**, 2017–	411–459	.472
Atl. Braves	Bobby Cox, 1978–81 and 1990–2010	2149–1709	.557
Bos. Braves	George Stallings, 1913–20	579–597	.492
Brk. Dodgers	Wilbert Robinson, 1914–31	1375–1341	.504
Chi. Cubs	Charlie Grimm, 1932–38, 1944–49, and 1960	946–784	.547
Cin. Reds	Sparky Anderson, 1970–78	863–586	.596
Col. Rockies	Clint Hurdle, 2002–09	534–625	.461
Mia. Marlins	Don Mattingly, 2016–22	443–587	.430
L.A. Dodgers	Walter Alston, 1958–76	1673–1355	.552
Mil. Braves	Fred Haney, 1956–59	341–231	.596
Mil. Brewers***	Craig Counsell**, 2015–	615–555	.526
Mon. Expos	Felipe Alou, 1992–2001	691–717	.491
N.Y. Giants	John McGraw, 1902–32	2658–1823	.593
N.Y. Mets	Davey Johnson, 1984–90	595–417	.588
Phi. Phillies	Charlie Manuel, 2005–13	780–636	.551
Pit. Pirates	Fred Clarke, 1900–15	1422–969	.595
St.L. Cardinals	Tony La Russa, 1996–2011	1408–1182	.544
S.D. Padres	Bruce Bochy, 1995–2006	951–975	.494
S.F. Giants	Bruce Bochy, 2007–19	1052–1054	.500
Was. Nationals	Dave Martinez**, 2018–	321–387	.453

* Played in NL from 1962–2012.

** Still active with team.

*** Played in AL from 1970–97.

Best Winning Percentage as Manager with One Team (Post-1900; Min. 150 Games)

Percentage		Wins–Losses
.664	Frank Chance, Chi. Cubs (NL), 1905–12	768–389
.642	Chuck Dressen, Brk. Dodgers (NL), 1951–53	298–166
.642	Billy Southworth, St.L. Cardinals (NL), 1939–45	620–346
.632	Dick Howser, N.Y. Yankees (AL), 1978 and 1980	103–60
.632	Dave Roberts*, L.A. Dodgers (NL), 2016–	653–381
.627	Joe McCarthy, N.Y. Yankees (AL), 1931–46	1460–867
.623	Casey Stengel, N.Y. Yankees (AL), 1949–60	1149–696
.622	Terry Francona, Bos. Red Sox (AL), 2004–11	744–552
.621	Jake Stahl, Bos. Red Sox (AL), 1912–13	144–88
.620	Bucky Harris, N.Y. Yankees (AL), 1947–48	191–117
.617	Al Lopez, Cle. Indians (AL), 1951–56	570–354
.606	Joe McCarthy, Bos. Red Sox (AL), 1948–50	223–145
.605	Joe Torre, N.Y. Yankees (AL), 1996–2007	1173–767

* Still active with team.

Managers with 500 Wins in Each League

2900	Tony La Russa	(1492 AL, 1408 NL)
2326	Joe Torre	(1173 AL, 1153 NL)
2194	Sparky Anderson	(1331 NL, 863 AL)
1905	Casey Stengel	(1149 AL, 756 NL)
1902	Gene Mauch	(1145 NL, 757 AL)
1835	Lou Piniella	(1264 AL, 571 NL)
1769	Jim Leyland	(700 AL, 1069 NL)
1571	Dick Williams	(854 AL, 717 NL)
1186	Bobby Valentine	(650 AL, 536 NL)
1160	John McNamara	(657 AL, 503 NL)
1129	Art Howe	(600 AL, 529 NL)

Played in 2000 Games, Managed in 2000 Games

	Games Played	Games Managed
Cap Anson	2276 (1876–97)	2296 (1879–98)
Charlie Grimm	2164 (1916, 1918–36)	2370 (1932–38, 1944–49, 1952–56, 1960)
Dusty Baker	2039 (1968–86)	3884 (1993–2006, 2008–13, 2016–17, 2020–)
Felipe Alou	2082 (1958–74)	2055 (1992–2001, 2003–06)
Frankie Frisch	2311 (1919–37)	2245 (1933–38, 1940–46, 1949–51)
Frank Robinson	2808 (1956–76)	2241 (1975–77, 1981–84, 1988–91, 2002–06)
Fred Clarke	2245 (1894–1915)	2822 (1897–1915)
Jimmy Dykes	2282 (1918–39)	2960 (1934–46, 1951–54, 1958–61)
Joe Cronin	2124 (1926–45)	2315 (1933–47)
Joe Torre	2209 (1960–77)	4329 (1977–84, 1990–2010)

Managers Managing 100-Loss Teams After 1000th Career Victory

Sparky Anderson, Det. Tigers (AL), 1989
Lou Boudreau, K.C. A's (AL), 1956
Leo Durocher, Chi. Cubs (NL), 1966
Jimmy Dykes, Bal. Orioles (AL), 1954
Ned Hanlon, Brk. Dodgers (NL), 1905
Ralph Houk, Det. Tigers (AL), 1975

Connie Mack, Phi. A's (AL), 1915–16, 1919–20, 1943, 1946, and 1950
Bill McKechnie, Bos. Braves (NL), 1935
Buck Showalter, Bal. Orioles (AL), 2018
Casey Stengel, N.Y. Mets (NL), 1962–64
Chuck Tanner, Pit. Pirates (NL), 1985
Ned Yost, K.C. Royals (AL), 2018

Managers with Both 100-Win and 100-Loss Seasons

	100 Wins	100 Losses
Bill Carrigan	Bos. Red Sox (AL), 1915	Bos. Red Sox (AL), 1927
Chuck Dressen	Brk. Dodgers (NL) 1953	Was. Senators (AL) 1955
Connie Mack	Phi. A's (AL), 1910, 1911, 1929, 1930, 1931	Phi. A's (AL), 1915, 1916, 1919, 1920, 1921, 1936, 1940, 1943, 1946, 1950
Bill McKechnie	Cin. Reds (NL), 1940	Bos. Braves (NL), 1935
Buck Showalter	Ari. D'backs (NL), 1999, N.Y. Mets (NL), 2022	Bal. Orioles (AL), 2018
Casey Stengel	N.Y. Yankees (AL), 1954	N.Y. Mets (NL), 1962, 1963, 1964

continued on next page

100 Wins		100 Losses
Gil Hodges..............N.Y. Mets (NL), 1969	....	Was. Senators (AL), 1964
Joe Maddon..............Chi. Cubs (NL), 2016	....	T.B. Devil Rays (AL), 2006
Leo Durocher ....Brk. Dodgers (NL) 1941, 1942	....	Chi. Cubs (NL) 1966
Ned Hanlon ....Brk. Superbas (NL), 1899	....	Brk. Superbas (NL), 1905
Ralph Houk .............N.Y. Yankees (AL), 1961, 1963	....	Det. Tigers (AL) 1975
Sparky Anderson......Cin. Reds (NL) 1970, 1975, 1976	....	Det. Tigers (AL), 1989

Former Pitchers Winning Pennants as Managers (Post-1900)

Eddie Dyer, St.L. Cardinals (NL), 1946
Dallas Green, Phi. Phillies (NL), 1980
Clark Griffith, Chi. White Sox (AL), 1901
Roger Craig, S.F. Giants (NL), 1989
John Farrell, Bos. Red Sox (AL), 2013

Fred Hutchinson, Cin. Reds (NL), 1961
Tommy Lasorda, L.A. Dodgers (NL), 1977–78, 1981, and 1988
Bob Lemon, N.Y. Yankees (AL), 1978 and 1981
Kid Gleason, Chi. White Sox (AL), 1919

Managers Taking Over World Series Teams in Midseason

American League

Season	Manager	Wins–Losses	Former Manager
1978	Bob Lemon, N.Y. Yankees*	48–20	Billy Martin (52–42), Dick Howser (0–1)
1981	Bob Lemon, N.Y. Yankees	13–15	Gene Michael (46–33)
1982	Harvey Kuenn, Mil. Brewers	72–49	Buck Rodgers (23–24)

National League

Season	Manager	Wins–Losses	Former Manager
1932	Charlie Grimm, Chi. Cubs	37–20	Rogers Hornsby (53–44)
1938	Gabby Hartnett, Chi. Cubs	44–27	Charlie Grimm (45–36)
1947	Burt Shotton, Brk. Dodgers	93–60	Clyde Sukeforth (1–0)
1983	Paul Owens, Phi. Phillies	47–30	Pat Corrales (43–42)
2003	Jack McKeon, Fla. Marlins*	75–49	Jeff Torborg (17–22)
2022	Rob Thomson, Phi. Phillies	65–46	Joe Girardi (22–29)

* World Series winner.

Managers Replaced While Team Was in First Place

Season	Team	Former Manager	Wins–Losses	New Manager	Wins–Losses
1947	Brk. Dodgers (NL)	Clyde Sukeforth	1–0	Burt Shotton	93–60
1983	Phi. Phillies (NL)	Pat Corrales	43–42	Paul Owens	47–30

Managers Winning Pennant in First Year as Manager of Team

American League

Clark Griffith, Chi. White Sox, 1901
Hughie Jennings, Det. Tigers, 1907
Kid Gleason, Chi. White Sox, 1919
Tris Speaker*, Cle. Indians, 1920
Bucky Harris, Was. Senators, 1924
Joe Cronin, Was. Senators, 1933
Mickey Cochrane, Det. Tigers, 1934
Ralph Houk, N.Y. Yankees, 1961
Yogi Berra, N.Y. Yankees, 1964
Dick Williams, Bos. Red Sox, 1967
Earl Weaver*, Bal. Orioles, 1969
Bob Lemon**, N.Y. Yankees, 1978
Jim Frey, K.C. Royals, 1980
Joe Torre, N.Y. Yankees, 1996
Terry Francona, Bos. Red Sox, 2004
Jim Leyland, Det. Tigers, 2006
John Farrell, Bos. Red Sox, 2013
Alex Cora*, Bos. Red Sox, 2018

* First full season as manager.
** Took over in mid-season.

National League

Frank Chance*, Chi. Cubs, 1906
Pat Moran, Phi. Phillies, 1915
Pat Moran, Cin. Reds, 1919
Charlie Grimm**, Chi. Cubs, 1932
Gabby Hartnett**, Chi. Cubs, 1938
Eddie Dyer, St.L. Cardinals, 1946
Burt Shotton, Brk. Dodgers, 1947
Tommy Lasorda*, L.A. Dodgers, 1977
Jim Leyland, Fla. Marlins, 1997
Bob Brenly*, Ari. D'backs, 2001
Jack McKeon**, Fla. Marlins, 2003
Rob Thomson**, Phi. Phillies, 2022

Managers Undefeated in World Series Play

George Stallings, Bos. Braves (NL), 1914 ....4–0 over Phi. A's (AL)
Hank Bauer, Bal. Orioles (AL), 1966 ....4–0 over L.A. Dodgers (NL)
Lou Piniella, Cin. Reds (NL), 1990..4–0 over Oak. A's (AL)
Ozzie Guillen, Chi. White Sox (AL), 2005 ....4–0 over Hou. Astros (NL)

Managers with Fewest Career Wins to Win World Series

	Wins		Wins
Bob Brenly, Ari. D'backs (NL), 2001	92	John Farrell, Bos. Red Sox (AL), 2013	251
Tom Kelly, Min. Twins (AL), 1987	97	Mike Scioscia, Ana. Angels (AL), 2002	256
Eddie Dyer, St.L. Cardinals (NL), 1946	98	Joe Girardi, N.Y. Yankees (AL), 2009	270
Alex Cora, Bos. Red Sox (AL), 2018	108	Pants Rowland, Chi. White Sox (AL), 1917	281
Dallas Green, Phi. Phillies (NL), 1980	110	Davey Johnson, N.Y. Mets (NL), 1986	296
Ed Barrow, Bos. Red Sox (AL), 1918	172	Lou Piniella, Cin. Reds (NL), 1990	315
Dave Martinez, Was. Nationals (NL), 2019	175	Johnny Keane, St.L. Cardinals (NL), 1964	317
Ozzie Guillen, Chi. White Sox (AL), 2005	182	Joe Altobelli, Bal. Orioles (AL), 1983	323
Mickey Cochrane, Det. Tigers (AL), 1935	194	Cito Gaston, Tor. Blue Jays, 1992	331
Gabby Street, St.L. Cardinals (NL), 1931	194	Bill Carrigan, Bos. Red Sox (AL), 1916	323
Jake Stahl, Bos. Red Sox (AL), 1912	224	A.J. Hinch, Hou. Astros (AL), 2017	360
Bill Carrigan, Bos. Red Sox (AL), 1915	232	A.J. Hinch, Hou. Astros (AL), 2017	360
Jimmy Collins, Bos. Red Sox (AL), 1903	247		

Managers with Most Career Wins *Never* to Manage a World Series Team (Post-1903)

	Wins	Seasons
Gene Mauch	1901	26 (1960–82, 1985–87)
Buck Showalter*	1652	21 (1992–95, 1998–2000, 2003–06, 2010–18 , 2020–)
Jimmy Dykes	1407	21 (1934–46, 1951–54, 1958–61)
Bob Melvin*	1435	19 (2003–09, 2011–)
Bill Rigney	1239	18 (1956–72, 1976)
Ron Gardenhire	1200	16 (2002–14, 2018–20)
Art Howe	1129	14 (1989–93, 1996–2004)
Bud Black*	1066	15 (2007–15, 2017–)
Frank Robinson	1065	14 (1975–77, 1981–84, 1988–91, 2002–06)
Felipe Alou	1033	14 (1992–2001, 2003–06)
Bill Virdon	995	13 (1972–84)
Paul Richards	923	12 (1951–61, 1976)
Jimy Williams	910	12 (1986–89, 1997–2004)
Don Zimmer	906	14 (1972–73, 1976–82, 1988–91, 1999)
Don Mattingly	889	12 (2011–15, 2017–22)
Jim Tracy	856	10 (2001–07, 2009–12)
Johnny Oates	797	11 (1991–2001)
John Gibbons	793	11 (2004–08, 2013–18)
Buck Rodgers	784	13 (1980–82, 1985–94)

* Still active.

Pennant-Winning Managers with Fewest Career Wins (Since 1900)

44 ...... Gabby Hartnett, 1938 Chi. Cubs (NL)
65 ...... Rob Thomson, 2022 Phi. Phillies (NL)
73 ...... Harvey Kuenn, 1982 Mil. Brewers (AL)
80 ...... Paul Owens, 1983 Phi. Phillies (NL)

101 ..... Mickey Cochrane, 1934 Det. Tigers (AL)
108 ..... Alex Cora, 2018 Bos. Red Sox (AL)*
109 ..... Ralph Houk, 1961 N.Y. Yankees (AL)*
110 ..... Dallas Green, 1980 Phi. Phillies (NL)*

continued on next page

88 ...... Kid Gleason, 1919 Chi. White Sox (AL)
92 ...... Bucky Harris, 1924 Was. Senators (AL)*
92 ...... Bob Brenly, 2001 Ari. D'backs (NL)*
93 ...... Gabby Street, 1930 St.L. Cardinals (NL)
97 ...... Jim Frey, 1980 K.C. Royals (AL)
98 ...... Eddie Dyer, 1946 St.L. Cardinals (NL)*
99 ...... Joe Cronin, 1933 Was. Senators (AL)
99 ...... Yogi Berra, 1964 N.Y. Yankees (AL)
* Won World Series.

172 ..... Ed Barow, 1918 Bos. Red Sox (AL)*
175 ..... Dave Martinez, 2019 Was. Nationals (NL)*
182 ..... Ozzie Guillen, 2005 Chi. White Sox (AL)*
188 ..... Bucky Harris, 1925 Was. Senators (AL)
194 ..... Gabby Street, 1931 St.L. Cardinals (NL)*
194 ..... Mickey Cochrane, 1935 Det. Tigers (AL)*
195 ..... Dave Roberts, 2017 L.A. Dodgers (NL)
205 ..... Ralph Houk, 1962 N.Y. Yankees (AL)

Most Times Managing the Same Club

5 .... Billy Martin, N.Y. Yankees, 1975–78, 1979, 1983, 1985, and 1988
4 .... Danny Murtaugh, Pit. Pirates, 1957–64, 1967, 1970–71, and 1973–76
3 .... Bucky Harris, Was. Senators, 1924–28, 1935–42, and 1950–54
3 .... Charlie Grimm, Chi. Cubs, 1932–38, 1944–49, and 1960

Managers with Best Winning Percentage for First Five Full Years of Managing

	Wins–Losses	Percentage
Frank Chance, Chi. Cubs (NL), 1906–10	530–235	.693
Al Lopez, Cle. Indians (AL), 1951–55	482–288	.626
Earl Weaver, Bal. Orioles (AL), 1969–73	495–303	.620
John McGraw, Bal. Orioles (NL), 1899; Bal. Orioles (AL), 1901; and N.Y. Giants (NL), 1903–05	449–277	.618
Davey Johnson, N.Y. Mets (NL), 1984–88	488–320	.604
Aaron Boone, N.Y. Yankees (AL), 2018–22	427–281	.603
Hughie Jennings, Det. Tigers (AL), 1907–11	455–308	.596
Leo Durocher, Brk. Dodgers (NL), 1939–43	457–310	.596
Sparky Anderson, Cin. Reds (NL), 1970–74	473–329	.590
Fielder Jones, Chi. White Sox (AL), 1904–07; and St.L. Terriers (FL), 1915	447–313	.588
Joe McCarthy, Chi. Cubs (NL), 1926–29; and N.Y. Yankees (AL), 1931	450–316	.587
Pat Moran, Phi. Phillies (NL), 1915–18; and Cin. Reds (NL), 1919	419–301	.582

Managers Never Experiencing a Losing Season (Post-1900; Min. Two Full Seasons)

	Winning Seasons	Wins–Losses	Percentage
Joe McCarthy (1926–46, 1948–50)	24	2136–1335	.614
Steve O'Neill (1935–37, 1943–48, 1950–54)	14	1039–819	.559
Dave Roberts* (2015–)	7	653–381	.632
Aaron Boone* (2018–)	5	427–281	.603
Eddie Dyer (1946–50)	5	446–325	.578
Grady Little (2002–03, 2006–07)	4	358–290	.552
Eddie Kasko (1970–73)	4	345–295	.539
Joe Morgan (1988–91)	4	255–231	.525
Mike Shildt (2018–21)	4	252–199	.559
Ossie Vitt (1938–40)	3	262–198	.570
Harvey Kuenn (1975, 1982–83)	3	160–118	.576
Dick Sisler (1964–65)	2	121–94	.563
Matt Williams (2014–15)	2	179–145	552
Eddie Collins (1925–26)	2	160–147	.521

* Still active.
+ Went 0–1 as an interim manager for the 2015 S.D. Padres.

Career One-Game Managers

American League

Bibb Falk, Cle. Indians, 1933 1–0

Marty Martinez, Sea. Mariners, 1986 0–1

Bob Schaefer, K.C. Royals, 1991 1–0

Jo-Jo White, Cle. Indians, 1960 1–0

Del Wilber, Tex. Rangers, 1973 1–0

Rudy York, Bos. Red Sox, 1959 0–1

Eddie Yost, Was. Senators II, 1963 0–1

National League

Vern Benson, Atl. Braves, 1977 1–0

Bill Burwell, Pit. Pirates, 1947 1–0

Andy Cohen, Phi. Phillies, 1960 1–0

Bill Holbert, Syr. Stars, 1879 0–1

Roy Johnson, Chi. Cubs, 1944 1–0

Tom Prince, Pit. Pirates, 2019 0–1

Ted Turner, Atl. Braves, 1977 0–1

Managers Managing in Civilian Clothes

Bill Armour, Cle. Indians (AL), 1902–04; and Det. Tigers (AL), 1905–06

Judge Emil Fuchs, Bos. Braves (NL), 1929

Connie Mack, Pit. Pirates (NL), 1894–96; and Phi. A's (AL), 1901–50

John McGraw, N.Y. Giants (NL), 1930–32

Burt Shotton, Phi. Phillies (NL), 1928–33; Cin. Reds (NL), 1934; and Brk. Dodgers (NL), 1947–48 and 1949–50

George Stallings, Phi. Phillies (NL), 1897–99; Det. Tigers (AL), 1901; N.Y. Yankees (AL), 1909–10; and Bos. Braves (NL), 1913–20

Managers Who Were Lawyers

Bill Armour, Cle. Indians (AL), 1902–04; Det. Tigers (AL), 1905–06

Judge Emil Fuchs, Bos. Braves (NL), 1929

Miller Huggins, St.L. Cardinals (NL), 1913–17; and N.Y. Yankees (AL), 1918–29

Hughie Jennings, Det. Tigers (AL), 1907–20

Tony La Russa, Chi. White Sox (AL), 1979–86 and 2021–22; Oak. A's (AL), 1986–88; St.L. Cardinals (NL), 1996–2011

Branch Rickey, St.L. Browns (AL), 1913–15; and St.L. Cardinals (NL), 1919–25

Muddy Ruel, St.L. Browns (AL), 1947

Monte Ward, N.Y. Gothams (NL), 1884; Brk. Wonders (PL), 1890; Brk. Bridegrooms (NL), 1891–92; and N.Y. Giants (NL), 1893–94

Pennant-Winning Managers Who Won Batting Titles

Manager of Pennant Winner	Batting Champion
Lou Boudreau...........Cle. Indians (AL), 1948	Cle. Indians (AL), 1944 (.327)
Rogers Hornsby........St.L. Cardinals (NL), 1926	St.L. Cardinals (NL), 1920 (.370), 1921 (.397), 1922 (.401), 1923 (.384), 1924 (.424), 1925 (.403) Bos. Braves (NL), 1928 (.387)
Harvey Kuenn..........Mil. Brewers (AL), 1982	Det. Tigers (AL), 1959 (.353)
Tris Speaker ....Cle. Indians (AL), 1920	Cle. Indians (AL), 1916 (.386)
Bill Terry ................N.Y. Giants (NL), 1933, 1936–37	N.Y. Giants (NL), 1930 (.401)
Joe Torre ................N.Y. Yankees (AL), 1996, 1998–2001, 2003	St.L. Cardinals (NL), 1971 (.363)

Managers with Same Initials as Team They Managed

Billy Barnie, Brk. Bridegrooms (1897–98)
Harry Craft, Hou. Colt .45s (1962)
Bill Dahlen, Brk. Dodgers (1910–13)
Dick Tracewski, Det. Tigers (1979)

Playing Managers After 1950

American League

Lou Boudreau (shortstop), Cle. Indians, 1950 (81 games)
Lou Boudreau (shortstop), Bos. Red Sox, 1952 (4 games)
Fred Hutchinson (pitcher), Det. Tigers, 1952–53 (12 games in 1952; 3 games in 1953)
Marty Marion (shortstop, third base), St.L. Browns, 1952–53 (67 games in 1952; 3 games in 1953)
Eddie Joost (infield), Phi. A's, 1954 (19 games)
Hank Bauer (outfield), K.C. A's, 1961 (43 games)
Frank Robinson (designated hitter), Cle. Indians, 1976 (36 games)
Don Kessinger (shortstop), Chi. White Sox, 1979 (56 games)

National League

Tommy Holmes (outfield), Bos. Braves, 1951 (27 games)
Phil Cavaretta (first base), Chi. Cubs, 1951–53 (89 games in 1951; 41 games in 1952; 27 games in 1953)
Eddie Stanky (second base), St.L. Cardinals, 1952–53 (53 games in 1952; 17 games in 1953)
Harry Walker (outfield), St.L. Cardinals, 1955 (11 games)
Solly Hemus (infield), St.L. Cardinals, 1959 (24 games)
El Tappe (catcher), Chi. Cubs, 1962 (26 games)
Joe Torre (first base, pinch hitter), N.Y. Mets, 1977 (26 games)
Pete Rose (first base), Cin. Reds, 1984–86 (26 games in 1984; 119 games in 1985; 72 games in 1986)

1000 Wins as Manager and 2000 Hits as Player

Felipe Alou...Manager (1992–2006) 1033 wins
Player (1958–74) 2101 hits
Cap Anson..Manager (1875, 1879–98) 2196 wins
Player (1871–97) 3435 hits
Fred Clarke...Manager (1897–15) 1602 wins
Player (1894–1915) 2678 hits
Joe Cronin...Manager (1933–47) 1236 wins
Player (1926–45) 2285 hits
Jimmy Dykes..Manager (1934–46, 1951–54, 1958–61) 1406 wins
Player (1918–38) 2256 hits
Frankie Frisch..Manager (1933–38, 1940–46, 1949–51) 1138 wins
Player (1919–37) 2880 hits
Charlie Grimm...Manager (1932–38, 1944–49, 1952–56, 1960) 1287 wins
Player (1916, 1918–36) 2299 hits
Frank Robinson..Manager (1975–77, 1981–84, 1988–91, 2002–06) 1065 wins
Player (1957–76) 2943 hits
Red Schoendienst...Manager (1965–76, 1980, 1990) 1041 wins
Player (1945–63) 2449 hits
Joe Torre..Manager (1977–84, 1990–2010) 2326 wins
Player (1960–77) 2342 hits

6

FIELDING

Most Games Played by Position, Career

First Base .... 2413 .... Eddie Murray (1977–97)
Second Base .... 2650 .... Eddie Collins (1906, 1908–28)
Third Base .... 2870 .... Brooks Robinson (1955–77)
Shortstop... 2709 .... Omar Vizquel (1989–2012)
Left Field... 2715 .... Barry Bonds (1986–2007)
Centerfield... 2829 .... Willie Mays (1951–52, 1954–73)
Right Field .... 2305 .... Roberto Clemente (1955–72)
Catcher.. 2427 .... Ivan Rodriguez (1991–2011)
Pitcher... 1252 .... Jesse Orosco (1979, 1981–2004)
Designated Hitter... 2029 ....David Ortiz (1997–2016)

Most Consecutive Games Played at Each Position

American League

First Base .... 885 .... Lou Gehrig, N.Y. Yankees, 1925–30
Second Base .... 798 .... Nellie Fox, Chi. White Sox, 1955–60
Third Base .... 576 .... Eddie Yost, Was. Senators, 1951–55
Shortstop... 2216 .... Cal Ripken Jr., Bal. Orioles, 1983–95
Outfield .... 511 .... Clyde Milan, Was. Senators, 1910–13
Catcher.. 312 .... Frankie Hayes, St.L. Browns–Phi. A's–Cle. Indians, 1943–46
Pitcher... 13 ....Dale Mohoric, Tex. Rangers, 1986

National League

First Base .... 652 .... Frank McCormick, Cin. Reds, 1938–42
Second Base .... 443 ....Dave Cash, Pit. Pirates–Phi. Phillies, 1973–76
Third Base .... 364 ....Ron Santo, Chi. Cubs, 1964–66
Shortstop... 584 .... Roy McMillan, Cin. Reds, 1951–55
Outfield .... 897 .... Billy Williams, Chi. Cubs, 1963–69
Catcher.. 217 .... Ray Mueller, Cin. Reds, 1943–44
Pitcher... 13 .... Mike Marshall, L.A. Dodgers, 1974

Players Who Played 1000 Games at Two Positions, Career

Ernie Banks.....................................1125 at shortstop, 1259 at first base
Rod Carew................................1130 at second base, 1184 at first base
Ron Fairly ....1218 at first base, 1037 in the outfield
Stan Musial.................................1890 in the outfield, 1016 at first base
Alex Rodriguez............................. 1272 at shortstop, 1194 at third base
Robin Yount......................................1479 at shortstop, 1160 in center field
Babe Ruth ....1054 in left field, 1133 in right field

Unassisted Triple Plays

Neal Ball, shortstop, Cle. Indians (vs. Bos. Red Sox) (AL), Jul. 19, 1909, 2nd inning; Batter: Amby McConnell
Ball spears McConnell's line drive, comes down on second to double up Heinie Wagner, and tags out Jake Stahl, coming from first.

Bill Wambsganss, second base, Cle. Indians (vs. Brk. Dodgers) (AL), Oct. 10, 1920*, 5th inning; Batter: Clarence Mitchell
"Wamby" catches Mitchell's liner, steps on second to retire Pete Kilduff, and wheels around to tag Otto Miller, coming down from first.

George H. Burns, first base, Bos. Red Sox (vs. Cle. Indians) (AL), Sep. 14, 1923, 2nd inning; Batter: Frank Brower
Burns takes Brower's line drive, reaches out and tags Walter Lutzke, who was on first base, and then rushes down to second to tag the base before base runner Joe Stephenson can return.

Ernie Padgett, shortstop, Bos. Braves (vs. Phi. Phillies) (NL), Oct. 6, 1923, 4th inning; Batter: Walter Holke
Padgett takes Holke's line drive, tags second to retire Cotton Tierney, and then tags out Cliff Lee, coming into second.

Glenn Wright, shortstop, Pit. Pirates (vs. St.L. Cardinals) (NL), May 7, 1925, 9th inning; Batter: Jim Bottomley
Wright snares Bottomley's liner, touches second to retire Jimmy Cooney, and then tags out Rogers Hornsby, on his way into second.

Jimmy Cooney, shortstop, Chi. Cubs (vs. Pit. Pirates) (NL), May 30, 1927, 4th inning; Batter: Paul Waner
Cooney grabs Waner's line drive, doubles Lloyd Waner off second, and then tags out Clyde Barnhart, coming down from first.

Johnny Neun, first base, Det. Tigers (vs. Cle. Indians) (AL), May 31, 1927, 9th inning; Batter: Homer Summa
Neun snares Summa's liner, tags first to double up Charlie Jamieson, and then races down toward second to tag out base runner Glenn Myatt before he can return to second, ending the game.

Ron Hansen, shortstop, Was. Senators II (vs. Cle. Indians) (AL), Jul. 29, 1968, 1st inning; Batter: Joe Azcue
Hansen grabs Azcue's liner, steps on second to double up Dave Nelson, and then tags out Russ Snyder, barreling down from first.

Mickey Morandini, second base, Phi. Phillies (vs. Pit. Pirates) (NL), Sep. 20, 1992, 6th inning; Batter: Jeff King
Morandini makes a diving catch of King's line drive, runs to second to double off Andy Van Slyke, and then tags out Barry Bonds running down from first.

John Valentin, shortstop, Bos. Red Sox (vs. Sea. Mariners) (AL), Jul. 8, 1994, 6th inning; Batter: Marc Newfield
Valentin catches Newfield's line drive, steps on second to double up Mike Blowers, and then tags out Kevin Mitchell coming down from first.

Randy Velarde, second base, Oak. A's (vs. N.Y. Yankees) (AL), May 29, 2000, 6th inning; Batter: Shane Spencer
Velarde catches Spencer's liner, tags Jorge Posada running from first to second, and then runs over to step on second to retire Tino Martinez.

Rafael Furcal, shortstop, Atl. Braves (vs. St.L. Cardinals) (NL), Aug. 10, 2003, 6th inning; Batter: Woody Williams
Furcal grabs Williams's liner, steps on second to retire Mike Matheny, and then tags Orlando Palmeiro coming down the line from first.

Troy Tulowitzki, shortstop, Col. Rockies (vs. Atl. Braves) (NL), Apr. 29, 2007, 7th inning; Batter: Chipper Jones
Jones hits a line drive to Tulowitzki, who then steps on second to double up Kelly Johnson and tags Edgar Renteria between first and second base.

Asdrubal Cabrera, second base, Cle. Indians (vs. Tor. Blue Jays) (AL), May 12, 2008, 5th inning; Batter: Lyle Overbay
Overbay hits a line drive that is caught by a diving Cabrera, who steps on second to double up Kevin Mench and then tags out Marco Scutaro.

Eric Bruntlett, second base, Phi. Phillies (vs. N.Y. Mets) (NL), Aug. 23, 2009, 9th inning; Batter: Jeff Francoeur
Francoeur hits a line drive to Bruntlett, who steps on second to double up Luis Castillo and then tags Daniel Murphy between first and second, ending the game.

* World Series game.

Most No-Hitters Caught

	Catcher	Pitcher
4	Jason Varitek, Bos. Red Sox (AL)	Hideo Nomo, Apr. 4, 2001, vs. Bal. Orioles, 3–0
		Derek Lowe, Apr. 27, 2002, vs. T.B. Devil Rays, 10–0
		Clay Buchholz, Sep. 1, 2007, vs. Bal. Orioles, 10–0
		Jon Lester, May 19, 2008, vs. K.C. Royals, 7–0

continued on next page

	Catcher	Pitcher
4	Carlos Ruiz, Phi. Phillies (NL)	Roy Halladay, May 29, 2010, vs. Fla. Marlins, 1–0 (perfect game)
		Roy Halladay, Oct. 6, 2010, vs. Cin. Reds, 4–0 (Division Series)
		Cole Hamels, Jake Diekman, Ken Giles, Jonathan Papelbon, Sep. 1, 2014, vs. Atl. Braves, 7–0
		Cole Hamels, Jul. 25, 2015, vs. Chi. Cubs, 5–0
3	Ed McFarland, Phi. Phillies (NL)	Red Donahue, Jul. 8, 1898, vs. Bos. Beaneaters, 5–0
	Chi. White Sox (AL)	Nixey Callahan, Sep. 20, 1902, vs. Det. Tigers, 3–0
		Frank Smith, Sep. 6, 1905, vs. Det. Tigers, 15–0
3	Lou Criger, Bos. Red Sox (AL)	Cy Young, May 5, 1904, vs. Phi. A's, 3–0 (perfect game)
		Bill Dinneen, Sep. 27, 1905, vs. Chi. White Sox, 2–0
		Cy Young, Jun. 30, 1908, vs. N.Y. Highlanders, 8–0
3	Bill Carrigan, Bos. Red Sox (AL)	Smoky Joe Wood, Jul. 29, 1911, vs. St.L. Browns, 5–0
		Rube Foster, Jun. 16, 1916, vs. N.Y. Yankees, 2–0
		Dutch Leonard, Aug. 30, 1916, vs. St.L. Browns, 4–0
3	Ray Schalk, Chi. White Sox (AL)	Joe Benz, May 31, 1914, vs. Cle. Indians, 6–1
		Jim Scott, May 14, 1914, vs. Was. Senators, 0–1*
		Eddie Cicotte, Apr. 14, 1917, vs. St.L. Browns, 11–0
		Charlie Robertson, Apr. 30, 1922, vs. Det. Tigers, 2–0 (perfect game)
3	Val Picinich, Phi. A's (AL)	Joe Bush, Aug. 26, 1916, vs. Cle. Indians, 5–0
	Was. Senators (AL)	Walter Johnson, Jul. 1, 1920, vs. Bos. Red Sox, 1–0
	Bos. Red Sox (AL)	Howard Ehmke, Sep. 7, 1923, vs. Phi. A's, 4–0
3	Luke Sewell, Cle. Indians (AL)	Wes Ferrell, Apr. 29, 1931, vs. St.L. Browns, 9–0
	Chi. White Sox (AL)	Vern Kennedy, Aug. 31, 1935, vs. Cle. Indians, 5–0
		Bill Dietrich, Jun. 1, 1937, vs. St.L. Browns, 8–0
3	Jim Hegan, Cle. Indians (AL)	Don Black, Jul. 10, 1947, vs. Phi. A's, 3–0
		Bob Lemon, Jun. 30, 1948, vs. Det. Tigers, 2–0
		Bob Feller, Jul. 1, 1951, vs. Det. Tigers, 2–1
3	Yogi Berra, N.Y. Yankees (AL)	Allie Reynolds, Jul. 12, 1951, vs. Cle. Indians, 1–0
		Allie Reynolds, Sep. 28, 1951, vs. Bos. Red Sox, 8–0
		Don Larsen, Oct. 8, 1956, vs. Brk. Dodgers, 2–0 (World Series, perfect game)
3	Roy Campanella, Brk. Dodgers (NL)	Carl Erskine, Jun. 19, 1952, vs. Chi. Cubs, 5–0
		Carl Erskine, May 12, 1956, vs. N.Y. Giants, 3–0
		Sal Maglie, Sep. 25, 1956, vs. Phi. Phillies, 5–0
3	Del Crandall, Mil. Braves (NL)	Jim Wilson, Jun. 12, 1954, vs. Phi. Phillies, 2–0
		Lew Burdette, Aug. 18, 1960, vs. Phi. Phillies, 1–0
		Warren Spahn, Sep. 16, 1960, vs. Phi. Phillies, 4–0
3	Jeff Torborg, L.A. Dodgers (NL)	Sandy Koufax, Sep. 9, 1965, vs. Chi. Cubs, 1–0 (perfect game)
		Bill Singer, Jul. 20, 1970, vs. Phi. Phillies, 5–0
	Cal. Angels (AL)	Nolan Ryan, May 15, 1973, vs. K.C. Royals, 3–0
3	Alan Ashby, Hou. Astros (NL)	Ken Forsch, Apr. 7, 1979, vs. Atl. Braves, 6–0
		Nolan Ryan, Sep. 26, 1981, vs. L.A. Dodgers, 5–0
		Mike Scott, Sep. 25, 1986, vs. S.F. Giants, 2–0
3	Charles Johnson, Fla. Marlins (NL)	Al Leiter, May 11, 1996, vs. Col. Rockies, 11–0
		Kevin Brown, Jun. 10, 1997, vs. S.F. Giants, 9–0
		A.J. Burnett, May 12, 2001, vs. S.D. Padres, 3–0
3	Buster Posey, S.F. Giants (NL)	Matt Cain, Jun. 13, 2012, vs. Hou. Astros, 10–0 (perfect game)
		Tim Lincecum, Jul. 13, 2013, vs. S.D. Padres, 9–0
		Chris Heston, Jun. 9, 2015, vs. N.Y. Mets, 5–0
3	Wilson Ramos, Was. Nationals (NL)	Jordan Zimmermann, Sep. 28, 2014, vs. Mia. Marlins, 1–0
		Max Scherzer, Jun. 20, 2015, vs. Pit. Pirates, 6–0
		Max Scherzer, Oct. 3, 2015, vs. N.Y. Mets, 2–0

Games Caught by Left-Handed Catchers

1073	Jack Clements, 1884–1900
272	Sam Trott, 1880–85 and 1887–88
202	Pop Tate, 1885–90
186	Sy Sutcliffe, 1885, 1888–91
125	Bill Harbridge, 1876–78, 1880–83
99	Mike Hines, 1883–85, 1888
75	John Humphries, 1883–84
71	Fred Tenney, 1894–96, 1898, 1901
62	Phil Baker, 1883–84, 1886
52	Art Twineham, 1893–94
45	Jiggs Donahue, 1900–02
35	Dave Oldfield, 1883, 1885–86
34	Charlie Householder, 1882, 1884
21	Fergy Malone, 1876, 1884
16	Jack McMahon, 1892–93

12	Charlie Krehmeyer, 1884–85
7	Joe Wall, 1901–02
5	Elmer Foster, 1884
3	Homer Hillebrand, 1905
3	Benny Distefano, 1989
2	Jim Egan, 1882
2	Dale Long, 1958
2	Mike Squires, 1980
1	John Mullen, 1876
1	Billy Redmond, 1878
1	Charlie Eden, 1879
1	Martin Powell, 1881
1	John Cassidy, 1887
1	Lefty Marr, 1889
1	Chris Short, 1961

Players Pitching and Catching, Same Game

American League

Frank Isbell, Chi. White Sox	Sep. 28, 1902
Sam Mertes, Chi. White Sox	Sep. 28, 1902
Joe Sugden, St.L. Browns	Sep. 28, 1902
Bert Campaneris, K.C. A's	Sep. 8, 1965
Cesar Tovar, Min. Twins	Sep. 22, 1968
Jeff Newman, Oak. A's	Sep. 14, 1977
Rick Cerone, N.Y. Yankees	Jul. 19 and Aug. 9, 1987
Scott Sheldon, Tex. Rangers	Sep. 6, 2000
Shane Halter, Det. Tigers	Oct. 1, 2000
Jamie Burke, Sea. Mariners	Jul. 6, 2008
Jake Elmore, Hou. Astros	Aug. 19, 2013
Chris Gimenez, Min. Twins	Jun. 6 and Jun. 22, 2017
Jeff Mathis, Tor. Blue Jays	Jul. 25, 2012; Jul. 8, 2018
Francisco Arcia, L.A. Angels	Sep. 20, 2018
Tom Murphy, Sea. Mariners	May 1, 2019
Kevin Plawecki, Cle. Indians	May 5, 2019
Luke Maile, Tor. Blue Jays	May 25, 2019
Tim Federowicz, Tex. Rangers	Jul. 17, 2019
Kevin Plawecki, Bos. Red Sox	Aug. 13, 2020
Willians Astudillo, Min. Twins	May 17, 2021
Francisco Mejia, T.B. Rays	Jul. 17 and Aug. 11, 2021
Christian Bethancourt, T.B. Rays	Aug. 23 and Aug. 28, 2022

National League (Post-1900)

Frank Bowerman, N.Y. Giants	Sep. 23, 1904
Roger Bresnahan, St.L. Cardinals	Aug. 3, 1910
Dee Moore, Cin. Reds	Sep. 27, 1936
Rick Dempsey, Mil. Brewers	Jul. 2, 1991
Wiki Gonzalez, S.D. Padres	May 15, 2003
Rob Johnson, N.Y. Mets	May 18, 2012
Christian Bethancourt, S.D. Padres	May 31, 2016
Erik Kratz, Mil. Brewers	Jun. 30 and Aug. 2, 2018
Jeff Mathis, Ari. D'backs	Jul. 8, 2018
Alex Avila, Ari. D'backs	Jul. 11, 2018; Aug. 17, 2019
John Ryan Murphy, Ari. D'backs	May 6, 2019
Caleb Joseph, Ari. D'backs	Jun. 16, 2019
Russell Martin, L.A. Dodgers	Jun. 26, 2019
Taylor Davis, Chi. Cubs	Aug. 6, 2019
Kyle Farmer, Cin. Reds	Aug. 8, 2019
Carson Kelly, Ari. D'backs	Aug. 9, 2020; Apr. 10, Jul. 12, and Sep. 16, 2022
Tyler Heineman, S.F. Giants	Aug. 16, 2020
Sandy Leon, Mia. Marlins	Jun. 4 and Aug. 6, 2021
Bryan Holaday, Ari. D'backs	Aug. 1, 2021

7

Father-Son Combinations with 250 Home Runs, Career

Total	Father	Home Runs	Son	Home Runs
1094	Bobby Bonds (1968–81)	332	Barry Bonds (1986–2007)	762
782	Ken Griffey Sr. (1973–91)	152	Ken Griffey Jr. (1989–2010)	639
638	Cecil Fielder (1985–88, 1990–98)	319	Prince Fielder (2005–16)	319
553	Vladimir Guerrero Sr. (1996–2011)	449	Vladimir Guerrero Jr. (2019–)	104
538	Felipe Alou (1958–74)	206	Moises Alou (1990,1992–98, 2000–08)	332
458	Tony Perez (1964–86)	374	Eduardo Perez (1993–2000, 2002–06)	74
440	Randy Hundley (1964–77)	238	Todd Hundley (1990–2003)	202
407	Gus Bell (1950–64)	206	Buddy Bell (1972–88)	201
407	Yogi Berra (1946–65)	358	Dale Berra (1977–87)	49
369	Jose Cruz (1970–88)	165	Jose Cruz Jr. (1997–2008)	204
357	Bob Boone (1972–89)	105	Bret Boone (1992–2005)	252
343	Dante Bichette (1988–2001	274	Bo Bichette (2019–)	69
342	Gary Matthews Sr. (1972–87)	234	Gary Matthews Jr. (1999–2010)	108
328	Craig Biggio (1988–2007)	291	Cavan Biggio (2019–)	37
324	Buddy Bell (1972–88)	201	David Bell (1995–2006)	123
309	Raul Mondesi (1993–05)	271	Adalberto Mondesi (2016–)	38
299	Earl Averill Sr. (1929–41)	255	Earl Averill Jr. (1956–63)	44
283	Mike Cameron (1995–2011)	278	Daz Cameron (2020–)	5
265	Steve Swisher (1974–82)	20	Nick Swisher (2004–15)	245
264	Jose Tartabull (1962–70)	2	Danny Tartabull (1984–97)	262
264	Tim Wallach (1980–96)	260	Chad Wallach (2017–)	4
257	Jesse Barfield (1981–92)	241	Josh Barfield (2006–09)	16
257	Dolph Camilli (1933–45)	239	Doug Camilli (1960–69)	18
256	Ray Boone (1948–60)	151	Bob Boone (1972–89)	105
252	Jeff Burroughs (1970–85)	240	Sean Burroughs (2002–06, 2011–12)	12
247	John Mayberry Sr. (1968–82)	191	John Mayberry Jr. (2009–15)	56

Brother Batteries*

Jim and Ed Bailey................Cin. Reds (NL), 1959
Dick and Bill Conway................Bal. Orioles (AA), 1886
Mort and Walker Cooper................St.L. Cardinals (NL), 1940–45; and N.Y. Giants (NL), 1947
Ed and Bill Dugan................Rich. Virginians (AA), 1884
John and Buck Ewing................N.Y. Giants (NL), 1890–91
Wes and Rick Ferrell................Bos. Red Sox (AL), 1934–37; and Was. Senators (AL), 1937–38
Milt and Alex Gaston................Bos. Red Sox (AL), 1929
Mike and John O'Neill................St.L. Cardinals (NL), 1902–03
Elmer and Johnny Riddle................Cin. Reds (NL), 1941 and 1944–45; and Pit. Pirates (NL), 1948

continued on next page

Bobby and Billy Shantz .... Phi. A's (AL), 1954; K.C. A's (AL), 1955; and N.Y. Yankees (AL), 1960
Larry and Norm Sherry .... L.A. Dodgers (NL), 1960–62
Tom and Homer Thompson .... N.Y. Yankees (AL), 1912
Lefty and Fred Tyler .... Bos. Braves (NL), 1914
Will and Deacon White .... Bos. Red Caps (NL), 1877; and Cin. Reds (NL), 1878–79
Pete and Fred Wood .... Buff. Bisons (NL), 1885

* Pitcher listed first; catcher second.

Twins Who Played Major League Baseball

Canseco .... Jose, outfield (1985–2001)
               Ozzie, outfield (1990, 1992–93)
Cliburn .... Stan, catcher (1980)
               Stu, pitcher (1984–85)
Edwards .... Marshall, outfield (1981–83)
               Mike, second base (1977–80)
Grimes .... Ray, first base (1920–26)
               Roy, second base (1920)
Hunter .... Bill, outfield (1912)
               George, outfield and pitcher (1909–10)
Minor .... Ryan, first base (1998–2001)
               Damon, first base (2000–04)

Jonnard .... Bubber, catcher (1920, 1922, 1926–27, 1929, 1935)
               Claude, pitcher (1921–24, 1926, 1929)
O'Brien .... Eddie, shortstop, outfield, and pitcher (1953, 1955–58)
               Johnny, infield and pitcher (1953, 1955–59)
Reccius .... John, outfield and pitcher (1882–88, 1890)
               Phil, infield, outfield, and pitcher (1882–83)
Rogers .... Taylor, pitcher (2016–)
               Tyler, pitcher (2019–)
Shannon .... Joe, outfield and second base (1915)
               Red, shortstop (1915, 1917–21, 1926)

Hall of Famers Whose Sons Played in Majors

Father	Sons
Earl Averill Sr. (1929–41)	Earl Averill Jr. (1956, 1958–63)
Yogi Berra (1946–63, 1965)	Dale Berra (1977–87)
Craig Biggio (1998–2007)	Cavan Biggio (2019–)
Eddie Collins Sr. (1906–30)	Eddie Collins Jr. (1939, 1941–42)
Tony Gwynn Sr. (1982–2001)	Tony Gwynn Jr. (2006–12, 2014)
Vladimir Guerrero Sr. (1996–2001)	Vladimir Guerrero Jr. (2019–)
Freddie Lindstrom (1924–36)	Charlie Lindstrom (1958)
Connie Mack (1886–96)	Earle Mack (1910–11, 1914)
Jim O'Rourke (1876–93, 1904)	Queenie O'Rourke (1908)
Tony Perez (1964–86)	Eduardo Perez (1993–2000, 2002–06)
Ivan Rodriguez (1991–2011)	Dereck Rodriguez (2018–20, 2022–)
George Sisler (1915–22, 1924–30)	Dick Sisler (1946–53)
	Dave Sisler (1956–62)
Ed Walsh Sr. (1904–17)	Ed Walsh Jr. (1928–30)

Players with Two Sons Who Played in Majors

Father	Sons
Sandy Alomar (1964–78)	Roberto Alomar (1988–2004)
	Sandy Alomar Jr. (1988–2007)
Buddy Bell (1972–89)	David Bell (1995–2006)
	Mike Bell (2000)
Bob Boone (1972–90)	Bret Boone (1992–2005)
	Aaron Boone (1997–2009)
Jimmy Cooney (1890–92)	Jimmy Cooney (1917, 1919, 1924–28)
	Johnny Cooney (1921–44)

continued on next page

Father	Sons
Chris Cron (1991–22	C.J. Kron* (2014–)
	Kevin Cron (2019–20)
Dave Duncan (1964–76)	Chris Duncan (2005–09)
	Shelley Duncan (2007–13)
Larry Gilbert (1914–15)	Charlie Gilbert (1940–43, 1946–47)
	Tookie Gilbert (1950, 1953)
Tom Gordon (1988–1999, 2001–09)	Dee Strange-Gordon* (2011–20, 2022–)
	Nick Gordon* (2021–)
Sam Hairston (1951)	John Hairston (1969)
	Jerry Hairston (1973–88)
Jerry Hairston (1973–88)	Jerry Hairston Jr. (1998–2013)
	Scott Hairston (2004–14)
Dave LaRoche (1970–83)	Adam LaRoche (2004–15)
	Andy LaRoche (2007–11, 2013)
Manny Mota (1962–82)	Andy Mota (1991)
	Jose Mota (1991–95)
Tony Pena (1980–97)	Tony Pena (2006–09)
	Francisco Pena (2014–18)
Kevin Romine (1985–91)	Andrew Romine (2010–18, 2020–21)
	Austin Romine* (2011, 2013–)
George Sisler (1915–22, 1924–30)	Dick Sisler (1946–53)
	Dave Sisler (1956–62)
Mel Stottlemyre (1964–74)	Todd Stottlemyre (1988–2002)
	Mel Stottlemyre Jr. (1990)
Dixie Walker (1909–12)	Dixie Walker (1931, 1933–49)
	Harry Walker (1940–43, 1946–55)

* Still active.

Brother Double-Play Combinations

Garvin Hamner, second base, and Granny Hamner, shortstop, Phi. Phillies (NL), 1945
Eddie O'Brien, shortstop, and Johnny O'Brien, second base, Pit. Pirates (NL), 1953, 1955–56
Billy Ripken, second base, and Cal Ripken Jr., shortstop, Bal. Orioles (AL), 1987–92

Most Home Runs, Brothers

Total	Brothers	Home Runs
768	Hank Aaron (1954–76)	755
	Tommie Aaron (1962–63, 1965, 1968–71)	13
573	Joe DiMaggio (1936–42, 1946–51)	361
	Vince DiMaggio (1937–46)	125
	Dom DiMaggio (1940–42, 1946–53)	87
508	Eddie Murray (1977–97)	504
	Rich Murray (1980, 1983)	4
492	Jason Giambi (1995–2014)	440
	Jeremy Giambi (1998–2003)	52
489	Justin Upton* (2007–)	325
	Melvin Upton (2004, 2006–16)	164
462	Jose Canseco (1985–2001)	462
	Ozzie Canseco (1990, 1992–93)	0
451	Cal Ripken Jr. (1981–2001)	431
	Billy Ripken (1987–98)	20

continued on next page

Total	Brothers	Home Runs
444	Ken Boyer (1955–69)	282
	Clete Boyer (1955–71)	162
444	Lee May (1965–82)	354
	Carlos May (1968–77)	90
406	Graig Nettles (1967–88)	390
	Jim Nettles (1970–72, 1974, 1979, 1981)	16
378	Bret Boone (1992–2005)	252
	Aaron Boone (1997–2009)	126
365	J.D. Drew (1998–2011)	242
	Stephen Drew (2006–17)	123
363	Brian Giles (1995–2009)	287
	Marcus Giles (2001–07)	76
358	Dick Allen (1963–77)	351
	Hank Allen (1966–70, 1972–73)	6
	Ron Allen (1972)	1
346	Bob Johnson (1933–45)	288
	Roy Johnson (1929–38)	58
332	Sandy Alomar (1988–2007)	112
	Roberto Alomar (1988–2004)	210

* Still active.

Pitching Brothers Each Winning 20 Games in Same Season

1970	Gaylord Perry, S.F. Giants (NL)	23–13
	Jim Perry, Min. Twins (AL)	24–12
1979	Joe Niekro, Hou. Astros (NL)	21–11
	Phil Niekro, Atl. Braves (NL)	21–20

Hall of Famers' Brothers Who Played 10 or More Seasons in Majors (Post-1900)

Hall of Famer	Brother
Roberto Alomar (1988–2004)	Sandy Alomar Jr. (1988–2007)
George Brett (1973–93)	Ken Brett (1967, 1969–81)
Ed Delahanty (1888–1903)	Jim Delahanty (1901–02, 1904–12, 1914–15)
Joe DiMaggio (1936–42, 1946–51)	Dom DiMaggio (1940–42, 1946–53)
Joe DiMaggio (1936–42, 1946–51)	Vince DiMaggio (1937–46)
Rick Ferrell (1929–45, 1947)	Wes Ferrell (1927–41)
Tony Gwynn (1982–2001)	Chris Gwynn (1987–96)
Greg Maddux (1986–2008)	Mike Maddux (1986–2000)
Pedro Martinez (1992–2009)	Ramon Martinez (1998–2001)
Phil Niekro (1964–87)	Joe Niekro (1967–88)
Gaylord Perry (1962–83)	Jim Perry (1959–75)
Cal Ripken Jr. (1981–2001)	Billy Ripken (1987–98)
Joe Sewell (1920–33)	Luke Sewell (1921–39, 1942)
Lloyd Waner (1927–42, 1944–45)	Paul Waner (1926–45)
Paul Waner (1926–45)	Lloyd Waner (1927–42, 1944–45)

Father-Son Tandems Who Both Played for Same Manager

		Manager
Brucker	Earle Sr., Phi. A's (AL), 1937–40 and 1943	Connie Mack
	Earle Jr., Phi. A's (AL), 1948	
Collins	Eddie Sr., Phi. A's (AL), 1906–14	Connie Mack
	Eddie Jr., Phi. A's (AL), 1939 and 1941–42	
Hairston	Sam, Chi. White Sox (AL), 1951	Paul Richards
	Jerry, Chi. White Sox (AL), 1976	
Griffey	Ken Sr., Sea. Mariners (AL), 1990–91	Jim Lefebvre
	Ken Jr., Sea. Mariners (AL), 1989–91	
Raines	Tim Sr., Bal. Orioles (AL), 2001	Mike Hargrove
	Tim Jr., Bal. Orioles (AL), 2001	

Sons Who Played for Their Fathers

Son	Father-Manager
Moises Alou, Mon. Expos (NL), 1992–96; S.F. Giants (NL), 2005	Felipe Alou
Dale Berra, N.Y. Yankees (AL), 1985	Yogi Berra
Aaron Boone, Cin. Reds (NL), 2001–03	Bob Boone
Earle Mack, Phi. A's (AL), 1910–11 and 1914	Connie Mack
Brian McRae, K.C. Royals (AL), 1991–94	Hal McRae
Billy Ripken, Bal. Orioles (AL), 1987–88	Cal Ripken Sr.
Cal Ripken Jr., Bal. Orioles (AL), 1985 and 1987–88	Cal Ripken Sr.

Best Won–Lost Percentage for Pitching Brothers

Percentage	Brothers	Wins–Losses	Total
1.000	George Kelly (1917)	1–0	1–0
	Ren Kelly (1923)	0–0	
.800	Joe Hovlik (1909–11)	2–0	4–1
	Hick Hovlik (1918–19)	2–1	
.664	Christy Mathewson (1900–16)	373–188	373–189
	Henry Mathewson (1906–07)	0–1	
.660	Larry Corcoran (1880–87)	177–90	177–91
	Mike Corcoran (1884)	0–1	
.653	Ramon Martinez (1988–2001)	135–88	354–188
	Pedro Martinez (1992–2009)	219–100	
.639	Mickey Hughes (1888–90)	39–28	122–69
	Jim Hughes (1898–99, 1901–02)	83–41	
.631	Dizzy Dean (1930, 1932–41, 1947)	150–83	200–117
	Paul Dean (1934–41, 1943)	50–34	
.623	John Clarkson (1882, 1884–94)	328–178	385–233
	Dad Clarkson (1891–96)	39–39	
	Walter Clarkson (1904–08)	18–16	
.616	Old Hoss Radbourn (1880–91)	301–191	309–193
	George Radbourn (1883)	1–2	
.600	Harry Coveleski (1907–10, 1014–18)	81–55	296–197
	Stan Coveleski (1912, 1916–28)	215–142	
.599	Greg Maddux (1986–2008)	355–227	394–264
	Mike Maddux (1986–2000)	39–37	
.591	Vean Gregg (1911–16, 1918, 1925)	91–63	91–63
	Dave Gregg (1913)	0–0	
.588	Cy Ferry (1904–05)	0–1	10–7
	Jack Ferry (1910–13)	10–6	
.583	Snake Wiltse (1901–03)	30–31	169–121
	Hooks Wiltse (1904–15)	139–90	
.580	George Pipgras (1923–24, 1927–35)	102–73	102–74
	Ed Pipgras (1932)	0–1	
.580	Deacon White (1876, 1890)	0–0	229–166
	Will White (1877–86)	229–166	
.576	Gene Ford (1905)	0–1	98–72
	Russ Ford (1909–15)	98–71	
.565	Erskine Mayer (1912–19)	91–70	91–70
	Sam Mayer (1915)	0–0	
.563	Johnny Morrison (1920–27, 1929–30)	103–80	103–80
	Phil Morrison (1921)	0–0	

continued on next page

Percentage	Brothers	Wins-Losses	Total
.558	Howie Camnitz (1904, 1906-15)	133-106	134-106
	Harry Camnitz (1909, 1911)	1-0	
.556	Tom Gettinger (1895)	0-0	15-12
	Charlie Getting (1896-99)	15-12	
.556	Earl Johnson (1940-41, 1946-51)	40-32	40-32
	Chet Johnson (1946)	0-0	
.556	Jay Sborz (2010)	0-0	5-4
	Josh Sborz (2019-)	5-4	
.554	Big Jeff Pfeffer (1905-08, 1910-11)	31-40	189-152
	Jeff Pfeffer (1911, 1913-24)	158-112	
.546	Jim Perry (1959-75)	215-174	529-439
	Gaylord Perry (1962-83)	314-265	
.544	Lindy McDaniel (1955-75)	141-119	148-124
	Von McDaniel (1957-58)	7-5	
.542	Ad Gumbert (1888-96)	122-101	129-109
	Billy Gumbert (1890, 1892-93)	7-8	
.539	Jeff Weaver (1999-2007, 2009-10)	104-119	254-217
	Jered Weaver (2006-17)	150-98	
.539	Pud Galvin (1879-92)	365-310	365-312
	Lou Galvin (1884)	0-2	
.538	Jim O'Toole (1958-67)	98-84	98-84
	Denny O'Toole (1969-73)	0-0	
.535	Vicente Romo (1968-74, 1982)	32-33	76-66
	Enrique Romo (1977-82)	44-33	
.531	Ken Forsch (1970-84, 1986)	114-113	282-249
	Bob Forsch (1974-89)	168-136	
.531	Gus Weyhing (1887-96, 1898-1901)	264-232	267-236
	John Weyhing (1888-89)	3-4	
.530	Phil Niekro (1964-87)	318-274	539-478
	Joe Niekro (1967-88)	221-204	
.526	Rick Reuschel (1972-81, 1983-91)	214-191	230-207
	Paul Reuschel (1975-79)	16-16	
.525	Livan Hernandez (1996-2012)	178-177	268-242
	Orlando Hernandez (1998-2007)	90-65	
.524	Andy Benes (1989-2002)	155-139	184-167
	Alan Benes (1995-97, 1999-2003)	29-28	
.522	Al Lary (1954-55)	0-1	128-117
	Frank Lary (1954-65)	128-116	
.514	Jesse Fowler (1924)	1-1	55-52
	Art Fowler (1954-57, 1959, 1961-64)	54-51	
.514	Taylor Rogers (2016-)	21-26	36-34
	Tyler Rogers (2019-)	15-8	
.509	Matt Kilroy (1886-94, 1898)	142-134	142-137
	Mike Kilroy (1888, 1890)	0-3	
.507	Jesse Barnes (1915-27)	153-149	214-208
	Virgil Barnes (1919-20, 1922-28)	61-59	
.507	Frank Foreman (1884-85, 1889-93, 1895-96, 1901-02)	98-93	109-106
	Brownie Foreman (1895-96)	11-13	
.506	Carlos Pascual (1950)	1-1	175-171
	Camilo Pascual (1954-71)	174-170	
.500	Diomedes Olivo (1960, 1962-63)	5-6	12-12
	Chi Chi Olivo (1961, 1964-66)	7-6	
.500	Trevor Megill (2021-)	5-5	13-13
	Tylor Megill (2021-)	8-8	

Most Total Combined Career Wins for Pitching Brothers

Total	Brothers	Wins
539	Phil Niekro (1964–87)	318
	Joe Niekro (1967–88)	221
529	Jim Perry (1959–75)	215
	Gaylord Perry (1962–83)	314
394	Greg Maddux (1986–2008)	355
	Mike Maddux (1986–2000)	39
385	John Clarkson (1882–94)	328
	Dad Clarkson (1891–96)	39
	Walter Clarkson (1904–08)	18
373	Christy Mathewson (1900–16)	373
	Henry Mathewson (1906–07)	0
365	Pud Galvin (1879–92)	365
	Lou Galvin (1884)	0
354	Ramon Martinez (1988–2001)	135
	Pedro Martinez (1992–2009)	219
296	Harry Coveleski (1907–10, 1914–18)	81
	Stan Coveleski (1912, 1916–28)	215
282	Ken Forsch (1970–84, 1986)	114
	Bob Forsch (1974–89)	168
268	Livan Hernandez (1996–2012)	178
	Orlando Hernandez (1998–2007)	90
254	Jeff Weaver (1999–2007, 2009–10)	104
	Jered Weaver (2006–17)	150
230	Rick Reuschel (1972–89)	214
	Paul Reuschel (1975–79)	16
214	Jesse Barnes (1905–27)	153
	Virgil Barnes (1919–20, 1922–28)	61
200	Dizzy Dean (1930, 1932–41, 1947)	150
	Paul Dean (1934–41, 1947)	50

Pitching Brothers Facing Each Other, Regular Season

Frank Foreman, Cin. Reds (NL), vs. Brownie Foreman, Pit. Pirates (NL), 1896*

Stan Coveleski, Cle. Indians (AL), vs. Harry Coveleski, Det. Tigers (AL), 1916*

Virgil Barnes, N.Y. Giants (NL), vs. Jesse Barnes, Bos. Braves (NL), 1923

Virgil Barnes, N.Y. Giants (NL), vs. Jesse Barnes, Brk. Dodgers (NL), 1927

Phil Niekro, Atl. Braves (NL), vs. Joe Niekro, Chi. Cubs (NL), 1968

* Same game but not at same time.

** Interleague play.

Gaylord Perry, Cle. Indians (AL), vs. Jim Perry, Det. Tigers (AL), 1973

Bob Forsch, St.L. Cardinals (NL), vs. Ken Forsch, Hou. Astros (NL), 1974

Tom Underwood, Tor. Blue Jays (AL), vs. Pat Underwood, Det. Tigers (AL), 1979

Greg Maddux, Chi. Cubs (NL), vs. Mike Maddux, Phi. Phillies (NL), 1986

Greg Maddux, Chi. Cubs (NL), vs. Mike Maddux, Phi. Phillies (NL), 1988

Jeff Weaver, L.A. Dodgers (NL), vs. Jered Weaver, L.A. Angels (AL), 2009**

Jeff Weaver, L.A. Dodgers (NL), vs. Jered Weaver, L.A. Angels (AL), 2010**

Most Career Victories by Father-Son Combination (Post-1900)

Total	Father	Wins	Son	Wins
302	Mel Stottlemyre (1964–74)	164	Todd Stottlemyre (1988–2002)	138
258	Dizzy Trout (1939–52, 1957)	170	Steve Trout (1978–89)	88
224	Jim Bagby Sr. (1912, 1916–23)	127	Jim Bagby Jr. (1938–47)	97
206	Ed Walsh Sr. (1904–17)	195	Ed Walsh Jr. (1928–30, 1932)	11
194	Joe Coleman Sr. (1942, 1946–51, 1953–55)	52	Joe Coleman Jr. (1965–79)	142
171	Floyd Bannister (1977–89, 1991–92)	134	Brian Bannister (2006–10)	37
168	Clyde Wright (1966–75)	100	Jaret Wright (1997–2007)	68
163	Doug Drabek (1986–98)	155	Kyle Drabek (2010–16)	8
157	Thornton Lee (1933–48)	117	Don Lee (1957–58, 1960–66)	40
150	Joe Coleman (1965–79)	142	Casey Coleman (2010–12, 2014)	8
140	Charlie Leibrandt (1979–82, 1984–93)	140	Brandon Leibrandt (2020)	0
124	Ross Grimsley Sr. (1951)	0	Ross Grimsley Jr. (1971–80, 1982)	124
123	Julio Navarro (1962–70)	7	Jaime Navarro (1989–2000)	116
117	Smoky Joe Wood (1908–15, 1917, 1919–20)	117	Joe Wood Jr. (1944)	0
116	Dick Ellsworth (1958, 1960–71)	115	Steve Ellsworth (1988)	1
99	Paul Quantrill (1992–2005)	68	Cal Quantrill (2019–)	31
93	Steve Bedrosian (1981–91, 1993–95)	76	Cam Bedrosian (2014–2021)	17
77	David Weathers (1991–2009)	73	Ryan Weathers (2021–)	4
73	Lew Krausse Sr. (1931–32)	5	Lew Krausse Jr. (1961, 1964–74)	68
72	Herman Pillette (1917, 1922–24)	34	Duane Pillette (1949–56)	38
70	Mark Leiter Sr. (1990–99, 2001)	65	Mark Leiter Jr. (2017–)	5
68	Jeff Russell (1983–96)	56	James Russell (2010–16)	10
61	Bruce Ruffin (1986–97)	60	Chance Ruffin (2011, 2013)	1

Brothers Who Played Together on Three Major League Teams

Sandy Jr. and Roberto Alomar . . . . .S.D. Padres (NL), 1988–89
Cle. Indians (AL), 1999–2000
Chi. White Sox (AL), 2003–04

Arthur and John Irwin . . . . .Worc. Brown Stockings (NL), 1882
Was. Statesmen (NL), 1889
Bos. Reds (AA), 1891

Paul and Lloyd Waner . . . . .Pit. Pirates (NL), 1927–40
Bos. Braves (NL), 1941
Brk. Dodgers (NL), 1944

8
WORLD SERIES

Teams Never to Trail in a World Series

1963..L.A. Dodgers (NL) vs. N.Y. Yankees (AL)
1966.. Bal. Orioles (AL) vs. L.A. Dodgers (NL)
1989...Oak. A's (AL) vs. S.F. Giants (NL)
2004.. Bos. Red Sox (AL) vs. St.L. Cardinals (NL)

Highest Batting Average for a World Series Team

American League	National League

Batting Average	Batting Average
.338...N.Y. Yankees, 1960*	.323...Pit. Pirates, 1979
.333... Bos. Red Sox, 2007	.317...Cin. Reds, 1990
.316... Phi. A's, 1910	.309..N.Y. Giants, 1922
.313..N.Y. Yankees, 1932	.300..Brk. Dodgers, 1953
.311...Tor. Blue Jays, 1993	
.310.. Ana. Angels, 2002	
.309..N.Y. Yankees, 1998	
.309... Oak. A's, 1989	
.302..N.Y. Yankees, 1936	

* Lost World Series.

Lowest Batting Average for a World Series Team

American League	National League

Batting Average	Batting Average
.146...Bal. Orioles, 1969	.142...L.A. Dodgers, 1966
.149..Det. Tigers, 2006	.163.. Phi. Phillies, 2022
.161... Phi. A's, 1905	.175...N.Y. Giants, 1911
.172... Phi. A's, 1914	.180...L.A. Dodgers, 2018
.177.. Oak. A's, 1988	.182.. Phi. Phillies, 1915
.179..Cle. Indians, 1995	.182..Brk. Dodgers, 1941
.183...St.L. Browns, 1944	.185..St.L. Cardinals, 1985
.183..N.Y. Yankees, 2001	.190...St.L. Cardinals, 2004
.186.. Bos. Red Sox, 1918*	.193.. N.Y. Mets, 2015
.190..Cle. Indians, 1954	.195..Brk. Dodgers, 1956
.190...Tex. Rangers, 2010	.195.. Phi. Phillies, 1983
.197... Phi. A's, 1930*	.196.. Chi. Cubs, 1906
.198...Chi. White Sox, 1906*	
.199..Cle. Indians, 1948*	
.199..N.Y. Yankees, 1962*	

* Won World Series.

Most Regular Season Losses, Reaching World Series

American League	National League
Losses	**Losses**
77 ....1987 Min. Twins* (Record: 85–77)	79 ....1973 N.Y. Mets (Record: 82–79)
75 ....1997 Cle. Indians (Record: 86–75)	78 ....2006 St.L. Cardinals* (Record: 83–78)
74 ....2000 N.Y. Yankees* (Record: 87–74)	75 ....2022 Phi. Phillies (Record: 87–75)
74 ....2012 Det. Tigers (Record: 88–74)	74 ....2014 S.F. Giants* (Record: 88–74)
73 ....2014 K.C. Royals (Record: 89–73)	73 ....2005 Hou. Astros (Record: 89–73)
72 ....1974 Oak. A's* (Record: 90–72)	73 ....2007 Col. Rockies (Record: 90–73)
72 ....2010 Tex. Rangers (Record: 90–72)	73 ....2021 Atl. Braves* (Record: 88–73)
71 ....1985 K.C. Royals* (Record: 91–71)	72 ....1983 Phi. Phillies* (Record: 90–72)
70 ....1967 Bos. Red Sox (Record: 92–70)	72 ....2011 St.L. Cardinals* (Record: 90–72)
70 ....1996 N.Y. Yankees* (Record: 92–70)	72 ....2015 N.Y. Mets (Record: 90–72)
68 ....1973 Oak. A's* (Record: 94–68)	71 ....1980 Phi. Phillies* (Record: 91–71)
67 ....1982 Mil. Brewers (Record: 95–67)	71 ....1990 Cin. Reds* (Record: 91–71)
67 ....1991 Min. Twins* (Record: 95–67)	71 ....2003 Fla. Marlins* (Record: 91–71)
67 ....1993 Tor. Blue Jays* (Record: 95–67)	71 ....2018 L.A. Dodgers* (Record: 92–71)
67 ....2016 Cle. Indians (Record: 94–67)	70 ....1982 St.L. Cardinals* (Record: 92–70)
67 ....2021 Hou. Astros (Record: 95–67)	70 ....1984 S.D. Padres (Record: 92–70)
* Won World Series.	70 ....1989 S.F. Giants (Record: 92–70)
	70 ....1997 Fla. Marlins* (Record: 92–70)
	70 ....2001 Ari. D'backs* (Record: 92–70)
	70 ....2008 Phi. Phillies* (Record: 92–70)
	70 ....2010 S.F. Giants* (Record: 92–70)
	69 ....1964 St.L. Cardinals (Record: 93–69)
	69 ....2009 Phi. Phillies (Record: 93–69)
	69 ....2019 Was. Nationals* (Record: 93–69)
	68 ....1959 L.A. Dodgers* (Record: 88–68)
	68 ....1991 Atl. Braves (Record: 94–68)
	68 ....2000 N.Y. Mets (Record: 94–68)
	68 ....2012 S.F. Giants* (Record: 94–68)
	67 ....1966 L.A. Dodgers (Record: 95–67)
	67 ....1978 L.A. Dodgers (Record: 95–67)
	67 ....1987 St.L. Cardinals (Record: 95–67)
	67 ....1988 L.A. Dodgers* (Record: 95–67)

Teams with Lowest Batting Average (Season), Winning World Series

Avg.	Team	Record	Avg.	Team	Record
.230	Chi. White Sox, 1906	93–58	.248	Bos. Red Sox, 1916	91–63
.235	Det. Tigers, 1968	103–59	.248	L.A. Dodgers, 1988	94–67
.240	Oak. A's, 1972	93–62	.249	Chi. Cubs, 1908	99–55
.242	N.Y. Mets, 1969	100–62	.249	Bos. Red Sox, 1918	75–51
.244	Atl. Braves, 2021	88–73	.250	Chi. Cubs, 1907	107–45
.245	L.A. Dodgers, 1965	97–65	.250	Atl. Braves, 1995	90–54
.247	Oak. A's, 1974	90–72			

Teams Winning World Series a Year After Finishing with a Losing Record

Team	WS-Winning Season	Losing Season
Bos. Braves (NL)	1914 (94–59)	1913 (69–82)
Was. Senators (AL)	1924 (92–62)	1923 (75–78)
N.Y. Giants (NL)	1954 (97–57)	1953 (70–84)
L.A. Dodgers (NL)	1959 (88–68)	1958 (71–83)
L.A. Dodgers (NL)	1965 (97–65)	1964 (80–82)
N.Y. Mets (NL)	1969 (100–62)	1968 (73–89)
Min. Twins (AL)	1987 (85–77)	1986 (71–91)
L.A. Dodgers (NL)	1988 (94–67)	1987 (73–89)
Cin. Reds (NL)	1990 (91–71)	1989 (75–87)
Min. Twins (AL)	1991 (95–67)	1990 (74–88)*
Ana. Angels (AL)	2002 (99–63)	2001 (75–87)

continued on next page

Team	WS-Winning Season	Losing Season
Fla. Marlins (NL)	2003 (91–71)	2002 (79–83)
Bos. Red Sox (AL)	2013 (97–65)	2012 (69–93)*
S.F. Giants (NL)	2014 (88–74)	2013 (76–86)

* Finished in last place.

World Series Champions with More Errors Than League Average

Year	Team	Team Total	League Average
1925	Pit. Pirates	224	206
1926	St.L. Cardinals	198	196
1928	N.Y. Yankees	199	187
1932	N.Y. Yankees	190	183
1933	N.Y. Giants	178	170
1954	N.Y. Giants	154	142
1963	L.A. Dodgers	159	146
1964	St.L. Cardinals	172	142
1967	St.L. Cardinals	140	137
1971	Pit. Pirates	133	130
1986	N.Y. Mets	138	133
1988	L.A. Dodgers	142	125
2004	Bos. Red Sox	118	105
2011	St.L. Cardinals	116	102
2012	S.F. Giants	115	94
2014	S.F. Giants	100	97
2016	Chi. Cubs	101	95
2020	L.A. Dodgers	40	36*

* COVID-shortened season.

Players Hitting .500 in World Series (Min. 10 At-Bats)

Billy Hatcher, Cin. Reds (NL), 1990	9-for-12	.750
David Ortiz, Bos. Red Sox (AL), 2013	11-for-16	.688
Babe Ruth, N.Y. Yankees (AL), 1928	10-for-16	.625
Hideki Matsui, N.Y. Yankees (AL), 2009	8-for-13	.615
Ricky Ledee, N.Y. Yankees (AL), 1998	6-for-10	.600
Chris Sabo, Cin. Reds (NL), 1990	9-for-16	.563
Hank Gowdy, Bos. Braves (NL), 1914	6-for-11	.545
Lou Gehrig, N.Y. Yankees (AL), 1928	6-for-11	.545
Bret Boone*, Atl. Braves (NL), 1999	7-for-13	.538
Johnny Bench, Cin. Reds (NL), 1976	8-for-15	.533
Lou Gehrig, N.Y. Yankees (AL), 1932	9-for-17	.529
Thurman Munson*, N.Y. Yankees (AL), 1976	9-for-17	.529
Dane Iorg, St.L. Cardinals (NL), 1982	9-for-17	.529
Larry McLean, N.Y. Giants (NL), 1913	6-for-12	.500
Dave Robertson, N.Y. Giants (NL), 1917	11-for-22	.500
Mark Koenig, N.Y. Yankees (AL), 1927	9-for-18	.500
Pepper Martin, St.L. Cardinals (NL), 1931	12-for-24	.500
Joe Gordon, N.Y. Yankees (AL), 1941	7-for-14	.500
Billy Martin, N.Y. Yankees (AL), 1953	12-for-24	.500
Vic Wertz*, Cle. Indians (AL), 1954	8-for-16	.500
Phil Garner, Pit. Pirates (NL), 1979	12-for-24	.500
Paul Molitor, Tor. Blue Jays (AL), 1993	12-for-24	.500
Tony Gwynn*, S.D. Padres (NL), 1998	8-for-16	.500
Pablo Sandoval, S.F. Giants (NL), 2012	8-for-16	.500

* Member of losing team.

0-for-the Series (Min. 10 At-Bats)

Dal Maxvill, St.L. Cardinals (NL), 1968	0-for-22	Dick Green, Oak. A's (AL), 1974	0-for-13
Jimmy Sheckard, Chi. Cubs (NL), 1906	0-for-21	Pat Burrell, S.F. Giants (NL), 2010	0-for-13
Billy Sullivan, Chi. White Sox (AL), 1906	0-for-21	Carl Reynolds, Chi. Cubs (NL), 1938	0-for-12
Red Murray, N.Y. Giants (NL), 1911	0-for-21	Joe Collins, N.Y. Yankees (AL), 1952	0-for-12
Gil Hodges, Brk. Dodgers (NL), 1952	0-for-21	Barbaro Garbey, Det. Tigers (AL), 1984	0-for-12
Lonny Frey, Cin. Reds (NL), 1939	0-for-17	Birdie Tebbetts, Det. Tigers (AL), 1940	0-for-11
Flea Clifton, Det. Tigers (AL), 1935	0-for-16	Davey Williams, N.Y. Giants (NL), 1954	0-for-11
Mike Epstein, Oak. A's (AL), 1972	0-for-16	Jim Rivera, Chi. White Sox (AL), 1959	0-for-11

continued on next page

Rafael Belliard, Atl. Braves (NL), 1995................. 0-for-16
Bill Dahlen, N.Y. Giants (NL), 1905...................... 0-for-15
Wally Berger, Cin. Reds (NL), 1939.................... 0-for-15
Scott Rolen, St.L. Cardinals (NL), 2004 .... 0-for-15
Bryson Stott, Phi. Phillies (NL), 2022.................. 0-for-14
Hal Wagner, Bos. Red Sox (AL), 1946 .... 0-for-13

Roy Howell, Mil. Brewers (AL), 1982..................... 0-for-11
Austin Barnes, L.A. Dodgers (NL), 2018................. 0-for-11
Hippo Vaughn, Chi. Cubs (NL), 1918.................... 0-for-10
Lefty Grove, Phi. A's (AL), 1931........................ 0-for-10
Felix Mantilla, Mil. Braves (NL), 1957.................. 0-for-10
Jim Leyritz, S.D. Padres (NL), 1998 .... 0-for-10
Pete Kozma, St.L. Cardinals (NL), 2013 .... 0-for-10

Players on World Series–Winning Teams in Both Leagues

	American League	National League
Rick Aguilera	Min. Twins, 1991	N.Y. Mets, 1986
Doug Bair	Det. Tigers, 1984	St.L. Cardinals, 1982
Mookie Betts	Bos. Red Sox, 2018	L.A. Dodgers, 2020
Josh Beckett	Bos. Red Sox, 2007	Fla. Marlins, 2003
Joe Blanton	K.C. Royals, 2015*	Phi. Phillies, 2008
Bert Blyleven	Min. Twins, 1987	Pit. Pirates, 1979
A.J. Burnett	N.Y. Yankees, 2009	Fla. Marlins, 2003*
Terry Crowley	Bal. Orioles, 1970	Cin. Reds, 1975
Mike Cuellar	Bal. Orioles, 1970	St.L. Cardinals, 1964*
Vic Davalillo	Oak. A's, 1973	Pit. Pirates, 1971
Murry Dickson	N.Y. Yankees, 1958	St.L. Cardinals, 1942 and 1946
Mariano Duncan	N.Y. Yankees, 1996	Cin. Reds, 1990
Leo Durocher	N.Y. Yankees, 1928	St.L. Cardinals, 1934
David Eckstein	Ana. Angels, 2002	St.L. Cardinals, 2006
Lonny Frey	N.Y. Yankees, 1947	Cin. Reds, 1940
Billy Gardner	N.Y. Yankees, 1961	N.Y. Giants, 1954*
Kirk Gibson	Det. Tigers, 1984	L.A. Dodgers, 1988
Dwight Gooden	N.Y. Yankees, 1996*	N.Y. Mets, 1986
Terrance Gore	K.C. Royals, 2015	Atl. Braves, 2021*
Alfredo Griffin	Tor. Blue Jays, 1992–93	L.A. Dodgers, 1988
Don Gullett	N.Y. Yankees, 1977	Cin. Reds, 1975–76
Mule Haas	Phi. A's, 1929–30	Pit. Pirates, 1925*
Johnny Hopp	N.Y. Yankees, 1950–51	St.L. Cardinals, 1942 and 1944
Dane Iorg	K.C. Royals, 1985	St.L. Cardinals, 1982
Danny Jackson	K.C. Royals, 1985	Cin. Reds, 1990
Howard Johnson	Det. Tigers, 1984	N.Y. Mets, 1986
Jay Johnstone	N.Y. Yankees, 1978	L.A. Dodgers, 1981
David Justice	N.Y. Yankees, 2000	Atl. Braves, 1995
Joe Kelly	Bos. Red Sox, 2018	L.A. Dodgers, 2020
Byung-Hyun Kim	Bos. Red Sox, 2004*	Ari. D'backs, 2001
John Lackey	Ana. Angels, 2002; and Bos. Red Sox, 2013	Chi. Cubs, 2016
Al Leiter	Tor. Blue Jays, 1993	Fla. Marlins, 1997
Jon Lester	Bos. Red Sox, 2007	Chi. Cubs, 2016
Javier Lopez	Bos. Red Sox, 2007	S.F. Giants, 2010, 2012* and 2014
Mike Lowell	Bos. Red Sox, 2007	Fla. Marlins, 2003
Ryan Madsen	K.C. Royals, 2015	Phi. Phillies, 2008
Roger Maris	N.Y. Yankees, 1960–61	St.L. Cardinals, 1967
Eddie Mathews	Det. Tigers, 1968	Mil. Braves, 1957
Dal Maxvill	Oak. A's, 1972* and 1974	St.L. Cardinals, 1964 and 1967
Stuffy McInnis	Phi. A's, 1911 and 1913; and Bos. Red Sox, 1918	Pit. Pirates, 1925
Don McMahon	Det. Tigers, 1968	Mil. Braves, 1957
Paul O'Neill	N.Y. Yankees, 1996 and 1998–2000	Cin. Reds, 1990
Dave Parker	Pit. Pirates, 1979	Oak. A's, 1989
Jake Peavy	Bos. Red Sox, 2013	S.F. Giants, 2014
Paul Richards	Det. Tigers, 1945	N.Y. Giants, 1933*
David Robertson	N.Y. Yankees, 2009	Phi. Phillies, 2022
David Ross	Bos. Red Sox, 2013	Chi. Cubs, 2016
Dutch Ruether	N.Y. Yankees, 1927*	Cin. Reds, 1919
Rosy Ryan	N.Y. Yankees, 1928*	N.Y. Giants, 1921* and 1923
Curt Schilling	Bos. Red Sox, 2004 and 2007	Ari. D'backs, 2001
John Shelby	Bal. Orioles, 1983	L.A. Dodgers, 1988
Bill Skowron	N.Y. Yankees, 1956, 1958, and 1961–62	L.A. Dodgers, 1963
Enos Slaughter	N.Y. Yankees, 1956 and 1958	St.L. Cardinals, 1942 and 1944

continued on next page

American League	National League
Lonnie Smith ............K.C. Royals, 1985..Phi. Phillies, 1980, and St.L. Cardinals, 1982
Scott Spiezio ....Ana. Angels, 2002...St.L. Cardinals, 2006
Dave Stewart...........Oak. A's, 1989...L.A. Dodgers, 1981
Darryl Strawberry.....N.Y. Yankees, 1996 and 1999* ..............................N.Y. Mets, 1986
Gene Tenace ....Oak. A's, 1972–74...St.L. Cardinals, 1982
Dick Tracewski ....Det. Tigers, 1968..L.A. Dodgers, 1963 and 1965
Juan Uribe...............Chi. White Sox, 2005 ....S.F. Giants, 2010
Bob Welch ....Oak. A's, 1989..L.A. Dodgers, 1981
Devon White ....Tor. Blue Jays, 1992–93..Fla. Marlins, 1997
Ben Zobrist..............K.C. Royals, 2015..Chi. Cubs, 2016

* Did not play.

Pitchers in World Series with Highest Slugging Percentage

Slugging %	Pitcher	Games	At-Bats	Hits	Doubles	Triples	Home Runs	Batting Avg.
1.667	Orel Hershiser	2	3	3	2	0	0	1.000
.833	Ken Holtzman	8	12	4	3	0	1	.333
.800	Joe Blanton	2	7	1	0	0	1	.200
.818	Dutch Ruether	7	11	4	1	2	0	.364
.777	Pop Haines	6	9	4	0	0	2	.444
.750	Jack Bentley	10	12	5	1	0	1	.417
.667	Mike Moore	2	3	1	1	0	0	.333
.500	Dave McNally	9	16	2	0	0	2	.125
.467	Dizzy Dean	6	15	5	2	0	0	.333
.375	Jack Coombs	6	24	8	1	0	0	.333
.375	Johnny Podres	7	16	5	1	0	0	.313
.357	Bob Gibson	9	28	4	0	0	2	.143
.346	Allie Reynolds	15	26	8	1	0	0	.308
.316	Burleigh Grimes	9	19	6	0	0	0	.316

World Series–Ending Hits

1912....... Bos. Red Sox (AL) Larry Gardner hits a deep sacrifice drive to N.Y. Giant (NL) right fielder Josh Devore to score Boston second baseman Steve Yerkes with the winning run in the eighth game of the Series (one had ended in a tie) as Boston scored two in the bottom of the 10th inning for a comeback 3–2 win to win Series 4 games to 3.

1924....... Earl McNeeley's single over Freddie Lindstrom's head in the 12th inning of Game 7 drives in Muddy Ruel with the winning run as the Was. Senators (AL) beat the N.Y. Giants (NL), 4 games to 3.

1929....... Bing Miller's double in the 9th inning of Game 5 drives in Al Simmons with the winning run as the Phi. A's (AL) beat the Chi. Cubs (NL), 4 games to 1.

1935....... Goose Goslin's single in the ninth inning drives in Charlie Gehringer with the winning run as the Det. Tigers (AL) beat the Chi. Cubs (NL), 4 games to 2.

1953....... Billy Martin's 12th hit of the Series, a single, drives in Hank Bauer with the winning run as the N.Y. Yankees (AL) beat the Brk. Dodgers (NL), 4 games to 2.

1960....... Bill Mazeroski's lead-off home run in the bottom of the 9th inning of Game 7 wins the Series for the Pittsburgh Pirates (NL) over the N.Y. Yankees (AL), 4 games to 3.

1991....... Pinch-hitter Gener Larkin singles into the outfield off pitcher Alejandro Pena to drive in Dan Gladden to give the Minnesota Twins (AL) the Game 7 victory over the Atlanta Braves (NL), 1–0.

1993....... Joe Carter's bottom-of-the-ninth home run off pitcher Mitch Williams with Rickey Henderson and Paul Molitor aboard gives the Tor. Blue Jays (AL) an 8–6 victory over the Phi. Phillies (NL) (and their second straight World Championship), 4 games to 2.

1997....... Edgar Renteria's ground-ball single up the middle scored Craig Counsell as the Fla. Marlins (NL) rallied with two in the 11th inning against the Cle. Indians (AL) to win Game 7, 3–2.

2001....... Luis Gonzalez's bloop single over a drawn-in N.Y. Yankees (AL) infield in the bottom of the 9th inning of Game 7 wins the Series for the Ari. D'backs (NL), 4 games to 3.

Pitchers in World Series with 300 Career Wins

	Wins		Wins
Cy Young, Bos. Red Sox (AL), 1903	379	Pete Alexander, St.L. Cardinals (NL), 1928	364
Christy Mathewson, N.Y. Giants (NL), 1912	312	Steve Carlton, Phi. Phillies (NL), 1983	300
Christy Mathewson, N.Y. Giants (NL), 1913	337	Roger Clemens, N.Y. Yankees (AL), 2003	310
Walter Johnson, Was. Senators (AL), 1924	377	Hou. Astros (NL), 2005	341
Walter Johnson, Was. Senators (AL), 1925	397		
Pete Alexander, St.L. Cardinals (NL), 1926	327		

Players on World Series Teams in Three Decades

Yogi Berra	N.Y. Yankees (AL)	1947 and 1949
	N.Y. Yankees (AL)	1950–53 and 1955–58
	N.Y. Yankees (AL)	1960–61 and 1963
Roger Clemens	Bos. Red Sox (AL)	1986
	N.Y. Yankees (AL)	1999
	N.Y. Yankees (AL)	2000–01, 2003
	Hou. Astros (NL)	2005
Bill Dickey	N.Y. Yankees (AL)	1928*
	N.Y. Yankees (AL)	1932 and 1936–39
	N.Y. Yankees (AL)	1941–43
Joe DiMaggio	N.Y. Yankees (AL)	1936–39
	N.Y. Yankees (AL)	1941–42, 1947, and 1949
	N.Y. Yankees (AL)	1950–51
Leo Durocher	N.Y. Yankees (AL)	1928
	St.L. Cardinals (NL)	1934
	Brk. Dodgers (NL)	1941*
Willie Mays	N.Y. Giants (NL)	1951 and 1954
	S.F. Giants (NL)	1962
	N.Y. Mets (NL)	1973
Tug McGraw	N.Y. Mets (NL)	1969*
	N.Y. Mets (NL)	1973
	Phi. Phillies (NL)	1980
Jim Palmer	Bal. Orioles (AL)	1966 and 1969
	Bal. Orioles (AL)	1970–71 and 1979
	Bal. Orioles (AL)	1983
Herb Pennock	Phi. A's (AL)	1913* and 1914
	N.Y. Yankees (AL)	1923 and 1926–28*
	N.Y. Yankees (AL)	1932
Billy Pierce	Det. Tigers (AL)	1945*
	Chi. White Sox (AL)	1959
	S.F. Giants (NL)	1962
Luis Polonia	Oak. A's (AL)	1988
	Atl. Braves (NL)	1995 and 1996
	N.Y. Yankees (AL)	2000
Edgar Renteria	Fla. Marlins (NL	1997
	St.L. Cardinals (NL)	2004
	S.F. Giants (NL)	2010
Babe Ruth	Bos. Red Sox (AL)	1915–16 and 1918
	N.Y. Yankees (AL)	1921–23 and 1926–28
	N.Y. Yankees (AL)	1932
Wally Schang	Phi. A's (AL)—Bos. Red Sox (AL)	1913–14 and 1918
	N.Y. Yankees (AL)	1921–23
	Phi. A's (AL)	1930*
Justin Verlander	Det. Tigers (AL)	2006 and 2012
	Det. Tigers (AL)—Hou. Astros (AL)	2017
	Hou. Astros (AL)	2019 and 2022
Bob Welch	L.A. Dodgers (NL)	1978
	L.A. Dodgers (NL)	1981
	Oak. A's (AL)	1990

continued on next page

Matt Williams	S.F. Giants (NL)	1989
	Cle. Indians (AL)	1997
	Ari. D'backs (NL)	2001
Jimmy Wilson	St.L. Cardinals (NL)	1928
	St.L. Cardinals (NL)	1930–31
	Cin. Reds (NL)	1940

* Did not play.

Players with World Series Home Runs in Three Decades

Yogi Berra	N.Y. Yankees (AL)	1947
	N.Y. Yankees (AL)	1950, 1952–53, and 1955–57
	N.Y. Yankees (AL)	1960–61
Joe DiMaggio	N.Y. Yankees (AL)	1937–39
	N.Y. Yankees (AL)	1947 and 1949
	N.Y. Yankees (AL)	1950–51
Matt Williams	S.F. Giants (NL)	1989
	Cle. Indians (AL)	1997
	Ari. D'backs (NL)	2001
Eddie Murray	Bal. Orioles (AL)	1979
	Bal. Orioles (AL)	1983
	Cle. Indians (AL)	1995

Player-Managers on World Series–Winning Teams

Jimmy Collins	Bos. Red Sox (AL), 1903	Bucky Harris	Was. Senators (AL), 1924
John McGraw	N.Y. Giants (NL), 1905	Rogers Hornsby	St.L. Cardinals (NL), 1926
Fielder Jones	Chi. White Sox (AL), 1906	Gabby Street	St.L. Cardinals (NL), 1931
Frank Chance	Chi. Cubs (NL), 1907, 1908	Bill Terry	N.Y. Giants (NL), 1933
Fred Clarke	Pit. Pirates (NL), 1909	Frankie Frisch	St.L. Cardinals (NL), 1934
Jake Stahl	Bos. Red Sox (AL), 1912	Mickey Cochrane	Det. Tigers (AL), 1935
John Carrigan	Bos. Red Sox (AL), 1915 and 1916	Lou Boudreau	Cle. Indians (AL), 1948
Tris Speaker	Cle. Indians (AL), 1920		

World Series–Winning Managers Who Never Played in Majors

Ed Barrow	Bos. Red Sox (AL)	1918
Johnny Keane	St.L. Cardinals (NL)	1964
Jim Leyland	Fla. Marlins (NL)	1997
Joe Maddon	Chi. Cubs (NL)	2016
Joe McCarthy	N.Y. Yankees (AL)	1932, 1936, 1937, 1938, 1939, 1941, and 1943
Jack McKeon	Fla. Marlins (NL)	2003
Pants Rowland	Chi. White Sox (AL)	1917
Brian Snitker	Atl. Braves (NL)	2021
Earl Weaver	Bal. Orioles (AL)	1970

Leaders in Offensive Categories, Never Appearing in World Series (Post-1903)

Games	Rafael Palmeiro	2831
Base Hits	Ichiro Suzuki	3089
Runs	Rafael Palmeiro	1663
Singles	Ichiro Suzuki	2514
Doubles	Rafael Palmeiro	585
Triples	George Sisler	164
Home Runs	Ken Griffey Jr.	630
Grand Slams	Carlos Lee	17
Pinch-Hit Home Runs	Dave Hansen	15
Total Bases	Rafael Palmeiro	5388

continued on next page

Extra-Base Hits	Rafael Palmeiro	1192
	Ken Griffery Jr.	1192
RBIs	Ken Griffey Jr.	1836
Walks	Frank Thomas	1667
Strikeouts	Adam Dunn	2379
Slugging Percentage (Min. 4000 Total Bases)	Frank Thomas	.555
Batting Average (Min. 10 Seasons)	Lefty O'Doul	.349
.300 Seasons	Luke Appling	16
Stolen Bases	Ichiro Suzuki	509

Most Seasons, Never Appearing in World Series (Post-1903)

24 ....Phil Niekro, pitcher (1964–87)
23 .... Julio Franco, first base (1982–94, 1996–97,1999, 2001–07)
22 .... Harold Baines, outfield and designated hitter (1980–2001)
22 .... Gaylord Perry, pitcher (1962–83)
22 .... Ken Griffey Jr., outfield (1989–2010)
21 .... Tom Gordon, pitcher (1988–1999, 2001–09)
21 .... Ted Lyons, pitcher (1923–42, 1946)
21 .... Lindy McDaniel, pitcher (1955–75)
21 .... Danny Darwin, pitcher (1978–98)
21 .... Frank Tanana, pitcher (1973–93)
20 .... Johnny Cooney, outfield (1921–30, 1935–44)
20 .... Mel Harder, pitcher (1928–47)
20 .... Luke Appling, shortstop (1930–43, 1945–50)
20 .... Dutch Leonard, pitcher (1933–36, 1938–53)
20..............Mickey Vernon, first base (1939–43, 1946–60)
20..............Elmer Valo, outfield (1940–43, 1946–61)
20..............Brian Downing, outfield (1973–92)
20..............Rafael Palmeiro, first base (1986–2005)
19..............Cy Williams, outfield (1912–30)
19..............Rube Bressler, outfield and pitcher (1914–32)
19..............Al Lopez, catcher (1928, 1930–47)
19..............Ernie Banks, shortstop and first base (1953–71)
19..............Tony Taylor, second base (1958–76)
19..............Ferguson Jenkins, pitcher (1965–83)
19..............Rod Carew, infield (1967–85)
19.............Gene Garber, pitcher (1969–70, 1972–88)
19.............Jose Cruz, outfield (1970–88)
19..............Torii Hunter, outfield (1997–2015)
19..............Mark McLemore, infield and outfield (1986–2004)
19..............Chris Speier, infield (1971–89)
19..............Andres Galarraga, first base (1985–2004)
19..............B.J. Surhoff, infield (1987–2005)
19..............Frank Thomas, first base (1990–2008)

Playing Most Games, Never Appearing in World Series (Post-1903)

Rafael Palmeiro (1986–2005)	2831	Billy Williams (1959–76)	2488
Ken Griffey Jr. (1989–2010)	2671	Rod Carew (1967–85)	2469
Ichiro Suzuki (2001–2018)	2651	Bobby Abreu (1996–2012, 2014)	2425
Andre Dawson (1976–86)	2627	Luke Appling (1930–43, 1945–50)	2422
Ernie Banks (1953–71)	2528	Mickey Vernon (1939–43, 1946–60)	2409
Julio Franco (1982–94, 1996–97, 1999, 2001–07)	2527	Buddy Bell (1972–89)	2405

Players with the Most Home Runs, Never Appearing in World Series

Ken Griffey Jr. (1989–2010)	630	Harold Baines (1980–2000)	384
Sammy Sosa (1989–2005, 2007)	609	Giancarlo Stanton* (2010–)	378
Rafael Palmeiro (1986–2005)	569	Rocky Colavito (1955–68)	374
Frank Thomas (1990–2008)	521	Ralph Kiner (1946–55)	369
Ernie Banks (1953–71)	512	Carlos Lee (1999–2012)	358
Carlos Delgado (1993–2009)	473	Torii Hunter (1997–2015)	353
Adam Dunn (2001–2014)	462	Ellis Burks (1987–2004)	352
Dave Kingman (1971–86)	442	Ryan Braun (2007–20)	352
Andre Dawson (1976–96)	438	Dick Allen (1963–77)	351
Juan Gonzalez (1990–2005)	434	Mike Trout* (2011–)	350
Billy Williams (1959–76)	426	Jose Bautista (2004–18)	344
Edwin Encarnacion (2005–20)	424	Ron Santo (1960–74)	342
Andres Galarraga (1985–2004)	399	Joey Votto* (2007–)	342
Dale Murphy (1976–93)	398	Bobby Bonds (1968–81)	332
Aramis Ramirez (1998–2015)	386		

* Still active.

Players with Highest Lifetime Batting Average, Never Appearing in World Series (Post-1903; Min. 10 Seasons)

Harry Heilmann (1914, 1916–30, 1932)	.342	Cecil Travis (1933–41, 1945–47)	.314
George Sisler (1915–22, 1924–30)	.340	Jack Fournier (1912–18, 1920–27)	.313
Nap Lajoie (1903–16)	.328	Nomar Garciaparra (1996–2009)	.313
Rod Carew (1967–85)	.328	Edgar Martinez (1987–2004)	.312
Fats Fothergill (1922–33)	.325	Baby Doll Jacobson (1915, 1917, 1919–27)	.311
Babe Herman (1926–37, 1945)	.324	Luke Appling (1930–43, 1945–50)	.311
Ken Williams (1915–29)	.319	Rip Radcliff (1934–43)	.311
Bibb Falk (1920–31)	.314	Ichiro Suzuki (2001–19)	.311

Players with Most Hits, Never Appearing in World Series (Post-1903)

Ichiro Suzuki (2001–18)	3089	Mickey Vernon (1939–43, 1946–60)	2495
Rod Carew (1967–85)	3053	Bobby Abreu (1996–2012, 2014)	2470
Rafael Palmeiro (1986–2005)	3020	Frank Thomas (1990–2008)	2468
George Sisler (1915–22, 1924–30)	2812	Torii Hunter (1997–2015)	2452
Ken Griffey Jr. (1989–2010)	2781	Sammy Sosa (1989–2007)	2408
Andre Dawson (1976–96)	2774	Miguel Tejada (1997–2011, 2013)	2407
Luke Appling (1930–43, 1945–50)	2749	Nick Markakis (2006–20)	2388
Billy Williams (1959–76)	2711	Ryne Sandberg (1981–97)	2386
Harry Heilmann (1914, 1916–30, 1932)	2660	Brett Butler (1981–97)	2375
Julio Franco (1982–94, 1996–97, 1999, 2001–07)	2586	Joe Torre (1960–77)	2342
Ernie Banks (1953–71)	2583	Andres Galarraga (1985–2004)	2333
Buddy Bell (1972–89)	2514		

Leaders in Pitching Categories, Never Pitching in World Series (Post-1903)

Victories	Phil Niekro (1964–87)	318
Games Pitched	Dan Plesac (1986–2003)	1064
Games Started	Phil Niekro (1964–87)	716
Complete Games	Ted Lyons (1923–42, 1946)	356
Innings Pitched	Phil Niekro (1964–87)	5404
ERA (Min. 2000 Innings)	Addie Joss (1903–10)	1.77
Hits Allowed	Phil Niekro (1964–87)	5044
Runs Allowed	Phil Niekro (1964–87)	2337
Losses	Phil Niekro (1964–87)	274
Grand Slams Allowed	Ned Garver (1948–61)	9
	Milt Pappas (1957–73)	9
	Tom Gordon (1988–99, 2001–09)	9
	Lee Smith (1980–97)	9
20-Win Seasons	Ferguson Jenkins (1965–83)	7
Saves	Lee Smith (1980–97)	478
Shutouts	Gaylord Perry (1962–83)	53
Walks	Phil Niekro (1964–87)	1809
Strikeouts	Gaylord Perry (1962–83)	3534

Pitchers with Most Wins, Never Appearing in World Series (Post-1903)

Phil Niekro (1964–87)	318	Joe Niekro (1967–88)	221
Gaylord Perry (1961–83)	314	Jerry Reuss (1969–90)	220
Ferguson Jenkins (1965–83)	284	Wilbur Cooper (1912–26)	216
Ted Lyons (1923–42, 1946)	260	Jim Perry (1959–75)	215

continued on next page

Frank Tanana (1973–93)...240
Jim Bunning (1955–71)...224
Hooks Dauss (1912–26)..223
Mel Harder (1928–47) 223

Milt Pappas (1957–73) 209
Roy Halladay (1998–2013) 203
George Uhle (1919–34, 1936) 200
Chuck Finley (1986–2003) 200

Pitchers with World Series Wins in Both Leagues

Josh Beckett....................................Fla. Marlins (NL), 2003; Bos. Red Sox (AL), 2007
Hank Borowy...................................N.Y. Yankees (AL), 1943; Chi. Cubs (NL), 1945
Jack Coombs ....Phi. A's (AL), 1910, 1911; Brk. Robins (NL), 1916
Don Larsen .....................................N.Y. Yankees (AL), 1956, 1957, 1958; S.F. Giants (NL), 1962
Jon Lester ....Bos. Red Sox (AL), 2007, 2013; Chi. Cubs (NL), 2016
Johnny Sain....................................Bos. Braves (NL), 1948; N.Y. Yankees (AL), 1953
Curt Schilling...................................Phi. Phillies (NL), 1993; Ari. D'backs (NL), 2001; Bos. Red Sox (AL), 2004

Pitchers with World Series Losses in Both Leagues

Al Downing .....................................N.Y. Yankees (AL), 1963, 1964; L.A. Dodgers (NL), 1974
Dock Ellis ....Pit. Pirates (NL), 1971; N.Y. Yankees (AL), 1976
Don Gullett......................................Cin. Reds (NL), 1975; N.Y. Yankees (AL), 1976, 1977
Danny Jackson ...............................K.C. Royals (AL), 1985; Phi. Phillies (NL), 1993
Charlie Leibrandt.............................K.C. Royals (AL), 1985; Atl. Braves (NL), 1991, 1992
John Lackey.....................................Bos. Red Sox (AL), 2013; Chi. Cubs (NL), 2016
Pat Malone......................................Chi. Cubs (NL), 1929; N.Y. Yankees (AL), 1936
Johnny Sain.....................................Bos. Braves (NL), 1948; N.Y. Yankees (AL), 1952
Don Sutton ......................................L.A. Dodgers (NL) 1978; Mil. Brewers (AL), 1982

Players Whose Home Run Won World Series Game 1–0

Casey Stengel, N.Y. Giants (NL), 1923, Game 3, 7th inning, off Sam Jones, N.Y. Yankees (AL)
Tommy Henrich, N.Y. Yankees (AL), 1949, Game 1, 9th inning, off Don Newcombe, Brk. Dodgers (NL)
Paul Blair, Bal. Orioles (AL), 1966, Game 3, 5th inning, off Claude Osteen, L.A. Dodgers (NL)
Frank Robinson, Bal. Orioles (AL), 1966, Game 4 (final game), 4th inning, off Don Drysdale, L.A. Dodgers (NL)
David Justice, Atl. Braves (NL), 1995, Game 6 (final game), 6th inning, off Jim Poole, Cle. Indians (AL)

Brothers Who Were World Series Teammates

Felipe Alou, outfield, and Matty Alou, outfield, S.F. Giants (NL), 1962
Jesse Barnes, pitcher, and Virgil Barnes, pitcher, N.Y. Giants (NL), 1922
George Brett, third base, and Ken Brett, pitcher, K.C. Royals (AL), 1980
Mort Cooper, pitcher, and Walker Cooper, catcher, St.L. Cardinals (NL), 1942–44
Dizzy Dean, pitcher, and Paul Dean, pitcher, St.L. Cardinals (NL), 1934
Lloyd Waner, outfield, and Paul Waner, outfield, Pit. Pirates (NL), 1927

Brothers Facing Each Other in World Series

Clete Boyer, third base, N.Y. Yankees (AL), and Ken Boyer, third base, St.L. Cardinals (NL), 1964
Doc Johnston, first base, Cle. Indians (AL), and Jimmy Johnston, third base, Brk. Dodgers (NL), 1920
Bob Meusel, outfield, N.Y. Yankees (AL), and Irish Meusel, outfield, N.Y. Giants (NL), 1921–23

Fathers and Sons in World Series Competition

Father   **Son**

Felipe Alou, outfield, S.F. Giants (NL), 1962 ....Moises Alou, outfield, Fla. Marlins (NL), 1997
Jim Bagby Sr., pitcher, Cle. Indians (AL), 1920 ....Jim Bagby Jr., pitcher, Bos. Red Sox (AL), 1946

continued on next page

Father	Son
Clay Bellinger, outfielder, N.Y. Yankees (AL), 1999–2001	Cody Bellinger, first base and outfield, L.A. Dodgers (NL), 2017–18, 2020
Pedro Borbon, pitcher, Cin. Reds (NL), 1972, 1975–76	Pedro Borbon Jr., pitcher, Atl. Braves (NL), 1995
Ray Boone, pinch hitter, Cle. Indians (AL), 1948	Bob Boone, catcher, Phi. Phillies (NL), 1980
Bob Boone, catcher, Phi. Phillies (NL), 1980	Aaron Boone, third base, N.Y. Yankees (AL), 2003
Sal Butera, catcher, Min. Twins (AL), 1987	Drew Butera, catcher, K.C. Royals (AL), 2015
Cecil Fielder, first base and designated hitter, N.Y. Yankees (AL), 1996	Prince Fielder, first base, Det. Tigers (AL), 2012
Dave Duncan, catcher, Oak. A's (AL), 1972	Chris Duncan, outfield, St.L. Cardinals (NL), 2006
Jim Hegan, catcher, Cle. Indians (AL), 1948 and 1954	Mike Hegan, pinch hitter and first base, N.Y. Yankees (AL), 1964; Oak. A's (AL), 1972
Julian Javier, second base and pinch hitter, St.L. Cardinals (NL), 1964, 1967–68; Cin. Reds (NL), 1972	Stan Javier, outfield and pinch runner, Oak. A's (AL), 1988–89
Ernie Johnson, shortstop, N.Y. Yankees (AL), 1923	Don Johnson, second base, Chi. Cubs (NL), 1945
Bob Kennedy, outfield, Cle. Indians (AL), 1948	Terry Kennedy, catcher, S.D. Padres (NL), 1984
Mel Stottlemyre, pitcher, N.Y. Yankees (AL), 1964	Todd Stottlemyre, pitcher, Tor. Blue Jays (AL), 1992–93
Ed Spiezio, infield, St.L. Cardinals (NL), 1967–68	Scott Spiezio, infield, Ana. Angels (AL) 2002; St.L. Cardinals (NL), 2006
Billy Sullivan Sr., catcher, Chi. White Sox (AL), 1906	Billy Sullivan Jr., catcher, Det. Tigers (AL), 1940

Batting Average of .400 Hitters in World Series Play

.345... Joe Jackson, 1919 World Series, Chi. White Sox .... .408 in 1910

.295... Bill Terry, 1924, 1933, and 1934 World Series, N.Y. Giants .... .401 in 1930

.262... Ty Cobb, 1907, 1908 and 1909 World Series, Det. Tigers .... .420 in 1911, .410 in 1912, .401 in 1922

.245... Rogers Hornsby, 1926 World Series, St.L. Cardinals;

1929 World Series Chi. Cubs .... .401 in 1922, .424 in 1924, .403 in 1925

.200... Ted Williams, 1946 World Series, Bos. Red Sox .... .406 in 1941

Batting Averages of .400 in World Series Play, Career

Career Leaders

	BA	PA		BA	PA		BA	PA
Phil Garner	.500	28	David Ortiz	.455	59	Pablo Sandoval	.426	50
Amos Otis	.478	26	Bobby Brown	.439	46	Paul Molitor	.418	61
Barry Bonds	.471	30	Jake Powell	.435	27	Pepper Martin	.418	60
Max Carey	.458	31	Marty Barrett	.433	35			

Highest Batting Average in a Single World Series

Single-Series Leaders

Billy Hatcher	.750	15	1990 World Series
David Ortiz	.688	25	2013 World Series
Babe Ruth	.625	17	1928 World Series
Hideki Matsui	.615	14	2009 World Series
Ricky Ledee	.600	13	1998 World Series
Danny Bautista	.583	13	2001 World Series
Ivey Wingo	.571	11	1919 World Series
Chris Sabo	.562	18	1990 World Series
Lou Gehrig	.545	17	1928 World Series
Hank Gowdy	.545	16	1914 World Series

Players Hitting World Series Home Runs in Each League

American League	National League
Mookie Betts.................Bos. Red Sox, 2018	L.A, Dodgers, 2020
Miguel Cabrera ....Det. Tigers, 2012	Fla. Marlins, 2003
Kirk Gibson ....Det. Tigers, 1984	L.A. Dodgers, 1988
Roger Maris ................N.Y. Yankees, 1960–62 and 1964	St.L. Cardinals, 1967
Frank Robinson ....Bal. Orioles, 1966 and 1969–71	Cin. Reds, 1961
Bill Skowron .................N.Y. Yankees, 1955–56, 1958, and 1960–61	L.A. Dodgers, 1963
Enos Slaughter..............N.Y. Yankees, 1956	St.L. Cardinals, 1942 and 1946
Matt Williams ....Cle. Indians, 1997	S.F. Giants, 1989; Ari. D'backs, 2001
Reggie Smith ....Bos. Red Sox, 1967	St.L. Cardinals, 1977–78

World Series Inside-The-Park Home Runs

	HRs		Player's Team	Opponent
1903	1	Jimmy Sebrig	Pit. Pirates	Bos. Americans
1903	1	Patsy Dougherty	Bos. Americans	Pit. Pirates
1915	1	Duffy Lewis	Bos. Red Sox	Phi. Phillies
1916	1	Hy Myers	Brk. Robins	Bos. Red Sox
1916	1	Larry Gardner	Bos. Red Sox	Brk. Robins
1923	1	Casey Stengel	N.Y. Giants	N.Y. Yankees
1926	1	Tommy Thevenow	St.L. Cardinals	N.Y. Yankees
1928	1	Lou Gehrig	N.Y. Yankees	St.L. Cardinals
1929	2	Mule Haas	Phi. A's	Chi. Cubs
2015	1	Alcides Escobar	K.C. Royals	N.Y. Mets

World Series Teams Using Six Different Starting Pitchers

Brk. Dodgers (NL), 1947	Game 1	Ralph Branca (lost)
	Games 2 and 6	Vic Lombardi (lost and won)
	Game 3	Joe Hatten (won)
	Game 4	Harry Taylor (won)
	Game 5	Rex Barney (lost)
	Game 7	Hal Gregg (lost)
Brk. Dodgers (NL), 1955	Game 1	Don Newcombe (lost)
	Game 2	Billy Loes (lost)
	Games 3 and 7	Johnny Podres (won and won)
	Game 4	Carl Erskine (won)
	Game 5	Roger Craig (won)
	Game 6	Karl Spooner (lost)
Pit. Pirates (NL), 1971	Game 1	Dock Ellis (lost)
	Game 2	Bob Johnson (lost)
	Games 3 and 7	Steve Blass (won and won)
	Game 4	Luke Walker (won)
	Game 5	Nelson Briles (won)
	Game 6	Bob Moose (lost)

Rookies Starting Seventh Game of World Series

Babe Adams, Pit. Pirates (NL) (vs. Det. Tigers, AL), 1909.........................Pitched complete game and wins 8–0

Hugh Bedient, Bos. Red Sox (AL) (vs. N.Y. Giants, NL), 1912...................Pitched 7 innings, no decision* (Bos. wins 3–2)

Spec Shea, N.Y. Yankees (AL) (vs. Brk. Dodgers, NL), 1947.....................Pitched 1⅓ innings, no decision (N.Y. wins 5–2)

Joe Black, Brk. Dodgers (NL) (vs. N.Y. Yankees, AL), 1952 ....Pitched 5⅓ innings and loses 4–2

continued on next page

Mel Stottlemyre, N.Y. Yankees (AL) (vs. St.L. Cardinals, NL), 1964.............Pitched 4 innings and loses 7–5

Joe Magrane, St.L. Cardinals (NL) (vs. Min. Twins, AL), 1987 ....Pitched 4⅓ innings, no decision (Min. wins 4–2)

John Lackey, Ana. Angels (AL) (vs. S.F. Giants, NL), 2002 ....Pitched 5 innings and wins 4–1

* Started last game of eight-game Series.

Players Playing Four Different Positions in World Series Competition, Career

Elston Howard..........Left field, right field, first base, catcher

Tony Kubek..............Left field, third base, center field, shortstop

Jackie Robinson........First base, second base, left field, third base

Pete Rose.................Right field, left field, third base, first base

Babe Ruth................Pitcher, left field, right field, first base

Players Stealing Home in World Series Game

Bill Dahlen, N.Y. Giants (NL) (vs. Phi. A's, AL), 1905, Game 3, 5th inning*

George Davis, Chi. White Sox (AL) (vs. Chi. Cubs, NL), 1906, Game 5, 3rd inning*

Jimmy Slagle, Chi. Cubs (NL) (vs. Det. Tigers, AL), 1907, Game 4, 7th inning*

Ty Cobb, Det. Tigers (AL) (vs. Pit. Pirates, NL), 1909, Game 2, 3rd inning

Buck Herzog, N.Y. Giants (NL) (vs. Bos. Red Sox, AL), 1912, Game 6, 1st inning

Butch Schmidt, Bos. Braves (NL) (vs. Phi. A's, AL), 1914, Game 1, 8th inning*

Mike McNally, N.Y. Yankees (AL) (vs. N.Y. Giants, NL), 1921, Game 1, 5th inning

Bob Meusel, N.Y. Yankees (AL) (vs. N.Y. Giants, NL), 1921, Game 2, 8th inning

Bob Meusel, N.Y. Yankees (AL) (vs. St.L. Cardinals, NL), 1928, Game 3, 6th inning*

Hank Greenberg, Det. Tigers (AL) (vs. St.L. Cardinals, NL), 1934, Game 4, 8th inning*

Monte Irvin, N.Y. Giants (NL) (vs. N.Y. Yankees, AL),1951, Game 1, 1st inning

Jackie Robinson, Brk. Dodgers (NL) (vs. N.Y. Yankees, AL), 1955, Game 1, 8th inning

Tim McCarver, St.L. Cardinals (NL) (vs. N.Y. Yankees, AL), 1964, Game 7, 4th inning*

Brad Fullmer, Ana. Angels (AL) (vs. S.F. Giants, NL), 2002, Game 2, 1st inning

* Front end of double steal.

Pitchers Hitting Home Runs in World Series Play

Jim Bagby Sr., Cle. Indians (AL) (vs. Brk. Dodgers, NL), 1920, Game 5

Rosy Ryan, N.Y. Giants (NL) (vs. Was. Senators, AL), 1924, Game 3

Jack Bentley, N.Y. Giants (NL) (vs. Was. Senators, AL), 1924, Game 5

Jesse Haines, St.L. Cardinals (NL) (vs. N.Y. Yankees, AL), 1926, Game 3

Bucky Walters, Cin. Reds (NL) (vs. Det. Tigers, AL), 1940, Game 6

Lew Burdette, Mil. Braves (NL) (vs. N.Y. Yankees, AL), 1958, Game 2

Mudcat Grant, Min. Twins (AL) (vs. L.A. Dodgers, NL), 1965, Game 6

Jose Santiago, Bos. Red Sox (AL) (vs. St.L. Cardinals, NL), 1967, Game 1*

Bob Gibson, St.L. Cardinals (NL) (vs. Bos. Red Sox, AL), 1967, Game 4

Mickey Lolich, Det. Tigers (AL) (vs. St.L. Cardinals, NL), 1968, Game 2

Dave McNally, Bal. Orioles (AL) (vs. N.Y. Mets, NL), 1969, Game 5*

Dave McNally**, Bal. Orioles (AL) (vs. Cin. Reds, NL), 1970, Game 3

Ken Holtzman, Oak. A's (AL) (vs. L.A. Dodgers, NL), 1974, Game 4

Joe Blanton, Phi. Phillies (NL) (vs. T.B. Rays, AL), 2008, Game 4

* Hit home run in losing effort.
** Hit grand slam home run.

Cy Young Winners Facing Each Other in World Series Games

Denny McLain, Det. Tigers (AL), vs. Bob Gibson, St.L. Cardinals (NL), 1968, Games 1 and 4

Mike Cuellar, Bal. Orioles (AL), vs. Tom Seaver, N.Y. Mets (NL), 1969, Games 1 and 4

Catfish Hunter, Oak. A's (AL), vs. Mike Marshall, L.A. Dodgers (NL), 1974, Games 1 and 3

World Series in Which Neither Team Had a 20-Game Winner

Bos. Red Sox (AL) vs. Cin. Reds (NL), 1975

N.Y. Yankees (AL) vs. Cin. Reds (NL), 1976

N.Y. Yankees (AL) vs. L.A. Dodgers (NL), 1981

Mil. Brewers (AL) vs. St.L. Cardinals (NL), 1982

Bal. Orioles (AL) vs. Phi. Phillies (NL), 1983

Det. Tigers (AL) vs. S.D. Padres (NL), 1984

Det. Tigers (AL) vs. St.L. Cardinals (NL), 2006

Bos. Red Sox (AL) vs. Col. Rockies (NL), 2007

T.B. Rays (AL) vs. Phi. Phillies (NL), 2008

N.Y. Yankees (AL) vs. Phi. Phillies (NL), 2009

Tex. Rangers (AL) vs. S.F. Giants (NL), 2010

Tex. Rangers (AL) vs. St.L. Cardinals (NL), 2011

Min. Twins (AL) vs. St.L. Cardinals (NL), 1987

Tor. Blue Jays (AL) vs. Phi. Phillies (NL), 1993

Cle. Indians (AL) vs. Atl. Braves (NL), 1995

Cle. Indians (AL) vs. Fla. Marlins (NL), 1997

N.Y. Yankees (AL) vs. N.Y. Mets (NL), 2000

Ana. Angels (AL) vs. S.F. Giants (NL), 2002

Det. Tigers (AL) vs. S.F. Giants (NL), 2012

Bos. Red Sox (AL) vs. St.L. Cardinals (NL), 2013

K.C. Royals (AL) vs. S.F. Giants (NL), 2014

K.C. Royals (AL) vs. N.Y. Mets (NL), 2015

Cle. Indians (AL), vs. Chi. Cubs (NL), 2016

Hou. Astros (AL) vs. L.A. Dodgers (NL), 2017

Bos. Red Sox (AL) vs. L.A. Dodgers (NL), 2018

Hou. Astros (AL) vs. Was, Nationals (NL), 2019

T.B. Rays (AL) vs. L.A. Dodgers (NL), 2020

Hou. Astros (AL) vs. Atl. Braves NL), 2021

Hou. Astros (AL) vs. Phi. Phillies (NL), 2022

Pitchers with Lowest ERA in Total World Series Play (Min. 25 Innings)

Career Leaders

	ERA	IP
Madison Bumgarner	0.25	36
Jack Billingham	0.36	25⅓
Harry Brecheen	0.83	32⅔
Claude Osteen	0.86	21
Babe Ruth	0.87	31
Sherry Smith	0.89	30⅓
Sandy Koufax	0.95	57
Christy Mathewson	0.97	101⅔
Mariano Rivera	0.99	36⅓
Hippo Vaughn	1.00	27

Single-Series Leaders

	ERA	IP	
Christy Mathewson	0.00	27	1905 World Series
Waite Hoyt	0.00	27	1921 World Series
Carl Hubbell	0.00	20	1933 World Series
Whitey Ford	0.00	18	1960 World Series
Joe McGinnity	0.00	17	1905 World Series
Duster Mails	0.00	15⅔	1920 World Series
Rube Benton	0.00	14	1917 World Series
Whitey Ford	0.00	14	1961 World Series
Jack Billingham	0.00	13⅔	1972 World Series
Joe Dobson	0.00	12⅔	1946 World Series
Allie Reynolds	0.00	12⅓	1949 World Series
Clem Labine	0.00	12	1956 World Series
Mordecai Brown	0.00	11	1908 World Series
Bill James	0.00	11	1914 World Series
Jack Kramer	0.00	11	1944 World Series
Gene Bearden	0.00	10⅔	1948 World Series
Don Larsen	0.00	10⅔	1956 World Series

World Series Grand Slams

Elmer Smith, Cle. Indians (AL), 1920, Game 5, 1st inning,
off Burleigh Grimes, Brk. Dodgers (NL)

Tony Lazzeri, N.Y. Yankees (AL), 1936, Game 2,
3rd inning, off Dick Coffman, N.Y. Giants (NL)

Gil McDougald, N.Y. Yankees (AL), 1951, Game 5,
3rd inning, off Larry Jansen, N.Y. Giants (NL)

Mickey Mantle, N.Y. Yankees (AL), 1953, Game 5,
3rd inning, off Russ Meyer, Brk. Dodgers (NL)

Yogi Berra, N.Y. Yankees (AL), 1956, Game 2, 2nd inning,
off Don Newcombe, Brk. Dodgers (NL)

Bill Skowron, N.Y. Yankees (AL), 1956, Game 7,
7th inning, off Roger Craig, Brk. Dodgers (NL)

Bobby Richardson, N.Y. Yankees (AL), 1960, Game 3,
1st inning, off Clem Labine, Pit. Pirates (NL)

Chuck Hiller, S.F. Giants (NL), 1962, Game 4, 7th inning,
off Marshall Bridges, N.Y. Yankees (AL)

Ken Boyer, St.L. Cardinals (NL), 1964, Game 4, 6th inning,
off Al Downing, N.Y. Yankees (AL)

Joe Pepitone, N.Y. Yankees (AL), 1964, Game 6,
8th inning, off Gordie Richardson, St.L. Cardinals (NL)

Jim Northrup, Det. Tigers (AL), 1968, Game 6, 3rd inning,
off Larry Jaster, St.L. Cardinals (NL)

Dave McNally, Bal. Orioles (AL), 1970, Game 3, 6th inning,
off Wayne Granger, Cin. Reds (NL)

Dan Gladden, Min. Twins (AL), 1987, Game 1, 4th inning,
off Bob Forsch, St.L. Cardinals (NL)

Kent Hrbek, Min. Twins (AL), 1987, Game 6, 6th inning,
off Ken Dayley, St.L. Cardinals (NL)

Jose Canseco, Oak. A's (AL), 1988, Game 1, 2nd inning,
off Tim Belcher, L.A. Dodgers (NL)

Lonnie Smith, Atl. Braves (NL), 1992, Game 5, 5th inning,
off Jack Morris, Tor. Blue Jays (AL)

Tino Martinez, N.Y. Yankees (AL), 1998, Game 1, 7th inning,
off Mark Langston, S.D. Padres (NL)

Paul Konerko, Chi. White Sox (AL), 2005, Game 2,
7th inning, off Chad Qualls, Hou. Astros (NL)

Addison Russell, Chi. Cubs (NL), 2016, Game 6,
3rd inning, off Dan Otero, Cle. Indians (AL)

Alex Bregman, Hou. Astros (AL), 2019, Game 4,
7th inning, off Fernando Rodney, Was. Nationals (NL)

Adam Duvall, Atl. Braves (NL), 2021, Game 5, 1st inning,
off Framber Valdez, Hou. Astros (AL)

Players on Three Different World Series Clubs

Don Baylor................................ Bos. Red Sox (AL), 1986
Min. Twins (AL), 1987
Oak. A's (AL), 1988

Joe Bush...Phi. A's (AL), 1913–14
Bos. Red Sox (AL), 1918
N.Y. Yankees (AL), 1922–23

Bobby Byrne....................................Pit. Pirates (NL), 1909
Phi. Phillies (NL), 1915
Chi. White Sox (AL), 1917*

Roger Clemens........................... Bos. Red Sox (AL), 1986
N.Y. Yankees (AL), 1999–2001, 2003
Hou. Astros (NL), 2005

Vic Davalillo...................................Pit. Pirates (NL), 1971
Oak. A's (AL), 1973
L.A. Dodgers (NL), 1977–78

Paul Derringer...........................St.L. Cardinals (NL), 1931
Cin. Reds (NL), 1939–40
Chi. Cubs (NL), 1945

Leo Durocher .... N.Y. Yankees (AL), 1928
St.L. Cardinals (NL), 1934
Brk. Dodgers (NL), 1941*

Mike Gonzalez ..........................N.Y. Giants (NL), 1921*
Chi. Cubs (NL), 1929
St.L. Cardinals (NL), 1931*

Stuffy McInnis ....Phi. A's (AL), 1910*–1911, 1913–14
Bos. Red Sox (AL), 1918
Pit. Pirates (NL), 1925

Fred Merkle............................ N.Y. Giants (NL), 1911–13
Brk. Dodgers (NL), 1916
Chi. Cubs (NL), 1918
N.Y. Yankees (AL), 1926*

Jack Morris.....................................Det. Tigers (AL), 1984
Min. Twins (AL), 1991
Tor. Blue Jays (AL), 1992–1993*

Andy Pafko.....................................Chi. Cubs (NL), 1945
Brk. Dodgers (NL), 1952
Mil. Braves (NL), 1957–58

Billy Pierce ....Det. Tigers (AL), 1945*
Chi. White Sox (AL), 1959
S.F. Giants (NL), 1962

Edgar Renteria............................Fla. Marlins (NL), 1997
St.L. Cardinals (NL), 2004
S.F. Giants (NL), 2010

Dutch Ruether ....Cin. Reds (NL), 1919
Was. Senators (AL), 1925
N.Y. Yankees (AL), 1926–1927*

Wally Schang ....Phi. A's (AL), 1913–14, 1930*
Bos. Red Sox (AL), 1918
N.Y. Yankees (AL), 1921–22

continued on next page

Burleigh Grimes .... Brk. Dodgers (NL), 1920
St.L. Cardinals (NL), 1930–31
Chi. Cubs (NL), 1932
Heinie Groh .... N.Y. Giants (NL), 1912*, 1922–24
Cin. Reds (NL), 1919
Pit. Pirates (NL), 1927
Pinky Higgins .... Phi. A's (AL), 1930*
Det. Tigers (AL), 1940
Bos. Red Sox (AL), 1946
Grant Jackson .... Bal. Orioles (AL), 1971
N.Y. Yankees (AL), 1976
Pit. Pirates (NL), 1979
Mark Koenig .... N.Y. Yankees (AL), 1926–28
Chi. Cubs (NL), 1932
N.Y. Giants (NL), 1936
John Lackey .... Ana. Angels (AL), 2002
Bos. Red Sox (AL), 2013
Chi. Cubs (NL), 2016
Ryan Madson .... Phi. Phillies (NL), 2008–09
K.C. Royals (AL), 2015
L.A. Dodgers (NL), 2018
Mike McCormick .... Cin. Reds (NL), 1940
Bos. Braves (NL), 1948
Brk. Dodgers (NL), 1949

Everett Scott .... Bos. Red Sox (AL), 1915–16, 1918
N.Y. Yankees (AL), 1922–23
Was. Senators (AL), 1925*
Earl Smith .... N.Y. Giants (NL), 1921–22
Pit. Pirates (NL), 1925, 1927
St.L. Cardinals (NL), 1928
Lonnie Smith .... Phi. Phillies (NL), 1980
St.L. Cardinals (NL), 1982
K.C. Royals (AL), 1985
Tuck Stainback .... Chi. Cubs (NL), 1935*
Det. Tigers (AL), 1940*
N.Y. Yankees (AL), 1942–43
Matt Williams .... S.F. Giants (NL), 1989
Cle. Indians (AL), 1997
Ari. D'backs (NL), 2001
Eddie Stanky .... Brk. Dodgers (NL), 1947
Bos. Braves (NL), 1948
N.Y. Giants (NL), 1951

* Did not play in Series.

Players Playing for Two Different World Series Champions in Successive Years

Allie Clark, outfield .... 1947 N.Y. Yankees; 1948 Cle. Indians
Clem Labine, pitcher .... 1959 L.A. Dodgers; 1960 Pit. Pirates
Moose Skowron, first base .... 1962 N.Y. Yankees; 1963 L.A. Dodgers
Don Gullett, pitcher .... 1976 Cin. Reds; 1977 N.Y. Yankees
Jack Morris, pitcher .... 1991 Min. Twins; 1992 Tor. Blue Jays
Jake Peavy, pitcher .... 2013 Bos. Red Sox; 2014 S.F. Giants
Joc Pederson, outfield .... 2020 L.A. Dodgers; 2021 Atl. Braves
Ryan Theriot, second base .... 2011 St.L. Cardinals; 2012 S.F. Giants
Ben Zobrist, infield and outfield .... 2015 K.C. Royals; 2016 Chi. Cubs

Players with Same Lifetime Batting Average as Their World Series Overall Average

	Lifetime/World Series Batting Average	World Series Appearance(s)
Aubrey Huff (2000–12)	.278	2010 and 2012
Duffy Lewis (1910–17, 1919–21)	.284	1912 and 1915–16
Phil Linz (1962–68)	.235	1963–64
Danny Murphy (1900–15)	.288	1905 and 1910–11
Paul Waner (1926–45)	.333	1927

Batting Champions Facing Each Other in World Series

Ty Cobb (.377), Det. Tigers (AL) and Honus Wagner (.339), Pit. Pirates (NL), 1909
Al Simmons (.390), Phi. A's (AL) and Chick Hafey (.349), St.L. Cardinals (NL), 1931
Bobby Avila (.341), Cle. Indians (AL) and Willie Mays (.345), N.Y. Giants (NL), 1954
Miguel Cabrera (.330), Det. Tigers (AL) and Buster Posey (.336), S.F. Giants (NL), 2012

Home Run Champions Facing Each Other in World Series

Babe Ruth (59), N.Y. Yankees (AL) and George Kelly (23), N.Y. Giants (NL), 1921
Babe Ruth (54), N.Y. Yankees (AL) and Jim Bottomley (31), St.L. Cardinals (NL), 1928
Lou Gehrig (49), N.Y. Yankees (AL) and Mel Ott (33), N.Y. Giants (NL), 1936
Joe DiMaggio (46), N.Y. Yankees (AL) and Mel Ott (31), N.Y. Giants (NL), 1937
Mickey Mantle (52), N.Y. Yankees (AL) and Duke Snider (43), Brk. Dodgers (NL), 1956

Players Hitting Home Run in First World Series At-Bat

Joe Harris, Was. Senators (AL), 1925
George Watkins, St.L. Cardinals (NL), 1930
Mel Ott, N.Y. Giants (NL), 1933
George Selkirk, N.Y. Yankees (AL), 1936
Dusty Rhodes, N.Y. Giants (NL), 1954
Elston Howard, N.Y. Yankees (AL), 1955
Roger Maris, N.Y. Yankees (AL), 1960
Don Mincher, Min. Twins (AL), 1965
Brooks Robinson, Bal. Orioles (AL), 1966
Jose Santiago, Bos. Red Sox (AL), 1967
Mickey Lolich, Det. Tigers (AL), 1968
Don Buford, Bal. Orioles (AL), 1969
Gene Tenace*, Oak. A's (AL), 1972
Jim Mason, N.Y. Yankees (AL), 1976
Doug DeCinces, Bal. Orioles (AL), 1979
Amos Otis, K.C. Royals (AL), 1980
Bob Watson, N.Y. Yankees (AL), 1981
Jim Dwyer, Bal. Orioles (AL), 1983
Jose Canseco, Oak. A's (AL), 1988

Mickey Hatcher, L.A. Dodgers (NL), 1988
Bill Bathe, S.F. Giants (NL), 1989
Eric Davis, Cin. Reds (NL), 1990
Ed Sprague Jr., Tor. Blue Jays (AL), 1992
Fred McGriff, Atl. Braves (NL), 1995
Andruw Jones, Atl. Braves (NL), 1996
Troy Glaus. Ana. Angels (AL), 2002
Barry Bonds, S.F. Giants (NL), 2002
David Ortiz, Bos. Red Sox (AL), 2004
Mike Lamb, Hou. Astros (NL), 2005
Geoff Blum, Chi. White Sox (AL), 2005
Bobby Kielly, Bos. Red Sox (AL), 2007
Dustin Pedroia, Bos. Red Sox (AL), 2007
Chase Utley, Phi. Phillies (NL), 2008
Chris Taylor, L.A. Dodgers (NL), 2017
Matt Kemp, L.A. Dodgers (NL), 2018
Eduardo Nunez, Bos. Red Sox (AL), 2018
Ryan Zimmerman, Was. Nationals (NL), 2019
Michael A. Taylor, Was. Nationals (NL), 2019

* Hit home runs in first two times at bat in World Series.

World Series Pitchers with Most Losses, Season

American League		National League	
George Mullin, Det. Tigers, 1907	20	Larry French, Chi. Cubs, 1938	19
Ken Holtzman, Oak. A's, 1974	17	Pat Malone, Chi. Cubs, 1932	17
Dennis Martinez, Bal. Orioles, 1979	16	Don Drysdale, L.A. Dodgers, 1963	17
Dennis Martinez, Bal. Orioles, 1983	16	Don Drysdale, L.A. Dodgers, 1966	16
Joe Bush, Bos. Red Sox, 1918	15	Jon Matlack, N.Y. Mets, 1973	16
Joe Bush, N.Y. Yankees, 1923	15	Steve Carlton, Phi. Phillies, 1983	16
Tom Zachary, Was. Senators, 1925	15	Livan Hernandez, S.F. Giants, 2002	16
General Crowder, Was. Senators, 1933	15	Jason Marquis, St.L. Cardinals, 2006	16
Dizzy Trout, Det. Tigers, 1945	15	Joe McGinnity, N.Y. Giants, 1905	15
Bob Feller, Cle. Indians, 1948	15	Erskine Mayer, Phi. Phillies, 1915	15
Billy Pierce, Chi. White Sox, 1959	15	Harry Brecheen, St.L. Cardinals, 1946	15
Ralph Terry, N.Y. Yankees, 1963	15	Johnny Sain, Bos. Braves, 1948	15
Vida Blue, Oak. A's, 1974	15	Claude Osteen, L.A. Dodgers, 1965	15
Catfish Hunter, N.Y. Yankees, 1976	15	Jerry Koosman, N.Y. Mets, 1973	15
Bud Black, K.C. Royals, 1985	15	Tim Lincecum, S.F. Giants, 2012	15
Mike Moore, Oak. A's, 1990	15		

Teams Winning a World Series in First Year in New Ballpark

Team	Ballpark	Opponent	Series
Pit. Pirates (NL)	Forbes Field, 1909	Det. Tigers (AL)	4 games to 3
Bos. Red Sox (AL)	Fenway Park, 1912	N.Y. Giants (NL)	4 games to 3

continued on next page

Team	Ballpark	Opponent	Series
N.Y. Yankees (AL)............................	Yankee Stadium I, 1923	N.Y. Giants (NL)	4 games to 2
St.L. Cardinals (NL)	Busch Stadium III, 2006	Det. Tigers (AL)	4 games to 2
N.Y. Yankees (AL)............................	Yankee Stadium II, 2009	Phi. Phillies (NL)......................	4 games to 2

Pitchers on World Series–Winning Teams, Both Winning 20 Games and *All* of Their Team's Series Victories

American League

1903 Cy Young (28 season wins, 2 Series wins) and Bill Dinneen (21 season wins, 3 Series wins), Bos. Americans
1910 Jack Coombs (31 season wins, 3 Series wins) and Chief Bender (23 season wins, 1 Series win), Phi. A's
1912 Smoky Joe Wood (34 season wins, 3 Series wins) and Hugh Bedient (20 season wins, 1 Series win), Bos. Red Sox
1930 Lefty Grove (28 season wins, 2 Series wins) and George Earnshaw (22 season wins, 2 Series wins), Phi. A's

National League

1905 Christy Mathewson (31 season wins, 3 Series wins) and Joe McGinnity (21 season wins, 1 Series win), N.Y. Giants
1914 Bill James (26 season wins, 2 Series wins) and Dick Rudolph (26 season wins, 2 Series wins), Bos. Braves
1940 Bucky Walters (22 season wins, 2 Series wins) and Paul Derringer (20 season wins, 2 Series wins), Cin. Reds
2001 Curt Schilling (22 season wins, 1 Series win) and Randy Johnson (21 season wins, 3 Series wins), Ari. D'backs

Teams' Overall Won–Lost Percentage in World Series Games Played

American League

	Games Won–Lost	Percentage
Tor. Blue Jays (2 appearances, 2–0)............................	8–4	.667
Bos. Red Sox (13 appearances, 9–4)............................	49–29–1	.620
N.Y. Yankees (40 appearances, 27–13)............................	1131–85–1	.606
Bal. Orioles (6 appearances, 3–3)............................	19–14	.576
Ana. Angels (1 appearance, 1–0)	4–3	.571
Chi. White Sox (5 appearances, 3–2)............................	17–13	.567
Phi. A's (8 appearances, 5–3)............................	24–19	.558
Oak. A's (6 appearances, 4–2)............................	17–15	.531
Min. Twins (3 appearances, 2–1)............................	11–10	.524
K.C. Royals (4 appearances, 2–2)............................	13–12	.520
Cle. Indians (6 appearances, 2–4)............................	17–20	.459
Det. Tigers (11 appearances, 4–7)............................	27–37–1	.450
Hou. Astros* (5 appearances, 2–3)............................	13–17	.433
Was. Senators (3 appearances, 1–2)............................	8–11	.421
St.L. Browns (1 appearance, 0–1)............................	2–4	.333
Tex. Rangers (2 appearances, 0–2)............................	4–8	.333
T.B. Rays (2 appearances, 0–2)............................	3–8	.272

* Were in National League from 1962–2012.

National League

	Games Won–Lost	Percentage
Fla.–Mia. Marlins (2 appearances, 2–0)............................	8–5	.615
Bos. Braves (2 appearances, 1–1)............................	6–4	.600
Ari. D'backs (1 appearance, 1–0)............................	4–3	.571
Was. Nationals (1 appearance, 1–0)............................	4–3	.571
S.F. Giants (6 appearances, 3–3)............................	18–16	.529
Cin. Reds (9 appearances, 5–4)............................	26–25	.510

continued on next page

	Games Won–Lost	Percentage
Mil. Braves (2 appearances, 1–1)	7–7	.500
L.A. Dodgers (12 appearances, 6–6)	33–34	.493
St.L. Cardinals (19 appearances, 11–8)	58–60	.492
Pit. Pirates (7 appearances, 5–2)	23–24	.489
N.Y. Giants (14 appearances, 5–9)	39–41–2	.488
N.Y. Mets (5 appearances, 2–3)	13–16	.448
Atl. Braves (6 appearances, 2–4)	15–20	.429
Mil. Brewers* (1 appearance, 0–1)	3–4	.429
Chi. Cubs (11 appearances, 3–8)	23–36–1	.383
Phi. Phillies (8 appearances, 2–6)	16–27	.372
Brk. Dodgers (9 appearances, 1–8)	20–36	.357
S.D. Padres (2 appearances, 0–2)	1–8	.111
Col. Rockies (1 appearance, 0–1)	0–4	.000

* Were in American League from 1970–97.

Oldest Players to Appear in World Series

47 years, 3 months	Jack Quinn, Phi. A's, 1929, pitcher
46 years, 10 months	Jamie Moyer, Phi. Phillies, 2009, pitcher
46 years, 3 months	Jack Quinn, Phi. A's, 1930, pitcher
45 years, 10 months	Jamie Moyer, Phi. Phillies, 2008, pitcher
42 years, 5 months	Bartolo Colon, N.Y. Mets, 2015, pitcher
42 years, 3 months	Satchel Paige, Cle. Indians, 1948, pitcher
42 years, 1 month	Chuck Hostetler, Det. Tigers, 1945, pinch hitter
42 years, 0 months	Arthur Rhodes, St.L. Cardinals, 2011, pitcher
41 years, 9 months	Pete Alexander, St.L. Cardinals, 1928, pitcher
41 years, 0 months	Darren Oliver, Tex. Rangers, 2011, pitcher
40 years, 6 months	Carlos Beltran, Hou. Astros, 2017, pinch hitter
40 years, 5 months	Rick Reuschel, S.F. Giants, 1989, pitcher
40 years, 3 months	Freddie Fitzsimmons, Brk. Dodgers, 1941, pitcher
40 years, 3 months	Bobo Newsom, N.Y. Yankees, 1947, pitcher
40 years, 0 months	Darren Oliver, Tex. Rangers, 2010, pitcher

Players with 3000 Hits Playing in World Series

	Number of Hits at Time
Willie Mays (1973 N.Y. Mets)	3283
Pete Rose (1980 Phi. Phillies)	3557
Pete Rose (1983 Phi. Phillies)	3990
Eddie Murray (1995 Cle. Indians)	3071

9

ALL-STAR GAME

Players Who Made All-Star Roster After Starting Season in Minors

Don Newcombe, Brk. Dodgers (NL), 1949..Started season with Montreal (IL)
Don Schwall, Bos. Red Sox (AL), 1961..Started season with Seattle (PCL)
Alvin Davis, Sea. Mariners (AL), 1984 ....Started season with Salt Lake City (PCL)
Evan Longoria, T.B. Rays (AL), 2008 ....Started season with Durham (IL)
Mike Trout, L.A. Angels (AL), 2012..Started season with Salt Lake (PCL)
Kris Bryant, Chi. Cubs (NL), 2015..Started season with Iowa (PCL)
Mike Soroka, Atl. Braves (NL), 2019 ....Started season with Gwinnett (IL)

Pitchers Winning All-Star Game and World Series Game, Same Season

Lefty Gomez, N.Y. Yankees (AL), 1937

Paul Derringer, Cin. Reds (NL), 1940

Spec Shea, N.Y. Yankees (AL), 1947

Vern Law, Pit. Pirates (NL), 1960

Sandy Koufax, L.A. Dodgers (NL), 1965

Don Sutton, L.A. Dodgers (NL), 1977

John Smoltz, Atl. Braves (NL), 1996

Josh Beckett, Bos. Red Sox (AL), 2007

Corey Kluber, Cle. Indians (AL), 2016

Pitchers Who Pitched More Than Three Innings in One All-Star Game

Lefty Gomez (AL), 1935 6

Mel Harder (AL), 1934 5

Al Benton (AL), 1942 5

Larry Jansen (NL), 1950.. 5

Catfish Hunter (AL), 1967.. 5

Lon Warneke (NL), 1933.. 4

Hal Schumacher (NL), 1935 4

Spud Chandler (AL), 1942 4

Johnny Antonelli (NL), 1956.. 4

Lew Burdette (NL), 1957.. 4

Bob Feller (AL), 1939.. 3⅔

Frank Sullivan (AL), 1955 .... 3⅓

Joe Nuxhall (NL), 1955.. 3⅓

Ray Narleski (AL), 1958.. 3⅓

All-Star Game Managers Who Never Managed in World Series

Paul Richards, Bal. Orioles (AL), 1961 ....Replaced Casey Stengel, N.Y. Yankees

Gene Mauch, Phi. Phillies (NL), 1965 ....Replaced Johnny Keane, St.L. Cardinals

Brad Mills, Cle. Indians (AL), 2017..Replaced Terry Francona, Cle. Indians

Brothers Selected to Play in All-Star Game, Same Season

Sandy Alomar Jr., Cle. Indians (AL) and Roberto Alomar, S.D. Padres (NL) and Bal. Orioles (AL), 1990, 1996–98

Felipe Alou, Atl. Braves (NL) and Matty Alou, Pit. Pirates (NL), 1968

Aaron Boone, Cin. Reds (NL) and Bret Boone, Sea. Mariners (AL), 2003

Mort Cooper, St.L. Cardinals (NL) and Walker Cooper, St.L. Cardinals (NL), 1942–43

William Contreras, Atl. Braves (NL) and Willson Contreras, Chi. Cubs (NL), 2022

Joe DiMaggio, N.Y. Yankees (AL) and Dom DiMaggio, Bos. Red Sox (AL), 1941–42, 1946, and 1949–51

Carlos May, Chi. White Sox (AL) and Lee May, Cin. Reds (NL), 1969 and 1971

Gaylord Perry, S.F. Giants (NL) and Jim Perry, Min. Twins (AL), 1970

Dixie Walker, Brk. Dodgers (NL) and Harry Walker, St.L. Cardinals and Phi. Phillies (NL), 1943 and 1947

Players Hitting Home Runs in All-Star Game and World Series, Same Season

Joe Medwick, St.L. Cardinals (NL), 1934

Lou Gehrig, N.Y. Yankees (AL), 1936

Lou Gehrig, N.Y. Yankees (AL), 1937

Joe DiMaggio, N.Y. Yankees (AL), 1939

Jackie Robinson, Brk. Dodgers (NL), 1952

Mickey Mantle, N.Y. Yankees (AL), 1955

continued on next page

Mickey Mantle, N.Y. Yankees (AL), 1956

Ken Boyer, St.L. Cardinals (NL), 1964

Harmon Killebrew, Min. Twins (AL), 1965

Roberto Clemente, Pit. Pirates (NL), 1971

Frank Robinson, Bal. Orioles (AL), 1971

Steve Garvey, L.A. Dodgers (NL), 1977

Sandy Alomar, Cle. Indians (AL), 1997

Barry Bonds, S.F. Giants (NL), 2002

David Ortiz, Bos. Red Sox (AL), 2004

Manny Ramirez, Bos. Red Sox (AL), 2004

Kris Bryant, Chi. Cubs (NL), 2016

Fathers and Sons, Both of Whom Played in All-Star Games

Father	Son
Sandy Alomar Sr., Cal. Angels (AL), 1970	Roberto Alomar, S.D. Padres (NL), 1990; Tor. Blue Jays (AL), 1991–95; Bal. Orioles (AL), 1996–98; Cle. Indians (AL), 1999–2001
	Sandy Alomar Jr., Cle. Indians (AL), 1990–92 and 1996–98
Felipe Alou, S.F. Giants (NL), 1962; Atl. Braves (NL), 1966 and 1968	Moises Alou, Mon. Expos (NL), 1994; Fla. Marlins (NL), 1997; Hou. Astros (NL), 1998 and 2001
Gus Bell, Cin. Reds (NL), 1953–54 and 1956–57	Buddy Bell, Cle. Indians (AL), 1973; Tex. Rangers (AL), 1980–82 and 1984
Dante Bichette, Col. Rockies (NL), 1994–96 and 1998	Bo Bichette, Tor. Blue Jays (AL), 2021
Bobby Bonds, S.F. Giants (NL), 1971 and 1973; N.Y. Yankees (AL), 1975	Barry Bonds, Pit. Pirates (NL), 1990 and 1992; S.F. Giants (NL), 1993–98 and 2000–04
Bob Boone, Phi. Phillies (NL), 1976 and 1978–79; Cal. Angels (AL), 1983	Aaron Boone, Cin. Reds (NL), 2003
	Bret Boone, Cin. Reds (NL), 1998; Sea. Mariners (AL), 2001 and 2003
Ray Boone, Det. Tigers (AL), 1954 and 1956	Bob Boone, Phi. Phillies (NL), 1976 and 1978–79; Cal. Angels (AL), 1983
Tom Gordon, Bos. Red Sox (AL), 1998; N.Y. Yankees (AL), 2004; Phi. Phillies (NL), 2008	Dee Strange-Gordon, L.A. Dodgers (NL), 2014; Mia. Marlins (NL), 2015
Cecil Fielder, Det. Tigers (AL), 1990–91 and 1993	Prince Fielder, Mil. Brewers (NL), 2007–2008 and 2011; Det. Tigers, 2012–13; Tex. Rangers (AL), 2015
Ken Griffey Sr., Cin. Reds (NL), 1976–77 and 1980	Ken Griffey Jr., Sea. Mariners (AL), 1990–99; Cin. Reds (NL), 2000
Vladimir Guerrero, Mon. Expos (NL), 1999–2002; Ana.–L.A. Angels (AL), 2004–07; Tex. Rangers, 2010	Vladimir Guerrero Jr., Tor. Blue Jays (AL), 2021–22
Jim Hegan, Cle. Indians (AL), 1947 and 1949–52	Mike Hegan, Sea. Pilots (AL), 1969
Randy Hundley, Chi. Cubs (NL), 1969	Todd Hundley, N.Y. Mets (NL), 1996–97
Vern Law, Pit. Pirates (NL), 1960	Vance Law, Chi. Cubs (NL), 1988
Gary Matthews Sr., Atl. Braves (NL), 1979	Gary Matthews Jr., Tex. Rangers (AL), 2006
Steve Swisher, Chi. Cubs (NL), 1976	Nick Swisher, N.Y. Yankees (AL), 2010

Pitchers with No Victories, Named to All-Star Team

Dave LaRoche, Cle. Indians (AL), 1976

Tom Henke, Tor. Blue Jays (AL), 1987

John Hudek, Hou. Astros (NL), 1994

Lee Smith, Cal. Angels (AL), 1995

Troy Percival, Cal. Angels (AL), 1996

Kazuhiro Sasaki, Sea. Mariners (AL), 2001

John Smoltz, Atl. Braves (NL), 2003

Danny Kolb, Mil. Brewers (NL), 2004

Bob Wickman, Cle. Indians (AL), 2005

Trevor Hoffman, S.D. Padres (NL), 2006

Francisco Cordero, Mil. Brewers (NL), 2007

Billy Wagner, N.Y. Mets (NL), 2008

Chris Perez, Cle. Indians (AL), 2012

Jason Grilli, Pit. Pirates (NL), 2013

continued on next page

Craig Kimbrel, Atl. Braves (NL), 2014
Aroldis Chapman, Cin. Reds (NL), 2014
Kenley Jansen, L.A. Dodgers (NL), 2018
Edwin Diaz, Sea. Mariners (AL), 2018

Kirby Yates, S.D. Padres (NL), 2019
Shane Greene, Det. Tigers (AL), 2019
Josh Hader. Mil. Brewers (NL), 2021

Oldest Players Named to All-Star Team

Satchel Paige, pitcher, St.L. Browns (AL), 1953 .... 47 years, 7 days
Satchel Paige, pitcher, Cle. Indians (AL), 1952.. 46 years, 1 day
Pete Rose, first baseman, Cin. Reds (NL), 1985... 44 years, 93 days
Carl Yastrzemski, designated hitter, Bos. Red Sox (AL), 1983 .... 43 years, 318 days
Mariano Rivera, pitcher, N.Y. Yankees (AL), 2013 .... 43 years, 229 days
Carlton Fisk, catcher, Chi. White Sox (AL), 1991 .... 43 years, 195 days
Bartolo Colon, pitcher, N.Y. Mets (NL), 2016.. 43 years, 49 days
Barry Bonds, outfielder, S.F. Giants (NL), 2007 .... 42 years, 351 days
Roger Clemens, pitcher, Hou. Astros (NL), 2005.. 42 years, 342 days
Carl Yastrzemski, designated hitter, Bos. Red Sox (AL), 1982 .... 42 years, 325 days
Stan Musial, outfielder, St.L. Cardinals (NL), 1963 .... 42 years, 230 days
Albert Pujols, designated hitter, St.L. Cardinals (NL), 2022 .... 42 years, 184 days
Nolan Ryan, pitcher, Tex. Rangers (AL), 1989... 42 years, 161 days
Willie Mays, outfielder, N.Y. Mets (NL), 1973... 42 years, 79 days

10

T E A M S

Teams' Won–Lost Percentage by Decade

1901–09

American League	Wins	Losses	%
Phi. A's	734	568	.564
Chi. White Sox	744	575	.564
Cle. Blues–Bronchos–Naps	609	632	.525
Bos. Americans–Red Sox	691	634	.522
Det. Tigers	683	632	.519
N.Y. Highlanders	520	518	.501
Mil. Brewers–St.L. Browns*	599	721	.454
Bal. Orioles	118	153	.435
Was. Senators	480	834	.365

* Milwaukee moved to St. Louis in 1902.

National League	Wins	Losses	%
Pit. Pirates	859	478	.642
Chi. Orphans–Cubs	814	517	.612
N.Y. Giants	763	567	.574
Cin. Reds	642	691	.482
Phi. Phillies	634	689	.479
Brk. Superbas	567	755	.429
Bos. Beaneaters–Doves	521	805	.393
St.L. Cardinals	515	813	.388

1910–19

American League	Wins	Losses	%
Bos. Red Sox	857	624	.579
Chi. White Sox	796	692	.535
Det. Tigers	790	704	.529
Was. Senators	755	737	.506
Cle. Naps–Indians	742	749	.498
Phi. A's	710	774	.478
N.Y. Highlanders–Yankees	701	780	.473
St.L. Browns	597	892	.401

National League	Wins	Losses	%
N.Y. Giants	889	597	.598
Chi. Cubs	826	668	.553
Phi. Phillies	762	717	.515
Pit. Pirates	736	751	.495
Cin. Reds	717	779	.479
Brk. Superbas–Dodgers	696	787	.469
Bos. Doves–Rustlers–Braves	666	815	.450
St.L. Cardinals	652	830	.440

continued on next page

1920–29

American League	Wins	Losses	%
N.Y. Yankees	933	602	.608
Was. Senators	791	735	.518
Cle. Indians	786	749	.512
Phi. A's	770	754	.505
St.L. Browns	762	769	.496
Det. Tigers	760	778	.494
Chi. White Sox	731	804	.476
Bos. Red Sox	595	938	.388

National League	Wins	Losses	%
N.Y. Giants	890	639	.582
Pit. Pirates	887	656	.572
St.L. Cardinals	822	712	.536
Chi. Cubs	807	728	.526
Cin. Reds	798	736	.520
Brk. Dodgers	765	768	.499
Bos. Braves	603	928	.394
Phi. Phillies	566	962	.370

1930–39

American League	Wins	Losses	%
N.Y. Yankees	970	554	.636
Cle. Indians	824	708	.538
Det. Tigers	818	716	.533
Was. Senators	806	722	.527
Phi. A's	723	795	.476
Bos. Red Sox	705	815	.464
Chi. White Sox	678	841	.446
St.L. Browns	578	951	.378

National League	Wins	Losses	%
Chi. Cubs	889	646	.579
N.Y. Giants	868	657	.569
St.L. Cardinals	869	665	.566
Pit. Pirates	812	718	.531
Brk. Dodgers	724	793	.477
Bos. Braves	700	829	.458
Cin. Reds	664	866	.434
Phi. Phillies	581	943	.381

1940–49

American League	Wins	Losses	%
N.Y. Yankees	929	609	.604
Bos. Red Sox	754	683	.556
Det. Tigers	834	705	.542
Cle. Indians	800	731	.523
Chi. White Sox	707	820	.463
St.L. Browns	698	833	.456
Was. Senators	677	858	.441
Phi. A's	638	898	.415

National League	Wins	Losses	%
St.L. Cardinals	960	580	.623
Brk. Dodgers	894	646	.581
Cin. Reds	767	769	.499
Pit. Pirates	756	776	.493
Chi. Cubs	736	802	.479
N.Y. Giants	724	808	.473
Bos. Braves	719	808	.470
Phi. Phillies	584	951	.380

1950–59

American League	Wins	Losses	%
N.Y. Yankees	955	582	.621
Cle. Indians	904	634	.588
Chi. White Sox	847	693	.550
Bos. Red Sox	814	725	.529
Det. Tigers	738	802	.479
Was. Senators	640	898	.416
St.L. Browns–Bal. Orioles*	632	905	.412
Phi.–K.C. A's**	624	915	.405

* St. Louis franchise moved to Baltimore in 1954.

** Philadelphia franchise moved to Kansas City in 1955.

National League	Wins	Losses	%
Brk.–L.A. Dodgers*	913	630	.592
Bos.–Mil. Braves**	854	687	.554
N.Y.–S.F. Giants***	822	721	.531
St.L. Cardinals	776	763	.504
Phi. Phillies	767	773	.498
Cin. Reds	741	798	.481
Chi. Cubs	672	866	.437
Pit. Pirates	616	923	.400

* Brooklyn franchise moved to Los Angeles in 1958.

** Boston franchise moved to Milwaukee in 1953.

*** New York franchise moved to San Francisco in 1958.

continued on next page

1960–69

American League

	Wins	Losses	%
Bal. Orioles	911	698	.566
N.Y. Yankees	887	720	.552
Det. Tigers	882	729	.547
Was. Senators–Min. Twins*	852	747	.536
Chi. White Sox	783	760	.529
Cle. Indians	764	826	.487
Bos. Red Sox	685	845	.475
L.A.–Cal. Angels**	685	770	.471
K.C.–Oak. A's***	686	922	.427
K.C. Royals****	69	93	.426
Was. Senators**	607	844	.418
Sea. Pilots–Mil. Brewers****	64	98	.395

* Original Washington Senators franchise moved to Minnesota in 1961.

** New team awarded to Washington by League as expansion team in 1961, along with Los Angeles.

*** Kansas City franchise moved to Oakland in 1968.

**** Kansas City and Seattle (now Milwaukee) joined the League as expansion teams in 1961.

National League

	Wins	Losses	%
S.F. Giants	902	704	.562
St.L. Cardinals	884	718	.552
L.A. Dodgers	878	729	.546
Cin. Reds	860	742	.537
Mil.–Atl. Braves*	851	753	.531
Pit. Pirates	848	755	.529
Phi. Phillies	759	843	.474
Chi. Cubs	735	868	.459
Hou. Astros**	555	739	.429
N.Y. Mets**	494	799	.382
Mon. Expos***	52	110	.321
S.D. Padres***	52	110	.321

* Milwaukee franchise moved to Atlanta in 1966.

** Houston and New York joined League as expansion teams in 1962.

*** San Diego and Montreal joined League as expansion teams in 1969.

1970–79

American League

	Wins	Losses	%
Bal. Orioles	944	656	.590
Bos. Red Sox	895	714	.556
N.Y. Yankees	892	715	.555
K.C. Royals	851	760	.528
Oak. A's	838	772	.520
Min. Twins	812	794	.506
Det. Tigers	789	820	.490
Cal. Angels	781	831	.484
Chi. White Sox	752	853	.469
Was. Senators–Tex. Rangers*	747	860	.465
Cle. Indians	737	866	.460
Mil. Brewers	838	873	.458
Sea. Mariners**	187	297	.386
Tor. Blue Jays**	166	318	.343

* The second edition of the Washington Senators moved to Texas in 1972.

** The Seattle Mariners and Toronto Blue Jays joined the League as expansion teams in 1977.

National League

	Wins	Losses	%
Cin. Reds	953	657	.592
Pit. Pirates	916	695	.569
L.A. Dodgers	910	701	.565
Phi. Phillies	812	801	.503
St.L. Cardinals	800	813	.496
S.F. Giants	794	818	.493
Hou. Astros	793	817	.493
Chi. Cubs	785	827	.487
N.Y. Mets	763	850	.473
Mon. Expos	748	862	.465
Atl. Braves	725	883	.451
S.D. Padres	667	942	.415

continued on next page

1980-89

American League

	Wins	Losses	%
N.Y. Yankees	854	708	.547
Det. Tigers	839	727	.536
K.C. Royals	826	734	.529
Bos. Red Sox	821	742	.525
Tor. Blue Jays	817	746	.523
Mil. Brewers	804	760	.514
Bal. Orioles	800	761	.512
Oak. A's	803	764	.512
Cal. Angels	783	783	.500
Chi. White Sox	758	802	.486
Min. Twins	733	833	.468
Tex. Rangers	720	839	.462
Cle. Indians	710	849	.455
Sea. Mariners	673	893	.430

National League

	Wins	Losses	%
St.L. Cardinals	825	734	.529
L.A. Dodgers	825	741	.527
N.Y. Mets	816	743	.523
Hou. Astros	819	750	.522
Mon. Expos	811	752	.519
Phi. Phillies	783	780	.501
Cin. Reds	781	783	.499
S.F. Giants	773	795	.493
S.D. Padres	762	805	.486
Chi. Cubs	735	821	.472
Pit. Pirates	732	825	.470
Atl. Braves	712	845	.457

1990-99

American League

	Wins	Losses	%
N.Y. Yankees	851	702	.548
Cle. Indians	823	728	.531
Chi. White Sox	816	735	.526
Bos. Red Sox	814	741	.523
Tex. Rangers	807	747	.519
Tor. Blue Jays	801	754	.515
Bal. Orioles	794	757	.512
Oak. A's	773	781	.497
Sea. Mariners	764	787	.493
Mil. Brewers*	594	636	.483
Ana. Angels	738	817	.475
K.C. Royals	725	825	.468
Min. Twins	718	833	.463
Det. Tigers	702	852	.452
T.B. Devil Rays**	132	192	.407

* Milwaukee Brewers switched to National League in 1998.
** Tampa Bay joined League as expansion team in 1998.

National League

	Wins	Losses	%
Atl. Braves	925	629	.595
Hou. Astros	813	742	.523
Cin. Reds	809	746	.520
L.A. Dodgers	797	757	.513
Ari. D'backs*	165	159	.509
S.F. Giants	790	766	.508
Mon. Expos	776	777	.499
Pit. Pirates	774	779	.498
N.Y. Mets	767	786	.494
St.L. Cardinals	758	794	.488
S.D. Padres	758	799	.486
Col. Rockies**	512	559	.478
Chi. Cubs	739	813	.476
Phi. Phillies	732	823	.471
Mil. Brewers	148	175	.458
Fla. Marlins**	472	596	.442

* Arizona joined League as expansion team in 1998.
** Colorado and Florida joined League as expansion teams in 1993.

2000-09

American League

	Wins	Losses	%
N.Y. Yankees	965	651	.597
Bos. Red Sox	920	699	.568
L..A. Angels	900	720	.556
Oak. A's	890	728	.550
Min. Twins	863	758	.532
Chi. White Sox	857	764	.529
Sea. Mariners	837	783	.517
Cle. Indians	816	804	.504
Tor. Blue Jays	805	814	.497
Tex. Rangers	776	844	.479
Det. Tigers	729	891	.450
Bal. Orioles	698	920	.431
T.B. Rays	694	923	.429
K.C. Royals	672	948	.415

National League

	Wins	Losses	%
St.L. Cardinals	913	706	.564
Atl. Braves	892	726	.551
L.A. Dodgers	862	758	.532
S.F. Giants	855	762	.529
Phi. Phillies	850	769	.525
Hou. Astros	832	787	.514
N.Y. Mets	815	803	.504
Fla. Marlins	811	807	.501
Chi. Cubs	807	811	.499
Ari. D'backs	805	815	.497
Col. Rockies	769	852	.474
S.D. Padres	769	852	.474
Cin. Reds	751	869	.464
Mil. Brewers	741	878	.458
Mon. Expos–Was. Nationals*	711	908	.439
Pit. Pirates	681	936	.421

* Montreal franchise moved to Washington in 2005.

continued on next page

2010–19

American League	Wins	Losses	%
N.Y. Yankees	921	699	.569
Bos. Red Sox	872	748	.538
T.B. Rays	860	761	.531
Cle. Indians	855	763	.528
Tex. Rangers	843	778	.520
Oak. A's	839	781	.518
L.A. Angels	822	798	.507
Tor. Blue Jays	794	826	.490
Hou. Astros	789	831	.487
Det. Tigers	782	835	.484
Min. Twins	765	855	.472
K.C. Royals	758	862	.468
Sea. Mariners	758	862	.468
Bal. Orioles	755	865	.466
Chi. White Sox	743	876	.459

* Houston Astros switched to American League in 2013.

National League	Wins	Losses	%
L.A. Dodgers	919	701	.567
St. L. Cardinals	899	721	.555
Was. Nationals	879	740	.543
Atl. Braves	843	776	.521
Mil. Brewers	824	797	.508
S.F. Giants	821	799	.507
Chi. Cubs	817	803	.504
Ari. D'Backs	793	827	.490
N.Y. Mets	793	827	.490
Pit. Pirates	792	826	.489
Phi. Phillies	787	833	.486
Cin. Reds	775	845	.478
Col. Rockies	752	869	.464
S.D. Padres	739	881	.456
Fla.-Mia. Marlins	707	911	.437

2020–22

American League	Wins	Losses	%
Hou. Astros	230	154	.599
T.B. Rays	226	158	.589
N.Y. Yankees	224	160	.583
Tor. Blue Jays	215	169	.560
Chi. White Sox	209	175	.544
Cle. Indians-Guardians	207	177	.539
Sea. Mariners	207	177	.539
Bos. Red Sox	194	190	.505
Min. Twins	187	197	.487
Oak. A's	182	202	.474
L.A. Angels	176	208	.458
Det. Tigers	166	216	.435
K.C. Royals	165	219	.430
Bal. Orioles	160	224	.417
Tex. Rangers	150	234	.391

National League	Wins	Losses	%
L.A. Dodgers	260	124	.677
Atl. Braves	224	159	.585
S.F. Giants	217	167	.565
St. L. Cardinals	213	169	.558
Mil. Brewers	210	174	.547
S.D. Padres	205	179	.534
N.Y. Mets	204	180	.531
Phi. Phillies	197	187	.513
Chi. Cubs	179	205	.466
Cin. Reds	176	208	.458
Col. Rockies	168	215	.439
Mia. Marlins	167	217	.435
Ari. D'Backs	151	233	.393
Was. Nationals	146	238	.380
Pit. Pirates	142	242	.370

Clubs Winning 100 Games, Not Winning Pennant

American League

Wins

116 .... Sea. Mariners, 2001 (116–46, .716)
(Lost League Championship Series to N.Y. Yankees)
103 .... N.Y. Yankees, 1954 (103–51, .667)
(Finished second to Cle. Indians by 8 games)
103 .... N.Y. Yankees, 1980 (103–59, .636)
(Lost League Championship Series to K.C. Royals)
103 .... N.Y. Yankees, 2002 (103–58, .640)
(Lost Division Series to Ana. Angels)
103 .... Oak. A's, 2002 (103–59, .636)
(Lost Division Series to Min. Twins)
103 .... Hou. Astros, 2018 (103–59, .636)
(Lost League Championship Series to Bos. Red Sox)
103 .... N.Y. Yankees, 2019 (103–59, .636)
(Lost League Championship Series to Hou. Astros)

National League

Wins

111 .... L.A. Dodgers, 2022 (111–51, .685)
(Lost Division Series to S.D. Padres)
107 .... S.F. Giants, 2021 (107–55, .660)
(Lost Division Series to L.A. Dodgers)
106 .... Atl. Braves, 1998 (106–56, .654)
(Lost League Championship Series to S.D. Padres)
106 .... L.A. Dodgers, 2019 (106–56, 654)
(Lost Division Series to Was. Nationals)
106 .... LA Dodgers, 2021 (106–56, .654)
(Lost League Championship Series to Atl. Braves)
104 .... Chi. Cubs, 1909 (104–49, .680)
(Finished second to Pit. Pirates by 6.5 games)
104 .... Brk. Dodgers, 1942 (104–50, .675)
(Finished second to St.L. Cardinals by 2 games)

continued on next page

Wins

102 .... K.C. Royals, 1977 (102–60, .630)
    (Lost League Championship Series to N.Y. Yankees)
102 .... Oak. A's, 2001 (102–60, .630)
    (Lost Division Series to N.Y. Yankees)
102 ....Cle. Indians, 2017 (102–60, .630)
    (Lost Division Series to N.Y. Yankees)
101 ....Det. Tigers, 1961 (101–61, .623)
    (Finished second to N.Y. Yankees by 8 games)
101 .... Oak. A's, 1971 (101–60, .627)
    (Lost League Championship Series to Bal. Orioles)
101 .... N.Y. Yankees, 2004 (101–61, .623)
    (Lost League Championship Series to Bos. Red Sox)
101 ....Min. Twins, 2019 (101–61, .623)
    (Lost Division Series to N.Y. Yankees)
100 ....Det. Tigers, 1915 (100–54, .649)
    (Finished second to Bos. Red Sox by 2.5 games)
100 ....Bal. Orioles, 1980 (100–62, .617)
    (Finished second in AL East to N.Y. Yankees by 3 games)
100 ............................L.A. Angels, 2008 (100–62, .617)
    (Lost Division Series to Bos. Red Sox)
100 .... N.Y. Yankees, 2018 (100–62, .617)
    (Lost Division Series to Bos. Red Sox)
100 ............................T.B. Rays, 2021 (100–62, .617)
    (Lost Division Series to Bos. Red Sox)

Wins

104..............................Atl. Braves, 1993 (104–58, .642)
    (Lost League Championship Series to Phi. Phillies)
103............................. S.F. Giants, 1993 (103–59, .636)
    (Finished second in NL West to Atl. Braves by 1 game)
102......................... L.A. Dodgers, 1962 (102–63, .618)
    (Lost Pennant Playoff to S.F. Giants)
102 .... Hou. Astros, 1998 (102–60, .630)
    (Lost Division Series to S.D. Padres)
102............................Phi. Phillies, 2011 (102–60, .630)
    (Lost Division Series to St.L. Cardinals)
102............................Cle. Indians, 2017 (102–60, .630
    (Lost Division Series to N.Y. Yankees)
101............................Phi. Phillies, 1976 (101–61, .623)
    (Lost League Championship Series to Cin. Reds)
101............................Phi. Phillies, 1977 (101–61, .623)
    (Lost League Championship Series to L.A. Dodgers)
101..............................Atl. Braves, 2002 (101–59, .631)
    (Lost Division Series to S.F. Giants)
101..............................Atl. Braves, 2003 (101–61, .623)
    (Lost Division Series to Chi. Cubs)
101..............................Atl. Braves, 2022 (101–61, .623)
    (Lost Division Series to Phi. Phillies)
101..............................N.Y. Mets, 2022 (101–61, .623)
    (Lost Wild Card Series to S.D. Padres)
100..............................N.Y. Mets, 1988 (100–60, .625)
    (Lost League Championship Series to L.A. Dodgers)
100.......................... Ari. D'backs, 1999 (100–62, .617)
    (Lost Division Series to St.L. Cardinals)
100........................ S.F. Giants, 2003 (100–62, .617)
    (Lost Division Series to Chi. Cubs)
100........................ St.L. Cardinals, 2005 (100–62, .617)
    (Lost Division Series to Hou. Astros)
100........................ St.L. Cardinals, 2015 (100–62, .617)
    (Lost Division Series to Chi. Cubs)

Pennant Winners One Year, Losing Record Next (Post-1900)

American League

Won Pennant		Losing Record	%
1914	Phi. A's	1915: 43–109	.283
1917	Chi. White Sox	1918: 57–67	.460
1918	Bos. Red Sox*	1919: 66–71	.482
1933	Was. Senators	1934: 66–86	.434
1964	N.Y. Yankees	1965: 77–85	.475
1966	Bal. Orioles*	1967: 76–85	.472
1980	K.C. Royals	1981: 50–53	.485
1981	N.Y. Yankees	1982: 79–83	.488
1985	K.C. Royals*	1986: 76–86	.469
1986	Bos. Red Sox	1987: 78–84	.481
1993	Tor. Blue Jays*	1994: 55–60	.478
2002	Ana. Angels*	2003: 77–85	.475
2013	Bos. Red Sox*	2014: 71–91	.438
2019	Hou. Astros	2020: 29–31	.483

National League

Won Pennant		Losing Record	%
1916	Brk. Dodgers	1917: 70–81	.464
1931	St.L. Cardinals*	1932: 72–82	.468
1948	Bos. Braves	1949: 75–79	.487
1950	Phi. Phillies	1951: 73–81	.474
1960	Pit. Pirates*	1961: 75–79	.487

continued on next page

Won Pennant		Losing Record	%
1963	L.A. Dodgers*	1964: 80–82	.494
1964	St.L. Cardinals*	1965: 80–81	.497
1966	L.A. Dodgers	1967: 73–89	.451
1970	Cin. Reds	1971: 79–83	.488
1973	N.Y. Mets	1974: 71–91	.438
1978	L.A. Dodgers	1979: 79–83	.488
1982	St.L. Cardinals*	1983: 79–83	.488
1985	St.L. Cardinals	1986: 79–83	.488
1987	St.L. Cardinals	1988: 76–86	.469
1990	Cin. Reds	1991: 74–88	.457
1993	Phi. Phillies	1994: 54–61	.470
1997	Fla. Marlins*	1998: 54–108	.333
1998	S.D. Padres	1999: 74–88	.457
2006	St.L. Cardinals*	2007: 78–84	.481
2007	Col. Rockies	2008: 74–88	.457
2012	S.F. Giants*	2013: 76–86	.469
2019	Was. Nationals*	2020: 26–34	.433

* World Series winner.

Pennant-Winning Season After Losing Record Year Before

American League

Won Pennant		Losing Record	%
1907	Det. Tigers	1906: 71–78	.477
1919	Chi. White Sox	1918: 57–67	.460
1924	Was. Senators*	1923: 75–78	.490
1926	N.Y. Yankees	1925: 69–85	.448
1934	Det. Tigers	1933: 75–79	.487
1944	St.L. Browns	1943: 72–80	.474
1946	Bos. Red Sox	1945: 71–83	.461
1965	Min. Twins	1964: 79–83	.488
1967	Bos. Red Sox	1966: 72–90	.444
1987	Min. Twins*	1986: 71–91	.438
1991	Min. Twins*	1990: 74–88	.457
2002	Ana. Angels*	2001: 75–87	.463
2006	Det. Tigers	2005: 71–91	.438
2008	T.B. Rays	2007: 66–96	.407
2013	Bos. Red Sox*	2012: 69–93	.425
2021	Hou. Astros	2020: 29–31	.433

National League

Won Pennant		Losing Record	%
1914	Bos. Braves*	1913: 69–82	.457
1915	Phi. Phillies	1914: 74–80	.481
1918	Chi. Cubs	1917: 74–80	.481
1920	Bkly. Dodgers	1919: 69–71	.493
1933	N.Y. Giants*	1932: 72–82	.468
1945	Chi. Cubs	1944: 75–79	.487
1954	N.Y. Giants*	1953: 70–84	.455
1959	L.A. Dodgers*	1958: 71–83	.461
1961	Cin. Reds	1960: 67–87	.435
1965	L.A. Dodgers*	1964: 80–82	.494
1969	N.Y. Mets*	1968: 73–89	.451
1972	Cin. Reds	1971: 77–83	.481
1987	St.L. Cardinals	1986: 76–82	.491
1988	L.A. Dodgers*	1987: 73–89	.451
1990	Cin. Reds*	1989: 75–87	.463
1991	Atl. Braves	1990: 65–97	.401
1993	Phi. Phillies	1992: 70–92	.432
1997	Fla. Marlins*	1996: 80–82	.494

continued on next page

Won Pennant		Losing Record	%
1998	S.D. Padres	1997: 76-86	.469
2003	Fla. Marlins*	2002: 79-83	.488
2007	Col. Rockies	2006: 76-86	.469
2014	S.F. Giants*	2013: 76-86	.469
2015	N.Y. Mets	2016: 79-83	.488

* World Series winner.

Teams Winning 100 Games in a Season, Three Years in a Row

American League		National League	
1929-31 Phi. A's	1929: 104 wins	1942-44 St.L. Cardinals	1942: 106 wins
	1930: 102 wins		1943: 106 wins
	1931: 107 wins		1944: 105 wins
1969-71 Bal. Orioles	1969: 109 wins	1997-99 Atl. Braves	1997: 101 wins
	1970: 108 wins		1998: 106 wins
	1971: 101 wins		1999: 103 wins
2002-04 N.Y. Yankees	2002: 103 wins		
	2003: 101 wins		
	2004: 101 wins		

Largest Increase in Games Won by Team Next Season

American League

Wins

+34 ....Cle. Indians, 1995 (100 wins vs. 66 wins in 1994)*
+33 ....Bos. Red Sox, 1946 (104 wins vs. 71 wins in 1945)
+33 ...... Bal. Orioles, 1989 (87 wins vs. 54 wins in 1988)
+32 ....Bos. Red Sox, 1995 (86 wins vs. 54 wins in 1994)*
+31 ....Chi. White Sox, 1919 (88 wins vs. 57 wins in 1918)*
+31 ......Cal. Angels, 1995 (78 wins vs. 47 wins in 1994)*
+31 .... T.B. Rays, 2008 (97 wins vs. 66 wins in 2007)
+31 ...... Bal. Orioles, 2022 (83 wins vs. 52 wins in 2021)
+30 .... Det. Tigers, 1961 (101 wins vs. 71 wins in 1960)
+30 ..... Bos. Red Sox, 1967 (92 wins vs. 72 wins in 1966)
+30 .....Sea. Mariners, 1995 (79 wins vs. 49 wins in 1994)*

* 1994 was a strike-shortened season; 1918 was shortened by WWI.

National League (Post-1900)

Wins

+36 .......N.Y. Giants, 1903 (84 wins vs. 48 wins in 1902)
+35 ....Ari. D'backs, 1999 (100 wins vs. 65 wins in 1998)
+34 .... Phi. Phillies, 1962 (81 wins vs. 47 wins in 1961)
+33 .... Bos. Braves, 1936 (71 wins vs. 38 wins in 1935)
+32 ...St.L. Cardinals, 1904 (75 wins vs. 43 wins in 1903)
+31 .... Phi. Phillies, 1905 (83 wins vs. 52 wins in 1904)
+31 ...... S.F. Giants, 1993 (103 wins vs. 72 wins in 1992)
+30 ...St.L. Cardinals, 1914 (81 wins vs. 51 wins in 1913)

Largest Decrease in Games Won by Team Next Season

American League

Wins

−56 .... Phi. A's, 1915 (43 wins vs. 99 wins in 1914)
−47 .....K.C. Royals, 1981 (50 wins vs. 97 wins in 1980)*
−44 .......N.Y. Yankees, 1981 (59 wins vs. 103 wins in 1980)*
−43 .....Chi. White Sox, 1918 (57 wins vs. 100 wins in 1917)
−41 ....Bal. Orioles, 1981 (59 wins vs. 100 wins in 1980)*
−40 ...Tor. Blue Jays, 1994 (55 wins vs. 95 wins in 1993)*
−36 ...... Min. Twins, 1981 (41 wins vs. 77 wins in 1980)*
−35 .... Cle. Naps, 1914 (51 wins vs. 86 wins in 1913)
−34 ....Tex. Rangers, 1994 (52 wins vs. 86 wins in 1993)*
−34 ....Chi. White Sox, 1921 (62 wins vs. 96 wins in 1920)
−33 ......Was. Senators, 1934 (66 wins vs. 99 wins in 1933)
−33 ..Sea. Mariners, 1994 (49 wins vs. 82 wins in 1993)*
−32 ...... Det. Tigers, 1994 (53 wins vs. 85 wins in 1993)*

* 1981 and 1994 were strike-shortened seasons; 1918 was shortened by WWI.

National League

Wins

−48 ... S.F. Giants, 1994 (55 wins vs. 103 wins in 1993)*
−43 .... Phi. Phillies, 1994 (54 wins vs. 97 wins in 1993)*
−40 ....Bos. Braves, 1935 (38 wins vs. 78 wins in 1934)
−38 .... Fla. Marlins, 1998 (54 wins vs. 92 wins in 1997)
−37 ......Pit. Pirates, 1981 (46 wins vs. 83 wins in 1980)*
−36 .. Atl. Braves, 1994 (68 wins vs. 104 wins in 1993)*
−35 ...... Chi. Cubs, 1994 (49 wins vs. 84 wins in 1993)*
−34 ...St.L. Cardinals, 1994 (53 wins vs. 87 wins in 1993)*
−33 .. Ari. D'backs, 2004 (51 wins vs. 84 wins in 2003)
−32 .....Phi. Phillies, 1918 (55 wins vs. 87 wins in 1917)
−32 ....Hou. Astros, 1981 (61 wins vs. 93 wins in 1980)*
−32 .... Phi. Phillies, 1981 (59 wins vs. 91 wins in 1980)*
−32 ....S.D. Padres, 1981 (41 wins vs. 73 wins in 1980)*

Teams with Worst Won–Lost Percentage

American League

	Wins–Losses	Percentage
Phi. A's, 1916	36–117	.235
Was. Senators, 1904	38–113	.252
Phi. A's, 1919	36–104	.257
Det. Tigers, 2003	43–119	.265
Was. Senators, 1909	42–110	.276
Bos. Red Sox, 1932	43–111	.279
St.L. Browns, 1939	43–111	.279
Phi. A's, 1915	43–109	.283
Bal. Orioles, 2018	47–115	.290
St.L. Browns, 1911	45–107	.296
St.L. Browns, 1937	46–108	.299

National League (Post-1900)

	Wins–Losses	Percentage
Bos. Braves, 1935	38–115	.248
N.Y. Mets, 1962	40–120	.250
Pit. Pirates, 1952	42–112	.273
Phi. Phillies, 1942	42–109	.278
Phi. Phillies, 1941	43–111	.279
Phi. Phillies, 1928	43–109	.283
Bos. Rustlers, 1911	44–107	.291
Bos. Doves, 1909	45–108	.294
Phi. Phillies, 1939	45–106	.298
Phi. Phillies, 1945	46–108	.299
Phi. Phillies, 1938	45–105	.300

Teams Hitting .300

American League		National League (Post-1900)	
St.L. Browns, 1920	.308	St.L. Cardinals, 1921	.308
Cle. Indians, 1920	.303	Pit. Pirates, 1922	.308
Det. Tigers, 1921	.316	N.Y. Giants, 1922	.305
Cle. Indians, 1921	.308	St.L. Cardinals, 1922	.301
St.L. Browns, 1921	.304	N.Y. Giants, 1924	.300
N.Y. Yankees, 1921	.300	Pit. Pirates, 1925	.307
St.L. Browns, 1922	.313	Pit. Pirates, 1927	.305
Det. Tigers, 1922	.305	Pit. Pirates, 1928	.309
Cle. Indians, 1923	.301	Phi. Phillies, 1929	.309
Det. Tigers, 1923	.300	Chi. Cubs, 1929	.303
Phi. A's, 1925	.307	Pit. Pirates, 1929	.303
Was. Senators, 1925	.303	N.Y. Giants, 1930	.319
Det. Tigers, 1925	.302	Phi. Phillies, 1930	.315
N.Y. Yankees, 1927	.307	St.L. Cardinals, 1930	.314
Phi. A's, 1927	.303	Chi. Cubs, 1930	.309
N.Y. Yankees, 1930	.309	Brk. Dodgers, 1930	.304
Cle. Indians, 1930	.304	Pit. Pirates, 1930	.303
Was. Senators, 1930	.302		
Det. Tigers, 1934	.300		
Cle. Indians, 1936	.304		
Det. Tigers, 1936	.300		
N.Y. Yankees, 1936	.300		
Bos. Red Sox, 1950	.302		

Teams with Three 20-Game Winners

American League

Bos. Americans, 1903 .... Cy Young (28), Bill Dinneen (21), Long Tom Hughes (20)

Bos. Americans, 1904 .... Cy Young (27), Bill Dinneen (23), Jesse Tannehill (21)

Cle. Indians, 1906 .... Otto Hess (22), Addie Joss (21), Bob Rhoads (21)

Chi. White Sox, 1907 .... Doc White (27), Ed Walsh (25), Frank Smith (23)

Det. Tigers, 1907 ....Bill Donovan (25), Ed Killian (25), George Mullin (20)

Chi. White Sox, 1920* .... Red Faber (23), Lefty Williams (22), Eddie Cicotte (21), Dickie Kerr (21)

Cle. Indians, 1920 ....Jim Bagby Sr. (31), Stan Coveleski (24), Ray Caldwell (20)

Phi. A's, 1931 ....Lefty Grove (31), George Earnshaw (21), Rube Walberg (20)

Cle. Indians, 1951 ....Bob Feller (22), Mike Garcia (20), Early Wynn (20)

Cle. Indians, 1952 .... Early Wynn (23), Mike Garcia (22), Bob Lemon (22)

Cle. Indians, 1956 .... Bob Lemon (20), Herb Score (20), Early Wynn (20)

Bal. Orioles, 1970 ....Mike Cuellar (24), Dave McNally (24), Jim Palmer (20)

Bal. Orioles, 1971* .... Dave McNally (21), Mike Cuellar (20), Pat Dobson (20), Jim Palmer (20)

Oak. A's, 1973..Ken Holtzman (21), Catfish Hunter (21), Vida Blue (20)

National League

Pit. Pirates, 1902 ....Jack Chesbro (28), Deacon Phillippe (20), Jesse Tannehill (20)

Chi. Cubs, 1903... Jack Taylor (21), Jake Weimer (21), Bob Wicker (20)**

N.Y. Giants, 1904 ....Joe McGinnity (35), Christy Mathewson (33), Dummy Taylor (21)

N.Y. Giants, 1905 .... Christy Mathewson (31), Red Ames (22), Joe McGinnity (21)

Chi. Cubs, 1906...Mordecai Brown (26), Ed Reulbach (20), Jack Taylor (20)***

N.Y. Giants, 1913 .... Christy Mathewson (25), Rube Marquard (23), Jeff Tesreau (22)

N.Y. Giants, 1920 .... Art Nehf (21), Fred Toney (21), Jesse Barnes (20)

Cin. Reds, 1923 .... Dolf Luque (27), Pete Donohue (21), Eppa Rixey (20)

* Four 20-game winners on staff.

** Wicker started 1903 season with St.L. Cardinals (1 game, 0–0).

*** Taylor started 1906 season with St.L. Cardinals (17 games, 8–9).

Teams with 30-Game Winners, Not Winning Pennant

American League

Team	Pitcher	Finish
Bos. Americans, 1901	Cy Young (33)	2nd, 4 games behind Chi. White Sox
Bos. Americans, 1902	Cy Young (32)	3rd, 6.5 games behind Phi. A's
N.Y. Highlanders, 1904	Jack Chesbro (41)	2nd, 1.5 games behind Bos. Red Sox
Chi. White Sox, 1908	Ed Walsh (40)	3rd, 1.5 games behind Det. Tigers
Was. Senators, 1912	Walter Johnson (32)	2nd, 14 games behind Bos. Red Sox
Was. Senators, 1913	Walter Johnson (36)	2nd, 6.5 games behind Phi. A's

National League

Team	Pitcher	Finish
N.Y. Giants, 1903	Joe McGinnity (31), Christy Mathewson (30)	2nd, 6.5 games behind Pit. Pirates
N.Y. Giants, 1908	Christy Mathewson (37)	2nd, 1 game behind Chi. Cubs
Phi. Phillies, 1916	Pete Alexander (33)	2nd, 2.5 games behind Brk. Dodgers
Phi. Phillies, 1917	Pete Alexander (30)	2nd, 10 games behind N.Y. Giants

Teams Leading or Tied for First Place Entire Season

American League		National League	
1927	N.Y. Yankees (Record: 110–44)	1923	N.Y. Giants (Record: 95–58)
1984	Det. Tigers (Record: 104–58)	1955	Brk. Dodgers (Record: 98–55)

continued on next page

American League	**National League**
1997....................................Bal. Orioles (Record: 98–64)	1990 ....Cin. Reds (Record: 91–71)
1998....................................Cle. Indians (Record: 89–73)	2003 .... S.F. Giants (Record: 100–61)
2001............................Sea. Mariners (Record: 116–46)	
2005..............................Chi. White Sox (Record: 99–63)	

Teams Scoring in Every Inning (Post-1900)

American League

Bos. Americans vs. Cle. Indians, Sep. 16, 1903.......................................Cle. Indians.................043000000–7
Bos. Red Sox 22311311X–14

Cle. Indians vs. Bos. Red Sox, Jul. 7, 1923* ....Bos. Red Sox 000200001–3
Cle. Indians.................3231 2(13)1 2X–27

N.Y. Yankees vs. St.L. Browns, Jul. 26, 1939 ....St.L. Browns.................000000010–1
N.Y. Yankees 21141311X–14

Chi. White Sox vs. Bos. Red Sox, May 11, 1949.....................................Bos. Red Sox 000501020–8
Chi. White Sox 11212113X–12

K.C. Royals vs. Oak. A's, Sep. 14, 1998 ....Oak. A's.......................100050000–6
K.C. Royals 11311324X–16

N.Y. Yankees vs. Tor. Blue Jays, Apr. 29, 2006....................................Tor. Blue Jays...............203010000–6
N.Y. Yankees 41223131X–17

Det. Tigers vs. Col. Rockies (NL), Aug. 3, 2014 ....Col. Rockies.................020000003–5
Det. Tigers...................11123111X–11

Chi. White Sox vs. Cle. Indians, Sep. 12, 2016.......................................Cle. Indians.................030000010–4
Chi. White Sox 11121122X–11

National League (Post-1900)

N.Y. Giants @ Phi. Phillies, Jun. 1, 1923...N.Y. Giants 421155121–22
Phi. Phillies...................140110010–8

St.L. Cardinals vs. Chi. Cubs, Jun. 9, 1935 ....Chi. Cubs....................000011000–2
St.L. Cardinals 11121223X–13

St.L. Cardinals vs. Chi. Cubs, Sep. 13, 1964...St.L. Cardinals 212221311–15
Chi. Cubs.....................100001000–2

Chi. Cubs vs. Hou. Astros, Sep. 1, 1978 ....Hou. Astros 060300110–11
Chi. Cubs.....................51111212X–14

Col. Rockies @ Chi. Cubs, May 5, 1999..Col. Rockies.................111121222–13
Chi. Cubs.....................023000010–6

Col. Rockies vs. S.D. Padres, Sep. 24, 2001 ....S.D. Padres.................1 01204021–11
Col. Rockies 12212511X–15

Mil. Brewers vs. Atl. Braves, Aug. 11, 2016..Atl. Braves...................000002100–3
Mil. Brewers 21111311X–11

* First game of doubleheader.

Most Lopsided Shutouts

American League	**National League**
22–0.........Cle. Indians over N.Y. Yankees, Aug. 31, 2004	22–0..............Pit. Pirates over Chi. Cubs, Sep. 16, 1975
21–0................Det. Tigers over Cle. Blues, Sep. 15, 1901	20–0...........Mil. Brewers over Pit. Pirates, Apr. 22, 2010
21–0............... N.Y. Yankees over Phi. A's, Aug. 13, 1939	

11

Players with Both Little League and Major League World Series Teams

Boog Powell	1954 (Lakeland, Florida)	1966 World Series
Jim Barbieri	1954 (Schenectady, New York)	1966 World Series
Rick Wise	1958 (Portland, Oregon)	1975 World Series, 1988 World Series
Carney Lansford	1969 (Santa Clara, California)	1990 World Series
Ed Vosberg	1973 (Tucson, Arizona)	1997 World Series
Charlie Hayes	1977 (Hattiesburg, Mississippi)	1996 World Series
Dwight Gooden	1979 (Tampa, Florida) 1980 (Tampa, Florida)	1986 World Series
Gary Sheffield	1980 (Tampa, Florida)	1997 World Series
Derek Bell	1981 (Tampa, Florida)	1992 World Series
Jason Varitek	1984 (Altamonte Springs, Florida)	2004 World Series, 2007 World Series
Jason Marquis	1991 (Staten Island, New York)	2004 World Series
Yusmeiro Petit	1994 (Maracaibo, Venezuela)	2014 World Series
Lance Lynn	1999 (Brownsburg, Indiana)	2011 World Series, 2013 World Series
Michael Conforto	2004 (Redmond, Washington)	2015 World Series
Cody Bellinger	2007 (Chandler, Arizona)	2017 World Series, 2018 World Series, 2020 World Series

Olympians (in Sports Other Than Baseball) Who Played Major League Baseball

Ed "Cotton" Minahan, pitcher, Cin. Reds (NL), 1907 .... Track and field, Paris, 1900

Al Spalding, pitcher, Chi. Cubs (NL), 1876–78 .... Shooting, Paris, 1900

Jim Thorpe, outfield, N.Y. Giants (NL), 1913–15 and 1917–18; Cin. Reds (NL), 1917;
   Bos. Braves (NL), 1919 .... Decathlon, Stockholm, 1912

Four-Decade Players

1870s–1900s

Dan Brouthers, first base (1879–96, 1904)   Jim O'Rourke, outfield (1876–93, 1904)

1880s–1910s

Kid Gleason, pitcher and second base (1888–1908, 1912)   Jack O'Connor, catcher (1887–1904, 1906–07, 1910)

Deacon McGuire, catcher (1884–88, 1890–1908, 1910, 1912)   John Ryan, catcher (1889–91, 1894–96, 1898–1903, 1912–13)

1890s–1920s

Nick Altrock, pitcher (1898, 1902–09, 1912–15, 1918–19, 1924, 1929, 1931, 1933)*

1900s–30s

Eddie Collins, second base (1906–30)   Jack Quinn, pitcher (1909–15, 1918–33)

continued on next page

1910s–40s

[No player]

1920s–50s

Bobo Newsom, pitcher (1929–30, 1932, 1934–48, 1952–53)

1930s–60s

Elmer Valo, outfield (1939–43, 1946–61)**   Ted Williams, outfield (1939–42, 1946–60)
Mickey Vernon, first base (1939–43, 1946–60)   Early Wynn, pitcher (1939, 1941–44, 1946–63)

1940s–70s

Minnie Minoso, outfield (1949, 1951–64, 1976, 1980)*

1950s–80s

Jim Kaat, pitcher (1959–83)   Willie McCovey, first base (1959–80)
Tim McCarver, catcher (1959–61, 1963–80)

1960s–90s

Bill Buckner, outfield and first base (1969–90)   Jerry Reuss, pitcher (1969–90)
Rick Dempsey, catcher (1969–92)   Nolan Ryan, pitcher (1966, 1968–93)
Carlton Fisk, catcher (1969, 1971–90)

1970s–2000s

Rickey Henderson, outfield (1979–2003)   Jesse Orosco, pitcher (1979, 1981–2003)
Mike Morgan, pitcher (1979, 1982–83, 1985–2002)   Tim Raines, outfield (1979–99, 2001–02)

1980s–2010s

Ken Griffey Jr., outfield (1989–2010)   Omar Vizquel, shortstop (1989–2012)
Jamie Moyer, pitcher (1986–91, 1993–2010, 2012)

* Played five decades.
** Played in last game of 1939 season for Phi. A's (AL), but manager Connie Mack kept his name off the official line-up card.

First Players Chosen in Draft by Expansion Teams

American League	National League
K.C. Royals ....Roger Nelson, pitcher	Ari. D'backs.................................. Brian Anderson, pitcher
L.A. Angels... Eli Grba, pitcher	Col. Rockies...................................... David Nied, pitcher
Sea. Pilots ....Don Mincher, first base	Fla. Marlins .... Nigel Wilson, outfield
Sea. Mariners................................Ruppert Jones, outfield	Hou. Colt .45s ....Ed Bressoud, shortstop
T.B. Devil Rays ....Tony Saunders, pitcher	Mon. Expos ....Manny Mota, outfield
Tor. Blue Jays................................... Bob Bailor, shortstop	N.Y. Mets ....,............... Hobie Landrith, catcher
Was. Senators II............................Bobby Shantz, pitcher	S.D. Padres...................................... Ollie Brown, outfield

Last Active Player Once Playing for . . .

Brk. Dodgers (NL)...Bob Aspromonte (played for Brk. Dodgers in 1956; active until 1971)
N.Y. Giants (NL) ....Willie Mays (played for N.Y. Giants in 1957; active until 1973)
Bos. Braves (NL)....................................... Eddie Mathews (played for Bos. Braves in 1952; active until 1968)
Phi. A's (AL)... Vic Power (played for Phi. A's in 1954; active until 1965)
St.L. Browns (AL) .... Don Larsen (played for St.L. Browns in 1953; active until 1967)
Mil. Braves (NL) .... Phil Niekro (played for Mil. Braves in 1965; active until 1987)
K.C. A's (AL).. Reggie Jackson (played for K.C. A's in 1967; active until 1987)
Hou. Colt .45s (NL) ....Rusty Staub (played for Hou. Astros in 1964; active until 1985)
Sea. Pilots (AL) ....Fred Stanley (played for Sea. Pilots in 1969; active until 1982)
Was. Senators (AL) ....Jim Kaat (played for Was. Senators in 1960; active until 1983)
Was. Senators II (AL) ....Toby Harrah (played for Was. Senators II in 1971; active until 1986)
Mon. Expos (NL) ....Bartolo Colon (played for Mon. Expos in 2002; active until 2018)

Last Players Born in Nineteenth Century to Play in Majors

American League

Fred Johnson, pitcher (b. Mar. 5, 1894)...Played in 1939 with St.L. Browns

Jimmy Dykes, third base (b. Nov. 10, 1896)...Played in 1939 with Chi. White Sox

National League

Hod Lisenbee, pitcher (b. Sep. 23, 1898)...Played in 1945 with Cin. Reds

Charlie Root, pitcher (b. Mar. 17, 1899)...Played in 1941 with Chi. Cubs

First Players Born in Twentieth Century to Play in Majors

American League

Ed Corey, pitcher (b. Jul. 13, 1900) ....Played in 1918 with Chi. White Sox

National League

John Cavanaugh, third base (b. Jun. 5, 1900) ....Played in 1919 with Phi. Phillies

First Players Born in Twenty-First Century to Play in Majors

American League

Elvis Luciano, pitcher (b. February 15, 2000)...Played in 2019 with Tor. Blue Jays

National League

Luis Garcia, second baseman (b. May 16, 2000)..Played in 2020 for Was. Nationals

Second African American to Play for Each of
16 Original Major League Teams

American League

	Second African American	First African American
Bos. Red Sox	Earl Wilson, pitcher, 1959	Pumpsie Green, infield, 1959
Chi. White Sox	Sammy Hairston, catcher, 1951	Minnie Minoso, outfield, 1951
Cle. Indians	Satchel Paige, pitcher, 1948	Larry Doby, outfield, 1947
Det. Tigers	Larry Doby, outfield, 1959	Ozzie Virgil, third base, 1958
N.Y. Yankees	Harry "Suitcase" Simpson, outfield, 1957	Elston Howard, catcher, 1955
Phi. A's	Vic Power, outfield and first base, 1954	Bob Trice, pitcher, 1953
St.L. Browns	Willard Brown, outfield, 1947	Hank Thompson, second base, 1947
Was. Senators	Joe Black, pitcher, 1957	Carlos Paula, outfield, 1954

National League

	Second African American	First African American
Bos. Braves	Luis Marquez, outfield, 1951	Sam Jethroe, outfield, 1950
Brk. Dodgers	Dan Bankhead, pitcher, 1947	Jackie Robinson, first base, 1947
Chi. Cubs	Gene Baker, second base, 1953	Ernie Banks, shortstop, 1953
Cin. Reds	Chuck Harmon, infield, 1954	Nino Escalera, outfield, 1954
N.Y. Giants	Monte Irvin, outfield, 1949	Hank Thompson, second base, 1949
Phi. Phillies	Chuck Harmon, infield, 1957	John Kennedy, third base, 1957
Pit. Pirates	Sam Jethroe, outfield, 1954	Curt Roberts, second base, 1954
St.L. Cardinals	Brooks Lawrence, pitcher, 1954	Tom Alston, first base, 1954

Players and Managers Having Same Number Retired on Two Different Clubs

Hank Aaron..Atl. Braves (NL) and Mil. Brewers (AL).. 44

Rod Carew..Cal. Angels (AL) and Min. Twins (AL) 29

continued on next page

Rollie Fingers	Mil. Brewers (NL) and Oak. A's (AL)		34
Greg Maddux	Atl. Braves (NL) and Chi. Cubs (NL)		31
Willie Mays	N.Y. Mets (NL) and S.F. Giants (NL		24
Frank Robinson	Bal. Orioles (AL) and Cin. Reds (NL)		20
Nolan Ryan	Hou. Astros (AL) and Tex. Rangers (AL)		34
Casey Stengel	N.Y. Mets (NL) and N.Y. Yankees (AL)		37

Major Leaguers Who Played Pro Football in Same Year(s)

	Baseball Team	Year(s)	Football Team
Red Badgro, outfield	St.L. Browns (AL)	1929–30	N.Y. Giants
Charlie Berry, catcher	Phi. A's (AL)	1925	Pottsville (PA) Maroons
Joe Berry, second base	N.Y. Giants (NL)	1921	Rochester (NY) Jeffs
Garland Buckeye, pitcher	Cle. Indians (AL)	1926	Chi. Bulls
Bruce Caldwell, outfield	Cle. Indians (AL)	1928	N.Y. Giants
Chuck Corgan, infield	Brk. Dodgers (NL)	1925	K.C. Cowboys
	Brk. Dodgers (NL)	1927	N.Y. Giants
Steve Filipowicz, outfield	N.Y. Giants (NL)	1945	N.Y. Giants
	Cin. Reds (NL)	1946	N.Y. Giants
Walter French, outfield	Phi. A's (AL)	1925	Pottsville (PA) Maroons
George Halas, outfield	N.Y. Yankees (AL)	1919	Decatur (IL) Staleys
Bo Jackson, outfield	K.C. Royals (AL)	1987–90	L.A. Raiders
Vic Janowicz, catcher	Pit. Pirates (NL)	1954	Was. Redskins
Bert Kuczynski, pitcher	Phi. A's (AL)	1943	Det. Lions
Pete Layden, outfield	St.L. Browns (AL)	1948	N.Y. Yankees
Christy Mathewson, pitcher	N.Y. Giants (NL)	1902	Pit. Pros
John Mohardt, second base	Det. Tigers (AL)	1922	Chi. Cardinals
Ernie Nevers, pitcher	St.L. Browns (AL)	1926–27	Duluth Eskimos
Ace Parker, shortstop	Phi. A's (AL)	1937–38	Brk. Dodgers
Al Pierotti, pitcher	Bos. Braves (NL)	1920	Cle. Tigers
	Bos. Braves (NL)	1921	N.Y. Giants
Pid Purdy, outfield	Cin. Reds (NL), Chi. White Sox (AL)	1926–27	G.B. Packers
Dick Reichle, outfield	Bos. Red Sox (AL)	1923	Mil. Badgers
Deion Sanders, outfield	N.Y. Yankees (AL)	1989–90	Atl. Falcons
	Atl. Braves (NL)	1991–94	Atl. Falcons (until 1993)
	Cin. Reds (NL)	1994–95, 1997	S.F. 49ers (1994)
	S.F. Giants (NL)	1995	Dal. Cowboys
John Scalzi, outfield	Bos. Braves (NL)	1931	Brk. Dodgers
Red Smith, catcher	N.Y. Giants (NL)	1927	G.B. Packers
Jim Thorpe, outfield	N.Y. Giants (NL)	1915, 1917	Canton Bulldogs
	Cin. Reds (NL)	1917	Canton Bulldogs
	Bos. Braves (NL)	1919	Canton Bulldogs
Ernie Vick, catcher	St.L. Cardinals (NL)	1925	Det. Panthers
Rube Waddell, pitcher	Phi. A's (AL)	1902	Pit. Pros
Tom Whelan, first base	Bos. Braves (NL)	1920	Canton Bulldogs

Performances by Oldest Players

Pitched	Satchel Paige, K.C. A's (AL), Sep. 25, 1965		59 years, 2 months
Batted (0-for-1)	Satchel Paige, K.C. A's (AL), Sep. 25, 1965		59 years, 2 months
Caught	Jim O'Rourke, N.Y. Giants (NL), Sep. 20, 1904		52 years, 1 month
At-Bat	Nick Altrock, Was. Senators (AL), Sep. 30, 1933		57 years, 0 months
Base Hit	Minnie Minoso, Chi. White Sox (AL), Sep. 12, 1976		53 years, 9 months
Double	Julio Franco, Atl. Braves (NL), Jul. 27, 2007		48 years, 11 months
Triple	Nick Altrock, Was. Senators (AL), Sep. 30, 1924		48 years, 0 months

continued on next page

Home Run	Julio Franco, N.Y. Mets (NL), May 4, 2007	48 years, 9 months
Grand Slam Home Run	Julio Franco, Atl. Braves (NL), Jun. 3, 2004	45 years, 10 months
Run Scored	Charlie O'Leary, St.L. Browns (AL), Sep. 30, 1934	52 years, 11 months
RBI	Julio Franco, Atl. Braves (NL), Sep. 27, 2007	49 years, 1 months
Stolen Base	Arlie Latham, N.Y. Giants (NL), Aug. 18, 1909	50 years, 5 months
100 Games, Season	Cap Anson, Chi. Colts (NL), 1897	45 years, 0 months
Game Won, Relief	Jack Quinn, Brk. Dodgers (NL), Aug. 14, 1932	48 years, 1 month
Game Lost, Relief	Hoyt Wilhelm, L.A. Dodgers (NL), Jun. 24, 1972	48 years, 11 months
Complete Game	Phil Niekro, N.Y. Yankees (AL), Oct. 6, 1985	46 years, 6 months
Shutout	Phil Niekro, N.Y. Yankees (AL), Oct. 6, 1985	46 years, 6 months
No-Hitter	Cy Young, Bos. Red Sox (AL), Jun. 30, 1908	41 years, 3 months
Perfect Game	Randy Johnson, Ari. D'backs (NL), May 18, 2004	39 years, 8 months

Oldest Players, by Position

First Base	Julio Franco, Atl. Braves (NL), 2007	48
Second Base	Arlie Latham, N.Y. Giants (NL), 1909	49
Third Base	Jimmy Austin, St.L. Browns (AL), 1929	49
Shortstop	Bobby Wallace, St.L. Cardinals (NL), 1918	44
Outfield	Sam Thompson, Det. Tigers (AL), 1906	46
Catcher	Jim O'Rourke, N.Y. Giants (NL), 1904	52
Pitcher	Satchel Paige, K.C. A's (AL), 1965	59
Designated Hitter	Minnie Minoso, Chi. White Sox (AL), 1976	53
Pinch Hitter	Nick Altrock, Was. Senators (AL), 1933	57

Youngest Players to Play in Majors

Fred Chapman, pitcher, Phi. A's (AA), Jul. 22, 1887	14 years, 8 months
Joe Nuxhall, pitcher, Cin. Reds (NL), Jun. 10, 1944	15 years, 10 months
Willie McGill, pitcher, Cle. Infants (PL), May 8, 1890	16 years, 6 months
Joe Stanley, outfield, Was. Senators (NL), Sep. 11, 1897	16 years, 6 months
Carl Scheib, pitcher, Phi. A's (AL), Sep. 6, 1943	16 years, 8 months
Tommy Brown, shortstop, Brk. Dodgers (NL) Aug. 3, 1944	16 years, 8 months
Milton Scott, first base, Chi. Cubs (NL), Sep. 30, 1882	16 years, 9 months
Putsy Caballero, third base, Phi. Phillies (NL), Sep. 14, 1944	16 years, 10 months
Jim Derrington, pitcher, Chi. White Sox (AL), Sep. 30, 1956	16 years, 10 months
Rogers McKee, pitcher, Phi. Phillies (NL), Aug. 18, 1943	16 years, 11 months
Alex George, shortstop, K.C. A's (AL), Sep. 16, 1955	16 years, 11 months
Merito Acosta, outfield, Was. Senators (AL), Jun. 5, 1913	17 years, 0 months

Youngest Players, by Position

First Base	Milton Scott, Chi. Cubs (NL), 1882	16
Second Base	Ted Sepkowski, Cle. Indians (AL), 1942	18
Third Base	Putsy Caballero, Phi. Phillies (NL), 1944	16
Shortstop	Tommy Brown, Brk. Dodgers (NL), 1944	16
Outfield	Merito Acosta, Was. Senators (AL), 1913	17
	Mel Ott, N.Y. Giants (NL), 1926	17
	Willie Crawford, L.A. Dodgers (NL), 1964	17
Catcher	Jimmie Foxx, Phi. A's (AL), 1925	17
Right-Handed Pitcher	Fred Chapman, Phi. A's (AA), 1887	14
Left-Handed Pitcher	Joe Nuxhall, Cin. Reds (NL), 1944	15

Players Who Played During Most Presidential Administrations

Cap Anson (1876–97)..8..Ulysses S. Grant (1876–77)
Rutherford B. Hayes (1887–81)
James A. Garfield (1881)
Chester A. Arthur (1881–85)
Grover Cleveland (1885–89)
Benjamin Harrison (1889–93)
Grover Cleveland (1893–97)
William McKinley (1897)

Jim O'Rourke (1876–93, 1904) ....8..Ulysses S. Grant (1876–77)
Rutherford B. Hayes (1877–81)
James A. Garfield (1881)
Chester A. Arthur (1881–85)
Grover Cleveland (1885–89)
Benjamin Harrison (1889–93)
Grover Cleveland (1893–97)
Theodore Roosevelt (1904)

Nick Altrock (1898, 1902–09, 1912–15, 1918–19,
1924, 1929, 1931, 1933) ....7..William McKinley (1898)
Theodore Roosevelt (1902–09)
William Howard Taft (1909–13)
Woodrow Wilson (1913–19)
Calvin Coolidge (1924)
Herbert Hoover (1929, 1931)
Franklin D. Roosevelt (1933)

Jim Kaat (1959–83)......................................7.........................Dwight D. Eisenhower (1959–61)
John F. Kennedy (1961–63)
Lyndon B. Johnson (1963–69)
Richard M. Nixon (1969–74)
Gerald Ford (1974–77)
Jimmy Carter (1977–81)
Ronald Reagan (1981–83)

Nolan Ryan (1966, 1968–93) ....7.............................Lyndon B. Johnson (1966, 1968)
Richard M. Nixon (1969–74)
Gerald Ford (1974–77)
Jimmy Carter (1977–81)
Ronald Reagan (1981–89)
George H.W. Bush (1980–93)
Bill Clinton (1993)

Players Playing Most Seasons with One Address (One Club, One City in Majors)

23 ....Brooks Robinson, Bal. Orioles (AL), 1955–77
23 ....Carl Yastrzemski, Bos. Red Sox (AL), 1961–83
22 ....Cap Anson, Chi. Cubs (Colts) (NL), 1876–97
22 ....Al Kaline, Det. Tigers (AL), 1953–74
22 ....Stan Musial, St.L. Cardinals (NL), 1941–44 and 1946–63
22 ....Mel Ott, N.Y. Giants (NL), 1926–47
21 ....George Brett, K.C. Royals (AL), 1973–93
21 ....Walter Johnson, Was. Senators (AL), 1907–27
21 ....Ted Lyons, Chi. White Sox (AL), 1923–42 and 1946
21 ....Cal Ripken Jr., Bal. Orioles (AL), 1981–2001
21 ....Willie Stargell, Pit. Pirates (NL), 1962–82
20 ....Luke Appling, Chi. White Sox (AL), 1930–43 and 1945–50

continued on next page

20	Red Faber, Chi. White Sox (AL), 1914–33
20	Tony Gwynn, S.D. Padres (NL), 1982–2001
20	Mel Harder, Cle. Indians (AL), 1928–47
20	Alan Trammell, Det. Tigers (AL), 1977–96
20	Robin Yount, Mil. Brewers (AL), 1974–93
20	Derek Jeter, N.Y. Yankees (AL), 1995–2014

Players Who Played 2500 Games in One Uniform (Post-1900)

3308	Carl Yastrzemski, Bos. Red Sox (AL), 1961–83
3026	Stan Musial, St.L. Cardinals (NL), 1941–44 and 1946–63
3001	Cal Ripken Jr., Bal. Orioles (AL), 1981–2001
2896	Brooks Robinson, Bal. Orioles (AL), 1955–77
2856	Robin Yount, Mil. Brewers (AL), 1974–93
2850	Craig Biggio, Hou. Astros (NL), 1988–2007
2834	Al Kaline, Det. Tigers (AL), 1953–74
2747	Derek Jeter, N.Y. Yankees, (AL), 1995–2004
2732	Mel Ott, N.Y. Giants (NL), 1926–47
2707	George Brett, K.C. Royals (AL), 1973–93
2528	Ernie Banks, Chi. Cubs (NL), 1953–71

Players Playing Most Seasons in City of Birth

22	Phil Cavarretta, Chi. Cubs (NL), 1934–53, and Chi. White Sox (AL), 1954–55
19	Pete Rose, Cin. Reds (NL), 1963–78 and 1984–86
19	Barry Larkin, Cin. Reds (NL), 1986–2004
18	Ed Kranepool, N.Y. Mets (NL), 1962–79
17	Lou Gehrig, N.Y. Yankees (AL), 1923–39
16	Harry Davis, Phi. A's (AL), 1901–11 and 1913–17
16	Whitey Ford, N.Y. Yankees (AL), 1950 and 1953–67

Players with Same Surname as Town of Birth

Loren Bader, pitcher (1912, 1917–18), born in Bader, Illinois
Verne Clemons, catcher (1916, 1919–24), born in Clemons, Iowa
Estel Crabtree, outfield (1929, 1931–33, 1941–44), born in Crabtree, Ohio
Charlie Gassaway, pitcher, (1944–46), born in Gassaway, Tennessee
Elmer "Slim" Love, pitcher, (1913, 1916–20), born in Love, Missouri
Jack Ogden, pitcher, (1918, 1928–29, 1931–32), born in Ogden, Pennsylvania
Curly Ogden, pitcher, (1922–26), born in Ogden, Pennsylvania
Steve Phoenix, pitcher (1984–95), born in Phoenix, Arizona
Happy Townsend, pitcher (1901–06), born in Townsend, Delaware
George Turbeville, pitcher (1935–37), born in Turbeville, South Carolina

Players with Longest Given Names

Alan Mitchell Edward George Patrick Henry Gallagher ("Al"), third base (1970–73)	45 characters
Christian Frederick Albert John Henry David Betzel ("Bruno"), infield (1914–18)	44 characters
Calvin Coolidge Julius Caesar Tuskahoma McLish ("Cal"), pitcher, (1944, 1946–49, 1951, 1956–64)	41 characters

Players with Palindromic Surnames*

Dean Anna, pitcher (2014–15)	Dave Otto, pitcher (1987–94)
Truck Hannah, catcher (1918–20)	Johnny Reder, first base (1932)
Toby Harrah, infield (1969, 1971–80)	Mark Salas, catcher (1984–91)
Eddie Kazak, shortstop (1948–52)	Juan Salas, pitcher (2006–08)
Dick Nen, first base (1963, 1965–68, 1970)	Marino Salas, pitcher (2008)
Robb Nen, pitcher (1993–2002)	Fernando Salas, pitcher (2010–19)

* Last name spelled the same forward and backward.

Most Common Last Names in Baseball History*

Smith	168	Brown	89
Johnson	115	Williams	82
Jones	104	Wilson	78
Miller	92	Davis	77

* From 1871 through 2022.

Number of Major League Players by First Letter of Last Name*

A	642	N	360
B	1930	O	381
C	1573	P	974
D	996	Q	53
E	370	R	1129
F	726	S	1992
G	1116	T	676
H	1461	U	64
I	63	V	286
J	527	W	1128
K	747	X	0
L	931	Y	125
M	2119	Z	100

* From 1871 through 2022.

Third Basemen on Tinker-to-Evers-to-Chance Chicago Cubs Teams*

Doc Casey	1903–05	388 games
Harry Steinfeldt	1906–10	729 games
Heinie Zimmerman	1908, 1910	23 games
Solly Hoffman	1905–08	20 games
Otto Williams	1903–04	7 games
John Kane	1909–10	7 games
Tommy Raub	1903	4 games
George Moriarty	1903–04	3 games
Bobby Lowe	1903	1 game
Broadway Aleck Smith	1904	1 game

* Famed Hall of Fame double-play combination for the Chi. Cubs, 1903–10.

First Designated Hitter for Each Major League Team

American League

Bal. Orioles	Terry Crowley (vs. Mil. Brewers), Apr. 6, 1973	2-for-4
Bos. Red Sox	Orlando Cepeda (vs. N.Y. Yankees), Apr. 6, 1973	0-for-6
Cal. Angels	Tom McCraw (vs. K.C. Royals), Apr. 6, 1973	1-for-4
Chi. White Sox	Mike Andrews (vs. Tex. Rangers), Apr. 7, 1973	1-for-3
Cle. Indians	John Ellis (vs. Det. Tigers), Apr. 7, 1973	0-for-4
Det. Tigers	Gates Brown (vs. Cle. Indians), Apr. 7, 1973	0-for-4
K.C. Royals	Ed Kirkpatrick (vs. Cal. Angels), Apr. 6, 1973	0-for-3
Mil. Brewers	Ollie Brown (vs. Bal. Orioles), Apr. 6, 1973	0-for-3
Min. Twins	Tony Oliva (vs. Oak. A's), Apr. 6, 1973	2-for-4
N.Y. Yankees	Ron Blomberg* (vs. Bos. Red Sox), Apr. 6, 1973	1-for-3
Oak. A's	Bill North (vs. Min. Twins), Apr. 6, 1973	2-for-5

continued on next page

Sea. Mariners	Dave Collins (vs. Cal. Angels), Apr. 6, 1977	0-for-4
T.B. Devil Rays	Paul Sorrento (vs. Det. Tigers), Mar. 31, 1998	1-for-5
Tex. Rangers	Rico Carty (vs. Chi. White Sox), Apr. 7, 1973	1-for-4
Tor. Blue Jays	Otto Velez (vs. Chi. White Sox), Apr. 7, 1977	2-for-4

National League

Ari. D'backs	Kelly Stinnett (vs. Oak. A's, AL), Jun. 5, 1998	1-for-3
Atl. Braves	Keith Lockhart (vs. Tor. Blue Jays, AL), Jun. 16, 1997	0-for-4
Chi. Cubs	Dave Clark (vs. Chi. White Sox, AL), Jun. 16, 1997	1-for-4
Cin. Reds	Eddie Taubensee (vs. Cle. Indians, AL), Jun. 16, 1997	0-for-3
Col. Rockies	Dante Bichette (vs. Sea. Mariners, AL), Jun. 12, 1997	3-for-5
Fla. Marlins	Jim Eisenreich (vs. Det. Tigers, AL), Jun. 16, 1997	1-for-5
Hou. Astros	Sean Berry (vs. K.C. Royals, AL), Jun. 16, 1997	1-for-4
L.A. Dodgers	Mike Piazza (vs. Oak. A's, AL), Jun. 12, 1997	3-for-4
Mon. Expos	Jose Vidro (vs. Bal. Orioles, AL), Jun. 16, 1997	0-for-4
N.Y. Mets	Butch Huskey (vs. N.Y. Yankees, AL), Jun. 16, 1997	2-for-4
Phi. Phillies	Darren Daulton (vs. Bos. Red Sox, AL), Jun. 16, 1997	1-for-5
Pit. Pirates	Mark Smith (vs. Min. Twins, AL), Jun. 16, 1997	1-for-4
St.L. Cardinals	Dmitri Young (vs. Mil. Brewers, AL), Jun. 16, 1997	1-for-4
S.D. Padres	Rickey Henderson (vs. Ana. Angels, AL), Jun. 12, 1997	2-for-5
S.F. Giants	Glenallen Hill** (vs. Tex. Rangers, AL), Jun. 12, 1997	0-for-3

* First AL designated hitter.

** First NL designated hitter.

Players Killed as Direct Result of Injuries Sustained in Major League Games

Maurice "Doc" Powers, catcher, Phi. A's (AL) .... Died Apr. 26, 1909, after three operations for "intestinal problems" after running into railing on Apr. 12, 1909, at Shibe Park inaugural game.

Ray Chapman, shortstop, Cle. Indians (AL) .... Died Aug. 17, 1920, after being hit by pitch thrown by N.Y. Yankees pitcher Carl Mays at the Polo Grounds on Aug. 16, 1920.

Players Who Played for Three New York Teams

Dan Brouthers .... Tro. Trojans (NL), 1879–80
Buff. Bisons (NL), 1881–85
N.Y. Giants (NL), 1904

Jack Doyle.. N.Y. Giants (NL), 1893–95, 1898–1900, and 1902
Brk. Dodgers (NL), 1903–04
N.Y. Yankees (AL), 1905

Dude Esterbrook... Buff. Bisons (NL), 1880
N.Y. Metropolitans (AA), 1883–84 and 1887
N.Y. Gothams–Giants (NL), 1885–86 and 1890
Brk. Dodgers (NL), 1891

Burleigh Grimes .... Brk. Dodgers (NL), 1918–26
N.Y. Giants (NL), 1927
N.Y. Yankees (AL), 1934

Benny Kauff... N.Y. Yankees (AL), 1912
Brk. Tip-Tops (FL), 1915
N.Y. Giants (NL), 1916–20

Willie Keeler .... N.Y. Giants (NL), 1892–93 and 1910
Brk. Dodgers (NL), 1893 and 1899–1902
N.Y. Yankees (AL), 1903–09

continued on next page

Tony Lazzeri ....N.Y. Yankees (AL), 1926–37
Brk. Dodgers (NL), 1939
N.Y. Giants (NL), 1939
Sal Maglie ....N.Y. Giants (NL), 1945 and 1950–55
Brk. Dodgers (NL), 1956–57
N.Y. Yankees (AL), 1957–58
Fred Merkle ....N.Y. Giants (NL), 1907–16
Brk. Dodgers (NL), 1916–17
N.Y. Yankees (AL), 1925–26
Jack Nelson ..../........... Tro. Trojans (NL), 1879
N.Y. Metropolitans (AA), 1883–87
N.Y. Giants (NL), 1887
Brk. Bridegrooms (AA), 1890
Lefty O'Doul ....N.Y. Yankees (AL), 1919–20 and 1922
N.Y. Giants (NL), 1928 and 1933–34
Brk. Dodgers (NL), 1931–33
Dave Orr ....N.Y. Gothams (NL), 1883
N.Y. Metropolitans (AA), 1884–87
Brk. Bridegrooms (AA), 1888
Brk. Wonders (PL), 1890
Jack Taylor ....Brk. Dodgers (NL), 1920–25 and 1935
N.Y. Giants (NL), 1927
N.Y. Yankees (AL), 1934
Monte Ward..N.Y. Gothams–Giants (NL), 1883–89 and 1893–94
Brk. Wonders (PL), 1890
Brk. Bridegrooms (NL), 1891–92

Players Who Played for Both Original and Expansion Washington Senators

Rudy Hernandez, pitcher ....Original Senators, 1960 ....Expansion Senators, 1961
Hector Maestri, pitcher...............................Original Senators, 1960 ....Expansion Senators, 1961
Pedro Pamos, pitcher ....Original Senators, 1955–60 ....Expansion Senators, 1970
Camilo Pascual, pitcher...............................Original Senators, 1954–60 ....Expansion Senators, 1967–69
Zoilo Versalles, shortstop ....Original Senators, 1959–60 ....Expansion Senators, 1969

Players Who Played for Both Kansas City Athletics and Kansas City Royals

Moe Drabowsky, pitcher.............................K.C. A's, 1963–65 .... K.C. Royals, 1969–70
Aurelio Monteagudo, pitcher......................K.C. A's, 1963–66 .... K.C. Royals, 1970
Ken Sanders, pitcher...................................K.C. A's, 1964, 1966 .... K.C. Royals, 1976
Dave Wickersham, pitcher..........................K.C. A's, 1960–63 .... K.C. Royals, 1969

Players Who Played for Both Milwaukee Braves and Milwaukee Brewers

Hank Aaron, outfield and designated hitter............................Mil. Braves, 1954–65..................... Mil. Brewers, 1975–76
Felipe Alou, outfield...Mil. Braves, 1964–65............................Mil. Brewers, 1974
Phil Roof, catcher ....Mil. Braves, 1961 and 1964............ Mil. Brewers, 1970–71

Pitchers Who Gave Up Most Hits to Pete Rose

Phil Niekro	64	Claude Osteen	38
Don Sutton	60	Ron Reed	38
Juan Marichal	42	Bob Gibson	36
Gaylord Perry	42	Ferguson Jenkins	36
Joe Niekro	39		

Pitchers Who Gave Up Home Runs to Both Mark McGwire and Barry Bonds in Their Record-Breaking Seasons (1998 and 2001)

Scott Elarton .... Pitching for Hou. Astros (NL), gave up #40 to McGwire
Pitching for Col. Rockies (NL), gave up #61 and #62 to Bonds
Bobby Jones .... Pitching for N.Y. Mets (NL), gave up #47 to McGwire
Pitching for S.D. Padres (NL), gave up #30 to Bonds
John Thomson .... Pitching for Col. Rockies (NL), gave up #25 and #44 to McGwire
Pitching for Col. Rockies (NL), gave up #25 and #57 to Bonds
Steve Trachsel .... Pitching for Chi. Cubs (NL), gave up #62 to McGwire
Pitching for N.Y. Mets (NL), gave up #15 to Bonds

Players Born on Leap Year Day (February 29)

	Year of Birth		Year of Birth
Dickey Pearce, shortstop (1871–77)	1836	Al Autry, pitcher (1976)	1952
Sadie Houck, shortstop (1879–81, 1883–87)	1856	Jerry Fry, catcher (1978)	1956
Ed Appleton, pitcher (1913, 1916)	1892	Bill Long, pitcher (1985, 1987–91)	1960
Roy Parker, pitcher (1919)	1896	Terrence Long, outfield (1999–2006)	1976
Ralph Miller, infield (1920–21, 1924)	1896	Gerardo Concepcion, pitcher (2016)	1992
Pepper Martin, outfield (1928, 1930–40, 1944)	1904	Stefan Crichton, pitcher (2017)	1992
Al Rosen, third base (1947–56)	1924	Bligh Madris, outfield (2022)	1996
Steve Mingori, pitcher (1970–79)	1944		

Players Who Played on Four of California's Five Major League Teams

Mike Aldrete .... S.F. Giants, 1986–88; S.D. Padres, 1991; Oak. A's, 1993–95; and Cal. Angels, 1995–96
Trevor Cahill .... Oak A's, 2009–11, 2018; S.D. Padres, 2017; L.A, Angels, 2019; and S.F. Giants, 2020
John D'Acquisto .... S.F. Giants, 1973–76; S.D. Padres, 1977–80; Cal. Angels, 1981; and Oak. A's, 1982
Steve Finley .... S.D. Padres ,1995–98; L.A. Dodgers, 2004; L.A. Angels, 2005, and S.F. Giants, 2006
Rickey Henderson .... Oak. A's, 1979–84, 1989–93, 1994–95, and 1998; S.D. Padres, 1996–97;
Ana. Angels, 1997; and L.A. Dodgers, 2003
Stan Javier .... Oak. A's, 1986–90 and 1994–95; L.A. Dodgers, 1990–92; Cal. Angels, 1993; and S.F. Giants, 1996–99
Jay Johnstone .... Cal. Angels, 1966–70; Oak. A's, 1973; S.D. Padres, 1979; and L.A. Dodgers, 1980–82 and 1985
Scott Kazmir .... L.A. Angels, 2009–11; Oak A's, 2014–15; L.A. Dodgers, 2016; and S.F. Giants, 2021
Dave Kingman .... S.F. Giants, 1971–74; S.D. Padres, 1977; Cal. Angels, 1977; and Oak. A's, 1984–86
Elias Sosa .... S.F. Giants, 1972–74; L.A. Dodgers, 1976–77; Oak. A's, 1978; and S.D. Padres, 1983
Derrel Thomas.... S.D. Padres, 1972–74 and 1978; S.F. Giants, 1975–77; L.A. Dodgers, 1979–83; and Cal. Angels, 1984
Brett Tomko .... S.D. Padres, 2002, 2007–08; S.F. Giants, 2004–05; L.A. Dodgers, 2006–07; and Oak. A's, 2009

Tallest Players in Major League History

6'8" .... Mark Acre, pitcher (1994–97)
Dellin Betances, pitcher (2011, 2013–21)
Darren Clarke, pitcher (2007)
Tony Clark, first base (1995–2009)
Gene Conley, pitcher (1952, 1954–63)
Steve Ellsworth, pitcher (1988)
Doug Fister, pitcher (2009–18)
Brian Flynn, pitcher (2013–14, 2016–19)
Nate Freiman, first base (2013–14)
Tyler Glasnow*, pitcher (2016–)
Tayron Guerrero, pitcher (2016, 2018–19)
Lee Guetterman, pitcher (1984, 1986–93, 1995–96)
Jason Hirsh, pitcher (2006–08)
Gabe Klobosits, pitcher (2021)
Graeme Lloyd, pitcher (1993–2003)
Kameron Loe, pitcher (2004–08, 2010–13)
Brandon McCarthy, pitcher (2005–09, 2011–18)
Trevor Megill*, pitcher (2021–)
Chris Martin*, pitcher (2014–15, 2018–)

continued on next page

6'8" ....Nate Minchey, pitcher (1993–97)
Mike Naymick, pitcher (1939–40, 1943–44)
Jeff Nelson, pitcher (1992–2006)
Logan Ondrusek pitcher (2010–14, 2016)
Angel Pedermo, pitcher (2020–21)
Max Povse, pitcher (2017)
J.R. Richard, pitcher (1971–80)
Stephen Ridings, pitcher (2021)
Adam Russell pitcher (2008–11)
Michael Schwimer pitcher (2011–12)
Mike Smithson, pitcher (1982–89)
Kyle Snyder, pitcher (2003–2008)
Phil Stockman, pitcher (2006–2008)
Billy Taylor, pitcher (1994, 1996–98)
Joe Vitko, pitcher (1992)
Chris Volstad, pitcher (2008–13, 2015, 2017–18)
Tyler Wells, pitcher (2021–)
Sean West, pitcher (2009–10)
Stefan Wever, pitcher (1982)
Brad Wieck, pitcher (2018–21)
6'9" ....Terry Bross, pitcher (1991, 1993)
Johnny Gee, pitcher (1939, 1941, 1943–46)
Mark Hendrickson, pitcher (2002–11)
John Holdzkom, pitcher (2014)
Adam McCreery, pitcher (2018)
Alex Meyer, pitcher (2015–17)
Kam Mickolio, pitcher (2008–11)
Jeff Niemann, pitcher (2008–12)
Bailey Ober*, pitcher (2021–)
Johan Quezada, pitcher (2020)
6'10" ....Andrew Brackman, pitcher (2011)
Eric Hillman, pitcher (1992–94)
Sean Hjelle*, pitcher (2022–)
Randy Johnson, pitcher (1988–2009)
Andy Sisco, pitcher (2005–07)
Aaron Slegers, pitcher (2017–21)
Chris Young, pitcher (2004–17)
6'11" ....Jon Rauch, pitcher (2002, 2004–13)
* Still active.

Shortest Players in Major League History

3'7" ....Eddie Gaedel, pinch hitter (1951)
5'3" ....Jess Cortazzo, pinch hitter (1923)
Yo-Yo Davalillo, shortstop (1953)
Bob Emmerich, outfield (1923)
Bill Finley, outfield/catcher (1886)
Stubby Magner, infield (1911)
Mike McCormick, third base (1904)
Tom Morrison, infield (1895–96)
Yale Murphy, shortstop/outfield (1894–95, 1897)
Dickey Pearce, shortstop (1871–77)
Frank Shannon, infield (1892, 1896)
Cub Stricker, second base (1882–85, 1887–93)

Teammates the Longest

19 years	Derek Jeter (shortstop) and Mariano Rivera (pitcher), N.Y. Yankees, 1995–2013
18 years	Joe Judge (first base) and Sam Rice (outfield), Was. Senators; 1915–32
18 years	Alan Trammell (shortstop) and Lou Whitaker (second base), Det. Tigers, 1977–95
17 years	Derek Jeter (shortstop) and Jorge Posada (catcher), N.Y. Yankees, 1995–2011
17 years	Jorge Posada (catcher) and Mariano Rivera (pitcher), N.Y. Yankees, 1995–2011
15 years	Derek Jeter (shortstop) and Andy Pettitte (pitcher), N.Y. Yankees, 1995–2003, 2007–10, 2012–13
15 years	Andy Pettitte (pitcher) and Mariano Rivera (pitcher), N.Y. Yankees, 1995–2003, 2007–10, 2012–13
15 years	Jeff Bagwell (first base) and Craig Biggio (second base/outfield), Hou. Astros, 1991–2005
14 years	Duke Snider (outfield) and Carl Furillo (outfield), Brk.–L.A. Dodgers, 1947–60
13 years	Joe Judge (first base) and Walter Johnson (pitcher), Was. Senators, 1915–27
13 years	Andy Pettitte (pitcher) and Jorge Posada (catcher), N.Y. Yankees, 1995–2003, 2007–10

Teammates with 300 Wins and 500 Home Runs

Lefty Grove (pitcher) and Jimmie Foxx (batter) ....1941 Bos. Red Sox (AL)

Warren Spahn (pitcher) and Willie Mays (batter) ....1965 S.F. Giants (NL)

Don Sutton (pitcher) and Reggie Jackson (batter) ....1985 Cal. Angels (AL)

Greg Maddux (pitcher) and Sammy Sosa (batter)..2004 Chi. Cubs (NL)

New Baseball Stadiums Built Since 2005

Team	Stadium	Opened	Capacity	Surface	Approximate Cost (in millions)	Center Field Distance
Mia. Marlins	loanDepot Park	2012	37,422	Grass	$515	415' (126 m)
Min. Twins	Target Field	2010	40,000	Grass	$522	404' (124 m)
N.Y. Mets	Citi Field	2009	41,800	Grass	$850	408' (124 m)
N.Y. Yankees	Yankee Stadium	2009	52,325	Grass	$1300	408' (124.3 m)
Was. Nationals	Nationals Park	2008	41,888	Grass	$611	402' (122.5 m)
St.L. Cardinals	Busch Stadium	2006	46,861	Grass	$346	400' (122 m)
Atl. Braves	Truist Park	2017	41,149	Grass	$622	400' (122 m)
Tex. Rangers	Globe Life Field	2020	40,300	Artificial Turf	$1100	407' (124 m)

Players Traded for Themselves

Harry Chiti (Apr. 26, 1962 and Jun. 15, 1962)

Archie Corbin (Nov. 20, 1992 and Feb. 5, 1993)

Clint Courtney (Jan. 24, 1961 and Mar. 14, 1961)

Brad Gulden (Nov. 18, 1980 and May 18, 1981)

John MacDonald (Jul. 22, 2005 and Nov. 10, 2005)

Dickie Noles (Sep. 22, 1987 and Oct. 23, 1987)

Mark Ross (Dec. 9, 1985 and Mar. 31, 1986)

Players Wearing Numbers "0" and "00"

"0"

Brandon Barnes, Cle. Indians (2018)

Alex Blandino, Cin. Reds (2021)

Austin Dean, St. L. Cardinals (2020–21)

Delino DeShields, Cle. Indians (2020)

Yunel Escobar, L.A. Angels (2016–17)

Kent Emanuel, Hou. Astros (2021)

Mario Feliciano, Mil. Brewers (2021–22)

Oscar Gamble, Chi. White Sox (1985)

Andres Gimenez, Cle. Indians–Guardians (2012–22)

Terrance Gore, K.C. Royals (2014)

Sam Haggerty, Sea. Mariners (2021–22)

Billy Hamilton, Chi. White Sox, Min. Twins (2020–21)

Nick Heath, K.C. Royals (2020)

L.J. Hoes, Hou. Astros (2014–15)

Rafael Lopez, S.D. Padres (2018)

Candy Maldonado, Tor. Blue Jays (1995)

Jordy Mercer, N.Y. Yankees (2020)

Terry McDaniel, N.Y. Mets (1991)

Oddibe McDowell, Tex. Rangers (1985–88)

Al Oliver, L.A. Dodgers, S.F. Giants, Mon. Expos, Phi. Phillies, Tex. Rangers, Tor. Blue Jays (1978–85)

Omar Quintanilla, N.Y. Mets (2014)

Junior Ortiz, Pit. Pirates, Min. Twins, Cle. Indians, Tex. Rangers (1989–94)

Adam Ottavino, Col. Rockies (2013–)

Rey Ordonez, N.Y. Mets (1996–97)

Brandon Phillips, Bos. Red Sox (2018)

Kerry Robinson, St.L. Cardinals (2002–03)

Mark Ryal, Chi. White Sox (1985)

George Scott, K.C. Royals (1979)

Mallex Smith, T.B. Rays, Sea. Mariners (2017–20)

Marcus Stroman, N.Y. Mets, Chi. Cubs (2021–22)

Franklin Stubbs, Mil. Brewers (1991–92)

Taylor Walls, T.B. Rays (2022)

U.L. Washington, Pit. Pirates (1986)

"00"

Don Baylor, Oak. A's (1988)

Brennen Boesch, L.A. Angels (2014)

Bobby Bonds, St.L. Cardinals (1980)

Jose Canseco, Tor. Blue Jays (1998)

Jack Clark, S.D. Padres (1990)

Tony Clark, N.Y. Mets (2003)

Paul Dade, Cle. Indians (1977–79)

Curtis Goodwin, Cin. Reds (1996–97)

Cliff Johnson, Tor. Blue Jays (1985–86)

Jeff Leonard, Mil. Brewers, S.F. Giants, Sea. Mariners (1987–90)

Curt Leskanic, Mil. Brewers (2000–01)

John Mayberry, Hou. Astros (1968)

Eddie Milner, Cin. Reds (1988)

Bobo Newsom, Was. Senators (1943, 1946–47)

Omar Olivares, St.L. Cardinals, Phi. Phillies (1993, 1995)

Joe Page, Pit. Pirates (1954)

Kerry Robinson, Cin. Reds (1999)

Brandon Watson, Cin. Reds, Was. Nationals (2005–07)

Rick White, Cle. Indians, Pit. Pirates, Cin. Reds, Phi. Phillies (2004–06)

Brian Wilson, L.A. Dodgers (2013–14)

Taijuan Walker, Tor. Blue Jays (2020)

PART 2
Team-by-Team Histories

Baltimore Orioles

Dates of Operation: 1954–present (69 years)
Overall Record: 5466 wins, 5398 losses (.503)
Stadiums: Memorial Stadium, 1954–91; Oriole Park at Camden Yards, 1992–present (capacity: 45,971)

Year-by-Year Finishes

Year	Finish	Wins	Losses	Percentage	Games Behind	Manager	Attendance
1954	7th	54	100	.351	57.0	Jimmy Dykes	1,060,910
1955	7th	57	97	.370	39.0	Paul Richards	852,039
1956	6th	69	85	.448	28.0	Paul Richards	901,201
1957	5th	76	76	.500	21.0	Paul Richards	1,029,581
1958	6th	74	79	.484	17.5	Paul Richards	829,991
1959	6th	74	80	.481	20.0	Paul Richards	891,926
1960	2nd	89	65	.578	8.0	Paul Richards	1,187,849
1961	3rd	95	67	.586	14.0	Paul Richards, Luman Harris	951,089
1962	7th	77	85	.475	19.0	Billy Hitchcock	790,254
1963	4th	86	76	.531	18.5	Billy Hitchcock	774,343
1964	3rd	97	65	.599	2.0	Hank Bauer	1,116,215
1965	3rd	94	68	.580	8.0	Hank Bauer	781,649
1966	1st	97	63	.606	+9.0	Hank Bauer	1,203,366
1967	6th (Tie)	76	85	.472	15.5	Hank Bauer	955,053
1968	2nd	91	71	.562	12.0	Hank Bauer, Earl Weaver	943,977
East Division							
1969	1st	109	53	.673	+19.0	Earl Weaver	1,058,168
1970	1st	108	54	.667	+15.0	Earl Weaver	1,057,069
1971	1st	101	57	.639	+12.0	Earl Weaver	1,023,037
1972	3rd	80	74	.519	5.0	Earl Weaver	899,950
1973	1st	97	65	.599	+8.0	Earl Weaver	958,667
1974	1st	91	71	.562	+2.0	Earl Weaver	962,572
1975	2nd	90	69	.566	4.5	Earl Weaver	1,002,157
1976	2nd	88	74	.543	10.5	Earl Weaver	1,058,609
1977	2nd (Tie)	97	64	.602	2.5	Earl Weaver	1,195,769
1978	4th	90	71	.559	9.0	Earl Weaver	1,051,724
1979	1st	102	57	.642	+8.0	Earl Weaver	1,681,009
1980	2nd	100	62	.617	3.0	Earl Weaver	1,797,438
1981*	2nd/4th	59	46	.562	2.0/2.0	Earl Weaver	1,024,652
1982	2nd	94	68	.580	1.0	Earl Weaver	1,613,031
1983	1st	98	64	.605	+6.0	Joe Altobelli	2,042,071
1984	5th	85	77	.525	19.0	Joe Altobelli	2,045,784
1985	4th	83	78	.516	16.0	Joe Altobelli, Earl Weaver	2,132,387

Year	Finish	Wins	Losses	Percentage	Games Behind	Manager	Attendance
1986	7th	73	89	.451	22.5	Earl Weaver	1,973,176
1987	6th	67	95	.414	31.0	Cal Ripken Sr.	1,835,692
1988	7th	54	107	.335	34.5	Cal Ripken Sr., Frank Robinson	1,660,738
1989	2nd	87	75	.537	2.0	Frank Robinson	2,535,208
1990	5th	76	85	.472	11.5	Frank Robinson	2,415,189
1991	6th	67	95	.414	24.0	Frank Robinson, Johnny Oates	2,552,753
1992	3rd	89	73	.549	7.0	Johnny Oates	3,567,819
1993	3rd (Tie)	85	77	.525	10.0	Johnny Oates	3,644,965
1994	2nd	63	49	.563	6.5	Johnny Oates	2,535,359
1995	3rd	71	73	.493	15.0	Phil Regan	3,098,475
1996	2nd	88	74	.543	4.0	Davey Johnson	3,646,950
1997	1st	98	64	.605	+2.0	Davey Johnson	3,711,132
1998	4th	79	83	.488	35.0	Ray Miller	3,685,194
1999	4th	78	84	.481	20.0	Ray Miller	3,433,150
2000	4th	74	88	.457	13.5	Mike Hargrove	3,295,128
2001	4th	63	98	.391	32.5	Mike Hargrove	3,094,841
2002	4th	67	95	.414	36.5	Mike Hargrove	2,682,917
2003	4th	71	91	.438	30.0	Mike Hargrove	2,454,523
2004	3rd	78	84	.481	23.0	Lee Mazzilli	2,747,573
2005	4th	74	88	.457	21.0	Lee Mazzilli, Sam Perlozzo	2,624,740
2006	4th	70	92	.432	27.0	Sam Perlozzo	2,153,139
2007	4th	69	93	.426	27.0	Sam Perlozzo, Dave Trembley	2,164,822
2008	5th	68	93	.422	28.5	Dave Trembley	1,950,075
2009	5th	64	98	.395	39.0	Dave Trembley	1,907,163
2010	5th	66	96	.407	30.0	Dave Trembley, Juan Samuel, Buck Showalter	1,733,019
2011	5th	69	93	.425	28.0	Buck Showalter	1,755,461
2012	2nd	93	69	.574	2.0	Buck Showalter	2,102,240
2013	3rd	85	77	.525	12.0	Buck Showalter	2,357,561
2014	1st	96	66	.593	+12.0	Buck Showalter	2,464,473
2015	3rd	81	81	.500	12.0	Buck Showalter	2,281,202
2016	2nd(Tie)	89	73	.549	4.0	Buck Showalter	2,172,344
2017	5th	75	87	.463	18.0	Buck Showalter	2,028,424
2018	5th	47	115	.290	61.0	Buck Showalter	1,564,192
2019	5th	54	108	.333	49.0	Brandon Hyde	1,307,807
2020	4th	25	35	.417	15.0	Brandon Hyde	0
2021	5th	52	110	.321	48.0	Brandon Hyde	793,229
2022	4th	83	79	.512	16.0	Brandon Hyde	1,368,367

* Split season.

Awards

Most Valuable Player

Brooks Robinson, third base, 1964

Frank Robinson, outfield, 1966

Boog Powell, first base, 1970

Cal Ripken Jr., shortstop, 1983

Cal Ripken Jr., shortstop, 1991

Rookie of the Year

Ron Hansen, shortstop, 1960

Curt Blefary, outfield, 1965

Al Bumbry, outfield, 1973

Eddie Murray, first base, 1977

Cal Ripken Jr., shortstop and third base, 1982

Gregg Olson, pitcher, 1989

Cy Young

Mike Cuellar (co-winner), 1969

Jim Palmer, 1973

Jim Palmer, 1975

Jim Palmer, 1976

Mike Flanagan, 1979

Steve Stone, 1980

Manager of the Year (Since 1983)

Frank Robinson, 1989

Davey Johnson, 1997

Buck Showalter, 2014

Hall of Famers Who Played for the Orioles

Luis Aparicio, shortstop, 1963–67

Harold Baines, designated hitter,

1993–95, 1997–99, 2000

Vladimir Guerrero, designated hitter, 2011

Reggie Jackson, outfield, 1976

George Kell, third base, 1956–57

Eddie Murray, first base and designated hitter, 1977–88 and 1996

Mike Mussia, pitcher, 1991–2000

Jim Palmer, pitcher, 1965–84

Tim Raines, outfield, 2001

Cal Ripken Jr., shortstop and third base, 1981–2001

Robin Roberts, pitcher, 1962–65

Brooks Robinson, third base, 1955–77

Frank Robinson, outfield, 1966–71

Lee Smith, pitcher, 1994

Jim Thome, designated hitter, 2012

Hoyt Wilhelm, pitcher, 1958–62

Retired Numbers

4 ....Earl Weaver
5 ....Brooks Robinson
8 ....Cal Ripken Jr.
20 ....Frank Robinson
22 ....Jim Palmer
33 ....Eddie Murray

League Leaders, Batting

Batting Average, Season

Frank Robinson, 1966 .... .316

Home Runs, Season

Frank Robinson, 1966 49
Eddie Murray, 1981 ....22 (Tie)
Chris Davis, 2013 53
Nelson Cruz, 2014 40
Chris Davis, 2015 47
Mark Trumbo, 2016 47

RBIs, Season

Brooks Robinson, 1964 118
Frank Robinson, 1966 122
Lee May, 1976 109
Eddie Murray, 1981 78
Miguel Tejada, 2004 150
Chris Davis, 2013 138

Stolen Bases, Season

Luis Aparicio, 1963 40
Luis Aparicio, 1964 57
Brady Anderson, 1992 53
Brian Roberts, 2008 50
Jorge Mateo, 2022 35

Total Bases, Season

Frank Robinson, 1966 367
Cal Ripken Jr., 1991...................368
Chris Davis, 2013......................370

Most Hits, Season

Cal Ripken Jr., 1983...................211

Most Runs, Season

Frank Robinson, 1966 122
Don Buford, 1971 99
Cal Ripken Jr., 1983...................121

Batting Feats

Triple Crown Winners

Frank Robinson, 1966 (.316 BA,
   49 HRs, 122 RBIs)

Hitting for the Cycle

Brooks Robinson, Jul. 15, 1960
Cal Ripken Jr., May 6, 1984
Aubrey Huff, Jun. 29, 2007
Felix Pie, Aug. 14, 2009
Jonathan Villar, Aug. 5, 2019
Austin Hays, Jun. 22, 2022

Six Hits in a Game

Cal Ripken Jr., Jun. 13, 1999

40 or More Home Runs, Season

53 .... Chris Davis, 2013
50 ....Brady Anderson, 1996
49 .... Frank Robinson, 1966
47 .... Chris Davis, 2015
47 .... Mark Trumbo, 2016
46 .... Jim Gentile, 1961
43 .... Rafael Palmeiro, 1998
40 ....Nelson Cruz, 2014

League Leaders, Pitching

Most Wins, Season

Chuck Estrada, 1960.............18 (Tie)
Mike Cuellar, 1970 ....24 (Tie)
Dave McNally, 1970 ....24 (Tie)
Jim Palmer, 1975 ....23 (Tie)
Jim Palmer, 1976 22
Jim Palmer, 1977 ....20 (Tie)
Mike Flanagan, 1979 23
Steve Stone, 1980.........................25
Dennis Martinez, 1981 ....14 (Tie)
Mike Boddicker, 1984 20
Mike Mussina, 1995 19

Most Strikeouts, Season

Bob Turley, 1954 185

Lowest ERA, Season

Hoyt Wilhelm, 1959..................2.19
Jim Palmer, 1973 ....2.40
Jim Palmer, 1975 ....2.09
Mike Boddicker, 1984 ....2.79

Most Saves, Season

Lee Smith, 1994...........................33
Randy Myers, 1997......................45
Jim Johnson, 2012 51
Jim Johnson, 2013 50
Zach Britton, 2016.......................47

Best Won–Lost Percentage, Season

Wally Bunker, 1964 .. 19–5....... .792
Jim Palmer, 1969 ...... 16–4...... .800
Mike Cuellar, 1970 ... 24–8...... .750
Dave McNally, 1971 . 21–5...... .808
Mike Cuellar, 1974 . 22–10...... .688
Mike Torrez, 1975 .... 20–9...... .690
Steve Stone, 1980..... 25–7...... .781
Mike Mussina, 1992 . 18–5...... .783

Pitching Feats

20 Wins, Season

Steve Barber, 1963 20–13
Dave McNally, 1968 22–10
Mike Cuellar, 1969 23–11
Dave McNally, 1969 20–7
Mike Cuellar, 1970 24–8
Dave McNally, 1970 24–9
Jim Palmer, 1970 20–10
Dave McNally, 1971 21–5
Pat Dobson, 1971 20–8
Mike Cuellar, 1971 20–9
Jim Palmer, 1971 20–9
Jim Palmer, 1972 21–10
Jim Palmer, 1973 22–9
Mike Cuellar, 1974 22–10
Jim Palmer, 1975 23–11
Mike Torrez, 1975 20–9
Jim Palmer, 1976 22–13
Wayne Garland, 1976 20–7
Jim Palmer, 1977 20–11
Jim Palmer, 1978 21–12
Mike Flanagan, 1979 23–9
Steve Stone, 1980.................... 25–7
Scott McGregor, 1980 20–8
Mike Boddicker, 1984 20–11

No-Hitters

Hoyt Wilhelm (vs. N.Y. Yankees),
   Sep. 2, 1958 (final: 1–0)
Steve Barber and Stu Miller (vs. Det.
   Tigers), Apr. 30, 1967 (final: 1–2)
Tom Phoebus (vs. Bos. Red Sox),
   Apr. 27, 1968 (final: 6–0)
Jim Palmer (vs. Oak. A's),
   Aug. 13, 1969 (final: 8–0)
Bob Milacki, Mike Flanagan,
   Mark Williamson, and Gregg Olson
   (vs. Oak. A's), Jul. 13, 1991(final: 2–0)
John Means (vs. Sea. Mariners),
   May 5, 2021 (final: 6–0)

No-Hitters Pitched Against

Bo Belinsky, L.A. Angels,
  May 5, 1962 (final: 2–0)

Nolan Ryan, Cal. Angels,
  Jun. 1, 1975 (final: 1–0)

Juan Nieves, Mil. Brewers (AL),
  Apr. 15, 1987 (final: 7–0)

Wilson Alvarez, Chi. White Sox,
  Aug. 11, 1991 (final: 7–0)

Hideo Nomo, Bos. Red Sox,
  Apr. 4, 2001 (final: 3–0)

Clay Buchholz, Bos. Red Sox,
  Sep. 1, 2007 (final: 10–0)

Hisashi Iwakuma, Sea. Mariners,
  Aug. 12, 2015 (final: 3–0)

Postseason Play

1966 World Series vs. L.A. Dodgers
    (NL), won 4 games to 0

1969 League Championship Series vs.
    Min. Twins, won 3 games to 0

World Series vs. N.Y. Mets (NL),
  lost 4 games to 1

1970 League Championship Series vs.
    Min. Twins, won 3 games to 0

World Series vs. Cin. Reds (NL),
  won 4 games to 1

1971 League Championship Series vs.
    Oak. A's, won 3 games to 0

World Series vs. Pit. Pirates (NL),
  lost 4 games to 3

1973 League Championship Series vs.
    Oak. A's, lost 3 games to 2

1974 League Championship Series vs.
    Oak. A's, lost 3 games to 1

1979 League Championship Series vs.
    Cal. Angels, won 3 games to 1

World Series vs. Pit. Pirates (NL),
  lost 4 games to 3

1983 League Championship Series vs.
    Chi. White Sox, won 3
    games to 1

World Series vs. Phi. Phillies
  (NL), won 4 games to 1

1996 Division Series vs. Cle. Indians,
    won 3 games to 1

League Championship Series vs.
  N.Y. Yankees, lost 4 games to 1

1997 Division Series vs. Sea.
    Mariners,
    won 3 games to 1

League Championship Series vs.
  Cle. Indians, lost 4 games
  to 2

2012 AL Wild Card Playoff Game vs.
    Tex. Rangers, won

Division Series vs. N.Y. Yankees,
  lost 3 games to 2

2014 Division Series vs. Det. Tigers,
    won 3 games to 0

League Championship Series vs.
  K.C. Royals, lost 4 games to 0

2016 AL Wild Card Playoff Game vs.
    Tor. Blue Jays, lost

Boston Red Sox

Dates of Operation: 1901–present (122 years)
Overall Record: 9797 wins, 9098 losses (.518)
Stadiums: Huntington Avenue Baseball Grounds, 1901–11; Braves Field, 1915–16 World Series
and 1929–32 (Sundays only); Fenway Park, 1912–present (capacity: 37,673)
Other Names: Americans, Puritans, Pilgrims, Plymouth Rocks, Somersets

Year-by-Year Finishes

Year	Finish	Wins	Losses	Percentage	Games Behind	Manager	Attendance
1901	2nd	79	57	.581	4.0	Jimmy Collins	289,448
1902	3rd	77	60	.562	6.5	Jimmy Collins	348,567
1903	1st	91	47	.659	+14.5	Jimmy Collins	379,338
1904	1st	95	59	.617	+1.5	Jimmy Collins	623,295
1905	4th	78	74	.513	16.0	Jimmy Collins	468,828
1906	8th	49	105	.318	45.5	Jimmy Collins, Chick Stahl	410,209
1907	7th	59	90	.396	32.5	George Huff, Bob Unglaub, Deacon McGuire	436,777
1908	5th	75	79	.487	15.5	Deacon McGuire, Fred Lake	473,048
1909	3rd	88	63	.583	9.5	Fred Lake	668,965
1910	4th	81	72	.529	22.5	Patsy Donovan	584,619
1911	5th	78	75	.510	24.0	Patsy Donovan	503,961
1912	1st	105	47	.691	+14.0	Jake Stahl	597,096
1913	4th	79	71	.527	15.5	Jake Stahl, Bill Carrigan	437,194
1914	2nd	91	62	.595	8.5	Bill Carrigan	481,359
1915	1st	101	50	.669	+2.5	Bill Carrigan	539,885
1916	1st	91	63	.591	+2.0	Bill Carrigan	496,397
1917	2nd	90	62	.592	9.0	Jack Barry	387,856
1918	1st	75	51	.595	+2.5	Ed Barrow	249,513
1919	6th	66	71	.482	20.5	Ed Barrow	417,291
1920	5th	72	81	.471	25.5	Ed Barrow	402,445
1921	5th	75	79	.487	23.5	Hugh Duffy	279,273
1922	8th	61	93	.396	33.0	Hugh Duffy	259,184
1923	8th	61	91	.401	37.0	Frank Chance	229,668
1924	7th	67	87	.435	25.0	Lee Fohl	448,556
1925	8th	47	105	.309	49.5	Lee Fohl	267,782
1926	8th	46	107	.301	44.5	Lee Fohl	285,155
1927	8th	51	103	.331	59.0	Bill Carrigan	305,275
1928	8th	57	96	.373	43.5	Bill Carrigan	396,920
1929	8th	58	96	.377	48.0	Bill Carrigan	394,620
1930	8th	52	102	.338	50.0	Heinie Wagner	444,045
1931	6th	62	90	.408	45.0	Shano Collins	350,975
1932	8th	43	111	.279	64.0	Shano Collins, Marty McManus	182,150
1933	7th	63	86	.423	34.5	Marty McManus	268,715
1934	4th	76	76	.500	24.0	Bucky Harris	610,640
1935	4th	78	75	.510	16.0	Joe Cronin	558,568
1936	6th	74	80	.481	28.5	Joe Cronin	626,895
1937	5th	80	72	.526	21.0	Joe Cronin	559,659
1938	2nd	88	61	.591	9.5	Joe Cronin	646,459
1939	2nd	89	62	.589	17.0	Joe Cronin	573,070
1940	4th (Tie)	82	72	.532	8.0	Joe Cronin	716,234

Year	Finish	Wins	Losses	Percentage	Games Behind	Manager	Attendance
1941	2nd	84	70	.545	17.0	Joe Cronin	718,497
1942	2nd	93	59	.612	9.0	Joe Cronin	730,340
1943	7th	68	84	.447	29.0	Joe Cronin	358,275
1944	4th	77	77	.500	12.0	Joe Cronin	506,975
1945	7th	71	83	.461	17.5	Joe Cronin	603,794
1946	1st	104	50	.675	+12.0	Joe Cronin	1,416,944
1947	3rd	83	71	.539	14.0	Joe Cronin	1,427,315
1948	2nd	96	59	.619	1.0	Joe McCarthy	1,558,798
1949	2nd	96	58	.623	1.0	Joe McCarthy	1,596,650
1950	3rd	94	60	.610	4.0	Joe McCarthy, Steve O'Neill	1,344,080
1951	3rd	87	67	.565	11.0	Steve O'Neill	1,312,282
1952	6th	76	78	.494	19.0	Lou Boudreau	1,115,750
1953	4th	84	69	.549	16.0	Lou Boudreau	1,026,133
1954	4th	69	85	.448	42.0	Lou Boudreau	931,127
1955	4th	84	70	.545	12.0	Pinky Higgins	1,203,200
1956	4th	84	70	.545	13.0	Pinky Higgins	1,137,158
1957	3rd	82	72	.532	16.0	Pinky Higgins	1,181,087
1958	3rd	79	75	.513	13.0	Pinky Higgins	1,077,047
1959	5th	75	79	.487	19.0	Pinky Higgins, Billy Jurges	984,102
1960	7th	65	89	.422	32.0	Billy Jurges, Pinky Higgins	1,129,866
1961	6th	76	86	.469	33.0	Pinky Higgins	850,589
1962	8th	76	84	.475	19.0	Pinky Higgins	733,080
1963	7th	76	85	.472	28.0	Johnny Pesky	942,642
1964	8th	72	90	.444	27.0	Johnny Pesky, Billy Herman	883,276
1965	9th	62	100	.383	40.0	Billy Herman	652,201
1966	9th	72	90	.444	26.0	Billy Herman, Pete Runnels	811,172
1967	1st	92	70	.568	+1.0	Dick Williams	1,727,832
1968	4th	86	76	.531	17.0	Dick Williams	1,940,788

East Division

Year	Finish	Wins	Losses	Percentage	Games Behind	Manager	Attendance
1969	3rd	87	75	.537	22.0	Dick Williams, Eddie Popowski	1,833,246
1970	3rd	87	75	.537	21.0	Eddie Kasko	1,595,278
1971	3rd	85	77	.525	18.0	Eddie Kasko	1,678,732
1972	2nd	85	70	.548	0.5	Eddie Kasko	1,441,718
1973	2nd	89	73	.549	8.0	Eddie Kasko	1,481,002
1974	3rd	84	78	.519	7.0	Darrell Johnson	1,556,411
1975	1st	95	65	.594	+4.5	Darrell Johnson	1,748,587
1976	3rd	83	79	.512	15.5	Darrell Johnson, Don Zimmer	1,895,846
1977	2nd (Tie)	97	64	.602	2.5	Don Zimmer	2,074,549
1978	2nd	99	64	.607	1.0	Don Zimmer	2,320,643
1979	3rd	91	69	.569	11.5	Don Zimmer	2,353,114
1980	4th	83	77	.519	19.0	Don Zimmer, Johnny Pesky	1,956,092
1981*	5th/2nd (Tie)	59	49	.546	4.0/1.5	Ralph Houk	1,060,379
1982	3rd	89	73	.549	6.0	Ralph Houk	1,950,124
1983	6th	78	84	.481	20.0	Ralph Houk	1,782,285
1984	4th	86	76	.531	18.0	Ralph Houk	1,661,618
1985	5th	81	81	.500	18.5	John McNamara	1,786,633
1986	1st	95	66	.590	+5.5	John McNamara	2,147,641
1987	5th	78	84	.481	20.0	John McNamara	2,231,551
1988	1st	89	73	.549	+1.0	John McNamara, Joe Morgan	2,464,851
1989	3rd	83	79	.512	6.0	Joe Morgan	2,510,012
1990	1st	88	74	.543	+2.0	Joe Morgan	2,528,986
1991	2nd (Tie)	84	78	.519	7.0	Joe Morgan	2,562,435
1992	7th	73	89	.451	23.0	Butch Hobson	2,468,574
1993	5th	80	82	.494	15.0	Butch Hobson	2,422,021
1994	4th	54	61	.470	17.0	Butch Hobson	1,775,818

Year	Finish	Wins	Losses	Percentage	Games Behind	Manager	Attendance
1995	1st	86	58	.597	+7.0	Kevin Kennedy	2,164,410
1996	3rd	85	77	.525	7.0	Kevin Kennedy	2,315,231
1997	4th	78	84	.481	20.0	Jimy Williams	2,226,136
1998	2nd	92	70	.568	22.0	Jimy Williams	2,343,947
1999	2nd	94	68	.580	4.0	Jimy Williams	2,446,162
2000	2nd	85	77	.525	2.5	Jimy Williams	2,586,032
2001	2nd	82	79	.509	13.5	Jimy Williams, Joe Kerrigan	2,625,333
2002	2nd	93	69	.574	10.5	Grady Little	2,650,063
2003	2nd	95	67	.586	6.0	Grady Little	2,724,165
2004	2nd	98	64	.605	3.0	Terry Francona	2,837,304
2005	1st (Tie)	95	67	.586	—	Terry Francona	2,847,888
2006	3rd	86	76	.531	11.0	Terry Francona	2,967,508
2007	1st	96	66	.593	+2.0	Terry Francona	2,971,025
2008	2nd	95	67	.586	2.0	Terry Francona	3,048,250
2009	2nd	95	67	.586	8.0	Terry Francona	3,062,699
2010	3rd	89	73	.549	7.0	Terry Francona	3,046,445
2011	3rd	90	72	.556	7.0	Terry Francona	3,054,001
2012	5th	69	93	.426	26.0	John Farrell	3,043,003
2013	1st	97	65	.599	+5.5	John Farrell	2,833,333
2014	5th	71	91	.438	25.0	John Farrell	2,956,089
2015	5th	78	84	.481	15.0	John Farrell	2,880,694
2016	1st	98	64	.574	+4.0	John Farrell	2,955,434
2017	1st	93	69	.574	+2.0	John Farrell	2,917,678
2018	1st	108	54	.667	+8.0	Alex Cora	2,895,575
2019	3rd	84	78	.519	19.0	Alex Cora	2,915,502
2020	5th	24	36	.400	16.0	Ron Roenicke	0
2021	2nd (Tie)	92	70	.568	8.0	Alex Cora	1,725,323
2022	5th	78	84	.481	21.0	Alex Cora	2,625,089

* Split season.

Awards

Most Valuable Player

Tris Speaker, outfield, 1912
Jimmie Foxx, first base, 1938
Ted Williams, outfield, 1946
Ted Williams, outfield, 1949
Jackie Jensen, outfield, 1958
Carl Yastrzemski, outfield, 1967
Fred Lynn, outfield, 1975
Jim Rice, outfield, 1978
Roger Clemens, pitcher, 1986
Mo Vaughn, first base, 1995
Dustin Pedroia, second base, 2008
Mookie Betts, outfield, 2018

Rookie of the Year

Walt Dropo, first base, 1950
Don Schwall, pitcher, 1961
Carlton Fisk, catcher, 1972
Fred Lynn, outfield, 1975
Nomar Garciaparra, shortstop, 1997
Dustin Pedroia, second base, 2007

Cy Young

Jim Lonborg, 1967
Roger Clemens, 1986
Roger Clemens, 1987
Roger Clemens, 1991
Pedro Martinez, 1999
Pedro Martinez, 2000
Rick Porcello, 2016

Manager of the Year (Since 1983)

John McNamara, 1986
Jimy Williams, 1999

Hall of Famers Who Played for the Red Sox

Luis Aparicio, shortstop, 1971–73
Wade Boggs, third base, 1982–92
Lou Boudreau, shortstop, 1951–52
Jesse Burkett, outfield, 1905
Orlando Cepeda, designated hitter, 1973
Jack Chesbro, pitcher, 1909
Jimmy Collins, third base, 1901–07
Joe Cronin, shortstop, 1935–45
Andre Dawson, outfield and designated hitter, 1993–94
Bobby Doerr, second base, 1937–44 and 1946–51
Dennis Eckersley, pitcher, 1978–84 and 1998
Rick Ferrell, catcher, 1933–37
Carlton Fisk, catcher, 1969–80
Jimmie Foxx, first base, 1936–42
Lefty Grove, pitcher, 1934–41
Rickey Henderson, outfield, 2002
Harry Hooper, outfield, 1909–20
Waite Hoyt, pitcher, 1919–20
Ferguson Jenkins, pitcher, 1976–77
George Kell, third base, 1952–54
Heinie Manush, outfield, 1936
Juan Marichal, pitcher, 1974
Pedro Martinez, pitcher, 1998–2004
David Ortiz, designated hitter and first base, 2003–16
Herb Pennock, pitcher, 1915–22
Tony Perez, first base, 1980–82
Jim Rice, outfield, 1974–89

Red Ruffing, pitcher, 1924–30
Babe Ruth, pitcher and outfield, 1914–19
Tom Seaver, pitcher, 1986
Al Simmons, outfield, 1943
Lee Smith, pitcher, 1988–90
John Smoltz, pitcher, 2009
Tris Speaker, outfield, 1907–15
Ted Williams, outfield, 1939–42 and
    1946–60
Carl Yastrzemski, outfield, 1961–83
Cy Young, pitcher, 1901–08

Retired Numbers

1	Bobby Doerr
4	Joe Cronin
6	Johnny Pesky
8	Carl Yastrzemski
9	Ted Williams
14	Jim Rice
26	Wade Boggs
27	Carlton Fisk
34	David Ortiz
45	Pedro Martinez

League Leaders, Batting

Batting Average, Season

Dale Alexander*, 1932 .... .367
Jimmie Foxx, 1938 .... .349
Ted Williams, 1941 .... .406
Ted Williams, 1942 .... .356
Ted Williams, 1947 .... .343
Ted Williams, 1948 .... .369
Billy Goodman, 1950 .... .354
Ted Williams, 1957 .... .388
Ted Williams, 1958 .... .328
Pete Runnels, 1960 .... .320
Pete Runnels, 1962 .... .326
Carl Yastrzemski, 1963 .... .321
Carl Yastrzemski, 1967 .... .326
Carl Yastrzemski, 1968 .... .301
Fred Lynn, 1979 .... .333
Carney Lansford, 1981 .... .336
Wade Boggs, 1983 .... .361
Wade Boggs, 1985 .... .368
Wade Boggs, 1986 .... .357
Wade Boggs, 1987 .... .363
Wade Boggs, 1988 .... .366
Nomar Garciaparra, 1999 .... .357
Nomar Garciaparra, 2000 .... .372
Manny Ramirez, 2002 .... .349
Bill Mueller, 2003 .... .326
Mookie Betts, 2018 .... .346
* .250 with Det. Tigers and .372 with Bos.
    Red Sox.

Home Runs, Season

Buck Freeman, 1903 13
Jake Stahl, 1910........................... 10
Tris Speaker, 1912 .... 10 (Tie)
Babe Ruth, 1918 .... 11 (Tie)
Babe Ruth, 1919 29
Jimmie Foxx, 1939 35
Ted Williams, 1941 37
Ted Williams, 1942 36
Ted Williams, 1947 32
Ted Williams, 1949 43
Tony Conigliaro, 1965................. 32
Carl Yastrzemski, 1967 .... 44 (Tie)
Jim Rice, 1977............................. 39
Jim Rice, 1978............................. 46
Dwight Evans, 1981 .... 22 (Tie)
Jim Rice, 1983............................. 39
Tony Armas, 1984........................ 43
Manny Ramirez, 2004 43
David Ortiz, 2006 54

RBIs, Season

Babe Ruth, 1919.........................112
Jimmie Foxx, 1938 175
Ted Williams, 1939....................145
Ted Williams, 1942....................137
Ted Williams, 1947....................114
Vern Stephens, 1949 .... 159 (Tie)
Ted Williams, 1949............. 159 (Tie)
Walt Dropo, 1950 .... 144 (Tie)
Vern Stephens, 1950 .... 144 (Tie)
Jackie Jensen, 1955 .... 116 (Tie)
Jackie Jensen, 1958 122
Jackie Jensen, 1959 112
Dick Stuart, 1963.......................118
Carl Yastrzemski, 1967 121
Ken Harrelson, 1968 109
Jim Rice, 1978............................139
Jim Rice, 1983....................126 (Tie)
Tony Armas, 1984.......................123
Mo Vaughn, 1995 .... 126 (Tie)
David Ortiz, 2005 148
David Ortiz, 2006 137
David Ortiz, 2016 .... 127 (Tie)
J.D. Martinez, 2018 130

Stolen Bases, Season

Buddy Myer, 1928 30
Billy Werber, 1934......................40
Billy Werber, 1935......................29
Ben Chapman*, 1937 .... 35 (Tie)
Dom DiMaggio, 1950 15
Jackie Jensen, 1954 22
Tommy Harper, 1973...................54

Jacoby Ellsbury, 2008..................50
Jacoby Ellsbury, 2009..................70
Jacoby Ellsbury, 2013..................52
* 8 with Was. Senators and 27 with Bos.
    Red Sox.

Total Bases, Season

Buck Freeman, 1902 287
Buck Freeman, 1903 281
Tris Speaker, 1914.....................287
Babe Ruth, 1919.........................284
Jimmie Foxx, 1938 398
Ted Williams, 1939....................344
Ted Williams, 1942....................338
Ted Williams, 1946....................343
Ted Williams, 1947....................335
Ted Williams, 1949....................368
Walt Dropo, 1950 326
Ted Williams, 1951....................295
Dick Stuart, 1963.......................319
Carl Yastrzemski, 1967 360
Carl Yastrzemski, 1970 335
Reggie Smith, 1971....................302
Jim Rice, 1977............................382
Jim Rice, 1978............................406
Jim Rice, 1979............................369
Dwight Evans, 1981 215
Jim Rice, 1983............................344
Tony Armas, 1984.......................339
David Ortiz, 2006 355
Jacoby Ellsbury, 2011................364
Mookie Betts, 2016 359
J.D. Martinez, 2018 358
Rafael Devers, 2019...................359

Most Hits, Season

Patsy Dougherty, 1903................195
Tris Speaker, 1914.....................193
Joe Vosmik, 1938.......................201
Doc Cramer, 1940 .... 200 (Tie)
Johnny Pesky, 1942....................205
Johnny Pesky, 1946....................208
Johnny Pesky, 1947....................207
Carl Yastrzemski, 1963 183
Carl Yastrzemski, 1967 189
Jim Rice, 1978............................213
Wade Boggs, 1985.....................240
Nomar Garciaparra, 1997..........209
Dustin Pedroia, 2008........... 213 (Tie)
Adrian Gonzalez, 2011........213 (tie)

Most Runs, Season

Patsy Dougherty, 1903................108
Babe Ruth, 1919.........................103

Ted Williams, 1940 134
Ted Williams, 1941 135
Ted Williams, 1942 141
Ted Williams, 1946 142
Ted Williams, 1947 125
Ted Williams, 1949 150
Dom DiMaggio, 1950 131
Dom DiMaggio, 1951 113
Carl Yastrzemski, 1967 112
Carl Yastrzemski, 1970 125
Carl Yastrzemski, 1974 93
Fred Lynn, 1975 103
Dwight Evans, 1984 121
Wade Boggs, 1988 128
Wade Boggs, 1989 .... 113 (Tie)
Dustin Pedroia, 2008 118
Dustin Pedroia, 2009 115
Mookie Betts, 2018 .... 129 (Tie)
Mookie Betts, 2019 135

Batting Feats

Triple Crown Winners

Ted Williams, 1942 (.356 BA, 35 HRs, 137 RBIs)
Ted Williams, 1947 (.343 BA, 32 HRs, 114 RBIs)
Carl Yastrzemski, 1967 (.326 BA, 44 HRs (Tie), 121 RBIs)

Hitting for the Cycle

Buck Freeman, Jul. 21, 1903
Patsy Dougherty, Jul. 29, 1903
Tris Speaker, Jun. 9, 1912
Roy Carlyle, Jul. 21, 1925
Moose Solters, Aug. 19, 1934
Joe Cronin, Aug. 2, 1940
Leon Culberson, Jul. 3, 1943
Bobby Doerr, May 17, 1944
Bob Johnson, Jul. 6, 1944
Ted Williams, Jul. 21, 1946
Bobby Doerr, May 13, 1947
Lou Clinton, Jul. 13, 1962
Carl Yastrzemski, May 14, 1965
Bob Watson, Sep. 15, 1979
Fred Lynn, May 13, 1980
Dwight Evans, Jun. 28, 1984
Rich Gedman, Sep. 18, 1985
Mike Greenwell, Sep. 14, 1988
Scott Cooper, Apr. 12, 1994
John Valentin, Jun. 6, 1996
Brock Holt, Jun. 16, 2015
Mookie Betts, Aug. 9, 2018
Brock Holt, Oct. 9, 2018*
* Hit cycle in playoffs.

Six Hits in a Game

Jimmy Piersall, Jun. 10, 1953
Pete Runnels, Aug. 30, 1960*
Jerry Remy, Sep. 3, 1981*
Nomar Garciaparra, Jun. 21, 2003*
Rafael Devers, Aug. 13, 2019*
* Extra-inning game.

40 or More Home Runs, Season

54	David Ortiz, 2006
50	Jimmie Foxx, 1938
47	David Ortiz, 2005
46	Jim Rice, 1978
45	Manny Ramirez, 2005
44	Carl Yastrzemski, 1967
	Mo Vaughn, 1996
43	Ted Williams, 1949
	Tony Armas, 1984
	Manny Ramirez, 2004
	J.D. Martinez, 2018
42	Dick Stuart, 1963
41	Jimmie Foxx, 1936
	Manny Ramirez, 2001
	David Ortiz, 2004
40	Rico Petrocelli, 1969
	Carl Yastrzemski, 1969
	Carl Yastrzemski, 1970
	Mo Vaughn, 1998

League Leaders, Pitching

Triple Crown Winner

Cy Young, 1901 (33–10, 1.62 ERA, 150 SO)
Pedro Martinez, 1999 (23–4, 2.07 ERA, 313 SO)

Most Wins, Season

Cy Young, 1901 33
Cy Young, 1902 32
Cy Young, 1903 28
Smoky Joe Wood, 1912 34
Wes Ferrell, 1935 25
Tex Hughson, 1942 22
Mel Parnell, 1949 25
Frank Sullivan, 1955 18
Jim Lonborg, 1967 .... 22 (Tie)
Roger Clemens, 1986 24
Roger Clemens, 1987 .... 20 (Tie)
Curt Schilling, 2004 21
Josh Beckett, 2007 20
Rick Porcello, 2016 22

Most Strikeouts, Season

Cy Young, 1901 158
Tex Hughson, 1942 .... 113 (Tie)
Jim Lonborg, 1967 246
Roger Clemens, 1988 291
Roger Clemens, 1991 241
Roger Clemens, 1996 257
Pedro Martinez, 1999 313
Pedro Martinez, 2000 284
Hideo Nomo, 2001 220
Pedro Martinez, 2002 239
Chris Sale, 2017 308

Lowest ERA, Season

Dutch Leonard, 1914 .... 1.00
Smoky Joe Wood, 1915 .... 1.49
Babe Ruth, 1916 .... 1.75
Lefty Grove, 1935 .... 2.70
Lefty Grove, 1936 .... 2.81
Lefty Grove, 1938 .... 3.07
Lefty Grove, 1939 .... 2.54
Mel Parnell, 1949 .... 2.78
Luis Tiant, 1972 .... 1.91
Roger Clemens, 1986 .... 2.48
Roger Clemens, 1990 .... 1.93
Roger Clemens, 1991 .... 2.62
Roger Clemens, 1992 .... 2.41
Pedro Martinez, 1999 .... 2.07
Pedro Martinez, 2000 .... 1.74
Pedro Martinez, 2002 .... 2.26
Pedro Martinez, 2003 .... 2.22

Most Saves, Season

Bill Campbell, 1977 31
Tom Gordon, 1998 46
Derek Lowe, 2000 .... 42 (Tie)

Best Won–Lost Percentage, Season

Cy Young, 1903 .... 28–9 .757
Jesse Tannehill, 1905 ...... 22–9 .710
Smoky Joe Wood, 1912 .. 34–5 .872
Smoky Joe Wood, 1915 .. 15–5 .750
Sad Sam Jones, 1918 ..... 16–5 .762
Lefty Grove, 1939 .... 15–4 .789
Tex Hughson, 1944 .... 18–5 .783
Dave Ferriss, 1946 .... 25–6 .806
Jack Kramer, 1948 .... 18–5 .783
Ellis Kinder, 1949 .... 23–6 .793
Roger Clemens, 1986 ..... 24–4 .857
Roger Clemens, 1987 ..... 20–9 .690
Pedro Martinez, 1999 ..... 23–4 .852
Pedro Martinez, 2002 ..... 20–4 .833
Curt Schilling, 2004 .... 21–6 .778

Pitching Feats

20 Wins, Season

Cy Young, 1901	33–10
Cy Young, 1902	32–11
Bill Dinneen, 1902	21–21
Cy Young, 1903	28–9
Bill Dinneen, 1903	21–13
Tom Hughes, 1903	20–7
Cy Young, 1904	26–16
Bill Dinneen, 1904	23–14
Jesse Tannehill, 1904	21–11
Jesse Tannehill, 1905	22–9
Cy Young, 1907	22–15
Cy Young, 1908	21–11
Smoky Joe Wood, 1911	23–17
Smoky Joe Wood, 1912	34–5
Hugh Bedient, 1912	20–9
Buck O'Brien, 1912	20–13
Ray Collins, 1914	20–13
Babe Ruth, 1916	23–12
Babe Ruth, 1917	24–13
Carl Mays, 1917	22–9
Carl Mays, 1918	21–13
Sad Sam Jones, 1921	23–16
Howard Ehmke, 1923	20–17
Wes Ferrell, 1935	25–14
Lefty Grove, 1935	20–12
Wes Ferrell, 1936	20–15
Tex Hughson, 1942	22–6
Dave Ferriss, 1945	21–10
Dave Ferriss, 1946	25–6
Tex Hughson, 1946	20–11
Mel Parnell, 1949	25–7
Ellis Kinder, 1949	23–6
Mel Parnell, 1953	21–8
Bill Monbouquette, 1963	20–10
Jim Lonborg, 1967	22–9
Luis Tiant, 1973	20–13
Luis Tiant, 1974	22–13
Luis Tiant, 1976	21–12
Dennis Eckersley, 1978	20–8
Roger Clemens, 1986	24–4
Roger Clemens, 1987	20–9
Roger Clemens, 1990	21–6
Pedro Martinez, 1999	23–4
Derek Lowe, 2002	21–8
Pedro Martinez, 2002	20–4
Curt Schilling, 2004	21–6
Josh Beckett, 2007	20–7
Rick Porcello, 2016	22–4

No-Hitters

Cy Young (vs. Phi. A's), May 5, 1904 (final: 3–0) (perfect game)

Jesse Tannehill (vs. Chi. White Sox), Aug. 17, 1904 (final: 6–0)

Bill Dinneen (vs. Chi. White Sox), Sep. 27, 1905 (final: 2–0)

Cy Young (vs. N.Y. Yankees), Jun. 30, 1908 (final: 8–0)

Smoky Joe Wood (vs. St.L. Browns), Jul. 29, 1911 (final: 5–0)

George Foster (vs. N.Y. Yankees), Jun. 21, 1916 (final: 2–0)

Hub Leonard (vs. St.L. Browns), Aug. 30, 1916 (final: 4–0)

Babe Ruth and Ernie Shore (vs. Was. Senators), Jun. 23, 1917 (final: 4–0)

Hub Leonard (vs. Det. Tigers), Jun. 3, 1918 (final: 5–0)

Ray Caldwell (vs. N.Y. Yankees), Sep. 10, 1919 (final: 3–0)

Howard Ehmke (vs. Phi. A's), Sep. 7, 1923 (final: 4–0)

Mel Parnell (vs. Chi. White Sox), Jul. 14, 1956 (final: 4–0)

Earl Wilson (vs. L.A. Angels), Jun. 26, 1962 (final: 2–0)

Bill Monbouquette (vs. Chi. White Sox), Aug. 1, 1962 (final: 1–0)

Dave Morehead (vs. Cle. Indians), Sep. 16, 1965 (final: 2–0)

Hideo Nomo (vs. Bal. Orioles), Apr. 4, 2001 (final: 3–0)

Derek Lowe (vs. T.B. Devil Rays), Apr. 27, 2002 (final: 10–0)

Clay Buchholz (vs. Bal. Orioles), Sep. 1, 2007 (final: 10–0)

Jon Lester (vs. K.C. Royals), May 19, 2008 (final 7–0)

No-Hitters Pitched Against

Ed Walsh, Chi. White Sox, Aug. 27, 1911 (final: 5–0)

George Mogridge, N.Y. Yankees, Apr. 24, 1917 (final: 2–1)

Walter Johnson, Was. Senators, Jul. 1, 1920 (final: 1–0)

Ted Lyons, Chi. White Sox, Aug. 21, 1926 (final: 6–0)

Bob Burke, Was. Senators, Aug. 8, 1931 (final: 5–0)

Allie Reynolds, N.Y. Yankees, Sep. 28,

1951 (final: 8–0)

Jim Bunning, Det. Tigers, Jul. 20, 1958 (final: 3–0)

Tom Phoebus, Bal. Orioles, Apr. 27, 1968 (final: 6–0)

Dave Righetti, N.Y. Yankees, Jul. 4, 1983 (final: 4–0)

Chris Bosio, Sea. Mariners, Apr. 22, 1993 (final: 7–0)

Sean Manaea, Oak. A's, Apr. 21, 2018 (final: 3–0)

Postseason Play

1903 World Series vs. Pit. Pirates (NL), won 5 games to 3

1912 World Series vs. N.Y. Giants (NL), won 4 games to 3

1915 World Series vs. Phi. Phillies (NL), won 4 games to 1

1916 World Series vs. Brk. Dodgers (NL), won 4 games to 1

1918 World Series vs. Chi. Cubs (NL), won 4 games to 2

1946 World Series vs. St.L. Cardinals (NL), lost 4 games to 3

1948 Pennant Playoff Game vs. Cle. Indians, lost

1967 World Series vs. St.L. Cardinals (NL), lost 4 games to 3

1975 League Championship Series vs. Oak. A's, won 3 games to 0
World Series vs. Cin. Reds (NL), lost 4 games to 3

1978 East Division Playoff Game vs. N.Y. Yankees, lost

1986 League Championship Series vs. Cal. Angels, won 4 games to 3
World Series vs. N.Y. Mets (NL), lost 4 games to 3

1988 League Championship Series vs. Oak. A's, lost 4 games to 0

1990 League Championship Series vs. Oak. A's, lost 4 games to 0

1995 Division Series vs. Cle. Indians, lost 3 games to 0

1998 Division Series vs. Cle. Indians, lost 3 games to 1

1999 Division Series vs. Cle. Indians, won 3 games to 2
League Championship Series vs. N.Y. Yankees, lost 4 games to 1

2003 Division Series vs. Oak. A's, won 3 games to 2

League Championship Series vs. N.Y. Yankees, lost 4 games to 3

2004 Division Series vs. Ana. Angels, won 3 games to 0

League Championship Series vs. N.Y. Yankees, won 4 games to 3

World Series vs. St.L. Cardinals (NL), won 4 games to 0

2005 Division Series vs. Chi. White Sox, lost 3 games to 0

2007 Division Series vs. L.A. Angels, won 3 games to 0

League Championship Series vs. Cle. Indians, won 4 games to 3

World Series vs. Col. Rockies (NL), won 4 games to 0

2008 Division Series vs. L.A. Angels, won 3 games to 1

League Championship Series vs. T.B. Rays, lost 4 games to 3

2009 Division Series vs. L.A. Angels, lost 3 games to 0

2013 Division Series vs. T.B. Rays, won 3 games to 1

League Championship Series vs Det. Tigers, won 4 games to 2

World Series vs. St.L. Cardinals (NL), won 4 games to 2

2016 Division Series vs. Cle. Indians, lost 3 games to 0

2017 Division Series vs. Hou. Astros, lost 3 games to 1

2018 Division Series vs. N.Y. Yankees, won 3 games to 1

League Championship Series vs. Hou. Astros, won 4 games to 1

World Series vs. L.A. Dodgers (NL), won 4 games to 1

2021 AL Wild Card vs. N.Y. Yankees, won

Division Series vs. T.B. Rays, won 3 games to 1

League Championship Series vs. Hou. Astros, lost 4 games to 2

Chicago White Sox

Dates of Operation: 1901–present (122 years)
Overall Record: 9492 wins, 9390 losses (.503)
Stadiums: South Side Park (also known as White Stocking Park, 1901–03; White Sox Park, 1904–10), 1901–10; Comiskey Park (also known as White Sox Park, 1910–12, 1962–75), 1910–90; Milwaukee County Stadium, 1968–69; Guaranteed Rate Field (formerly Comiskey Park II, 1991–2002, U.S. Cellular Field, 2003–16), 1991–present (capacity: 40,615)
Other Name: White Stockings

Year-by-Year Finishes

Year	Finish	Wins	Losses	Percentage	Games Behind	Manager	Attendance
1901	1st	83	53	.610	+4.0	Clark Griffith	354,350
1902	4th	74	60	.552	8.0	Clark Griffith	337,898
1903	7th	60	77	.438	30.5	Nixey Callahan	286,183
1904	3rd	89	65	.578	6.0	Nixey Callahan, Fielder Jones	557,123
1905	2nd	92	60	.605	2.0	Fielder Jones	687,419
1906	1st	93	58	.616	+3.0	Fielder Jones	585,202
1907	3rd	87	64	.576	5.5	Fielder Jones	666,307
1908	3rd	88	64	.579	1.5	Fielder Jones	636,096
1909	4th	78	74	.513	20.0	Billy Sullivan	478,400
1910	6th	68	85	.444	35.5	Hugh Duffy	552,084
1911	4th	77	74	.510	24.0	Hugh Duffy	583,208
1912	4th	78	76	.506	28.0	Nixey Callahan	602,241
1913	5th	78	74	.513	17.5	Nixey Callahan	644,501
1914	6th (Tie)	70	84	.455	30.0	Nixey Callahan	469,290
1915	3rd	93	61	.604	9.5	Pants Rowland	539,461
1916	2nd	89	65	.578	2.0	Pants Rowland	679,923
1917	1st	100	54	.649	+9.0	Pants Rowland	684,521
1918	6th	57	67	.460	17.0	Pants Rowland	195,081
1919	1st	88	52	.629	+3.5	Kid Gleason	627,186
1920	2nd	96	58	.623	2.0	Kid Gleason	833,492
1921	7th	62	92	.403	36.5	Kid Gleason	543,650
1922	5th	77	77	.500	17.0	Kid Gleason	602,860
1923	7th	69	85	.448	30.0	Kid Gleason	573,778
1924	8th	66	87	.431	25.5	Johnny Evers	606,658
1925	5th	79	75	.513	18.5	Eddie Collins	832,231
1926	5th	81	72	.529	9.5	Eddie Collins	710,339
1927	5th	70	83	.458	29.5	Ray Schalk	614,423
1928	5th	72	82	.468	29.0	Ray Schalk, Lena Blackburne	494,152
1929	7th	59	93	.388	46.0	Lena Blackburne	426,795
1930	7th	62	92	.403	40.0	Donie Bush	406,123
1931	8th	56	97	.366	51.0	Donie Bush	403,550
1932	7th	49	102	.325	56.5	Lew Fonseca	233,198
1933	6th	67	83	.447	31.0	Lew Fonseca	397,789
1934	8th	53	99	.349	47.0	Lew Fonseca, Jimmy Dykes	236,559
1935	5th	74	78	.487	19.5	Jimmy Dykes	470,281
1936	3rd	81	70	.536	20.0	Jimmy Dykes	440,810
1937	3rd	86	68	.558	16.0	Jimmy Dykes	589,245
1938	6th	65	83	.439	32.0	Jimmy Dykes	338,278
1939	4th	85	69	.552	22.5	Jimmy Dykes	594,104
1940	4th (Tie)	82	72	.532	8.0	Jimmy Dykes	660,336
1941	3rd	77	77	.500	24.0	Jimmy Dykes	677,077

Year	Finish	Wins	Losses	Percentage	Games Behind	Manager	Attendance
1942	6th	66	82	.446	34.0	Jimmy Dykes	425,734
1943	4th	82	72	.532	16.0	Jimmy Dykes	508,962
1944	7th	71	83	.461	18.0	Jimmy Dykes	563,539
1945	6th	71	78	.477	15.0	Jimmy Dykes	657,981
1946	5th	74	80	.481	30.0	Jimmy Dykes, Ted Lyons	983,403
1947	6th	70	84	.455	27.0	Ted Lyons	876,948
1948	8th	51	101	.336	44.5	Ted Lyons	777,844
1949	6th	63	91	.409	34.0	Jack Onslow	937,151
1950	6th	60	94	.390	38.0	Jack Onslow, Red Corriden	781,330
1951	4th	81	73	.526	17.0	Paul Richards	1,328,234
1952	3rd	81	73	.526	14.0	Paul Richards	1,231,675
1953	3rd	89	65	.578	11.5	Paul Richards	1,191,353
1954	3rd	94	60	.610	17.0	Paul Richards, Marty Marion	1,231,629
1955	3rd	91	63	.591	5.0	Marty Marion	1,175,684
1956	3rd	85	69	.552	12.0	Marty Marion	1,000,090
1957	2nd	90	64	.584	8.0	Al Lopez	1,135,668
1958	2nd	82	72	.532	10.0	Al Lopez	797,451
1959	1st	94	60	.610	+5.0	Al Lopez	1,423,144
1960	3rd	87	67	.565	10.0	Al Lopez	1,644,460
1961	4th	86	76	.531	23.0	Al Lopez	1,146,019
1962	5th	85	77	.525	11.0	Al Lopez	1,131,562
1963	2nd	94	68	.580	10.5	Al Lopez	1,158,848
1964	2nd	98	64	.605	1.0	Al Lopez	1,250,053
1965	2nd	95	67	.586	7.0	Al Lopez	1,130,519
1966	4th	83	79	.512	15.0	Eddie Stanky	990,016
1967	4th	89	73	.549	3.0	Eddie Stanky	985,634
1968	8th (Tie)	67	95	.414	36.0	Eddie Stanky, Al Lopez	803,775

West Division

Year	Finish	Wins	Losses	Percentage	Games Behind	Manager	Attendance
1969	5th	68	94	.420	29.0	Al Lopez, Don Gutteridge	589,546
1970	6th	56	106	.346	42.0	Don Gutteridge, Chuck Tanner	495,355
1971	3rd	79	83	.488	22.5	Chuck Tanner	833,891
1972	2nd	87	67	.565	5.5	Chuck Tanner	1,177,318
1973	5th	77	85	.475	17.0	Chuck Tanner	1,302,527
1974	4th	80	80	.500	9.0	Chuck Tanner	1,149,596
1975	5th	75	86	.466	22.5	Chuck Tanner	750,802
1976	6th	64	97	.398	25.5	Paul Richards	914,945
1977	3rd	90	72	.556	12.0	Bob Lemon	1,657,135
1978	5th	71	90	.441	20.5	Bob Lemon, Larry Doby	1,491,100
1979	5th	73	87	.456	14.0	Don Kessinger, Tony La Russa	1,280,702
1980	5th	70	90	.438	26.0	Tony La Russa	1,200,365
1981*	3rd/6th	54	52	.509	2.5/7.0	Tony La Russa	946,651
1982	3rd	87	75	.537	6.0	Tony La Russa	1,567,787
1983	1st	99	63	.611	+20.0	Tony La Russa	2,132,821
1984	5th (Tie)	74	88	.457	10.0	Tony La Russa	2,136,988
1985	3rd	85	77	.525	6.0	Tony La Russa	1,669,888
1986	5th	72	90	.444	20.0	Tony La Russa, Jim Fregosi	1,424,313
1987	5th	77	85	.475	8.0	Jim Fregosi	1,208,060
1988	5th	71	90	.441	32.5	Jim Fregosi	1,115,749
1989	7th	69	92	.429	29.5	Jeff Torborg	1,045,651
1990	2nd	94	68	.580	9.0	Jeff Torborg	2,002,357
1991	2nd	87	75	.537	8.0	Jeff Torborg	2,934,154
1992	3rd	86	76	.531	10.0	Gene Lamont	2,681,156
1993	1st	94	68	.580	+8.0	Gene Lamont	2,581,091

Year	Finish	Wins	Losses	Percentage	Games Behind	Manager	Attendance
					Central Division		
1994	1st	67	46	.593	+1.0	Gene Lamont	1,697,398
1995	3rd	68	76	.472	32.0	Gene Lamont, Terry Bevington	1,609,773
1996	2nd	85	77	.525	14.5	Terry Bevington	1,676,403
1997	2nd	80	81	.497	6.0	Terry Bevington	1,864,782
1998	2nd	80	82	.494	9.0	Jerry Manuel	1,391,146
1999	2nd	75	86	.466	21.5	Jerry Manuel	1,338,851
2000	1st	95	67	.586	+5.0	Jerry Manuel	1,947,799
2001	3rd	83	79	.512	8.0	Jerry Manuel	1,766,172
2002	2nd	81	81	.500	13.5	Jerry Manuel	1,676,804
2003	2nd	86	76	.531	4.0	Jerry Manuel	1,939,524
2004	2nd	83	79	.512	9.0	Ozzie Guillen	1,930,537
2005	1st	99	63	.611	+6.0	Ozzie Guillen	2,342,833
2006	3rd	90	72	.556	6.0	Ozzie Guillen	2,057,411
2007	4th	72	90	.444	24.5	Ozzie Guillen	2,684,395
2008	1st	89	74	.546	+1.0	Ozzie Guillen	2,501,103
2009	3rd	79	83	.488	7.5	Ozzie Guillen	2,284,164
2010	2nd	88	74	.543	6.0	Ozzie Guillen	2,194,378
2011	3rd	79	83	.488	16.0	Ozzie Guillen	2,001,117
2012	2nd	85	77	.525	3.0	Robin Ventura	1,965,955
2013	5th	63	99	.389	30.0	Robin Ventura	1,768,413
2014	4th	73	89	.451	17.0	Robin Ventura	1,650,821
2015	4th	76	86	.469	19.0	Robin Ventura	1,755,810
2016	4th	78	84	.481	16.5	Robin Ventura	1,746,293
2017	4th	67	95	.414	35.0	Robin Ventura	1,629,470
2018	4th	62	100	.383	29.0	Rick Renteria	1,608,817
2019	3rd	72	89	.447	28.5	Rick Renteria	1,649,775
2020	3rd (Tie)	35	25	.583	1.0	Rick Renteria	0
2021	1st	93	69	.574	+13.0	Tony La Russa	1,596,385
2022	2nd	81	81	.500	11.0	Tony La Russa	2,009,359

* Split season.

Awards

Most Valuable Player
Nellie Fox, second base, 1959
Dick Allen, first base, 1972
Frank Thomas, first base, 1993
Frank Thomas, first base, 1994
Jose Abreu, first base, 2020

Rookie of the Year
Luis Aparicio, shortstop, 1956
Gary Peters, pitcher, 1963
Tommie Agee, outfield, 1966
Ron Kittle, outfield, 1983
Ozzie Guillen, shortstop, 1985
Jose Abreu, first base, 2014

Cy Young
Early Wynn, 1959
LaMarr Hoyt, 1983
Jack McDowell, 1993

Manager of the Year (Since 1983)
Tony La Russa, 1983
Jeff Torborg, 1990
Gene Lamont, 1993
Jerry Manuel, 2000
Ozzie Guillen, 2005

Hall of Famers Who Played for the White Sox
Roberto Alomar, second base, 2003–04
Luis Aparicio, shortstop, 1956–62
Luke Appling, shortstop, 1930–43 and 1945–50
Harold Baines, outfield and designated hitter, 1980–89, 1996, 2000–01
Chief Bender, pitcher, 1925
Steve Carlton, pitcher, 1986
Eddie Collins, second base, 1915–26
Jocko Conlan, outfield, 1934–35
George Davis, shortstop, 1902 and 1904–09

Larry Doby, outfield, 1956–57 and 1959
Johnny Evers, second base, 1922
Red Faber, pitcher, 1914–33
Carlton Fisk, catcher, 1981–93
Nellie Fox, second base, 1950–63
Goose Gossage, pitcher, 1972–76
Ken Griffey Jr., outfield, 2008
Clark Griffith, pitcher, 1901–02
Harry Hooper, outfield, 1921–25
Jim Kaat, pitcher, 1973–75
George Kell, third base, 1954–56
Ted Lyons, pitcher, 1923–42 and 1946
Minnie Minoso, outfield and infield, 1949, 1951, 1958–59
Tim Raines, outfield, 1991–95
Edd Roush, outfield, 1913
Red Ruffing, pitcher, 1947
Ron Santo, third base, 1974
Ray Schalk, catcher, 1912–28
Tom Seaver, pitcher, 1984–86

Al Simmons, outfield, 1933–35
Frank Thomas, first base and designated
  hitter, 1990–2005
Jim Thome, designated hitter, 2006–08
Ed Walsh, pitcher, 1904–16
Hoyt Wilhelm, pitcher, 1963–68
Early Wynn, pitcher, 1958–62

Retired Numbers

2 ....Nellie Fox
3 .... Harold Baines
4 ....Luke Appling
9 .... Minnie Minoso
11 ....Luis Aparicio
14 ....Paul Konerko
16 ....Ted Lyons
19 ....Billy Pierce
35 ....Frank Thomas
56 ....Mark Buehrle
72 .... Carlton Fisk

League Leaders, Batting

Batting Average, Season

Luke Appling, 1936...................388
Luke Appling, 1943...................328
Frank Thomas, 1997.................347
Tim Anderson, 2019.................335

Home Runs, Season

Braggo Roth*, 1915......................7
Gus Zernial**, 1951...................33
Bill Melton, 1971 33
Dick Allen, 1972............................37
Dick Allen, 1974............................32
* 4 with Cle. Indians and 3 with Chi. White
  Sox.
** 33 with Phi. A's and 0 with Chi. White Sox.

RBIs, Season

Gus Zernial*, 1951................... 129
Dick Allen, 1972....................... 113
Jose Abreu, 2019 123
Jose Abreu, 2020 60
* 125 with Phi. A's and 4 with Chi. White Sox.

Stolen Bases, Season

Frank Isbell, 1901 48
Patsy Dougherty, 1908...............47
Eddie Collins, 1919 33
Eddie Collins, 1923 49
Eddie Collins, 1924 42
Johnny Mostil, 1925 43
Johnny Mostil, 1926 35

Minnie Minoso*, 1951 31
Minnie Minoso, 1952...................22
Minnie Minoso, 1953 25
Jim Rivera, 1955...........................25
Luis Aparicio, 1956.....................21
Luis Aparicio, 1957.....................28
Luis Aparicio, 1958.....................29
Luis Aparicio, 1959.....................56
Luis Aparicio, 1960.....................51
Luis Aparicio, 1961.....................53
Luis Aparicio, 1962.....................31
Juan Pierre, 2010 68
* 0 with Cle. Indians and 31 with Chi.
  White Sox.

Total Bases, Season

Joe Jackson, 1916......................293
Minnie Minoso, 1954 304
Albert Belle, 1998......................399
Jose Abreu, 2017 343
Jose Abreu, 2020 148

Most Hits, Season

Nellie Fox, 1952 192
Nellie Fox, 1954 .... 201 (Tie)
Nellie Fox, 1957 196
Nellie Fox, 1958 187
Minnie Minoso, 1960 184
Lance Johnson, 1995..................186
Jose Abreu, 2020 76

Most Runs, Season

Johnny Mostil, 1925 135
Frank Thomas, 1994...................106
Tim Anderson, 2020............. 45 (Tie)

Batting Feats

Triple Crown Winners

[No player]

Hitting for the Cycle

Ray Schalk, Jun. 27, 1922
Jack Brohamer, Sep. 24, 1977
Carlton Fisk, May 16, 1984
Jose Abreu, Sep. 9, 2017
Chris Singleton, Jul. 6, 1999
Jose Valentin, Apr. 27, 2000

Six Hits in a Game

Ray Radcliffe, Jul. 18, 1936
Hank Steinbacher, Jun. 22, 1938
Floyd Robinson, Jul. 22, 1962

Lance Johnson, Sep. 23, 1995
Alex Rios, Jul. 9, 2013

40 or More Home Runs, Season

49 ....Albert Belle, 1998
44 ....Jermaine Dye, 2006
43 ....Frank Thomas, 2000
42 ....Frank Thomas, 2003
           Jim Thome, 2006
41 ....Frank Thomas, 1993
           Paul Konerko, 2004
           Adam Dunn, 2012
40 ....Frank Thomas, 1995
           Frank Thomas, 1996
           Paul Konerko, 2005
           Todd Frazier, 2016

League Leaders, Pitching

Most Wins, Season

Doc White, 1907.................27 (Tie)
Ed Walsh, 1908 40
Eddie Cicotte, 1917 28
Eddie Cicotte, 1919 29
Ted Lyons, 1925 .... 21 (Tie)
Ted Lyons, 1927 .... 22 (Tie)
Billy Pierce, 1957 .... 20 (Tie)
Early Wynn, 1959 22
Gary Peters, 1964 .... 20 (Tie)
Wilbur Wood, 1972.............. 24 (Tie)
Wilbur Wood, 1973......................24
LaMarr Hoyt, 1982 19
LaMarr Hoyt, 1983 24
Jack McDowell, 1993 22

Most Strikeouts, Season

Ed Walsh, 1908 269
Frank Smith, 1909 177
Ed Walsh, 1911 255
Billy Pierce, 1953 186
Early Wynn, 1958 179
Esteban Loaiza, 2003.................207
Chris Sale, 2015 274

Lowest ERA, Season

Eddie Cicotte, 1917 ....1.53
Red Faber, 1921.......................2.47
Red Faber, 1922.......................2.80
Thornton Lee, 1941 ....2.37
Ted Lyons, 1942 ....2.10
Saul Rogovin*, 1951..................2.78
Billy Pierce, 1955 ....1.97
Frank Baumann, 1960 ....2.68

Gary Peters, 1963 .... 2.33
Gary Peters, 1966 .... 1.98
Joe Horlen, 1967 .... 2.06
* 5.25 with Det. Tigers and 2.48 with Chi.
White Sox.

Most Saves, Season

Terry Forster, 1974 24
Goose Gossage, 1975 26
Bobby Thigpen, 1990 57
Liam Hendriks, 2021 38

Best Won–Lost Percentage, Season

Clark Griffith, 1901 ... 24–7 ...... .774
Ed Walsh, 1908 .... 40–15 ..... .727
Eddie Cicotte, 1916 .. 15–7 ...... .682
Reb Russell, 1917 ..... 15–5 ...... .750
Eddie Cicotte, 1919 .. 29–7 ...... .806
Sandy Consuegra,
    1954 .... 16–3 ...... .842
Dick Donovan, 1957 ...... 16–6 .727 (Tie)
Bob Shaw, 1959 .... 18–6 ...... .750
Ray Herbert, 1962 .... 20–9 ...... .690
Joe Horlen, 1967 ...... 19–7 ...... .731
Rich Dotson, 1983 .... 22–7 ...... .759
Jason Bere, 1994 ...... 12–2 ...... .857

Pitching Feats

20 Wins, Season

Clark Griffith, 1901 24–7
Roy Patterson, 1902 20–12
Frank Owen, 1904 21–15
Nick Altrock, 1905 24–12
Frank Owen, 1905 21–13
Frank Owen, 1906 22–13
Nick Altrock, 1906 20–13
Doc White, 1907 27–13
Ed Walsh, 1907 24–18
Frank Smith, 1907 23–10
Ed Walsh, 1908 40–15
Frank Smith, 1909 25–17
Ed Walsh, 1911 27–18
Ed Walsh, 1912 27–17
Reb Russell, 1913 22–16
Jim Scott, 1913 20–20
Jim Scott, 1915 24–11
Red Faber, 1915 24–14
Eddie Cicotte, 1917 28–12
Eddie Cicotte, 1919 29–7
Lefty Williams, 1919 23–11
Red Faber, 1920 23–13
Lefty Williams, 1920 22–14

Dickie Kerr, 1920 21–9
Eddie Cicotte, 1920 21–10
Red Faber, 1921 25–15
Red Faber, 1922 21–17
Sloppy Thurston, 1924 20–14
Ted Lyons, 1925 21–11
Ted Lyons, 1927 22–14
Ted Lyons, 1930 22–15
Vern Kennedy, 1936 21–9
Thornton Lee, 1941 22–11
Virgil Trucks, 1953 .... 20–10*
Billy Pierce, 1956 20–9
Billy Pierce, 1957 20–12
Early Wynn, 1959 22–10
Ray Herbert, 1962 20–9
Gary Peters, 1964 20–8
Wilbur Wood, 1971 22–13
Wilbur Wood, 1972 24–17
Stan Bahnsen, 1972 21–16
Wilbur Wood, 1973 24–20
Wilbur Wood, 1974 20–19
Jim Kaat, 1974 21–13
Jim Kaat, 1975 20–14
LaMarr Hoyt, 1983 24–10
Rich Dotson, 1983 22–7
Jack McDowell, 1992 20–10
Jack McDowell, 1993 22–10
Esteban Loaiza, 2003 21–9
* 15–6 with Chi. White Sox and 5–4 with
    St.L. Browns.

No-Hitters

Jimmy Callahan (vs. Det. Tigers),
    Sep. 20, 1902 (final: 3–0)
Frank Smith (vs. Det. Tigers), Sep.
    6, 1905 (final: 15–0)
Frank Smith (vs. Phi. A's), Sep. 20,
    1908 (final: 1–0)
Ed Walsh (vs. Bos. Red Sox), Aug.
    27, 1911 (final: 5–0)
Joe Benz (vs. Cle. Indians), May 31,
    1914 (final: 6–1)
Eddie Cicotte (vs. St.L. Browns),
    Apr. 14, 1917 (final: 11–0)
Charlie Robertson (vs. Det. Tigers),
    Apr. 30, 1922 (final: 2–0)
    (perfect game)
Ted Lyons (vs. Bos. Red Sox),
    Aug. 21, 1926 (final: 6–0)
Vern Kennedy (vs. St.L. Browns),
    Aug. 31, 1935 (final: 5–0)
Bill Dietrich (vs. St.L. Browns), Jun.
    1, 1937 (final: 8–0)

Bob Keegan (vs. Was. Senators),
    Aug. 20, 1957 (final: 6–0)
Joe Horlen (vs. Det. Tigers),
    Sep. 10, 1967 (final: 6–0)
Blue Moon Odom and Francisco
    Barrios (vs. Oak. A's), Jul. 28, 1976
    (final: 6–0)
Joe Cowley (vs. Cal. Angels),
    Sep. 19, 1986 (final: 7–1)
Wilson Alvarez (vs. Bal. Orioles),
    Aug. 11, 1991 (final: 7–0)
Mark Buehrle (vs. Tex. Rangers),
    Apr. 18, 2007 (final: 6–0)
Mark Buehrle (vs. T.B. Rays), Jul. 23,
    2009 (final: 5–0) (perfect game)
Philip Humber (vs. Sea Mariners),
    Apr. 21, 2012 (final: 4–0)
    (perfect game)
Lucas Giolito (vs. Pit. Pirates),
    Aug. 25, 2020 (final: 4–0)
Carlos Rodon (vs. Cle. Indians),
    Apr. 14, 2021 (final: 8–0)

No-Hitters Pitched Against

Jesse Tannehill, Bos. Red Sox,
    Aug. 17, 1904 (final: 6–0)
Bill Dinneen, Bos. Red Sox, Sep. 27,
    1905 (final: 2–0)
Bob Rhoads, Cle. Indians, Sep. 18,
    1908 (final: 2–0)
Addie Joss, Cle. Indians, Oct. 2,
    1908 (final: 1–0) (perfect game)
Addie Joss, Cle. Indians, Apr. 20,
    1910 (final: 1–0)
Ernie Koob, St.L. Browns, May 5,
    1917 (final: 1–0)
Bob Groom, St.L. Browns, May 6,
    1917 (final: 3–0)
Bob Feller, Cle. Indians, Apr. 16,
    1940 (final: 1–0)
Mel Parnell, Bos. Red Sox, Jul. 14,
    1956 (final: 4–0)
Bill Monbouquette, Bos. Red Sox,
    Aug. 1, 1962 (final: 1–0)
Mike Warren, Oak. A's, Sep. 29, 1983
    (final: 3–0)
Jack Morris, Det. Tigers, Apr. 7, 1984
    (final: 4–0)
Bret Saberhagen, K.C. Royals,
    Aug. 26, 1991 (final: 7–0)
Francisco Liriano, Min. Twins,
    May 3, 2011 (final 1–0)

Postseason Play

1906   World Series vs. Chi. Cubs (NL),
won 4 games to 2

1917   World Series vs. N.Y. Giants (NL),
won 4 games to 2

1919   World Series vs. Cin. Reds (NL),
lost 5 games to 3

1959   World Series vs. L.A. Dodgers
(NL), lost 4 games to 2

1983   League Championship Series vs.
Bal. Orioles, lost 3 games to 1

1993   League Championship Series vs.
Tor. Blue Jays, lost 4 games
to 2

2000   Division Series vs. Sea. Mariners,
lost 3 games to 0

2005   Division Series vs. Bos. Red Sox,
won 3 games to 0
League Championship Series vs.
L.A. Angels, won 4 games to 1
World Series vs. Hou. Astros (NL),
won 4 games to 0

2008   AL Central Playoff Game vs.
Min. Twins, won
Division Series vs. T.B. Rays, lost 3
games to 1

2020   Wild Card Series vs.
Oak. A's, lost 2 games to 1

2021   Division Series vs. Hou. Astros,
lost 3 games to 1

Cleveland Guardians

Dates of Operation: 1901–present (122 years)
Overall Record: 9686 wins, 9214 losses (.512)
Stadiums: League Park, 1901–09; League Park II (also called Dunn Field, 1916–27), 1910–32 and 1934–36; Cleveland Stadium (formerly Lakefront Stadium, 1932–33, and Municipal Stadium, 1936–93), 1932–93; Progressive Field (formerly Jacobs Field, 1994–2007), 1994–present (capacity: 37,675)
Other Names: Blues, Broncos (or Bronchos), Molly Maguires, Naps, Indians

Year-by-Year Finishes

Year	Finish	Wins	Losses	Percentage	Games Behind	Manager	Attendance
1901	7th	54	82	.397	29.0	Jimmy McAleer	131,380
1902	5th	69	67	.507	14.0	Bill Armour	275,395
1903	3rd	77	63	.550	15.0	Bill Armour	311,280
1904	4th	86	65	.570	7.5	Bill Armour	264,749
1905	5th	76	78	.494	19.0	Nap Lajoie	316,306
1906	3rd	89	64	.582	5.0	Nap Lajoie	325,733
1907	4th	85	67	.559	8.0	Nap Lajoie	382,046
1908	2nd	90	64	.584	0.5	Nap Lajoie	422,242
1909	6th	71	82	.464	27.5	Nap Lajoie, Deacon McGuire	354,627
1910	5th	71	81	.467	32.0	Deacon McGuire	293,456
1911	3rd	80	73	.523	22.0	Deacon McGuire, George Stovall	406,296
1912	5th	75	78	.490	30.5	Harry Davis, Joe Birmingham	336,844
1913	3rd	86	66	.566	9.5	Joe Birmingham	541,000
1914	8th	51	102	.333	48.5	Joe Birmingham	185,997
1915	7th	57	95	.375	44.5	Joe Birmingham, Lee Fohl	159,285
1916	6th	77	77	.500	14.0	Lee Fohl	492,106
1917	3rd	88	66	.571	12.0	Lee Fohl	477,298
1918	2nd	73	54	.575	2.5	Lee Fohl	295,515
1919	2nd	84	55	.604	3.5	Lee Fohl, Tris Speaker	538,135
1920	1st	98	56	.636	+2.0	Tris Speaker	912,832
1921	2nd	94	60	.610	4.5	Tris Speaker	748,705
1922	4th	78	76	.506	16.0	Tris Speaker	528,145
1923	3rd	82	71	.536	16.5	Tris Speaker	558,856
1924	6th	67	86	.438	24.5	Tris Speaker	481,905
1925	6th	70	84	.455	27.5	Tris Speaker	419,005
1926	2nd	88	66	.571	3.0	Tris Speaker	627,426
1927	6th	66	87	.431	43.5	Jack McAllister	373,138
1928	7th	62	92	.403	39.0	Roger Peckinpaugh	375,907
1929	3rd	81	71	.533	24.0	Roger Peckinpaugh	536,210
1930	4th	81	73	.526	21.0	Roger Peckinpaugh	528,657
1931	4th	78	76	.506	30.0	Roger Peckinpaugh	483,027
1932	4th	87	65	.572	19.0	Roger Peckinpaugh	468,953
1933	4th	75	76	.497	23.5	Roger Peckinpaugh, Walter Johnson	387,936
1934	3rd	85	69	.552	16.0	Walter Johnson	391,338
1935	3rd	82	71	.536	12.0	Walter Johnson, Steve O'Neill	397,615
1936	5th	80	74	.519	22.5	Steve O'Neill	500,391
1937	4th	83	71	.539	19.0	Steve O'Neill	564,849
1938	3rd	86	66	.566	13.0	Ossie Vitt	652,006
1939	3rd	87	67	.565	20.5	Ossie Vitt	563,926
1940	2nd	89	65	.578	1.0	Ossie Vitt	902,576
1941	4th (Tie)	75	79	.487	26.0	Roger Peckinpaugh	745,948

Year	Finish	Wins	Losses	Percentage	Games Behind	Manager	Attendance
1942	4th	75	79	.487	28.0	Lou Boudreau	459,447
1943	3rd	82	71	.536	15.5	Lou Boudreau	438,894
1944	5th (Tie)	72	82	.468	17.0	Lou Boudreau	475,272
1945	5th	73	72	.503	11.0	Lou Boudreau	558,182
1946	6th	68	86	.442	36.0	Lou Boudreau	1,057,289
1947	4th	80	74	.519	17.0	Lou Boudreau	1,521,978
1948	1st	97	58	.626	+1.0	Lou Boudreau	2,620,627
1949	3rd	89	65	.578	8.0	Lou Boudreau	2,233,771
1950	4th	92	62	.597	6.0	Lou Boudreau	1,727,464
1951	2nd	93	61	.604	5.0	Al Lopez	1,704,984
1952	2nd	93	61	.604	2.0	Al Lopez	1,444,607
1953	2nd	92	62	.597	8.5	Al Lopez	1,069,176
1954	1st	111	43	.721	+8.0	Al Lopez	1,335,472
1955	2nd	93	61	.604	3.0	Al Lopez	1,221,780
1956	2nd	88	66	.571	9.0	Al Lopez	865,467
1957	6th	76	77	.497	21.5	Kerby Farrell	722,256
1958	4th	77	76	.503	14.5	Bobby Bragan, Joe Gordon	663,805
1959	2nd	89	65	.578	5.0	Joe Gordon	1,497,976
1960	4th	76	78	.494	21.0	Joe Gordon, Jimmy Dykes	950,985
1961	5th	78	83	.484	30.5	Jimmy Dykes	725,547
1962	6th	80	82	.494	16.0	Mel McGaha	716,076
1963	5th (Tie)	79	83	.488	25.5	Birdie Tebbetts	562,507
1964	6th (Tie)	79	83	.488	20.0	Birdie Tebbetts	653,293
1965	5th	87	75	.537	15.0	Birdie Tebbetts	934,786
1966	5th	81	81	.500	17.0	Birdie Tebbetts, George Strickland	903,359
1967	8th	75	87	.463	17.0	Joe Adcock	662,980
1968	3rd	86	75	.534	16.5	Alvin Dark	857,994

East Division

Year	Finish	Wins	Losses	Percentage	Games Behind	Manager	Attendance
1969	6th	62	99	.385	46.5	Alvin Dark	619,970
1970	5th	76	86	.469	32.0	Alvin Dark	729,752
1971	6th	60	102	.370	43.0	Alvin Dark, Johnny Lipon	591,361
1972	5th	72	84	.462	14.0	Ken Aspromonte	626,354
1973	6th	71	91	.438	26.0	Ken Aspromonte	615,107
1974	4th	77	85	.475	14.0	Ken Aspromonte	1,114,262
1975	4th	79	80	.497	15.5	Frank Robinson	977,039
1976	4th	81	78	.509	16.0	Frank Robinson	948,776
1977	5th	71	90	.441	28.5	Frank Robinson, Jeff Torborg	900,365
1978	6th	69	90	.434	29.0	Jeff Torborg	800,584
1979	6th	81	80	.503	22.0	Jeff Torborg, Dave Garcia	1,011,644
1980	6th	79	81	.494	23.0	Dave Garcia	1,033,827
1981*	6th/5th	52	51	.505	5.0/5.0	Dave Garcia	661,395
1982	6th (Tie)	78	84	.481	17.0	Dave Garcia	1,044,021
1983	7th	70	92	.432	28.0	Mike Ferraro, Pat Corrales	768,941
1984	6th	75	87	.463	29.0	Pat Corrales	734,079
1985	7th	60	102	.370	39.5	Pat Corrales	655,181
1986	5th	84	78	.519	11.5	Pat Corrales	1,471,805
1987	7th	61	101	.377	37.0	Pat Corrales, Doc Edwards	1,077,898
1988	6th	78	84	.481	11.0	Doc Edwards	1,411,610
1989	6th	73	89	.451	16.0	Doc Edwards, John Hart	1,285,542
1990	4th	77	85	.475	11.0	John McNamara	1,225,240
1991	7th	57	105	.352	34.0	John McNamara, Mike Hargrove	1,051,863

Year	Finish	Wins	Losses	Percentage	Games Behind	Manager	Attendance
1992	4th (Tie)	76	86	.469	20.0	Mike Hargrove	1,224,274
1993	6th	76	86	.469	19.0	Mike Hargrove	2,177,908
				Central Division			
1994	2nd	66	47	.584	1.0	Mike Hargrove	1,995,174
1995	1st	100	44	.694	+30.0	Mike Hargrove	2,842,745
1996	1st	99	62	.615	+14.5	Mike Hargrove	3,318,174
1997	1st	86	75	.534	+6.0	Mike Hargrove	3,404,750
1998	1st	89	73	.549	+9.0	Mike Hargrove	3,467,299
1999	1st	97	65	.599	+21.5	Mike Hargrove	3,468,456
2000	2nd	90	72	.556	5.0	Charlie Manuel	3,456,278
2001	1st	91	71	.562	+6.0	Charlie Manuel	3,175,523
2002	3rd	74	88	.457	20.5	Charlie Manuel, Joel Skinner	2,616,940
2003	4th	68	94	.420	22.0	Eric Wedge	1,730,002
2004	3rd	80	82	.494	12.0	Eric Wedge	1,814,401
2005	2nd	93	69	.574	6.0	Eric Wedge	2,013,763
2006	4th	78	84	.481	18.0	Eric Wedge	1,997,995
2007	1st	96	66	.593	+8.5	Eric Wedge	2,275,916
2008	3rd	81	81	.500	7.5	Eric Wedge	2,169,760
2009	4th	65	97	.401	21.5	Eric Wedge	1,766,242
2010	4th	69	93	.416	25.0	Manny Acta	1,391,644
2011	2nd	80	82	.494	15.0	Manny Acta	1,840,835
2012	4th	68	94	.420	20.0	Manny Acta, Sandy Alomar	1,603,596
2013	2nd	92	70	.568	1.0	Terry Francona	1,572,926
2014	3rd	85	77	.525	5.0	Terry Francona	1,437,393
2015	3rd	81	80	.503	13.5	Terry Francona	1,388,905
2016	1st	94	67	.584	+8.0	Terry Francona	1,591,667
2017	1st	102	60	.630	+17.0	Terry Francona	2,048,138
2018	1st	91	71	.562	+13.0	Terry Francona	1,926,701
2019	2nd	93	69	.572	8.0	Terry Francona	1,738,642
2020	2nd (Tie)	35	25	.578	1.0	Terry Francona	0
2021	2nd	80	82	.494	13.0	Terry Francona	1,114,368
				Cle. Guardians			
2022	1st	92	70	.568	+11.0	Terry Francona	1,295,870

* Split season.

Awards

Most Valuable Player
George H. Burns, first base, 1926
Lou Boudreau, shortstop, 1948
Al Rosen, third base, 1953

Rookie of the Year
Herb Score, pitcher, 1955
Chris Chambliss, first base, 1971
Joe Charboneau, outfield, 1980
Sandy Alomar Jr., catcher, 1990

Cy Young
Gaylord Perry, 1972
CC Sabathia, 2007
Cliff Lee, 2008
Corey Kluber, 2014

Corey Kluber, 2017
Shane Bieber, 2020

Manager of the Year (Since 1983)
Eric Wedge, 2007
Terry Francona, 2013
Terry Francona, 2016
Terry Francona, 2022

Hall of Famers Who Played for the Indians
Roberto Alomar, second base, 1999–2001
Earl Averill, outfield, 1929–39
Harold Baines, designated hitter, 1999
Lou Boudreau, shortstop, 1938–50
Steve Carlton, pitcher, 1987

Stan Coveleski, pitcher, 1916–24
Larry Doby, outfield, 1947–55 and 1958
Dennis Eckersley, pitcher, 1975–77
Bob Feller, pitcher, 1936–41 and 1945–56
Elmer Flick, outfield, 1902–10
Joe Gordon, second base, 1947–50
Addie Joss, pitcher, 1902–10
Ralph Kiner, outfield, 1955
Nap Lajoie, second base, 1902–14
Bob Lemon, pitcher, 1941–42 and 1946–58
Al Lopez, catcher, 1947
Minnie Minoso, outfield and infield, 1949, 1951, 1958–59
Jack Morris, pitcher, 1994

Eddie Murray, designated hitter, 1994–96

Hal Newhouser, pitcher, 1954–55

Phil Niekro, pitcher, 1986–87

Satchel Paige, pitcher, 1948–49

Gaylord Perry, pitcher, 1972–75

Sam Rice, outfield, 1934

Frank Robinson, designated hitter, 1974–76

Joe Sewell, shortstop, 1920–30

Billy Southworth, outfield, 1913 and 1915

Tris Speaker, outfield, 1916–26

Jim Thome, first base and third base, 1991–2002, 2011

Hoyt Wilhelm, pitcher, 1957–58

Dave Winfield, designated hitter, 1995

Early Wynn, pitcher, 1949–57

Cy Young, pitcher, 1890–98 and 1909–11

Retired Numbers

3	Earl Averill
5	Lou Boudreau
14	Larry Doby
18	Mel Harder
19	Bob Feller
20	Frank Robinson
21	Bob Lemon
25	Jim Thome
455	The Fans (consecutive sellouts)

League Leaders, Batting

Batting Average, Season

Nap Lajoie, 1903	.355
Nap Lajoie, 1904	.381
Elmer Flick, 1905	.308
Tris Speaker, 1916	.386
Lew Fonseca, 1929	.369
Lou Boudreau, 1944	.327
Roberto Avila, 1954	.341

Home Runs, Season

Braggo Roth*, 1915	7
Al Rosen, 1950	37
Larry Doby, 1952	32
Al Rosen, 1953	43
Larry Doby, 1954	32
Rocky Colavito, 1959	42 (Tie)
Albert Belle, 1995	50

* 3 with Chi. White Sox and 4 with Cle. Indians.

RBIs, Season

Hal Trosky, 1936	162
Al Rosen, 1952	105
Al Rosen, 1953	145
Larry Doby, 1954	126
Rocky Colavito, 1965	108
Joe Carter, 1986	121
Albert Belle, 1993	129
Albert Belle, 1995	126 (Tie)
Albert Belle, 1996	148
Manny Ramirez, 1999	165

Stolen Bases, Season

Harry Bay, 1903	46
Harry Bay, 1904	42 (Tie)
Elmer Flick, 1904	42 (Tie)
Elmer Flick, 1906	39 (Tie)
George Case, 1946	28
Minnie Minoso*, 1951	31
Kenny Lofton, 1992	66
Kenny Lofton, 1993	70
Kenny Lofton, 1994	60
Kenny Lofton, 1995	54
Kenny Lofton, 1996	75
Rajai Davis, 2016	43

* 31 with Chi. White Sox and 0 with Cle. Indians.

Total Bases, Season

Nap Lajoie, 1904	304
Nap Lajoie, 1910	304
Joe Jackson, 1912	331
Hal Trosky, 1936	405
Al Rosen, 1952	297
Al Rosen, 1953	367
Rocky Colavito, 1959	301
Albert Belle, 1994	294
Albert Belle, 1995	377

Most Hits, Season

Charlie Hickman*, 1902	194
Nap Lajoie, 1904	211
Nap Lajoie, 1906	214
Nap Lajoie, 1910	227
Joe Jackson, 1913	197
Tris Speaker, 1916	211
Charlie Jamieson, 1923	222
George Burns, 1926	216 (Tie)
Johnny Hodapp, 1930	225
Joe Vosmik, 1935	216
Earl Averill, 1936	232
Dale Mitchell, 1949	203

Kenny Lofton, 1994 160
* 32 with Bos. Red Sox and 161 with Cle. Indians.

Most Runs, Season

Elmer Flick, 1906	98
Ray Chapman, 1918	84
Larry Doby, 1952	104
Al Rosen, 1953	115
Al Smith, 1955	123
Albert Belle, 1995	121 (Tie)
Roberto Alomar, 1999	138
Grady Sizemore, 2006	134
Francisco Lindor, 2018	129 (Tie)
Jose Ramirez, 2020	45 (Tie)

Batting Feats

Triple Crown Winners

[No player]

Hitting for the Cycle

Bill Bradley, Sep. 24, 1903

Earl Averill, Aug. 17, 1933

Odell Hale, Jul. 12, 1938

Larry Doby, Jun. 4, 1952

Tony Horton, Jul. 2, 1970

Andre Thornton, Apr. 22, 1978

Travis Hafner, Aug. 14, 2003

Rajai Davis, Jul. 2, 2016

Jake Bauers, Jun. 14, 2019

Six Hits in a Game

Zaza Harvey, Apr. 25, 1902

Frank Brower, Aug. 7, 1923

George H. Burns, Jun. 19, 1924

Johnny Burnett, Jul. 10, 1932*
(9 hits in game)

Bruce Campbell, Jul. 2, 1936

Jim Fridley, Apr. 29, 1952

Jorge Orta, Jun. 15, 1980

Carlos Baerga, Apr. 11, 1992*

Omar Vizquel, Aug. 31, 2004

* Extra-inning game.

40 or More Home Runs, Season

52	Jim Thome, 2002
50	Albert Belle, 1995
49	Jim Thome, 2001
48	Albert Belle, 1996
45	Manny Ramirez, 1998
44	Manny Ramirez, 1999
43	Al Rosen, 1953

42 ....Hal Trosky, 1936
　　　　　　Rocky Colavito, 1959
　　　　　　Travis Hafner, 2006
41 .... Rocky Colavito, 1958
　　　　　　David Justice*, 2000
40 ....Jim Thome, 1997
* 20 with N.Y. Yankees and 21 with
　Cle. Indians.

League Leaders, Pitching

Triple Crown Winner

Bob Feller, 1940 (27–11, 2.61 ERA, 261 SO)

Most Wins, Season

Addie Joss, 1907 .... 27 (Tie)
Jim Bagby Sr., 1920 31
George Uhle, 1923 26
George Uhle, 1926 27
Bob Feller, 1939 24
Bob Feller, 1940 27
Bob Feller, 1941 25
Bob Feller, 1946 .... 26 (Tie)
Bob Feller, 1947 20
Bob Lemon, 1950 23
Bob Lemon, 1951 22
Bob Lemon, 1954 .... 23 (Tie)
Early Wynn, 1954 .... 23 (Tie)
Bob Lemon, 1955 .... 18 (Tie)
Jim Perry, 1960 .... 18 (Tie)
Gaylord Perry, 1972 .... 24 (Tie)
Cliff Lee, 2008 22
Corey Kluber, 2014 .... 18 (Tie)
Corey Kluber, 2017 .... 18 (Tie)
Carlos Carrasco, 2017 .... 18 (Tie)
Shane Bieber, 2020 8

Most Strikeouts, Season

Stan Coveleski, 1920 133
Bob Feller, 1938 240
Bob Feller, 1939 246
Bob Feller, 1940 261
Bob Feller, 1941 260
Allie Reynolds, 1943 151
Bob Feller, 1946 348
Bob Feller, 1947 196
Bob Feller, 1948 164
Bob Lemon, 1950 170
Herb Score, 1955 245
Herb Score, 1956 263
Early Wynn, 1957 184
Sam McDowell, 1965 325
Sam McDowell, 1966 225
Sam McDowell, 1968 283
Sam McDowell, 1969 279
Sam McDowell, 1970 304

Len Barker, 1980 187
Len Barker, 1981 127
Bert Blyleven*, 1985 206
Shane Bieber, 2020 122
* 77 with Min. Twins and 129 with Cle. Indians.

Lowest ERA, Season

Stan Coveleski, 1923 .... 2.76
Monte Pearson, 1933 .... 2.33
Bob Feller, 1940 .... 2.62
Gene Bearden, 1948 .... 2.43
Early Wynn, 1950 .... 3.20
Mike Garcia, 1954 .... 2.64
Sam McDowell, 1965 .... 2.18
Luis Tiant, 1968 .... 1.60
Rick Sutcliffe, 1982 .... 2.96
Kevin Millwood, 2005 .... 2.64
Cliff Lee, 2008 .... 2.54
Corey Kluber, 2017 .... 2.25
Shane Bieber, 2020 .... 1.63

Most Saves, Season

Jose Mesa, 1995 46
Bob Wickman, 2005 .... 45 (Tie)
Joe Borowski, 2007 45
Brad Hand, 2020 16
Emmanuel Clase, 2022 42

Best Won–Lost Percentage, Season

Bill Bernhard*, 1902 .... 18–5 .... .783
Jim Bagby, 1920 .... 31–12 .... .721
George Uhle, 1926 .... 27–11 .... .711
Johnny Allen, 1937 ...... 15–1 .... .938
Bob Feller, 1951 .... 22–8 .... .733
Jim Perry, 1960 .... 18–10 .... .643
Sonny Siebert, 1966 .... 16–8 .... .667
Charles Nagy, 1996 ... 17–5 .... .773
Cliff Lee, 2005 .... 18–5 .... .783
Cliff Lee, 2008 .... 22–3 .... .880
Corey Kluber, 2017 .... 18–4 .... .818
Shane Bieber, 2020 .... 8–1 .... .889
* 1–0 (1.000) with Phi. A's and 17–5 (.773)
　with Cle. Indians.

Pitching Feats

20 Wins, Season

Bill Bernhard, 1904 23–13
Addie Joss, 1905 20–12
Bob Rhoads, 1906 22–10
Addie Joss, 1906 21–9
Otto Hess, 1906 20–17
Addie Joss, 1907 27–10

Addie Joss, 1908 24–11
Vean Gregg, 1911 23–7
Vean Gregg, 1912 20–13
Cy Falkenberg, 1913 23–10
Vean Gregg, 1913 20–13
Jim Bagby, 1917 23–13
Stan Coveleski, 1918 22–13
Stan Coveleski, 1919 23–12
Jim Bagby, 1920 31–12
Stan Coveleski, 1920 24–14
Ray Caldwell, 1920 20–10
Stan Coveleski, 1921 23–13
George Uhle, 1922 22–16
George Uhle, 1923 26–16
Joe Shaute, 1924 20–17
George Uhle, 1926 27–11
Wes Ferrell, 1929 21–10
Wes Ferrell, 1930 25–13
Wes Ferrell, 1931 22–12
Wes Ferrell, 1932 23–13
Mel Harder, 1934 20–12
Mel Harder, 1935 22–11
Johnny Allen, 1936 20–10
Bob Feller, 1937 24–9
Bob Feller, 1940 27–11
Bob Feller, 1941 25–13
Bob Feller, 1946 26–15
Bob Feller, 1947 20–11
Gene Bearden, 1948 20–7
Bob Lemon, 1948 20–14
Bob Lemon, 1949 22–10
Bob Lemon, 1950 23–11
Bob Feller, 1951 22–8
Mike Garcia, 1951 20–13
Early Wynn, 1951 20–13
Early Wynn, 1952 23–12
Mike Garcia, 1952 22–11
Bob Lemon, 1952 22–11
Bob Lemon, 1953 21–15
Bob Lemon, 1954 23–7
Early Wynn, 1954 23–11
Herb Score, 1956 20–9
Early Wynn, 1956 20–9
Bob Lemon, 1956 20–14
Dick Donovan, 1962 20–10
Luis Tiant, 1968 21–9
Sam McDowell, 1970 20–12
Gaylord Perry, 1972 24–16
Gaylord Perry, 1974 21–13
Cliff Lee, 2008 22–3
Corey Kluber, 2018 20–7

No-Hitters

Bob Rhoads (vs. Chi. White Sox), Sep. 18, 1908 (final: 2–0)

Addie Joss (vs. Chi. White Sox), Oct. 2, 1908 (final: 1–0) (perfect game)

Addie Joss (vs. Chi. White Sox), Apr. 20, 1910 (final: 1–0)

Ray Caldwell (vs. N.Y. Yankees), Sep. 10, 1919 (final: 3–0)

Wes Ferrell (vs. St.L. Browns), Apr. 29, 1931 (final: 9–0)

Bob Feller (vs. Chi. White Sox), Apr. 16, 1940 (final: 1–0)

Bob Feller (vs. N.Y. Yankees), Apr. 30, 1946 (final: 1–0)

Don Black (vs. Phi. A's), Jul. 10, 1947 (final: 3–0)

Bob Lemon (vs. Det. Tigers), Jun. 30, 1948 (final: 2–0)

Bob Feller (vs. Det. Tigers), Jul. 1, 1951 (final: 2–1)

Sonny Siebert (vs. Was. Senators II), Jun. 10, 1966 (final: 2–0)

Dick Bosman (vs. Oak. A's), Jul. 19, 1974 (final: 4–0)

Dennis Eckersley (vs. Cal. Angels), May 30, 1977 (final: 1–0)

Len Barker (vs. Tor. Blue Jays), May 15, 1981 (final: 3–0) (perfect game)

No-Hitters Pitched Against

Chief Bender, Phi. A's, May 12, 1910 (final: 4–0)

Joe Benz, Chi. White Sox, May 31, 1914 (final: 6–1)

Joe Bush, Phi. A's, Aug. 26, 1916

(final: 5–0)

Monte Pearson, N.Y. Yankees, Aug. 27, 1938 (final: 13–0)

Allie Reynolds, N.Y. Yankees, Jul. 12, 1951 (final: 1–0)

Dave Morehead, Bos. Red Sox, Sep. 16, 1965 (final: 2–0)

Dean Chance, Min. Twins, Aug. 25, 1967 (final: 2–1)

Jim Abbott, N.Y. Yankees, Sep. 4, 1993 (final: 4–0)

Ervin Santana, L.A. Angels, Jul. 27, 2011 (final: 3–1)

Postseason Play

1920　World Series vs. Brk. Dodgers (NL), won 5 games to 2

1948　Pennant Playoff Game vs. Bos. Red Sox, won

World Series vs. Bos. Braves (NL), won 4 games to 2

1954　World Series vs. N.Y. Giants (NL), lost 4 games to 0

1995　Division Series vs. Bos. Red Sox, won 3 games to 0

League Championship Series vs. Sea. Mariners, won 4 games to 2

World Series vs. Atl. Braves (NL), lost 4 games to 2

1996　Division Series vs. Bal. Orioles, lost 3 games to 1

1997　Division Series vs. N.Y. Yankees, won 3 games to 2

League Championship Series vs.

Bal. Orioles, won 4 games to 2

World Series vs. Fla. Marlins (NL), lost 4 games to 3

1998　Division Series vs. Bos. Red Sox, won 3 games to 1

League Championship Series vs. N.Y. Yankees, lost 4 games to 2

1999　Division Series vs. Bos. Red Sox, lost 3 games to 2

2001　Division Series vs. Sea. Mariners, lost 3 games to 2

2007　Division Series vs. N.Y. Yankees, won 3 games to 1

League Championship Series vs. Bos. Red Sox, lost 4 games to 3

2013　AL Wild Card Playoff Game vs T.B. Rays, lost

2016　Division Series vs. Bos. Red Sox, won 3 games to 0

League Championship Series vs. Tor. Blue Jays, won 4 games to 1

World Series vs. Chi. Cubs (NL), lost 4 games to 3

2017　Division Series vs. N.Y. Yankees, lost 3 games to 2

2018　Division Series vs. Hou. Astros, lost 3 games to 0

2020　Wild Card Series vs. N.Y. Yankees, lost 2 games to 0

2022　Wild Card Series vs. T.B. Rays, won 2 games to 0

Division Series vs. N.Y. Yankees, lost 3 games to 2

Detroit Tigers

Dates of Operation: 1901–present (122 years)
Overall Record: 9512 wins, 9407 losses (.503)
Stadiums: Bennett Park, 1901–11; Burns Park, 1901–02 (Sundays only); Tiger Stadium, 1912–
1999 (formerly Navin Field, 1912–37, and Briggs Stadium, 1938–60); Comerica Park,
2000–present (capacity: 41,574)

Year-by-Year Finishes

Year	Finish	Wins	Losses	Percentage	Games Behind	Manager	Attendance
1901	3rd	74	61	.548	8.5	George Stallings	259,430
1902	7th	52	83	.385	30.5	Frank Dwyer	189,469
1903	5th	65	71	.478	25.0	Ed Barrow	224,523
1904	7th	62	90	.408	32.0	Ed Barrow, Bobby Lowe	177,796
1905	3rd	79	74	.516	15.5	Bill Armour	193,384
1906	6th	71	78	.477	21.0	Bill Armour	174,043
1907	1st	92	58	.613	+1.5	Hughie Jennings	297,079
1908	1st	90	63	.588	+0.5	Hughie Jennings	436,199
1909	1st	98	54	.645	+3.5	Hughie Jennings	490,490
1910	3rd	86	68	.558	18.0	Hughie Jennings	391,288
1911	2nd	89	65	.578	13.5	Hughie Jennings	484,988
1912	6th	69	84	.451	36.5	Hughie Jennings	402,870
1913	6th	66	87	.431	30.0	Hughie Jennings	398,502
1914	4th	80	73	.523	19.5	Hughie Jennings	416,225
1915	2nd	100	54	.649	2.5	Hughie Jennings	476,105
1916	3rd	87	67	.565	4.0	Hughie Jennings	616,772
1917	4th	78	75	.510	21.5	Hughie Jennings	457,289
1918	7th	55	71	.437	20.0	Hughie Jennings	203,719
1919	4th	80	60	.571	8.0	Hughie Jennings	643,805
1920	7th	61	93	.396	37.0	Hughie Jennings	579,650
1921	6th	71	82	.464	27.0	Ty Cobb	661,527
1922	3rd	79	75	.513	15.0	Ty Cobb	861,206
1923	2nd	83	71	.539	16.0	Ty Cobb	911,377
1924	3rd	86	68	.558	6.0	Ty Cobb	1,015,136
1925	4th	81	73	.526	16.5	Ty Cobb	820,766
1926	6th	79	75	.513	12.0	Ty Cobb	711,914
1927	4th	82	71	.536	27.5	George Moriarty	773,716
1928	6th	68	86	.442	33.0	George Moriarty	474,323
1929	6th	70	84	.455	36.0	Bucky Harris	869,318
1930	5th	75	79	.487	27.0	Bucky Harris	649,450
1931	7th	61	93	.396	47.0	Bucky Harris	434,056
1932	5th	76	75	.503	29.5	Bucky Harris	397,157
1933	5th	75	79	.487	25.0	Del Baker	320,972
1934	1st	101	53	.656	+7.0	Mickey Cochrane	919,161
1935	1st	93	58	.616	+3.0	Mickey Cochrane	1,034,929
1936	2nd	83	71	.539	19.5	Mickey Cochrane	875,948
1937	2nd	89	65	.578	13.0	Mickey Cochrane	1,072,276
1938	4th	84	70	.545	16.0	Mickey Cochrane, Del Baker	799,557
1939	5th	81	73	.526	26.5	Del Baker	836,279
1940	1st	90	64	.584	+1.0	Del Baker	1,112,693
1941	4th (Tie)	75	79	.487	26.0	Del Baker	684,915
1942	5th	73	81	.474	30.0	Del Baker	580,087
1943	5th	78	76	.506	20.0	Steve O'Neill	606,287

Year	Finish	Wins	Losses	Percentage	Games Behind	Manager	Attendance
1944	2nd	88	66	.571	1.0	Steve O'Neill	923,176
1945	1st	88	65	.575	+1.5	Steve O'Neill	1,280,341
1946	2nd	92	62	.597	12.0	Steve O'Neill	1,722,590
1947	2nd	85	69	.552	12.0	Steve O'Neill	1,398,093
1948	5th	78	76	.506	18.5	Steve O'Neill	1,743,035
1949	4th	87	67	.565	10.0	Red Rolfe	1,821,204
1950	2nd	95	59	.617	3.0	Red Rolfe	1,951,474
1951	5th	73	81	.474	25.0	Red Rolfe	1,132,641
1952	8th	50	104	.325	45.0	Red Rolfe, Fred Hutchinson	1,026,846
1953	6th	60	94	.390	40.5	Fred Hutchinson	884,658
1954	5th	68	86	.442	43.0	Fred Hutchinson	1,079,847
1955	5th	79	75	.513	17.0	Bucky Harris	1,181,838
1956	5th	82	72	.532	15.0	Bucky Harris	1,051,182
1957	4th	78	76	.506	20.0	Jack Tighe	1,272,346
1958	5th	77	77	.500	15.0	Jack Tighe, Bill Norman	1,098,924
1959	4th	76	78	.494	18.0	Bill Norman, Jimmy Dykes	1,221,221
1960	6th	71	83	.461	26.0	Jimmy Dykes, Billy Hitchcock, Joe Gordon	1,167,669
1961	2nd	101	61	.623	8.0	Bob Scheffing	1,600,710
1962	4th	85	76	.528	10.5	Bob Scheffing	1,207,881
1963	5th (Tie)	79	83	.488	25.5	Bob Scheffing, Chuck Dressen	821,952
1964	4th	85	77	.525	14.0	Chuck Dressen	816,139
1965	4th	89	73	.549	13.0	Chuck Dressen, Bob Swift	1,029,645
1966	3rd	88	74	.543	10.0	Chuck Dressen, Bob Swift, Frank Skaff	1,124,293
1967	2nd (Tie)	91	71	.562	1.0	Mayo Smith	1,447,143
1968	1st	103	59	.636	+12.0	Mayo Smith	2,031,847

East Division

Year	Finish	Wins	Losses	Percentage	Games Behind	Manager	Attendance
1969	2nd	90	72	.556	19.0	Mayo Smith	1,577,481
1970	4th	79	83	.488	29.0	Mayo Smith	1,501,293
1971	2nd	91	71	.562	12.0	Billy Martin	1,591,073
1972	1st	86	70	.551	+0.5	Billy Martin	1,892,386
1973	3rd	85	77	.525	12.0	Billy Martin, Joe Schultz	1,724,146
1974	6th	72	90	.444	19.0	Ralph Houk	1,243,080
1975	6th	57	102	.358	37.5	Ralph Houk	1,058,836
1976	5th	74	87	.460	24.0	Ralph Houk	1,467,020
1977	4th	74	88	.457	26.0	Ralph Houk	1,359,856
1978	5th	86	76	.531	13.5	Ralph Houk	1,714,893
1979	5th	85	76	.528	18.0	Les Moss, Dick Tracewski, Sparky Anderson	1,630,929
1980	5th	84	78	.519	19.0	Sparky Anderson	1,785,293
1981*	4th/2nd (Tie)	60	49	.550	3.5/1.5	Sparky Anderson	1,149,144
1983	2nd	92	70	.568	6.0	Sparky Anderson	1,829,636
1984	1st	104	58	.642	+15.0	Sparky Anderson	2,704,794
1985	3rd	84	77	.522	15.0	Sparky Anderson	2,286,609
1986	3rd	87	75	.537	8.5	Sparky Anderson	1,899,437
1987	1st	98	64	.605	+2.0	Sparky Anderson	2,061,830
1988	2nd	88	74	.543	1.0	Sparky Anderson	2,081,162
1989	7th	59	103	.364	30.0	Sparky Anderson	1,543,656
1990	3rd	79	83	.488	9.0	Sparky Anderson	1,495,785
1991	2nd	84	78	.519	7.0	Sparky Anderson	1,641,661
1992	6th	75	87	.463	21.0	Sparky Anderson	1,423,963
1993	3rd (Tie)	85	77	.525	10.0	Sparky Anderson	1,971,421

Year	Finish	Wins	Losses	Percentage	Games Behind	Manager	Attendance
					Central Division		
1994	5th	53	62	.461	18.0	Sparky Anderson	1,184,783
1995	4th	60	84	.417	26.0	Sparky Anderson	1,180,979
1996	5th	53	109	.327	39.0	Buddy Bell	1,168,610
1997	3rd	79	83	.488	19.0	Buddy Bell	1,365,157
1998	5th	65	97	.401	24.0	Buddy Bell, Larry Parrish	1,409,391
1999	3rd	69	92	.429	27.5	Larry Parrish	2,026,441
2000	3rd	79	83	.488	16.0	Phil Garner	2,533,752
2001	4th	66	96	.407	25.0	Phil Garner	1,921,305
2002	4th	55	106	.342	39.0	Phil Garner, Luis Pujols	1,503,623
2003	5th	43	119	.265	47.0	Alan Trammell	1,368,245
2004	4th	72	90	.444	20.0	Alan Trammell	1,917,004
2005	4th	71	91	.438	28.0	Alan Trammell	2,024,485
2006	2nd	95	67	.586	1.0	Jim Leyland	2,595,937
2007	2nd	88	74	.543	8.5	Jim Leyland	3,047,139
2008	5th	74	88	.457	14.5	Jim Leyland	3,202,645
2009	2nd	86	77	.528	1.0	Jim Leyland	2,567,185
2010	3rd	81	81	.500	13.0	Jim Leyland	2,461,237
2011	1st	95	67	.586	+15.0	Jim Leyland	2,642,045
2012	1st	88	74	.543	+3.0	Jim Leyland	3,028,033
2013	1st	93	69	.574	+1.0	Jim Leyland	3,083,397
2014	1st	90	72	.556	+1.0	Brad Ausmus	2,917,209
2015	5th	74	87	.460	20.5	Brad Ausmus	2,726,048
2016	2nd	86	75	.518	8.0	Brad Ausmus	2,493,859
2017	5th	64	98	.395	38.0	Brad Ausmus	2,321,599
2018	3rd	64	98	.395	27.0	Ron Gardenhire	1,856,970
2019	5th	47	114	.292	53.5	Ron Gardenhire	1,501,430
2020	5th	23	35	.397	12.0	Ron Gardenhire, Lloyd McClendon	0
2021	3rd	77	85	.463	16.0	A.J. Hinch	1,102,621
2022	4th	66	96	.407	26.0	A.J. Hinch	1,575,544

* Split season.

Awards

Most Valuable Player
Ty Cobb, outfield, 1911
Mickey Cochrane, catcher, 1934
Hank Greenberg, first base, 1935
Charley Gehringer, second base, 1937
Hank Greenberg, outfield, 1940
Hal Newhouser, pitcher, 1944
Hal Newhouser, pitcher, 1945
Denny McLain, pitcher, 1968
Willie Hernandez, pitcher, 1984
Justin Verlander, pitcher, 2011
Miguel Cabrera, third base, 2012
Miguel Cabrera, third base, 2013

Rookie of the Year
Harvey Kuenn, shortstop, 1953
Mark Fidrych, pitcher, 1976
Lou Whitaker, second base, 1978
Justin Verlander, pitcher, 2006
Michael Fullmer, pitcher, 2016

Cy Young
Denny McLain, 1968
Denny McLain (co-winner), 1969
Willie Hernandez, 1984
Justin Verlander, 2011
Max Scherzer, 2013

Manager of the Year (Since 1983)
Sparky Anderson, 1984
Sparky Anderson, 1987
Jim Leyland, 2006

Hall of Famers Who Played for the Tigers
Earl Averill, outfield, 1939–40
Jim Bunning, pitcher, 1955–63
Ty Cobb, outfield, 1905–26
Mickey Cochrane, catcher, 1934–37
Sam Crawford, outfield, 1903–17
Larry Doby, outfield, 1959
Charlie Gehringer, second base, 1924–42
Goose Goslin, outfield, 1934–37
Hank Greenberg, first base and outfield, 1930, 1933–41, and 1945–46
Bucky Harris, second base, 1929 and 1931
Harry Heilmann, outfield, 1914 and 1916–29
Waite Hoyt, pitcher, 1930–31
Hughie Jennings, infield, 1907, 1909, 1912, and 1918
Al Kaline, outfield, 1953–74
George Kell, third base, 1946–52
Heinie Manush, outfield, 1923–27
Eddie Mathews, third base, 1967–68
Jack Morris, pitcher, 1977–90
Hal Newhouser, pitcher, 1939–53
Ivan Rodriguez, catcher, 2009
Al Simmons, outfield, 1936
Alan Trammel, shortstop, 1977–96

Retired Numbers

TC...Ty Cobb
EH .... Ernie Harwell
1 ....Lou Whitaker
2 .... Charlie Gehringer
3 ....Alan Trammell
5 ....Hank Greenberg
6 .... Al Kaline
11 .... Sparky Anderson
16 .... Hal Newhouser
23 .... Willie Horton
47 .... Jack Morris

League Leaders, Batting

Batting Average, Season

Ty Cobb, 1907 .... .350
Ty Cobb, 1908 .... .324
Ty Cobb, 1909 .... .377
Ty Cobb, 1910 .... .385
Ty Cobb, 1911 .... .420
Ty Cobb, 1912 .... .410
Ty Cobb, 1913 .... .390
Ty Cobb, 1914 .... .368
Ty Cobb, 1915 .... .369
Ty Cobb, 1917 .... .383
Ty Cobb, 1918 .... .382
Ty Cobb, 1919 .... .384
Harry Heilmann, 1921.............. .394
Harry Heilmann, 1923.............. .403
Harry Heilmann, 1925.............. .393
Heinie Manush, 1926................ .378
Harry Heilmann, 1927.............. .398
Dale Alexander*, 1932 .... .367
Charlie Gehringer, 1937........... .371
George Kell, 1949 .... .343
Al Kaline, 1955 .... .340
Harvey Kuenn, 1959 .... .353
Norm Cash, 1961..................... .361
Maglio Ordonez, 2007 .... .363
Miguel Cabrera, 2011.............. .344
Miguel Cabrera, 2012.............. .330
Miguel Cabrera, 2013.............. .348
Miguel Cabrera, 2015.............. .338

* .372 with Bos. Red Sox and .250 with
Det. Tigers.

Home Runs, Season

Sam Crawford, 1908 7
Ty Cobb, 1909 9
Hank Greenberg, 1935 ....36 (Tie)
Hank Greenberg, 1938 58

Hank Greenberg, 1940 41
Rudy York, 1943 34
Hank Greenberg, 1946 44
Darrell Evans, 1985 40
Cecil Fielder, 1990 51
Cecil Fielder, 1991 44
Miguel Cabrera, 2008...........37 (Tie)
Miguel Cabrera, 2012 44

RBIs, Season

Ty Cobb, 1907 116
Ty Cobb, 1908 101
Ty Cobb, 1909 115
Sam Crawford, 1910 115
Ty Cobb, 1911 144
Sam Crawford, 1914 112
Sam Crawford, 1915 116
Bobby Veach, 1917 115
Bobby Veach, 1918 ....74 (Tie)
Hank Greenberg, 1935 170
Hank Greenberg, 1937 183
Hank Greenberg, 1940 150
Rudy York, 1943........................118
Hank Greenberg, 1946 127
Ray Boone, 1955................ 116 (Tie)
Cecil Fielder, 1990 132
Cecil Fielder, 1991 133
Cecil Fielder, 1992 124
Miguel Cabrera, 2010................126
Miguel Cabrera, 2012................139

Stolen Bases, Season

Ty Cobb, 1907 49
Ty Cobb, 1909 76
Ty Cobb, 1911 83
Ty Cobb, 1915 96
Ty Cobb, 1916 68
Ty Cobb, 1917 55
Charlie Gehringer, 1929..............27
Marty McManus, 1930.................23
Ron LeFlore, 1978.......................68
Brian Hunter, 1997 74
Brian Hunter*, 1999 44
* 44 with Sea. Mariners and 0 with Det. Tigers.

Total Bases, Season

Ty Cobb, 1907 286
Ty Cobb, 1908 276
Ty Cobb, 1909 296
Ty Cobb, 1911 367
Sam Crawford, 1913 298
Ty Cobb, 1915 274

Ty Cobb, 1917 336
Hank Greenberg, 1935 389
Hank Greenberg, 1940 384
Rudy York, 1943 301
Al Kaline, 1955 321
Rocky Colavito, 1962 309
Cecil Fielder, 1990 339
Miguel Cabrera, 2008...........331 (Tie)
Miguel Cabrera, 2012............... 377

Most Hits, Season

Ty Cobb, 1907 212
Ty Cobb, 1908 188
Ty Cobb, 1909 216
Ty Cobb, 1911 248
Ty Cobb, 1912 227
Ty Cobb, 1915 208
Ty Cobb, 1917 225
Ty Cobb, 1919 .... 191 (Tie)
Bobby Veach, 1919 .... 191 (Tie)
Harry Heilmann, 1921................237
Dale Alexander, 1929 .... 215 (Tie)
Charlie Gehringer, 1929...... 215 (Tie)
Charlie Gehringer, 1934............214
Barney McCosky, 1940........ 200 (Tie)
Dick Wakefield, 1943.................200
George Kell, 1950......................218
George Kell, 1951......................191
Harvey Kuenn, 1953 209
Harvey Kuenn, 1954 .... 201 (Tie)
Al Kaline, 1955.........................200
Harvey Kuenn, 1956 196
Harvey Kuenn, 1959 198
Norm Cash, 1961......................193

Most Runs, Season

Sam Crawford, 1907 102
Matty McIntyre, 1908.................105
Ty Cobb, 1909 116
Ty Cobb, 1910 106
Ty Cobb, 1911 147
Ty Cobb, 1915 144
Ty Cobb, 1916 113
Donie Bush, 1917 112
Charlie Gehringer, 1929............131
Charlie Gehringer, 1935............134
Hank Greenberg, 1938 144
Eddie Yost, 1959 115
Dick McAuliffe, 1968 95
Ron LeFlore, 1978.....................126
Tony Phillips, 1992.....................114

Batting Feats

Triple Crown Winners
Ty Cobb, 1909 (.377 BA, 9 HRs, 115 RBIs)
Miguel Cabrera, 2012 (.330 BA, 44 HRs, 139 RBIs)

Hitting for the Cycle
Bobby Veach, Sep. 17, 1920
Fats Fothergill, Sep. 26, 1926
Gee Walker, Apr. 20, 1937
Charlie Gehringer, May 27, 1939
Vic Wertz, Sep. 14, 1947
George Kell, Jun. 2, 1950
Hoot Evers, Sep. 7, 1950
Travis Fryman, Jul. 28, 1993
Damion Easley, Jun. 8, 2001
Carlos Guillen, Aug. 1, 2006

Six Hits in a Game
Doc Nance, Jul. 13, 1901
Bobby Veach, Sep. 17, 1920*
Ty Cobb, May 5, 1925
George Kell, Sep. 20, 1946
Rocky Colavito, Jun. 24, 1962*
  (7 hits in game)
Jim Northrup, Aug. 28, 1969*
Cesar Gutierrez, Jun. 21, 1970*
  (7 hits in game)
Damion Easley, Aug. 8, 2001
Carlos Pena, May 27, 2004
* Extra-inning game.

40 or More Home Runs, Season
58	Hank Greenberg, 1938
51	Cecil Fielder, 1990
45	Rocky Colavito, 1961
44	Hank Greenberg, 1946
	Cecil Fielder, 1991
	Miguel Cabrera, 2012
	Miguel Cabrera, 2013
41	Hank Greenberg 1940
	Norm Cash 1961
40	Hank Greenberg 1937
	Darrell Evans, 1985

League Leaders, Pitching

Most Wins, Season
George Mullin, 1909 29
Tommy Bridges, 1936 23
Dizzy Trout, 1943 .... 20 (Tie)
Hal Newhouser, 1944 29
Hal Newhouser, 1945 25
Hal Newhouser, 1946 .... 26 (Tie)
Hal Newhouser, 1948 21
Frank Lary, 1956 21
Jim Bunning, 1957 .... 20 (Tie)
Earl Wilson, 1967 .... 22 (Tie)
Denny McLain, 1968 31
Denny McLain, 1969 24
Mickey Lolich, 1971 25
Jack Morris, 1981 .... 14 (Tie)
Bill Gullickson, 1991 .... 20 (Tie)
Justin Verlander, 2009 .... 19 (Tie)
Justin Verlander, 2011 24
Max Scherzer, 2013 21
Max Scherzer, 2014 .... 18 (Tie)

Most Strikeouts, Season
Tommy Bridges, 1935 163
Tommy Bridges, 1936 175
Hal Newhouser, 1944 187
Hal Newhouser, 1945 212
Virgil Trucks, 1949 153
Jim Bunning, 1959 201
Jim Bunning, 1960 201
Mickey Lolich, 1971 308
Jack Morris, 1983 232
Justin Verlander, 2009 269
Justin Verlander, 2011 250
Justin Verlander, 2012 239
Justin Verlander, 2016 254

Lowest ERA, Season
Dizzy Trout, 1944 .... 2.12
Hal Newhouser, 1945 .... 1.81
Hal Newhouser, 1946 .... 1.94
Hank Aguirre, 1962 .... 2.21
Mark Fidrych, 1976 .... 2.34
Justin Verlander, 2011 .... 2.40
Anibal Sanchez, 2013 .... 2.56
David Price*, 2015 .... 2.45
* 2.30 with Tor. Blue Jays and 2.53 with Det. Tigers.

Most Saves, Season
John Hiller, 1973 38
Todd Jones, 2000 .... 42 (Tie)
Jose Valverde, 2011 49

Best Won–Lost Percentage, Season
Bill Donovan, 1907 ...... 25–4... .862
George Mullin, 1909.... 29–8... .784
Eldon Auker, 1935 .... 18–7... .720
Schoolboy Rowe, 1940. 16–3... .842
Hal Newhouser, 1945 .. 25–9... .735
Denny McLain, 1968 .... 31–6... .838
Justin Verlander, 2009 .. 18–6... .750
Justin Verlander, 2011 .. 24–5... .828
Max Scherzer, 2013..... 21–3... .875

Pitching Feats

Triple Crown Winner
Hal Newhouser, 1945 (25–9, 1.81 ERA, 212 SO)
Justin Verlander, 2011 (24–5, 2.40 ERA, 250 SO)

20 Wins, Season
Roscoe Miller, 1901 23–13
Ed Killian, 1905 23–13
George Mullin, 1905............. 21–20
George Mullin, 1906 21–18
Bill Donovan, 1907 25–4
Ed Killian, 1907 25–13
George Mullin, 1907............. 20–20
Ed Summers, 1908 24–12
George Mullin, 1909 29–8
Ed Willett, 1909 21–10
George Mullin, 1910 21–12
Harry Coveleski, 1914 22–12
Hooks Dauss, 1915 24–13
Harry Coveleski, 1915 22–13
Harry Coveleski, 1916 21–11
Hooks Dauss, 1919 21–9
Hooks Dauss, 1923 21–13
Schoolboy Rowe, 1934............ 24–8
Tommy Bridges, 1934 22–11
Tommy Bridges, 1935 21–10
Tommy Bridges, 1936 23–11
Bobo Newsom, 1939 ....20–11*
Bobo Newsom, 1940 21–5
Dizzy Trout, 1943 20–12
Hal Newhouser, 1944 29–9
Dizzy Trout, 1944 27–14
Hal Newhouser, 1945 25–9
Hal Newhouser, 1946 26–9
Hal Newhouser, 1948 21–12
Frank Lary, 1956 21–13
Billy Hoeft, 1956 20–14
Jim Bunning, 1957 20–8
Frank Lary, 1961 23–9
Denny McLain, 1966 20–14
Earl Wilson, 1967................. 22–11
Denny McLain, 1968 31–6
Denny McLain, 1969 24–9
Mickey Lolich, 1971 25–14
Joe Coleman, 1971 20–9

Mickey Lolich, 1972 22–14
Joe Coleman, 1973 23–15
Jack Morris, 1983 20–13
Jack Morris, 1986 21–8
Bill Gullickson, 1991 20–9
Justin Verlander, 2011 24–5
Max Scherzer, 2013 21–3
* 17–10 with Det. Tigers and 3–1 with
St.L. Browns.

No-Hitters

George Mullin (vs. St.L. Browns),
Jul. 4, 1912 (final: 7–0)
Virgil Trucks (vs. Was. Senators), May
15, 1952 (final: 1–0)
Virgil Trucks (vs. N.Y. Yankees),
Aug. 25, 1952 (final: 1–0)
Jim Bunning (vs. Bos. Red Sox),
Jul. 20, 1958 (final: 3–0)
Jack Morris (vs. Chi. White Sox),
Apr. 7, 1984 (final: 4–0)
Justin Verlander (vs. Mil. Brewers), Jun.
12, 2007 (final: 4–0)
Justin Verlander (vs. Tor. Blue Jays),
May 7, 2011 (final: 9–0)
Spencer Turnbull (vs. Sea. Mariners),
May 18, 2021 (final: 5–0)

No-Hitters Pitched Against

Jimmy Callahan, Chi. White Sox,
Sep. 20, 1902 (final: 3–0)
Frank Smith, Chi. White Sox, Sep. 6,
1905 (final: 15–0)
Earl Hamilton, St.L. Browns, Aug. 30,
1912 (final: 5–1)
Hub Leonard, Bos. Red Sox, Jun. 3,
1918 (final: 5–0)

Charlie Robertson, Chi. White Sox, Apr.
30, 1922 (final: 2–0) (perfect game)
Bob Lemon, Cle. Indians, Jun. 30,
1948 (final: 2–0)
Bob Feller, Cle. Indians, Jul. 1, 1951
(final: 2–1)
Steve Barber and Stu Miller, Bal.
Orioles, Apr. 30, 1967 (final: 1–2)
Joe Horlen, Chi. White Sox, Sep. 10,
1967 (final: 6–0)
Steve Busby, K.C. Royals, Apr. 27,
1973 (final: 3–0)
Nolan Ryan, Cal. Angels, Jul. 15,
1973 (final: 6–0)
Randy Johnson, Sea. Mariners, Jun. 2,
1990 (final: 2–0)
Dave Stieb, Tor. Blue Jays, Sep. 2,
1990 (final: 3–0)
Matt Garza, T.B. Rays, Jul. 26, 2010
(final: 5–0)
Henderson Alvarez, Mia. Marlins, Sep.
29, 2013 (final: 1–0)

Postseason Play

1907 World Series vs. Chi. Cubs (NL),
lost 4 games to 0, 1 tie
1908 World Series vs. Chi. Cubs (NL),
lost 4 games to 1
1909 World Series vs. Pit. Pirates (NL),
lost 4 games to 3
1934 World Series vs. St.L. Cardinals
(NL), lost 4 games to 3
1935 World Series vs. Chi. Cubs (NL),
won 4 games to 2
1940 World Series vs. Cin. Reds (NL),
lost 4 games to 3

1945 World Series vs. Chi. Cubs (NL),
won 4 games to 3
1968 World Series vs. St.L. Cardinals
(NL), won 4 games to 3
1972 League Championship Series vs.
Oak. A's, lost 3 games to 2
1984 League Championship Series vs.
K.C. Royals, won 3 games to
0
World Series vs. S.D. Padres (NL),
won 4 games to 1
1987 League Championship Series vs.
Min. Twins, lost 4 games to 1
2006 Division Series vs. N.Y. Yankees,
won 3 games to 1
League Championship Series vs.
Oak. A's, won 4 games to 0
World Series vs. St.L. Cardinals
(NL), lost 4 games to 1
2009 AL Central Playoff Game vs.
Min. Twins, lost
2011 Division Series vs. N.Y. Yankees,
won 3 games to 2
2011 League Championship Series vs.
Tex. Rangers, lost 4 games to 2
2012 Division Series vs. Oak. A's, won
3 games to 2
League Championship Series vs.
N.Y. Yankees, won 4 games to 0
World Series vs. S.F. Giants
(NL), lost 4 games to 0
2013 Division Series vs. Oak. A's, won
3 games to 2
League Championship Series vs.
Bos. Red Sox, lost 4 games to 2
2014 Division Series vs. Bal. Orioles,
lost 3 games to 0

Houston Astros

Dates of Operation: NL: 1962–2012 (51 years); AL: 2013–present (10 years)
Overall Record: NL: 3999 wins, 4134 losses (.491); AL: 832 wins, 686 losses (.548);
combined: 4494 wins, 4611 losses (.501)
Stadiums: Colt Stadium, 1962–64; The Astrodome, 1965–99; Minute Maid Park (formerly Enron
Field, 2000–02, and Astros Field, 2002), 2000–present (capacity: 41,574)
Other Name: Colt .45s

Year-by-Year Finishes

Year	Finish	Wins	Losses	Percentage	Games Behind	Manager	Attendance
1962	8th	64	96	.400	36.5	Harry Craft	924,456
1963	9th	66	96	.407	33.0	Harry Craft	719,502
1964	9th	66	96	.407	27.0	Harry Craft, Luman Harris	725,773
1965	9th	65	97	.401	32.0	Luman Harris	2,151,470
1966	8th	72	90	.444	23.0	Grady Hatton	1,872,108
1967	9th	69	93	.426	32.5	Grady Hatton	1,348,303
1968	10th	72	90	.444	25.0	Grady Hatton, Harry Walker	1,312,887
West Division							
1969	5th	81	81	.500	12.0	Harry Walker	1,442,995
1970	4th	79	83	.488	23.0	Harry Walker	1,253,444
1971	4th (Tie)	79	83	.488	11.0	Harry Walker	1,261,589
1972	2nd	84	69	.549	10.5	Harry Walker, Salty Parker, Leo Durocher	1,469,247
1973	4th	82	80	.506	17.0	Leo Durocher, Preston Gomez	1,394,004
1974	4th	81	81	.500	21.0	Preston Gomez	1,090,728
1975	6th	64	97	.398	43.5	Preston Gomez, Bill Virdon	858,002
1976	3rd	80	82	.494	22.0	Bill Virdon	886,146
1977	3rd	81	81	.500	17.0	Bill Virdon	1,109,560
1978	5th	74	88	.457	21.0	Bill Virdon	1,126,145
1979	2nd	89	73	.549	1.5	Bill Virdon	1,900,312
1980	1st	93	70	.571	+1.0	Bill Virdon	2,278,217
1981*	3rd/1st	61	49	.555	8.0/+1.5	Bill Virdon	1,321,282
1982	5th	77	85	.475	12.0	Bill Virdon, Bob Lillis	1,558,555
1983	3rd	85	77	.525	6.0	Bob Lillis	1,351,962
1984	2nd (Tie)	80	82	.494	12.0	Bob Lillis	1,229,862
1985	3rd (Tie)	83	79	.512	12.0	Bob Lillis	1,184,314
1986	1st	96	66	.593	+10.0	Hal Lanier	1,734,276
1987	3rd	76	86	.469	14.0	Hal Lanier	1,909,902
1988	5th	82	80	.506	12.5	Hal Lanier	1,933,505
1989	3rd	86	76	.531	6.0	Art Howe	1,834,908
1990	4th (Tie)	75	87	.463	16.0	Art Howe	1,310,927
1991	6th	65	97	.401	29.0	Art Howe	1,196,152
1992	4th	81	81	.500	17.0	Art Howe	1,211,412
1993	3rd	85	77	.525	19.0	Art Howe	2,084,546
Central Division							
1994	2nd	66	49	.574	0.5	Terry Collins	1,561,136
1995	2nd	76	68	.528	9.0	Terry Collins	1,363,801
1996	2nd	82	80	.506	6.0	Terry Collins	1,975,888
1997	1st	84	78	.519	+5.0	Larry Dierker	2,046,781

Year	Finish	Wins	Losses	Percentage	Games Behind	Manager	Attendance
1998	1st	102	60	.630	+12.5	Larry Dierker	2,450,451
1999	1st	97	65	.599	+1.5	Larry Dierker	2,706,017
2000	4th (Tie)	72	90	.444	23.0	Larry Dierker	3,056,139
2001	1st (Tie)	93	69	.574	—	Larry Dierker	2,904,280
2002	2nd	84	78	.519	13.0	Jimy Williams	2,517,407
2003	2nd	87	75	.537	1.0	Jimy Williams	2,454,241
2004	2nd	92	70	.568	13.0	Jimy Williams, Phil Garner	3,087,872
2005	2nd	89	73	.552	11.0	Phil Garner	2,804,760
2006	2nd	82	80	.506	1.5	Phil Garner	3,022,763
2007	4th	73	89	.451	12.0	Phil Garner, Cecil Cooper	3,020,405
2008	3rd	86	75	.534	11.0	Cecil Cooper	2,779,287
2009	5th	74	88	.457	17.0	Cecil Cooper, Dave Clark	2,521,076
2010	4th	76	86	.469	15.0	Brad Mills	2,331,490
2011	6th	56	106	.345	40.0	Brad Mills	2,067,016

American League Central Division

Year	Finish	Wins	Losses	Percentage	Games Behind	Manager	Attendance
2012	6th	55	107	.340	42.0	Brad Mills, Tony DeFrancesco	1,607,733
2013	5th	51	111	.315	45.0	Bo Porter	1,651,883
2014	4th	70	92	.432	28.0	Bo Porter, Tom Lawless	1,751,829
2015	2nd	86	76	.531	2.0	A.J. Hinch	2,153,585
2016	3rd	84	78	.515	11.0	A.J. Hinch	2,306,623
2017	1st	101	61	.623	+21.0	A.J. Hinch	2,403,671
2018	1st	103	59	.636	+6.0	A.J. Hinch	2,980,549
2019	1st	107	55	.000	+10.0	A.J. Hinch	2,857,367
2020	2nd	29	31	.483	7.0	Dusty Baker	0
2021	1st	95	67	.586	+5.0	Dusty Baker	2,068,509
2022	1st	106	56	.654	+16.0	Dusty Baker	2,688,998

* Split season.

Awards

Most Valuable Player
Jeff Bagwell, first base, 1994
Jose Altuve, second base, 2017

Rookie of the Year
Jeff Bagwell, first base, 1991
Carlos Correa, shortstop, 2015
Yordan Alvarez, designated hitter, 2019

Cy Young
Mike Scott, 1986
Roger Clemens, 2004
Dallas Keuchel, 2015
Justin Verlander, 2019
Justin Verlander, 2022

Manager of the Year (Since 1983)
Hal Lanier, 1986
Larry Dierker, 1998

Hall of Famers Who Played for the Astros
Jeff Bagwell, first base, 1991–2005
Craig Biggio, second base, 1988–2007

Nellie Fox, second base, 1964–65
Randy Johnson, pitcher, 1998
Eddie Mathews, third base, 1967
Joe Morgan, second base, 1963–71 and 1980
Robin Roberts, pitcher, 1965–66
Ivan Rodriguez, catcher, 2009
Nolan Ryan, pitcher, 1980–88
Don Sutton, pitcher, 1981–82

Retired Numbers

5	Jeff Bagwell
7	Craig Biggio
24	Jimmy Wynn
25	Jose Cruz
32	Jim Umbricht
33	Mike Scott
34	Nolan Ryan
40	Don Wilson
49	Larry Dierker

League Leaders, Batting

Batting Average, Season
Jose Altuve, 2014 .... .341
Jose Altuve, 2016 .... .338
Jose Altuve, 2017 .... .346
Yuli Gurriel, 2021 .... .319

Home Runs, Season
[No player]

RBIs, Season
Jeff Bagwell, 1994 116
Lance Berkman, 2002 128

Stolen Bases, Season
Craig Biggio, 1994 39
Michael Bourn, 2009 61
Michael Bourn, 2010 52
Jose Altuve, 2014 56
Jose Altuve, 2015 38

Total Bases, Season
Jeff Bagwell, 1994 300

Most Hits, Season
Jose Cruz, 1983 .... 189 (Tie)
Jose Altuve, 2014 225
Jose Altuve, 2015 200
Jose Altuve, 2016 216
Jose Altuve, 2017 204

Most Runs, Season

Jeff Bagwell, 1994	104
Craig Biggio, 1995	123
Craig Biggio, 1997	146
Jeff Bagwell, 1999	143
Jeff Bagwell, 2000	152

Batting Feats

Triple Crown Winners

[No player]

Hitting for the Cycle

Cesar Cedeno, Aug. 2, 1972
Cesar Cedeno, Aug. 9, 1976
Bob Watson, Jun. 24, 1977
Andujar Cedeno, Aug. 25, 1992
Jeff Bagwell, Jul. 18, 2001
Craig Biggio, Apr. 8, 2002
Luke Scott, Jul. 28, 2006
Brandon Barnes, Jul. 19, 2013

Six Hits in a Game

Joe Morgan, Jul. 8, 1965*
George Springer, May 7, 2018
* Extra-inning game.

40 or More Home Runs, Season

47	Jeff Bagwell, 2000
45	Lance Berkman, 2006
44	Richard Hidalgo, 2000
43	Jeff Bagwell, 1997
42	Jeff Bagwell, 1999
	Lance Berkman, 2002
41	Alex Bregman, 2019

League Leaders, Pitching

Most Wins, Season

Joe Niekro, 1979	21 (Tie)
Mike Scott, 1989	20
Roy Oswalt, 2004	20
Dallas Keuchel, 2015	20
Justin Verlander, 2019	21
Justin Verlander, 2022	18

Most Strikeouts, Season

J.R. Richard, 1978	303
J.R. Richard, 1979	313
Mike Scott, 1986	306
Nolan Ryan, 1987	270
Nolan Ryan, 1988	228
Justin Verlander, 2018	290
Gerrit Cole, 2019	326

Lowest ERA, Season

J.R. Richard, 1979	2.71
Nolan Ryan, 1981	1.69
Mike Scott, 1986	2.22
Nolan Ryan, 1987	2.76
Danny Darwin, 1990	2.21
Roger Clemens, 2005	1.87
Roy Oswalt, 2006	2.98
Gerrit Cole, 2019	2.50
Justin Verlander, 2022	1.75

Most Saves, Season

Fred Gladding, 1969	29
Jose Valverde, 2008	44
Roberto Osuna, 2019	38

Best Won–Lost Percentage, Season

Mark Portugal, 1993	18–4	.818
Mike Hampton, 1999	22–4	.846
Roger Clemens, 2004	18–4	.818
Charlie Morton, 2018	15–3	.833
Justin Verlander, 2022	18–4	.818

Pitching Feats

20 Wins, Season

Larry Dierker, 1969	20–13
J.R. Richard, 1976	20–15
Joe Niekro, 1979	21–11
Joe Niekro, 1980	20–12
Mike Scott, 1989	20–10
Mike Hampton, 1999	22–4
Jose Lima, 1999	21–10
Roy Oswalt, 2004	20–10
Roy Oswalt, 2005	20–12
Dallas Keuchel, 2015	20–8
Justin Verlander, 2019	21–6
Gerrit Cole, 2019	20–5

No-Hitters

Don Nottebart (vs. Phi. Phillies), May 17, 1963 (final: 4–1)
Ken Johnson (vs. Cin. Reds), Apr. 23, 1964 (final: 0–1)
Don Wilson (vs. Atl. Braves), Jun. 18, 1967 (final: 2–0)
Don Wilson (vs. Cin. Reds), May 1, 1969 (final: 4–0)
Larry Dierker (vs. Mon. Expos), Jul. 9, 1976 (final: 6–0)
Ken Forsch (vs. Atl. Braves), Apr. 7, 1979 (final: 6–0)

Nolan Ryan (vs. L.A. Dodgers), Sep. 26, 1981 (final: 5–0)
Mike Scott (vs. S.F. Giants), Sep. 25, 1986 (final: 2–0)
Darryl Kile (vs. N.Y. Mets), Sep. 8, 1993 (final: 7–1)
Roy Oswalt, Pete Munro, Kirk Saarloos, Brad Lidge, Octavio Dotel, and Billy Wagner (vs. N.Y. Yankees, AL), Jun. 11, 2003 (final: 8–0)
Mike Fiers (vs. L.A. Dodgers), Aug. 21, 2015 (final: 3–0)
Aaron Sanchez, Will Harris, Joe Biagini, and Chris Devenski (vs. Sea. Mariners), Aug. 3, 2019 (final: 9–0)
Justin Verlander (vs. Tor. Blue Jays), Sep. 1, 2019 (final: 2–0)
Cristian Javier, Hector Neris, and Ryan Pressly (vs. N.Y. Yankees), Jun. 25, 2022 (final: 3–0)
Cristian Javier, Bryan Abreu, Rafael Montero, Ryan Pressly, (vs. Phi. Phillies), Nov. 2, 2022 (final: 5–0) (World Series)

No-Hitters Pitched Against

Juan Marichal, S.F. Giants, Jun. 15, 1963 (final: 1–0)
Jim Maloney, Cin. Reds, Apr. 30, 1969 (final: 1–0)
Francisco Cordova and Ricardo Rincon, Pit. Pirates, Jul. 12, 1997 (final: 3–0)
Carlos Zambrano, Chi. Cubs, Sep. 14, 2008 (final: 5–0)
Matt Cain, S.F. Giants, Jun. 13, 2012 (final: 10–0) (perfect game)

Postseason Play

1980	NL West Playoff Game vs. L.A. Dodgers, won
	League Championship Series vs. Phi. Phillies, lost 3 games to 2
1981	First-Half Division Playoff Series vs. L.A. Dodgers, lost 3 games to 2
1986	League Championship Series vs. N.Y. Mets, lost 4 games to 2

1997 Division Series vs. Atl. Braves,
lost 3 games to 0

1998 Division Series vs. S.D. Padres,
lost 3 games to 1

1999 Division Series vs. Atl. Braves,
lost 3 games to 1

2001 Division Series vs. Atl. Braves,
lost 3 games to 0

2004 Division Series vs. Atl. Braves,
won 3 games to 2

League Championship Series vs.
St.L. Cardinals, lost 4 games
to 3

2005 Division Series vs. Atl. Braves,
won 3 games to 1

League Championship Series vs.
St.L. Cardinals, won 4 games
to 2

World Series vs. Chi. White Sox
(AL), lost 4 games to 0

2015 AL Wild Card Playoff Game vs.
N.Y. Yankees, won

Division Series vs. K.C. Royals,
lost 3 games to 2

2017 Division Series vs. Bos. Red Sox,
won 3 games to 1

League Championship Series vs.
N.Y. Yankees, won 4 games
to 3

World Series vs. L.A. Dodgers
(NL), won 4 games to 3

2018 Division Series vs. Cle. Indians,
won 3 games to 0

League Championship Series vs.
Bos. Red Sox, lost 4 games
to 1

2019 Division Series vs. T.B. Rays, won
3 games to 2

League Championship Series vs.
N.Y. Yankees, won 4 games
to 2

World Series vs. Was. Nationals
(NL), lost 4 games to 3

2020 Wild Card Series vs. Min. Twins,
won 2 games to 0

Division Series vs. Oak. A's, won
3 games to 1

League Championship Series vs.
T.B. Rays, lost 4 games to 3

2021 Division Series vs. Chi. White
Sox, won 3 games to 1

League Championship Series vs.
Bos. Red Sox, won 4 games
to 2

World Series vs. Atl. Braves (NL),
lost 4 games to 2

2022 Division Series vs. Sea.
Mariners, won 3 games to 0

League Championship Series vs.
N.Y. Yankees, won 4 games
to 0

World Series vs. Phi. Phillies
(NL), won 4 games to 2

Kansas City Royals

Dates of Operation: 1969–present (54 years)
Overall Record: 4066 wins, 4441 losses (.478)
Stadiums: Municipal Stadium, 1969–72; Kauffman Stadium (formerly Royals Stadium, 1973–93), 1973–present (capacity: 37,903)

Year-by-Year Finishes

Year	Finish	Wins	Losses	Percentage	Games Behind	Manager	Attendance
					West Division		
1969	4th	69	93	.426	28.0	Joe Gordon	902,414
1970	4th (Tie)	65	97	.401	33.0	Charlie Metro, Bob Lemon	693,047
1971	2nd	85	76	.528	16.0	Bob Lemon	910,784
1972	4th	76	78	.494	16.5	Bob Lemon	707,656
1973	2nd	88	74	.543	6.0	Jack McKeon	1,345,341
1974	5th	77	85	.475	13.0	Jack McKeon	1,173,292
1975	2nd	91	71	.562	7.0	Jack McKeon, Whitey Herzog	1,151,836
1976	1st	90	72	.556	+2.5	Whitey Herzog	1,680,265
1977	1st	102	60	.630	+8.0	Whitey Herzog	1,852,603
1978	1st	92	70	.568	+5.0	Whitey Herzog	2,255,493
1979	2nd	85	77	.525	3.0	Whitey Herzog	2,261,845
1980	1st	97	65	.599	+14.0	Jim Frey	2,288,714
1981*	5th/1st	50	53	.485	12.0/+1.0	Jim Frey, Dick Howser	1,279,403
1982	2nd	90	72	.556	3.0	Dick Howser	2,284,464
1983	2nd	79	83	.488	20.0	Dick Howser	1,963,875
1984	1st	84	78	.519	+3.0	Dick Howser	1,810,018
1985	1st	91	71	.562	+1.0	Dick Howser	2,162,717
1986	3rd (Tie)	76	86	.469	16.0	Dick Howser, Mike Ferraro	2,320,794
1987	2nd	83	79	.512	2.0	Billy Gardner, John Wathan	2,392,471
1988	3rd	84	77	.522	19.5	John Wathan	2,350,181
1989	2nd	92	70	.568	7.0	John Wathan	2,477,700
1990	6th	75	86	.466	27.5	John Wathan	2,244,956
1991	6th	82	80	.506	13.0	John Wathan, Hal McRae	2,161,537
1992	5th (Tie)	72	90	.444	24.0	Hal McRae	1,867,689
1993	3rd	84	78	.519	10.0	Hal McRae	1,934,578
					Central Division		
1994	3rd	64	51	.557	4.0	Hal McRae	1,400,494
1995	2nd	70	74	.486	30.0	Bob Boone	1,233,530
1996	5th	75	86	.466	24.0	Bob Boone	1,435,997
1997	5th	67	94	.416	19.0	Bob Boone, Tony Muser	1,517,638
1998	3rd	72	89	.447	16.5	Tony Muser	1,494,875
1999	4th	64	97	.398	32.5	Tony Muser	1,506,068
2000	4th	77	85	.475	18.0	Tony Muser	1,677,915
2001	5th	65	97	.401	26.0	Tony Muser	1,536,371
2002	4th	62	100	.383	32.5	Tony Muser, Tony Pena	1,323,034
2003	3rd	83	79	.512	7.0	Tony Pena	1,779,895
2004	5th	58	104	.358	34.0	Tony Pena	1,661,478
2005	5th	56	106	.346	43.0	Tony Pena, Bob Schaefer, Buddy Bell	1,371,181
2006	5th	62	100	.383	34.0	Buddy Bell	1,372,638
2007	5th	69	93	.426	27.5	Buddy Bell	1,616,867
2008	4th	75	87	.463	13.5	Trey Hillman	1,578,922

Year	Finish	Wins	Losses	Percentage	Games Behind	Manager	Attendance
2009	4th	65	97	.401	21.5	Trey Hillman	1,797,887
2010	5th	67	95	.414	27.0	Trey Hillman, Ned Yost	1,615,327
2011	4th	71	91	.438	24.0	Ned Yost	1,724,450
2012	3rd	72	90	.444	16.0	Ned Yost	1,739,859
2013	3rd	86	76	.531	7.0	Ned Yost	1,750,754
2014	2nd	89	73	.549	10.0	Ned Yost	1,956,482
2015	1st	95	67	.586	+12.0	Ned Yost	2,708,549
2016	3rd	81	81	.500	13.5	Ned Yost	2,557,712
2017	3rd	80	82	.494	22.0	Ned Yost	2,220,370
2018	5th	58	104	.358	33.0	Ned Yost	1,665,107
2019	4th	59	103	.364	42.0	Ned Yost	1,479,659
2020	4th	26	34	.433	10.0	Ned Yost	0
2021	4th	74	88	.457	19.0	Mike Matheny	1,159,613
2022	5th	65	97	.401	27.0	Mike Matheny	1,277,686

* Split season.

Awards

Most Valuable Player
George Brett, third base, 1980

Rookie of the Year
Lou Piniella, outfield, 1969
Bob Hamelin, designated hitter, 1994
Carlos Beltran, outfield, 1999
Angel Berroa, shortstop, 2003

Cy Young
Bret Saberhagen, 1985
Bret Saberhagen, 1989
David Cone, 1994
Zack Greinke, 2009

Manager of the Year (Since 1983)
Tony Pena, 2003

Hall of Famers Who Played for the Royals
George Brett, infield, 1973–93
Orlando Cepeda, designated hitter, 1974
Harmon Killebrew, designated hitter, 1975
Gaylord Perry, pitcher, 1983

Retired Numbers
5 .... George Brett
10 .... Dick Howser
20 .... Frank White

League Leaders, Batting

Batting Average, Season
George Brett, 1976 .... .333
George Brett, 1980 .... .390
Willie Wilson, 1982 .... .332
George Brett, 1990 .... .329

Home Runs, Season
Jorge Soler, 2019 48
Salvador Perez, 2021 ....48 (Tie)

RBIs, Season
Hal McRae, 1982 133
Salvador Perez, 2021 121

Stolen Bases, Season
Amos Otis, 1971 52
Freddie Patek, 1977 53
Willie Wilson, 1979 83
Johnny Damon, 2000 46
Whit Merrifield, 2017 34
Whit Merrifield, 2018 45
Whit Merrifield, 2019 206
Adalberto Mondesi, 2020 24
Whit Merrifield, 2021 40

Total Bases, Season
George Brett, 1976 298

Most Hits, Season
George Brett, 1975 195
George Brett, 1976 215
George Brett, 1979 212
Willie Wilson, 1980 230
Kevin Seitzer, 1987 .... 207 (Tie)
Whit Merrifield, 2018 192
Whit Merrifield, 2019 206

Most Runs, Season
Willie Wilson, 1980 133

Johnny Damon, 2000 136

Batting Feats

Triple Crown Winners
[No player]

Hitting for the Cycle
Freddie Patek, Jul. 9, 1971
John Mayberry, Aug. 5, 1977
George Brett, May 28, 1979
Frank White, Sep. 26, 1979
Frank White, Aug. 3, 1982
George Brett, Jul. 25, 1990

Six Hits in a Game
Bob Oliver, May 4, 1969
Kevin Seitzer, Aug. 2, 1987
Joe Randa, Sep. 9, 2004

40 or More Home Runs, Season
48 .... Jorge Soler, 2019
Salvador Perez, 2021

League Leaders, Pitching

Most Wins, Season
Dennis Leonard, 1977 .... 20 (Tie)
Bret Saberhagen, 1989 23
Jason Vargas, 2017 .... 18 (Tie)

Most Strikeouts, Season
[No player]

Lowest ERA, Season
Bret Saberhagen, 1989 .... 2.16
Kevin Appier, 1993 .... 2.56
Zack Greinke, 2009 .... 2.16

Most Saves, Season

Dan Quisenberry, 1980 .... 33 (Tie)
Dan Quisenberry, 1982 35
Dan Quisenberry, 1983 45
Dan Quisenberry, 1984 44
Dan Quisenberry, 1985 37
Jeff Montgomery, 1993 .... 45 (Tie)
Greg Holland, 2014 46

Best Won–Lost Percentage, Season

Paul Splittorff, 1977 .. 16–6 ...... .727
Bret Saberhagen, 1981. 23–6 ...... .793

Pitching Feats

20 Wins, Season

Paul Splittorff, 1973 20–11
Steve Busby, 1974 22–14
Dennis Leonard, 1977 20–12
Dennis Leonard, 1978 21–17
Dennis Leonard, 1980 20–11
Bret Saberhagen, 1985............. 20–6
Mark Gubicza, 1988................ 20–8
Bret Saberhagen, 1989............ 23–6

No-Hitters

Steve Busby (vs. Det. Tigers), Apr. 27,
1973 (final: 3–0)

Steve Busby (vs. Mil. Brewers), Jun.
19, 1974 (final: 2–0)
Jim Colborn (vs. Tex. Rangers), May
14, 1977 (final: 6–0)
Bret Saberhagen (vs. Chi. White Sox),
Aug. 26, 1991 (final: 7–0)

No-Hitters Pitched Against

Nolan Ryan, Cal. Angels, May 15, 1973
(final: 3–0)
Jon Lester, Bos. Red Sox, May 19,
2008 (final: 7–0)

Postseason Play

1976 League Championship Series vs.
N.Y. Yankees, lost 3 games to 2
1977 League Championship Series vs.
N.Y. Yankees, lost 3 games to 2
1978 League Championship Series vs.
N.Y. Yankees, lost 3 games to 1
1980 League Championship Series vs.
N.Y. Yankees, won 3 games
to 0
World Series vs. Phi. Phillies
(NL), lost 4 games to 2

1981 First-Half Division Playoff vs.
Oak.
A's, lost 3 games to 0
1984 League Championship Series vs.
Det. Tigers, lost 3 games to 0
1985 League Championship Series vs.
Tor. Blue Jays, won 4 games
to 3
World Series vs. St.L. Cardinals
(NL), won 4 games to 3
2014 AL Wild Card Playoff Game vs.
Oak. A's, won
Division Series vs. L.A. Angels,
won 3 games to 0
League Championship Series vs.
Bal. Orioles, won 4 games to 0
World Series vs. S.F. Giants
(NL), lost 4 games to 3
2015 Division Series vs. Hou. Astros,
won 3 games to 2
League Championship Series vs.
Tor. Blue Jays, won 4 games to 2
World Series vs. N.Y. Mets (NL),
won 4 games to 1

Los Angeles Angels

Dates of Operation: 1961–present (62 years)

Overall Record: 4885 wins, 4927 losses (.498)

Stadiums: Wrigley Field, 1961; Chavez Ravine (also known as Dodger Stadium), 1962–65; Angel Stadium of Anaheim (formerly Anaheim Stadium, 1996–97, Edison International Field 1998–2003), 1966–present (capacity: 45,957)

Other Names: Los Angeles Angels (1961–64), California Angels (1965–96), Anaheim Angels (1996–2004), Los Angeles Angels of Anaheim (2005–15)

Year-by-Year Finishes

Year	Finish	Wins	Losses	Percentage	Games Behind	Manager	Attendance
1961	8th	70	91	.435	38.5	Bill Rigney	603,510
1962	3rd	86	76	.531	10.0	Bill Rigney	1,144,063
1963	9th	70	91	.435	34.0	Bill Rigney	821,015
1964	5th	82	80	.506	17.0	Bill Rigney	760,439
1965	7th	75	87	.463	27.0	Bill Rigney	566,727
1966	6th	80	82	.494	18.0	Bill Rigney	1,400,321
1967	5th	84	77	.522	7.5	Bill Rigney	1,317,713
1968	8th	67	95	.414	36.0	Bill Rigney	1,025,956
				West Division			
1969	3rd	71	91	.438	26.0	Bill Rigney, Lefty Phillips	758,388
1970	3rd	86	76	.531	12.0	Lefty Phillips	1,077,741
1971	4th	76	86	.469	25.5	Lefty Phillips	926,373
1972	5th	75	80	.484	18.0	Del Rice	744,190
1973	4th	79	83	.488	15.0	Bobby Winkles	1,058,206
1974	6th	68	94	.420	22.0	Bobby Winkles, Dick Williams	917,269
1975	6th	72	89	.447	25.5	Dick Williams	1,058,163
1976	4th (Tie)	76	86	.469	14.0	Dick Williams, Norm Sherry	1,006,774
1977	5th	74	88	.457	28.0	Norm Sherry, Dave Garcia	1,432,633
1978	2nd (Tie)	87	75	.537	5.0	Dave Garcia, Jim Fregosi	1,755,386
1979	1st	88	74	.543	+3.0	Jim Fregosi	2,523,575
1980	6th	65	95	.406	31.0	Jim Fregosi	2,297,327
1981*	4th/7th	51	59	.464	6.0/8.5	Jim Fregosi, Gene Mauch	1,441,545
1982	1st	93	69	.574	+3.0	Gene Mauch	2,807,360
1983	5th (Tie)	70	92	.432	29.0	John McNamara	2,555,016
1984	2nd (Tie)	81	81	.500	3.0	John McNamara	2,402,997
1985	2nd	90	72	.556	1.0	Gene Mauch	2,567,427
1986	1st	92	70	.568	+5.0	Gene Mauch	2,655,872
1987	6th (Tie)	75	87	.463	10.0	Gene Mauch	2,696,299
1988	4th	75	87	.463	29.0	Cookie Rojas	2,340,925
1989	3rd	91	71	.562	8.0	Doug Rader	2,647,291
1990	4th	80	82	.494	23.0	Doug Rader	2,555,688
1991	7th	81	81	.500	14.0	Doug Rader, Buck Rodgers	2,416,236
1992	5th (Tie)	72	90	.444	24.0	Buck Rodgers	2,065,444
1993	5th (Tie)	71	91	.438	23.0	Buck Rodgers	2,057,460
1994	4th	47	68	.409	5.5	Buck Rodgers, Marcel Lachemann	1,512,622
1995	2nd	78	67	.538	1.0	Marcel Lachemann	1,748,680
1996	4th	70	91	.435	19.5	Marcel Lachemann, John McNamara, Joe Maddon	1,820,521
1997	2nd	84	78	.519	6.0	Terry Collins	1,767,330
1998	2nd	85	77	.525	3.0	Terry Collins	2,519,210
1999	4th	70	92	.432	25.0	Terry Collins, Joe Maddon	2,253,123
2000	3rd	82	80	.506	9.5	Mike Scioscia	2,066,977
2001	3rd	75	87	.463	41.0	Mike Scioscia	2,000,917
2002	2nd	99	63	.611	4.0	Mike Scioscia	2,305,565

Year	Finish	Wins	Losses	Percentage	Games Behind	Manager	Attendance
2003	3rd	77	85	.475	19.0	Mike Scioscia	3,061,094
2004	1st	92	70	.568	+1.0	Mike Scioscia	3,375,677
2005	1st	95	67	.586	+7.0	Mike Scioscia	3,404,686
2006	2nd	89	73	.649	4.0	Mike Scioscia	3,406,790
2007	1st	94	68	.580	+6.5	Mike Scioscia	3,365,632
2008	1st	100	62	.617	+21.0	Mike Scioscia	3,336,744
2009	1st	97	65	.599	+10.0	Mike Scioscia	3,240,386
2010	3rd	80	82	.494	10.0	Mike Scioscia	3,250,814
2011	2nd	86	76	.531	10.0	Mike Scioscia	3,166,321
2012	3rd	89	73	.549	5.0	Mike Scioscia	3,061,770
2013	3rd	78	84	.481	18.0	Mike Scioscia	3,019,505
2014	1st	98	64	.605	+5.0	Mike Scioscia	3,095,935
2015	3rd	85	77	.525	3.0	Mike Scioscia	3,012,765
2016	4th	74	88	.494	21.0	Mike Scioscia	3,016,142
2017	2nd	80	82	.494	21.0	Mike Scioscia	3,019,585
2018	4th	80	82	.494	23.0	Mike Scioscia	3,020,216
2019	4th	72	90	.444	35.0	Brad Ausmus	3,023,012
2020	4th	26	34	.433	10.0	Joe Maddon	0
2021	4th	77	85	.475	18.0	Joe Maddon	1,515,689
2022	3rd	73	89	.451	33.0	Joe Maddon, Phil Nevin	2,457,461

* Split season.

Awards

Most Valuable Player

Don Baylor, outfield, 1979

Vladimir Guererro, outfield, 2004

Mike Trout, outfield, 2014

Mike Trout, outfield, 2016

Mike Trout, outfield, 2019

Shohei Ohtani, pitcher and designated hitter, 2021

Rookie of the Year

Tim Salmon, outfield, 1993

Mike Trout, outfield, 2012

Shohei Ohtani, pitcher and designated hitter, 2018

Manager of the Year (Since 1983)

Mike Scioscia, 2002

Mike Scioscia, 2009

Cy Young

Dean Chance, 1964

Bartolo Colon, 2005

Hall of Famers Who Played for the Angels

Rod Carew, infield, 1979–85

Vladimir Guerrero, outfield, 2004–09

Rickey Henderson, outfield, 1997

Reggie Jackson, designated hitter and outfield, 1982–86

Eddie Murray, designated hitter, 1997

Frank Robinson, designated hitter, 1973–74

Nolan Ryan, pitcher, 1972–79

Lee Smith, pitcher, 1995–96

Don Sutton, pitcher, 1985–87

Hoyt Wilhelm, pitcher, 1969

Dave Winfield, outfield and designated hitter, 1990–91

Retired Numbers

11 .... Jim Fregosi

26 .... Gene Autry

29 .... Rod Carew

30 .... Nolan Ryan

50 .... Jimmy Reese

League Leaders, Batting

Batting Average, Season

Alex Johnson, 1970 .... .329

Home Runs, Season

Bobby Grich, 1981 .... 22 (Tie)

Reggie Jackson, 1982 .... 39 (Tie)

Troy Glaus, 2000 47

RBIs, Season

Don Baylor, 1979 139

Mike Trout, 2014 111

Stolen Bases, Season

Mickey Rivers, 1975 70

Chone Figgins, 2005 62

Mike Trout, 2012 49

Total Bases, Season

Vladimir Guerrero, 2004 366

Mike Trout, 2014 338

Most Hits, Season

Darin Erstad, 2000 240

Most Runs, Season

Albie Pearson, 1962 115

Don Baylor, 1979 120

Vladimir Guerrero, 2004 124

Mike Trout, 2012 129

Mike Trout, 2013 109

Mike Trout, 2014 115

Mike Trout, 2016 123

Batting Feats

Triple Crown Winners

[No player]

Hitting for the Cycle

Jim Fregosi, Jul. 28, 1964

Jim Fregosi, May 20, 1968

Dan Ford, Aug. 10, 1979

Dave Winfield, Jun. 24, 1991

Jeff DaVanon, Aug. 25, 2004

Chone Figgins, Sep. 16, 2006
Mike Trout, May 21, 2013
Shohei Ohtani, Jun. 13, 2019
Jared Walsh, Jun. 11, 2022

Six Hits in a Game
Garret Anderson, Sep. 27, 1996*
C.J. Cron, Jul. 2, 2016
* Extra-inning game.

40 or More Home Runs, Season
47 ....Troy Glaus, 2000
46 ....Shohei Ohtani, 2021
45 ....Mike Trout, 2019
41 ....Troy Glaus, 2001
40 ....Mike Trout, 2022

League Leaders, Pitching

Most Wins, Season
Dean Chance, 1964..............20 (Tie)
Bartolo Colon, 2005 21
Jered Weaver, 2012..............20 (Tie)
Jered Weaver, 2014..............18 (Tie)

Most Strikeouts, Season
Nolan Ryan, 1972 329
Nolan Ryan, 1973 383
Nolan Ryan, 1974 367
Frank Tanana, 1975 269
Nolan Ryan, 1976 327
Nolan Ryan, 1977 341
Nolan Ryan, 1978 260
Nolan Ryan, 1979 223
Jered Weaver, 2010...................233

Lowest ERA, Season
Dean Chance, 1964..................1.65
Frank Tanana, 1977 ....2.54
John Lackey, 2007 ....3.01

Most Saves, Season
Bryan Harvey, 1991.....................46
Francisco Rodriguez, 2005.....45 (Tie)
Francisco Rodriguez, 2006...........47
Francisco Rodriguez, 2007...........62
Brian Fuentes, 2008 48

Best Won–Lost Percentage, Season
Jered Weaver, 2012....20–5.. .800 (Tie)
Matt Shoemaker, 2014....16–4..... .800

Pitching Feats

20 Wins, Season
Dean Chance, 1964................. 20–9
Clyde Wright, 1970 22–12
Andy Messersmith, 1971......... 20–13
Nolan Ryan, 1973 21–16
Bill Singer, 1973..................... 20–14
Nolan Ryan, 1974 22–16
Bartolo Colon, 2005 21–8
Jered Weaver, 2012................. 20–5

No-Hitters
Bo Belinsky (vs. Bal. Orioles), May 5, 1962 (final: 2–0)
Clyde Wright (vs. Oak. A's), Jul. 3, 1970 (final: 4–0)
Nolan Ryan (vs. K.C. Royals), May 15, 1973 (final: 3–0)
Nolan Ryan (vs. Det. Tigers), Jul. 15, 1973 (final: 6–0)
Nolan Ryan (vs. Min. Twins), Sep. 28, 1974 (final: 4–0)
Nolan Ryan (vs. Bal. Orioles), Jun. 1, 1975 (final: 1–0)
Mike Witt (vs. Tex. Rangers), Sep. 30, 1984 (final: 1–0) (perfect game)
Mark Langston and Mike Witt (vs. Sea. Mariners), Apr. 11, 1990 (final: 1–0)
Jered Weaver (vs. Min. Twins), May 2, 2012 (final: 9–0)
Taylor Cole and Felix Pena (vs. Sea. Mariners), Jul. 12, 2019 (final: 13–0)
Reid Detmers (vs. T.B. Rays), May 10, 2022 (final: 12–0)

No-Hitters Pitched Against
Earl Wilson, Bos. Red Sox, Jun. 26, 1962 (final: 2–0)
Vida Blue, Glenn Abbott, Paul Lindblad, and Rollie Fingers, Oak. A's, Sep. 28, 1975 (final: 5–0)
Dennis Eckersley, Cle. Indians, May 30, 1977 (final: 1–0)

Bert Blyleven, Tex. Rangers, Sep. 22, 1977 (final: 6–0)
Joe Cowley, Chi. White Sox, Sep. 19, 1986 (final: 7–1)
Kenny Rogers, Tex. Rangers, Jul. 28, 1994 (final: 4–0) (perfect game)
Eric Milton, Min. Twins, Sep. 11, 1999 (final: 7–0)

Postseason

1979 League Championship Series vs. Bal. Orioles, lost 3 games to 1
1982 League Championship Series vs. Mil. Brewers, lost 3 games to 2
1986 League Championship Series vs. Bos. Red Sox, lost 4 games to 3
1995 AL West Playoff Game vs. Sea. Mariners, lost
2002 Division Series vs. N.Y. Yankees, won 3 games to 1
League Championship Series vs. Min. Twins, won 4 games to 1
World Series vs. S.F. Giants (NL), won 4 games to 3
2004 Division Series vs. Bos. Red Sox, lost 3 games to 0
2005 Division Series vs. N.Y. Yankees, won 3 games to 2
League Championship Series vs. Chi. White Sox, lost 4 games to 1
2007 Division Series vs. Bos. Red Sox, lost 3 games to 0
2008 Division Series vs. Bos. Red Sox, lost 3 games to 1
2009 Division Series vs. Bos. Red Sox, won 3 games to 0
League Championship Series vs. N.Y. Yankees, lost 4 games to 2
2014 Division Series vs. K.C. Royals, lost 3 games to 0

Minnesota Twins

Dates of Operation: 1961–present (62 years)
Overall Record: 4867 wins, 4936 losses (.496)
Stadiums: Metropolitan Stadium, 1961–81; Hubert H. Humphrey Metrodome (also known as The Metrodome), 1982–2009; Target Field, 2010–present (capacity: 39,021)

Year-by-Year Finishes

Year	Finish	Wins	Losses	Percentage	Games Behind	Manager	Attendance
1961	7th	70	90	.438	38.0	Cookie Lavagetto, Sam Mele	1,256,723
1962	2nd	91	71	.562	5.0	Sam Mele	1,433,116
1963	3rd	91	70	.565	13.0	Sam Mele	1,406,652
1964	6th (Tie)	79	83	.488	20.0	Sam Mele	1,207,514
1965	1st	102	60	.630	+7.0	Sam Mele	1,463,258
1966	2nd	89	73	.549	9.0	Sam Mele	1,259,374
1967	2nd (Tie)	91	71	.562	1.0	Sam Mele, Cal Ermer	1,483,547
1968	7th	79	83	.488	24.0	Cal Ermer	1,143,257

West Division

Year	Finish	Wins	Losses	Percentage	Games Behind	Manager	Attendance
1969	1st	97	65	.599	+9.0	Billy Martin	1,349,328
1970	1st	98	64	.605	+9.0	Bill Rigney	1,261,887
1971	5th	74	86	.463	26.5	Bill Rigney	940,858
1972	3rd	77	77	.500	15.5	Bill Rigney, Frank Quilici	797,901
1973	3rd	81	81	.500	13.0	Frank Quilici	907,499
1974	3rd	82	80	.506	8.0	Frank Quilici	662,401
1975	4th	76	83	.478	20.5	Frank Quilici	737,156
1976	3rd	85	77	.525	5.0	Gene Mauch	715,394
1977	4th	84	77	.522	17.5	Gene Mauch	1,162,727
1978	4th	73	89	.451	19.0	Gene Mauch	787,878
1979	4th	82	80	.506	6.0	Gene Mauch	1,070,521
1980	3rd	77	84	.478	19.5	Gene Mauch, Johnny Goryl	769,206
1981*	7th/4th	41	68	.376	18.0/6.0	Johnny Goryl, Billy Gardner	469,090
1982	7th	60	102	.370	33.0	Billy Gardner	921,186
1983	5th (Tie)	70	92	.432	29.0	Billy Gardner	858,939
1984	2nd (Tie)	81	81	.500	3.0	Billy Gardner	1,598,422
1985	4th (Tie)	77	85	.475	14.0	Billy Gardner, Ray Miller	1,651,814
1986	6th	71	91	.438	21.0	Ray Miller, Tom Kelly	1,255,453
1987	1st	85	77	.525	+2.0	Tom Kelly	2,081,976
1988	2nd	91	71	.562	13.0	Tom Kelly	3,030,672
1989	5th	80	82	.494	19.0	Tom Kelly	2,277,438
1990	7th	74	88	.457	29.0	Tom Kelly	1,751,584
1991	1st	95	67	.586	+8.0	Tom Kelly	2,293,842
1992	2nd	90	72	.556	6.0	Tom Kelly	2,482,428
1993	5th (Tie)	71	91	.438	23.0	Tom Kelly	2,048,673

Central Division

Year	Finish	Wins	Losses	Percentage	Games Behind	Manager	Attendance
1994	4th	53	60	.469	14.0	Tom Kelly	1,398,565
1995	5th	56	88	.389	44.0	Tom Kelly	1,057,667
1996	4th	78	84	.481	21.5	Tom Kelly	1,437,352
1997	4th	68	94	.420	18.5	Tom Kelly	1,411,064
1998	4th	70	92	.432	19.0	Tom Kelly	1,165,980
1999	5th	63	97	.394	33.0	Tom Kelly	1,202,829
2000	5th	69	93	.426	26.0	Tom Kelly	1,059,715
2001	2nd	85	77	.525	6.0	Tom Kelly	1,782,926
2002	1st	94	67	.584	+13.5	Ron Gardenhire	1,924,473
2003	1st	90	72	.556	+4.0	Ron Gardenhire	1,946,011

Year	Finish	Wins	Losses	Percentage	Games Behind	Manager	Attendance
2004	1st	92	70	.568	+9.0	Ron Gardenhire	1,911,418
2005	3rd	83	79	.512	16.0	Ron Gardenhire	2,034,243
2006	1st	96	66	.593	+1.0	Ron Gardenhire	2,285,018
2007	3rd	79	83	.488	17.5	Ron Gardenhire	2,296,347
2008	2nd	88	75	.540	1.0	Ron Gardenhire	2,302,431
2009	1st	87	76	.534	+1.0	Ron Gardenhire	2,416,237
2010	1st	94	68	.580	+6.0	Ron Gardenhire	3,223,640
2011	5th	63	99	.389	32.0	Ron Gardenhire	3,168,116
2012	5th	66	96	.407	22.0	Ron Gardenhire	2,776,354
2013	4th	66	96	.407	27.0	Ron Gardenhire	2,477,644
2014	5th	70	92	.432	20.0	Ron Gardenhire	2,250,606
2015	2nd	83	79	.512	12.0	Paul Molitor	2,220,054
2016	5th	59	103	.364	35.5	Paul Molitor	1,963,912
2017	2nd	85	77	.525	17.0	Paul Molitor	2,051,279
2018	2nd	78	84	.481	13.0	Paul Molitor	1,959,197
2019	1st	101	61	.623	+8.0	Rocco Baldelli	2,303,299
2020	1st	36	24	.600	+1.0	Rocco Baldelli	0
2021	5th	73	89	.451	20.0	Rocco Baldelli	1,310,199
2022	3rd	78	84	.481	14.0	Rocco Baldelli	1,801,128

* Split season.

Awards

Most Valuable Player
Zoilo Versalles, shortstop, 1965
Harmon Killebrew, infield, 1969
Rod Carew, first base, 1977
Justin Morneau, first base, 2006
Joe Mauer, catcher, 2009

Rookie of the Year
Tony Oliva, outfield, 1964
Rod Carew, second base, 1967
John Castino (co-winner), third base, 1979
Chuck Knoblauch, second base, 1991
Marty Cordova, outfield, 1995

Cy Young
Jim Perry, 1970
Frank Viola, 1988
Johan Santana, 2004
Johan Santana, 2006

Manager of the Year (Since 1983)
Tom Kelly, 1991
Ron Gardenhire, 2010
Paul Molitor, 2017
Rocco Baldelli, 2019

Hall of Famers Who Played for the Twins
Rod Carew, infield, 1967–78
Steve Carlton, pitcher, 1987–88
Jim Kaat, pitcher, 1961–73
Harmon Killebrew, infield and outfield, 1961–74
Paul Molitor, shortstop, second base, designated hitter, 1996–98
Jack Morris, pitcher, 1991
Tony Oliva, outfield, 1962–76
David Ortiz, first base and designated hitter, 1997–2002
Kirby Puckett, outfield, 1984–95
Jim Thome, designated hitter, 2010–11
Dave Winfield, designated hitter, 1993–94

Retired Numbers
3 .... Harmon Killebrew
6 .... Tony Oliva
7 .... Joe Mauer
10 .... Tom Kelly
14 .... Kent Hrbek
28 .... Bert Blyleven
29 .... Rod Carew
34 .... Kirby Puckett
36 .... Jim Kaat

League Leaders, Batting

Batting Average, Season
Tony Oliva, 1964 .... .323
Tony Oliva, 1965 .... .321
Rod Carew, 1969 .... .332
Tony Oliva, 1971 .... .337
Rod Carew, 1972 .... .318
Rod Carew, 1973 .... .350
Rod Carew, 1974 .... .364
Rod Carew, 1975 .... .359
Rod Carew, 1977 .... .388
Rod Carew, 1978 .... .333
Kirby Puckett, 1989 .... .339
Joe Mauer, 2006 .... .347
Joe Mauer, 2008 .... .328
Joe Mauer, 2009 .... .365
Luis Arraez, 2022 .... .316

Home Runs, Season
Harmon Killebrew, 1962 48
Harmon Killebrew, 1963 45
Harmon Killebrew, 1964 49
Harmon Killebrew, 1967 .... 44 (Tie)
Harmon Killebrew, 1969 49

RBIs, Season
Harmon Killebrew, 1962 126
Harmon Killebrew, 1969 140
Harmon Killebrew, 1971 119
Larry Hisle, 1977 119
Kirby Puckett, 1994 112

Stolen Bases, Season
[No player]

Total Bases, Season
Tony Oliva, 1964 374

Zoilo Versalles, 1965.................308
Kirby Puckett, 1988...................358
Kirby Puckett, 1992...................313

Most Hits, Season
Tony Oliva, 1964.....................217
Tony Oliva, 1965.....................185
Tony Oliva, 1966.....................191
Tony Oliva, 1969.....................197
Tony Oliva, 1970.....................204
Cesar Tovar, 1971 204
Rod Carew, 1973 203
Rod Carew, 1974 218
Rod Carew, 1977 239
Kirby Puckett, 1987............207 (Tie)
Kirby Puckett, 1988..................234
Kirby Puckett, 1989..................215
Kirby Puckett, 1992..................210
Paul Molitor, 1996 225

Most Runs, Season
Bob Allison, 1963........................99
Tony Oliva, 1964.....................109
Zoilo Versalles, 1965.................126
Rod Carew, 1977 128

Batting Feats

Triple Crown Winners
[No player]

Hitting for the Cycle
Rod Carew, May 20, 1970
Cesar Tovar, Sep. 19, 1972
Larry Hisle, Jun. 4, 1976
Lyman Bostock, Jul. 24, 1976
Mike Cubbage, Jul. 27, 1978
Gary Ward, Sep. 18, 1980
Kirby Puckett, Aug. 1, 1986
Carlos Gomez, May 7, 2008
Jason Kubel, Apr. 17, 2009
Michael Cuddyer, May 22, 2009
Jorge Polanco, Apr. 5, 2019

Six Hits in a Game
Kirby Puckett, Aug. 30, 1987
Kirby Puckett, May 23, 1991*
* Extra-inning game.

40 or More Home Runs, Season
49 .... Harmon Killebrew, 1964
              Harmon Killebrew, 1969
48 .... Harmon Killebrew, 1962

46 .... Harmon Killebrew, 1961
45 .... Harmon Killebrew, 1963
44 .... Harmon Killebrew, 1967
42 ....Brian Dozier, 2016
41 .... Harmon Killebrew, 1970
              Nelson Cruz, 2019

League Leaders, Pitching

Most Wins, Season
Mudcat Grant, 1965 21
Jim Kaat, 1966.............................25
Jim Perry, 1970 24
Frank Viola, 1988.,.......................24
Scott Erickson, 1991..............20 (Tie)
Johan Santana, 2006 ....19 (Tie)

Most Strikeouts, Season
Camilo Pascual, 1961 221
Camilo Pascual, 1962 206
Camilo Pascual, 1963 202
Bert Blyleven*, 1985 206
Johan Santana, 2004 265
Johan Santana, 2005 238
Johan Santana, 2006 245
* 129 with Cle. Indians and 77 with Min. Twins.

Lowest ERA, Season
Allan Anderson, 1988 ....2.45
Johan Santana, 2004 ....2.61
Johan Santana, 2006 ....2.77

Most Saves, Season
Ron Perranoski, 1969 31
Ron Perranoski, 1970 34
Mike Marshall, 1979....................32
Eddie Guardado, 2002 45

Best Won–Lost Percentage, Season
Mudcat Grant, 1965...21–7...... .750
Bill Campbell, 1976....17–5...... .773
Frank Viola, 1988 ......24–7...... .774
Scott Erickson, 1991 ...20–8...... .714
Johan Santana, 2003..12–3...... .800
Francisco Liriano, 2006 12–3...... .800

Pitching Feats

Triple Crown Winner
Johan Santana, 2006 (19–6, 2.77 ERA, 245 SO)

20 Wins, Season
Camilo Pascual, 1962 20–11

Camilo Pascual, 1963 21–9
Mudcat Grant, 1965 21–7
Jim Kaat, 1966...................... 25–13
Dean Chance, 1967............... 20–14
Jim Perry, 1969 20–6
Dave Boswell, 1969 20–12
Jim Perry, 1970 24–12
Bert Blyleven, 1973................ 20–17
Dave Goltz, 1977 20–11
Jerry Koosman, 1979 20–13
Frank Viola, 1988.................... 24–7
Scott Erickson, 1991 20–8
Brad Radke, 1997.................. 20–10
Johan Santana, 2004 20–6

No-Hitters
Jack Kralick (vs. K.C. A's), Aug. 26, 1962 (final: 1–0)
Dean Chance (vs. Cle. Indians), Aug. 25, 1967 (final: 2–1)
Scott Erickson (vs. Mil. Brewers), Apr. 27, 1994 (final: 6–0)
Eric Milton (vs. Ana. Angels), Sep. 11, 1999 (final: 7–0)
Francisco Liriano (vs. Cle. Indians), May 3, 2011 (final 1–0)

No-Hitters Pitched Against
Catfish Hunter, Oak. A's, May 8, 1968 (final: 4–0) (perfect game)
Vida Blue, Oak. A's, Sep. 21, 1970 (final: 6–0)
Nolan Ryan, Cal. Angels, Sep. 28, 1974 (final: 4–0)
David Wells, N.Y. Yankees, May 17, 1998 (final: 4–0) (perfect game)
Jered Weaver, L.A. Angels, May 2, 2012 (final: 4–0)

Postseason Play

1965 World Series vs. L.A. Dodgers (NL), lost 4 games to 3
1969 Championship Series vs. Bal. Orioles, lost 3 games to 0
1970 Championship Series vs. Bal. Orioles, lost 3 games to 0
1987 Championship Series vs. Det. Tigers, won 3 games to 1
       World Series vs. St.L. Cardinals (NL), won 4 games to 3
1991 Championship Series vs. Tor. Blue Jays, won 4 games to 1

World Series vs. Atl. Braves (NL), won 4 games to 3

2002 Division Series vs. Oak. A's, won 3 games to 2

Championship Series vs. Ana. Angels, lost 4 games to 1

2003 Division Series vs. N.Y. Yankees, lost 3 games to 1

2004 Division Series vs. N.Y. Yankees, lost 3 games to 1

2006 Division Series vs. Oak. A's, lost 3 games to 0

2008 AL Central Playoff Game vs. Chi White Sox, lost

2009 AL Central Playoff Game vs. Det. Tigers, won

Division Series vs. N.Y. Yankees, lost 3 games to 0

2010 Division Series vs. N.Y. Yankees, lost 3 games to 0

2017 AL Wild Card Playoff Game vs. N.Y. Yankees, lost

2019 Division Series vs. N.Y. Yankees, lost 3 games to 0

2020 Wild Card Series vs. Hou. Astros, lost 2 games to 0

New York Yankees

Dates of Operation: 1903–present (120 years)
Overall Record: 10,602 wins, 8000 losses (.570)
Stadiums: Hilltop Park, 1903–12; Polo Grounds, 1912, 1913–22; Harrison Field, 1918 (Sundays only); Yankee Stadium, 1923–73, 1976–2008; Shea Stadium, 1974–75; Yankee Stadium II, 2009–present (capacity: 49,642)
Other Name: Hilltoppers, Highlanders

Year-by-Year Finishes

Year	Finish	Wins	Losses	Percentage	Games Behind	Manager	Attendance
1903	4th	72	62	.537	17.0	Clark Griffith	211,808
1904	2nd	92	59	.609	1.5	Clark Griffith	438,919
1905	6th	71	78	.477	21.5	Clark Griffith	309,100
1906	2nd	90	61	.596	3.0	Clark Griffith	434,709
1907	5th	70	78	.473	21.0	Clark Griffith	350,020
1908	8th	51	103	.331	39.5	Clark Griffith, Kid Elberfeld	305,500
1909	5th	74	77	.490	23.5	George Stallings	501,000
1910	2nd	88	63	.583	14.5	George Stallings, Hal Chase	355,857
1911	6th	76	76	.500	25.5	Hal Chase	302,444
1912	8th	50	102	.329	55.0	Harry Wolverton	242,194
1913	7th	57	94	.377	38.0	Frank Chance	357,551
1914	6th (Tie)	70	84	.455	30.0	Frank Chance, Roger Peckinpaugh	359,477
1915	5th	69	83	.454	32.5	Bill Donovan	256,035
1916	4th	80	74	.519	11.0	Bill Donovan	469,211
1917	6th	71	82	.464	28.5	Bill Donovan	330,294
1918	4th	60	63	.488	13.5	Miller Huggins	282,047
1919	3rd	80	59	.576	7.5	Miller Huggins	619,164
1920	3rd	95	59	.617	3.0	Miller Huggins	1,289,422
1921	1st	98	55	.641	+4.5	Miller Huggins	1,230,696
1922	1st	94	60	.610	+1.0	Miller Huggins	1,026,134
1923	1st	98	54	.645	+16.0	Miller Huggins	1,007,066
1924	2nd	89	63	.586	2.0	Miller Huggins	1,053,533
1925	7th	69	85	.448	30.0	Miller Huggins	697,267
1926	1st	91	63	.591	+3.0	Miller Huggins	1,027,095
1927	1st	110	44	.714	+19.0	Miller Huggins	1,164,015
1928	1st	101	53	.656	+2.5	Miller Huggins	1,072,132
1929	2nd	88	66	.571	18.0	Miller Huggins, Art Fletcher	960,148
1930	3rd	86	68	.558	16.0	Bob Shawkey	1,169,230
1931	2nd	94	59	.614	13.5	Joe McCarthy	912,437
1932	1st	107	47	.695	+13.0	Joe McCarthy	962,320
1933	2nd	91	59	.607	7.0	Joe McCarthy	728,014
1934	2nd	94	60	.610	7.0	Joe McCarthy	854,682
1935	2nd	89	60	.597	3.0	Joe McCarthy	657,508
1936	1st	102	51	.667	+19.5	Joe McCarthy	976,913
1937	1st	102	52	.662	+13.0	Joe McCarthy	998,148
1938	1st	99	53	.651	+9.5	Joe McCarthy	970,916
1939	1st	106	45	.702	+17.0	Joe McCarthy	859,785
1940	3rd	88	66	.571	2.0	Joe McCarthy	988,975
1941	1st	101	53	.656	+17.0	Joe McCarthy	964,722
1942	1st	103	51	.669	+9.0	Joe McCarthy	988,251
1943	1st	98	56	.636	+13.5	Joe McCarthy	645,006

Year	Finish	Wins	Losses	Percentage	Games Behind	Manager	Attendance
1944	3rd	83	71	.539	6.0	Joe McCarthy	822,864
1945	4th	81	71	.533	6.5	Joe McCarthy	881,846
1946	3rd	87	67	.565	17.0	Joe McCarthy, Bill Dickey, Johnny Neun	2,265,512
1947	1st	97	57	.630	+12.0	Bucky Harris	2,178,937
1948	3rd	94	60	.610	2.5	Bucky Harris	2,373,901
1949	1st	97	57	.630	+1.0	Casey Stengel	2,281,676
1950	1st	98	56	.636	+3.0	Casey Stengel	2,081,380
1951	1st	98	56	.636	+5.0	Casey Stengel	1,950,107
1952	1st	95	59	.617	+2.0	Casey Stengel	1,629,665
1953	1st	99	52	.656	+8.5	Casey Stengel	1,537,811
1954	2nd	103	51	.669	8.0	Casey Stengel	1,475,171
1955	1st	96	58	.623	+3.0	Casey Stengel	1,490,138
1956	1st	97	57	.630	+9.0	Casey Stengel	1,491,784
1957	1st	98	56	.636	+8.0	Casey Stengel	1,497,134
1958	1st	92	62	.597	+10.0	Casey Stengel	1,428,438
1959	3rd	79	75	.513	15.0	Casey Stengel	1,552,030
1960	1st	97	57	.630	+8.0	Casey Stengel	1,627,349
1961	1st	109	53	.673	+8.0	Ralph Houk	1,747,725
1962	1st	96	66	.593	+5.0	Ralph Houk	1,493,574
1963	1st	104	57	.646	+10.5	Ralph Houk	1,308,920
1964	1st	99	63	.611	+1.0	Yogi Berra	1,305,638
1965	6th	77	85	.475	25.0	Johnny Keane	1,213,552
1966	10th	70	89	.440	26.5	Johnny Keane, Ralph Houk	1,124,648
1967	9th	72	90	.444	20.0	Ralph Houk	1,259,514
1968	5th	83	79	.512	20.0	Ralph Houk	1,185,666
East Division							
1969	5th	80	81	.497	28.5	Ralph Houk	1,067,996
1970	2nd	93	69	.574	15.0	Ralph Houk	1,136,879
1971	4th	82	80	.506	21.0	Ralph Houk	1,070,771
1972	4th	79	76	.510	6.5	Ralph Houk	966,328
1973	4th	80	82	.494	17.0	Ralph Houk	1,262,103
1974	2nd	89	73	.549	2.0	Bill Virdon	1,273,075
1975	3rd	83	77	.519	12.0	Bill Virdon, Billy Martin	1,288,048
1976	1st	97	62	.610	+10.5	Billy Martin	2,012,434
1977	1st	100	62	.617	+2.5	Billy Martin	2,103,092
1978	1st	100	63	.613	+1.0	Billy Martin, Dick Howser, Bob Lemon	2,335,871
1979	4th	89	71	.556	13.5	Bob Lemon, Billy Martin	2,537,765
1980	1st	103	59	.636	+3.0	Dick Howser	2,627,417
1981*	1st/6th	59	48	.551	+2.0/5.0	Gene Michael, Bob Lemon	1,614,533
1982	5th	79	83	.488	16.0	Bob Lemon, Gene Michael, Clyde King	2,041,219
1983	3rd	91	71	.562	7.0	Billy Martin	2,257,976
1984	3rd	87	75	.537	17.0	Yogi Berra	1,821,815
1985	2nd	97	64	.602	2.0	Yogi Berra, Billy Martin	2,214,587
1986	2nd	90	72	.556	5.5	Lou Piniella	2,268,030
1987	4th	89	73	.549	9.0	Lou Piniella	2,427,672
1988	5th	85	76	.528	3.5	Billy Martin, Lou Piniella	2,633,701
1989	5th	74	87	.460	14.5	Dallas Green, Bucky Dent	2,170,485

Year	Finish	Wins	Losses	Percentage	Games Behind	Manager	Attendance
1990	7th	67	95	.414	21.0	Bucky Dent, Stump Merrill	2,006,436
1991	5th	71	91	.438	20.0	Stump Merrill	1,863,733
1992	4th (Tie)	76	86	.469	20.0	Buck Showalter	1,748,733
1993	2nd	88	74	.543	7.0	Buck Showalter	2,416,965
1994	1st	70	43	.619	+6.5	Buck Showalter	1,675,556
1995	2nd	79	65	.549	7.0	Buck Showalter	1,705,263
1996	1st	92	70	.568	+4.0	Joe Torre	2,250,877
1997	2nd	96	66	.593	2.0	Joe Torre	2,580,325
1998	1st	114	48	.704	+22.0	Joe Torre	2,949,734
1999	1st	98	64	.605	+4.0	Joe Torre	3,292,736
2000	1st	87	74	.540	+2.5	Joe Torre	3,227,657
2001	1st	95	65	.594	+13.5	Joe Torre	3,264,777
2002	1st	103	58	.640	+10.5	Joe Torre	3,461,644
2003	1st	101	61	.623	+6.0	Joe Torre	3,465,600
2004	1st	101	61	.623	+3.0	Joe Torre	3,775,292
2005	1st (Tie)	95	67	.585	—	Joe Torre	4,090,692
2006	1st	97	65	.599	+10.0	Joe Torre	4,243,780
2007	2nd	94	68	.580	2.0	Joe Torre	4,271,083
2008	3rd	89	73	.549	8.0	Joe Girardi	4,298,655
2009	1st	103	59	.636	+8.0	Joe Girardi	3,719,358
2010	2nd	95	67	.586	1.0	Joe Girardi	3,765,807
2011	1st	97	65	.599	+6.0	Joe Girardi	3,653,680
2012	1st	95	67	.586	+2.0	Joe Girardi	3,542,406
2013	3rd	85	77	.525	12.0	Joe Girardi	3,279,589
2014	2nd	84	78	.519	12.0	Joe Girardi	3,401,624
2015	2nd	87	75	.537	6.0	Joe Girardi	3,193,795
2016	4th	84	78	.519	9.0	Joe Girardi	3,063,405
2017	2nd	91	71	.562	2.0	Joe Girardi	3,146,966
2018	2nd	100	62	.617	8.0	Aaron Boone	3,482,855
2019	1st	103	59	.636	+0.0	Aaron Boone	3,304,404
2020	2nd	33	27	.550	7.0	Aaron Boone	0
2021	2nd (Tie)	92	70	.568	8.0	Aaron Boone	1,959,854
2022	1st	99	63	.611	+7.0	Aaron Boone	3,136,207

* Split season.

Awards

Most Valuable Player

Babe Ruth, outfield, 1923
Lou Gehrig, first base, 1927
Lou Gehrig, first base, 1936
Joe DiMaggio, outfield, 1939
Joe DiMaggio, outfield, 1941
Joe Gordon, second base, 1942
Spud Chandler, pitcher, 1943
Joe DiMaggio, outfield, 1947
Phil Rizzuto, shortstop, 1950
Yogi Berra, catcher, 1951
Yogi Berra, catcher, 1954

Yogi Berra, catcher, 1955
Mickey Mantle, outfield, 1956
Mickey Mantle, outfield, 1957
Roger Maris, outfield, 1960
Roger Maris, outfield, 1961
Mickey Mantle, outfield, 1962
Elston Howard, catcher, 1963
Thurman Munson, catcher, 1976
Don Mattingly, first base, 1985
Alex Rodriguez, third base, 2005
Alex Rodriguez, third base, 2007
Aaron Judge, outfield, 2022

Rookie of the Year

Gil McDougald, infield, 1951
Bob Grim, pitcher, 1954
Tony Kubek, infield, 1957
Tom Tresh, shortstop and outfield, 1962
Stan Bahnsen, pitcher, 1968
Thurman Munson, catcher, 1970
Dave Righetti, pitcher, 1981
Derek Jeter, shortstop, 1996
Aaron Judge, outfield, 2017

Cy Young

Bob Turley, 1958
Whitey Ford, 1961

Sparky Lyle, 1977
Ron Guidry, 1978
Roger Clemens, 2001

Manager of the Year (Since 1983)
Buck Showalter, 1994
Joe Torre, 1996 (Tie)
Joe Torre, 1998

Hall of Famers Who Played for the Yankees
Home Run Baker, third base, 1916–19 and 1921–22
Yogi Berra, catcher and outfield, 1946–63 and 1965
Wade Boggs, third base, 1993–97
Frank Chance, first base, 1913–14
Jack Chesbro, pitcher, 1903–09
Earle Combs, outfield, 1924–35
Stan Coveleski, pitcher, 1928
Bobby Cox, third base, 1968–69
Bill Dickey, catcher, 1928–43 and 1946
Joe DiMaggio, outfield, 1936–42 and 1946–51
Leo Durocher, shortstop, 1925 and 1928–29
Whitey Ford, pitcher, 1950 and 1953–67
Lou Gehrig, first base, 1923–39
Lefty Gomez, pitcher, 1930–42
Joe Gordon, second base, 1938–43 and 1946
Goose Gossage, pitcher, 1978–83 and 1989
Clark Griffith, pitcher, 1903–07
Burleigh Grimes, pitcher, 1934
Rickey Henderson, outfield, 1985–89
Waite Hoyt, pitcher, 1921–30
Catfish Hunter, pitcher, 1975–79
Reggie Jackson, outfield, 1977–81
Derek Jeter, shortstop, 1995–2014
Randy Johnson, pitcher, 2005–06
Jim Kaat, pitcher, 1979–80
Wee Willie Keeler, outfield, 1903–09
Tony Lazzeri, second base, 1926–37
Mickey Mantle, outfield, 1951–68
Bill McKechnie, infield, 1913
Johnny Mize, first base and pinch hitter, 1949–53
Mike Mussina, pitcher, 2001–08
Phil Niekro, pitcher, 1984–85
Herb Pennock, pitcher, 1923–33

Gaylord Perry, pitcher, 1980
Tim Raines, outfield and designated hitter, 1996–98
Branch Rickey, outfield and catcher, 1907
Mariano Rivera, pitcher, 1995–2013
Phil Rizzuto, shortstop, 1941–42 and 1946–56
Ivan Rodriguez, catcher, 2008
Red Ruffing, pitcher, 1930–42 and 1945–46
Babe Ruth, outfield, 1920–34
Joe Sewell, third base, 1931–33
Enos Slaughter, outfield, 1954–55 and 1956–59
Lee Smith, pitcher, 1993
Dazzy Vance, pitcher, 1915
Paul Waner, pinch hitter, 1944–45
Dave Winfield, outfield, 1981–90

Retired Numbers

1	Billy Martin
2	Derek Jeter
3	Babe Ruth
4	Lou Gehrig
5	Joe DiMaggio
6	Joe Torre
7	Mickey Mantle
8	Yogi Berra
8	Bill Dickey
9	Roger Maris
10	Phil Rizzuto
15	Thurman Munson
16	Whitey Ford
20	Jorge Posada
21	Paul O'Neill
23	Don Mattingly
32	Elston Howard
37	Casey Stengel
42	Mariano Rivera
44	Reggie Jackson
46	Andy Pettitte
49	Ron Guidry
51	Bernie Williams

League Leaders, Batting

Batting Average, Season

Babe Ruth, 1924	.378
Lou Gehrig, 1934	.363
Joe DiMaggio, 1939	.381
Joe DiMaggio, 1940	.352
Snuffy Stirnweiss, 1945	.309
Mickey Mantle, 1956	.353

Don Mattingly, 1984	.343
Paul O'Neill, 1994	.359
Bernie Williams, 1998	.339
DJ LeMahieu, 2020	.364

Home Runs, Season

Wally Pipp, 1916	12
Wally Pipp, 1917	9
Babe Ruth, 1920	54
Babe Ruth, 1921	59
Babe Ruth, 1923	41
Babe Ruth, 1924	46
Bob Meusel, 1925	33
Babe Ruth, 1926	47
Babe Ruth, 1927	60
Babe Ruth, 1928	54
Babe Ruth, 1929	46
Babe Ruth, 1930	49
Babe Ruth, 1931	46 (Tie)
Lou Gehrig, 1931	46 (Tie)
Lou Gehrig, 1934	49
Lou Gehrig, 1936	49
Joe DiMaggio, 1937	46
Nick Etten, 1944	22
Joe DiMaggio, 1948	39
Mickey Mantle, 1955	37
Mickey Mantle, 1956	52
Mickey Mantle, 1958	42
Mickey Mantle, 1960	40
Roger Maris, 1961	61
Graig Nettles, 1976	32
Reggie Jackson, 1980	41 (Tie)
Alex Rodriguez, 2005	48
Alex Rodriguez, 2007	54
Mark Teixeira, 2009	39 (Tie)
Aaron Judge, 2017	52
Luke Voit, 2020	22
Aaron Judge, 2022	62

RBIs, Season

Wally Pipp, 1916	99
Babe Ruth, 1920	137
Babe Ruth, 1921	171
Babe Ruth, 1923	131
Bob Meusel, 1925	138
Babe Ruth, 1926	145
Lou Gehrig, 1927	175
Lou Gehrig, 1928	142 (Tie)
Babe Ruth, 1928	142 (Tie)
Lou Gehrig, 1930	174
Lou Gehrig, 1931	184
Lou Gehrig, 1934	165
Joe DiMaggio, 1941	125

Nick Etten, 1945 111
Joe DiMaggio, 1948 155
Mickey Mantle, 1956 130
Roger Maris, 1960.....................112
Roger Maris, 1961.....................142
Reggie Jackson, 1973 117
Don Mattingly, 1985 145
Alex Rodriguez, 2007 156
Mark Teixeira, 2009..................122
Curtis Granderson, 2011 119
Aaron Judge, 2022 131

Stolen Bases, Season

Fritz Maisel, 1914 74
Ben Chapman, 1931 61
Ben Chapman, 1932 38
Ben Chapman, 1933 27
Frankie Crosetti, 1938 27
Snuffy Stirnweiss, 1944 55
Snuffy Stirnweiss, 1945 33
Rickey Henderson, 1985 80
Rickey Henderson, 1986 87
Rickey Henderson, 1988 93
Rickey Henderson*, 1989 77
Alfonso Soriano, 2002 41
* 52 with Oak. A's and 25 with N.Y. Yankees.

Total Bases, Season

Babe Ruth, 1921........................457
Babe Ruth, 1923........................399
Babe Ruth, 1924........................391
Babe Ruth, 1926........................365
Lou Gehrig, 1927 447
Babe Ruth, 1928........................380
Lou Gehrig, 1930 419
Lou Gehrig, 1931 410
Lou Gehrig, 1934 409
Joe DiMaggio, 1937 418
Joe DiMaggio, 1941 348
Johnny Lindell, 1944 297
Snuffy Stirnweiss, 1945 301
Joe DiMaggio, 1948 355
Mickey Mantle, 1956 376
Mickey Mantle, 1958 307
Mickey Mantle, 1960 294
Roger Maris, 1961 366
Bobby Murcer, 1972 314
Don Mattingly, 1985 370
Don Mattingly, 1986 388
Alex Rodriguez, 2007 376
Mark Teixeira, 2009...................344
Aaron Judge, 2022 391

Most Hits, Season

Earle Combs, 1927 231
Lou Gehrig, 1931 211
Red Rolfe, 1939.........................213
Snuffy Stirnweiss, 1944 205
Snuffy Stirnweiss, 1945 195
Bobby Richardson, 1962.............209
Don Mattingly, 1984 207
Don Mattingly, 1986 238
Derek Jeter, 1999.......................219
Alfonso Soriano, 2002 209
Derek Jeter, 2012.......................216

Most Runs, Season

Patsy Dougherty*, 1904 113
Babe Ruth, 1920........................158
Babe Ruth, 1921........................177
Babe Ruth, 1923........................151
Babe Ruth, 1924........................143
Babe Ruth, 1926........................139
Babe Ruth, 1927........................158
Babe Ruth, 1928........................163
Lou Gehrig, 1931 163
Lou Gehrig, 1933 138
Lou Gehrig, 1935 125
Lou Gehrig, 1936 167
Joe DiMaggio, 1937 151
Red Rolfe, 1939.........................139
Snuffy Stirnweiss, 1944 125
Snuffy Stirnweiss, 1945 107
Tommy Henrich, 1948..................138
Mickey Mantle, 1954 129
Mickey Mantle, 1956 132
Mickey Mantle, 1957 121
Mickey Mantle, 1958 127
Mickey Mantle, 1960 119
Mickey Mantle, 1961 ....132 (Tie)
Roger Maris, 1961..............132 (Tie)
Bobby Murcer, 1972 102
Roy White, 1976 104
Rickey Henderson, 1985.............146
Rickey Henderson, 1986 130
Rickey Henderson**, 1989 ..113 (Tie)
Derek Jeter, 1998.......................127
Alfonso Soriano, 2002 128
Alex Rodriguez, 2005 124
Alex Rodriguez, 2007 143
Mark Teixeira, 2010....................113
Curtis Granderson, 2011 136
Aaron Judge, 2017 128
Aaron Judge, 2022 133
* 33 with Bos. Red Sox and 80 with N.Y. Yankees.
** 72 with Oak. A's and 41 with N.Y. Yankees.

Batting Feats

Triple Crown Winners

Lou Gehrig, 1934 (.363 BA, 49 HRs, 165 RBIs)
Mickey Mantle, 1956 (.353 BA, 52 HRs, 130 RBIs)

Hitting for the Cycle

Bert Daniels, Jul. 25, 1912
Bob Meusel, May 7, 1921
Bob Meusel, Jul. 3, 1922
Bob Meusel, Jul. 26, 1928
Tony Lazzeri, Jun. 3, 1932
Lou Gehrig, Jun. 25, 1934
Joe DiMaggio, Jul. 9, 1937
Lou Gehrig, Aug. 1, 1937
Buddy Rosar, Jul. 19, 1940
Joe Gordon, Sep. 8, 1940
Joe DiMaggio, May 20, 1948
Mickey Mantle, Jul. 23, 1957
Bobby Murcer, Aug. 29, 1972
Tony Fernandez, Sep. 3, 1995
Johnny Damon, Jun. 7, 2008
Melky Cabrera, Aug. 2, 2009

Six Hits in a Game

Myril Hoag, Jun. 6, 1934
Gerald Williams, May 1, 1996*
* Extra-inning game.

40 or More Home Runs, Season

62 ....Aaron Judge, 2022
61 ....Roger Maris, 1961
60 ....Babe Ruth, 1927
59 ....Babe Ruth, 1921
54 ....Babe Ruth, 1920
                           Babe Ruth, 1928
                       Mickey Mantle, 1961
                        Alex Rodriguez, 2005
52 ....Mickey Mantle, 1956
                          Aaron Judge, 2017
49 ....Babe Ruth, 1930
                             Lou Gehrig, 1934
                             Lou Gehrig, 1936
48 ....Alex Rodriguez, 2007
47 ....Babe Ruth, 1926
                             Lou Gehrig, 1927
46 ....Babe Ruth, 1924
                             Babe Ruth, 1929
                             Lou Gehrig, 1931
                             Babe Ruth, 1931
                          Joe DiMaggio, 1937

44 ....Tino Martinez, 1997
43 .... Curtis Granderson, 2012
42 ....Mickey Mantle, 1958
41 .... Babe Ruth, 1923
Lou Gehrig, 1930
Babe Ruth, 1932
Reggie Jackson, 1980
David Justice*, 2000
Jason Giambi, 2002
Jason Giambi, 2003
Curtis Granderson, 2011
40 ....Mickey Mantle, 1960
* 20 with Cle. Indians and 21 with N.Y. Yankees.

League Leaders, Pitching

Most Wins, Season
Jack Chesbro, 1904 41
Al Orth, 1906 27
Carl Mays, 1921 .... 27 (Tie)
Waite Hoyt, 1927 .... 22 (Tie)
George Pipgras, 1928 ....24 (Tie)
Lefty Gomez, 1934 26
Lefty Gomez, 1937 21
Red Ruffing, 1938 21
Spud Chandler, 1943 .... 20 (Tie)
Whitey Ford, 1955 .... 18 (Tie)
Bob Turley, 1958 21
Whitey Ford, 1961 25
Ralph Terry, 1962 23
Whitey Ford, 1963 24
Ron Guidry, 1978 25
Ron Guidry, 1985 22
Jimmy Key, 1994 17
Andy Pettitte, 1996 21
David Cone, 1998 .... 20 (Tie)
Chien-Ming Wang, 2006 19
CC Sabathia, 2009............... 19 (Tie)
CC Sabathia, 2010.......................21
Gerrit Cole, 2020 16

Most Strikeouts, Season
Red Ruffing, 1932 190
Lefty Gomez, 1933 163
Lefty Gomez, 1934 158
Lefty Gomez, 1937 194
Vic Rashi, 1951 164
Allie Reynolds, 1952 160
Al Downing, 1964 217
Gerrit Cole, 2022 257

Lowest ERA, Season
Bob Shawkey, 1920 ....2.45
Wiley Moore, 1927 ....2.28

Lefty Gomez, 1934 ....2.33
Lefty Gomez, 1937 ....2.33
Spud Chandler, 1943 ....1.64
Spud Chandler, 1947 ....2.46
Allie Reynolds, 1952 ....2.07
Eddie Lopat, 1953 ....2.43
Whitey Ford, 1956 ....2.47
Bobby Shantz, 1957 ....2.45
Whitey Ford, 1958 ....2.01
Ron Guidry, 1978 ....1.74
Ron Guidry, 1979 ....2.78
Rudy May, 1980 ....2.47

Most Saves, Season
Sparky Lyle, 1972 35
Sparky Lyle, 1976 23
Goose Gossage, 1978 27
Goose Gossage, 1980 ....33 (Tie)
Dave Righetti, 1986 46
John Wetteland, 1996 43
Mariano Rivera, 1999 45
Mariano Rivera, 2001 50
Mariano Rivera, 2004 53

Best Won–Lost Percentage, Season
Jack Chesbro, 1904 ... 41–13... .759
Carl Mays, 1921 .... 27–9... .750
Joe Bush, 1922............. 26–7... .788
Herb Pennock, 1923 .... 19–6... .760
Waite Hoyt, 1927 .... 22–7... .759
Johnny Allen, 1932 ...... 17–4... .810
Lefty Gomez, 1934 ...... 26–5... .839
Monte Pearson, 1936 ... 19–7... .731
Red Ruffing, 1938........ 21–7... .750
Lefty Gomez, 1941 ...... 15–5... .750
Tiny Bonham, 1942 ...... 21–5... .808
Spud Chandler, 1943 ... 20–4... .833
Allie Reynolds, 1947 .... 19–8... .704
Vic Raschi, 1950 .... 21–8... .724
Eddie Lopat, 1953 .... 16–4... .800
Tommy Byrne, 1955 ..... 16–5... .762
Whitey Ford, 1956 ...... 19–6... .760
Tom Sturdivant, 1957... 16–6. .727 (Tie)
Bob Turley, 1958 .... 21–7... .750
Whitey Ford, 1961 ..... 25–4... .862
Whitey Ford, 1963 ..... 24–7... .774
Ron Guidry, 1978 .... 25–3... .893
Ron Guidry, 1985 .... 22–6... .786
Jimmy Key, 1993 .... 18–6... .750
David Wells, 1998 .... 18–4... .818
Roger Clemens, 2001 ... 20–3... .870
Nathan Eovaldi, 2015... 14–3... .824
Domingo German, 2019.. 18–4... .818

Pitching Feats
Triple Crown Winner
Lefty Gomez, 1934 (26–5, 2.33 ERA, 158 SO)
Lefty Gomez, 1935 (21–11, 2.33 ERA, 194 SO)

20 Wins, Season
Jack Chesbro, 1903 21–15
Jack Chesbro, 1904 41–13
Jack Powell, 1904.................. 23–19
Al Orth, 1906 27–17
Jack Chesbro, 1906 24–16
Russ Ford, 1910 26–6
Russ Ford, 1911 22–11
Bob Shawkey, 1916 24–14
Bob Shawkey, 1919 20–13
Carl Mays, 1920 26–11
Bob Shawkey, 1920 20–13
Carl Mays, 1921 27–9
Joe Bush, 1922........................ 26–7
Bob Shawkey, 1922 20–12
Sad Sam Jones, 1923............... 21–8
Herb Pennock, 1924 21–9
Herb Pennock, 1927 23–11
Waite Hoyt, 1927 22–7
George Pipgras, 1928 24–13
Waite Hoyt, 1928 23–7
Lefty Gomez, 1931 21–9
Lefty Gomez, 1932 24–7
Lefty Gomez, 1934 26–5
Red Ruffing, 1936 20–12
Lefty Gomez, 1937 21–11
Red Ruffing, 1937.................. 20–7
Red Ruffing, 1938.................. 21–7
Red Ruffing, 1939.................. 21–7
Tiny Bonham, 1942................. 21–5
Spud Chandler, 1943 20–4
Spud Chandler, 1946 20–8
Vic Raschi, 1949 21–10
Vic Raschi, 1950 21–8
Ed Lopat, 1951 21–9
Vic Raschi, 1951 21–10
Allie Reynolds, 1952 20–8
Bob Grim, 1954 20–6
Bob Turley, 1958 21–7
Whitey Ford, 1961 25–4
Ralph Terry, 1962 23–12
Whitey Ford, 1963 24–7
Jim Bouton, 1963 21–7
Mel Stottlemyre, 1965 20–9
Mel Stottlemyre, 1968 21–12
Mel Stottlemyre, 1969 20–14

Fritz Peterson, 1970 20–11
Catfish Hunter, 1975 23–14
Ron Guidry, 1978 25–3
Ed Figueroa, 1978 20–9
Tommy John, 1979 21–9
Tommy John, 1980 22–9
Ron Guidry, 1983 21–9
Ron Guidry, 1985 22–6
Andy Pettitte, 1996 21–8
David Cone, 1998 20–7
Roger Clemens, 2001 20–3
Andy Pettitte, 2003 21–8
Mike Mussina, 2008 20–9
CC Sabathia, 2010 21–7

No-Hitters

George Mogridge (vs. Bos. Red Sox),
  Apr. 24, 1917 (final: 2–1)
Sam Jones (vs. Phi. A's), Sep. 4,
  1923 (final: 4–0)
Monte Pearson (vs. Cle. Indians),
  Aug. 27, 1938 (final: 13–0)
Allie Reynolds (vs. Cle. Indians), Jul.
  12, 1951 (final: 1–0)
Allie Reynolds (vs. Bos. Red Sox), Sep.
  28, 1951 (final: 8–0)
Don Larsen (vs. Brk. Dodgers, NL),
  Oct. 8, 1956 (final: 2–0) (World
  Series, perfect game)
Dave Righetti (vs. Bos. Red Sox), Jul.
  4, 1983 (final: 4–0)
Jim Abbott (vs. Cle. Indians), Sep. 4,
  1993 (final: 4–0)
Dwight Gooden (vs. Sea. Mariners),
  May 14, 1996 (final: 2–0)
David Wells (vs. Min. Twins), May 17,
  1998 (final: 4–0) (perfect game)
David Cone (vs. Mon. Expos, NL), Jul.
  18, 1999 (final: 6–0) (perfect game)
Corey Kluber (vs. Tex. Rangers),
  May 19, 2021 (final: 2–0)

No-Hitters Pitched Against

Cy Young, Bos. Red Sox, Jun. 30,
  1908 (final: 8–0)
George Foster, Bos. Red Sox, Jun. 21,
  1916 (final: 2–0)
Ray Caldwell, Bos. Red Sox, Sep. 10,
  1919 (final: 3–0)
Bob Feller, Cle. Indians, Apr. 30,
  1946 (final: 1–0)
Virgil Trucks, Det. Tigers, Aug. 25,
  1952 (final: 1–0)

Hoyt Wilhelm, Bal. Orioles, Sep. 2,
  1958 (final: 1–0)
Roy Oswalt, Pete Munro, Kirk Saarloos,
  Brad Lidge, Octavio Dotel, and Billy
  Wagner, Hou. Astros (NL), Jun. 11,
  2003 (final: 8–0)

Postseason Play

1921 World Series vs. N.Y. Giants
      (NL), lost 5 games to 3
1922 World Series vs. N.Y. Giants
      (NL), lost 4 games to 0, 1 tie
1923 World Series vs. N.Y. Giants
      (NL), won 4 games to 2
1926 World Series vs. St.L. Cardinals
      (NL), lost 4 games to 3
1927 World Series vs. Pit. Pirates (NL),
      won 4 games to 0
1928 World Series vs. St.L. Cardinals
      (NL), won 4 games to 0
1932 World Series vs. Chi. Cubs (NL),
      won 4 games to 0
1936 World Series vs. N.Y. Giants
      (NL), won 4 games to 2
1937 World Series vs. N.Y. Giants
      (NL), won 4 games to 1
1938 World Series vs. Chi. Cubs (NL),
      won 4 games to 0
1939 World Series vs. Cin. Reds (NL),
      won 4 games to 0
1941 World Series vs. Brk. Dodgers
      (NL), won 4 games to 1
1942 World Series vs. St.L. Cardinals
      (NL), lost 4 games to 1
1943 World Series vs. St.L. Cardinals
      (NL), won 4 games to 1
1947 World Series vs. Brk. Dodgers
      (NL), won 4 games to 3
1949 World Series vs. Brk. Dodgers
      (NL), won 4 games to 1
1950 World Series vs. Phi. Phillies (NL),
      won 4 games to 0
1951 World Series vs. N.Y. Giants
      (NL), won 4 games to 2
1952 World Series vs. Brk. Dodgers
      (NL), won 4 games to 3
1953 World Series vs. Brk. Dodgers
      (NL), won 4 games to 2
1955 World Series vs. Brk. Dodgers
      (NL), lost 4 games to 3
1956 World Series vs. Brk. Dodgers
      (NL), won 4 games to 3
1957 World Series vs. Mil. Braves (NL),
      lost 4 games to 3

1958 World Series vs. Mil. Braves (NL),
      won 4 games to 3
1960 World Series vs. Pit. Pirates (NL),
      lost 4 games to 3
1961 World Series vs. Cin. Reds (NL),
      won 4 games to 1
1962 World Series vs. S.F. Giants (NL),
      won 4 games to 3
1963 World Series vs. L.A. Dodgers
      (NL), lost 4 games to 0
1964 World Series vs. St.L. Cardinals
      (NL), lost 4 games to 3
1976 League Championship Series vs.
      K.C. Royals, won 3 games to 2
      World Series vs. Cin. Reds (NL),
      lost 4 games to 0
1977 League Championship Series vs.
      K.C. Royals, won 3 games to 2
      World Series vs. L.A. Dodgers
      (NL), won 4 games to 2
1978 Pennant Playoff Game vs. Bos.
      Red Sox, won
      League Championship Series vs.
      K.C. Royals, won
      3 games to 1
      World Series vs. L.A. Dodgers
      (NL), won 4 games to 2
1980 League Championship Series vs.
      K.C. Royals, lost 3 games to 0
1981 Second-Half Division Playoff vs.
      Mil. Brewers, won 3
      games to 2
      League Championship Series vs.
      Oak. A's, won 3 games to 0
      World Series vs. L.A. Dodgers
      (NL), lost 4 games to 2
1995 Division Series vs. Sea. Mariners,
      lost 3 games to 2
1996 Division Series vs. Tex. Rangers,
      won 3 games to 1
      League Championship Series vs.
      Bal. Orioles, won 4 games to 1
      World Series vs. Atl. Braves (NL),
      won 4 games to 2
1997 Division Series vs. Cle. Indians,
      lost 3 games to 2
1998 Division Series vs. Tex. Rangers,
      won 3 games to 0
      League Championship Series vs.
      Cle. Indians, won 4 games
      to 2
      World Series vs. S.D. Padres
      (NL), won 4 games to 0
1999 Division Series vs. Tex. Rangers,
      won 3 games to 0

League Championship Series vs. Bos. Red Sox, won 4 games to 1

World Series vs. Atl. Braves (NL), won 4 games to 0

2000 Division Series vs. Oak. A's, won 3 games to 2

League Championship Series vs. Sea. Mariners, won 4 games to 2

World Series vs. N.Y. Mets (NL), won 4 games to 1

2001 Division Series vs. Oak. A's, won 3 games to 2

League Championship Series vs. Sea. Mariners, won 4 games to 1

World Series vs. Ari. D'backs (NL), lost 4 games to 3

2002 Division Series vs. Ana. Angels, lost 3 games to 1

2003 Division Series vs. Min. Twins, won 3 games to 1

League Championship Series vs. Bos. Red Sox, won 4 games to 3

World Series vs. Fla. Marlins (NL), lost 4 games to 2

2004 Division Series vs. Min. Twins, won 3 games to 1

League Championship Series vs. Bos. Red Sox, lost 4 games to 3

2005 Division Series vs. L.A. Angels, lost 3 games to 2

2006 Division Series vs. Det. Tigers, lost 3 games to 1

2007 Division Series vs. Cle. Indians, lost 3 games to 1

2009 Division Series vs. Min. Twins, won 3 games to 0

League Championship Series vs. L.A. Angels, won 4 games to 2

World Series vs. Phi. Phillies (NL), won 4 games to 2

2010 Division Series vs. Min. Twins, won 3 games to 0

League Championship Series vs. Tex. Rangers, lost 4 games to 2

2011 Division Series vs. Det. Tigers, lost 3 games to 2

2012 Division Series vs. Bal. Orioles, won 3 games to 2

League Championship Series vs. Det. Tigers, lost 4 games to 0

2015 AL Wild Card Playoff Game vs. Hou. Astros, lost

2017 AL Wild Card Playoff Game vs. Min. Twins, won

Division Series vs. Cle. Indians, won 3 games to 2

League Championship Series vs. Hou. Astros, lost 4 games to 3

2018 AL Wild Card Playoff Game vs. Oak. A's, won

Division Series vs. Bos. Red Sox, lost 3 games to 1

2019 Division Series vs. Min. Twins, won 3 games to 0

League Championship Series vs. Hou. Astros, lost 4 games to 2

2020 Wild Card Series vs. Cle. Indians, won 2 games to 0

Division Series vs. T.B. Rays, lost 3 games to 2

2021 AL Wild Card vs. Bos. Red Sox, lost

2022 Division Series vs. Cle. Guardians, won 3 games to 2

League Championship Series vs. Hou. Astros, lost 4 games to 0

Oakland Athletics (formerly the Kansas City Athletics)

Dates of Operation: (as the Kansas City Athletics) 1955–67 (13 years)
Overall Record: 829 wins, 1224 losses (.404)
Stadium: Municipal Stadium, 1955–67
Other Name: A's

Dates of Operation: (as the Oakland Athletics) 1968–present (55 years)
Overall Record: 4495 wins, 4182 losses (.518)
Stadium: Oakland-Alameda County Coliseum (formerly UMax Coliseum, 1997–98, Network Associates Coliseum, 1998–2004, McAfee Coliseum, 2004–08, O.co Coliseum, also known as Overstock.com Coliseum, 2001–15), 1968–present (capacity: 35,067)
Other Name: A's

Year-by-Year Finishes

Year	Finish	Wins	Losses	Percentage	Games Behind	Manager	Attendance
					K.C. Athletics		
1955	6th	63	91	.409	33.0	Lou Boudreau	1,393,054
1956	8th	52	102	.338	45.0	Lou Boudreau	1,015,154
1957	7th	59	94	.386	38.5	Lou Boudreau, Harry Craft	901,067
1958	7th	73	81	.474	19.0	Harry Craft	925,090
1959	7th	66	88	.429	28.0	Harry Craft	963,683
1960	8th	58	96	.377	39.0	Bob Elliott	774,944
1961	9th (Tie)	61	100	.379	47.5	Joe Gordon, Hank Bauer	683,817
1962	9th	72	90	.444	24.0	Hank Bauer	635,675
1963	8th	73	89	.451	31.5	Ed Lopat	762,364
1964	10th	57	105	.352	42.0	Ed Lopat, Mel McGaha	642,478
1965	10th	59	103	.364	43.0	Mel McGaha, Haywood Sullivan	528,344
1966	7th	74	86	.463	23.0	Alvin Dark	773,929
1967	10th	62	99	.385	29.5	Alvin Dark, Luke Appling	726,639
					Oak. Athletics		
1968	6th	82	80	.506	21.0	Bob Kennedy	837,466
					West Division		
1969	2nd	88	74	.543	9.0	Hank Bauer, John McNamara	778,232
1970	2nd	89	73	.549	9.0	John McNamara	778,355
1971	1st	101	60	.627	+16.0	Dick Williams	914,993
1972	1st	93	62	.600	+5.5	Dick Williams	921,323
1973	1st	94	68	.580	+6.0	Dick Williams	1,000,763
1974	1st	90	72	.556	+5.0	Alvin Dark	845,693
1975	1st	98	64	.605	+7.0	Alvin Dark	1,075,518
1976	2nd	87	74	.540	2.5	Chuck Tanner	780,593
1977	7th	63	98	.391	38.5	Jack McKeon, Bobby Winkles	495,599
1978	6th	69	93	.426	23.0	Bobby Winkles, Jack McKeon	526,999
1979	7th	54	108	.333	34.0	Jim Marshall	306,763
1980	2nd	83	79	.512	14.0	Billy Martin	842,259
1981*	1st/2nd	64	45	.587	+1.5/1.0	Billy Martin	1,304,054
1982	5th	68	94	.420	25.0	Billy Martin	1,735,489
1983	4th	74	88	.457	25.0	Steve Boros	1,294,941
1984	4th	77	85	.475	7.0	Steve Boros, Jackie Moore	1,353,281
1985	4th (Tie)	77	85	.475	14.0	Jackie Moore	1,334,599

Year	Finish	Wins	Losses	Percentage	Games Behind	Manager	Attendance
1986	3rd (Tie)	76	86	.469	16.0	Jackie Moore, Tony La Russa	1,314,646
1987	3rd	81	81	.500	4.0	Tony La Russa	1,678,921
1988	1st	104	58	.642	+13.0	Tony La Russa	2,287,335
1989	1st	99	63	.611	+7.0	Tony La Russa	2,667,225
1990	1st	103	59	.636	+9.0	Tony La Russa	2,900,217
1991	4th	84	78	.519	11.0	Tony La Russa	2,713,493
1992	1st	96	66	.593	+6.0	Tony La Russa	2,494,160
1993	7th	68	94	.420	26.0	Tony La Russa	2,035,025
1994	2nd	51	63	.447	1.0	Tony La Russa	1,242,692
1995	4th	67	77	.465	11.5	Tony La Russa	1,174,310
1996	3rd	78	84	.481	12.0	Art Howe	1,148,380
1997	4th	65	97	.401	25.0	Art Howe	1,264,218
1998	4th	74	88	.457	14.0	Art Howe	1,232,339
1999	2nd	87	75	.537	8.0	Art Howe	1,434,610
2000	1st	91	70	.565	+0.5	Art Howe	1,728,888
2001	2nd	102	60	.630	14.0	Art Howe	2,133,277
2002	1st	103	59	.636	+4.0	Art Howe	2,169,811
2003	1st	96	66	.593	+3.0	Ken Macha	2,216,596
2004	2nd	91	71	.562	1.0	Ken Macha	2,201,516
2005	2nd	88	74	.543	7.0	Ken Macha	2,109,118
2006	1st	93	69	.574	+4.0	Ken Macha	1,976,625
2007	3rd	76	86	.469	18.0	Bob Geren	1,921,834
2008	3rd	75	86	.466	24.5	Bob Geren	1,665,256
2009	4th	75	87	.463	22.0	Bob Geren	1,408,783
2010	2nd	81	81	.500	9.0	Bob Geren	1,418,391
2011	3rd	74	88	.457	22.0	Bob Geren, Bob Melvin	1,476,791
2012	1st	94	68	.580	+1.0	Bob Melvin	1,679,013
2013	1st	96	66	.593	+5.5	Bob Melvin	1,809,302
2014	2nd	88	74	.543	10.0	Bob Melvin	2,003,628
2015	5th	68	94	.420	20.0	Bob Melvin	1,768,175
2016	5th	69	93	.426	26.0	Bob Melvin	1,521,506
2017	5th	75	87	.463	26.0	Bob Melvin	1,475,721
2018	2nd	97	65	.599	6.0	Bob Melvin	1,573,616
2019	2nd	97	65	.599	10.0	Bob Melvin	1,670,734
2020	1st	36	24	.600	+7.0	Bob Melvin	0
2021	3rd	86	76	.531	9.0	Bob Melvin	701,430
2022	5th	60	102	.370	46.0	Mark Kotsay	787,902

* Split season.

Awards

Most Valuable Player
Vida Blue, pitcher, 1971
Reggie Jackson, outfield, 1973
Jose Canseco, outfield, 1988
Rickey Henderson, outfield, 1990
Dennis Eckersley, pitcher, 1992
Jason Giambi, first base, 2000
Miguel Tejada, shortstop, 2002

Rookie of the Year
Jose Canseco, outfield, 1986
Mark McGwire, first base, 1987
Walt Weiss, shortstop, 1988
Ben Grieve, outfield, 1998
Bobby Crosby, shortstop, 2004
Huston Street, pitcher, 2005
Andrew Bailey, pitcher, 2009

Cy Young
Vida Blue, 1971
Catfish Hunter, 1974
Bob Welch, 1990
Dennis Eckersley, 1992
Barry Zito, 2002

Manager of the Year (Since 1983)
Tony La Russa, 1988
Tony La Russa, 1992
Bob Melvin, 2002
Bob Melvin, 2018

Hall of Famers Who Played for the Athletics
Harold Baines, designated hitter, 1991–92
Dennis Eckersley, pitcher, 1987–95
Rollie Fingers, pitcher, 1968–76
Goose Gossage, pitcher, 1992–93
Rickey Henderson, outfield, 1979–84, 1989–93, 1994–95, and 1998
Catfish Hunter, pitcher, 1965–74
Reggie Jackson, outfield, 1967–75 and 1987
Tony La Russa, second base and shortstop, 1963 (K.C.) and 1968–71
Willie McCovey, designated hitter, 1976
Joe Morgan, second base, 1984
Satchel Paige, pitcher, 1965 (K.C.)
Mike Piazza, designated hitter, 2007
Tim Raines, outfield, 1999
Enos Slaughter, outfield, 1955–56 (K.C.)
Don Sutton, pitcher, 1985
Frank Thomas, first base and designated hitter, 2006 and 2008

Retired Numbers

WH .... Walter Haas
9 .... Reggie Jackson
24 .... Rickey Henderson
27 .... Catfish Hunter
34 .... Rollie Fingers
43 .... Dennis Eckersley

League Leaders, Batting

Batting Average, Season
[No player]

Home Runs, Season
Reggie Jackson, 1973 32
Reggie Jackson, 1975 .... 36 (Tie)
Tony Armas, 1981 .... 22 (Tie)
Mark McGwire, 1987 49
Jose Canseco, 1988 42
Jose Canseco, 1991 .... 44 (Tie)
Mark McGwire, 1996 52
Khris Davis, 2018 48

RBIs, Season
Jose Canseco, 1988 124

Stolen Bases, Season
Bert Campaneris, 1965 (K.C.) 51
Bert Campaneris, 1966 (K.C.) 52
Bert Campaneris, 1967 (K.C.) 55
Bert Campaneris, 1968 62
Bert Campaneris, 1970 42
Bert Campaneris, 1972 52
Billy North, 1974 54
Billy North, 1976 75
Rickey Henderson, 1980 100
Rickey Henderson, 1981 56
Rickey Henderson, 1982 130
Rickey Henderson, 1983 108
Rickey Henderson, 1984 66
Rickey Henderson*, 1989 77
Rickey Henderson, 1990 65
Rickey Henderson, 1991 58
Rickey Henderson, 1998 66
Coco Crisp, 2011 .... 49 (Tie)
* 25 with N.Y. Yankees and 52 with Oak. A's.

Total Bases, Season
Sal Bando, 1973 .... 295 (Tie)
Joe Rudi, 1974 287

Most Hits, Season
Bert Campaneris, 1968 177
Joe Rudi, 1972 181
Rickey Henderson, 1981 135

Batting Feats

Triple Crown Winners
[No player]

Hitting for the Cycle
Tony Phillips, May 16, 1986
Mike Blowers, May 18, 1998
Eric Chavez, Jun. 21, 2000
Miguel Tejada, Sep. 29, 2001
Eric Byrnes, Jun. 29, 2003
Mark Ellis, Jun. 4, 2007

Six Hits in a Game
Joe DeMaestri, Jul. 8, 1955* (K.C.)
* Extra-inning game.

40 or More Home Runs, Season
52 .... Mark McGwire, 1996
49 .... Mark McGwire, 1987
48 .... Khris Davis, 2018
47 ....Reggie Jackson, 1969
44 .... Jose Canseco, 1991
43 ....Jason Giambi, 2000
                    Khris Davis, 2017
42 .... Jose Canseco, 1988
                    Mark McGwire, 1992
                    Khris Davis, 2016

League Leaders, Pitching

Most Wins, Season
Catfish Hunter, 1974 .... 25 (Tie)
Catfish Hunter, 1975 .... 23 (Tie)
Steve McCatty, 1981 .... 14 (Tie)
Dave Stewart, 1987 .... 20 (Tie)
Bob Welch, 1990 27

Most Strikeouts, Season
[No player]

Lowest ERA, Season
Diego Segui, 1970 .... 2.56
Vida Blue, 1971 .... 1.82
Catfish Hunter, 1974 .... 2.49
Steve McCatty, 1981 .... 2.32
Steve Ontiveros, 1994 .... 2.65

Most Saves, Season
Dennis Eckersley, 1988 45
Dennis Eckersley, 1992 51
Keith Foulke, 2003 43

Best Won–Lost Percentage, Season
Catfish Hunter, 1972 ...21–7 .... .750
Catfish Hunter, 1973 ...21–5 .... .808
Bob Welch, 1982 ....27–6 .... .818
Tim Hudson, 2000 ......20–6 .... .769
Chris Bassitt, 2021 ......12–4 .... .750

Pitching Feats

20 Wins, Season
Vida Blue, 1971 24–8
Catfish Hunter, 1971 21–11
Catfish Hunter, 1972 21–7
Catfish Hunter, 1973 21–5
Ken Holtzman, 1973 21–13
Vida Blue, 1973 20–9
Catfish Hunter, 1974 25–12
Vida Blue, 1975 22–11
Mike Norris, 1980 22–9
Dave Stewart, 1987 20–13
Dave Stewart, 1988 21–12
Dave Stewart, 1989 21–9
Bob Welch, 1990 27–6
Dave Stewart, 1990 22–11
Tim Hudson, 2000 20–6
Mark Mulder, 2001 21–8
Barry Zito, 2002 23–5

No-Hitters
Catfish Hunter (vs. Min. Twins),
    May 8, 1968 (final: 4–0) (perfect game)
Vida Blue (vs. Min. Twins), Sep. 21,
    1970 (final: 6–0)
Vida Blue, Glenn Abbott, Paul Lindblad,
    and Rollie Fingers (vs. Cal. Angels),
    Sep. 28, 1975 (final: 5–0)
Mike Warren (vs. Chi. White Sox),
    Sep. 29, 1983 (final: 3–0)
Dave Stewart (vs. Tor. Blue Jays),
    Jun. 29, 1990 (final: 5–0)
Dallas Braden (v.s. T.B. Rays), May 9,
    2010 (final: 4–0) (perfect game)
Sean Manaea, (vs. Bos. Red Sox),
    Apr. 21, 2018 (final: 3–0)
Mike Fiers (vs. Cin. Reds),
    May 7, 2019 (final: 2–0)

No-Hitters Pitched Against
Jack Kralick, Min. Twins (vs. K.C.),
    Aug. 26, 1962 (final: 1–0)

Most Runs, Season
Reggie Jackson, 1969 123
Reggie Jackson, 1973 99
Rickey Henderson, 1981 89
Rickey Henderson*, 1989 .... 113 (Tie)
Rickey Henderson, 1990 119
* 41 with N.Y. Yankees and 72 with Oak. A's.

Jim Palmer, Bal. Orioles, Aug. 13, 1969 (final: 8–0)

Clyde Wright, Cal. Angels, Jul. 3, 1970 (final: 4–0)

Jim Bibby, Tex. Rangers, Jul. 30, 1973 (final: 6–0)

Dick Bosman, Cle. Indians, Jul. 19, 1974 (final: 4–0)

Blue Moon Odom and Francisco Barrios, Chi. White Sox, Jul. 28, 1976 (final: 6–0)

Nolan Ryan, Tex. Rangers, Jun. 11, 1990 (final: 5–0)

Bob Milacki, Mike Flanagan, Mark Williamson, and Gregg Olson, Bal. Orioles, Jul. 13, 1991 (final: 2–0)

Postseason Play

1971 League Championship Series vs. Bal. Orioles, lost 3 games to 0

1972 League Championship Series vs. Det. Tigers, won 3 games to 2
World Series vs. Cin. Reds (NL), won 4 games to 3

1973 League Championship Series vs. Bal. Orioles, won 3 games to 2

World Series vs. N.Y. Mets (NL), won 4 games to 3

1974 League Championship Series vs. Bal. Orioles, won 3 games to 1
World Series vs. L.A. Dodgers (NL), won 4 games to 1

1975 League Championship Series vs. Bos. Red Sox, lost 3 games to 0

1981 First-Half Pennant Playoff vs. K.C. Royals, won 3 games to 0
League Championship Series vs. N.Y. Yankees, lost 3 games to 0

1988 League Championship Series vs. Bos. Red Sox, won 4 games to 0
World Series vs. L.A. Dodgers (NL), lost 4 games to 1

1989 League Championship Series vs. Tor. Blue Jays, won 4 games to 1
World Series vs. S.F. Giants (NL), won 4 games to 0

1990 League Championship Series vs. Bos. Red Sox, won 4 games to 0
World Series vs. Cin. Reds (NL), lost 4 games to 0

1992 League Championship Series vs. Tor. Blue Jays, lost 4 games to 2

2000 Division Series vs. N.Y. Yankees, lost 3 games to 2

2001 Division Series vs. N.Y. Yankees, lost 3 games to 2

2002 Division Series vs. Min. Twins, lost 3 games to 2

2003 Division Series vs. Bos. Red Sox, lost 3 games to 2

2006 Division Series vs. Min. Twins, won 3 games to 0
League Championship Series vs. Det. Tigers, lost 4 games to 0

2012 Division Series vs. Det. Tigers, lost 3 games to 2

2013 Division Series vs. Det. Tigers, lost 3 games to 2

2014 AL Wild Card Playoff Game vs. K.C. Royals, lost

2018 AL Wild Card Playoff Game vs. N.Y. Yankees, lost

2019 AL Wild Card vs. T.B. Rays, lost

2020 AL Wild Card vs. Chi. White Sox, won 2 games to 1
Division Series vs. Hou. Astros, lost 3 games to 1

Seattle Mariners

Dates of Operation: 1977–present (46 years)
Overall Record: 3426 wins, 3799 losses (.474)
Stadiums: Kingdome, 1977–99; Safeco Field (also known as King County Stadium), 1999–present
(capacity: 47,574)

Year-by-Year Finishes

Year	Finish	Wins	Losses	Percentage	Games Behind	Manager	Attendance
					West Division		
1977	6th	64	98	.395	38.0	Darrell Johnson	1,338,511
1978	7th	56	104	.350	35.0	Darrell Johnson	877,440
1979	6th	67	95	.414	21.0	Darrell Johnson	844,447
1980	7th	59	103	.364	38.0	Darrell Johnson, Maury Wills	836,204
1981*	6th/5th	44	65	.404	14.5/6.5	Maury Wills, Rene Lachemann	636,276
1982	4th	76	86	.469	17.0	Rene Lachemann	1,070,404
1983	7th	60	102	.370	39.0	Rene Lachemann, Del Crandall	813,537
1984	5th (Tie)	74	88	.457	10.0	Del Crandall, Chuck Cottier	870,372
1985	6th	74	88	.457	17.0	Chuck Cottier	1,128,696
1986	7th	67	95	.414	25.0	Chuck Cottier, Marty Martinez, Dick Williams	1,029,045
1987	4th	78	84	.481	7.0	Dick Williams	1,134,255
1988	7th	68	93	.422	35.5	Dick Williams, Jim Snyder	1,022,398
1989	6th	73	89	.451	26.0	Jim Lefebvre	1,298,443
1990	5th	77	85	.475	26.0	Jim Lefebvre	1,509,727
1991	5th	83	79	.512	12.0	Jim Lefebvre	2,147,905
1992	7th	64	98	.395	32.0	Bill Plummer	1,651,398
1993	4th	82	80	.506	12.0	Lou Piniella	2,051,853
1994	3rd	49	63	.438	2.0	Lou Piniella	1,104,206
1995	1st	79	66	.545	+1.0	Lou Piniella	1,643,203
1996	2nd	85	76	.528	4.5	Lou Piniella	2,732,850
1997	1st	90	72	.556	+6.0	Lou Piniella	3,192,237
1998	3rd	76	85	.472	11.5	Lou Piniella	2,644,166
1999	3rd	79	83	.488	16.0	Lou Piniella	2,916,346
2000	2nd	91	71	.562	0.5	Lou Piniella	3,148,317
2001	1st	116	46	.716	+14.0	Lou Piniella	3,507,975
2002	3rd	93	69	.574	10.0	Lou Piniella	3,540,482
2003	2nd	93	69	.574	3.0	Bob Melvin	3,268,509
2004	4th	63	99	.389	29.0	Bob Melvin	2,940,731
2005	4th	69	93	.426	26.0	Mike Hargrove	2,725,549
2006	4th	78	84	.481	15.0	Mike Hargrove	2,481,375
2007	2nd	88	75	.540	6.5	Mike Hargrove, John McLaren	2,672,485
2008	4th	61	101	.377	39.0	John McLaren, Jim Riggleman	2,329,702
2009	3rd	85	77	.525	12.0	Don Wakamatsu	2,195,284
2010	4th	61	101	.377	29.0	Don Wakamatsu, Darren Brown	2,085,630
2011	4th	67	95	.414	29.0	Eric Wedge	1,939,421
2012	4th	75	87	.463	19.0	Eric Wedge	1,721,920
2013	4th	71	91	.438	25.0	Eric Wedge	1,761,546
2014	3rd	87	75	.537	11.0	Lloyd McClendon	2,064,334
2015	4th	76	86	.469	12.0	Lloyd McClendon	2,193,581
2016	2nd	86	76	.531	9.0	Scott Servais	2,267,928
2017	3rd	78	84	.481	23.0	Scott Servais	2,135,445

Year	Finish	Wins	Losses	Percentage	Games Behind	Manager	Attendance
2018	3rd	89	73	.549	14.0	Scott Servais	2,299,489
2019	5th	68	94	.420	39.0	Scott Servais	1,791,109
2020	3rd	27	33	.450	9.0	Scott Servais	0
2021	2nd	90	72	.556	5.0	Scott Servais	1,215,985
2022	2nd	90	72	.556	16.0	Scott Servais	2,287,267

* Split season.

Awards

Most Valuable Player
Ken Griffey Jr., outfield, 1997
Ichiro Suzuki, outfield, 2001

Rookie of the Year
Alvin Davis, first base, 1984
Kazuhiro Sasaki, pitcher, 2000
Ichiro Suzuki, outfield, 2001
Kyle Lewis, outfield, 2020
Julio Rodriguez, outfield, 2022

Cy Young
Randy Johnson, 1995
Felix Hernandez, 2010

Manager of the Year (Since 1983)
Lou Piniella, 1995
Lou Piniella, 2001

Hall of Famers Who Played for the Mariners
Goose Gossage, pitcher, 1994
Ken Griffey Jr., outfield and designated hitter, 1989–99 and 2009–10
Randy Johnson, pitcher, 1989–98
Edgar Martinez, infield and designated hitter, 1987–2004
Gaylord Perry, pitcher, 1982–83

Retired Numbers
11 ....Edgar Martinez
24 ....Ken Griffey Jr.

League Leaders, Batting

Batting Average, Season
Edgar Martinez, 1992 .... .343
Edgar Martinez, 1995 .... .356
Alex Rodriguez, 1996 .... .358
Ichiro Suzuki, 2001 .... .350
Ichiro Suzuki, 2004 .... .372

Home Runs, Season
Ken Griffey Jr., 1994 40
Ken Griffey Jr., 1997 56

Ken Griffey Jr., 1998 56
Ken Griffey Jr., 1999 48

RBIs, Season
Ken Griffey Jr., 1997 147
Edgar Martinez, 2000 145
Bret Boone, 2001 141
Nelson Cruz, 2017 119

Stolen Bases, Season
Harold Reynolds, 1987.................60
Brian Hunter*, 1999 44
Ichiro Suzuki, 2001 56
Mallex Smith, 2019......................46
* 0 with Det. Tigers and 44 with Sea. Mariners.

Total Bases, Season
Ken Griffey Jr., 1993..................359
Alex Rodriguez, 1996 379
Ken Griffey Jr., 1997..................393

Most Hits, Season
Alex Rodriguez, 1998 213
Ichiro Suzuki, 2001 242
Ichiro Suzuki, 2004....................262
Ichiro Suzuki, 2006....................224
Ichiro Suzuki, 2007....................238
Ichiro Suzuki, 2008.............213 (Tie)
Ichiro Suzuki, 2009....................225
Ichiro Suzuki, 2010....................214

Most Runs, Season
Edgar Martinez, 1995.........121 (Tie)
Alex Rodriguez, 1996 141
Ken Griffey Jr., 1997..................125

Batting Feats

Triple Crown Winners
[No player]

Hitting for the Cycle
Jay Buhner, Jul. 23, 1993
Alex Rodriguez, Jun. 5, 1997
John Olerud, Jun. 16, 2001
Adrian Beltre, Sep. 1, 2008

Six Hits in a Game
Raul Ibanez, Sep. 22, 2004

40 or More Home Runs, Season
56 ....Ken Griffey Jr., 1997
               Ken Griffey Jr., 1998
49 ....Ken Griffey Jr., 1996
48 ....Ken Griffey Jr., 1999
45 ....Ken Griffey Jr., 1993
44 ....Jay Buhner, 1996
43 ....Nelson Cruz, 2016
42 ....Alex Rodriguez, 1998
               Alex Rodriguez, 1999
41 ....Alex Rodriguez, 2000
40 ....Ken Griffey Jr., 1994
               Jay Buhner, 1995
               Jay Buhner, 1997

League Leaders, Pitching

Most Wins, Season
Felix Hernandez, 2009 .... 19 (Tie)

Most Strikeouts, Season
Floyd Bannister, 1982.................209
Mark Langston, 1984 204
Mark Langston, 1986 245
Mark Langston, 1987 262
Randy Johnson, 1992 241
Randy Johnson, 1993 308
Randy Johnson, 1994 204
Randy Johnson, 1995 294
Lowest ERA, Season
Randy Johnson, 1995 ....2.48
Freddy Garcia, 2001 ....3.05
Felix Hernandez, 2010.............2.27
Felix Hernandez, 2014.............2.14

Most Saves, Season
Edwin Diaz, 2018........................57

Best Won–Lost Percentage, Season
Randy Johnson, 1995 ... 18–2 ... .900
Randy Johnson, 1997 ... 20–4 ... .833
Felix Hernandez, 2009 ...19–5... .792

Pitching Feats

20 Wins, Season
Randy Johnson, 1997 20–4
Jamie Moyer, 2001 20–6
Jamie Moyer, 2003 21–7

No-Hitters

Randy Johnson (vs. Det. Tigers), Jun. 2, 1990 (final: 2–0)

Chris Bosio (vs. Bos. Red Sox), Apr. 22, 1993 (final: 7–0)

Kevin Millwood, Charlie Furbush, Stephen Pryor, Lucas Luetge, Brandon League, Tom Wilhelmsen (vs. L.A. Dodgers), Jun. 8, 2012 (final: 1–0)

Felix Hernandez (vs. T.B. Rays), Aug. 15, 2012 (final: 1–0) (perfect game)

Hisashi Iwakuma (vs. Bal. Orioles), Aug. 12, 2015 (final: 3–0)

James Paxton (vs. Tor. Blue Jays), May 8, 2018 (final: 5–0)

No-Hitters Pitched Against

Mark Langston and Mike Witt, Cal. Angels, Apr. 11, 1990 (final: 1–0)

Dwight Gooden, N.Y. Yankees, May 14, 1996 (final: 2–0)

Philip Humber, Chi. White Sox, Apr. 21, 2012 (final: 4–0) (perfect game)

Postseason Play

1995   Division Playoff Game vs. Cal. Angels, won
Division Series vs. N.Y. Yankees, won 3 games to 2
League Championship Series vs. Cle. Indians, lost 4 games to 2

1997   Division Series vs. Bal. Orioles, lost 3 games to 1

2000   Division Series vs. Chi. White Sox, won 3 games to 0
League Championship Series vs. N.Y. Yankees, lost 4 games to 2

2001   Division Series vs. Cle. Indians, won 3 games to 2
League Championship Series vs. N.Y. Yankees, lost 4 games to 1

2022   Wild Card Series vs. Tor. Blue Jays, won 2 games to 0
Division Series vs. Hou. Astros, lost 3 games to 0

Tampa Bay Rays

Dates of Operation: 1998–present (25 years)
Overall Record: 1912 wins, 2034 losses (.485)
Stadium: Tropicana Field, 1998–present (capacity: 31,042)
Other Name: Devil Rays

Year-by-Year Finishes

Year	Finish	Wins	Losses	Percentage	Games Behind	Manager	Attendance
					East Division		
1998	5th	63	99	.389	51.0	Larry Rothschild	2,261,158
1999	5th	69	93	.426	29.0	Larry Rothschild	1,562,827
2000	5th	69	92	.429	18.0	Larry Rothschild	1,549,052
2001	5th	62	100	.383	34.0	Larry Rothschild, Hal McRae	1,227,673
2002	5th	55	106	.342	48.0	Hal McRae	1,065,762
2003	5th	63	99	.389	38.0	Lou Piniella	1,058,695
2004	4th	70	91	.435	30.0	Lou Piniella	1,275,011
2005	5th	67	95	.414	28.0	Lou Piniella	1,152,793
2006	5th	61	101	.377	36.0	Joe Maddon	1,370,963
2007	5th	66	96	.407	30.0	Joe Maddon	1,387,603
2008	1st	97	65	.599	+2.0	Joe Maddon	1,780,791
2009	3rd	84	78	.519	19.0	Joe Maddon	1,874,962
2010	1st	96	66	.593	+1.0	Joe Maddon	1,864,999
2011	2nd	91	71	.562	6.0	Joe Maddon	1,529,188
2012	3rd	90	72	.556	5.0	Joe Maddon	1,559,681
2013	2nd	92	71	.564	5.5	Joe Maddon	1,510,300
2014	4th	77	85	.475	19.0	Joe Maddon	1,446,464
2015	4th	80	82	.494	13.0	Kevin Cash	1,287,054
2016	5th	68	94	.420	25.0	Kevin Cash	1,286,163
2017	3rd	80	82	.494	13.0	Kevin Cash	1,253,619
2018	3rd	90	72	.556	18.0	Kevin Cash	1,154,973
2019	2nd	96	66	.593	0.0	Kevin Cash	1,178,735
2020	1st	40	20	.667	+7.0	Kevin Cash	0
2021	1st	100	62	.617	+8.0	Kevin Cash	761,072
2022	3rd	86	76	.531	13.0	Kevin Cash	1,128,127

Awards

Most Valuable Player
[No player]

Rookie of the Year
Evan Longoria, third base, 2008
Jeremy Hellickson, pitcher, 2011
Wil Myers, outfield, 2013
Randy Arozarena, outfield, 2021

Cy Young
David Price, 2012
Blake Snell, 2018

Manager of the Year (Since 1983)
Joe Maddon, 2008
Joe Maddon, 2011
Kevin Cash, 2020
Kevin Cash, 2021

Hall of Famer Who Played for the Rays
Wade Boggs, third base, 1998–99
Fred McGriff, first base and designated
   hitter, 1998–2001, 2004

Retired Numbers
12 ....Wade Boggs
66 ....Don Zimmer

League Leaders, Batting

Batting Average, Season
[No player]

Home Runs, Season
Carlos Pena, 2009 ....39 (Tie)

RBIs, Season
[No player]

Stolen Bases, Season
Carl Crawford, 2003....................55
Carl Crawford, 2004....................59
Carl Crawford, 2006....................58
Carl Crawford, 2007.............50 (Tie)

Total Bases, Season
[No player]

Most Hits, Season
[No player]

Most Runs, Season
[No player]

Batting Feats

Triple Crown Winners
[No player]

Hitting for the Cycle
Melvin Upton, Oct. 2, 2009
Evan Longoria, Aug. 1, 2017

Six Hits in a Game
[No player]

40 or More Home Runs, Season
46 .... Carlos Pena, 2007

League Leaders, Pitching

Most Wins, Season
David Price, 2012.................20 (Tie)
Blake Snell, 2018...........................21

Most Strikeouts, Season
Scott Kazmir, 2007 239
David Price, 2014.......................271

Lowest ERA, Season
David Price, 2012.......................2.56
Blake Snell, 2018 ....1.89

Most Saves, Season
Rafael Soriano, 2010 45
Brad Boxberger, 2015 41
Alex Colome, 2017......................47

Pitching Feats

Best Won–Lost Percentage, Season
David Price, 2012..... 20–5...... .800 (Tie)
20 Wins, Season
David Price, 2012 20–5
Blake Snell, 2018 21–5

No-Hitters
Matt Garza (vs. Det. Tigers), Jul. 26, 2010 (final 5–0)

No-Hitters Pitched Against
Derek Lowe, Bos. Red Sox, Apr. 27, 2002 (final: 10–0)
Mark Buehrle, Chi. White Sox, Jul. 23, 2009 (final: 5–0) (perfect game)
Dallas Braden, Oak. A's, May 9, 2010 (final: 4–0) (perfect game)
Edwin Jackson, Ari. D'backs (NL), Jun. 25, 2010 (final 1–0)
Felix Hernandez, Sea. Mariners, Aug. 15, 2015 (final:1–0) (perfect game)

Postseason Play

2008 Division Series vs. Chi. White Sox, won 3 games to 1
League Championship Series vs. Bos. Red Sox, won 4 games to 3
World Series vs. Phi. Phillies (NL), lost 4 games to 1

2010 Division Series vs. Tex. Rangers, lost 3 games to 2
2011 Division Series vs. Tex. Rangers, lost 3 games to 1
2013 AL Wild Card tiebreaker Game vs. Tex. Rangers, won
AL Wild Card Playoff Game vs. Cle. Indians, won
Division Series vs. Bos. Red Sox, lost 3 games to 1
2019 AL Wild Card vs. Oak. A's, won
Division Series vs. Hou. Astros, lost 3 games to 2
2020 Wild Card Series vs. Tor. Blue Jays, won 2 games to 0
Division Series vs. N.Y. Yankees, won 3 games to 2
League Championship Series vs. Hou. Astros, won 4 games to 3
World Series vs. L.A. Dodgers (NL), lost 4 games to 2
2021 Division Series vs. Bos. Red Sox, lost 3 games to 1
2022 Wild Card Series vs. Cle. Guardians, lost 2 games to 0

Texas Rangers

Dates of Operation: 1972–present (51 years)

Overall Record: 4650 wins, 5146 losses (.475)

Stadiums: Arlington Stadium, 1972–93; Globe Life Park in Arlington (formerly The Ballpark in Arlington, 1994–2004, and Ameriquest Field in Arlington, 2004–06, and Rangers Ballpark in Arlington, 2007–13), 1994–present (capacity: 48,114)

Year-by-Year Finishes

Year	Finish	Wins	Losses	Percentage	Games Behind	Manager	Attendance
					West Division		
1972	6th	54	100	.351	38.5	Ted Williams	662,974
1973	6th	57	105	.352	37.0	Whitey Herzog, Del Wilber, Billy Martin	686,085
1974	2nd	84	76	.525	5.0	Billy Martin	1,193,902
1975	3rd	79	83	.488	19.0	Billy Martin, Frank Lucchesi	1,127,924
1976	4th (Tie)	76	86	.469	14.0	Frank Lucchesi	1,164,982
1977	2nd	94	68	.580	8.0	Frank Lucchesi, Eddie Stanky, Connie Ryan, Billy Hunter	1,250,722
1978	2nd (Tie)	87	75	.537	5.0	Billy Hunter, Pat Corrales	1,447,963
1979	3rd	83	79	.512	5.0	Pat Corrales	1,519,671
1980	4th (Tie)	76	85	.472	20.5	Pat Corrales	1,198,175
1981*	2nd/3rd	57	48	.543	1.5/4.5	Don Zimmer	850,076
1982	6th	64	98	.395	29.0	Don Zimmer, Darrell Johnson	1,154,432
1983	3rd	77	85	.475	22.0	Doug Rader	1,363,469
1984	7th	69	92	.429	14.5	Doug Rader	1,102,471
1985	7th	62	99	.385	28.5	Doug Rader, Bobby Valentine	1,112,497
1986	2nd	87	75	.537	5.0	Bobby Valentine	1,692,002
1987	6th (Tie)	75	87	.463	10.0	Bobby Valentine	1,763,053
1988	6th	70	91	.435	33.5	Bobby Valentine	1,581,901
1989	4th (Tie)	83	79	.512	16.0	Bobby Valentine	2,043,993
1990	3rd	83	79	.512	20.0	Bobby Valentine	2,057,911
1991	3rd	85	77	.525	10.0	Bobby Valentine	2,297,720
1992	4th (Tie)	77	85	.475	19.0	Bobby Valentine, Toby Harrah	2,198,231
1993	2nd	86	76	.531	8.0	Kevin Kennedy	2,244,616
1994	1st	52	62	.456	+1.0	Kevin Kennedy	2,503,198
1995	3rd	74	70	.514	4.5	Johnny Oates	1,985,910
1996	1st	90	72	.556	+4.5	Johnny Oates	2,889,020
1997	3rd	77	85	.475	13.0	Johnny Oates	2,945,228
1998	1st	88	74	.543	+3.0	Johnny Oates	2,927,409
1999	1st	95	67	.586	+8.0	Johnny Oates	2,771,469
2000	4th (Tie)	71	91	.438	20.5	Johnny Oates	2,800,147
2001	4th (Tie)	73	89	.451	43.0	Johnny Oates, Jerry Narron	2,831,111
2002	4th (Tie)	72	90	.444	31.0	Jerry Narron	2,352,447
2003	4th	71	91	.438	25.0	Buck Showalter	2,094,394
2004	3rd	89	73	.549	3.0	Buck Showalter	2,513,685
2005	3rd	79	83	.488	16.0	Buck Showalter	2,525,221
2006	3rd	80	82	.494	13.0	Buck Showalter	2,388,757
2007	4th	75	87	.463	19.0	Ron Washington	2,353,862
2008	2nd	79	83	.488	21.0	Ron Washington	1,945,677
2009	2nd	87	75	.537	10.0	Ron Washington	2,156,016
2010	1st	90	72	.556	+9.0	Ron Washington	2,505,171
2011	1st	96	65	.593	+10.0	Ron Washington	2,946,949
2012	2nd	93	69	.574	1.0	Ron Washington	3,460,280
2013	2nd	91	72	.558	5.5	Ron Washington	3,178,273
2014	5th	67	95	.414	31.0	Ron Washington, Tim Bogar	2,718,733
2015	1st	88	74	.543	+2.0	Jeff Banister	2,491,875
2016	1st	95	67	.586	+9.0	Jeff Banister	2,710,402
2017	3rd	78	84	.481	23.0	Jeff Banister	2,507,760
2018	5th	67	95	.414	36.0	Jeff Banister, Don Wakamatsu	2,107,107

Year	Finish	Wins	Losses	Percentage	Games Behind	Manager	Attendance
2019	3rd	78	84	.481	29.0	Chris Woodward	2,132,994
2020	5th	22	38	.367	14.0	Chris Woodward	0
2021	5th	60	102	.370	35.0	Chris Woodward	2,110,258
2022	4th	68	94	.420	38.0	Chris Woodward, Tony Beasley	2,011,381

* Split season.

Awards

Most Valuable Player
Jeff Burroughs, outfield, 1974
Juan Gonzalez, outfield, 1996
Juan Gonzalez, outfield, 1998
Ivan Rodriguez, catcher, 1999
Alex Rodriguez, shortstop, 2003
Josh Hamilton, outfield, 2010

Rookie of the Year
Mike Hargrove, first base, 1974
Neftali Feliz, pitcher, 2010

Cy Young
[No player]

Manager of the Year (Since 1983)
Johnny Oates, 1996 (Tie)
Buck Showalter, 2004
Jeff Banister, 2015

Hall of Famers Who Played for the Rangers
Harold Baines, designated hitter, 1989–90
Goose Gossage, picher, 1993
Vladimir Guerrero, designated hitter, 2010
Ferguson Jenkins, pitcher, 1974–75 and 1978–81
Gaylord Perry, pitcher, 1975–77 and 1980
Ivan Rodriguez, catcher, 1991–2002, 2009
Nolan Ryan, pitcher, 1989–93

Retired Numbers
7 .... Ivan Rodriguez
10 .... Michael Young
26 .... Johnny Oates
29 .... Adrian Beltre
34 .... Nolan Ryan

League Leaders, Batting

Batting Average, Season
Julio Franco, 1991 .... .341
Michael Young, 2005 .... .331
Josh Hamilton, 2010 .... .359

Home Runs, Season
Juan Gonzalez, 1992 43
Juan Gonzalez, 1993 46
Alex Rodriguez, 2001 52
Alex Rodriguez, 2002 57
Alex Rodriguez, 2003 47

RBIs, Season
Jeff Burroughs, 1974 118
Ruben Sierra, 1989 119
Juan Gonzalez, 1998 157
Alex Rodriguez, 2002 142
Josh Hamilton, 2008 130

Stolen Bases, Season
[No player]

Total Bases, Season
Ruben Sierra, 1989 344
Alex Rodriguez, 2001 393
Alex Rodriguez, 2002 389
Mark Teixeira, 2005 370
Josh Hamilton, 2008 .... 331 (Tie)

Most Hits, Season
Rafael Palmeiro, 1990 191
Michael Young, 2005 221
Michael Young, 2011 .... 213 (Tie)
Adrian Beltre, 2013 199

Most Runs, Season
Rafael Palmeiro, 1993 124
Alex Rodriguez, 2001 133
Alex Rodriguez, 2003 124

Batting Feats

Triple Crown Winners
[No player]

Hitting for the Cycle
Oddibe McDowell, Jul. 23, 1985
Mark Teixeira, Aug. 17, 2004
Gary Matthews Jr., Sep. 13, 2006
Ian Kinsler, Apr. 15, 2005
Bengie Molina, Jul. 16, 2010
Adrian Beltre, Aug. 24, 2012
Alex Rios, Sep. 23, 2013
Adrian Beltre, Aug. 3, 2015
Shin-Soo Choo, Jul. 21, 2015
Carlos Gomez, Apr. 29, 2017

Six Hits in a Game
Alfonso Soriano, May 8, 2004
Ian Kinsler, Apr. 15, 2005

40 or More Home Runs, Season
57 .... Alex Rodriguez, 2002
52 .... Alex Rodriguez, 2001
47 .... Juan Gonzalez, 1996
          Rafael Palmeiro, 1999
          Rafael Palmeiro, 2001
          Alex Rodriguez, 2003
46 .... Juan Gonzalez, 1993
45 .... Juan Gonzalez, 1998
43 .... Juan Gonzalez, 1992
          Rafael Palmeiro, 2002
          Mark Teixeira, 2005
          Josh Hamilton, 2012
42 .... Juan Gonzalez, 1997
41 .... Joey Gallo, 2017
40 .... Joey Gallo, 2018

League Leaders, Pitching

Most Wins, Season
Ferguson Jenkins, 1974.......... 25 (Tie)
Kevin Brown, 1992 .... 21 (Tie)
Rick Helling, 1998 .... 20 (Tie)

Most Strikeouts, Season
Nolan Ryan, 1989 301
Nolan Ryan, 1990 232
Yu Darvish, 2013 277

Lowest ERA, Season
Rick Honeycutt, 1983 .... 2.42

Most Saves, Season
Jeff Russell, 1989 38

Best Won–Lost Percentage, Season
Tommy Hunter, 2010 .... .765

Pitching Feats

20 Wins, Season
Ferguson Jenkins, 1974.......... 25–12
Kevin Brown, 1992 21–11
Rich Helling, 1998 20–7

No-Hitters
Jim Bibby (vs. Oak. A's), Jul. 30, 1973 (final: 6–0)
Bert Blyleven (vs. Cal. Angels), Sep. 22, 1977 (final: 6–0)
Nolan Ryan (vs. Oak. A's), Jun. 11, 1990 (final: 5–0)

Nolan Ryan (vs. Tor. Blue Jays), May
1, 1991 (final: 3–0)

Kenny Rogers (vs. Cal. Angels), Jul.
28, 1994 (final: 4–0) (perfect game)

No-Hitters Pitched Against

Jim Colborn, K.C. Royals, May 14,
1977 (final: 6–0)

Mike Witt, Cal. Angels, Sep. 30, 1984
(final: 1–0) (perfect game)

Mark Buehrle, Chi. White Sox, Apr. 18,
2007 (final: 6–0)

Postseason Play

1996 Division Series vs. N.Y. Yankees,
lost 3 games to 1

1999 Division Series vs. N.Y. Yankees,
lost 3 games to 0

1998 Division Series vs. N.Y. Yankees,
lost 3 games to 0

2010 Division Series vs. T.B. Rays,
won 3 games to 2
League Championship Series vs.
N.Y. Yankees, won 4 games to 2
World Series vs. S. F. Giants
(NL), lost 4 games to 1

2011 Division Series vs. T.B. Rays,
won 3 games to 1
League Championship Series vs.
Det. Tigers, won 4 games to 2
World Series vs. St.L. Cardinals
(NL) lost 4 games to 3

2012 AL Wild Card Playoff Game vs.

Bal. Orioles, lost

2013 AL Wild Card tiebreaker Game
vs. T.B. Rays, lost

2015 Division Series vs. Tor. Blue
Jays, lost 3 games to 2

2016 Division Series vs. Tor. Blue
Jays, lost 3 games to 0

Toronto Blue Jays

Dates of Operation: 1977–present (46 years)
Overall Record: 3598 wins, 3627 losses (.498)
Stadiums: Exhibition Stadium, 1977–89; Rogers Centre (formerly Skydome, 1989–2004), 1989–present (capacity: 49,282)

Year-by-Year Finishes

Year	Finish	Wins	Losses	Percentage	Games Behind	Manager	Attendance
					East Division		
1977	7th	54	107	.335	45.5	Roy Hartsfield	1,701,052
1978	7th	59	102	.366	40.0	Roy Hartsfield	1,562,585
1979	7th	53	109	.327	50.5	Roy Hartsfield	1,431,651
1980	7th	67	95	.414	36.0	Bobby Mattick	1,400,327
1981*	7th/7th	37	69	.349	19.0/7.5	Bobby Mattick	755,083
1982	6th (Tie)	78	84	.481	17.0	Bobby Cox	1,275,978
1983	4th	89	73	.549	9.0	Bobby Cox	1,930,415
1984	2nd	89	73	.549	15.0	Bobby Cox	2,110,009
1985	1st	99	62	.615	+2.0	Bobby Cox	2,468,925
1986	4th	86	76	.531	9.5	Jimy Williams	2,455,477
1987	2nd	96	66	.593	2.0	Jimy Williams	2,778,429
1988	3rd (Tie)	87	75	.537	2.0	Jimy Williams	2,595,175
1989	1st	89	73	.549	+2.0	Jimy Williams, Cito Gaston	3,375,883
1990	2nd	86	76	.531	2.0	Cito Gaston	3,885,284
1991	1st	91	71	.562	+7.0	Cito Gaston	4,001,527
1992	1st	96	66	.593	+4.0	Cito Gaston	4,028,318
1993	1st	95	67	.586	+7.0	Cito Gaston	4,057,947
1994	3rd	55	60	.478	16.0	Cito Gaston	2,907,933
1995	5th	56	88	.389	30.0	Cito Gaston	2,826,483
1996	4th	74	88	.457	18.0	Cito Gaston	2,559,573
1997	5th	76	86	.469	22.0	Cito Gaston, Mel Queen	2,589,297
1998	3rd	88	74	.543	26.0	Tim Johnson	2,454,183
1999	3rd	84	78	.519	14.0	Jim Fregosi	2,163,464
2000	3rd	83	79	.512	4.5	Jim Fregosi	1,819,886
2001	3rd	80	82	.494	16.0	Buck Martinez	1,915,438
2002	3rd	78	84	.481	25.5	Buck Martinez, Carlos Tosca	1,636,904
2003	3rd	86	76	.531	15.0	Carlos Tosca	1,799,458
2004	5th	67	94	.416	33.5	Carlos Tosca, John Gibbons	1,900,041
2005	3rd	80	82	.494	15.0	John Gibbons	2,014,987
2006	2nd	87	75	.537	10.0	John Gibbons	2,302,212
2007	3rd	83	79	.512	13.0	John Gibbons	2,360,648
2008	4th	86	76	.531	11.0	John Gibbons, Cito Gaston	2,399,786
2009	4th	75	87	.463	28.0	Cito Gaston	1,876,129
2010	4th	85	77	.525	11.0	Cito Gaston	1,495,482
2011	4th	81	81	.500	16.0	John Farrell	1,818,103
2012	4th	73	89	.451	22.0	John Farrell	2,099,663
2013	5th	74	88	.457	23.0	John Gibbons	2,536,562
2014	3rd	83	79	.512	13.0	John Gibbons	2,375,525
2015	1st	93	69	.574	+6.0	John Gibbons	2,794,891
2016	2nd	89	73	.549	4.0	John Gibbons	3,392,099
2017	4th	76	86	.469	17.0	Jay Gibbons	3,203,886
2018	4th	73	89	.451	35.0	Jay Gibbons	2,325,281

Year	Finish	Wins	Losses	Percentage	Games Behind	Manager	Attendance
2019	4th	67	95	.414	36.0	Charlie Montovo	1,750,144
2020	3rd	32	28	.533	8.0	Charlie Montovo	0
2021	4th	91	71	.562	9.0	Charlie Montovo	805,901
2022	2nd	92	70	.568	7.0	Charlie Montovo, John Schneider	2,653,830

* Split season.

Awards

Most Valuable Player
George Bell, outfield, 1987
Josh Donaldson, third base, 2015

Rookie of the Year
Alfredo Griffin (co-winner), shortstop, 1979
Eric Hinske, third base, 2002

Cy Young
Pat Hentgen, 1996
Roger Clemens, 1997
Roger Clemens, 1998
Roy Halladay, 2003
Robbie Ray, 2021

Manager of the Year (Since 1983)
Bobby Cox, 1985

Hall of Famers Who Played for the Blue Jays
Roberto Alomar, second base, 1991–95
Roy Halladay, pitcher, 1998–2009
Rickey Henderson, outfield, 1993
Fred McGriff, first base and designated hitter, 1986–90
Paul Molitor, designated hitter, 1993–95
Jack Morris, pitcher, 1992–93
Phil Niekro, pitcher, 1987
Scott Rolen, third base, 2008–09
Frank Thomas, first base and designated hitter, 2007–08
Dave Winfield, designated hitter, 1992

Retired Numbers
12 .... Roberto Alomar
32 .... Roy Halladay

League Leaders, Batting

Batting Average, Season
John Olerud, 1993 .... .363

Home Runs, Season
Jesse Barfield, 1986 40
Fred McGriff, 1989 36
Jose Bautista, 2010 54
Jose Bautista, 2011 43
Vladimir Guerrero Jr., 2021 .... 48 (Tie)

RBIs, Season
George Bell, 1987 134
Carlos Delgado, 2003 145
Josh Donaldson, 2015 123
Edwin Encarnacion, 2016 .... 127 (Tie)

Stolen Bases, Season
[No player]

Total Bases, Season
George Bell, 1987 369
Shawn Green, 1999 361
Carlos Delgado, 2000 378
Vernon Wells, 2003 373
Jose Bautista, 2010 351
Josh Donaldson, 2015 352
Vladimir Guerrero Jr., 2021 363

Most Hits, Season
Paul Molitor, 1993 211
Vernon Wells, 2003 215
Bo Bichette, 2021 191
Bo Bichette, 2022 189

Most Runs, Season
Josh Donaldson, 2015 122
Vladimir Guerrero Jr., 2021 123

Batting Feats

Triple Crown Winners
[No player]

Hitting for the Cycle
Kelly Gruber, Apr. 16, 1989
Jeff Frye, Aug. 17, 2001
Cavan Biggio, Sep. 17, 2019

Six Hits in a Game
Frank Catalanotto, May 1, 2004
Lourdes Gurriel Jr., Jul. 22, 2022

40 or More Home Runs, Season
54 .... Jose Bautista, 2010
48 ....Vladimir Guerrero Jr.
47 .... George Bell, 1987
46 .... Jose Canseco, 1998
45 ....Marcus Semien, 2021
44 .... Carlos Delgado, 1999
43 .... Jose Bautista, 2011
42 .... Shawn Green, 1999
Carlos Delgado, 2003
Edwin Encarnacion, 2012
Edwin Encarnacion, 2016
41 .... Tony Batista, 2000
Carlos Delgado, 2000
40 .... Jesse Barfield, 1986

League Leaders, Pitching

Most Wins, Season
Jack Morris, 1992 .... 21 (Tie)
Roger Clemens, 1997 21
Roger Clemens, 1998 .... 20 (Tie)

Most Strikeouts, Season
Roger Clemens, 1997 292
Roger Clemens, 1998 271
A.J. Burnett, 2008 231
Robbie Ray, 2021 248

Lowest ERA, Season
Dave Stieb, 1985 .... 2.48
Jimmy Key, 1987 .... 2.76
Juan Guzman, 1996 .... 2.93
Roger Clemens, 1997 .... 2.05
Roger Clemens, 1998 .... 2.65
David Price, 2015 .... 2.45*
Aaron Sanchez, 2016 .... 3.00
Robbie Ray, 2021 .... 2.84

* 2.53 with Det. Tigers and 2.30 with Tor. Blue Jays.

Most Saves, Season
Tom Heinke, 1987 34
Duane Ward, 1993 .... 45 (Tie)

Best Won–Lost Percentage, Season
Doyle Alexander, 1984.. 17–6 ..... .739
Roy Halladay, 2003 ......22–7 .... .759
Aaron Sanchez, 2016 ...15–2 .... .882

Pitching Feats

Triple Crown Winner
Roger Clemens, 1997 (21–7, 2.05 ERA, 292 SO)
Roger Clemens, 1998 (20–6, 2.65 ERA, 271 SO)

20 Wins, Season

Jack Morris, 1992 21–6
Pat Hentgen, 1996 20–10
Roger Clemens, 1997 21–7
Roger Clemens, 1998 20–6
David Wells, 2000 20–8
Roy Halladay, 2003 22–7
Roy Halladay, 2008 20–11
J.A. Happ, 2016 20–4

No-Hitters

Dave Stieb (vs. Det. Tigers),
    Sep. 2, 1990 (final: 3–0)

No-Hitters Pitched Against

Len Barker, Cle. Indians, May 15,
    1981 (final: 3–0) (perfect game)
Dave Stewart, Oak. A's, Jun. 29, 1990
    (final: 5–0)

Nolan Ryan, Tex. Rangers, May 1, 1991
    (final: 3–0)
Justin Verlander, Det. Tigers,
    May 7, 2011 (final: 9–0)
James Paxton, Sea. Mariners, May 8,
    2018 (final: 5–0)

Postseason Play

1985   League Championship Series vs.
        K.C. Royals, lost 4 games to 3
1989   League Championship Series vs.
        Oak. A's, lost 4 games to 1
1991   League Championship Series vs.
        Min. Twins, lost 4 games to 1
1992   League Championship Series vs.
        Oak. A's, won 4 games to 2
        World Series vs. Atl. Braves (NL),
        won 4 games to 2

1993   League Championship Series vs.
        Chi. White Sox, won 4
        games to 2
        World Series vs. Phi. Phillies
        (NL), won 4 games to 2
2015   Division Series vs. Tex. Rangers,
        won 3 games to 2
        League Championship Series vs.
        K.C. Royals, lost 4 games to 2
2016   AL Wild Card Playoff Game vs.
        Bal. Orioles, won
        Division Series vs. Tex. Rangers,
        won 3 games to 0
        League Championship Series vs.
        Cle. Indians, lost 4 games to 1
2020   Wild Card Series vs. T.B. Rays,
        lost 2 games to 0
2022   Wild Card Series vs. Sea.
        Mariners, lost 2 games to 0

Arizona Diamondbacks

Dates of Operation: 1998–present (25 years)
Overall Record: 1914 wins, 2034 losses (.485)
Stadium: Chase Field (formerly Bank One Ballpark (The BOB), 1998–2005), 1998–present (capacity: 48,519)
Other Name: D'backs

Year-by-Year Finishes

Year	Finish	Wins	Losses	Percentage	Games Behind	Manager	Attendance
					West Division		
1998	5th	65	97	.401	33.0	Buck Showalter	3,600,412
1999	1st	100	62	.617	+14.0	Buck Showalter	3,019,654
2000	3rd	85	77	.525	12.0	Buck Showalter	2,942,516
2001	1st	92	70	.556	+2.0	Bob Brenly	2,740,554
2002	1st	98	64	.605	+2.5	Bob Brenly	3,200,725
2003	3rd	84	78	.519	16.5	Bob Brenly	2,805,542
2004	5th	51	111	.315	42.0	Bob Brenly, Al Pedrique	2,519,560
2005	2nd	77	85	.465	5.0	Bob Melvin	2,058,718
2006	4th	76	86	.469	12.0	Bob Melvin	2,092,189
2007	1st	90	72	.556	+0.5	Bob Melvin	2,325,414
2008	2nd	82	80	.506	2.0	Bob Melvin	2,509,924
2009	5th	70	92	.432	25.0	Bob Melvin, A. J. Hinch	2,129,183
2010	5th	65	97	.401	27.0	A.J. Hinch, Kirk Gibson	2,056,697
2011	1st	94	68	.580	+8.0	Kirk Gibson	2,105,432
2012	3rd	81	81	.500	13.0	Kirk Gibson	2,177,617
2013	2nd	81	81	.500	11.0	Kirk Gibson	2,134,895
2014	5th	64	98	.395	30.0	Kirk Gibson, Alan Trammell	2,073,730
2015	3rd	79	83	.488	13.0	Chip Hale	2,080,145
2016	4th	69	93	.426	22.0	Chip Hale	2,036,216
2017	2nd	93	69	.574	11.0	Torey Lovullo	2,134,375
2018	3rd	82	80	.506	9.0	Torey Lovullo	2,242,695
2019	2nd	85	77	.477	28.0	Torey Lovullo	2,135,510
2020	5th	25	35	.417	18.0	Torey Lovullo	0
2021	5th	52	110	.321	55.0	Torey Lovullo	1,043,010
2022	4th	74	88	.457	37.0	Torey Lovullo	1,605,199

Awards

Most Valuable Player
[No player]

Rookie of the Year
[No player]

Cy Young
Randy Johnson, 1999
Randy Johnson, 2000
Randy Johnson, 2001
Randy Johnson, 2002
Brandon Webb, 2006

Manager of the Year (Since 1983)
Bob Melvin, 2007
Kirk Gibson, 2011
Torey Lovullo, 2017

Hall of Famers Who Played for the Diamondbacks

Roberto Alomar, second base, 2004
Randy Johnson, pitcher, 1999–2004

Retired Numbers
20 .... Luis Gonzalez
51 .... Randy Johnson

League Leaders, Batting

Batting Average, Season
[No player]

Home Runs, Season
Paul Goldschmidt, 2013............36 (Tie)
RBIs, Season
Paul Goldschmidt, 2013................. 125

Stolen Bases, Season
Tony Womack, 1999 72

Total Bases, Season
Paul Goldschmidt, 2013................. 332

Most Hits, Season
Luis Gonzalez, 1999 206
Jean Segura, 2016.....................203

Most Runs, Season
[No player]

Batting Feats

Triple Crown Winners
[No player]

Hitting for the Cycle
Luis Gonzalez, Jul. 5, 2000
Greg Colbrunn, Sep. 18, 2002
Stephen Drew, Sep. 1, 2008
Kelly Johnson, Jul. 13, 2010
Aaron Hill, Jun. 18, 2012
Aaron Hill, Jun. 29, 2012

Six Hits in a Game
[No player]

40 or More Home Runs, Season
57 .... Luis Gonzalez, 2001
44 .... Mark Reynolds, 2009
40 ....Adam Dunn*, 2008
* 32 for Cin. Reds and 8 for Ari. D'backs.

League Leaders, Pitching

Most Wins, Season
Randy Johnson, 2002 24
Brandon Webb, 2006............ 16 (Tie)
Brandon Webb, 2008...................22
Ian Kennedy, 2011................ 21 (Tie)

Most Strikeouts, Season
Randy Johnson, 1999 364
Randy Johnson, 2000 347
Randy Johnson, 2001 372
Randy Johnson, 2002 334
Randy Johnson, 2004 290

Lowest ERA, Season
Randy Johnson, 1999 .... 2.48
Randy Johnson, 2001 .... 2.49
Randy Johnson, 2002 .... 2.32

Most Saves, Season
Jose Valverde, 2007 47

Best Won–Lost Percentage, Season
Randy Johnson, 2000 ...19–7 ... .731
Curt Schilling, 2001 .....22–6 ... .786
Randy Johnson, 2002 ...24–5 ... .828
Ian Kennedy, 2011.......21–4 ... .840

Pitching Feats

Triple Crown Winner
Randy Johnson, 2002 (24–5, 2.32 ERA, 334 SO)

20 Wins, Season
Curt Schilling, 2001 22–6
Randy Johnson, 2001 21–6
Randy Johnson, 2002 24–5
Curt Schilling, 2002 23–7
Brandon Webb, 2008............... 22–7
Ian Kennedy, 2011................... 21–4

No-Hitters
Randy Johnson (vs. Atl. Braves), May 18, 2004 (final: 2–0) (perfect game)
Edwin Jackson (vs. T.B. Rays), Jun. 25, 2010 (final: 1–0)
Tyler Gilbert (vs. S.D. Padres), Aug. 14, 2021 (final: 7–0)

No-Hitters Pitched Against
Jose Jimenez, St.L. Cardinals, Jun. 25, 1999 (final: 1–0)
Anibal Sanchez, Fla. Marlins, Sep. 6, 2006 (final: 2–0)
Edinson Volquez, Mia. Marlins, Jun. 3, 2017 (final: 3–0)

Postseason Play

1999 Division Series vs. N.Y. Mets, lost 3 games to 1
2001 Division Series vs. St.L. Cardinals, won 3 games to 2
      League Championship Series vs. Atl. Braves, won 4 games to 1
      World Series vs. N.Y. Yankees (AL), won 4 games to 3
2002 Division Series vs. St.L. Cardinals, lost 3 games to 2
2007 Division Series vs. Chi. Cubs, won 3 games to 0
      League Championship Series vs. Col. Rockies, lost 4 games to 0
2011 Division Series vs. Mil. Brewers, lost 3 games to 2
2017 NL Wild Card Playoff Game vs. Col. Rockies, won
      Division Series vs. L.A. Dodgers, lost 3 games to 0

Atlanta Braves (formerly the Milwaukee Braves)

Dates of Operation: (as the Milwaukee Braves) 1953–65 (13 years)
Overall Record: 1146 wins, 890 losses (.563)
Stadium: Milwaukee County Stadium, 1953–65 (capacity: 44,091)

Dates of Operation: (as the Atlanta Braves) 1966–present (57 years)
Overall Record: 4657 wins, 4330 losses (.518)
Stadiums: Atlanta–Fulton County Stadium, 1966–96; Turner Field, 1997–2016;
Truist Park (known as SunTrust Park, 2017–19), 2017–present (capacity: 41,500)

Year-by-Year Finishes

Year	Finish	Wins	Losses	Percentage	Games Behind	Manager	Attendance
					Mil. Braves		
1953	2nd	92	62	.597	13.0	Charlie Grimm	1,826,397
1954	3rd	89	65	.578	8.0	Charlie Grimm	2,131,388
1955	2nd	85	69	.552	13.5	Charlie Grimm	2,005,836
1956	2nd	92	62	.597	1.0	Charlie Grimm, Fred Haney	2,046,331
1957	1st	95	59	.617	+8.0	Fred Haney	2,215,404
1958	1st	92	62	.597	+8.0	Fred Haney	1,971,101
1959	2nd	86	70	.551	2.0	Fred Haney	1,749,112
1960	2nd	88	66	.571	7.0	Chuck Dressen	1,497,799
1961	4th	83	71	.539	10.0	Chuck Dressen, Birdie Tebbetts	1,101,441
1962	5th	86	76	.531	15.5	Birdie Tebbetts	766,921
1963	6th	84	78	.519	15.0	Bobby Bragan	773,018
1964	5th	88	74	.543	5.0	Bobby Bragan	910,911
1965	5th	86	76	.531	11.0	Bobby Bragan	555,584
					Atl. Braves		
1966	5th	85	77	.525	10.0	Bobby Bragan, Billy Hitchcock	1,539,801
1967	7th	77	85	.475	24.5	Billy Hitchcock, Ken Silvestri	1,389,222
1968	5th	81	81	.500	16.0	Lum Harris	1,126,540
					West Division		
1969	1st	93	69	.574	+3.0	Lum Harris	1,458,320
1970	5th	76	86	.469	26.0	Lum Harris	1,078,848
1971	3rd	82	80	.506	8.0	Lum Harris	1,006,320
1972	4th	70	84	.455	25.0	Lum Harris, Eddie Mathews	752,973
1973	5th	76	85	.472	22.5	Eddie Mathews	800,655
1974	3rd	88	74	.543	14.0	Eddie Mathews, Clyde King	981,085
1975	5th	67	94	.416	40.5	Clyde King, Connie Ryan	534,672
1976	6th	70	92	.432	32.0	Dave Bristol	818,179
1977	6th	61	101	.377	37.0	Dave Bristol, Ted Turner	872,464
1978	6th	69	93	.426	26.0	Bobby Cox	904,494
1979	6th	66	94	.413	23.5	Bobby Cox	769,465
1980	4th	81	80	.503	11.0	Bobby Cox	1,048,411
1981*	4th/5th	50	56	.472	9.5/7.5	Bobby Cox	535,418
1982	1st	89	73	.549	+1.0	Joe Torre	1,801,985
1983	2nd	88	74	.543	3.0	Joe Torre	2,119,935
1984	2nd (Tie)	80	82	.494	12.0	Joe Torre	1,724,892
1985	5th	66	96	.407	29.0	Eddie Haas, Bobby Wine	1,350,137
1986	6th	72	89	.447	23.5	Chuck Tanner	1,387,181
1987	5th	69	92	.429	20.5	Chuck Tanner	1,217,402
1988	6th	54	106	.338	39.5	Chuck Tanner, Russ Nixon	848,089
1989	6th	63	97	.394	28.0	Russ Nixon	984,930
1990	6th	65	97	.401	26.0	Russ Nixon, Bobby Cox	980,129
1991	1st	94	68	.580	+1.0	Bobby Cox	2,140,217

Year	Finish	Wins	Losses	Percentage	Games Behind	Manager	Attendance
1992	1st	98	64	.605	+8.0	Bobby Cox	3,077,400
1993	1st	104	58	.642	+1.0	Bobby Cox	3,884,725
				East Division			
1994	2nd	68	46	.596	6.0	Bobby Cox	2,539,240
1995	1st	90	54	.625	+21.0	Bobby Cox	2,561,831
1996	1st	96	66	.593	+8.0	Bobby Cox	2,901,242
1997	1st	101	61	.623	+9.0	Bobby Cox	3,464,488
1998	1st	106	56	.654	+18.0	Bobby Cox	3,361,350
1999	1st	103	59	.636	+6.5	Bobby Cox	3,284,897
2000	1st	95	67	.586	+1.0	Bobby Cox	3,234,301
2001	1st	88	74	.543	+2.0	Bobby Cox	2,823,494
2002	1st	101	59	.631	+19.0	Bobby Cox	2,603,482
2003	1st	101	61	.623	+10.0	Bobby Cox	2,401,104
2004	1st	96	66	.593	+10.0	Bobby Cox	2,322,565
2005	1st	90	72	.556	+2.0	Bobby Cox	2,521,167
2006	3rd	79	83	.488	18.0	Bobby Cox	2,550,524
2007	3rd	84	78	.519	5.0	Bobby Cox	2,745,210
2008	4th	72	90	.444	20.0	Bobby Cox	2,532,834
2009	3rd	86	76	.531	7.0	Bobby Cox	2,373,631
2010	2nd	91	71	.562	6.0	Bobby Cox	2,510,119
2011	2nd	89	73	.549	13.0	Fredi Gonzalez	2,372,940
2012	2nd	94	68	.580	4.0	Fredi Gonzalez	2,420,171
2013	1st	96	66	.593	+10.0	Fredi Gonzalez	2,548,679
2014	2nd	79	83	.488	17.0	Fredi Gonzalez	2,354,305
2015	4th	67	95	.141	23.0	Fredi Gonzalez	2,001,392
2016	5th	68	93	.422	26.5	Fredi Gonzalez, Brian Snitker	2,020,914
2017	3rd	72	90	.444	25.0	Brian Snitker	2,505,252
2018	1st	90	72	.556	+8.0	Brian Snitker	2,555,781
2019	1st	97	65	.599	+4.0	Brian Snitker	2,654,920
2020	1st	35	25	.583	+4.0	Brian Snitker	0
2021	1st	88	73	.547	+6.5	Brian Snitker	2,299,647
2022	1st (Tie)	101	61	.623	—	Brian Snitker	3,129,931

* Split season.

Awards

Most Valuable Player

Hank Aaron, outfield, 1957 (Mil.)
Dale Murphy, outfield, 1982
Dale Murphy, outfield, 1983
Terry Pendleton, third base, 1991
Chipper Jones, third base, 1999
Ronald Acuna, outfield, 2018
Freddie Freeman, first base, 2020

Rookie of the Year

Bob Horner, third base, 1978
David Justice, outfield, 1990
Rafael Furcal, second base and shortstop, 2000
Craig Kimbrel, pitcher, 2011
Michael Harris, outfield, 2022

Cy Young

Warren Spahn, 1957 (Mil.)
Tom Glavine, 1991
Greg Maddux, 1993
Greg Maddux, 1994
Greg Maddux, 1995
John Smoltz, 1996
Tom Glavine, 1998

Manager of the Year (Since 1983)

Bobby Cox, 1991
Bobby Cox, 2004
Bobby Cox, 2005
Brian Snitker, 2018

Hall of Famers Who Played for the Braves

Hank Aaron, outfield, 1954–65 (Mil.)
and 1966–74 (Atl.)
Orlando Cepeda, first base, 1969–72
Tom Glavine, pitcher, 1987–2002
and 2008
Chipper Jones, third base and outfield, 1993, 1995–2012
Tony La Russa, second base, 1971
Greg Maddux, pitcher, 1993–2003
Eddie Mathews, third base, 1953–65 (Mil.) and 1966 (Atl.)
Fred McGriff, first base, 1993–97
Phil Niekro, pitcher, 1964–65 (Mil.) and 1966–83 (Atl.)
Gaylord Perry, pitcher, 1981
Ted Simmons, catcher, 1986–88
Red Schoendienst, infield, 1957–60 (Mil.)
Enos Slaughter, outfield, 1959 (Mil.)
John Smoltz, pitcher, 1988–2008
Warren Spahn, pitcher, 1953–64 (Mil.)

Bruce Sutter, pitcher, 1985–88

Joe Torre, catcher and first base, 1960–65 (Mil.) and 1966–68 (Atl.)

Hoyt Wilhelm, pitcher, 1969–70, 1971

Retired Numbers

3	Dale Murphy
6	Bobby Cox
10	Chipper Jones
21	Warren Spahn
29	John Smoltz
31	Greg Maddux
35	Phil Niekro
41	Eddie Mathews
44	Hank Aaron
47	Tom Glavine

League Leaders, Batting

Batting Average, Season

Hank Aaron, 1956 (Mil.)	.328
Hank Aaron, 1959 (Mil.)	.355
Rico Carty, 1970	.366
Ralph Garr, 1974	.353
Terry Pendleton, 1991	.319
Chipper Jones, 2008	.364

Home Runs, Season

Eddie Mathews, 1953 (Mil.)	47
Hank Aaron, 1957 (Mil.)	44
Eddie Mathews, 1959 (Mil.)	46
Hank Aaron, 1963 (Mil.)	44
Hank Aaron, 1966	44
Hank Aaron, 1967	39
Dale Murphy, 1984	36 (Tie)
Dale Murphy, 1985	37
Andruw Jones, 2005	51
Marcell Ozuna, 2020	18

RBIs, Season

Hank Aaron, 1957 (Mil.)	132
Hank Aaron, 1960 (Mil.)	126
Hank Aaron, 1963 (Mil.)	130
Hank Aaron, 1966	127
Dale Murphy, 1982	109 (Tie)
Dale Murphy, 1983	121
Andruw Jones, 2005	128
Marcell Ozuna, 2020	56
Adam Duvall, 2021*	113

* 68 with Mia. Marlins and 45 with Atl. Braves.

Stolen Bases, Season

Bill Bruton, 1953 (Mil.)	26
Bill Bruton, 1954 (Mil.)	34
Bill Bruton, 1955 (Mil.)	25
Michael Bourn*, 2011	61
Ronald Acuna, 2019	37

* 39 with Hou. Astros and 22 with Atl. Braves.

Total Bases, Season

Hank Aaron, 1956 (Mil.)	340
Hank Aaron, 1957 (Mil.)	369
Hank Aaron, 1959 (Mil.)	400
Hank Aaron, 1960 (Mil.)	334
Hank Aaron, 1961 (Mil.)	358
Hank Aaron, 1963 (Mil.)	370
Felipe Alou, 1966	355
Hank Aaron, 1967	344
Hank Aaron, 1969	332
Dale Murphy, 1984	332
Terry Pendleton, 1991	303 (Tie)
Marcell Ozuna, 2020	145
Austin Riley, 2022	325

Most Hits, Season

Hank Aaron, 1956 (Mil.)	200
Red Schoendienst*, 1957 (Mil.)	200
Hank Aaron, 1959 (Mil.)	223
Felipe Alou, 1966	218
Felipe Alou, 1968	210 (Tie)
Ralph Garr, 1974	214
Terry Pendleton, 1991	187
Terry Pendleton, 1992	199 (Tie)
Freddie Freeman, 2018	191
Ozzie Albies, 2019	189

* 78 with N.Y. Giants and 122 with Mil. Braves.

Most Runs, Season

Hank Aaron, 1957 (Mil.)	118
Bill Bruton, 1960 (Mil.)	112
Hank Aaron, 1963 (Mil.)	121
Felipe Alou, 1966	122
Hank Aaron, 1967	113 (Tie)
Dale Murphy, 1985	118
Ronald Acuna, 2019	127
Freddie Freeman, 2020	51
Freddie Freeman, 2021	120

Batting Feats

Triple Crown Winners

[No player]

Hitting for the Cycle

Albert Hall, Sep. 23, 1987

Mark Kotsay, Aug. 14, 2008

Freddie Freeman, Jun. 15, 2016

Freddie Freeman, Aug. 18, 2021

Eddie Rosario, Sep. 19, 2021

Six Hits in a Game

Felix Milan, Jul. 6, 1970

Willie Harris, Jul. 21, 2007

40 or More Home Runs, Season

51	Andruw Jones, 2005
47	Eddie Mathews, 1953 (Mil.)
	Hank Aaron, 1971
46	Eddie Mathews, 1959 (Mil.)
45	Hank Aaron, 1962 (Mil.)
	Chipper Jones, 1999
44	Hank Aaron, 1957 (Mil.)
	Hank Aaron, 1963 (Mil.)
	Hank Aaron, 1966
	Hank Aaron, 1969
	Dale Murphy, 1987
	Andres Galarraga, 1998
43	Davey Johnson, 1973
	Javy Lopez, 2003
41	Eddie Mathews, 1955 (Mil.)
	Darrell Evans, 1973
	Jeff Burroughs, 1977
	Andruw Jones, 2006
	Ronald Acuna, 2019
40	Eddie Mathews, 1954 (Mil.)
	Hank Aaron, 1960 (Mil.)
	Hank Aaron, 1973
	David Justice, 1993

League Leaders, Pitching

Most Wins, Season

Warren Spahn, 1957 (Mil.)	21
Warren Spahn, 1958 (Mil.)	22 (Tie)
Lew Burdette, 1959 (Mil.)	21 (Tie)
Warren Spahn, 1959 (Mil.)	21 (Tie)
Warren Spahn, 1960 (Mil.)	21 (Tie)
Warren Spahn, 1961 (Mil.)	21 (Tie)
Phil Niekro, 1974	20 (Tie)
Phil Niekro, 1979	21 (Tie)
Tom Glavine, 1991	20 (Tie)
Tom Glavine, 1992	20 (Tie)
Tom Glavine, 1993	22 (Tie)
Greg Maddux, 1994	16 (Tie)
Greg Maddux, 1995	19
John Smoltz, 1996	24
Denny Neagle, 1997	20
Tom Glavine, 1998	20
John Smoltz, 2006	16 (Tie)
Kyle Wright, 2022	21

Most Strikeouts, Season

Phil Niekro, 1977 262
John Smoltz, 1992 215
John Smoltz, 1996 276

Lowest ERA, Season

Warren Spahn, 1953 (Mil.) 2.10
Lew Burdette, 1956 (Mil.) 2.71
Warren Spahn, 1961 (Mil.) 3.01
Phil Niekro, 1967 .... 1.87
Buzz Capra, 1974 .... 2.28
Greg Maddux, 1993 .... 2.36
Greg Maddux, 1994 .... 1.56
Greg Maddux, 1995 .... 1.63
Greg Maddux, 1998 .... 2.22

Most Saves, Season

John Smoltz, 2002 55
Craig Kimbrel, 2011 .... 46 (Tie)
Craig Kimbrel, 2012 42
Craig Kimbrel, 2013 50
Craig Kimbrel, 2014 47
Kenley Jansen, 2022 41

Best Won–Lost Percentage, Season

Bob Buhl, 1957 (Mil.) ... 18–7 ... .720
Warren Spahn, 1958
(Mil.) 22–11 .... 667 (Tie)
Lew Burdette, 1958
(Mil.) .... 20–10 .667 (Tie)
Phil Niekro, 1982 .... 17–4 ... .810
Greg Maddux, 1995 .... 19–2 ... .905
John Smoltz, 1996 .... 24–8 ... .750
Greg Maddux, 1997 .... 19–4 ... .826
John Smoltz, 1998 .... 17–3 ... .850
Russ Ortiz, 2003 .... 21–7 ... .750
Jorge Sosa, 2005 .... 13–3 ... .813
Chuck James, 2006 ...... 11–4 ... .733
Max Fried, 2020 .... 7–0 .. 1.000

Pitching Feats

20 Wins, Season

Warren Spahn, 1953 (Mil.) 23–7
Warren Spahn, 1954 (Mil.) 21–12
Warren Spahn, 1956 (Mil.) 20–11
Warren Spahn, 1957 (Mil.) 21–11
Warren Spahn, 1958 (Mil.) 22–11
Lew Burdette, 1958 (Mil.) 20–10
Lew Burdette, 1959 (Mil.) 21–15
Warren Spahn, 1959 (Mil.) 21–15
Warren Spahn, 1960 (Mil.) 21–10

Warren Spahn, 1961 (Mil.) 21–13
Warren Spahn, 1963 (Mil.) 23–7
Tony Cloninger, 1965 (Mil.) 24–11
Phil Niekro, 1969 23–13
Phil Niekro, 1974 20–13
Phil Niekro, 1979 21–20
Tom Glavine, 1991 20–11
Tom Glavine, 1992 20–8
Tom Glavine, 1993 22–6
Greg Maddux, 1993 20–10
John Smoltz, 1996 24–8
Denny Neagle, 1997 20–5
Tom Glavine, 1998 20–6
Tom Glavine, 2000 21–9
Russ Ortiz, 2003 21–7
Kyle Wright, 2002 21–5

No-Hitters

Jim Wilson (vs. Phi. Phillies), Jun. 12,
1954 (final: 2–0) (Mil.)
Lew Burdette (vs. Phi. Phillies), Aug. 18,
1960 (final: 1–0) (Mil.)
Warren Spahn (vs. Phi. Phillies), Sep.
15, 1960 (final: 4–0) (Mil.)
Warren Spahn (vs. S.F. Giants), Apr. 28,
1961 (final: 1–0) (Mil.)
Phil Niekro (vs. S.D. Padres), Aug. 5,
1973 (final: 9–0)
Kent Mercker, Mark Wohlers, and
Alejandro Pena (vs. S.D. Padres), Sep.
11, 1991 (final: 1–0)
Kent Mercker (vs. L.A. Dodgers), Apr. 8,
1994 (final: 6–0)

No-Hitters Pitched Against

Don Wilson, Hou. Astros, Jun. 18,
1967 (final: 2–0)
Ken Holtzman, Chi. Cubs, Aug. 19,
1969 (final: 3–0)
John Montefusco, S.F. Giants, Sep. 29,
1976 (final: 9–0)
Ken Forsch, Hou. Astros, Apr. 7, 1979
(final: 6–0)
Randy Johnson, Ari. D'backs, May 18,
2004 (final: 2–0) (perfect game)
Ubaldo Jimenez, Col. Rockies, Apr. 17,
2010 (final: 4–0)
Cole Hamels, Jake Diekman, Ken Giles,
Jonathan Papelbon, Phi. Phillies, Sep.
1, 2014 (final: 7–0)

Postseason Play

1957 World Series vs. N.Y. Yankees
(AL), won 4 games to 3 (Mil.)
1958 World Series vs. N.Y. Yankees
(AL), lost 4 games to 3 (Mil.)
1959 Pennant Playoff Series vs. L.A.
Dodgers, lost 2 games to 0
(Mil.)
1969 League Championship Series vs.
N.Y. Mets, lost 3 games to 0
1982 League Championship Series vs.
St.L. Cardinals, lost 3 games to 0
1991 League Championship Series vs.
Pit. Pirates, won 4 games to 3
World Series vs. Min. Twins (AL),
lost 4 games to 3
1992 League Championship Series vs.
Pit. Pirates, won 4 games to 3
World Series vs. Tor. Blue Jays
(AL), lost 4 games to 2
1993 League Championship Series vs.
Phi. Phillies, lost 4 games to 2
1995 Division Series vs. Col. Rockies,
won 3 games to 1
League Championship Series vs.
Cin. Reds, won 4 games to 0
World Series vs. Cle. Indians
(AL), won 4 games to 2
1996 Division Series vs. L.A. Dodgers,
won 3 games to 0
League Championship Series vs.
St.L. Cardinals, won 4 games
to 3
World Series vs. N.Y. Yankees
(AL), lost 4 games to 2
1997 Division Series vs. Hou. Astros,
won 3 games to 0
League Championship Series vs.
Fla. Marlins, lost 4 games to
2
1998 Division Series vs. Chi. Cubs,
won 3 games to 0
League Championship Series vs.
S.D. Padres, lost 4 games to 2
1999 Division Series vs. Hou. Astros,
won 3 games to 1
League Championship Series vs.
N.Y. Mets, won 4 games to 2
World Series vs. N.Y. Yankees
(AL), lost 4 games to 0
2000 Division Series vs. St.L.
Cardinals, lost 3 games to 0

2001 Division Series vs. Hou. Astros,
won 3 games to 0
League Championship Series vs.
Ari. D'backs, lost 4 games
to 1
2002 Division Series vs. S.F. Giants, lost
3 games to 1
2003 Division Series vs. Chi. Cubs, lost
3 games to 2
2004 Division Series vs. Hou. Astros,
lost 3 games to 2
2005 Division Series vs. Hou. Astros,
lost 3 games to 1

2010 Division Series vs. S. F. Giants,
lost 3 games to 1
2012 NL Wild Card Playoff Game vs.
St.L. Cardinals, lost
2013 Division Series vs. L.A. Dodgers,
lost 3 games to 1
2018 Division Series vs. L.A. Dodgers,
lost 3 games to 1
2019 Division Series vs. St.L. Cardinals,
lost 3 games to 2
2020 Wild Card Series vs. Cin. Reds,
won 2 games to 0
Division Series vs. Miami Marlins,

won 3 games to 0
League Championship Series
vs. L.A. Dodgers, lost 4
games to 3
World Series vs. Hou. Astros
(AL), won 4 games to 2
2022 Division Series vs. Phi. Phillies,
lost 3 games to 1

Chicago Cubs

Dates of Operation: 1876–present (147 years)

Overall Record: 11,161 wins, 10,609 losses (.513)

Stadiums: 23rd Street Grounds, 1876–77; Lakefront Park, 1878–84; West Side Park, 1885–92; South Side Park, 1891–93 and 1897; New West Side Park (also called West Side Grounds), 1893–1915; Comiskey Park, 1918 (World Series only); Wrigley Field (formerly Weeghman Park, 1916–19, and Cubs Park, 1920–26), 1916–present (capacity: 42,495)

Other Names: Broncos, Colts, Cowboys, Orphans, White Stockings

Year-by-Year Finishes

Year	Finish	Wins	Losses	Percentage	Games Behind	Manager	Attendance
1876	1st	52	14	.788	+6.0	Al Spalding	not available
1877	5th	26	33	.441	15.5	Al Spalding	not available
1878	4th	30	30	.500	11.0	Robert Ferguson	not available
1879	3rd (Tie)	44	32	.579	10.0	Cap Anson	not available
1880	1st	67	17	.798	+15.0	Cap Anson	not available
1881	1st	56	28	.667	+9.0	Cap Anson	not available
1882	1st	55	29	.655	+3.0	Cap Anson	not available
1883	2nd	59	29	.602	4.0	Cap Anson	not available
1884	4th (Tie)	62	50	.554	22.0	Cap Anson	not available
1885	1st	87	25	.776	+2.0	Cap Anson	not available
1886	1st	90	34	.725	+2.5	Cap Anson	not available
1887	3rd	71	50	.587	6.5	Cap Anson	not available
1888	2nd	77	58	.578	9.0	Cap Anson	not available
1889	3rd	67	65	.508	19.0	Cap Anson	not available
1890	2nd	83	53	.610	6.5	Cap Anson	not available
1891	2nd	82	53	.607	3.5	Cap Anson	not available
1892	7th	70	76	.479	40.0	Cap Anson	not available
1893	9th	57	71	.445	28.0	Cap Anson	not available
1894	8th	57	75	.432	34.0	Cap Anson	not available
1895	4th	72	58	.554	15.0	Cap Anson	not available
1896	5th	71	57	.555	18.5	Cap Anson	not available
1897	9th	59	73	.447	34.0	Cap Anson	not available
1898	4th	85	65	.567	17.5	Tom Burns	not available
1899	8th	75	73	.507	22.0	Tom Burns	not available
1900	5th (Tie)	65	75	.464	19.0	Tom Loftus	not available
1901	6th	53	86	.381	37.0	Tom Loftus	205,071
1902	5th	68	69	.496	34.0	Frank Selee	263,700
1903	3rd	82	56	.594	8.0	Frank Selee	386,205
1904	2nd	93	60	.608	13.0	Frank Selee	439,100
1905	3rd	92	61	.601	13.0	Frank Selee, Frank Chance	509,900
1906	1st	116	36	.763	+20.0	Frank Chance	654,300
1907	1st	107	45	.704	+17.0	Frank Chance	422,550
1908	1st	99	55	.643	+1.0	Frank Chance	665,325
1909	2nd	104	49	.680	6.5	Frank Chance	633,480
1910	1st	104	50	.675	+13.0	Frank Chance	526,152
1911	2nd	92	62	.597	7.5	Frank Chance	576,000
1912	3rd	91	59	.607	11.5	Frank Chance	514,000
1913	3rd	88	65	.575	13.5	Johnny Evers	419,000
1914	4th	78	76	.506	16.5	Hank O'Day	202,516

Year	Finish	Wins	Losses	Percentage	Games Behind	Manager	Attendance
1915	4th	73	80	.477	17.5	Roger Bresnahan	217,058
1916	5th	67	86	.438	26.5	Joe Tinker	453,685
1917	5th	74	80	.481	24.0	Fred Mitchell	360,218
1918	1st	84	45	.651	+10.5	Fred Mitchell	337,256
1919	3rd	75	65	.536	21.0	Fred Mitchell	424,430
1920	5th (Tie)	75	79	.487	18.0	Fred Mitchell	480,783
1921	7th	64	89	.418	30.0	Johnny Evers, Bill Killefer	410,107
1922	5th	80	74	.519	13.0	Bill Killefer	542,283
1923	4th	83	71	.539	12.5	Bill Killefer	703,705
1924	5th	81	72	.529	12.0	Bill Killefer	716,922
1925	8th	68	86	.442	27.5	Bill Killefer, Rabbit Maranville, George Gibson	622,610
1926	4th	82	72	.532	7.0	Joe McCarthy	885,063
1927	4th	85	68	.556	8.5	Joe McCarthy	1,159,168
1928	3rd	91	63	.591	4.0	Joe McCarthy	1,143,740
1929	1st	98	54	.645	+10.5	Joe McCarthy	1,485,166
1930	2nd	90	64	.584	2.0	Joe McCarthy, Rogers Hornsby	1,463,624
1931	3rd	84	70	.545	17.0	Rogers Hornsby	1,086,422
1932	1st	90	64	.584	+4.0	Rogers Hornsby, Charlie Grimm	974,688
1933	3rd	86	68	.558	6.0	Charlie Grimm	594,112
1934	3rd	86	65	.570	8.0	Charlie Grimm	707,525
1935	1st	100	54	.649	+4.0	Charlie Grimm	692,604
1936	2nd (Tie)	87	67	.565	5.0	Charlie Grimm	699,370
1937	2nd	93	61	.604	3.0	Charlie Grimm	895,020
1938	1st	89	63	.586	+2.0	Charlie Grimm, Gabby Hartnett	951,640
1939	4th	84	70	.545	13.0	Gabby Hartnett	726,663
1940	5th	75	79	.487	25.5	Gabby Hartnett	534,878
1941	6th	70	84	.455	30.0	Jimmy Wilson	545,159
1942	6th	68	86	.442	38.0	Jimmy Wilson	590,872
1943	5th	74	79	.484	30.5	Jimmy Wilson	508,247
1944	4th	75	79	.487	30.0	Jimmy Wilson, Charlie Grimm	640,110
1945	1st	98	56	.636	+3.0	Charlie Grimm	1,036,386
1946	3rd	82	71	.536	14.5	Charlie Grimm	1,342,970
1947	6th	69	85	.448	25.0	Charlie Grimm	1,364,039
1948	8th	64	90	.416	27.5	Charlie Grimm	1,237,792
1949	8th	61	93	.396	36.0	Charlie Grimm, Frankie Frisch	1,143,139
1950	7th	64	89	.418	26.5	Frankie Frisch	1,165,944
1951	8th	62	92	.403	34.5	Frankie Frisch, Phil Cavarretta	894,415
1952	5th	77	77	.500	19.5	Phil Cavarretta	1,024,826
1953	7th	65	89	.422	40.0	Phil Cavarretta	763,658
1954	7th	64	90	.416	33.0	Stan Hack	748,183
1955	6th	72	81	.471	26.0	Stan Hack	875,800
1956	8th	60	94	.390	33.0	Stan Hack	720,118
1957	7th (Tie)	62	92	.403	33.0	Bob Scheffing	670,629
1958	5th (Tie)	72	82	.468	20.0	Bob Scheffing	979,904
1959	5th (Tie)	74	80	.481	13.0	Bob Scheffing	858,255
1960	7th	60	94	.390	35.0	Charlie Grimm, Lou Boudreau	809,770
1961	7th	64	90	.416	29.0	Vedie Himsl, Harry Craft, Elvin Tappe, Lou Klein	673,057
1962	9th	59	103	.364	42.5	Charlie Metro, Elvin Tappe, Lou Klein	609,802
1963	7th	82	80	.506	17.0	Bob Kennedy	979,551
1964	8th	76	86	.469	17.0	Bob Kennedy	751,647
1965	8th	72	90	.444	25.0	Bob Kennedy, Lou Klein	641,361
1966	10th	59	103	.364	36.0	Leo Durocher	635,891

Year	Finish	Wins	Losses	Percentage	Games Behind	Manager	Attendance
1967	3rd	87	74	.540	14.0	Leo Durocher	977,226
1968	3rd	84	78	.519	13.0	Leo Durocher	1,043,409
				East Division			
1969	2nd	92	70	.568	8.0	Leo Durocher	1,674,993
1970	2nd	84	78	.519	5.0	Leo Durocher	1,642,705
1971	3rd (Tie)	83	79	.512	14.0	Leo Durocher	1,653,007
1972	2nd	85	70	.548	11.0	Leo Durocher, Whitey Lockman	1,299,163
1973	5th	77	84	.478	5.0	Whitey Lockman	1,351,705
1974	6th	66	96	.407	22.0	Whitey Lockman, Jim Marshall	1,015,378
1975	5th (Tie)	75	87	.463	17.5	Jim Marshall	1,034,819
1976	4th	75	87	.463	26.0	Jim Marshall	1,026,217
1977	4th	81	81	.500	20.0	Herman Franks	1,439,834
1978	3rd	79	83	.488	11.0	Herman Franks	1,525,311
1979	5th	80	82	.494	18.0	Herman Franks, Joe Amalfitano	1,648,587
1980	6th	64	98	.395	27.0	Preston Gomez, Joe Amalfitano	1,206,776
1981*	6th/5th	38	65	.369	17.5/6.0	Joe Amalfitano	565,637
1982	5th	73	89	.451	19.0	Lee Elia	1,249,278
1983	5th	71	91	.438	19.0	Lee Elia, Charlie Fox	1,479,717
1984	1st	96	65	.596	+6.5	Jim Frey	2,107,655
1985	4th	77	84	.478	23.5	Jim Frey	2,161,534
1986	5th	70	90	.438	37.0	Jim Frey, John Vukovich, Gene Michael	1,859,102
1987	6th	76	85	.472	18.5	Gene Michael, Frank Lucchesi	2,035,130
1988	4th	77	85	.475	24.0	Don Zimmer	2,089,034
1989	1st	93	69	.574	+6.0	Don Zimmer	2,491,942
1990	4th	77	85	.475	18.0	Don Zimmer	2,243,791
1991	4th	77	83	.481	20.0	Don Zimmer, Joe Altobelli, Jim Essian	2,314,250
1992	4th	78	84	.481	18.0	Jim Lefebvre	2,126,720
1993	4th	84	78	.519	13.0	Jim Lefebvre	2,653,763
				Central Division			
1994	5th	49	64	.434	16.5	Tom Trebelhorn	1,845,208
1995	3rd	73	71	.570	12.0	Jim Riggleman	1,918,265
1996	4th	76	86	.469	12.0	Jim Riggleman	2,219,110
1997	5th	68	94	.420	16.0	Jim Riggleman	2,190,308
1998	2nd	90	73	.552	12.5	Jim Riggleman	2,623,000
1999	6th	67	95	.414	30.0	Jim Riggleman	2,813,854
2000	6th	65	97	.401	30.0	Don Baylor	2,789,511
2001	3rd	88	74	.543	5.0	Don Baylor	2,779,456
2002	5th	67	95	.414	30.0	Don Baylor, Bruce Kimm	2,693,071
2003	1st	88	74	.543	+1.0	Dusty Baker	2,962,630
2004	3rd	89	73	.549	16.0	Dusty Baker	3,170,184
2005	4th	79	83	.488	21.0	Dusty Baker	3,099,992
2006	6th	66	96	.407	17.5	Dusty Baker	3,123,215
2007	1st	85	77	.525	+2.0	Lou Piniella	3,123,215
2008	1st	97	64	.602	+7.5	Lou Piniella	3,300,200
2009	2nd	83	78	.516	7.5	Lou Piniella	3,168,859
2010	5th	75	87	.463	16.0	Lou Piniella, Mike Quade	3,062,973
2011	5th	71	91	.438	25.0	Mike Quade	3,017,966
2012	5th	61	101	.377	36.0	Dale Sveum	2,882,756
2013	5th	66	96	.407	31.0	Dale Sveum	2,642,682
2014	5th	73	89	.451	17.0	Rick Renteria	2,652,113
2015	3rd	97	65	.599	3.0	Joe Maddon	2,959,812
2016	1st	103	58	.640	+17.5	Joe Maddon	3,232,420
2017	1st	92	70	.568	+6.0	Joe Maddon	3,199,562
2018	2nd	95	68	.583	1.0	Joe Maddon	3,181,089
2019	3rd	84	78	.519	7.0	Joe Maddon	3,094,865

Year	Finish	Wins	Losses	Percentage	Games Behind	Manager	Attendance
2020	1st	34	26	.567	+3.0	David Ross	0
2021	4th	71	91	.438	24.0	David Ross	1,978,934
2022	3rd	74	88	.457	19.0	David Ross	2,616,780

* Split season.

Awards

Most Valuable Player

Frank Schulte, outfield, 1911
Rogers Hornsby, second base, 1929
Gabby Hartnett, catcher, 1935
Phil Cavarretta, first base, 1945
Hank Sauer, outfield, 1952
Ernie Banks, shortstop, 1958
Ernie Banks, shortstop, 1959
Ryne Sandberg, second base, 1984
Andre Dawson, outfield, 1987
Sammy Sosa, outfield, 1998
Kris Bryant, outfield, 2016

Rookie of the Year

Billy Williams, outfield, 1961
Ken Hubbs, second base, 1962
Jerome Walton, outfield, 1989
Kerry Wood, pitcher, 1998
Geovany Soto, catcher, 2008
Kris Bryant, third base, 2015

Cy Young

Ferguson Jenkins, 1971
Bruce Sutter, 1979
Rick Sutcliffe, 1984
Greg Maddux, 1992
Jake Arrieta, 2015

Manager of the Year (Since 1983)

Jim Frey, 1984
Don Zimmer, 1989
Lou Piniella, 2008
Joe Maddon, 2015

Hall of Famers Who Played for the Cubs

Pete Alexander, pitcher, 1918–26
Cap Anson, first base, 1876–97
Richie Ashburn, outfield, 1960–61
Ernie Banks, shortstop, 1953–71
Roger Bresnahan, catcher, 1900 and 1913–15
Lou Brock, outfield, 1961–64
Mordecai Brown, pitcher, 1904–12 and 1916
Frank Chance, first base, 1898–1912
John Clarkson, pitcher, 1884–87
Kiki Cuyler, outfield, 1928–35
Andre Dawson, outfield, 1987–92
Dizzy Dean, pitcher, 1938–41
Hugh Duffy, outfield, 1888–89
Dennis Eckersley, pitcher, 1984–86
Johnny Evers, second base, 1902–13
Jimmie Foxx, first base, 1942 and 1944
Goose Gossage, pitcher, 1988
Clark Griffith, pitcher, 1893–1900
Burleigh Grimes, pitcher, 1932–33
Gabby Hartnett, catcher, 1922–40
Billy Herman, second base, 1931–41
Rogers Hornsby, second base, 1929–32
Monte Irvin, outfield, 1956
Ferguson Jenkins, pitcher, 1966–73 and 1982–83
George Kelly, first base, 1930
King Kelly, outfield, 1880–86
Ralph Kiner, outfield, 1953–54
Chuck Klein, outfield, 1934–36
Tony La Russa, shortstop, 1973
Tony Lazzeri, second base, 1938
Fred Lindstrom, outfield, 1935
Greg Maddux, pitcher, 1986–92 and 2004–06
Rabbit Maranville, shortstop, 1925
Fred McGriff, first base, 2001–02
Robin Roberts, pitcher, 1966
Ryne Sandberg, second base, 1982–94, 1996–97
Ron Santo, third base, 1960–73
Lee Smith, pitcher, 1980–87
Al Spalding, pitcher, 1876–78
Bruce Sutter, pitcher, 1976–88
Joe Tinker, shortstop, 1902–12 and 1916
Rube Waddell, pitcher, 1901
Hoyt Wilhelm, pitcher, 1970
Billy Williams, outfield, 1959–74
Hack Wilson, outfield, 1926–31

Retired Numbers

10	Ron Santo
14	Ernie Banks
23	Ryne Sandberg
26	Billy Williams
31	Ferguson Jenkins
31	Greg Maddux

League Leaders, Batting (Post-1900)

Batting Average, Season

Heinie Zimmerman, 1912 .... .372
Phil Cavarretta, 1945 .... .355
Billy Williams, 1972 .... .333
Bill Madlock, 1975 .... .354
Bill Madlock, 1976 .... .339
Bill Buckner, 1980 .... .324
Derrek Lee, 2005 .... .335

Home Runs, Season

Frank Schulte, 1910 .... 10 (Tie)
Frank Schulte, 1911 21
Heinie Zimmerman, 1912 14
Cy Williams, 1916 .... 12 (Tie)
Hack Wilson, 1926 21
Hack Wilson, 1927 .... 30 (Tie)
Hack Wilson, 1928 .... 31 (Tie)
Hack Wilson, 1930 56
Bill Nicholson, 1943 29
Bill Nicholson, 1944 33
Hank Sauer, 1952 .... 37 (Tie)
Ernie Banks, 1958 47
Ernie Banks, 1960 41
Dave Kingman, 1979 48
Andre Dawson, 1987 49
Ryne Sandberg, 1990 40
Sammy Sosa, 2000 50
Sammy Sosa, 2002 49

RBIs, Season

Harry Steinfeldt, 1906 83
Frank Schulte, 1911 121
Heinie Zimmerman, 1912 98
Heinie Zimmerman*, 1916 83
Fred Merkle, 1918 71
Hack Wilson, 1929 159
Hack Wilson, 1930 191
Bill Nicholson, 1943 128
Bill Nicholson, 1944 122
Hank Sauer, 1952 121
Ernie Banks, 1958 129
Ernie Banks, 1959 143
Andre Dawson, 1987 137
Sammy Sosa, 1998 158
Sammy Sosa, 2001 160
Javier Baez, 2018 111

* 19 with N.Y. Giants and 64 with Chi. Cubs

Stolen Bases, Season

Frank Chance, 1903 .... 67 (Tie)
Billy Maloney, 1905 .... 59 (Tie)
Frank Chance, 1906 57
Kiki Cuyler, 1928 37

Kiki Cuyler, 1929.........................43
Kiki Cuyler, 1930.........................37
Augie Galan, 1935.....................22
Augie Galan, 1937.....................23
Stan Hack, 1938 16
Stan Hack, 1939 ....17 (Tie)

Total Bases, Season
Frank Schulte, 1911 308
Heinie Zimmerman, 1912...........318
Charlie Hollocher, 1918 202
Rogers Hornsby, 1929................409
Bill Nicholson, 1944 317
Ernie Banks, 1958......................379
Billy Williams, 1968...................321
Billy Williams, 1970...................373
Billy Williams, 1972...................348
Andre Dawson, 1987 353
Ryne Sandberg, 1990.................344
Sammy Sosa, 1998 416
Sammy Sosa, 1999 397
Sammy Sosa, 2001 425

Most Hits, Season
Harry Steinfeldt, 1906 176
Heinie Zimmerman, 1912............207
Charlie Hollocher, 1918 161
Billy Herman, 1935 227
Stan Hack, 1940 ....191 (Tie)
Stan Hack, 1941 186
Phil Cavarretta, 1944 ....197 (Tie)
Billy Williams, 1970...........205 (Tie)
Derrek Lee, 2005.......................199
Juan Pierre, 2006 204
Starlin Castro, 2011 207

Most Runs, Season
Frank Chance, 1906 ....103 (Tie)
Jimmy Sheckard, 1911................121
Tommy Leach, 1913 ....99 (Tie)
Rogers Hornsby, 1929 156
Augie Galan, 1935....................133
Bill Nicholson, 1944 116
Glenn Beckert, 1968 98
Billy Williams, 1970...................137
Ivan DeJesus, 1978 104
Ryne Sandberg, 1984.................114
Ryne Sandberg, 1989..........104 (Tie)
Ryne Sandberg, 1990.................116
Sammy Sosa, 1998 134
Sammy Sosa, 2001 146
Sammy Sosa, 2002 122
Kris Bryant, 2016.......................121

Batting Feats

Triple Crown Winners
Heinie Zimmerman, 1912 (.372 BA,
    14 HRs, 98 RBIs)

Hitting for the Cycle
Jimmy Ryan, Jul. 28, 1888
Jimmy Ryan, Jul. 1, 1891
Hack Wilson, Jun. 23, 1930
Babe Herman, Sep. 30, 1933
Roy Smalley, Jun. 28, 1950
Lee Walls, Jul. 2, 1957
Billy Williams, Jul. 17, 1966
Randy Hundley, Aug. 11, 1966
Ivan DeJesus, Apr. 22, 1980
Andre Dawson, Apr. 29, 1987
Mark Grace, May 9, 1993

Six Hits in a Game (Post-1900)
Frank Demaree, Jul. 5, 1937*
Don Kessinger, Jul. 17, 1971*
Bill Madlock, Jul. 26, 1975*
Jose Cardenal, May 2, 1976*
Sammy Sosa, Jul. 2, 1993
* Extra-inning game.

40 or More Home Runs, Season
66 ....Sammy Sosa, 1998
64 ....Sammy Sosa, 2001
63 ....Sammy Sosa, 1999
56 ....Hack Wilson, 1930
50 ....Sammy Sosa, 2000
49 ....Andre Dawson, 1987
            Sammy Sosa, 2002
48 ....Dave Kingman, 1979
47 ....Ernie Banks, 1958
46 ....Derrek Lee, 2005
45 ....Ernie Banks, 1959
44 ....Ernie Banks, 1955
43 ....Ernie Banks, 1957
42 ....Billy Williams, 1970
41 ....Hank Sauer, 1954
            Ernie Banks, 1960
40 ....Ryne Sandberg, 1990
            Sammy Sosa, 1996
            Sammy Sosa, 2003

League Leaders, Pitching (Post-1900)

Most Wins, Season
Mordecai Brown, 1909.................27
Larry Cheney, 1912 ....26 (Tie)
Hippo Vaughn, 1918....................22
Pete Alexander, 1920 27
Charlie Root, 1927 26
Pat Malone, 1929 22
Pat Malone, 1930 ....20 (Tie)
Lon Warneke, 1932 22
Bill Lee, 1938.............................22
Larry Jackson, 1964 24
Ferguson Jenkins, 1971................24
Rick Sutcliffe, 1987 18
Greg Maddux, 1992 ....20 (Tie)
Carlos Zambrano, 2006 ....16 (Tie)

Jake Arrieta, 2015 22
Jon Lester, 2018...................18 (Tie)
Yu Darvish, 2020...........................8

Most Strikeouts, Season
Fred Beebe*, 1906 171
Orval Overall, 1909 205
Hippo Vaughn, 1918..................148
Hippo Vaughn, 1919..................141
Pete Alexander, 1920 173
Pat Malone, 1929 166
Clay Bryant, 1938 135
Claude Passeau**, 1939.....137 (Tie)
Johnny Schmitz, 1946.................135
Sam Jones, 1955 198
Sam Jones, 1956 176
Ferguson Jenkins, 1969...............273
Kerry Wood, 2003.....................266
* 116 with St.L. Cardinals and 55 with Chi. Cubs.
** 29 with Phi. Phillies and 108 with Chi. Cubs.

Lowest ERA, Season
Hippo Vaughn, 1918..................1.74
Pete Alexander, 1919 ....1.72
Pete Alexander, 1920 ....1.91
Lon Warneke, 1932 ....2.37
Bill Lee, 1938...........................2.66
Hank Borowy, 1945 ....2.13
Kyle Hendricks, 2016 ....2.13

Most Saves, Season
Bruce Sutter, 1979 37
Bruce Sutter, 1980 28
Lee Smith, 1983..........................29
Randy Myers, 1993.....................53
Randy Myers, 1995.....................38

Best Won–Lost Percentage, Season
Ed Reulbach, 1906 ......19–4... .826
Ed Reulbach, 1907 ......17–4... .810
Ed Reulbach, 1908 ......24–7... .774
King Cole, 1910..........20–4... .833
Bert Humphries, 1913...16–4... .800
Claude Hendrix, 1918...20–7... .741
Charlie Root, 1929 ......19–6... .760
Lon Warneke, 1932 .....22–6... .786
Bill Lee, 1935.............20–6... .769
Bill Lee, 1938.............22–9... .710
Rick Sutcliffe, 1984 ......16–1... .941
Mike Bielecki, 1989 .....18–7... .720
Jon Lester, 2016..........19–5... .792

Pitching Feats

Triple Crown Winner
Hippo Vaughn, 1918 (22–10, 1.74
    ERA, 148 SO)
Pete Alexander, 1920 (27–14, 1.91
    ERA, 173 SO)

20 Wins, Season

Jack Taylor, 1902.................. 22–10
Jack Taylor, 1903.................. 21–14
Jake Weimer, 1903 20–8
Jake Weimer, 1904 20–14
Mordecai Brown, 1906............ 26–6
Jack Pfiester, 1906 20–8
Jack Taylor, 1906.................20–12*
Orval Overall, 1907 23–8
Mordecai Brown, 1907............ 20–6
Mordecai Brown, 1908............ 29–9
Ed Reulbach, 1908 24–7
Mordecai Brown, 1909............ 27–9
Orval Overall, 1909 20–11
Mordecai Brown, 1910.......... 25–14
King Cole, 1910..................... 20–4
Mordecai Brown, 1911.......... 21–11
Larry Cheney, 1912 26–10
Larry Cheney, 1913 21–14
Hippo Vaughn, 1914............. 21–13
Larry Cheney, 1914 20–18
Hippo Vaughn, 1915............. 20–12
Hippo Vaughn, 1917............. 23–13
Hippo Vaughn, 1918............. 22–10
Claude Hendrix, 1918............. 20–7
Hippo Vaughn, 1919............. 21–14
Pete Alexander, 1920............. 27–14
Pete Alexander, 1923............. 22–12
Charlie Root, 1927 26–15
Pat Malone, 1929.................. 22–10
Pat Malone, 1930.................... 20–9
Lon Warneke, 1932 22–6
Guy Bush, 1933 20–12
Lon Warneke, 1934 22–10
Bill Lee, 1935.......................... 20–6
Lon Warneke, 1935 20–13
Bill Lee, 1938.......................... 22–9
Claude Passeau, 1940........... 20–13
Hank Wyse, 1945 22–10
Hank Borowy, 1945 ....21–7**
Dick Ellsworth, 1963 22–10
Larry Jackson, 1964 24–11
Ferguson Jenkins, 1967........... 20–13
Ferguson Jenkins, 1968........... 20–15
Ferguson Jenkins, 1969........... 21–15
Bill Hands, 1969................... 20–14
Ferguson Jenkins, 1970........... 22–16
Ferguson Jenkins, 1971........... 24–13
Ferguson Jenkins, 1972........... 20–12
Rick Reuschel, 1977 20–10
Rick Sutcliffe, 1984 ....20–6***
Greg Maddux, 1992 20–11
Jon Lieber, 2001 20–6
Jake Arrieta, 2015 22–6

* 8–9 with St.L. Cardinals and 12–3 with Chi. Cubs.
** 10–5 with N.Y. Yankees and 11–2 with Chi. Cubs.
*** 4–5 with Cle. Indians and 16–1 with Chi. Cubs.

No-Hitters

Jimmy Lavender (vs. N.Y. Giants), Aug. 31, 1915 (final: 2–0)
Sam Jones (vs. Pit. Pirates), May 12, 1955 (final: 4–0)
Don Cardwell (vs. St.L. Cardinals), May 15, 1960 (final: 4–0)
Ken Holtzman (vs. Atl. Braves), Aug. 19, 1969 (final: 3–0)
Ken Holtzman (vs. Cin. Reds), Jun. 3, 1971 (final: 1–0)
Burt Hooton (vs. Phi. Phillies), Apr. 16, 1972 (final: 4–0)
Milt Pappas (vs. S.D. Padres), Sep. 2, 1972 (final: 8–0)
Carlos Zambrano (vs. Hou. Astros), Sep. 14, 2008 (final: 5–0)
Jake Arrieta (vs. L.A. Dodgers), Aug. 30, 2015 (final: 2–0)
Jake Arrieta (vs. Cin. Reds), Apr. 21, 2016 (final: 16–0)
Alec Mills (vs. Mil. Brewers) Sep. 13, 2020 (final: 12–0)
Zach Davies, Ryan Tepera, Andrew Chafin, Craig Kimbrel (vs. L.A. Dodgers), Jun. 24, 2021 (final 4–0)

No-Hitters Pitched Against

Chick Fraser, Phi. Phillies, Sep. 18, 1903 (final: 10–0)
Christy Mathewson, N.Y. Giants, Jun. 13, 1905 (final: 1–0)
Jim Toney, Cin. Reds, May 2, 1917 (final: 1–0) (10 innings)
Carl Erskine, Brk. Dodgers, Jun. 19, 1952 (final: 5–0)
Jim Maloney, Cin. Reds, Aug. 9, 1965 (final: 1–0) (10 innings)
Sandy Koufax, L.A. Dodgers, Sep. 9, 1965 (final: 1–0) (perfect game)
Cole Hamels, Phi. Phillies, Jul. 25, 2015 (final: 5–0)

Postseason Play

1906 World Series vs. Chi. White Sox (AL), lost 4 games to 2
1907 World Series vs. Det. Tigers (AL), won 4 games to 0, 1 tie
1908 Pennant Playoff Game vs. N.Y. Giants, won
World Series vs. Det. Tigers (AL), won 4 games to 1
1910 World Series vs. Phi. A's (AL), lost 4 games to 1
1918 World Series vs. Bos. Red Sox (AL), lost 4 games to 2
1929 World Series vs. Phi. A's (AL), lost 4 games to 1
1932 World Series vs. N.Y. Yankees (AL), lost 4 games to 0
1935 World Series vs. Det. Tigers (AL), lost 4 games to 2
1938 World Series vs. N.Y. Yankees (AL), lost 4 games to 0
1945 World Series vs. Det. Tigers (AL), lost 4 games to 3
1984 League Championship Series vs. S.D. Padres, lost 3 games to 2
1989 League Championship Series vs. S.F. Giants, lost 4 games to 1
1998 NL Wild Card Playoff Game vs. S.F. Giants, won
Division Series vs. Atl. Braves, lost 3 games to 0
2003 Division Series vs. Atl. Braves, won 3 games to 2
League Championship Series vs. Fla. Marlins, lost 4 games to 3
2007 Division Series vs. Ari. D'backs, lost 3 games to 0
2008 Division Series vs. L.A. Dodgers, lost 3 games to 0
2015 NL Wild Card Playoff Game vs. Pit. Pirates, won
Division Series vs. St.L. Cardinals, won 3 games to 1
League Championship Series vs. N.Y. Mets, lost 4 games to 0
2016 Division Series vs. S.F. Giants, won 3 games to 1
League Championship Series vs. L.A. Dodgers, won 4 games to 2
World Series vs. Cle. Indians (AL), won 4 games to 3
2017 Division Series vs. Was. Nationals, won 3 games to 2
League Championship Series vs. L.A. Dodgers, lost 4 games to 1
2018 NL Wild Card Playoff Game vs. Col. Rockies, lost
2020 Wild Card Series vs. Mia. Marlins, lost 2 games to 0

Cincinnati Reds

Dates of Operation: 1882–present (141 years)
Overall Record: 10,775 wins, 10,601 losses (.504)
Stadiums: League Park, 1884–1901; Palace of the Fans, 1902–11; Crosley Field (formerly Redland Field, 1912–33), 1912–70; Cinergy Field (formerly Riverfront Stadium, 1970–95), 1970–2002; Great American Ball Park, 2003–present (capacity: 42,319)
Other Names: Red Stockings, Redlegs

Year-by-Year Finishes

Year	Finish	Wins	Losses	Percentage	Games Behind	Manager	Attendance
					American Association		
1882	1st	55	25	.688	+11.5	Pop Snyder	not available
1883	3rd	61	37	.622	5.0	Pop Snyder	not available
1884	5th	68	41	.624	8.0	Will White, Pop Snyder	not available
1885	2nd	63	49	.563	16.0	Ollie Caylor	not available
1886	5th	65	73	.471	27.5	Ollie Caylor	not available
1887	2nd	81	54	.600	14.0	Gus Schmelz	not available
1888	4th	80	54	.597	11.5	Gus Schmelz	not available
1889	4th	76	63	.547	18.0	Gus Schmelz	not available
					National League		
1890	4th	78	55	.586	10.0	Tom Loftus	not available
1891	7th	56	81	.409	30.5	Tom Loftus	not available
1892	5th	82	68	.547	20.0	Charles Comiskey	not available
1893	6th	65	63	.508	20.0	Charles Comiskey	not available
1894	10th	54	75	.419	35.5	Charles Comiskey	not available
1895	8th	66	64	.508	21.0	Buck Ewing	not available
1896	3rd	77	50	.606	12.0	Buck Ewing	not available
1897	4th	76	56	.576	17.0	Buck Ewing	not available
1898	3rd	92	60	.605	11.5	Buck Ewing	not available
1899	6th	83	67	.553	15.0	Buck Ewing	not available
1900	7th	62	77	.446	21.5	Robert Allen	not available
1901	8th	52	87	.374	38.0	Bid McPhee	205,728
1902	4th	70	70	.500	33.5	Bid McPhee, Frank Bancroft, Joe Kelley	217,300
1903	4th	74	65	.532	16.5	Joe Kelley	351,680
1904	3rd	88	65	.575	18.0	Joe Kelley	391,915
1905	5th	79	74	.516	26.0	Joe Kelley	313,927
1906	6th	64	87	.424	51.5	Ned Hanlon	330,056
1907	6th	66	87	.431	41.5	Ned Hanlon	317,500
1908	5th	73	81	.474	26.0	John Ganzel	399,200
1909	4th	77	76	.503	33.5	Clark Griffith	424,643
1910	5th	75	79	.487	29.0	Clark Griffith	380,622
1911	6th	70	83	.458	29.0	Clark Griffith	300,000
1912	4th	75	78	.490	29.0	Hank O'Day	344,000
1913	7th	64	89	.418	37.5	Joe Tinker	258,000
1914	8th	60	94	.390	34.5	Buck Herzog	100,791
1915	7th	71	83	.461	20.0	Buck Herzog	218,878
1916	7th (Tie)	60	93	.392	33.5	Buck Herzog, Christy Mathewson	255,846
1917	4th	78	76	.506	20.0	Christy Mathewson	269,056
1918	3rd	68	60	.531	15.5	Christy Mathewson, Heinie Groh	163,009

Year	Finish	Wins	Losses	Percentage	Games Behind	Manager	Attendance
1919	1st	96	44	.686	+9.0	Pat Moran	532,501
1920	3rd	82	71	.536	10.5	Pat Moran	568,107
1921	6th	70	83	.458	24.0	Pat Moran	311,227
1922	2nd	86	68	.558	7.0	Pat Moran	493,754
1923	2nd	91	63	.591	4.5	Pat Moran	575,063
1924	4th	83	70	.542	10.0	Jack Hendricks	437,707
1925	3rd	80	73	.523	15.0	Jack Hendricks	464,920
1926	2nd	87	67	.565	2.0	Jack Hendricks	672,987
1927	5th	75	78	.490	18.5	Jack Hendricks	442,164
1928	5th	78	74	.513	16.0	Jack Hendricks	490,490
1929	7th	66	88	.429	33.0	Jack Hendricks	295,040
1930	7th	59	95	.383	33.0	Dan Howley	386,727
1931	8th	58	96	.377	43.0	Dan Howley	263,316
1932	8th	60	94	.390	30.0	Dan Howley	356,950
1933	8th	58	94	.382	33.0	Donie Bush	218,281
1934	8th	52	99	.344	42.0	Bob O'Farrell, Chuck Dressen	206,773
1935	6th	68	85	.444	31.5	Chuck Dressen	448,247
1936	5th	74	80	.481	18.0	Chuck Dressen	466,245
1937	8th	56	98	.364	40.0	Chuck Dressen, Bobby Wallace	411,221
1938	4th	82	68	.547	6.0	Bill McKechnie	706,756
1939	1st	97	57	.630	+4.5	Bill McKechnie	981,443
1940	1st	100	53	.654	+12.0	Bill McKechnie	850,180
1941	3rd	88	66	.571	12.0	Bill McKechnie	643,513
1942	4th	76	76	.500	29.0	Bill McKechnie	427,031
1943	2nd	87	67	.565	18.0	Bill McKechnie	379,122
1944	3rd	89	65	.578	16.0	Bill McKechnie	409,567
1945	7th	61	93	.396	37.0	Bill McKechnie	290,070
1946	6th	67	87	.435	30.0	Bill McKechnie	715,751
1947	5th	73	81	.474	21.0	Johnny Neun	899,975
1948	7th	64	89	.418	27.0	Johnny Neun, Bucky Walters	823,386
1949	7th	62	92	.403	35.0	Bucky Walters	707,782
1950	6th	66	87	.431	24.5	Luke Sewell	538,794
1951	6th	68	86	.442	28.5	Luke Sewell	588,268
1952	6th	69	85	.448	27.5	Luke Sewell, Rogers Hornsby	604,197
1953	6th	68	86	.442	37.0	Rogers Hornsby, Buster Mills	548,086
1954	5th	74	80	.481	23.0	Birdie Tebbetts	704,167
1955	5th	75	79	.487	23.5	Birdie Tebbetts	693,662
1956	3rd	91	63	.591	2.0	Birdie Tebbetts	1,125,928
1957	4th	80	74	.519	15.0	Birdie Tebbetts	1,070,850
1958	4th	76	78	.494	16.0	Birdie Tebbetts, Jimmy Dykes	788,582
1959	5th (Tie)	74	80	.481	13.0	Mayo Smith, Fred Hutchinson	801,289
1960	6th	67	87	.435	28.0	Fred Hutchinson	663,486
1961	1st	93	61	.604	+4.0	Fred Hutchinson	1,117,603
1962	3rd	98	64	.605	3.5	Fred Hutchinson	982,085
1963	5th	86	76	.531	13.0	Fred Hutchinson	858,805
1964	2nd (Tie)	92	70	.568	1.0	Fred Hutchinson, Dick Sisler	862,466
1965	4th	89	73	.549	8.0	Dick Sisler	1,047,824
1966	7th	76	84	.475	18.0	Don Heffner, Dave Bristol	742,958
1967	4th	87	75	.537	14.5	Dave Bristol	958,300
1968	4th	83	79	.512	14.0	Dave Bristol	733,354

West Division

Year	Finish	Wins	Losses	Percentage	Games Behind	Manager	Attendance
1969	3rd	89	73	.549	4.0	Dave Bristol	987,991
1970	1st	102	60	.630	+14.5	Sparky Anderson	1,803,568

Year	Finish	Wins	Losses	Percentage	Games Behind	Manager	Attendance
1971	4th (Tie)	79	83	.488	11.0	Sparky Anderson	1,501,122
1972	1st	95	59	.617	+10.5	Sparky Anderson	1,611,459
1973	1st	99	63	.611	+3.5	Sparky Anderson	2,017,601
1974	2nd	98	64	.605	4.0	Sparky Anderson	2,164,307
1975	1st	108	54	.667	+20.0	Sparky Anderson	2,315,603
1976	1st	102	60	.630	+10.0	Sparky Anderson	2,629,708
1977	2nd	88	74	.543	10.0	Sparky Anderson	2,519,670
1978	2nd	92	69	.571	2.5	Sparky Anderson	2,532,497
1979	1st	90	71	.559	+1.5	John McNamara	2,356,933
1980	3rd	89	73	.549	3.5	John McNamara	2,022,450
1981*	2nd/2nd	66	42	.611	0.5/1.5	John McNamara	1,093,730
1982	6th	61	101	.377	28.0	John McNamara, Russ Nixon	1,326,528
1983	6th	74	88	.457	17.0	Russ Nixon	1,190,419
1984	5th	70	92	.432	22.0	Vern Rapp, Pete Rose	1,275,887
1985	2nd	89	72	.553	5.5	Pete Rose	1,834,619
1986	2nd	86	76	.531	10.0	Pete Rose	1,692,432
1987	2nd	84	78	.519	6.0	Pete Rose	2,185,205
1988	2nd	87	74	.540	7.0	Pete Rose	2,072,528
1989	5th	75	87	.463	17.0	Pete Rose, Tommy Helms	1,979,320
1990	1st	91	71	.562	+5.0	Lou Piniella	2,400,892
1991	5th	74	88	.457	20.0	Lou Piniella	2,372,377
1992	2nd	90	72	.556	8.0	Lou Piniella	2,315,946
1993	5th	73	89	.451	31.0	Tony Perez, Davey Johnson	2,453,232
Central Division							
1994	1st	66	48	.579	+0.5	Davey Johnson	1,897,681
1995	1st	85	59	.590	+9.0	Davey Johnson	1,837,649
1996	3rd	81	81	.500	7.0	Ray Knight	1,861,428
1997	3rd	76	86	.469	8.0	Ray Knight, Jack McKeon	1,785,788
1998	4th	77	85	.475	25.0	Jack McKeon	1,793,679
1999	2nd	96	67	.589	1.5	Jack McKeon	2,061,222
2000	2nd	85	77	.525	10.0	Jack McKeon	2,577,351
2001	5th	66	96	.407	27.0	Bob Boone	1,882,732
2002	3rd	78	84	.481	19.0	Bob Boone	1,855,973
2003	5th	69	93	.426	19.0	Bob Boone, Dave Miley	2,355,259
2004	4th	76	86	.469	29.0	Dave Miley	2,287,250
2005	5th	73	89	.451	27.0	Dave Miley, Jerry Narron	1,943,068
2006	3rd	80	82	.494	3.5	Jerry Narron	2,134,633
2007	5th	72	90	.444	13.0	Jerry Narron, Pete Mackanin	2,058,632
2008	5th	74	88	.457	23.5	Dusty Baker	2,058,632
2009	4th	78	84	.481	13.0	Dusty Baker	1,747,919
2010	1st	91	71	.562	+5.0	Dusty Baker	2,060,550
2011	3rd	79	83	.488	17.0	Dusty Baker	2,213,588
2012	1st	97	65	.599	+9.0	Dusty Baker	2,347,251
2013	3rd	90	72	.556	7.0	Dusty Baker	2,492,101
2014	4th	76	86	.469	14.0	Bryan Price	2,476,664
2015	5th	64	98	.395	36.0	Bryan Price	2,419,506
2016	5th	68	94	.420	35.5	Bryan Price	1,894,085
2017	5th	68	94	.420	24.0	Bryan Price	1,836,917
2018	5th	67	95	.414	28.0	Bryan Price, Jim Riggleman	1,629,356
2019	4th	75	87	.463	16.0	David Bell	1,809,075
2020	3rd	31	29	.517	3.0	David Bell	0
2021	3rd	83	79	.512	12.0	David Bell	1,505,024
2022	4th (Tie)	62	100	.383	31.0	David Bell	1,395,770

* Split season.

Awards

Most Valuable Player

Ernie Lombardi, catcher, 1938
Bucky Walters, pitcher, 1939
Frank McCormick, first base, 1940
Frank Robinson, outfield, 1961
Johnny Bench, catcher, 1970
Johnny Bench, catcher, 1972
Pete Rose, outfield, 1973
Joe Morgan, second base, 1975
Joe Morgan, second base, 1976
George Foster, outfield, 1977
Barry Larkin, shortstop, 1995
Joey Votto, first base, 2010

Rookie of the Year

Frank Robinson, outfield, 1956
Pete Rose, second base, 1963
Tommy Helms, third base, 1966
Johnny Bench, catcher, 1968
Pat Zachry, pitcher, 1976 (co-winner)
Chris Sabo, third base, 1988
Scott Williamson, pitcher, 1999
Jonathan India, second base, 2021

Cy Young

Trevor Bauer, 2020

Manager of the Year (Since 1983)

Jack McKeon, 1999

Hall of Famers Who Played for the Reds

Jake Beckley, first base, 1897–1903
Johnny Bench, catcher, 1967–83
Jim Bottomley, first base, 1933–35
Mordecai Brown, pitcher, 1913
Sam Crawford, outfield, 1899–1902
Candy Cummings, pitcher, 1877
Kiki Cuyler, outfield, 1935–37
Leo Durocher, shortstop, 1930–33
Ken Griffey Jr., outfield, 2000–08
Clark Griffith, pitcher, 1909–10
Chick Hafey, outfield, 1932–35 and 1937
Jesse Haines, pitcher, 1918
Harry Heilmann, outfield, 1930–31
Miller Huggins, second base, 1904–09
Joe Kelley, outfield, 1902–06
George Kelly, first base, 1927–30
King Kelly, outfield, 1878–79
Barry Larkin, shortstop, 1986–2004
Ernie Lombardi, catcher, 1932–41

Rube Marquard, pitcher, 1921
Christy Mathewson, pitcher, 1916
Bill McKechnie, second base, 1916–17
Joe Morgan, second base, 1972–79
Tony Perez, first base, 1964–76 and 1984–86
Old Hoss Radbourn, pitcher, 1891
Eppa Rixey, pitcher, 1921–33
Frank Robinson, outfield, 1956–65
Scott Rolen, third base, 2009–12
Edd Roush, outfield, 1916–26, 1931
Amos Rusie, pitcher, 1901
Tom Seaver, pitcher, 1977–82
Al Simmons, outfield, 1939
Lee Smith, pitcher, 1996
Joe Tinker, shortstop, 1913
Dazzy Vance, pitcher, 1934
Lloyd Waner, outfield, 1941

Retired Numbers

1	Fred Hutchinson
5	Johnny Bench
8	Joe Morgan
10	Sparky Anderson
11	Barry Larkin
13	Dave Concepcion
14	Pete Rose
18	Ted Kluszewski
20	Frank Robinson
24	Tony Perez

League Leaders, Batting (Post-1900)

Batting Average, Season

Cy Seymour, 1905	.377
Hal Chase, 1916	.339
Edd Roush, 1917	.341
Edd Roush, 1919	.321
Bubbles Hargrave, 1926	.353
Ernie Lombardi, 1938	.342
Pete Rose, 1968	.335
Pete Rose, 1969	.348
Pete Rose, 1973	.338

Home Runs, Season

Sam Crawford, 1901	16
Fred Odwell, 1905	9
Ted Kluszewski, 1954	49
Johnny Bench, 1970	45
Johnny Bench, 1972	40
George Foster, 1977	52
George Foster, 1978	40

RBIs, Season

Frank McCormick, 1939	128
Ted Kluszewski, 1954	141
Deron Johnson, 1965	130
Johnny Bench, 1970	148
Johnny Bench, 1972	125
Johnny Bench, 1974	129
George Foster, 1976	121
George Foster, 1977	149
George Foster, 1978	120
Dave Parker, 1985	125

Stolen Bases, Season

Jimmy Barrett, 1900	46
Bob Bescher, 1909	54
Bob Bescher, 1910	70
Bob Bescher, 1911	81
Bob Bescher, 1912	67
Lonny Frey, 1940	22
Bobby Tolan, 1970	57

Total Bases, Season

Sam Crawford, 1902	256
Cy Seymour, 1905	325
Johnny Bench, 1974	315
George Foster, 1977	388
Dave Parker, 1985	350
Dave Parker, 1986	304

Most Hits, Season

Cy Seymour, 1905	219
Hal Chase, 1916	184
Heinie Groh, 1917	182
Frank McCormick, 1938	209
Frank McCormick, 1939	209
Frank McCormick, 1940	191 (Tie)
Ted Kluszewski, 1955	192
Vada Pinson, 1961	208
Vada Pinson, 1963	204
Pete Rose, 1965	209
Pete Rose, 1968	210 (Tie)
Pete Rose, 1970	205
Pete Rose, 1972	198
Pete Rose, 1973	230
Pete Rose, 1976	215

Most Runs, Season

Bob Bescher, 1912	120
Heinie Groh, 1918	88
Billy Werber, 1939	115
Frank Robinson, 1956	122
Vada Pinson, 1959	131

Frank Robinson, 1962 134
Tommy Harper, 1965 126
Pete Rose, 1969 .... 120 (Tie)
Joe Morgan, 1972 122
Pete Rose, 1974 110
Pete Rose, 1975 112
Pete Rose, 1976 130
George Foster, 1977 124

Batting Feats

Triple Crown Winners
[No player]

Hitting for the Cycle
John Reilly, Aug. 6, 1890
Tom Parrott, Sep. 28, 1894
Mike Mitchell, Aug. 19, 1911
Heinie Groh, Jul. 5, 1915
Harry Craft, Jun. 8, 1940
Frank Robinson, May 2, 1959
Eric Davis, Jun. 2, 1989

Six Hits in a Game (Post-1900)
Tony Cuccinello, Aug. 13, 1931
Ernie Lombardi, May 9, 1937
Walker Cooper, Jul. 6, 1949
Phil Ervin, Jul. 13, 2019

40 or More Home Runs, Season
52 .... George Foster, 1977
49 .... Ted Kluszewski, 1954
                     Eugenio Suarez, 2019
47 .... Ted Kluszewski, 1955
46 .... Adam Dunn, 2004
45 .... Johnny Bench, 1970
                     Greg Vaughn, 1999
40 .... Ted Kluszewski, 1953
                     Wally Post, 1955
                     Tony Perez, 1970
                     Johnny Bench, 1972
                     George Foster, 1978
                     Ken Griffey Jr., 2000
                     Adam Dunn, 2005
                     Adam Dunn, 2006
                     Adam Dunn, 2007
                     Adam Dunn*, 2008
* 8 with Ari. D'backs and 32 with
Cin. Reds.

League Leaders, Pitching (Post-1900)

Most Wins, Season
Eppa Rixey, 1922 25
Dolf Luque, 1923 27

Pete Donohue, 1926 .... 20 (Tie)
Bucky Walters, 1939 27
Bucky Walters, 1940 22
Elmer Riddle, 1943 .... 21 (Tie)
Bucky Walters, 1944 23
Ewell Blackwell, 1947 22
Joey Jay, 1961 .... 21 (Tie)
Tom Seaver, 1981 14
Danny Jackson, 1988 .... 23 (Tie)
Aaron Harang, 2006 .... 16 (Tie)

Most Strikeouts, Season
Noodles Hahn, 1901 233
Bucky Walters, 1939 .... 137 (Tie)
Johnny Vander Meer, 1941 202
Johnny Vander Meer, 1942 186
Johnny Vander Meer, 1943 174
Ewell Blackwell, 1947 193
Jose Rijo, 1993 227
Aaron Harang, 2006 216
Johnny Cueto, 2014 .... 242 (Tie)

Lowest ERA, Season
Dolf Luque, 1923 .... 1.93
Dolf Luque, 1925 .... 2.63
Bucky Walters, 1939 .... 2.29
Bucky Walters, 1940 .... 2.48
Elmer Riddle, 1941 .... 2.24
Ed Heusser, 1944 .... 2.38
Trevor Bauer, 2020 .... 1.73

Most Saves, Season
Wayne Granger, 1970 35
Clay Carroll, 1972 37
Rawly Eastwick, 1975 .... 22 (Tie)
Rawly Eastwick, 1977 26
John Franco, 1988 39
Jeff Brantley, 1996 44
Jeff Shaw, 1997 42

Best Won–Lost Percentage, Season
Dutch Ruether, 1919 .... 19–6 ... .760
Pete Donohue, 1922 .... 18–9 ... .667
Dolf Luque, 1923 .... 27–8 ... .771
Paul Derringer, 1939 .... 25–7 ... .781
Elmer Riddle, 1941 ...... 19–4 ... .826
Bob Purkey, 1962 .... 23–5 ... .821
Don Gullett, 1971 .... 16–6 ... .727
Gary Nolan, 1972 .... 15–5 ... .750
Don Gullett, 1975 .... 15–4 ... .789
Tom Seaver, 1979 .... 16–6 ... .727
Tom Seaver, 1981 .... 14–2 ... .875
Jose Rijo, 1991 .... 15–6 ... .714

Pitching Feats

Triple Crown Winner
Bucky Walters, 1939 (27–11,
   2.29 ERA, 137 SO)

20 Wins, Season
Noodles Hahn, 1901 22–19
Noodles Hahn, 1902 22–12
Noodles Hahn, 1903 22–12
Jack Harper, 1904 23–9
Bob Ewing, 1905 20–11
Jake Weimer, 1906 20–14
George Suggs, 1910 20–12
Fred Toney, 1917 24–16
Pete Schneider, 1917 20–19
Slim Sallee, 1919 21–7
Eppa Rixey, 1922 25–13
Dolf Luque, 1923 27–8
Pete Donohue, 1923 21–15
Eppa Rixey, 1923 20–15
Carl Mays, 1924 20–9
Eppa Rixey, 1925 21–11
Pete Donohue, 1925 21–14
Pete Donohue, 1926 20–14
Paul Derringer, 1935 22–13
Paul Derringer, 1938 21–14
Bucky Walters, 1939 27–11
Paul Derringer, 1939 25–7
Bucky Walters, 1940 22–10
Paul Derringer, 1940 20–12
Elmer Riddle, 1943 21–11
Bucky Walters, 1944 23–8
Ewell Blackwell, 1947 22–8
Joey Jay, 1961 21–10
Bob Purkey, 1962 23–5
Joey Jay, 1962 21–14
Jim Maloney, 1963 23–7
Sammy Ellis, 1965 22–10
Jim Maloney, 1965 20–9
Jim Merritt, 1970 20–12
Tom Seaver*, 1977 21–6
Tom Browning, 1985 20–9
Danny Jackson, 1988 23–8
Johnny Cueto, 2014 20–9
* 7–3 with N.Y. Mets and 14–3 with Cin. Reds.

No-Hitters
Jim Toney (vs. Chi. Cubs), May 2,
   1917 (final: 1–0) (10 innings)
Hod Eller (vs. St.L. Cardinals), May 11,
   1919 (final: 6–0)
Johnny Vander Meer (vs. Bos. Braves),
   Jun. 11, 1938 (final: 3–0)
Johnny Vander Meer (vs. Brk. Dodgers),

Jun. 15, 1938 (final: 6–0)

Clyde Shoun (vs. Bos. Braves), May 15, 1944 (final: 1–0)

Ewell Blackwell (vs. Bos. Braves), Jun. 18, 1947 (final: 6–0)

Jim Maloney (vs. Chi. Cubs), Aug. 9, 1965 (final: 1–0) (10 innings)

George Culver (vs. Phi. Phillies), Jul. 29, 1968 (final: 6–1)

Jim Maloney (vs. Hou. Astros), Apr. 30, 1969 (final: 1–0)

Tom Seaver (vs. St.L. Cardinals), Jun. 16, 1978 (final: 4–0)

Tom Browning (vs. L.A. Dodgers), Sep. 16, 1988 (final: 1–0) (perfect game)

Homer Bailey (vs. Pit. Pirates), Sep. 28, 2012 (final: 1–0)

Homer Bailey (vs. S.F. Giants), Jul. 2, 2013 (final: 3–0)

Wade Miley (vs. Cle. Indians), May 7, 2021 (final: 3–0)

No-Hitters Pitched Against

Fred Pfeffer, Bos. Doves, May 8, 1907 (final: 6–0)

Tex Carleton, Brk. Dodgers, Apr. 30, 1940 (final: 3–0)

Lon Warneke, St.L. Cardinals, Aug. 30, 1941 (final: 2–0)

Ken Johnson, Hou. Colt .45s, Apr. 23, 1964 (final: 0–1)

Don Wilson, Hou. Astros, May 1, 1969 (final: 4–0)

Ken Holtzman, Chi. Cubs, Jun. 3, 1971 (final: 1–0)

Rick Wise, Phi. Phillies, Jun. 23, 1971 (final: 4–0)

Roy Halladay, Phi. Phillies, Oct. 6, 2010 (final: 4–0) (Postseason game)

Jake Arrieta, Chi. Cubs, Apr. 21, 2016 (final: 16–0)

Mike Fiers, Oak. A's, May 7, 2019 (final: 2–0)

Postseason Play

1919 World Series vs. Chi. White Sox (AL), won 5 games to 3

1939 World Series vs. N.Y. Yankees (AL), lost 4 games to 0

1940 World Series vs. Det. Tigers (AL), won 4 games to 3

1961 World Series vs. N.Y. Yankees (AL), lost 4 games to 1

1970 League Championship Series vs. Pit. Pirates, won 3 games to 0

World Series vs. Bal. Orioles (AL), lost 4 games to 1

1972 League Championship Series vs. Pit. Pirates, won 3 games to 2

World Series vs. Oak. A's (AL), lost 4 games to 3

1973 League Championship Series vs. N.Y. Mets, lost 3 games to 2

1975 League Championship Series vs. Pit. Pirates, won 3 games to 0

World Series vs. Bos. Red Sox (AL), won 4 games to 3

1976 League Championship Series vs. Phi. Phillies, won 3 games to 0

World Series vs. N.Y. Yankees (AL), won 4 games to 0

1979 League Championship Series vs. Pit. Pirates, lost 3 games to 0

1990 League Championship Series vs. Pit. Pirates, won 4 games to 2

World Series vs. Oak. A's (AL), won 4 games to 0

1995 Division Series vs. L.A. Dodgers, won 3 games to 0

League Championship Series vs. Atl. Braves, lost 4 games to 0

1999 NL Wild Card Playoff Game vs. N.Y. Mets, lost

2010 Division Series vs. Phi. Phillies, lost 3 games to 0

2012 Division Series vs. S.F. Giants, lost 3 games to 2

2013 NL Wild Card Playoff Game vs. Pit. Pirates, lost

2020 Wild Card Series vs. Atl. Braves, lost 2 games to 0

Colorado Rockies

Dates of Operation: 1993–present (30 years)
Overall Record: 2201 wins, 2495 losses (.469)
Stadiums: Mile High Stadium, 1993–94; Coors Field, 1995–present (capacity: 50,398)

Year-by-Year Finishes

Year	Finish	Wins	Losses	Percentage	Games Behind	Manager	Attendance
					West Division		
1993	6th	67	95	.414	37.0	Don Baylor	4,483,350
1994	3rd	53	64	.453	6.5	Don Baylor	3,281,511
1995	2nd	77	67	.535	1.0	Don Baylor	3,390,037
1996	3rd	83	79	.512	8.0	Don Baylor	3,891,014
1997	3rd	83	79	.512	7.0	Don Baylor	3,888,453
1998	4th	77	85	.475	21.0	Don Baylor	3,789,347
1999	5th	72	90	.444	28.0	Jim Leyland	3,481,065
2000	4th	82	80	.506	15.0	Buddy Bell	3,285,710
2001	5th	73	89	.451	19.0	Buddy Bell	3,159,385
2002	4th	73	89	.451	25.0	Buddy Bell, Clint Hurdle	2,737,918
2003	4th	74	88	.457	26.5	Clint Hurdle	2,334,085
2004	4th	68	94	.420	25.0	Clint Hurdle	2,338,069
2005	5th	67	95	.414	15.0	Clint Hurdle	1,914,389
2006	4th	76	86	.469	12.0	Clint Hurdle	2,104,362
2007	2nd	90	73	.552	5.5	Clint Hurdle	2,376,250
2008	3rd	74	88	.457	10.0	Clint Hurdle	2,650,218
2009	2nd	92	70	.568	3.0	Clint Hurdle, Jim Tracy	2,665,080
2010	3rd	83	79	.512	9.0	Jim Tracy	2,875,245
2011	4th	73	84	.451	21.0	Jim Tracy	2,909,777
2012	5th	64	98	.395	30.0	Jim Tracy	2,630,458
2013	5th	74	88	.457	18.0	Walt Weiss	2,793,828
2014	4th	66	96	.407	28.0	Walt Weiss	2,680,329
2015	5th	68	94	.420	24.0	Walt Weiss	2,506,789
2016	3rd	75	87	.463	16.0	Walt Weiss	2,602,524
2017	3rd	87	75	.537	17.0	Bud Black	2,953,650
2018	2nd	91	72	.558	1.0	Bud Black	3,015,880
2019	4th	71	91	.438	35.0	Bud Black	2,993,244
2020	4th	26	34	.433	17.0	Bud Black	0
2021	4th	74	87	.460	32.5	Bud Black	1,938,645
2022	5th	68	94	.420	43.0	Bud Black	2,597,428

Awards

Most Valuable Player
Larry Walker, outfield, 1997

Rookie of the Year
Jason Jennings, pitcher, 2002

Cy Young
[No player]

Manager of the Year (Since 1983)
Don Baylor, 1995
Jim Tracy, 2009

Hall of Famers Who Played for the Rockies
Larry Walker, outfield, 1995–2004

Retired Numbers
17 .... Todd Helton

League Leaders, Batting

Batting Average, Season
Andres Galarraga, 1993 .... .370
Larry Walker, 1998 .... .363
Larry Walker, 1999 .... .379
Todd Helton, 2000 .... .372
Larry Walker, 2001 .... .350
Matt Holliday, 2007 .... .340
Carlos Gonzalez, 2010 .... .336
Michael Cuddyer, 2013 .... .331
Justin Morneau, 2014 .... .319
DJ LeMahieu, 2016 .... .348
Charlie Blackmon, 2017 .... .331

Home Runs, Season
Dante Bichette, 1995 40
Andres Galarraga, 1996 47
Larry Walker, 1997 49
Nolan Arenado, 2015 .... 42 (Tie)

Nolan Arenado, 2016 .... 41 (Tie)
Nolan Arenado, 2018 37

RBIs, Season
Dante Bichette, 1995 128
Andres Galarraga, 1996 150
Andres Galarraga, 1997 140
Todd Helton, 2000 147
Preston Wilson, 2003 141
Vinny Castilla, 2004 131
Matt Holliday, 2007 137
Nolan Arenado, 2015 130
Nolan Arenado, 2016 133

Stolen Bases, Season
Eric Young, 1996 53
Juan Pierre, 2001 .... 46 (Tie)
Willy Taveras, 2007 68
Eric Young Jr.*, 2013 46
Trevor Story, 2020 15
* 38 with N.Y. Mets and 8 with Col.
Rockies.

Total Bases, Season
Dante Bichette, 1995 359
Ellis Burks, 1996 392
Larry Walker, 1997 409
Todd Helton, 2000 405
Matt Holliday, 2007 386
Carlos Gonzalez, 2010 351
Nolan Arenado, 2015 354
Nolan Arenado, 2016 352
Charlie Blackmon, 2017 387

Most Hits, Season
Dante Bichette, 1995 .... 197 (Tie)
Dante Bichette, 1998 219
Todd Helton, 2000 216
Matt Holliday, 2007 216
Carlos Gonzalez, 2010 197
Charlie Blackmon, 2017 213

Most Runs, Season
Ellis Burks, 1996 142
Charlie Blackmon, 2017 137
Charlie Blackmon, 2018 119

Batting Feats

Triple Crown Winners
[No player]

Hitting for the Cycle
Dante Bichette, Jun. 10, 1998
Neifi Perez, Jul. 25, 1998
Todd Helton, Jun. 19, 1999
Mike Lansing, Jun. 18, 2000
Troy Tulowitzki, Aug. 10, 2009
Carlos Gonzalez, Jul. 31, 2010
Michael Cuddyer, Aug. 17, 2014
Nolan Arenado, Jun. 18, 2017
Charlie Blackmon, Sep. 30, 2018

Six Hits in a Game
Andres Galarraga, Jul. 3, 1995
Charlie Blackmon, Apr. 4, 2014

40 or More Home Runs, Season
49 .... Larry Walker, 1997
                            Todd Helton, 2001
47 ....Andres Galarraga, 1996
46 .... Vinny Castilla, 1998
42 .... Todd Helton, 2000
                            Nolan Arenado, 2015
41 ....Andres Galarraga, 1997
                            Nolan Arenado, 2016
                            Nolan Arenado, 2019
40 .... Dante Bichette, 1995
                            Ellis Burks, 1996
                            Vinny Castilla, 1996
                            Vinny Castilla, 1997

League Leaders, Pitching

Most Wins, Season
[No player]

Most Strikeouts, Season
[No player]

Lowest ERA, Season
[No player]

Most Saves, Season
Greg Holland, 2017 .... 41 (Tie)
Wade Davis, 2018 43

Best Won–Lost Percentage, Season
Marvin Freeman, 1994 .10–2 ... .833
Ubaldo Jimenez, 2010..19–8 ... .704

Pitching Feats

20 Wins, Season
[No player]

No-Hitters
Ubaldo Jimenez (vs. Atl. Braves), Apr.
17, 2010 (final: 4–0)

No-Hitters Pitched Against
Al Leiter, Fla. Marlins, May 11, 1996
(final: 11–0)
Hideo Nomo, L.A. Dodgers, Sep. 17,
1996 (final: 9–0)
Clayton Kershaw, L.A. Dodgers, Jun.
18, 2014 (final: 8–0)

Postseason Play

1995 Division Series vs. Atl. Braves,
        lost 3 games to 1
        NL Wild Card Playoff Game vs.
        S.D. Padres, won
2007 Division Series vs. Phi. Phillies,
        won 3 games to 0
        League Championship Series vs.
        Ari. D'backs, won 4 games to 0
        World Series vs. Bos. Red Sox
        (AL), lost 4 games to 0
2009 Division Series vs. Phi. Phillies, lost
        3 games to 0
2017 NL Wild Card Playoff Game vs.
        Ari. D'backs, lost
2018 NL Wild Card Playoff Game vs.
        Chi. Cubs, won
        Division Series vs. Mil. Brewers,
        lost 3 games to 0

Los Angeles Dodgers

Dates of Operation: 1958–present (65 years)
Overall Record: 5610 wins, 4662 losses (.546)
Stadiums: L.A. Memorial Coliseum, 1958–61; Dodger Stadium (also known as Chavez Ravine), 1962–present (capacity: 56,000)

Year-by-Year Finishes

Year	Finish	Wins	Losses	Percentage	Games Behind	Manager	Attendance
1958	7th	71	83	.461	21.0	Walter Alston	1,845,556
1959	1st	88	68	.564	+2.0	Walter Alston	2,071,045
1960	4th	82	72	.532	13.0	Walter Alston	2,253,887
1961	2nd	89	65	.578	4.0	Walter Alston	1,804,250
1962	2nd	102	63	.618	1.0	Walter Alston	2,755,184
1963	1st	99	63	.611	+6.0	Walter Alston	2,538,602
1964	6th (Tie)	80	82	.494	13.0	Walter Alston	2,228,751
1965	1st	97	65	.599	+2.0	Walter Alston	2,553,577
1966	1st	95	67	.586	+1.5	Walter Alston	2,617,029
1967	8th	73	89	.451	28.5	Walter Alston	1,664,362
1968	7th	76	86	.469	21.0	Walter Alston	1,581,093

West Division

Year	Finish	Wins	Losses	Percentage	Games Behind	Manager	Attendance
1969	4th	85	77	.525	8.0	Walter Alston	1,784,527
1970	2nd	87	74	.540	14.5	Walter Alston	1,697,142
1971	2nd	89	73	.549	1.0	Walter Alston	2,064,594
1972	3rd	85	70	.548	10.5	Walter Alston	1,860,858
1973	2nd	95	66	.590	3.5	Walter Alston	2,136,192
1974	1st	102	60	.630	+4.0	Walter Alston	2,632,474
1975	2nd	88	74	.543	20.0	Walter Alston	2,539,349
1976	2nd	92	70	.568	10.0	Walter Alston, Tommy Lasorda	2,386,301
1977	1st	98	64	.605	+10.0	Tommy Lasorda	2,955,087
1978	1st	95	67	.586	+2.5	Tommy Lasorda	3,347,845
1979	3rd	79	83	.488	11.5	Tommy Lasorda	2,860,954
1980	2nd	92	71	.564	1.0	Tommy Lasorda	3,249,287
1981*	1st/4th	63	47	.573	+0.5/6.0	Tommy Lasorda	2,381,292
1982	2nd	88	74	.543	1.0	Tommy Lasorda	3,608,881
1983	1st	91	71	.562	+3.0	Tommy Lasorda	3,510,313
1984	4th	79	83	.488	13.0	Tommy Lasorda	3,134,824
1985	1st	95	67	.586	+5.5	Tommy Lasorda	3,264,593
1986	5th	73	89	.451	23.0	Tommy Lasorda	3,023,208
1987	4th	73	89	.451	17.0	Tommy Lasorda	2,797,409
1988	1st	94	67	.584	+7.0	Tommy Lasorda	2,980,262
1989	4th	77	83	.481	14.0	Tommy Lasorda	2,944,653
1990	2nd	86	76	.531	5.0	Tommy Lasorda	3,002,396
1991	2nd	93	69	.574	1.0	Tommy Lasorda	3,348,170
1992	6th	63	99	.389	35.0	Tommy Lasorda	2,473,266
1993	4th	81	81	.500	23.0	Tommy Lasorda	3,170,392
1994	1st	58	56	.509	+3.5	Tommy Lasorda	2,279,355
1995	1st	78	66	.542	+1.0	Tommy Lasorda	2,766,251
1996	2nd	90	72	.556	1.0	Tommy Lasorda, Bill Russell	3,188,454
1997	2nd	88	74	.543	2.0	Bill Russell	3,319,504
1998	3rd	83	79	.512	15.0	Bill Russell, Glenn Hoffman	3,089,201
1999	3rd	77	85	.475	23.0	Davey Johnson	3,095,346
2000	2nd	86	76	.531	11.0	Davey Johnson	3,010,819
2001	3rd	86	76	.531	6.0	Jim Tracy	3,017,502
2002	3rd	92	70	.568	6.0	Jim Tracy	3,131,077
2003	2nd	85	77	.525	10.5	Jim Tracy	3,138,626

Year	Finish	Wins	Losses	Percentage	Games Behind	Manager	Attendance
2004	1st	93	69	.574	+2.0	Jim Tracy	3,488,283
2005	4th	71	91	.438	11.0	Jim Tracy	3,603,646
2006	1st (Tie)	88	74	.543	—	Grady Little	3,758,545
2007	4th	82	80	.506	8.0	Grady Little	3,857,036
2008	1st	84	78	.519	+2.0	Joe Torre	3,730,553
2009	1st	95	67	.586	+3.0	Joe Torre	3,761,669
2010	4th	80	82	.494	12.0	Joe Torre	3,562,310
2011	3rd	82	79	.509	11.5	Don Mattingly	2,935,139
2012	2nd	86	76	.531	8.0	Don Mattingly	3,324,246
2013	1st	92	70	.568	+11.0	Don Mattingly	3,743,527
2014	1st	94	68	.580	+6.0	Don Mattingly	3,782,337
2015	1st	92	70	.568	+8.0	Don Mattingly	3,764,815
2016	1st	91	71	.562	+4.0	Dave Roberts	3,703,312
2017	1st	104	58	.642	+11.0	Dave Roberts	3,765,856
2018	1st	92	71	.564	+1.0	Dave Roberts	3,857,500
2019	1st	106	56	.654	+21.0	Dave Roberts	3,974,309
2020	1st	43	17	.717	+6.0	Dave Roberts	0
2021	2nd	106	56	.654	1.0	Dave Roberts	2,804,693
2022	1st	111	51	.685	+22.0	Dave Roberts	3,861,408

* Split season.

Awards

Most Valuable Player
Maury Wills, shortstop, 1962
Sandy Koufax, pitcher, 1963
Steve Garvey, first base, 1974
Kirk Gibson, outfield, 1988
Clayton Kershaw, pitcher, 2014
Clay Bellinger, first base
and outfield, 2019

Rookie of the Year
Frank Howard, outfield, 1960
Jim Lefebvre, second base, 1965
Ted Sizemore, second base, 1969
Rick Sutcliffe, pitcher, 1979
Steve Howe, pitcher, 1980
Fernando Valenzuela, pitcher, 1981
Steve Sax, second base, 1982
Eric Karros, first base, 1992
Mike Piazza, catcher, 1993
Raul Mondesi, outfield, 1994
Hideo Nomo, pitcher, 1995
Todd Hollandsworth, outfield, 1996
Corey Seager, shortstop, 2016
Cody Bellinger, first base and outfield,
2017

Cy Young
Don Drysdale, 1962
Sandy Koufax, 1963
Sandy Koufax, 1965
Sandy Koufax, 1966
Mike Marshall, 1974
Fernando Valenzuela, 1981
Orel Hershiser, 1988

Eric Gagne, 2003
Clayton Kershaw, 2011
Clayton Kershaw, 2013
Clayton Kershaw, 2014

Manager of the Year (Since 1983)
Tommy Lasorda, 1983
Tommy Lasorda, 1988
Dave Roberts, 2016

**Hall of Famers Who Played for the
Los Angeles Dodgers**
Jim Bunning, pitcher, 1969
Gary Carter, catcher, 1991
Don Drysdale, pitcher, 1958–69
Rickey Henderson, outfield, 2003
Gil Hodges, first base, 1943, 1947–61
Sandy Koufax, pitcher, 1958–66
Greg Maddux, pitcher, 2006 and 2008
Juan Marichal, pitcher, 1975
Pedro Martinez, pitcher, 1992–93
Fred McGriff, first base, 2003
Eddie Murray, first base, 1989–91
and 1997
Mike Piazza, catcher, 1992–98
Pee Wee Reese, shortstop, 1958
Frank Robinson, outfield, 1972
Duke Snider, outfield, 1958–62
Don Sutton, pitcher, 1966–80 and 1988
Jim Thome, pinch hitter, 2009
Hoyt Wilhelm, pitcher, 1971–72

Retired Numbers
1 .... Pee Wee Reese
2 ....Tommy Lasorda
4 .... Duke Snider

14 .... Gil Hodges
19 .... Jim Gilliam
20 ....Don Sutton
24 .... Walter Alston
32 .... Sandy Koufax
39 .... Roy Campanella
42 ....Jackie Robinson
53 .... Don Drysdale

League Leaders, Batting

Batting Average, Season
Tommy Davis, 1962.................. .346
Tommy Davis, 1963................. .326
Trea Turner*, 2021 .... .328
* .322 with Was. Nationals and .338
with L.A. Dodgers.

Home Runs, Season
Adrian Beltre, 2004 48
Matt Kemp, 2011.......................39

RBIs, Season
Tommy Davis, 1962................... 153
Matt Kemp, 2011...................... 125
Adrian Gonzalez, 2014.............. 116

Stolen Bases, Season
Maury Wills, 1960......................50
Maury Wills, 1961......................35
Maury Wills, 1962....... 101
Maury Wills, 1963......................40
Maury Wills, 1964......................53
Maury Wills, 1965......................94

Davey Lopes, 1975 77
Davey Lopes, 1976 63
Dee Strange-Gordon, 2014 64
Trea Turner*, 2021 32

* 21 with Was. Nationals and 11 with L.A. Dodgers.

Total Bases, Season

Matt Kemp, 2011......................353
Trea Turner*, 2021 319

* 202 with Was. Nationals and 117 with L.A. Dodgers.

Most Hits, Season

Tommy Davis, 1962....................230
Steve Garvey, 1978 202
Steve Garvey, 1980 200
Trea Turner*, 2021 195
Freddie Freeman, 2022 199

* 125 with Was. Nationals and 70 with L.A. Dodgers.

Most Runs, Season

Brett Butler, 1990......................112
Matt Kemp, 2011......................115
Mookie Betts, 2022.............117 (Tie)
Freddie Freeman, 2022 ....117 (Tie)

Batting Feats

Triple Crown Winners

[No player]

Hitting for the Cycle

Wes Parker, May 7, 1970
Orlando Hudson, Apr. 13, 2009
Cody Bellinger, Jul. 15, 2017

Six Hits in a Game

Willie Davis, May 24, 1973*
Paul Lo Duca, May 28, 2001*
Shawn Green, May 23, 2002
Chase Utley, Jul. 6, 2016

* Extra-inning game.

40 or More Home Runs, Season

49 ....Shawn Green, 2001
48 ....Adrian Beltre, 2004
43 ....Gary Sheffield, 2000
42 ....Shawn Green, 2002
40 ....Mike Piazza, 1997

League Leaders, Pitching

Most Wins, Season

Don Drysdale, 1962......................25
Sandy Koufax, 1963 ....25 (Tie)

Sandy Koufax, 1965 26
Sandy Koufax, 1966 27
Andy Messersmith, 1974........20 (Tie)
Fernando Valenzuela, 1986............21
Orel Hershiser, 1988.............23 (Tie)
Derek Lowe, 2006.................16 (Tie)
Clayton Kershaw, 2011 ....21 (Tie)
Clayton Kershaw, 2014 21
Clayton Kershaw, 2017 18

Most Strikeouts, Season

Don Drysdale, 1959...................242
Don Drysdale, 1960...................246
Sandy Koufax, 1961 269
Don Drysdale, 1962...................232
Sandy Koufax, 1963 306
Sandy Koufax, 1965 382
Sandy Koufax, 1966 317
Fernando Valenzuela, 1981.........180
Hideo Nomo, 1995....................236
Clayton Kershaw, 2011 248
Clayton Kershaw, 2013 232
Clayton Kershaw, 2015 301

Lowest ERA, Season

Sandy Koufax, 1962 ....2.54
Sandy Koufax, 1963 ....1.88
Sandy Koufax, 1964 ....1.74
Sandy Koufax, 1965 ....2.04
Sandy Koufax, 1966 ....1.73
Don Sutton, 1980......................2.21
Alejandro Pena, 1984 ....2.48
Kevin Brown, 2000 ....2.58
Clayton Kershaw, 2011 ....2.28
Clayton Kershaw, 2012 ....2.53
Clayton Kershaw, 2013 ....1.83
Clayton Kershaw, 2014 ....1.77
Zack Greinke, 2015 ....1.66
Clayton Kershaw, 2017 ....2.31
Hyun Jin Ryu, 2019 ....2.32
Julio Urias, 2021 ....2.29
Julio Urias, 2022 ....2.16

Most Saves, Season

Mike Marshall, 1974...................21
Todd Worrell, 1996..............44 (Tie)
Eric Gagne, 2003 55
Kenley Jansen, 2017 ....41 (Tie)

Best Won–Lost Percentage, Season

Johnny Podres, 1961 ......18–5 . .783
Ron Perranoski, 1963 .....17–3 . .842
Sandy Koufax, 1964 ......19–5 . .792
Sandy Koufax, 1965 ......26–8 . .765

Tommy John, 1973 ....16–7 . .696
Andy Messersmith, 1974.. 20–6 . .769
Orel Hershiser, 1985 ....19–3 . .864
Brad Penny, 2007............16–4 . .800
Zack Greinke, 2013 ....15–4 . .789
Clayon Kershaw, 2014 .....21–3 . .875
Zack Greinke, 2015 ....19–3 . .864
Alex Wood, 2017 ....16–3 . .842
Walker Buehler, 2019 ......14–4 . .778
Julio Urias, 2021 ....20–3 . .870
Tony Gonsolin, 2022 ....16–1 . .941

Pitching Feats

Triple Crown Winner

Sandy Koufax, 1963 (25–5, 1.88 ERA, 306 SO)
Sandy Koufax, 1964 (26–8, 2.04 ERA, 382 SO)
Sandy Koufax, 1965 (27–9 1.73 ERA, 317 SO)
Clayton Kershaw, 2011 (21–5, 2.28 ERA, 248 SO)

20 Wins, Season

Don Drysdale, 1962.................25–9
Sandy Koufax, 1963 25–5
Sandy Koufax, 1965 26–8
Don Drysdale, 1965 23–12
Sandy Koufax, 1966 27–9
Bill Singer, 1969......................20–12
Claude Osteen, 1969 20–15
Al Downing, 1971 20–9
Claude Osteen, 1972................20–11
Andy Messersmith, 1974........20–6
Don Sutton, 1976....................21–10
Tommy John, 1977 20–7
Fernando Valenzuela, 1986.....21–11
Orel Hershiser, 1988................23–8
Ramon Martinez, 1990.............20–6
Clayton Kershaw, 2011 21–5
Clayton Kershaw, 2014 21–3
Julio Urias, 2021 20–3

No-Hitters

Sandy Koufax (vs. N.Y. Mets), Jun. 30, 1962 (final: 5–0)
Sandy Koufax (vs. S.F. Giants), May 11, 1963 (final: 8–0)
Sandy Koufax (vs. Phi. Phillies), Jun. 4, 1964 (final: 3–0)
Sandy Koufax (vs. Chi. Cubs), Sep. 9, 1965 (final: 1–0) (perfect game)

Bill Singer (vs. Phi. Phillies), Jul. 20, 1970 (final: 5–0)

Jerry Reuss (vs. S.F. Giants), Jun. 27, 1980 (final: 8–0)

Fernando Valenzuela (vs. St.L. Cardinals), Jun. 29, 1990 (final: 6–0)

Kevin Gross (vs. S.F. Giants), Aug. 17, 1992 (final: 2–0)

Ramon Martinez (vs. Fla. Marlins), Jul. 14, 1995 (final: 7–0)

Hideo Nomo (vs. Col. Rockies), Sep. 17, 1996 (final: 9–0)

Josh Beckett (vs. Phi. Phillies), May 25, 2014 (final: 6–0)

Clayton Kershaw (vs. Col. Rockies), Jun. 18, 2014 (final: 8–0)

Walker Buehler, Tony Cingrani, Yimi Garcia, Adam Liberatore (vs. S.D. Padres), May 4, 2018 (final: 4–0)

No-Hitters Pitched Against

John Candelaria, Pit. Pirates, Aug. 9, 1976 (final: 2–0)

Nolan Ryan, Hou. Astros, Sep. 26, 1981 (final: 5–0)

Tom Browning, Cin. Reds, Sep. 16, 1988 (final: 1–0) (perfect game)

Dennis Martinez, Mon. Expos, Jul. 28, 1991 (final: 2–0) (perfect game)

Kent Mercker, Atl. Braves, Apr. 8, 1994 (final: 6–0)

Kevin Millwood, Charlie Furbush, Stephen Pryor, Lucas Luetge, Brandon League, Tom Wilhelmsen, Sea. Mariners, Jun. 8, 2012 (final: 1–0)

Mike Fiers, Hou. Astros, Aug. 21, 2015 (final: 3–0)

Jake Arrieta, Chi. Cubs, Aug. 30, 2015 (final: 2–0)

Zach Davies, Ryan Tepera, Andrew Chafin, Craig Kimbrel, Chi. Cubs, Jun. 24, 2021 (final: 4–0)

Postseason Play

1959 Pennant Playoff Series vs. Mil. Braves, won 2 games to 0
World Series vs. Chi. White Sox (AL), won 4 games to 2

1962 Pennant Playoff Series vs. S.F. Giants, lost 2 games to 1

1963 World Series vs. N.Y. Yankees (AL), won 4 games to 0

1965 World Series vs. Min. Twins (AL), won 4 games to 3

1966 World Series vs. Bal. Orioles (AL), lost 4 games to 0

1974 League Championship Series vs. Pit. Pirates, won 3 games to 1
World Series vs. Oak. A's (AL) lost 4 games to 1

1977 League Championship Series vs. Phi. Phillies, won 3 games to 1
World Series vs. N.Y. Yankees (AL), lost 4 games to 2

1978 League Championship Series vs. Phi. Phillies, won 3 games to 1
World Series vs. N.Y. Yankees (AL), lost 4 games to 2

1980 NL West Playoff Game vs. Hou. Astros, lost

1981 First-Half Division Playoff Series vs. Hou. Astros, won 3 games to 2
League Championship Series vs. Mon. Expos, won 3 games to 2
World Series vs. N.Y. Yankees (AL), won 4 games to 2

1983 League Championship Series vs. Phi. Phillies, lost 3 games to 1

1985 League Championship Series vs. St.L. Cardinals, lost 4 games to 2

1988 League Championship Series vs. N.Y. Mets, won 4 games to 3
World Series vs. Oak. A's (AL), won 4 games to 1

1995 Division Series vs. Cin. Reds, lost 3 games to 0

1996 Division Series vs. Atl. Braves, lost 3 games to 0

2004 Division Series vs. St.L. Cardinals, lost 3 games to 1

2006 Division Series vs. N.Y. Mets, lost 3 games to 0

2008 Division Series vs. Chi. Cubs, won 3 games to 0
League Championship Series vs. Phi. Phillies, lost 4 games to 1

2009 Division Series vs. St.L. Cardinals, won 3 games to 0
League Championship Series vs. Phi. Phillies, lost 4 games to 1

2013 Division Series vs. Atl. Braves, won 3 games to 1
League Championship Series vs. St.L. Cardinals, lost 4 games to 2

2014 Division Series vs. St.L. Cardinals, lost 3 games to 1

2015 Division Series vs. N.Y. Mets, lost 3 games to 2

2016 Division Series vs. Was. Nationals, won 3 games to 2
League Championship Series vs. Chi. Cubs, lost 4 games to 2

2017 Division Series vs. Ari. D'backs, won 3 games to 0
League Championship Series vs. Chi. Cubs, won 4 games to 1
World Series vs. Hou. Astros (AL), lost 4 games to 3

2018 Division Series vs. Atl. Braves, won 3 games to 1
League Championship Series vs. Mil. Brewers, won 4 games to 3
World Series vs. Bos. Red Sox (AL), lost 4 games to 1

2019 Division Series vs. Was. Nationals, lost 3 games to 2

2020 Wild Card Series vs. Mil. Brewers, won 2 games to 0
Division Series vs. S.D. Padres, won 3 games to 0
League Championship Series vs. Atl. Braves, won 4 games to 3
World Series vs. T.B. Rays (AL), won 4 games to 2

2021 NL Wild Card Playoff Game vs. St.L. Cardinals, won
Division Series vs. S.F. Giants, won 3 games to 2
League Championship Series vs. Atl. Braves, lost 4 games to 2

2022 Division Series vs. S.D. Padres, lost 3 games to 1

Miami Marlins

Dates of Operation: 1993–present (30 years)
Overall Record: 2157 wins, 2531 losses (.460)
Stadium: Sun Life Stadium, 1993–2011; loanDepot Park (formerly Marlins Park, 2012–20),
   2012–present (capacity: 36,742)
Other Name: Florida Marlins (1993–2011)

Year-by-Year Finishes

Year	Finish	Wins	Losses	Percentage	Games Behind	Manager	Attendance
					East Division		
1993	6th	64	98	.395	33.0	Rene Lachemann	3,064,847
1994	5th	51	64	.443	23.5	Rene Lachemann	1,937,467
1995	4th	67	76	.469	22.5	Rene Lachemann	1,700,466
1996	3rd	80	82	.494	16.0	Rene Lachemann, John Boles	1,746,767
1997	2nd	92	70	.586	9.0	Jim Leyland	2,364,387
1998	5th	54	108	.333	52.0	Jim Leyland	1,750,395
1999	5th	64	98	.395	39.0	John Boles	1,369,421
2000	3rd	79	82	.491	15.5	John Boles	1,218,326
2001	4th	76	86	.469	12.0	John Boles, Tony Perez	1,261,220
2002	4th	79	83	.488	23.0	Jeff Torborg	813,111
2003	2nd	91	71	.562	10.0	Jeff Torborg, Jack McKeon	1,303,215
2004	3rd	83	79	.512	13.0	Jack McKeon	1,723,105
2005	3rd (Tie)	83	79	.512	7.0	Jack McKeon	1,852,608
2006	4th	78	84	.481	19.0	Joe Girardi	1,164,134
2007	5th	71	91	.438	18.0	Fredi Gonzalez	1,370,511
2008	3rd	84	77	.522	7.5	Fredi Gonzalez	1,335,075
2009	2nd	87	75	.537	6.0	Fredi Gonzalez	1,464,109
2010	3rd	80	82	.494	17.0	Fredi Gonzalez, Edwin Rodriguez	1,524,894
2011	5th	72	90	.444	30.0	Edwin Rodriguez, Brandon Hyde, Jack McKeon	1,477,462
2012	5th	69	93	.426	29.0	Ozzie Guillen	2,219,444
2013	5th	62	100	.383	34.0	Mike Redmond	1,586,322
2014	4th	77	85	.475	19.0	Mike Redmond	1,732,283
2015	3rd	71	91	.438	19.0	Mike Redmond, Dan Jennings	1,752,235
2016	3rd	79	82	.491	15.5	Don Mattingly	1,712,417
2017	2nd	77	85	.475	20.0	Don Mattingly	1,651,997
2018	5th	63	98	.391	26.5	Don Mattingly	811,104
2019	5th	57	105	.352	40.0	Don Mattingly	811,302
2020	2nd	31	29	.517	4.0	Don Mattingly	0
2021	4th	67	95	.414	21.5	Don Mattingly	642,617
2022	4th	69	93	.426	32.0	Don Mattingly	907,487

Awards

Most Valuable Player
Giancarlo Stanton, outfield, 2017

Rookie of the Year
Dontrelle Willis, pitcher, 2003
Hanley Ramirez, shortstop, 2006
Chris Coghlan, outfield, 2009
Jose Fernandez, pitcher, 2013

Cy Young
Sandy Alcantara, 2022

Manager of the Year (Since 1983)
Jack McKeon, 2003
Joe Girardi, 2006

Retired Numbers
[No player]

Hall of Famers Who Played for the Marlins
Andre Dawson, outfield, 1995–1996
Trevor Hoffman, pitcher, 1993
Mike Piazza, catcher, 1998
Tim Raines, outfield, 2002
Ivan Rodriguez, catcher, 2003

League Leaders, Batting

Batting Average, Season
Hanley Ramirez, 2009.............. .342
Dee Strange-Gordon, 2015 .... .333

Home Runs, Season
Giancarlo Stanton, 2014 37
Giancarlo Stanton, 2017 59

RBIs, Season
Giancarlo Stanton, 2017 132
Adam Duvall, 2021 ....113*

* 68 with Mia. Marlins and 45 with Atl.
Braves.

Stolen Bases, Season
Chuck Carr, 1993 58
Quilvio Veras, 1995 56
Luis Castillo, 2000 62
Luis Castillo, 2002 48
Juan Pierre, 2003 65
Dee Strange-Gordon, 2015 58
Dee Strange-Gordon, 2017 60
Jon Berti, 2022.............................41

Total Bases, Season
Giancarlo Stanton, 2014 299

Most Hits, Season
Juan Pierre, 2004 221
Dee Strange-Gordon, 2015 205

Most Runs, Season
Hanley Ramirez, 2008................125

Batting Feats

Triple Crown Winners
[No player]

Hitting for the Cycle
[No player]

Six Hits in a Game
[No player]

40 or More Home Runs, Season
59 ....Giancarlo Stanton, 2017
42 ....Gary Sheffield, 1996

League Leaders, Pitching

Most Wins, Season
Dontrelle Willis, 2005 22

Most Strikeouts, Season
[No player]

Lowest ERA, Season
Kevin Brown, 1996 ....1.89
Josh Johnson, 2010...................2.30

Most Saves, Season
Antonio Alfonseca, 2000 45
Armando Benitez, 2004.........47 (Tie)

Best Won–Lost Percentage, Season
[No player]

Pitching Feats

20 Wins, Season
Dontrelle Willis, 2005 22–10

No-Hitters
Al Leiter (vs. Col. Rockies), May 11,
1996 (final: 11–0)
Kevin Brown (vs. S.F. Giants), Jun. 10,
1997 (final: 9–0)
A.J. Burnett (vs. S.D. Padres), May 12,
2001 (final: 3–0)
Anibal Sanchez (vs. Ari. D'backs),
Sep. 6, 2006 (final: 2–0)
Henderson Alvarez (vs. Det. Tigers),
Sep. 29, 2013 (final: 1–0)
Edinson Volquez, (vs. Ari. D'backs),
Jun. 3, 2017 (final: 3–0)

No-Hitters Pitched Against
Ramon Martinez, L.A. Dodgers, Jul.
14, 1995 (final: 7–0)
Roy Halladay, Phi. Phillies, May 29,
2010 (final: 1–0) (perfect game)
Jordan Zimmermann, Was. Nationals,
Sep. 28, 2014 (final: 1–0)

Postseason Play

1997 Division Series vs. S.F. Giants,
      won 3 games to 0
      League Championship Series vs.
      Atl. Braves, won 4 games to 2
      World Series vs. Cle. Indians
      (AL), won 4 games to 3
2003 Division Series vs. S.F. Giants,
      won 3 games to 1
      League Championship Series vs.
      Chi. Cubs, won 4 games to 3
      World Series vs. N.Y. Yankees
      (AL), won 4 games to 2
2020 Wild Card Series vs. Chi. Cubs,
      won 2 games to 0
      Division Series vs. Atl. Braves,
      lost 3 games to 0

Milwaukee Brewers (formerly the Seattle Pilots)

Dates of Operation: (as the Seattle Pilots) 1969 (1 year)
Overall Record: 64 wins, 98 losses (.395)
Stadium: Sick's Stadium, 1969

Dates of Operation: (as the Milwaukee Brewers) AL: 1970–97 (28 years); NL: 1998–present (25 years)
Overall Record: AL: 2136 wins, 2269 losses (.485); NL: 1923 wins, 2024 losses (.487); combined: 4059 wins, 4293 losses (.486)
Stadiums: Milwaukee County Stadium, 1970–2000; American Family Field (formerly Miller Park, 2001–20), 2001–present (capacity: 41,900)

Year-by-Year Finishes

Year	Finish	Wins	Losses	Percentage	Games Behind	Manager	Attendance
				American League West Division			
				Sea. Pilots			
1969	6th	64	98	.395	33.0	Joe Schultz	677,944
				Mil. Brewers			
1970	4th	65	97	.401	33.0	Dave Bristol	933,690
1971	6th	69	92	.429	32.0	Dave Bristol	731,531
				American League East Division			
1972	6th	65	91	.417	21.0	Dave Bristol, Del Crandall	600,440
1973	5th	74	88	.457	23.0	Del Crandall	1,092,158
1974	5th	76	86	.469	15.0	Del Crandall	955,741
1975	5th	68	94	.420	28.0	Del Crandall	1,213,357
1976	6th	66	95	.410	32.0	Alex Grammas	1,012,164
1977	6th	67	95	.414	33.0	Alex Grammas	1,114,938
1978	3rd	93	69	.574	6.5	George Bamberger	1,601,406
1979	2nd	95	66	.590	8.0	George Bamberger	1,918,343
1980	3rd	86	76	.531	17.0	George Bamberger, Buck Rodgers	1,857,408
1981*	3rd/1st	62	47	.569	3.0/+1.5	Buck Rodgers	878,432
1982	1st	95	67	.586	+1.0	Buck Rodgers, Harvey Kuenn	1,978,896
1983	5th	87	75	.537	11.0	Harvey Kuenn	2,397,131
1984	7th	67	94	.416	36.5	Rene Lachemann	1,608,509
1985	6th	71	90	.441	28.0	George Bamberger	1,360,265
1986	6th	77	84	.478	18.0	George Bamberger, Tom Trebelhorn	1,265,041
1987	3rd	91	71	.562	7.0	Tom Trebelhorn	1,909,244
1988	3rd (Tie)	87	75	.537	2.0	Tom Trebelhorn	1,923,238
1989	4th	81	81	.500	8.0	Tom Trebelhorn	1,970,735
1990	6th	74	88	.457	14.0	Tom Trebelhorn	1,752,900
1991	4th	83	79	.512	8.0	Tom Trebelhorn	1,478,729
1992	2nd	92	70	.568	4.0	Phil Garner	1,857,314
1993	7th	69	93	.426	26.0	Phil Garner	1,688,080
				Central Division			
1994	5th	53	62	.461	15.0	Phil Garner	1,268,399
1995	4th	65	79	.451	35.0	Phil Garner	1,087,560
1996	3rd	80	82	.494	19.5	Phil Garner	1,327,155

Year	Finish	Wins	Losses	Percentage	Games Behind	Manager	Attendance
				National League Central Division			
1997	3rd	78	83	.484	8.0	Phil Garner	1,444,027
1998	5th	74	88	.457	28.0	Phil Garner	1,811,548
1999	5th	74	87	.460	22.5	Phil Garner, Jim Lefebvre	1,701,796
2000	3rd	73	89	.451	22.0	Davey Lopes	1,573,621
2001	4th	68	94	.420	25.0	Davey Lopes	2,811,041
2002	6th	56	106	.346	41.0	Davey Lopes, Jerry Royster	1,969,693
2003	6th	68	94	.420	20.0	Ned Yost	1,700,354
2004	6th	67	94	.416	37.5	Ned Yost	2,062,382
2005	3rd	81	81	.500	19.0	Ned Yost	2,211,023
2006	4th	75	87	.463	8.5	Ned Yost	2,335,643
2007	2nd	83	79	.512	2.0	Ned Yost	2,869,144
2008	2nd	90	72	.556	7.5	Ned Yost, Dale Sveum	3,068,458
2009	3rd	80	82	.494	11.0	Ken Macha	3,037,451
2010	3rd	77	85	.475	14.0	Ken Macha	2,776,531
2011	1st	96	66	.593	+6.0	Ron Roenicke	3,071,373
2012	3rd	83	79	.512	14.0	Ron Roenicke	2,831,385
2013	4th	74	88	.457	23.0	Ron Roenicke	2,531,105
2014	3rd	82	80	.506	8.0	Ron Roenicke	2,797,384
2015	4th	68	94	.420	32.0	Ron Roenicke, Craig Counsell	2,542,558
2016	4th	73	89	.451	30.5	Craig Counsell	2,314,614
2017	2nd	86	76	.531	6.0	Craig Counsell	2,627,705
2018	1st	96	67	.589	+1.0	Craig Counsell	2,850,875
2019	2nd	89	73	.549	2.0	Craig Counsell	2,923,333
2020	4th	29	31	.383	5.0	Craig Counsell	0
2021	1st	95	67	.586	+5.0	Craig Counsell	1,824,282
2022	2nd	86	76	.531	7.0	Craig Counsell	2,422,420

* Split season.

Awards

Most Valuable Player
Rollie Fingers, pitcher, 1981
Robin Yount, shortstop, 1982
Robin Yount, outfield, 1989
Ryan Braun, outfield, 2011
Christian Yelich, outfield, 2018

Rookie of the Year
Pat Listach, shortstop, 1992
Ryan Braun, third base, 2007
Devin Williams, pitcher, 2020

Cy Young
Rollie Fingers, 1981
Pete Vuckovich, 1982
Corbin Burnes, 2021

Manager of the Year (Since 1983)
[No manager]

Hall of Famers Who Played for the Brewers
Hank Aaron, designated hitter, 1975–76
Rollie Fingers, pitcher, 1981–82 and 1984–85
Trevor Hoffman, pitcher, 2009–10
Paul Molitor, infield and designated hitter, 1978–92
Ted Simmons, catcher, 1981–85
Don Sutton, pitcher, 1982–84
Robin Yount, shortstop and outfield, 1974–93

Retired Numbers
1 ....Bud Selig
4 ....Paul Molitor
19 ....Robin Yount
34 ....Rollie Fingers
44 ....Hank Aaron

League Leaders, Batting

Batting Average, Season
Christian Yelich, 2018 (NL)........... .323
Christian Yelich, 2019 (NL)........... .329

Home Runs, Season
George Scott, 1975 (AL) .... 36 (Tie)
Gorman Thomas, 1979 (AL) 45
Ben Oglivie, 1980 (AL) .... 41 (Tie)
Gorman Thomas, 1982 (AL) ... 39 (Tie)
Prince Fielder, 2007 (NL) 50
Ryan Braun, 2012 (NL) 41
Chris Carter, 2016 (NL) .... 41 (Tie)

RBIs, Season
George Scott, 1975 (AL) 109
Cecil Cooper, 1980 (AL) 122
Cecil Cooper, 1983 (AL) 126
Prince Fielder, 2009 (NL) ..... 141 (Tie)

Stolen Bases, Season
Tommy Harper, 1969 (Sea. Pilots) ..73
Scott Podsednik, 2004 (NL) 70
Jonathan Villan, 2016 (NL)............62

Total Bases, Season
Dave May, 1973 (AL) .... 295 (Tie)
George Scott, 1973 (AL) ...... 295 (Tie)
George Scott, 1975 (AL) 318
Cecil Cooper, 1980 (AL) 335
Robin Yount, 1982 (AL) 367
Ryan Braun, 2012 (NL) 356
Christian Yelich, 2018 (NL)............340

Most Hits, Season
Robin Yount, 1982 (AL) 210

Paul Molitor, 1991 (AL) 216
Ryan Braun, 2009 (NL) 203

Most Runs, Season
Paul Molitor, 1982 (AL) 136
Paul Molitor, 1987 (AL) 114
Paul Molitor, 1991 (AL) 133
Ryan Braun, 2012 (NL) 108

Batting Feats

Triple Crown Winners
[No player]

Hitting for the Cycle
Mike Hegan, Sep. 3 1976 (AL)
Charlie Moore, Oct. 1, 1980 (AL)
Robin Yount, Jun. 12, 1988 (AL)
Paul Molitor, May 15, 1991 (AL)
Chad Moeller, Apr. 27, 2004 (NL)
Jody Gerut, May 8, 2010 (NL)
George Kottaras, Sep. 3, 2011 (NL)
Christian Yelich, Aug. 29, 2018 (NL)
Christian Yelich, Sep. 17, 2018 (NL)

Six Hits in a Game
Johnny Briggs, Aug. 4, 1973 (AL)
Kevin Reimer, Aug. 24, 1993 (AL)
Jean Segura, May 28, 2013 (NL)
Christian Yelich, Aug. 29, 2018 (NL)
Christian Yelich, May 11, 2022 (NL)

40 or More Home Runs, Season
50 .... Prince Fielder, 2009 (NL)
46 .... Prince Fielder, 2007 (NL)
45 .... Gorman Thomas, 1979 (AL)
                Richie Sexson, 2001 (NL)
                Richie Sexson, 2003 (NL)

44 .... Christian Yelich, 2019 (NL)
41 .... Ben Oglivie, 1980 (AL)
                Ryan Braun, 2012 (NL)
                Chris Carter, 2016 (NL)

League Leaders, Pitching

Most Wins, Season
Pete Vuckovich, 1981 (AL) ...... 14 (Tie)

Most Strikeouts, Season
Corbin Burnes, 2022 243

Lowest ERA, Season
Corbin Burnes, 2021 (NL) 2.43

Most Saves, Season
Ken Sanders, 1971 (AL) 31
Rollie Fingers, 1981 (AL) 28
John Axford, 2011 (NL) .... 46 (Tie)
Josh Hader, 2020 (NL) 13

Best Won–Lost Percentage, Season
Mike Caldwell, 1979 (AL) ... 16–6 .727
Pete Vuckovich, 1981 (AL) ... 14–4 .778
Pete Vuckovich, 1982 (AL) ... 18–6 .750

Pitching Feats

20 Wins, Season
Jim Colborn, 1973 (AL) 20–12
Mike Caldwell, 1978 (AL) 22–9
Ted Higuera, 1986 (AL) 20–11

No-Hitters
Juan Nieves (AL) (vs. Bal. Orioles, AL),
   Apr. 15, 1987 (final: 7–0)
Corbin Burnes and Josh Hader (NL)
   (vs. Cle. Indians, AL), Sep. 11, 2021

No-Hitters Pitched Against
Steve Busby, K.C. Royals (AL), Jun. 19,
   1974 (final: 2–0)
Scott Erickson, Min. Twins (AL), Apr.
   27, 1994 (final: 6–0)
Justin Verlander, Det. Tigers (AL),
   Jun. 12, 2007 (final: 6–0)
Alec Mills, Chi Cubs (NL), Sep. 13,
   2020 (final: 12–0)

Postseason Play

1981   (AL) Second-Half Pennant Playoff
          Series vs. N.Y. Yankees, lost 3
          games to 2
1982   (AL) League Championship
          Series vs. Cal. Angels, won 3
          games to 2
          World Series vs. St.L. Cardinals
          (NL), lost 4 games to 3
2008   (NL) Division Series vs. Phi.
          Phillies, lost 3 games to 1
2011   (NL) Division Series vs. Ari.
          D'backs, won 3 games to 2
          (NL) League Championship
          Series vs. St.L. Cardinals, lost
          4 games to 2
2018   (NL) Division Series vs. Col.
          Rockies, won 3 games to 0
          (NL) League Championship
          Series vs. L.A. Dodgers, lost 4
          games to 3
2019   (NL) Wild Card Playoff Game vs.
          Was. Nationals, lost
2020   (NL) Wild Card Series vs. L.A.
          Dodgers, lost 2 games to 0
2021   (NL) Division Series vs. Atl.
          Braves, lost 3 games to 1

New York Mets

Dates of Operation: 1962–present (61 years)
Overall Record: 4652 wins, 4988 losses (.483)
Stadiums: Polo Grounds, 1962–63; Shea Stadium, 1964–2008; Citi Field, 2009–present
(capacity: 41,922)

Year-by-Year Finishes

Year	Finish	Wins	Losses	Percentage	Games Behind	Manager	Attendance
1962	10th	40	120	.250	60.5	Casey Stengel	922,530
1963	10th	51	111	.315	48.0	Casey Stengel	1,080,108
1964	10th	53	109	.327	40.0	Casey Stengel	1,732,597
1965	10th	50	112	.309	47.0	Casey Stengel, Wes Westrum	1,768,389
1966	9th	66	95	.410	28.5	Wes Westrum	1,932,693
1967	10th	61	101	.377	40.5	Wes Westrum, Salty Parker	1,565,492
1968	9th	73	89	.451	24.0	Gil Hodges	1,781,657

East Division

Year	Finish	Wins	Losses	Percentage	Games Behind	Manager	Attendance
1969	1st	100	62	.617	+8.0	Gil Hodges	2,175,373
1970	3rd	83	79	.512	6.0	Gil Hodges	2,697,479
1971	3rd (Tie)	83	79	.512	14.0	Gil Hodges	2,266,680
1972	3rd	83	73	.532	13.5	Yogi Berra	2,134,185
1973	1st	82	79	.509	+1.5	Yogi Berra	1,912,390
1974	5th	71	91	.438	17.0	Yogi Berra	1,722,209
1975	3rd (Tie)	82	80	.506	10.5	Yogi Berra, Roy McMillan	1,730,566
1976	3rd	86	76	.531	15.0	Joe Frazier	1,468,754
1977	6th	64	98	.395	37.0	Joe Frazier, Joe Torre	1,066,825
1978	6th	66	96	.407	24.0	Joe Torre	1,007,328
1979	6th	63	99	.389	35.0	Joe Torre	788,905
1980	5th	67	95	.414	24.0	Joe Torre	1,192,073
1981*	5th/4th	41	62	.398	15.0/5.5	Joe Torre	704,244
1982	6th	65	97	.401	27.0	George Bamberger	1,323,036
1983	6th	68	94	.420	22.0	George Bamberger, Frank Howard	1,112,774
1984	2nd	90	72	.556	6.5	Davey Johnson	1,842,695
1985	2nd	98	64	.605	3.0	Davey Johnson	2,761,601
1986	1st	108	54	.667	+21.5	Davey Johnson	2,767,601
1987	2nd	92	70	.568	3.0	Davey Johnson	3,034,129
1988	1st	100	60	.625	+15.0	Davey Johnson	3,055,445
1989	2nd	87	75	.537	6.0	Davey Johnson	2,918,710
1990	2nd	91	71	.562	4.0	Davey Johnson, Bud Harrelson	2,732,745
1991	5th	77	84	.478	20.5	Bud Harrelson, Mike Cubbage	2,284,484
1992	5th	72	90	.444	24.0	Jeff Torborg	1,779,534
1993	7th	59	103	.364	38.0	Jeff Torborg, Dallas Green	1,873,183
1994	3rd	55	58	.487	18.5	Dallas Green	1,151,471
1995	2nd (Tie)	69	75	.479	21.0	Dallas Green	1,273,183
1996	4th	71	91	.438	25.0	Dallas Green, Bobby Valentine	1,588,323
1997	3rd	88	74	.543	13.0	Bobby Valentine	1,766,174
1998	2nd	88	74	.543	18.0	Bobby Valentine	2,287,942
1999	2nd	97	66	.595	6.5	Bobby Valentine	2,725,668
2000	2nd	94	68	.580	1.0	Bobby Valentine	2,800,221
2001	3rd	82	80	.506	6.0	Bobby Valentine	2,658,279
2002	5th	75	86	.466	26.5	Bobby Valentine	2,804,838
2003	5th	66	95	.410	34.5	Art Howe	2,140,599
2004	4th	71	91	.438	25.0	Art Howe	2,318,321
2005	3rd	83	79	.512	7.0	Willie Randolph	2,829,931
2006	1st	97	65	.599	+12.0	Willie Randolph	3,379,535
2007	2nd	88	74	.543	1.0	Willie Randolph	3,853,949

Year	Finish	Wins	Losses	Percentage	Games Behind	Manager	Attendance
2008	2nd	89	73	.549	3.0	Willie Randolph, Jerry Manuel	4,042,047
2009	4th	70	92	.432	23.0	Jerry Manuel	3,154,262
2010	4th	79	83	.488	18.0	Jerry Manuel	2,559,738
2011	4th	77	85	.475	25.0	Terry Collins	2,352,596
2012	4th	74	88	.457	24.0	Terry Collins	2,242,803
2013	3rd	74	88	.457	22.0	Terry Collins	2,135,657
2014	2nd	79	83	.488	17.0	Terry Collins	2,148,808
2015	1st	90	72	.556	+7.0	Terry Collins	2,569,753
2016	2nd	87	75	.537	8.0	Terry Collins	2,789,602
2017	4th	70	92	.432	27.0	Terry Collins	2,460,622
2018	4th	77	85	.475	13.0	Mickey Callaway	2,224,995
2019	3rd	86	76	.531	11.0	Mickey Callaway	2,442,532
2020	4th	26	34	.433	9.0	Luis Rojas	0
2021	3rd	77	85	.475	11.5	Luis Rojas	1,511,926
2022	1st (Tie)	101	61	.623	—	Buck Showalter	2,564,737

* Split season.

Awards

Most Valuable Player
[No player]

Rookie of the Year
Tom Seaver, pitcher, 1967
Jon Matlack, pitcher, 1972
Darryl Strawberry, outfield, 1983
Dwight Gooden, pitcher, 1984
Jacob deGrom, pitcher, 2014
Pete Alonso, first base, 2019

Cy Young
Tom Seaver, 1969
Tom Seaver, 1973
Tom Seaver, 1975
Dwight Gooden, 1985
R.A. Dickey, 2012
Jacob deGrom, 2018
Jacob deGrom, 2019

Manager of the Year (Since 1983)
Buck Showalter, 2022

Hall of Famers Who Played for the Mets
Roberto Alomar, second base, 2002–03
Richie Ashburn, outfield, 1962
Yogi Berra, catcher, 1965
Gary Carter, catcher, 1985–89
Tom Glavine, pitcher, 2003–07
Rickey Henderson, outfield, 1999–2000
Gil Hodges, first base, 1962–63
Pedro Martinez, pitcher, 2005–08

Willie Mays, outfield, 1972–73
Eddie Murray, first base, 1992–93
Mike Piazza, catcher and first base, 1998–2005
Nolan Ryan, pitcher, 1966 and 1968–71
Tom Seaver, pitcher, 1967–77 and 1983
Duke Snider, outfield, 1963
Warren Spahn, pitcher, 1965
Joe Torre, first base and third base, 1975–77

Retired Numbers
14 .... Gil Hodges
17 .... Keith Hernandez
24 .... Willie Mays
31 .... Mike Piazza
36 .... Jerry Koosman
37 .... Casey Stengel
41 .... Tom Seaver

League Leaders, Batting

Batting Average, Season
Jose Reyes, 2011 .... .337
Jeff McNeil, 2022 .... .326

Home Runs, Season
Dave Kingman, 1982 37
Darryl Strawberry, 1988 39
Howard Johnson, 1991 38
Pete Alonso, 2019 53

RBIs, Season
Howard Johnson, 1991 117
Pete Alonso, 2022 131

Stolen Bases, Season
Jose Reyes, 2005 60
Jose Reyes, 2006 64
Jose Reyes, 2007 78
Eric Young, 2013 .... 46*
* 8 with Col. Rockies and 38 with N.Y. Mets.

Total Bases, Season
[No player]

Most Hits, Season
Lance Johnson, 1996 227
Jose Reyes, 2008 204

Most Runs, Season
Howard Johnson, 1989 .... 104 (Tie)
Pete Alonso, 2022 131

Batting Feats

Triple Crown Winners
[No player]

Hitting for the Cycle
Jim Hickman, Aug. 7, 1963
Tommie Agee, Jul. 6, 1970
Mike Phillips, Jun. 25, 1976
Keith Hernandez, Jul. 4, 1985
Kevin McReynolds, Aug. 1, 1989
Alex Ochoa, Jul. 3, 1996
John Olerud, Sep. 11, 1997
Eric Valent, Jul. 29, 2004
Jose Reyes, Jun. 21, 2006
Scott Hairston, Apr. 27, 2012
Eduardo Escobar, Jun. 6, 2022

Six Hits in a Game
Edgardo Alfonzo, Aug. 30, 1999
Wilmer Flores, Jul. 3, 2016

40 or More Home Runs, Season
53 .... Pete Alonso, 2019
41 ....Todd Hundley, 1996
Carlos Beltran, 2006
40 .... Mike Piazza, 1999
Pete Alonso, 2022

League Leaders, Pitching

Most Wins, Season
Tom Seaver, 1969 25
Tom Seaver, 1975 22
Dwight Gooden, 1985 24

Most Strikeouts, Season
Tom Seaver, 1970 283
Tom Seaver, 1971 289
Tom Seaver, 1973 251
Tom Seaver, 1975 243
Tom Seaver, 1976 235
Dwight Gooden, 1984 276
Dwight Gooden, 1985 268
David Cone, 1990 233
David Cone, 1991 241
R.A. Dickey, 2012 230
Jacob deGrom, 2019 255
Jacob deGrom, 2020 104

Lowest ERA, Season
Tom Seaver, 1970 ....2.81
Tom Seaver, 1971 ....1.76
Tom Seaver, 1973 ....2.08
Craig Swan, 1978 ....2.43
Dwight Gooden, 1985 ....1.53
Johan Santana, 2008 ....2.53
Jacob deGrom, 2018 ....1.70

Most Saves, Season
John Franco, 1990 33
John Franco, 1994 30
Jeurys Familia, 2016 51

Best Won–Lost Percentage, Season
Tom Seaver, 1969 ....25–7 ... .781
Bob Ojeda, 1986 ....18–5 ... .783

Dwight Gooden, 1987..15–7 ... .682
David Cone, 1988 ....20–3 ... .870

Pitching Feats
Triple Crown Winner
Dwight Gooden, 1985 (24–4,
1.53 ERA, 268 SO)
20 Wins, Season
Tom Seaver, 1969 25–7
Tom Seaver, 1971 20–10
Tom Seaver, 1972 21–12
Tom Seaver, 1975 22–9
Jerry Koosman, 1976 21–10
Dwight Gooden, 1985 24–4
David Cone, 1988 20–3
Frank Viola, 1990 20–12
R.A. Dickey, 2012 20–6

No-Hitters
Johan Santana (vs. St.L. Cardinals), Jun.
1, 2012 (final: 8–0)
Tylor Megill, Drew Smith, Joely
Rodriguez, Seth Lugo, Edwin Diaz
(vs. Phi. Phillies), Apr. 29, 2022
(final: 3–0)

No-Hitters Pitched Against
Sandy Koufax, L.A. Dodgers, Jun. 30,
1962 (final: 5–0)
Jim Bunning, Phi. Phillies, Jun. 21,
1964 (final: 6–0) (perfect game)
Bob Moose, Pit. Pirates, Sep. 20, 1969
(final: 4–0)
Bill Stoneman, Mon. Expos, Oct. 2,
1972 (final: 7–0)
Ed Halicki, S.F. Giants, Aug. 24, 1975
(final: 6–0)
Darryl Kile, Hou. Astros, Sep. 8, 1993
(final: 7–1)
Chris Heston, S.F. Giants, Jun. 9, 2015
(final: 5–0)
Max Scherzer, Was. Nationals,
Oct. 3, 2015 (final: 2–0)

Postseason Play
1969　League Championship Series vs.
　　　Atl. Braves, won 3 games to 0

　　　World Series vs. Bal. Orioles
　　　(AL), won 4 games to 1
1973　League Championship Series vs.
　　　Cin. Reds, won 3 games to 2
　　　World Series vs. Oak. A's (AL),
　　　lost 4 games to 3
1986　League Championship Series vs.
　　　Hou. Astros, won 4 games
　　　to 2
　　　World Series vs. Bos. Red Sox
　　　(AL), won 4 games to 3
1988　League Championship Series vs.
　　　L.A. Dodgers, lost 4 games
　　　to 3
1999　NL Wild Card Playoff Game vs.
　　　Cin. Reds, won
　　　Division Series vs. Ari. D'backs,
　　　won 3 games to 1
　　　League Championship Series vs.
　　　Atl. Braves, lost 4 games to 2
2000　Division Series vs. S.F. Giants,
　　　won 3 games to 1
　　　League Championship Series vs.
　　　St.L. Cardinals, won 4 games
　　　to 1
　　　World Series vs. N.Y. Yankees
　　　(AL), lost 4 games to 1
2006　Division Series vs. L.A. Dodgers,
　　　won 3 games to 0
　　　League Championship Series vs.
　　　St.L. Cardinals, lost 4 games
　　　to 3
2015　Division Series vs. L.A. Dodgers,
　　　won 3 games to 2
　　　League Championship Series vs.
　　　Chi. Cubs, won 4 games to 0
　　　World Series vs. K.C. Royals
　　　(AL), lost 4 games to 1
2016　NL Wild Card Playoff Game vs.
　　　S.F. Giants, lost
2022　Wild Card Series vs. S.D.
　　　Padres, lost 2 games to 1

Philadelphia Phillies

Dates of Operation: 1883–present (140 years)
Overall Record: 10,022 wins, 11,187 losses (.473)
Stadiums: Recreation Park, 1883–86; Huntington Grounds, 1887–94; University of Pennsylvania
Athletic Field, 1894; Baker Bowl, 1895–1938; Columbia Park, 1903; Shibe Park (also known
as Connie Mack Stadium), 1927; 1938–70; Veterans Stadium, 1971–2003; Citizens Bank
Park, 2004–present (capacity: 43,651)
Other Names: Quakers, Live Wires, Blue Jays

Year-by-Year Finishes

Year	Finish	Wins	Losses	Percentage	Games Behind	Manager	Attendance
1883	8th	17	81	.173	46.0	Robert Ferguson	not available
1884	6th	39	73	.348	45.0	Harry Wright	not available
1885	3rd	56	54	.509	30.0	Harry Wright	not available
1886	4th	71	43	.622	19.0	Harry Wright	not available
1887	2nd	75	48	.610	3.5	Harry Wright	not available
1888	3rd	69	61	.531	15.5	Harry Wright	not available
1889	4th	63	64	.496	20.5	Harry Wright	not available
1890	3rd	78	54	.591	9.5	Harry Wright	not available
1891	4th	68	69	.496	18.5	Harry Wright	not available
1892	4th	87	66	.569	16.5	Harry Wright	not available
1893	4th	72	57	.558	13.5	Harry Wright	not available
1894	4th	71	56	.559	17.5	Arthur Irwin	not available
1895	3rd	78	53	.595	9.5	Arthur Irwin	not available
1896	8th	62	68	.477	28.5	William Nash	not available
1897	10th	55	77	.417	38.0	George Stallings	not available
1898	6th	78	71	.523	24.0	George Stallings, Bill Shettsline	not available
1899	3rd	94	58	.618	5.0	Bill Shettsline	not available
1900	3rd	75	63	.543	8.0	Bill Shettsline	not available
1901	2nd	83	57	.593	7.5	Bill Shettsline	234,937
1902	7th	56	81	.409	46.0	Bill Shettsline	112,066
1903	7th	49	86	.363	39.5	Chief Zimmer	151,729
1904	8th	52	100	.342	53.5	Hugh Duffy	140,771
1905	4th	83	69	.546	21.5	Hugh Duffy	317,932
1906	4th	71	82	.464	45.5	Hugh Duffy	294,680
1907	3rd	83	64	.565	21.5	Bill Murray	341,216
1908	4th	83	71	.539	16.0	Bill Murray	420,660
1909	5th	74	79	.484	36.5	Bill Murray	303,177
1910	4th	78	75	.510	25.5	Red Dooin	296,597
1911	4th	79	73	.520	19.5	Red Dooin	416,000
1912	5th	73	79	.480	30.5	Red Dooin	250,000
1913	2nd	88	63	.583	12.5	Red Dooin	470,000
1914	6th	74	80	.481	20.5	Red Dooin	138,474
1915	1st	90	62	.592	+7.0	Pat Moran	449,898
1916	2nd	91	62	.595	2.5	Pat Moran	515,365
1917	2nd	87	65	.572	10.0	Pat Moran	354,428
1918	6th	55	68	.447	26.0	Pat Moran	122,266
1919	8th	47	90	.343	47.5	Jack Coombs, Gavvy Cravath	240,424
1920	8th	62	91	.405	30.5	Gavvy Cravath	330,998
1921	8th	51	103	.331	43.5	Bill Donovan, Kaiser Wilhelm	273,961
1922	7th	57	96	.373	35.5	Kaiser Wilhelm	232,471
1923	8th	50	104	.325	45.5	Art Fletcher	228,168

Year	Finish	Wins	Losses	Percentage	Games Behind	Manager	Attendance
1924	7th	55	96	.364	37.0	Art Fletcher	299,818
1925	6th (Tie)	68	85	.444	27.0	Art Fletcher	304,905
1926	8th	58	93	.384	29.5	Art Fletcher	240,600
1927	8th	51	103	.331	43.0	Stuffy McInnis	305,420
1928	8th	43	109	.283	51.0	Burt Shotton	182,168
1929	5th	71	82	.464	27.5	Burt Shotton	281,200
1930	8th	52	102	.338	40.0	Burt Shotton	299,007
1931	6th	66	88	.429	35.0	Burt Shotton	284,849
1932	4th	78	76	.506	12.0	Burt Shotton	268,914
1933	7th	60	92	.395	31.0	Burt Shotton	156,421
1934	7th	56	93	.376	37.0	Jimmie Wilson	169,885
1935	7th	64	89	.418	35.5	Jimmie Wilson	205,470
1936	8th	54	100	.351	38.0	Jimmie Wilson	249,219
1937	7th	61	92	.399	34.5	Jimmie Wilson	212,790
1938	8th	45	105	.300	43.0	Jimmie Wilson, Hans Lobert	166,111
1939	8th	45	106	.298	50.5	Doc Prothro	277,973
1940	8th	50	103	.327	50.0	Doc Prothro	207,177
1941	8th	43	111	.279	57.0	Doc Prothro	231,401
1942	8th	42	109	.278	62.5	Hans Lobert	230,183
1943	7th	64	90	.416	41.0	Bucky Harris, Fred Fitzsimmons	466,975
1944	8th	61	92	.399	43.5	Fred Fitzsimmons	369,586
1945	8th	46	108	.299	52.0	Fred Fitzsimmons, Ben Chapman	285,057
1946	5th	69	85	.448	28.0	Ben Chapman	1,045,247
1947	7th (Tie)	62	92	.403	32.0	Ben Chapman	907,332
1948	6th	66	88	.429	25.5	Ben Chapman, Dusty Cooke, Eddie Sawyer	767,429
1949	3rd	81	73	.526	16.0	Eddie Sawyer	819,698
1950	1st	91	63	.591	+2.0	Eddie Sawyer	1,217,035
1951	5th	73	81	.474	23.5	Eddie Sawyer	937,658
1952	4th	87	67	.565	9.5	Eddie Sawyer, Steve O'Neill	775,417
1953	3rd (Tie)	83	71	.539	22.0	Steve O'Neill	853,644
1954	4th	75	79	.487	22.0	Steve O'Neill, Terry Moore	738,991
1955	4th	77	77	.500	21.5	Mayo Smith	922,886
1956	5th	71	83	.461	22.0	Mayo Smith	934,798
1957	5th	77	77	.500	19.0	Mayo Smith	1,146,230
1958	8th	69	85	.448	23.0	Mayo Smith, Eddie Sawyer	931,110
1959	8th	64	90	.416	23.0	Eddie Sawyer	802,815
1960	8th	59	95	.383	36.0	Eddie Sawyer, Andy Cohen, Gene Mauch	862,205
1961	8th	47	107	.305	46.0	Gene Mauch	590,039
1962	7th	81	80	.503	20.0	Gene Mauch	762,034
1963	4th	87	75	.537	12.0	Gene Mauch	907,141
1964	2nd (Tie)	92	70	.568	1.0	Gene Mauch	1,425,891
1965	6th	85	76	.528	11.5	Gene Mauch	1,166,376
1966	4th	87	75	.537	8.0	Gene Mauch	1,108,201
1967	5th	82	80	.506	19.5	Gene Mauch	828,888
1968	7th (Tie)	76	86	.469	21.0	Gene Mauch, George Myatt, Bob Skinner	664,546

East Division

Year	Finish	Wins	Losses	Percentage	Games Behind	Manager	Attendance
1969	5th	63	99	.389	37.0	Bob Skinner, George Myatt	519,414
1970	5th	73	88	.453	15.5	Frank Lucchesi	708,247
1971	6th	67	95	.414	30.0	Frank Lucchesi	1,511,223
1972	6th	59	97	.378	37.5	Frank Lucchesi, Paul Owens	1,343,329

Year	Finish	Wins	Losses	Percentage	Games Behind	Manager	Attendance
1973	6th	71	91	.438	11.5	Danny Ozark	1,475,934
1974	3rd	80	82	.494	8.0	Danny Ozark	1,808,648
1975	2nd	86	76	.531	6.5	Danny Ozark	1,909,233
1976	1st	101	61	.623	+9.0	Danny Ozark	2,480,150
1977	1st	101	61	.623	+5.0	Danny Ozark	2,700,070
1978	1st	90	72	.556	+1.5	Danny Ozark	2,583,389
1979	4th	84	78	.519	14.0	Danny Ozark, Dallas Green	2,775,011
1980	1st	91	71	.562	+1.0	Dallas Green	2,651,650
1981*	1st/3rd	59	48	.551	+1.5/4.5	Dallas Green	1,638,752
1982	2nd	89	73	.549	3.0	Pat Corrales	2,376,394
1983	1st	90	72	.556	+6.0	Pat Corrales, Paul Owens	2,128,339
1984	4th	81	81	.500	15.5	Paul Owens	2,062,693
1985	5th	75	87	.463	26.0	John Felske	1,830,350
1986	2nd	86	75	.534	21.5	John Felske	1,933,335
1987	4th (Tie)	80	82	.494	15.0	John Felske, Lee Elia	2,100,110
1988	6th	65	96	.404	35.5	Lee Elia, John Vukovich	1,990,041
1989	6th	67	95	.414	26.0	Nick Leyva	1,861,985
1990	4th (Tie)	77	85	.475	18.0	Nick Leyva	1,992,484
1991	3rd	78	84	.481	20.0	Nick Leyva, Jim Fregosi	2,050,012
1992	6th	70	92	.432	26.0	Jim Fregosi	1,927,448
1993	1st	97	65	.599	+3.0	Jim Fregosi	3,137,674
1994	4th	54	61	.470	20.5	Jim Fregosi	2,290,971
1995	2nd (Tie)	69	75	.479	21.0	Jim Fregosi	2,043,598
1996	5th	67	95	.414	29.0	Jim Fregosi	1,801,677
1997	5th	68	94	.420	33.0	Terry Francona	1,490,638
1998	3rd	75	87	.463	31.0	Terry Francona	1,715,702
1999	3rd	77	85	.475	26.0	Terry Francona	1,825,337
2000	5th	65	97	.401	30.0	Terry Francona	1,612,769
2001	2nd	86	76	.531	2.0	Larry Bowa	1,782,460
2002	3rd	80	81	.497	21.5	Larry Bowa	1,618,141
2003	3rd	86	76	.531	15.0	Larry Bowa	2,259,940
2004	2nd	86	76	.531	10.0	Larry Bowa, Gary Varsho	3,250,092
2005	2nd	88	74	.543	2.0	Charlie Manuel	2,665,304
2006	2nd	85	77	.525	12.0	Charlie Manuel	2,701,815
2007	1st	89	73	.549	+1.0	Charlie Manuel	3,108,325
2008	1st	92	70	.568	+3.0	Charlie Manuel	3,422,583
2009	1st	93	69	.574	+6.0	Charlie Manuel	3,600,693
2010	1st	97	65	.599	+6.0	Charlie Manuel	3,377,322
2011	1st	102	60	.630	+13.0	Charlie Manuel	3,680,718
2012	3rd	81	81	.500	17.0	Charlie Manuel	3,565,718
2013	4th	73	89	.451	23.0	Charlie Manuel, Ryne Sandberg	3,012,403
2014	5th	73	89	.451	23.0	Ryne Sandberg	2,423,852
2015	5th	63	99	.389	27.0	Ryne Sandberg, Pete Mackanin	1,831,080
2016	4th	71	91	.438	24.0	Pete Mackanin	1,915,144
2017	5th	66	96	.407	31.0	Pete Mackanin	1,905,354
2018	3rd	80	82	.494	10.0	Gabe Kapler	2,158,124
2019	4th	81	81	.500	16.0	Gabe Kapler	2,727,421
2020	3rd	28	32	.467	7.0	Joe Girardi	0
2021	2nd	82	80	.506	6.5	Joe Girardi	1,515,890
2022	3rd	87	75	.537	14.0	Joe Girardi, Rob Thomson	2,276,736

* Split season.

Awards

Most Valuable Player
Chuck Klein, outfield, 1932
Jim Konstanty, pitcher, 1950
Mike Schmidt, third base, 1980
Mike Schmidt, third base, 1981
Mike Schmidt, third base, 1986
Ryan Howard, first base, 2006
Jimmy Rollins, shortstop, 2007
Bryce Harper, outfield, 2021

Rookie of the Year
Jack Sanford, pitcher, 1957
Dick Allen, third base, 1964
Scott Rolen, third base, 1997
Ryan Howard, first base, 2005

Cy Young
Steve Carlton, 1972
Steve Carlton, 1977
Steve Carlton, 1980
Steve Carlton, 1982
John Denny, 1983
Steve Bedrosian, 1987
Roy Halladay, 2010

Manager of the Year (Since 1983)
Larry Bowa, 2001

Hall of Famers Who Played for the Phillies
Pete Alexander, pitcher, 1911–17 and 1930
Richie Ashburn, outfield, 1948–59
Dave Bancroft, shortstop, 1915–20
Chief Bender, pitcher, 1916–17
Dan Brouthers, first base, 1896
Jim Bunning, pitcher, 1964–67 and 1970–71
Steve Carlton, pitcher, 1972–86
Roger Connor, first base, 1892
Ed Delahanty, outfield, 1888–89 and 1891–1901
Hugh Duffy, outfield, 1904–06
Johnny Evers, second base, 1917
Elmer Flick, outfield, 1898–1901
Jimmie Foxx, first base, 1945
Roy Halladay, 2010–13
Billy Hamilton, outfield, 1890–95
Ferguson Jenkins, pitcher, 1965–66
Hughie Jennings, infield, 1901–02
Jim Kaat, pitcher, 1976–79

Tim Keefe, pitcher, 1891–93
Chuck Klein, outfield, 1928–33, 1936–39, and 1940–44
Nap Lajoie, second base and first base, 1896–1900
Pedro Martinez, pitcher, 2009
Tommy McCarthy, outfield, 1886–87
Joe Morgan, second base, 1983
Kid Nichols, pitcher, 1905–06
Tony Perez, first base, 1983
Eppa Rixey, pitcher, 1912–17 and 1919–20
Robin Roberts, pitcher, 1948–61
Scott Rolen, third base, 1996–2002
Ryne Sandberg, shortstop, 1981
Mike Schmidt, third base, 1972–89
Casey Stengel, outfield, 1920–21
Jim Thome, first base, 2003–05, 2012
Sam Thompson, outfield, 1889–98
Lloyd Waner, outfield, 1942
Hack Wilson, outfield, 1934

Retired Numbers
PA ....Pete Alexander
HK .... Harry Kalas
CK .... Chuck Klein
1 .... Richie Ashburn
14 .... Jim Bunning
15 .... Dick Allen
20 .... Mike Schmidt
32 .... Steve Carlton
34 .... Roy Halladay
36 .... Robin Roberts

League Leaders, Batting (Post-1900)

Batting Average, Season
Sherry Magee, 1910 .... .331
Lefty O'Doul, 1929 .... .398
Chuck Klein, 1933 .... .368
Harry Walker*, 1947 .... .363
Richie Ashburn, 1955 .... .338
Richie Ashburn, 1958 .... .350
* .200 with St.L. Cardinals and .371 with Phi. Phillies.

Home Runs, Season
Gavvy Cravath, 1913 19
Gavvy Cravath, 1914 19
Gavvy Cravath, 1915 24
Gavvy Cravath, 1917 .... 12 (Tie)
Gavvy Cravath, 1918 8
Gavvy Cravath, 1919 12

Cy Williams, 1920 15
Cy Williams, 1923 41
Cy Williams, 1927 .... 30 (Tie)
Chuck Klein, 1929 43
Chuck Klein, 1931 31
Chuck Klein, 1932 .... 38 (Tie)
Chuck Klein, 1933 28
Mike Schmidt, 1974 36
Mike Schmidt, 1975 38
Mike Schmidt, 1976 38
Mike Schmidt, 1980 48
Mike Schmidt, 1981 31
Mike Schmidt, 1983 40
Mike Schmidt, 1984 .... 36 (Tie)
Mike Schmidt, 1986 37
Jim Thome, 2003 47
Ryan Howard, 2006 58
Ryan Howard, 2008 48
Kyle Schwarber, 2022 46

RBIs, Season
Sherry Magee, 1910 116
Gavvy Cravath, 1913 118
Sherry Magee, 1914 101
Gavvy Cravath, 1915 118
Chuck Klein, 1931 121
Don Hurst, 1932 143
Chuck Klein, 1933 120
Del Ennis, 1950 126
Greg Luzinski, 1975 120
Mike Schmidt, 1980 121
Mike Schmidt, 1981 91
Mike Schmidt, 1984 .... 106 (Tie)
Mike Schmidt, 1986 119
Darren Daulton, 1992 109
Ryan Howard, 2006 149
Ryan Howard, 2008 146
Ryan Howard, 2009 .... 141 (Tie)

Stolen Bases, Season
Chuck Klein, 1932 20
Danny Murtaugh, 1941 18
Richie Ashburn, 1948 32
Jimmy Rollins, 2001 .... 46 (Tie)

Total Bases, Season
Elmer Flick, 1900 305
Sherry Magee, 1910 263
Gavvy Cravath, 1913 298
Sherry Magee, 1914 277
Gavvy Cravath, 1915 266
Chuck Klein, 1930 445

Chuck Klein, 1931 347
Chuck Klein, 1932 420
Chuck Klein, 1933 365
Dick Allen, 1964............................352
Greg Luzinski, 1975 322
Mike Schmidt, 1976 306
Mike Schmidt, 1980 342
Mike Schmidt, 1981 228
Ryan Howard, 2006....................383

Most Hits, Season
Gavvy Cravath, 1913.................179
Sherry Magee, 1914 171
Lefty O'Doul, 1929.....................254
Chuck Klein, 1932 226
Chuck Klein, 1933 223
Richie Ashburn, 1951 221
Richie Ashburn, 1953 205
Richie Ashburn, 1958 215
Dave Cash, 1975 213
Pete Rose, 1981 140
Lenny Dykstra, 1990............192 (Tie)
Lenny Dykstra, 1993..................194
Ben Revere, 2014 ....184 (Tie)

Most Runs, Season
Roy Thomas, 1900 131
Sherry Magee, 1910 110
Gavvy Cravath, 1915...................89
Chuck Klein, 1930 158
Chuck Klein, 1931 ....121 (Tie)
Chuck Klein, 1932 152
Dick Allen, 1964..........................125
Mike Schmidt, 1981 78
Van Hayes, 1986................107 (Tie)
Lenny Dykstra, 1993..................143
Chase Utley, 2006 131
Jimmy Rollins, 2007 139

Batting Feats
Triple Crown Winners
Chuck Klein, 1933 (.368 BA, 28 HRs,
   120 RBIs)

Hitting for the Cycle
Lave Cross, Apr. 24, 1894
Sam Thompson, Aug. 17, 1894
Cy Williams, Aug. 5, 1927
Chuck Klein, Jul. 1, 1931
Chuck Klein, May 26, 1933
Johnny Callison, Jun. 27, 1963
Gregg Jefferies, Aug. 25, 1995
David Bell, Jun. 28, 2004

Six Hits in a Game (Post-1900)
Connie Ryan, Apr. 16, 1953

40 or More Home Runs, Season
58 ....Ryan Howard, 2006
48 ....Mike Schmidt, 1980
            Ryan Howard, 2008
47 ....Jim Thome, 2003
            Ryan Howard, 2007
46 ....Kyle Schwarber, 2022
45 ....Mike Schmidt, 1979
            Ryan Howard, 2009
43 ....Chuck Klein, 1929
42 ....Jim Thome, 2004
41 ....Cy Williams, 1923
40 ....Chuck Klein, 1930
            Dick Allen, 1966
            Mike Schmidt, 1983

League Leaders, Pitching (Post-1900)
Most Wins, Season
Pete Alexander, 1911 28
Tom Seaton, 1913.........................27
Pete Alexander, 1914.............27 (Tie)
Pete Alexander, 1915....................31
Pete Alexander, 1916....................33
Pete Alexander, 1917....................30
Jumbo Elliott, 1931 ....19 (Tie)
Robin Roberts, 1952.....................28
Robin Roberts, 1953.............23 (Tie)
Robin Roberts, 1954.....................23
Robin Roberts, 1955.....................23
Steve Carlton, 1972 27
Steve Carlton, 1977 23
Steve Carlton, 1980 24
Steve Carlton, 1982 23
John Denny, 1983 19
Roy Halladay, 2011 19

Most Strikeouts, Season
Pete Alexander, 1912..................195
Tom Seaton, 1913........................165
Pete Alexander, 1914..................214
Pete Alexander, 1915..................241
Pete Alexander, 1916..................167
Pete Alexander, 1917..................200
Kirby Higbe, 1940.......................137
Robin Roberts, 1953...................198
Robin Roberts, 1954...................185
Jack Sanford, 1957 188
Jim Bunning, 1967 253
Steve Carlton, 1972 310

Steve Carlton, 1974 240
Steve Carlton, 1980 286
Steve Carlton, 1982 286
Steve Carlton, 1983 275
Curt Schilling, 1997 319
Curt Schilling, 1998 300
Zack Wheeler, 2021 247

Lowest ERA, Season
Pete Alexander, 1915.................1.22
Pete Alexander, 1916.................1.55
Pete Alexander, 1917.................1.83
Steve Carlton, 1972 ....1.98

Most Saves, Season
Steve Bedrosian, 1987..................40

Best Won–Lost Percentage, Season
Pete Alexander, 1915...31–10.... .756
Steve Carlton, 1976 .....20–7 ... .741
John Denny, 1983 ....19–6 ... .760

Pitching Feats
Triple Crown Winner
Pete Alexander, 1915 (31–10,
   1.22 ERA, 241 SO)
Pete Alexander, 1916 (33–12,
   1.55 ERA, 167 SO)
Steve Carlton, 1972 (27–10,
   1.97 ERA, 310 SO)

20 Wins, Season
Al Orth, 1901 20–12
Frank Donahue, 1901............. 20–13
Togie Pittinger, 1905 23–14
Tully Sparks, 1907 22–8
George McQuillan, 1908........ 23–17
Earl Moore, 1910 22–15
Pete Alexander, 1911 28–13
Tom Seaton, 1913................... 27–12
Pete Alexander, 1913.............. 22–8
Pete Alexander, 1914............. 27–15
Erskine Mayer, 1914 21–19
Pete Alexander, 1915 31–10
Erskine Mayer, 1915 21–15
Pete Alexander, 1916 33–12
Eppa Rixey, 1916 22–10
Pete Alexander, 1917 30–13
Robin Roberts, 1950 20–11
Robin Roberts, 1951 21–15
Robin Roberts, 1952 28–7
Robin Roberts, 1953 23–16
Robin Roberts, 1954............... 23–15

Robin Roberts, 1955............... 23–14

Chris Short, 1966 20–10

Steve Carlton, 1972 27–10

Steve Carlton, 1976 20–7

Steve Carlton, 1977 23–10

Steve Carlton, 1980 24–9

Steve Carlton, 1982 23–11

Roy Halladay, 2010 21–10

No-Hitters

Chick Fraser (vs. Chi. Cubs), Sep. 18, 1903 (final: 10–0)

John Lush (vs. Brk. Dodgers), May 1, 1906 (final: 1–0)

Jim Bunning (vs. N.Y. Mets), Jun. 21, 1964 (final: 6–0) (perfect game)

Rick Wise (vs. Cin. Reds), Jun. 23, 1971 (final: 4–0)

Terry Mulholland (vs. S.F. Giants), Aug. 15, 1990 (final: 6–0)

Tommy Greene (vs. Mon. Expos), May 23, 1991 (final: 2–0)

Kevin Millwood (vs. S.F. Giants), Apr. 27, 2003 (final: 1–0)

Roy Halladay (vs. Fla. Marins), May 29, 2010 (final: 1–0) (Perfect Game)

Roy Halladay (vs. Cin. Reds), Oct. 6, 2010 (final: 4–0) (Postseason Game)

Cole Hamels, Jake Diekman, Ken Giles, Jonathan Papelbon (vs. Atl. Braves), Sep. 1, 2014 (final: 7–0)

Cole Hamels (vs. Chi. Cubs), Jul. 25, 2015 (final: 5–0)

No-Hitters Pitched Against

Hooks Wiltse, N.Y. Giants, Sep. 5, 1908 (final: 1–0) (10 innings)

Jeff Tesereau, N.Y. Giants, Sep. 6, 1912 (final: 3–0)

George Davis, Bos. Braves, Sep. 9, 1914 (final: 7–0)

Jesse Barnes, N.Y. Giants, May 7, 1922 (final: 6–0)

Dazzy Vance, Brk. Dodgers, Sep. 13, 1925 (final: 10–1)

Jim Wilson, Mil. Braves, Jun. 12, 1954 (final: 2–0)

Sal Maglie, Brk. Dodgers, Sep. 25, 1956 (final: 5–0)

Lew Burdette, Mil. Braves, Aug. 18, 1960 (final: 1–0)

Warren Spahn, Mil. Braves, Sep. 15, 1960 (final: 4–0)

Don Nottebart, Hou. Astros, May 17, 1963 (final: 4–1)

Sandy Koufax, L.A. Dodgers, Jun. 4, 1964 (final: 3–0)

George Culver, Cin. Reds, Jul. 29, 1968 (final: 6–1)

Bill Stoneman, Mon. Expos, Apr. 17, 1969 (final: 7–0)

Bill Singer, L.A. Dodgers, Jul. 20, 1970 (final: 5–0)

Burt Hooton, Chi. Cubs, Apr. 16, 1972 (final: 4–0)

Bob Forsch, St.L. Cardinals, Apr. 16, 1978 (final: 5–0)

Josh Beckett, L.A. Dodgers, May 25, 2014 (final: 6–0)

Tylor Megill, Drew Smith, Joely Rodriguez, Seth Lugo, Edwin Diaz, New York Mets, Apr. 29, 2022 (final: 3–0)

Cristian Javier, Bryan Abreu, Rafael Montero, Ryan Pressly, Hou. Astros, Nov. 2, 2022 (final: 5–0) (World Series)

Postseason Play

1915   World Series vs. Bos. Red Sox (AL), lost 4 games to 1

1950   World Series vs. N.Y. Yankees (AL), lost 4 games to 0

1976   League Championship Series vs. Cin. Reds, lost 3 games to 0

1977   League Championship Series vs. L.A. Dodgers, lost 3 games to 1

1978   League Championship Series vs. L.A. Dodgers, lost 3 games to 1

1980   League Championship Series vs. Hou. Astros, won 3 games to 2

World Series vs. K.C. Royals (AL), won 4 games to 2

1981   First-Half Division Playoff Series vs. Mon. Expos, lost 3 games to 2

1983   League Championship Series vs. L.A. Dodgers, won 3 games to 1

World Series vs. Bal. Orioles (AL), lost 4 games to 1

1993   League Championship Series vs. Atl. Braves, won 4 games to 2

World Series vs. Tor. Blue Jays (AL), lost 4 games to 2

2007   Division Series vs. Col. Rockies, lost 3 games to 0

2008   Division Series vs. Mil. Brewers, won 3 games to 1

League Championship vs. L.A. Dodgers, won 4 games to 1

World Series vs. T.B. Rays (AL), won 4 games to 1

2009   Division Series vs. Col. Rockies, won 3 games to 1

League Championship Series vs. L.A. Dodgers, won 4 games to 1

World Series vs. N.Y. Yankees (AL), lost 4 games to 2

2010   Division Series vs. Cin. Reds, won 3 games to 0

League Championship Series vs. S.F. Giants, lost 4 games to 2

2011   Division Series vs. St.L. Cardinals, lost 3 games to 2

2022   Wild Card Series vs. St.L. Cardinals, won 2 games to 0

Division Series vs. Atl. Braves, won 3 games to 1

League Championship Series vs. S.D. Padres, won 4 games to 1

World Series vs. Hou. Astros, lost 4 games to 2

Pittsburgh Pirates

Dates of Operation: 1882–present (141 years)
Overall Record: 10,687 wins, 10,647 losses (.501)
Stadiums: Exposition Park I, 1882–83; Exposition Park, 1883; Recreation Park, 1884–90;
  Exposition Park III, 1891–1909; Forbes Field, 1909–70; Three Rivers Stadium, 1970–2000;
  PNC Park, 2001–present (capacity: 38,362)
Other Names: Alleghenys, Innocents

Year-by-Year Finishes

Year	Finish	Wins	Losses	Percentage	Games Behind	Manager	Attendance
				American Association			
1882	4th	39	39	.500	15.0	Denny Driscoll	not available
1883	7th	31	67	.316	35.0	Al Pratt, Ormond Butler, Joe Battin	not available
1884	11th	30	78	.278	45.5	Denny McKnight, Bob Ferguson, Joe Battin, George Creamer, Horace Phillips	not available
1885	3rd	56	55	.505	22.5	Horace Phillips	not available
1886	2nd	80	57	.584	12.0	Horace Phillips	not available
				National League			
1887	6th	55	69	.444	24.0	Horace Phillips	not available
1888	6th	66	68	.493	19.5	Horace Phillips	not available
1889	5th	61	71	.462	25.0	Horace Phillips, Fred Dunlap, Ned Hanlon	not available
1890	8th	23	113	.169	66.5	Guy Hecker	not available
1891	8th	55	80	.407	30.5	Ned Hanlon, Bill McGunnigle	not available
1892	6th	80	73	.523	23.5	Tom Burns, Al Buckenberger	not available
1893	2nd	81	48	.628	4.5	Al Buckenberger	not available
1894	7th	65	65	.500	25.0	Al Buckenberger, Connie Mack	not available
1895	7th	71	61	.538	17.0	Connie Mack	not available
1896	6th	66	63	.512	24.0	Connie Mack	not available
1897	8th	60	71	.458	32.5	Patrick Donovan	not available
1898	8th	72	76	.486	29.5	Bill Watkins	not available
1899	7th	76	73	.510	15.5	Bill Watkins, Patsy Donovan	not available
1900	2nd	79	60	.568	4.5	Fred Clarke	not available
1901	1st	90	49	.647	+7.5	Fred Clarke	251,955
1902	1st	103	36	.741	+27.5	Fred Clarke	243,826
1903	1st	91	49	.650	+6.5	Fred Clarke	326,855
1904	4th	87	66	.569	19.0	Fred Clarke	340,615
1905	2nd	96	57	.627	9.0	Fred Clarke	369,124
1906	3rd	93	60	.608	23.5	Fred Clarke	394,877
1907	2nd	91	63	.591	17.0	Fred Clarke	319,506
1908	2nd (Tie)	98	56	.636	1.0	Fred Clarke	382,444
1909	1st	110	42	.724	+6.5	Fred Clarke	534,950
1910	3rd	86	67	.562	17.5	Fred Clarke	436,586
1911	3rd	85	69	.552	14.5	Fred Clarke	432,000
1912	2nd	93	58	.616	10.0	Fred Clarke	384,000
1913	4th	78	71	.523	21.5	Fred Clarke	296,000
1914	7th	69	85	.448	25.5	Fred Clarke	139,620
1915	5th	73	81	.474	18.0	Fred Clarke	225,743
1916	6th	65	89	.422	29.0	Jimmy Callahan	289,132
1917	8th	51	103	.331	47.0	Jimmy Callahan, Honus Wagner, Hugo Bezdek	192,807

Year	Finish	Wins	Losses	Percentage	Games Behind	Manager	Attendance
1918	4th	65	60	.520	17.0	Hugo Bezdek	213,610
1919	4th	71	68	.511	24.5	Hugo Bezdek	276,810
1920	4th	79	75	.513	14.0	George Gibson	429,037
1921	2nd	90	63	.588	4.0	George Gibson	701,567
1922	3rd (Tie)	85	69	.552	8.0	George Gibson, Bill McKechnie	523,675
1923	3rd	87	67	.565	8.5	Bill McKechnie	611,082
1924	3rd	90	63	.588	3.0	Bill McKechnie	736,883
1925	1st	95	58	.621	+8.5	Bill McKechnie	804,354
1926	3rd	84	69	.549	4.5	Bill McKechnie	798,542
1927	1st	94	60	.610	+1.5	Donie Bush	869,720
1928	4th	85	67	.559	9.0	Donie Bush	495,070
1929	2nd	88	65	.575	10.5	Donie Bush, Jewel Ens	491,377
1930	5th	80	74	.519	12.0	Jewel Ens	357,795
1931	5th	75	79	.487	26.0	Jewel Ens	260,392
1932	2nd	86	68	.558	4.0	George Gibson	287,262
1933	2nd	87	67	.565	5.0	George Gibson	288,747
1934	5th	74	76	.493	19.5	George Gibson, Pie Traynor	322,622
1935	4th	86	67	.562	13.5	Pie Traynor	352,885
1936	4th	84	70	.545	8.0	Pie Traynor	372,524
1937	3rd	86	68	.558	10.0	Pie Traynor	459,679
1938	2nd	86	64	.573	2.0	Pie Traynor	641,033
1939	6th	68	85	.444	28.5	Pie Traynor	376,734
1940	4th	78	76	.506	22.5	Frankie Frisch	507,934
1941	4th	81	73	.526	19.0	Frankie Frisch	482,241
1942	5th	66	81	.449	36.5	Frankie Frisch	448,897
1943	4th	80	74	.519	25.0	Frankie Frisch	604,278
1944	2nd	90	63	.588	14.5	Frankie Frisch	498,740
1945	4th	82	72	.532	16.0	Frankie Frisch	604,694
1946	7th	63	91	.409	34.0	Frankie Frisch, Spud Davis	749,962
1947	7th (Tie)	62	92	.403	32.0	Billy Herman, Bill Burwell	1,283,531
1948	4th	83	71	.539	8.5	Billy Meyer	1,517,021
1949	6th	71	83	.461	26.0	Billy Meyer	1,499,435
1950	8th	57	96	.373	33.5	Billy Meyer	1,166,267
1951	7th	64	90	.416	32.5	Billy Meyer	980,590
1952	8th	42	112	.273	54.5	Billy Meyer	686,673
1953	8th	50	104	.325	55.0	Fred Haney	572,757
1954	8th	53	101	.344	44.0	Fred Haney	475,494
1955	8th	60	94	.390	38.5	Fred Haney	469,397
1956	7th	66	88	.429	27.0	Bobby Bragan	949,878
1957	7th (Tie)	62	92	.403	33.0	Bobby Bragan, Danny Murtaugh	850,732
1958	2nd	84	70	.545	8.0	Danny Murtaugh	1,311,988
1959	4th	78	76	.506	9.0	Danny Murtaugh	1,359,917
1960	1st	95	59	.617	+7.0	Danny Murtaugh	1,705,828
1961	6th	75	79	.487	18.0	Danny Murtaugh	1,199,128
1962	4th	93	68	.578	8.0	Danny Murtaugh	1,090,648
1963	8th	74	88	.457	25.0	Danny Murtaugh	783,648
1964	6th (Tie)	80	82	.494	13.0	Danny Murtaugh	759,496
1965	3rd	90	72	.556	7.0	Harry Walker	909,279
1966	3rd	92	70	.568	3.0	Harry Walker	1,196,618
1967	6th	81	81	.500	20.5	Harry Walker, Danny Murtaugh	907,012
1968	6th	80	82	.494	17.0	Larry Shepard	693,485
					East Division		
1969	3rd	88	74	.543	12.0	Larry Shepard, Alex Grammas	769,369
1970	1st	89	73	.549	+5.0	Danny Murtaugh	1,341,947

Year	Finish	Wins	Losses	Percentage	Games Behind	Manager	Attendance
1971	1st	97	65	.599	+7.0	Danny Murtaugh	1,501,132
1972	1st	96	59	.619	+11.0	Bill Virdon	1,427,460
1973	3rd	80	82	.494	2.5	Bill Virdon, Danny Murtaugh	1,319,913
1974	1st	88	74	.543	+1.5	Danny Murtaugh	1,110,552
1975	1st	92	69	.571	+6.5	Danny Murtaugh	1,270,018
1976	2nd	92	70	.568	9.0	Danny Murtaugh	1,025,945
1977	2nd	96	66	.593	5.0	Chuck Tanner	1,237,349
1978	2nd	88	73	.547	1.5	Chuck Tanner	964,106
1979	1st	98	64	.605	+2.0	Chuck Tanner	1,435,454
1980	3rd	83	79	.512	8.0	Chuck Tanner	1,646,757
1981*	4th/6th	46	56	.451	5.5/9.5	Chuck Tanner	541,789
1982	4th	84	78	.519	8.0	Chuck Tanner	1,024,106
1983	2nd	84	78	.519	6.0	Chuck Tanner	1,225,916
1984	6th	75	87	.463	21.5	Chuck Tanner	773,500
1985	6th	57	104	.354	43.5	Chuck Tanner	735,900
1986	6th	64	98	.395	44.0	Jim Leyland	1,000,917
1987	4th (Tie)	80	82	.494	15.0	Jim Leyland	1,161,193
1988	2nd	85	75	.531	15.0	Jim Leyland	1,866,713
1989	5th	74	88	.457	19.0	Jim Leyland	1,374,141
1990	1st	95	67	.586	+4.0	Jim Leyland	2,049,908
1991	1st	98	64	.605	+14.0	Jim Leyland	2,065,302
1992	1st	96	66	.593	+9.0	Jim Leyland	1,829,395
1993	5th	75	87	.463	22.0	Jim Leyland	1,650,593

Central Division

Year	Finish	Wins	Losses	Percentage	Games Behind	Manager	Attendance
1994	3rd (Tie)	53	61	.465	13.0	Jim Leyland	1,222,520
1995	5th	58	86	.403	27.0	Jim Leyland	905,517
1996	5th	73	89	.451	15.0	Jim Leyland	1,332,150
1997	2nd	79	83	.488	5.0	Gene Lamont	1,657,022
1998	6th	69	93	.426	33.0	Gene Lamont	1,560,950
1999	3rd	78	83	.484	18.5	Gene Lamont	1,638,023
2000	5th	69	93	.426	26.0	Gene Lamont	1,748,908
2001	6th	62	100	.383	31.0	Lloyd McClendon	2,436,126
2002	4th	72	89	.447	24.5	Lloyd McClendon	1,784,993
2003	4th	75	87	.463	13.0	Lloyd McClendon	1,636,751
2004	5th	72	89	.447	32.5	Lloyd McClendon	1,583,031
2005	6th	67	95	.414	33.0	Lloyd McClendon, Pete Mackanin	1,817,245
2006	5th	67	95	.414	16.5	Jim Tracy	1,861,549
2007	6th	68	94	.420	17.0	Jim Tracy	1,749,142
2008	6th	67	95	.414	30.5	John Russell	1,609,076
2009	6th	62	99	.385	28.5	John Russell	1,577,853
2010	6th	57	105	.352	34.0	John Russell	1,613,399
2011	4th	72	90	.444	24.0	Clint Hurdle	1,940,429
2012	4th	79	83	.488	18.0	Clint Hurdle	2,091,918
2013	2nd	94	68	.580	2.0	Clint Hurdle	2,256,862
2014	2nd	88	74	.543	3.0	Clint Hurdle	2,442,564
2015	2nd	98	64	.605	2.0	Clint Hurdle	2,498,596
2016	3rd	78	83	.484	25.0	Clint Hurdle	2,249,201
2017	4th	75	87	.463	17.0	Clint Hurdle	1,919,447
2018	4th	82	80	.509	12.5	Clint Hurdle	1,465,316
2019	5th	69	93	.426	22.0	Clint Hurdle, Tom Prince	1,491,439
2020	5th	19	41	.317	15.0	Derek Shelton	0
2021	5th	61	101	.377	34.0	Derek Shelton	859,498
2022	4th (Tie)	62	100	.383	31.0	Derek Shelton	1,257,458

* Split season.

Awards

Most Valuable Player
Paul Waner, outfield, 1927
Dick Groat, shortstop, 1960
Roberto Clemente, outfield, 1966
Dave Parker, outfield, 1978
Willie Stargell (co-winner), first base, 1979
Barry Bonds, outfield, 1990
Barry Bonds, outfield, 1992
Andrew McCutchen, outfield, 2013

Rookie of the Year
Jason Bay, outfield, 2004

Cy Young
Vernon Law, 1960
Doug Drabek, 1990

Manager of the Year (Since 1983)
Jim Leyland, 1990
Jim Leyland, 1992
Clint Hurdle, 2013

Hall of Famers Who Played for the Pirates
Jake Beckley, first base, 1888–89 and 1891–96
Jim Bunning, pitcher, 1968–69
Max Carey, outfield, 1910–26
Jack Chesbro, pitcher, 1899–1902
Fred Clarke, outfield, 1900–11 and 1913–15
Roberto Clemente, outfield, 1955–72
Joe Cronin, infield, 1926–27
Kiki Cuyler, outfield, 1921–27
Pud Galvin, pitcher, 1887–89 and 1891–92
Goose Gossage, pitcher, 1977
Hank Greenberg, first base, 1947
Burleigh Grimes, pitcher, 1916–17, 1928–29, and 1934
Billy Herman, second base, 1947
Waite Hoyt, pitcher, 1933–37
Joe Kelley, outfield, 1891–92
George Kelly, first base, 1917
Ralph Kiner, outfield, 1946–53
Chuck Klein, outfield, 1939
Fred Lindstrom, outfield, 1933–34
Al Lopez, catcher, 1940–46
Connie Mack, catcher, 1891–96
Heinie Manush, outfield, 1938–39

Rabbit Maranville, shortstop, 1921–24
Bill Mazeroski, second base, 1956–72
Bill McKechnie, infield, 1907, 1910–12, 1918, and 1920
Billy Southworth, outfield, 1918–20
Willie Stargell, outfield and first base, 1962–82
Casey Stengel, outfield, 1918–19
Pie Traynor, third base, 1920–35 and 1937
Dazzy Vance, pitcher, 1915
Arky Vaughan, shortstop, 1932–41
Rube Waddell, pitcher, 1900–01
Honus Wagner, shortstop, 1900–17
Lloyd Waner, outfield, 1927–41 and 1944–45
Paul Waner, outfield, 1926–40
Vic Willis, pitcher, 1906–09

Retired Numbers
1	Billy Meyer
4	Ralph Kiner
8	Willie Stargell
9	Bill Mazeroski
11	Paul Waner
20	Pie Traynor
21	Roberto Clemente
33	Honus Wagner
40	Danny Murtaugh

League Leaders, Batting (Post-1900)

Batting Average, Season
Honus Wagner, 1900 .... .381
Ginger Beaumont, 1902 .... .357
Honus Wagner, 1903 .... .355
Honus Wagner, 1904 .... .349
Honus Wagner, 1906 .... .339
Honus Wagner, 1907 .... .350
Honus Wagner, 1908 .... .354
Honus Wagner, 1909 .... .339
Honus Wagner, 1911 .... .334
Paul Waner, 1927 .... .380
Paul Waner, 1934 .... .362
Arky Vaughan, 1935 .... .385
Paul Waner, 1936 .... .373
Debs Garms, 1940 .... .355
Dick Groat, 1960 .... .325
Roberto Clemente, 1961 .... .351
Roberto Clemente, 1964 .... .339
Roberto Clemente, 1965 .... .329
Matty Alou, 1966 .... .342

Roberto Clemente, 1967 .... .357
Dave Parker, 1977 .... .338
Dave Parker, 1978 .... .334
Bill Madlock, 1981 .... .341
Bill Madlock, 1983 .... .323
Freddy Sanchez, 2006 .... .344

Home Runs, Season
Tommy Leach, 1902 6
Ralph Kiner, 1946......................23
Ralph Kiner, 1947................51 (Tie)
Ralph Kiner, 1948................40 (Tie)
Ralph Kiner, 1949......................54
Ralph Kiner, 1950......................47
Ralph Kiner, 1951......................42
Ralph Kiner, 1952................37 (Tie)
Willie Stargell, 1971..................48
Willie Stargell, 1973..................44
Pedro Alvarez, 2013 ....36 (Tie)

RBIs, Season
Honus Wagner, 1907 91
Honus Wagner, 1908 106
Honus Wagner, 1909 102
Paul Waner, 1927....................131
Ralph Kiner, 1949....................127
Willie Stargell, 1973 119

Stolen Bases, Season
Honus Wagner, 1901 48
Honus Wagner, 1902 43
Honus Wagner, 1904 53
Honus Wagner, 1907 61
Honus Wagner, 1908 53
Max Carey, 1913 61
Max Carey, 1915 36
Max Carey, 1916 63
Max Carey, 1917 46
Max Carey, 1918 58
Max Carey, 1920 52
Max Carey, 1922 51
Max Carey, 1923 51
Max Carey, 1924 49
Max Carey, 1925 46
Kiki Cuyler, 1926......................35
Lee Handley, 1939............... 17 (Tie)
Johnny Barrett, 1944 28
Frank Tavaras, 1977 70
Omar Moreno, 1978..................71
Omar Moreno, 1979...................77
Tony Womack, 1997 60
Tony Womack, 1998 58

Total Bases, Season

Ginger Beaumont, 1903	272
Honus Wagner, 1904	255
Honus Wagner, 1906	237
Honus Wagner, 1907	264
Honus Wagner, 1908	308
Honus Wagner, 1909	242
Paul Waner, 1927	342
Ralph Kiner, 1947	361
Dave Parker, 1978	340

Most Hits, Season

Ginger Beaumont, 1902	194
Ginger Beaumont, 1903	209
Ginger Beaumont, 1904	185
Honus Wagner, 1908	201
Bobby Byrne, 1910	178 (Tie)
Honus Wagner, 1910	178 (Tie)
Paul Waner, 1927	237
Lloyd Waner, 1931	214
Paul Waner, 1934	217
Roberto Clemente, 1964	211 (Tie)
Roberto Clemente, 1967	209
Matty Alou, 1969	231
Dave Parker, 1977	215
Andy Van Slyke, 1992	199 (Tie)
Andrew McCutchen, 2012	194

Most Runs, Season

Honus Wagner, 1902	105
Ginger Beaumont, 1903	137
Honus Wagner, 1906	103 (Tie)
Tommy Leach, 1909	126
Max Carey, 1913	99 (Tie)
Kiki Cuyler, 1925	144
Kiki Cuyler, 1926	113
Lloyd Waner, 1927	133 (Tie)
Paul Waner, 1928	142
Paul Waner, 1934	122
Arky Vaughan, 1936	122
Arky Vaughan, 1940	113
Ralph Kiner, 1951	124 (Tie)
Barry Bonds, 1992	109

Batting Feats

Triple Crown Winners
[No player]

Hitting for the Cycle
Fred Carroll, May 2, 1887
Fred Clarke, Jul. 23, 1901
Fred Clarke, May 7, 1903

Chief Wilson, Jul. 3, 1910
Honus Wagner, Aug. 22, 1912
Dave Robertson, Aug. 30, 1921
Pie Traynor, Jul. 7, 1923
Kiki Cuyler, Jun. 4, 1925
Max Carey, Jun. 20, 1925
Arky Vaughan, Jun. 24, 1933
Arky Vaughan, Jul. 19, 1939
Bob Elliott, Jul. 15, 1945
Bill Salkeld, Aug. 4, 1945
Wally Westlake, Jul. 30, 1948
Wally Westlake, Jun. 14, 1949
Ralph Kiner, Jun. 25, 1950
Gus Bell, Jun. 4, 1951
Willie Stargell, Jul. 22, 1964
Richie Zisk, Jun. 9, 1974
Mike Easler, Jun. 12, 1980
Gary Redus, Aug. 25, 1989
Jason Kendall, May 19, 2000
Daryle Ward, May 27, 2004
John Jaso, Sep. 28, 2016

Six Hits in a Game (Post-1900)

Carson Bigbee, Aug. 22, 1917*
Max Carey, Jul. 7, 1922*
Johnny Gooch, Jul. 7, 1922*
Kiki Cuyler, Aug. 9, 1924
Paul Waner, Aug. 26, 1926
Lloyd Waner, Jun. 15, 1929
Johnny Hopp, May 14, 1950
Dick Groat, May 13, 1960
Rennie Stennett, Sep. 16, 1975
  (7 hits in game)
Wally Backman, Apr. 27, 1990
Freddy Sanchez, May 25, 2009
* Extra-inning game.

40 or More Home Runs, Season

54	Ralph Kiner, 1949
51	Ralph Kiner, 1947
48	Willie Stargell, 1971
47	Ralph Kiner, 1950
44	Willie Stargell, 1973
42	Ralph Kiner, 1951
40	Ralph Kiner, 1948

League Leaders, Pitching (Post-1900)

Most Wins, Season

Jack Chesbro, 1902	28
Wilbur Cooper, 1921	22 (Tie)
Roy Kremer, 1926	20 (Tie)

Lee Meadows, 1926	20 (Tie)
Burleigh Grimes, 1928	25 (Tie)
Ray Kremer, 1930	20 (Tie)
Heinie Meine, 1931	19 (Tie)
Rip Sewell, 1943	21 (Tie)
Bob Friend, 1958	22 (Tie)
Doug Drabek, 1990	22
John Smiley, 1991	20 (Tie)

Most Strikeouts, Season

Rube Waddell, 1900	133
Preacher Roe, 1945	148
Bob Veale, 1964	250

Lowest ERA, Season

Ray Kremer, 1926	2.61
Ray Kremer, 1927	2.47
Cy Blanton, 1935	2.59
Bob Friend, 1955	2.84
John Candelaria, 1977	2.34

Most Saves, Season

Dave Giusti, 1971	30
Mark Melancon, 2015	51

Best Won–Lost Percentage, Season

Jack Chesbro, 1901	21–9	.700
Jack Chesbro, 1902	28–6	.824
Sam Leever, 1903	25–7	.781
Sam Leever, 1905	20–5	.800
Howie Camnitz, 1909	25–6	.806 (Tie)
Claude Hendrix, 1912	24–9	.727
Emil Yde, 1924	16–3	.842
Ray Kremer, 1926	20–6	.769
Roy Face, 1959	18–1	.947
Steve Blass, 1968	18–6	.750
John Candelaria, 1977	20–5	.800
Jim Bibby, 1980	19–6	.760
Doug Drabek, 1990	22–6	.786
John Smiley, 1991	20–8	.714 (Tie)

Pitching Feats

20 Wins, Season

Jesse Tannehill, 1900	20–7
Deacon Phillippe, 1901	22–12
Jack Chesbro, 1901	21–9
Jack Chesbro, 1902	28–6
Jesse Tannehill, 1902	20–6
Deacon Phillippe, 1902	20–9
Sam Leever, 1903	25–7

Deacon Phillippe, 1903 25–9
Patsy Flaherty*, 1904............. 21–11
Sam Leever, 1905 20–5
Deacon Phillippe, 1905 20–13
Vic Willis, 1906 23–13
Sam Leever, 1906 22–7
Vic Willis, 1907 21–11
Lefty Leifield, 1907................ 20–16
Nick Maddox, 1908................. 23–8
Vic Willis, 1908 23–11
Howie Camnitz, 1909 25–6
Vic Willis, 1909 22–11
Babe Adams, 1911 22–12
Howie Camnitz, 1911 20–15
Claude Hendrix, 1912.............. 24–9
Howie Camnitz, 1912 22–12
Babe Adams, 1913 21–10
Al Mamaux, 1915................... 21–8
Al Mamaux, 1916.................. 21–15
Wilbur Cooper, 1920 24–15
Wilbur Cooper, 1921 22–14
Wilbur Cooper, 1922 23–14
Johnny Morrison, 1923 25–13
Wilbur Cooper, 1924 20–14
Ray Kremer, 1926.................... 20–6
Lee Meadows, 1926................. 20–9
Carmen Hill, 1927 22–11
Burleigh Grimes, 1928 25–14
Ray Kremer, 1930................. 20–12
Rip Sewell, 1943 21–9
Rip Sewell, 1944 21–12
Murry Dickson, 1951............. 20–16
Bob Friend, 1958................... 22–14
Vernon Law, 1960................... 20–9
John Candelaria, 1977 20–5
Doug Drabek, 1990 22–6
John Smiley, 1991.................... 20–8
* 2–2 with Chi. White Sox and 19–9 with
  Pit. Pirates.

No-Hitters

Nick Maddox (vs. Brk. Dodgers), Sep.
29, 1907 (final: 2–1)
Cliff Chambers (vs. Bos. Braves), May
6, 1951 (final: 3–0)
Bob Moose (vs. N.Y. Mets), Sep. 20,
1969 (final: 4–0)
Dock Ellis (vs. S.D. Padres), Jun. 12,
1970 (final: 2–0)
John Candelaria (vs. L.A. Dodgers),
Aug. 9, 1976 (final: 2–0)
Francisco Cordova and Ricardo Rincon
(vs. Hou. Astros), Jul. 12, 1997
(final: 3–0)

No-Hitters Pitched Against

Tom Hughes, Bos. Braves, Jun. 16,
1916 (final: 2–0)
Carl Hubbell, N.Y. Giants, May 8,
1929 (final: 11–0)
Sam Jones, Chi. Cubs, May 12, 1955
(final: 4–0)
Bob Gibson, St.L. Cardinals, Aug. 14,
1971 (final: 11–0)
Homer Bailey, Cin. Reds, Sep. 28,
2012 (final: 1–0)
Max Scherzer, Was. Nationals, Jun.
20, 2015 (final: 6–0)
Lucas Giolito, Chi. White Sox, Aug.
25, 2020 (final: 4–0)

Postseason Play

1903 World Series vs. Bos. Red Sox
      (AL), lost 5 games to 3
1909 World Series vs. Det. Tigers (AL),
      won 4 games to 3
1925 World Series vs. Was. Senators
      (AL), won 4 games to 3
1927 World Series vs. N.Y. Yankees
      (AL), lost 4 games to 0
1960 World Series vs. N.Y. Yankees
      (AL), won 4 games to 3
1970 League Championship Series vs.
      Cin. Reds, lost 3 games to 0
1971 League Championship Series vs.
      S.F. Giants, won 3 games to 1
      World Series vs. Bal. Orioles
      (AL), won 4 games to 3
1972 League Championship Series vs.
      Cin. Reds, lost 3 games to 2
1974 League Championship Series vs.
      L.A. Dodgers, lost 3 games
      to 1
1975 League Championship Series vs.
      Cin. Reds, lost 3 games to 0
1979 League Championship Series vs.
      Cin. Reds, won 3 games to 0
      World Series vs. Bal. Orioles
      (AL), won 4 games to 3
1990 League Championship Series vs.
      Cin. Reds, lost 4 games to 2
1991 League Championship Series vs.
      Atl. Braves, lost 4 games to 3
1992 League Championship Series vs.
      Atl. Braves, lost 4 games to 3
2013 NL Wild Card Playoff Game vs.
      Cin. Reds, won
      Division Series vs. St.L. Cardinals,
      lost 3 games to 2
2014 NL Wild Card Playoff Game vs.
      S.F. Giants, lost
2015 NL Wild Card Playoff Game vs.
      Chi. Cubs, lost

St. Louis Cardinals

Dates of Operation: 1882–present (141 years)
Overall Record: 11,131 wins, 10,232 losses (.521)
Stadiums: Sportsman's Park, 1876–92; Sportsman's Park II (formerly Robison Field and League
  Park, 1899–1911; Cardinal Field, 1918–20), 1892–1920; Sportsman's Park III (also known as
  Busch Stadium, 1954–66), 1920–66; Busch Memorial Stadium II, 1966–2005; Busch Stadium
  III, 2006–present (capacity: 43,975)
Other Names: Brown Stockings, Browns, Perfectos

Year-by-Year Finishes

Year	Finish	Wins	Losses	Percentage	Games Behind	Manager	Attendance
					American Association		
1882	5th	37	43	.463	18.0	Ned Cuthbert	not available
1883	2nd	65	33	.663	1.0	Ted Sullivan, Charles Comiskey	not available
1884	4th	67	40	.626	8.0	Jimmy Williams, Charles Comiskey	not available
1885	1st	79	33	.705	+16	Charles Comiskey	not available
1886	1st	93	46	.669	+12	Charles Comiskey	not available
1887	1st	95	40	.704	+14	Charles Comiskey	not available
1888	1st	92	43	.681	+6.5	Charles Comiskey	not available
1889	2nd	90	45	.667	2.0	Charles Comiskey	not available
1890	3rd	77	58	.570	12.5	Tommy McCarthy, John Kerins, James Roseman	not available
1891	2nd	85	51	.625	8.5	Charles Comiskey	not available
					National League		
1892	11th	56	94	.373	46.0	Chris Von der Ahe	not available
1893	10th	57	75	.432	29.0	Bill Watkins	not available
1894	9th	56	76	.424	35.0	George Miller	not available
1895	11th	39	92	.298	48.5	Al Buckenberger, Joe Quinn, Lew Phelan, Chris Von der Ahe	not available
1896	11th	40	90	.308	50.5	Harry Diddledock, Arlie Latham, Chris Von der Ahe, Roger Conner, Tommy Dowd	not available
1897	12th	29	102	.221	63.5	Tommy Dowd, Hugh Nicol, Bill Hallman, Chris Von der Ahe	not available
1898	12th	39	111	.260	63.5	Tim Hurst	not available
1899	5th	83	66	.557	9.5	Patsy Tebeau	not available
1900	5th (Tie)	65	75	.464	19.0	Patsy Tebeau, Louie Heilbroner	not available
1901	4th	76	64	.543	14.5	Patsy Donovan	379,988
1902	6th	56	78	.418	44.5	Patsy Donovan	226,417
1903	8th	43	94	.314	46.5	Patsy Donovan	226,538
1904	5th	75	79	.487	31.5	Kid Nichols	386,750
1905	6th	58	96	.377	47.5	Kid Nichols, Jimmy Burke, Matt Robison	292,800
1906	7th	52	98	.347	63.0	John McCloskey	283,770
1907	8th	52	101	.340	55.5	John McCloskey	185,377
1908	8th	49	105	.318	50.0	John McCloskey	205,129
1909	7th	54	98	.355	56.0	Roger Bresnahan	299,982
1910	7th	63	90	.412	40.5	Roger Bresnahan	355,668
1911	5th	75	74	.503	22.0	Roger Bresnahan	447,768
1912	6th	63	90	.412	41.0	Roger Bresnahan	241,759

Year	Finish	Wins	Losses	Percentage	Games Behind	Manager	Attendance
1913	8th	51	99	.340	49.0	Miller Huggins	203,531
1914	3rd	81	72	.529	13.0	Miller Huggins	256,099
1915	6th	72	81	.471	18.5	Miller Huggins	252,666
1916	7th (Tie)	60	93	.392	33.5	Miller Huggins	224,308
1917	3rd	82	70	.539	15.0	Miller Huggins	288,491
1918	8th	51	78	.395	33.0	Jack Hendricks	110,599
1919	7th	54	83	.394	40.5	Branch Rickey	167,059
1920	5th (Tie)	75	79	.487	18.0	Branch Rickey	326,836
1921	3rd	87	66	.569	7.0	Branch Rickey	384,773
1922	3rd (Tie)	85	69	.552	8.0	Branch Rickey	536,998
1923	5th	79	74	.516	16.0	Branch Rickey	338,551
1924	6th	65	89	.422	28.5	Branch Rickey	272,885
1925	4th	77	76	.503	18.0	Branch Rickey, Rogers Hornsby	404,959
1926	1st	89	65	.578	+2.0	Rogers Hornsby	668,428
1927	2nd	92	61	.601	1.5	Bob O'Farrell	749,340
1928	1st	95	59	.617	+2.0	Bill McKechnie	761,574
1929	4th	78	74	.513	20.0	Bill McKechnie, Billy Southworth	399,887
1930	1st	92	62	.597	+2.0	Gabby Street	508,501
1931	1st	101	53	.656	+13.0	Gabby Street	608,535
1932	6th (Tie)	72	82	.468	18.0	Gabby Street	279,219
1933	5th	82	71	.536	9.5	Gabby Street, Frankie Frisch	256,171
1934	1st	95	58	.621	+2.0	Frankie Frisch	325,056
1935	2nd	96	58	.623	4.0	Frankie Frisch	506,084
1936	2nd (Tie)	87	67	.565	5.0	Frankie Frisch	448,078
1937	4th	81	73	.526	15.0	Frankie Frisch	430,811
1938	6th	71	80	.470	17.5	Frankie Frisch, Mike Gonzalez	291,418
1939	2nd	92	61	.601	4.5	Ray Blades	400,245
1940	3rd	84	69	.549	16.0	Ray Blades, Mike Gonzalez, Billy Southworth	324,078
1941	2nd	97	56	.634	2.5	Billy Southworth	633,645
1942	1st	106	48	.688	+2.0	Billy Southworth	553,552
1943	1st	105	49	.682	+18.0	Billy Southworth	517,135
1944	1st	105	49	.682	+14.5	Billy Southworth	461,968
1945	2nd	95	59	.617	3.0	Billy Southworth	594,630
1946	1st	98	58	.628	+2.0	Eddie Dyer	1,061,807
1947	2nd	89	65	.578	5.0	Eddie Dyer	1,247,913
1948	2nd	85	69	.552	6.5	Eddie Dyer	1,111,440
1949	2nd	96	58	.623	1.0	Eddie Dyer	1,430,676
1950	5th	78	75	.510	12.5	Eddie Dyer	1,093,411
1951	3rd	81	73	.526	15.5	Marty Marion	1,013,429
1952	3rd	88	66	.571	8.5	Eddie Stanky	913,113
1953	3rd (Tie)	83	71	.539	22.0	Eddie Stanky	880,242
1954	6th	72	82	.468	25.0	Eddie Stanky	1,039,698
1955	7th	68	86	.442	30.5	Eddie Stanky, Harry Walker	849,130
1956	4th	76	78	.494	17.0	Fred Hutchinson	1,029,773
1957	2nd	87	67	.565	8.0	Fred Hutchinson	1,183,575
1958	5th (Tie)	72	82	.468	20.0	Fred Hutchinson, Stan Hack	1,063,730
1959	7th	71	83	.461	16.0	Solly Hemus	929,953
1960	3rd	86	68	.558	9.0	Solly Hemus	1,096,632
1961	5th	80	74	.519	13.0	Solly Hemus, Johnny Keane	855,305
1962	6th	84	78	.519	17.5	Johnny Keane	953,895
1963	2nd	93	69	.574	6.0	Johnny Keane	1,170,546
1964	1st	93	69	.574	+1.0	Johnny Keane	1,143,294

Year	Finish	Wins	Losses	Percentage	Games Behind	Manager	Attendance
1965	7th	80	81	.497	16.5	Red Schoendienst	1,241,201
1966	6th	83	79	.512	12.0	Red Schoendienst	1,712,980
1967	1st	101	60	.627	+10.5	Red Schoendienst	2,090,145
1968	1st	97	65	.599	+9.0	Red Schoendienst	2,011,167
				East Division			
1969	4th	87	75	.537	13.0	Red Schoendienst	1,682,783
1970	4th	76	86	.469	13.0	Red Schoendienst	1,629,736
1971	2nd	90	72	.556	7.0	Red Schoendienst	1,604,671
1972	4th	75	81	.481	21.5	Red Schoendienst	1,196,894
1973	2nd	81	81	.500	1.5	Red Schoendienst	1,574,046
1974	2nd	86	75	.534	1.5	Red Schoendienst	1,838,413
1975	3rd (Tie)	82	80	.506	10.5	Red Schoendienst	1,695,270
1976	5th	72	90	.444	29.0	Red Schoendienst	1,207,079
1977	3rd	83	79	.512	18.0	Vern Rapp	1,659,287
1978	5th	69	93	.426	21.0	Vern Rapp, Jack Krol, Ken Boyer	1,278,215
1979	3rd	86	76	.531	12.0	Ken Boyer	1,627,256
1980	4th	74	88	.457	17.0	Ken Boyer, Jack Krol, Whitey Herzog, Red Schoendienst	1,385,147
1981*	2nd/2nd	59	43	.578	1.5/0.5	Whitey Herzog	1,010,247
1982	1st	92	70	.568	+3.0	Whitey Herzog	2,111,906
1983	4th	79	83	.488	11.0	Whitey Herzog	2,317,914
1984	3rd	84	78	.519	12.5	Whitey Herzog	2,037,448
1985	1st	101	61	.623	+3.0	Whitey Herzog	2,637,563
1986	3rd	79	82	.491	28.5	Whitey Herzog	2,471,974
1987	1st	95	67	.586	+3.0	Whitey Herzog	3,072,122
1988	5th	76	86	.469	25.0	Whitey Herzog	2,892,799
1989	3rd	86	76	.531	7.0	Whitey Herzog	3,080,980
1990	6th	70	92	.432	25.0	Whitey Herzog, Red Schoendienst, Joe Torre	2,573,225
1991	2nd	84	78	.519	14.0	Joe Torre	2,448,699
1992	3rd	83	79	.512	13.0	Joe Torre	2,418,483
1993	3rd	87	75	.537	10.0	Joe Torre	2,844,328
				Central Division			
1994	3rd (Tie)	53	61	.465	13.0	Joe Torre	1,866,544
1995	4th	62	81	.434	22.5	Joe Torre, Mike Jorgensen	1,756,727
1996	1st	88	74	.543	+6.0	Tony La Russa	2,654,718
1997	4th	73	89	.451	11.0	Tony La Russa	2,634,014
1998	3rd	83	79	.512	19.0	Tony La Russa	3,194,092
1999	4th	75	86	.466	21.5	Tony La Russa	3,225,334
2000	1st	95	67	.586	+10.0	Tony La Russa	3,336,493
2001	1st (Tie)	93	69	.574	—	Tony La Russa	3,113,091
2002	1st	97	65	.599	+13.0	Tony La Russa	3,011,756
2003	3rd	85	77	.525	3.0	Tony La Russa	2,910,386
2004	1st	105	57	.648	+13.0	Tony La Russa	3,048,427
2005	1st	100	62	.617	+11.0	Tony La Russa	3,538,988
2006	1st	83	78	.516	+1.5	Tony La Russa	3,407,114
2007	3rd	78	84	.481	7.0	Tony La Russa	3,552,180
2008	4th	86	76	.531	11.5	Tony La Russa	3,430,660
2009	1st	91	71	.562	+7.5	Tony La Russa	3,343,252
2010	2nd	86	76	.531	5.0	Tony La Russa	3,301,218
2011	2nd	90	72	.556	6.0	Tony La Russa	3,093,954
2012	2nd	88	74	.543	9.0	Mike Matheny	3,262,109
2013	1st	97	65	.599	+3.0	Mike Matheny	3,369,769

Year	Finish	Wins	Losses	Percentage	Games Behind	Manager	Attendance
2014	1st	90	72	.556	+2.0	Mike Matheny	3,540,649
2015	1st	100	62	.617	+2.0	Mike Matheny	3,520,889
2016	2nd	86	76	.531	17.5	Mike Matheney	3,444,490
2017	3rd	83	79	.512	9.0	Mike Matheney	3,447,937
2018	3rd	88	74	.543	7.0	Mike Matheney, Mike Shildt	3,403,587
2019	1st	91	71	.562	+2.0	Mike Shildt	3,480,393
2020	2nd	30	28	.517	3.0	Mike Shildt	0
2021	2nd	90	72	.556	5.0	Mike Shildt	2,102,530
2022	1st	93	69	.574	+7.0	Oliver Marmol	3,320,551

* Split season.

Awards

Most Valuable Player

Rogers Hornsby, second base, 1925
Bob O'Farrell, catcher, 1926
Jim Bottomley, first base, 1928
Frankie Frisch, second base, 1931
Dizzy Dean, pitcher, 1934
Joe Medwick, outfield, 1937
Mort Cooper, pitcher, 1942
Stan Musial, outfield, 1943
Marty Marion, shortstop, 1944
Stan Musial, first base and outfield, 1946
Stan Musial, outfield, 1948
Ken Boyer, third base, 1964
Orlando Cepeda, first base, 1967
Bob Gibson, pitcher, 1968
Joe Torre, third base, 1971
Keith Hernandez (co-winner), first base, 1979
Willie McGee, outfield, 1985
Albert Pujols, first base, 2005
Albert Pujols, first base, 2008
Albert Pujols, first base, 2009
Paul Goldschmidt, first base, 2022

Rookie of the Year

Wally Moon, outfield, 1954
Bill Virdon, outfield, 1955
Bake McBride, outfield, 1974
Vince Coleman, outfield, 1985
Todd Worrell, pitcher, 1986
Albert Pujols, outfield, 2001

Cy Young

Bob Gibson, 1968
Bob Gibson, 1970
Chris Carpenter, 2005

Manager of the Year (Since 1983)

Whitey Herzog, 1985
Tony La Russa, 2002
Mike Shildt, 2019

Hall of Famers Who Played for the Cardinals

Pete Alexander, pitcher, 1926–29
Walter Alston, first base, 1936
Jake Beckley, first base, 1904–07
Jim Bottomley, first base, 1922–32
Roger Bresnahan, catcher, 1909–12
Lou Brock, outfield, 1964–79
Mordecai Brown, pitcher, 1903
Jesse Burkett, outfield, 1899–1901
Steve Carlton, pitcher, 1965–71
Orlando Cepeda, first base, 1966–68
Roger Connor, first base, 1894–97
Dizzy Dean, pitcher, 1930 and 1932–37
Leo Durocher, shortstop, 1933–37
Dennis Eckersley, pitcher, 1996–97
Frankie Frisch, second base, 1927–37
Pud Galvin, pitcher, 1892
Bob Gibson, pitcher, 1959–75
Burleigh Grimes, pitcher, 1930–31 and 1933–34
Chick Hafey, outfield, 1924–31
Jesse Haines, pitcher, 1920–37
Rogers Hornsby, second base, 1915–26 and 1933
Miller Huggins, second base, 1910–16
Jim Kaat, pitcher, 1980–83
Rabbit Maranville, shortstop, 1927–28
John McGraw, third base, 1900
Joe Medwick, outfield, 1932–40 and 1947–48
Minnie Minoso, outfield, 1962
Johnny Mize, first base, 1936–41
Stan Musial, outfield and first base, 1941–44 and 1946–63
Kid Nichols, pitcher, 1904–05
Wilbert Robinson, catcher, 1900
Scott Rolen, third base, 2002–07
Red Schoendienst, second base, 1945–56 and 1961–63
Ted Simmons, catcher, 1968–80
Enos Slaughter, outfield, 1938–42 and 1946–53
Lee Smith, pitcher, 1990–93
Ozzie Smith, shortstop, 1982–96
John Smoltz, pitcher, 2009
Billy Southworth, outfield, 1926–27 and 1929
Bruce Sutter, pitcher, 1981–84
Joe Torre, catcher, first base, third base, 1969–74
Dazzy Vance, pitcher, 1933–34
Larry Walker, outfield, 2004–05
Bobby Wallace, shortstop, 1899–1901 and 1917–18
Hoyt Wilhelm, pitcher, 1957
Vic Willis, pitcher, 1910
Cy Young, pitcher, 1899–1900

Retired Numbers

JB	Jack Buck
RH	Rogers Hornsby
1	Ozzie Smith
2	Red Schoendienst
6	Stan Musial
9	Enos Slaughter
10	Tony La Russa
14	Ken Boyer
17	Dizzy Dean
20	Lou Brock
23	Ted Simmons
24	Whitey Herzog
42	Bruce Sutter
45	Bob Gibson
85	August Busch Jr.

League Leaders, Batting (Post-1900)

Batting Average, Season

Jesse Burkett, 1901		.382
Rogers Hornsby, 1920		.370
Rogers Hornsby, 1921		.397
Rogers Hornsby, 1922		.401
Rogers Hornsby, 1923		.384
Rogers Hornsby, 1924		.424
Rogers Hornsby, 1925		.403

Chick Hafey, 1931 .... .349
Joe Medwick, 1937 .... .374
Johnny Mize, 1939 .... .349
Stan Musial, 1943 .... .357
Stan Musial, 1946 .... .365
Harry Walker*, 1947 .... .363
Stan Musial, 1948 .... .376
Stan Musial, 1950 .... .346
Stan Musial, 1951 .... .355
Stan Musial, 1952 .... .336
Stan Musial, 1957 .... .351
Joe Torre, 1971 .... .363
Keith Hernandez, 1979 .... .344
Willie McGee, 1985 .... .353
Willie McGee, 1990 .... .335
Albert Pujols, 2003 .... .359
* .371 with Phi. Phillies and .200 with St.L.
  Cardinals.

Home Runs, Season
Rogers Hornsby, 1922 42
Rogers Hornsby, 1925 39
Jim Bottomley, 1928 31
Rip Collins, 1934 .... 35 (Tie)
Joe Medwick, 1937 .... 31 (Tie)
Johnny Mize, 1939 28
Johnny Mize, 1940 43
Mark McGwire, 1988 70
Mark McGwire, 1999 65
Albert Pujols, 2009 47
Albert Pujols, 2010 42

RBIs, Season
Rogers Hornsby, 1920 .... 94 (Tie)
Rogers Hornsby, 1921 126
Rogers Hornsby, 1922 152
Rogers Hornsby, 1925 143
Jim Bottomley, 1926 120
Jim Bottomley, 1928 136
Joe Medwick, 1936 138
Joe Medwick, 1937 154
Joe Medwick, 1938 122
Johnny Mize, 1940 137
Enos Slaughter, 1946 130
Stan Musial, 1948 131
Stan Musial, 1956 109
Ken Boyer, 1964 119
Joe Torre, 1971 137
Mark McGwire, 1999 147
Albert Pujols, 2010 118

Stolen Bases, Season
Frankie Frisch, 1927 48
Frankie Frisch, 1931 28
Pepper Martin, 1933 26

Pepper Martin, 1934 23
Pepper Martin, 1936 23
Red Schoendienst, 1945 26
Lou Brock, 1966 74
Lou Brock, 1967 52
Lou Brock, 1968 62
Lou Brock, 1969 53
Lou Brock, 1971 64
Lou Brock, 1972 63
Lou Brock, 1973 70
Lou Brock, 1974 118
Vince Coleman, 1985 110
Vince Coleman, 1986 107
Vince Coleman, 1987 109
Vince Coleman, 1988 81
Vince Coleman, 1989 65
Vince Coleman, 1990 77

Total Bases, Season
Jesse Burkett, 1901 313
Rogers Hornsby, 1917 253
Rogers Hornsby, 1920 329
Rogers Hornsby, 1921 378
Rogers Hornsby, 1922 450
Rogers Hornsby, 1924 373
Rogers Hornsby, 1925 381
Jim Bottomley, 1926 305
Jim Bottomley, 1928 362
Rip Collins, 1934 369
Joe Medwick, 1935 365
Joe Medwick, 1936 367
Joe Medwick, 1937 406
Johnny Mize, 1938 326
Johnny Mize, 1939 353
Johnny Mize, 1940 368
Enos Slaughter, 1942 292
Stan Musial, 1943 347
Stan Musial, 1946 366
Stan Musial, 1948 429
Stan Musial, 1949 382
Stan Musial, 1951 355
Stan Musial, 1952 311
Joe Torre, 1971 352
Albert Pujols, 2003 394
Albert Pujols, 2004 389
Albert Pujols, 2008 342
Albert Pujols, 2009 374

Most Hits, Season
Jesse Burkett, 1901 228
Rogers Hornsby, 1920 218
Rogers Hornsby, 1921 235
Rogers Hornsby, 1922 250
Rogers Hornsby, 1924 227

Jim Bottomley, 1925 227
Joe Medwick, 1936 223
Joe Medwick, 1937 237
Enos Slaughter, 1942 188
Stan Musial, 1943 220
Stan Musial, 1944 .... 197 (Tie)
Stan Musial, 1946 228
Stan Musial, 1948 230
Stan Musial, 1949 207
Stan Musial, 1952 194
Curt Flood, 1964 .... 211 (Tie)
Joe Torre, 1971 230
Garry Templeton, 1979 211
Willie McGee, 1985 216
Albert Pujols, 2003 212
Matt Carpenter, 2013 199

Most Runs, Season
Jesse Burkett, 1901 139
Rogers Hornsby, 1921 131
Rogers Hornsby, 1922 141
Rogers Hornsby, 1924 .... 121 (Tie)
Pepper Martin, 1933 122
Joe Medwick, 1937 111
Stan Musial, 1946 124
Stan Musial, 1948 135
Stan Musial, 1951 .... 124 (Tie)
Stan Musial, 1952 .... 105 (Tie)
Solly Hemus, 1952 .... 105 (Tie)
Stan Musial, 1954 .... 120 (Tie)
Lou Brock, 1967 .... 113 (Tie)
Lou Brock, 1971 126
Keith Hernandez, 1979 116
Keith Hernandez, 1980 111
Lonnie Smith, 1982 120
Albert Pujols, 2003 137
Albert Pujols, 2004 133
Albert Pujols, 2005 129
Albert Pujols, 2009 124
Albert Pujols, 2010 115
Matt Carpenter, 2013 126

Batting Feats

Triple Crown Winners
Rogers Hornsby, 1922 (.401 BA,
  42 HRs, 152 RBIs)
Rogers Hornsby, 1925 (.403 BA,
  39 HRs, 143 RBIs)
Joe Medwick, 1937 (.374 BA, 31 HRs,
  153 RBIs)

Hitting for the Cycle
Fred Dunlap, May 24, 1886
Tip O'Neil, Apr. 30, 1887

Tip O'Neil, May 7, 1887
Tommy Dowd, Aug. 16, 1895
Cliff Heathcote, Jul. 13, 1918
Jim Bottomley, Jul. 15, 1927
Chick Hafey, Aug. 21, 1930
Pepper Martin, May 5, 1933
Joe Medwick, Jun. 29, 1935
Johnny Mize, Jul. 13, 1940
Stan Musial, Jul. 24, 1949
Bill White, Aug. 14, 1960
Ken Boyer, Sep. 14, 1961
Ken Boyer, Jun. 16, 1964
Joe Torre, Jun. 27, 1973
Lou Brock, May 27, 1975
Willie McGee, Jun. 23, 1984
Ray Lankford, Sep. 15, 1991
John Mabry, May 18, 1996
Mark Grudzielanek, Apr. 27, 2005
Nolan Arenado, Jul. 1, 2022

Six Hits in a Game (Post-1900)
Jim Bottomley, Sep. 16, 1924
Jim Bottomley, Aug. 5, 1931
Terry Moore, Sep. 5, 1935
Skip Schumaker, Jul. 26, 2008*
* Extra-inning game.

40 or More Home Runs, Season
70 ....Mark McGwire, 1998
65 ....Mark McGwire, 1999
49 ....Albert Pujols, 2006
47 ....Albert Pujols, 2009
46 ....Albert Pujols, 2004
43 ....Johnny Mize, 1940
        Albert Pujols, 2003
42 .... Rogers Hornsby, 1922
        Jim Edmonds, 2000
        Jim Edmonds, 2004
        Albert Pujols, 2010
41 ....Albert Pujols, 2005

League Leaders, Pitching (Post-1900)

Most Wins, Season
Flint Rhem, 1926................... 20 (Tie)
Bill Hallahan, 1931 .... 19 (Tie)
Dizzy Dean, 1934 30
Dizzy Dean, 1935 28
Mort Cooper, 1942......................22
Mort Cooper, 1943 .... 21 (Tie)
Red Barrett*, 1945 23
Howie Pollet, 1946 21
Ernie Broglio, 1960......................21 (Tie)
Bob Gibson, 1970 .... 23 (Tie)

Joaquin Andujar, 1984 20
Adam Wainwright, 2009 19
Adam Wainwright, 2013 ....19 (Tie)
Miles Mikolas, 2018 .... 18 (Tie)
* 2 with Bos. Beaneaters and 21 with
  St.L. Cardinals.

Most Strikeouts, Season
Fred Beebe*, 1906 171
Bill Hallahan, 1930....................177
Bill Hallahan, 1931 159
Dizzy Dean, 1932 191
Dizzy Dean, 1933 199
Dizzy Dean, 1934 195
Dizzy Dean, 1935 182
Harry Brecheen, 1948...............149
Sam Jones, 1958 225
Bob Gibson, 1968 268
Jose DeLeon, 1989.....................201
* 2 with Bos. Beaneaters and 21 with St.L.
  Cardinals.

Lowest ERA, Season
Bill Doak, 1914 ....1.72
Bill Doak, 1921 ....2.58
Mort Cooper, 1942 ....1.77
Howie Pollet, 1943 ....1.75
Howie Pollet, 1946 ....2.10
Harry Brecheen, 1948 ....2.24
Bob Gibson, 1968 ....1.12
John Denny, 1976.....................2.52
Joe Magrane, 1988 ....2.18
Chris Carpenter, 2009...............2.24

Most Saves, Season
Al Hrabosky, 1976...............22 (Tie)
Bruce Sutter, 1981 25
Bruce Sutter, 1982 36
Bruce Sutter, 1984 45
Todd Worrell, 1986.....................36
Lee Smith, 1991.........................47
Lee Smith, 1992.........................43
Jason Isringhausen, 2004.......47 (Tie)

Best Won–Lost Percentage, Season
Bill Doak, 1921 ....15–6 ... .714
Willie Sherdel, 1925....15–6 ... .714
Paul Derringer, 1931....18–8 ... .692
Dizzy Dean, 1934 ....30–7 ... .811
Mort Cooper, 1943 ......21–8 ... .724
Ted Wilks, 1944 ....17–4 ... .810
Harry Brecheen, 1945..15–4 ... .789
Murry Dickson, 1946....15–6 ... .714
Harry Brecheen, 1948 ..20–7 ... .741
Ernie Broglio, 1960......21–9 ... .700
Dick Hughes, 1967 ......16–6 ... .727
Bob Gibson, 1970 ....23–7 ... .767

Bob Tewksbury, 1992 ...16–5 ... .762
Chris Carpenter, 2009 ..17–4 ... .810
Kyle Lohse, 2012 ....16–3 ... .842
Miles Mikolas, 2018 ....18–4 ... .818

Pitching Feats

20 Wins, Season
Cy Young, 1900 20–18
Jack Harper, 1901 20–12
Bob Wicker*, 1903 20–9
Kid Nichols, 1904 21–13
Jack Taylor, 1904................... 20–19
Bob Harmon, 1911 23–16
Bill Doak, 1920 20–12
Jesse Haines, 1923 20–13
Flint Rhem, 1926...................... 20–7
Jesse Haines, 1927 24–10
Pete Alexander, 1927 21–10
Bill Sherdel, 1928 21–10
Jesse Haines, 1928 20–8
Dizzy Dean, 1933 20–18
Dizzy Dean, 1934 30–7
Dizzy Dean, 1935 28–12
Dizzy Dean, 1936 24–13
Curt Davis, 1939 22–16
Mort Cooper, 1942................... 22–7
Johnny Beazley, 1942............... 21–6
Mort Cooper, 1943 21–8
Mort Cooper, 1944................... 22–7
Red Barrett**, 1945 23–12
Howie Pollet, 1946 21–10
Howie Pollet, 1949 20–9
Harvey Haddix, 1953 20–9
Ernie Broglio, 1960................... 21–9
Ray Sadecki, 1964.................. 20–11
Bob Gibson, 1965 20–12
Bob Gibson, 1966 21–12
Bob Gibson, 1968 22–9
Bob Gibson, 1969 20–13
Bob Gibson, 1970 23–7
Steve Carlton, 1971 20–9
Bob Forsch, 1977 20–7
Joaquin Andujar, 1984 20–14
John Tudor, 1985 21–8
Joaquin Andujar, 1985 21–12
Darryl Kile, 2000..................... 20–9
Matt Morris, 2001 22–8
Chris Carpenter, 2005............. 21–5
Adam Wainwright, 2010 20–11
Adam Wainwright, 2014 , ... 20–9
* 0 0 with Chi. Cubs and 20–9 with
  St.L. Cardinals.
** 2–3 with Bos. Braves and 21–9 with
  St.L. Cardinals.

No-Hitters

Jesse Haines (vs. Bos. Braves),
Jul. 17, 1924 (final: 5–0)

Paul Dean (vs. Brk. Dodgers),
Sep. 21, 1934 (final: 3–0)

Lon Warneke (vs. Cin. Reds),
Aug. 30, 1941 (final: 2–0)

Ray Washburn (vs. S.F. Giants),
Sep. 18, 1968 (final: 2–0)

Bob Gibson (vs. Pit. Pirates),
Aug. 14, 1971 (final: 11–0)

Bob Forsch (vs. Phi. Phillies),
Apr. 16, 1978 (final: 5–0)

Bob Forsch (vs. Mon. Expos),
Sep. 26, 1983 (final: 3–0)

Jose Jimenez (vs. Ari. D'backs),
Jun. 25, 1999 (final: 1–0)

Bud Smith (vs. S.D. Padres),
Sep. 3, 2001 (final: 4–0)

No-Hitters Pitched Against

Christy Mathewson, N.Y. Giants,
Jul. 15, 1901 (final: 4–0)

Mal Eason, Brk. Dodgers,
Jul. 20, 1906 (final: 2–0)

Hod Eller, Cin. Reds, May 11, 1919
(final: 6–0)

Don Cardwell, Chi. Cubs,
May 15, 1960 (final: 4–0)

Gaylord Perry, S.F. Giants,
Sep. 17, 1968 (final: 1–0)

Tom Seaver, Cin. Reds, Jun. 16, 1978
(final: 4–0)

Fernando Valenzuela, L.A. Dodgers,
Jun. 29, 1990 (final: 6–0)

Johan Santana, N.Y. Mets,
Jun. 1, 2012 (final: 8–0)

Postseason Play

1926 World Series vs. N.Y. Yankees
(AL), won 4 games to 3

1928 World Series vs. N.Y. Yankees
(AL), lost 4 games to 0

1930 World Series vs. Phi. A's (AL), lost
4 games to 2

1931 World Series vs. Phi. A's (AL),
won 4 games to 3

1934 World Series vs. Det. Tigers (AL),
won 4 games to 3

1942 World Series vs. N.Y. Yankees
(AL), won 4 games to 1

1943 World Series vs. N.Y. Yankees
(AL), lost 4 games to 1

1944 World Series vs. St.L. Browns
(AL), won 4 games to 2

1946 Pennant Playoff Series vs. Brk.
Dodgers, won 2 games to 0
World Series vs. Bos. Red Sox
(AL), won 4 games to 3

1964 World Series vs. N.Y. Yankees
(AL), won 4 games to 3

1967 World Series vs. Bos. Red Sox
(AL), won 4 games to 3

1968 World Series vs. Det. Tigers (AL),
lost 4 games to 3

1982 League Championship Series vs.
Atl. Braves, won 3 games to 0
World Series vs. Mil. Brewers
(AL), won 4 games to 3

1985 League Championship Series vs.
L.A. Dodgers, won 4 games
to 2
World Series vs. K.C. Royals (AL),
lost 4 games to 3

1987 League Championship Series vs.
S.F. Giants, won 4 games to 3
World Series vs. Min. Twins (AL),
lost 4 games to 3

1996 Division Series vs. S.D. Padres,
won 3 games to 0
League Championship Series vs.
Atl. Braves, lost 4 games to 3

2000 Division Series vs. Atl. Braves,
won 3 games to 0
League Championship Series vs.
N.Y. Mets, lost 4 games to 1

2001 Division Series vs. Ari. D'backs,
lost 3 games to 2

2002 Division Series vs. Ari. D'backs,
won 3 games to 0
League Championship Series vs.
S.F. Giants, lost 4 games to 1

2004 Division Series vs. L.A. Dodgers,
won 3 games to 1
League Championship Series vs.
Hou. Astros, won 4 games
to 3
World Series vs. Bos. Red Sox
(AL), lost 4 games to 0

2005 Division Series vs. S.D. Padres,
won 3 games to 0
League Championship Series vs.
Hou. Astros, lost 4 games to 2

2006 Division Series vs. S.D. Padres,
won 3 games to 1
League Championship Series vs.
N.Y. Mets, won 4 games to 3
World Series vs. Det. Tigers (AL),
won 4 games to 1

2009 Division Series vs. L.A. Dodgers,
lost 3 games to 0

2011 Division Series vs. Phi. Phillies,
won 3 games to 2
League Championship Series vs.
Mil. Brewers, won 4 games
to 2
World Series vs. Tex. Rangers
(AL), won 4 games to 3

2012 NL Wild Card Playoff Game vs.
Atl. Braves, won
Division Series vs. Was.
Nationals, won 3 games to 2
League Championship Series vs.
S.F. Giants, lost 4 games to 3

2013 Division Series vs. Pit. Pirates,
won 3 games to 2
League Championship Series vs.
L.A. Dodgers, won 4 games to 2
World Series vs. Bos. Red Sox
(AL), lost 4 games to 2

2014 Division Series vs. L.A. Dodgers,
won 3 games to 1
League Championship Series vs.
S.F. Giants, lost 4 games to 1

2015 Division Series vs. Chi. Cubs, lost
3 games to 1

2019 Division Series vs. Atl. Braves,
won 3 games to 2
League Championship Series vs.
Was. Nationals, lost 4 games
to 0

2020 Wild Card Series vs. S.D.
Padres, lost 2 games to 1

2021 NL Wild Card Playoff Game vs.
L.A. Dodgers, lost

2022 Wild Card Series vs. Phi. Phillies,
lost 2 games to 0

San Diego Padres

Dates of Operation: 1969–present (54 years)

Overall Record: 3952 wins, 4568 losses (.464)

Stadiums: Qualcomm Stadium at Jack Murphy Field (formerly San Diego Stadium, 1969–79; San Diego–Jack Murphy Stadium, 1980; Jack Murphy Stadium, 1981–97), 1969–2003; Petco Park, 2004–present (capacity: 41,164)

Year-by-Year Finishes

Year	Finish	Wins	Losses	Percentage	Games Behind	Manager	Attendance
					West Division		
1969	6th	52	110	.321	41.0	Preston Gomez	512,970
1970	6th	63	99	.389	39.0	Preston Gomez	643,679
1971	6th	61	100	.379	28.5	Preston Gomez	557,513
1972	6th	58	95	.379	36.5	Preston Gomez, Don Zimmer	644,273
1973	6th	60	102	.370	39.0	Don Zimmer	611,826
1974	6th	60	102	.370	42.0	John McNamara	1,075,399
1975	4th	71	91	.438	37.0	John McNamara	1,281,747
1976	5th	73	89	.451	29.0	John McNamara	1,458,478
1977	5th	69	93	.426	29.0	John McNamara, Bob Skinner, Alvin Dark	1,376,269
1978	4th	84	78	.519	11.0	Roger Craig	1,670,107
1979	5th	68	93	.422	22.0	Roger Craig	1,456,967
1980	6th	73	89	.451	19.5	Jerry Coleman	1,139,026
1981*	6th/6th	41	69	.373	12.5/15.5	Frank Howard	519,161
1982	4th	81	81	.500	8.0	Dick Williams	1,607,516
1983	4th	81	81	.500	10.0	Dick Williams	1,539,815
1984	1st	92	70	.568	+12.0	Dick Williams	1,983,904
1985	3rd (Tie)	83	79	.512	12.0	Dick Williams	2,210,352
1986	4th	74	88	.457	22.0	Steve Boros	1,805,716
1987	6th	65	97	.401	25.0	Larry Bowa	1,454,061
1988	3rd	83	78	.516	11.0	Larry Bowa, Jack McKeon	1,506,896
1989	2nd	89	73	.549	3.0	Jack McKeon	2,009,031
1990	4th (Tie)	75	87	.463	16.0	Jack McKeon, Greg Riddoch	1,856,396
1991	3rd	84	78	.519	10.0	Greg Riddoch	1,804,289
1992	3rd	82	80	.506	16.0	Greg Riddoch, Jim Riggleman	1,722,102
1993	7th	61	101	.377	43.0	Jim Riggleman	1,375,432
1994	4th	47	70	.402	12.5	Jim Riggleman	953,857
1995	3rd	70	74	.486	8.0	Bruce Bochy	1,041,805
1996	1st	91	71	.562	+1.0	Bruce Bochy	2,187,886
1997	4th	76	86	.469	14.0	Bruce Bochy	2,089,333
1998	1st	98	64	.605	+9.5	Bruce Bochy	2,555,901
1999	4th	74	88	.457	26.0	Bruce Bochy	2,523,538
2000	5th	76	86	.469	21.0	Bruce Bochy	2,423,149
2001	4th	79	83	.488	13.0	Bruce Bochy	2,377,969
2002	5th	66	96	.407	32.0	Bruce Bochy	2,220,416
2003	5th	64	98	.395	36.5	Bruce Bochy	2,030,084
2004	3rd	87	75	.537	6.0	Bruce Bochy	3,016,752
2005	1st	82	80	.506	+5.0	Bruce Bochy	2,869,787
2006	1st (Tie)	88	74	.543	—	Bruce Bochy	2,659,754
2007	3rd	89	74	.546	1.5	Bud Black	2,790,074
2008	5th	63	99	.389	21.0	Bud Black	2,427,535
2009	4th	75	87	.463	20.0	Bud Black	1,922,600
2010	2nd	90	72	.556	2.0	Bud Black	2,131,774
2011	5th	71	91	.438	23.0	Bud Black	2,143,018
2012	4th	76	86	.469	18.0	Bud Black	2,123,721

Year	Finish	Wins	Losses	Percentage	Games Behind	Manager	Attendance
2013	3rd	76	86	.469	16.0	Bud Black	2,166,691
2014	3rd	77	85	.475	17.0	Bud Black	2,195,373
2015	4th	74	88	.457	18.0	Bud Black, Dave Roberts, Pat Murphy	2,459,742
2016	5th	68	94	.420	23.0	Andy Green	2,351,422
2017	4th	71	91	.438	33.0	Andy Green	2,138,491
2018	5th	66	96	.407	25.0	Andy Green	2,168,536
2019	5th	70	92	.432	36.0	Andy Green, Rod Barajas	2,396,399
2020	2nd	37	23	.617	6.0	Jayce Tingler	0
2021	3rd	79	83	.488	28.0	Jayce Tingler	2,191,950
2022	2nd	89	73	.549	22.0	Jayce Tingler	2,987,470

* Split season.

Awards

Most Valuable Player
Ken Caminiti, third base, 1996

Rookie of the Year
Butch Metzger (co-winner), pitcher, 1976
Benito Santiago, catcher, 1987

Cy Young
Randy Jones, 1976
Gaylord Perry, 1978
Mark Davis, 1989
Jake Peavy, 2007

Manager of the Year (Since 1983)
Bruce Bochy, 1996
Bud Black, 2010

Hall of Famers Who Played for the Padres
Rollie Fingers, pitcher, 1977–80
Goose Gossage, pitcher, 1984–87
Tony Gwynn, outfield, 1982–2001
Rickey Henderson, outfield, 1996–2001
Trevor Hoffman, pitcher, 1993–2008
Greg Maddux, pitcher, 2007–08
Willie McCovey, first base, 1974–76
Fred McGriff, first base, 1991–93
Gaylord Perry, pitcher, 1978–79
Mike Piazza, catcher, 2006
Ozzie Smith, shortstop, 1978–81
Dave Winfield, outfield, 1973–80

Retired Numbers
JC ....Jerry Coleman
RK.................................... Ray Kroc
6 .... Steve Garvey
19 ....Tony Gwynn
31 ....Dave Winfield
35 ....Randy Jones
51 ....Trevor Hoffman

League Leaders, Batting

Batting Average, Season
Tony Gwynn, 1984 .... .351
Tony Gwynn, 1987 .... .370
Tony Gwynn, 1988 .... .313
Tony Gwynn, 1989 .... .336
Gary Sheffield, 1992 .... .330
Tony Gwynn, 1994 .... .394
Tony Gwynn, 1995 .... .368
Tony Gwynn, 1996 .... .353
Tony Gwynn, 1997 .... .372

Home Runs, Season
Fred McGriff, 1992 35

RBIs, Season
Dave Winfield, 1979.................118
Chase Headley, 2012.................115

Stolen Bases, Season
Everth Cabrera, 2012...................44

Total Bases, Season
Dave Winfield, 1979.................333
Gary Sheffield, 1992 323

Most Hits, Season
Tony Gwynn, 1984 213
Tony Gwynn, 1986 211
Tony Gwynn, 1987 218
Tony Gwynn, 1989 203
Tony Gwynn, 1994 165
Tony Gwynn, 1995 .... 197 (Tie)
Tony Gwynn, 1997 220

Most Runs, Season
Tony Gwynn, 1986 .... 107 (Tie)

Batting Feats

Triple Crown Winners
[No player]

Hitting for the Cycle
Matt Kemp, Aug. 14, 2015
Wil Myers, Apr. 10, 2017

Six Hits in a Game
Gene Richards, Jul. 26, 1977*
Jim Lefebvre, Sep. 13, 1982*
Tony Gwynn, Aug. 4, 1993*
Adrian Gonzalez, Aug. 11, 2009
Jake Cronenworth, Jul. 16, 2021

* Extra-inning game.

40 or More Home Runs, Season
50 .... Greg Vaughn, 1998
42 ....Fernando Tatis Jr., 2021
41 ....Phil Nevin, 2001
40 .... Ken Caminiti, 1996
           Adrian Gonzalez, 2009

League Leaders, Pitching

Most Wins, Season
Randy Jones, 1976.......................22
Gaylord Perry, 1978 21
Jake Peavy, 2007.........................19

Most Strikeouts, Season
Andy Benes, 1994 189
Jake Peavy, 2005.......................216
Jake Peavy, 2007.......................240

Lowest ERA, Season
Randy Jones, 1975...................2.24
Jake Peavy, 2004......................2.27
Jake Peavy, 2007......................2.54

Most Saves, Season
Rollie Fingers, 1977 35
Rollie Fingers, 1978 37
Mark Davis, 1989........................44
Trevor Hoffman, 1998 53

Trevor Hoffman, 2006 46
Heath Bell, 2009 42
Kirby Yates, 2019 41
Mark Melancon, 2021..................39

Best Won–Lost Percentage, Season
Gaylord Perry, 1978 ....21–6... .778

Pitching Feats
Triple Crown Winner
Jake Peavy, 2007 (19–6, 2.54 ERA,
   240 SO)

20 Wins, Season
Randy Jones, 1975................. 20–12
Randy Jones, 1976................. 22–14
Gaylord Perry, 1978 21–6

No-Hitters
Joe Musgrove (vs. Tex Rangers), Apr. 9,
   2021 (final: 3–0)

No-Hitters Pitched Against
Dock Ellis, Pit. Pirates, Jun. 12, 1970
   (final: 2–0)
Milt Pappas, Chi. Cubs, Sep. 2, 1972
   (final: 8–0)

Phil Niekro, Atl. Braves, Aug. 5, 1973
   (final: 9–0)
Kent Mercker, Mark Wohlers, and
   Alejandro Pena, Atl. Braves, Sep.
   11, 1991 (final: 1–0)
A.J. Burnett, Fla. Marlins, May 12,
   2001 (final: 3–0)
Bud Smith, St.L. Cardinals, Sep. 3,
   2001 (final: 4–0)
Jonathan Sanchez, S.F. Giants, Jul. 10,
   2009 (final: 8–0)
Tim Lincecum, S.F. Giants, Jul. 13,
   2013 (final: 9–0)
Tim Lincecum, S.F. Giants, Jun. 25,
   2014 (final: 4–0)
Walker Buehler, Tony Cingrani, Yimi
   Garcia, Adam Liberatore, L.A.
   Dodgers, May 4, 2018 (final: 4–0)
Tyler Gilbert, Ari. D'backs, Aug. 14,
   2021 (final: 7–0)

Postseason Play
1984   League Championship Series vs.
        Chi. Cubs, won 3 games to 2

World Series vs. Det. Tigers (AL),
   lost 4 games to 1
1996   Division Series vs. St.L.
        Cardinals, lost 3 games to 0
1998   Division Series vs. Hou. Astros,
        won 3 games to 1
        League Championship Series vs.
        Atl. Braves, won 4 games to
        2
        World Series vs. N.Y. Yankees
        (AL), lost 4 games to 0
2005   Division Series vs. St.L.
        Cardinals, lost 3 games to 0
2006   Division Series vs. St.L.
        Cardinals, lost 3 games to 1
2007   NL Wild Card Playoff Game vs.
        Col. Rockies, lost
2020   Wild Card Series vs. St.L.
        Cardinals, won 2 games to 1
        Division Series vs. L.A. Dodgers,
        lost 3 games to 0

San Francisco Giants

Dates of Operation: 1958–present (65 years)
Overall Record: 5315 wins, 4956 losses (.517)
Stadiums: Seals Stadium, 1958–59; Candlestick Park (formerly 3Com Park, 1996–99), 1960–2000; Oracle Park (formerly Pacific Bell Park, or Pac Bell, 2000–03; SBC Park, 2004–05; AT&T Park, 2006–18), 2000–present (capacity: 41,915)

Year-by-Year Finishes

Year	Finish	Wins	Losses	Percentage	Games Behind	Manager	Attendance
1958	3rd	80	74	.519	12.0	Bill Rigney	1,272,625
1959	3rd	83	71	.539	4.0	Bill Rigney	1,422,130
1960	5th	79	75	.513	16.0	Bill Rigney, Tom Sheehan	1,795,356
1961	3rd	85	69	.552	8.0	Alvin Dark	1,390,679
1962	1st	103	62	.624	+1.0	Alvin Dark	1,592,594
1963	3rd	88	74	.543	11.0	Alvin Dark	1,571,306
1964	4th	90	72	.556	3.0	Alvin Dark	1,504,364
1965	2nd	95	67	.586	2.0	Herman Franks	1,546,075
1966	2nd	93	68	.578	1.5	Herman Franks	1,657,192
1967	2nd	91	71	.562	10.5	Herman Franks	1,242,480
1968	2nd	88	74	.543	9.0	Herman Franks	837,220
				West Division			
1969	2nd	90	72	.556	3.0	Clyde King	873,603
1970	3rd	86	76	.531	16.0	Clyde King, Charlie Fox	740,720
1971	1st	90	72	.556	+1.0	Charlie Fox	1,106,043
1972	5th	69	86	.445	26.5	Charlie Fox	647,744
1973	3rd	88	74	.543	11.0	Charlie Fox	834,193
1974	5th	72	90	.444	30.0	Charlie Fox, Wes Westrum	519,987
1975	3rd	80	81	.497	27.5	Wes Westrum	522,919
1976	4th	74	88	.457	28.0	Bill Rigney	626,868
1977	4th	75	87	.463	23.0	Joe Altobelli	700,056
1978	3rd	89	73	.549	6.0	Joe Altobelli	1,740,477
1979	4th	71	91	.438	19.5	Joe Altobelli, Dave Bristol	1,456,402
1980	5th	75	86	.466	17.0	Dave Bristol	1,096,115
1981*	5th/3rd	56	55	.505	10.0/3.5	Frank Robinson	632,274
1982	3rd	87	75	.537	2.0	Frank Robinson	1,200,948
1983	5th	79	83	.488	12.0	Frank Robinson	1,251,530
1984	6th	66	96	.407	26.0	Frank Robinson, Danny Ozark	1,001,545
1985	6th	62	100	.383	33.0	Jim Davenport, Roger Craig	818,697
1986	3rd	83	79	.512	13.0	Roger Craig	1,528,748
1987	1st	90	72	.556	+6.0	Roger Craig	1,917,168
1988	4th	83	79	.512	11.5	Roger Craig	1,785,297
1989	1st	92	70	.568	+3.0	Roger Craig	2,059,701
1990	3rd	85	77	.525	6.0	Roger Craig	1,975,528
1991	4th	75	87	.463	19.0	Roger Craig	1,737,478
1992	5th	72	90	.444	26.0	Roger Craig	1,561,987
1993	2nd	103	59	.636	1.0	Dusty Baker	2,606,354
1994	2nd	55	60	.478	3.5	Dusty Baker	1,704,608
1995	4th	67	77	.465	11.0	Dusty Baker	1,241,500
1996	4th	68	94	.420	23.0	Dusty Baker	1,413,922
1997	1st	90	72	.556	+2.0	Dusty Baker	1,690,869
1998	2nd	89	74	.546	9.5	Dusty Baker	1,925,634
1999	2nd	86	76	.531	14.0	Dusty Baker	2,078,399
2000	1st	97	65	.599	+11.0	Dusty Baker	3,315,330
2001	2nd	90	72	.556	2.0	Dusty Baker	3,277,244
2002	2nd	95	66	.590	2.5	Dusty Baker	3,253,205

Year	Finish	Wins	Losses	Percentage	Games Behind	Manager	Attendance
2003	1st	100	61	.621	+15.5	Felipe Alou	3,264,898
2004	2nd	91	71	.562	2.0	Felipe Alou	3,256,858
2005	3rd	75	87	.463	7.0	Felipe Alou	3,223,217
2006	3rd	76	85	.472	11.5	Felipe Alou	3,129,785
2007	5th	71	91	.438	19.0	Bruce Bochy	3,223,217
2008	4th	72	90	.444	12.0	Bruce Bochy	2,863,837
2009	3rd	88	74	.543	7.0	Bruce Bochy	2,861,113
2010	1st	92	70	.568	+2.0	Bruce Bochy	3,037,443
2011	2nd	86	76	.531	8.0	Bruce Bochy	3,387,303
2012	1st	94	68	.580	+8.0	Bruce Bochy	3,377,371
2013	3rd	76	86	.469	16.0	Bruce Bochy	3,369,106
2014	2nd	88	74	.543	6.0	Bruce Bochy	3,368,697
2015	2nd	84	78	.519	8.0	Bruce Bochy	3,375,882
2016	2nd	87	75	.537	40.0	Bruce Bochy	3,365,256
2017	5th	64	98	.395	40.0	Bruce Bochy	3,303,652
2018	4th	73	89	.451	18.0	Bruce Bochy	3,156,185
2019	3rd	77	85	.475	29.0	Bruce Bochy	2,707,760
2020	3rd	29	31	.483	14.0	Gabe Kapler	0
2021	1st	107	55	.660	+1.0	Gabe Kapler	1,679,484
2022	3rd	81	81	.500	30.0	Gabe Kapler	2,482,686

* Split season.

Awards

Most Valuable Player
Willie Mays, outfield, 1965
Willie McCovey, first base, 1969
Kevin Mitchell, outfield, 1989
Barry Bonds, outfield, 1993
Jeff Kent, second base, 2000
Barry Bonds, outfield, 2001
Barry Bonds, outfield, 2002
Barry Bonds, outfield, 2003
Barry Bonds, outfield, 2004
Busty Posey, catcher, 2012

Rookie of the Year
Orlando Cepeda, first base, 1958
Willie McCovey, first base, 1959
Gary Matthews, outfield, 1973
John Montefusco, pitcher, 1975
Buster Posey, catcher, 2010

Cy Young
Mike McCormick, 1967
Tim Lincecum, 2008
Tim Lincecum, 2009

Manager of the Year (Since 1983)
Dusty Baker, 1993
Dusty Baker, 1997
Dusty Baker, 2000
Gabe Kapler, 2021

Hall of Famers Who Played for the San Francisco Giants
Steve Carlton, pitcher, 1986
Gary Carter, catcher, 1990
Orlando Cepeda, first base, 1958–66
Goose Gossage, pitcher, 1989
Randy Johnson, pitcher, 2009
Juan Marichal, pitcher, 1960–73
Willie Mays, outfield, 1958–72
Willie McCovey, first base and outfield, 1959–73 and 1977–80
Joe Morgan, second base, 1981–82
Gaylord Perry, pitcher, 1962–71
Duke Snider, outfield, 1964
Warren Spahn, pitcher, 1965

Retired Numbers
CM .... Christy Mathewson
JM............................. John McGraw
RH .... Russ Hodges
LS .... Lon Simmons
3 ....Bill Terry
4 .... Mel Ott
11 .... Carl Hubbell
20 .... Monte Irvin
24 .... Willie Mays
25 .... Barry Bonds
27 .... Juan Marichal
30 .... Orlando Cepeda
36 .... Gaylord Perry
44 .... Willie McCovey

League Leaders, Batting

Batting Average, Season
Barry Bonds, 2002.................. .370
Barry Bonds, 2004.................. .363
Buster Posey, 2012.................. .336

Home Runs, Season
Orlando Cepeda, 1961 46
Willie Mays, 1962 49
Willie McCovey, 1963........... 44 (Tie)
Willie Mays, 1964 47
Willie Mays, 1965 52
Willie McCovey, 1968..................36
Willie McCovey, 1969..................45
Kevin Mitchell, 1989 47
Barry Bonds, 1993 46
Matt Williams, 1994 43
Barry Bonds, 2001......................73

RBIs, Season
Orlando Cepeda, 1961 142
Orlando Cepeda, 1967 111
Willie McCovey, 1968............. 105
Willie McCovey, 1969.............. 126
Will Clark, 1988 109
Kevin Mitchell, 1989 125
Matt Williams, 1990 122
Barry Bonds, 1993................... 123

Stolen Bases, Season
Willie Mays, 1958 31
Willie Mays, 1959 27

Total Bases, Season
Willie Mays, 1962 382
Willie Mays, 1965 360
Bobby Bonds, 1973 341
Kevin Mitchell, 1989 345
Will Clark, 1991 .... 303 (Tie)
Barry Bonds, 1993 365

Most Hits, Season
Willie Mays, 1960 190
Brett Butler, 1990 .... 192 (Tie)
Rich Aurilia, 2001 206

Most Runs, Season
Willie Mays, 1958 121
Willie Mays, 1961 129
Bobby Bonds, 1969 .... 120 (Tie)
Bobby Bonds, 1973 131
Brett Butler, 1988 109
Will Clark, 1989 .... 104 (Tie)

Batting Feats

Triple Crown Winners
[No player]

Hitting for the Cycle
Jim Ray Hart, Jul. 8, 1970
Dave Kingman, Apr. 16, 1972
Jeffrey Leonard, Jun. 27, 1985
Candy Maldonado, May 4, 1987
Chris Speier, Jul. 9, 1988
Robby Thompson, Apr. 22, 1991
Jeff Kent, May 3, 1999
Randy Winn, Aug. 15, 2005
Fred Lewis, May 13, 2007
Pablo Sandoval, Sep. 15, 2011

Six Hits in a Game
Jesus Alou, Jul. 10, 1964
Mike Benjamin, Jun. 14, 1995*
Randy Winn, Aug. 15, 2005
Fred Lewis, May 13, 2007
Brandon Crawford, Aug. 8, 2016
    (7 hits in game)
Andrew McCutchen, Apr. 7, 2018*
* Extra-inning game.

40 or More Home Runs, Season
73 .... Barry Bonds, 2001
52 .... Willie Mays, 1965
49 .... Willie Mays, 1962
                        Barry Bonds, 2000
47 .... Willie Mays, 1964
                        Kevin Mitchell, 1989

46 .... Orlando Cepeda, 1961
                Barry Bonds, 1993
                Barry Bonds, 2002
45 .... Willie McCovey, 1969
                Barry Bonds, 2003
                Barry Bonds, 2004
44 .... Willie McCovey, 1963
43 .... Matt Williams, 1994
42 .... Barry Bonds, 1996
40 .... Willie Mays, 1961
                Barry Bonds, 1997

League Leaders, Pitching

Most Wins, Season
Sam Jones, 1959 .... 21 (Tie)
Juan Marichal, 1963 .... 25 (Tie)
Mike McCormick, 1967 22
Juan Marichal, 1968 26
Gaylord Perry, 1970 .... 23 (Tie)
Ron Bryant, 1973 24
John Burnett, 1993 .... 22 (Tie)

Most Strikeouts, Season
Tim Lincecum, 2008 265
Tim Lincecum, 2009 261
Tim Lincecum, 2010 231

Lowest ERA, Season
Stu Miller, 1958 .... 2.47
Sam Jones, 1959 .... 2.82
Mike McCormick, 1960 .... 2.70
Juan Marichal, 1969 .... 2.10
Atlee Hammaker, 1983 .... 2.25
Scott Garrelts, 1989 .... 2.28
Bill Swift, 1992 .... 2.08
Jason Schmidt, 2003 .... 2.34

Most Saves, Season
Rob Nen, 2001 45
Brian Wilson, 2010 48

Best Won–Lost Percentage, Season
Juan Marichal, 1966 .... 25–6 ... .806
Jason Schmidt, 2003 .... 17–5 ... .773
Tim Lincecum, 2008 ..... 18–5 ... .783

Pitching Feats

20 Wins, Season
Sam Jones, 1959 21–15
Jack Sanford, 1962 24–7
Juan Marichal, 1963 25–8
Juan Marichal, 1964 21–8
Juan Marichal, 1965 22–13
Juan Marichal, 1966 25–6
Gaylord Perry, 1966 21–8
Mike McCormick, 1967 22–10
Juan Marichal, 1968 26–9
Juan Marichal, 1969 21–11
Gaylord Perry, 1970 23–13
Ron Bryant, 1973 24–12
Mike Krukow, 1986 20–9

John Burkett, 1993 22–7
Bill Swift, 1993 21–8

No-Hitters
Juan Marichal (vs. Hou. Astros), Jun. 15, 1963 (final: 1–0)
Gaylord Perry (vs. St.L. Cardinals), Sep. 17, 1968 (final: 1–0)
Ed Halicki (vs. N.Y. Mets), Aug. 24, 1975 (final: 6–0)
John Montefusco (vs. Atl. Braves), Sep. 29, 1976 (final: 9–0)
Jonathan Sanchez (vs. S.D. Padres), Jul. 10, 2009 (final 8–0)
Matt Cain (vs. Hou. Astros), Jun. 13, 2012 (final: 10–0) (perfect game)
Tim Lincecum (vs. S.D. Padres), Jul. 13, 2013 (final: 9–0)
Tim Lincecum (vs. S.D. Padres), Jun. 25, 2014 (final: 4–0)
Chris Heston (vs. N.Y. Mets), Jun. 9, 2015 (final: 5–0)

No-Hitters Pitched Against
Warren Spahn, Mil. Braves, Apr. 28, 1961 (final: 1–0)
Sandy Koufax, L.A. Dodgers, May 11, 1963 (final: 8–0)
Ray Washburn, St.L. Cardinals, Sep. 18, 1968 (final: 2–0)
Jerry Reuss, L.A. Dodgers, Jun. 27, 1980 (final: 8–0)
Charlie Lea, Mon. Expos, May 10, 1981 (final: 4–0)
Mike Scott, Hou. Astros, Sep. 25, 1986 (final: 2–0)
Terry Mulholland, Phi. Phillies, Aug. 15, 1990 (final: 6–0)
Kevin Gross, L.A. Dodgers, Aug. 17, 1992 (final: 2–0)
Kevin Brown, Fla. Marlins, Jun. 10, 1997 (final: 9–0)
Kevin Millwood, Phi. Phillies, Apr. 27, 2003 (final: 1–0)
Homer Bailey, Cin. Reds, Jul. 2, 2013 (final: 3–0)

Postseason Play

1962 Pennant Playoff Series vs. L.A. Dodgers, won 2 games to 1
    World Series vs. N.Y. Yankees (AL), lost 4 games to 3
1971 League Championship Series vs. Pit. Pirates, lost 3 games to 1
1987 League Championship Series vs. St.L. Cardinals, lost 4 games to 3
1989 League Championship Series vs. Chi. Cubs, won 4 games to 1
    World Series vs. Oak. A's (AL),

lost 4 games to 0

1997 Division Series vs. Fla. Marlins,
lost 3 games to 0

1998 NL Wild Card Playoff Game vs.
Chi. Cubs, lost

2000 Division Series vs. N.Y. Mets, lost
3 games to 1

2002 Division Series vs. Atl. Braves,
won 3 games to 1
League Championship Series vs.
St.L. Cardinals, won 4 games
to 1
World Series vs. Ana. Angels
(AL), lost 4 games to 3

2003 Division Series vs. Fla. Marlins,
lost 3 games to 1

2010 Division Series vs. Atl. Braves,
won 3 games to 1
League Championship Series vs.
Phi. Phillies, won 4 games to 2
World Series vs. Tex. Rangers
(AL), won 4 games to 1

2012 Division Series vs. Cin. Reds,
won 3 games to 2
League Championship Series vs. St.L.
Cardinals, won 4 games to 3
World Series vs. Det. Tigers (AL),
won 4 games to 0

2014 NL Wild Card Playoff Game vs.
Pit. Pirates, won
Division Series vs. Was.
Nationals, won 3 games to 1

League Championship Series vs. St.L.
Cardinals, won 4 games to 1
World Series vs. K.C. Royals
(AL), won 4 games to 3

2016 NL Wild Card Playoff Game vs.
N.Y. Mets, won
Division Series vs. Chi. Cubs, lost
3 games to 1

2021 Division Series vs. L.A, Dodgers,
lost 3 games to 2

Washington Nationals (formerly the Montreal Expos)

Dates of Operation: (as the Montreal Expos) 1969–2004 (36 years)
Overall Record: 2755 wins, 2943 losses (.484)
Stadiums: Jerry Park, 1969–76; Olympic Stadium, 1977–2004 (capacity: 46,500); Estadio Hiram
  Bithorn, San Juan, Puerto Rico (part of 2003 and 2004 seasons) (capacity: 18,000)

Dates of Operation: (as the Washington Nationals) 2005–present (18 years)
Overall Record: 1368 wins, 1444 losses (.486)
Stadiums: RFK Stadium, 2005–07; Nationals Park, 2008–present (capacity: 41,888)

Year-by-Year Finishes

Year	Finish	Wins	Losses	Percentage	Games Behind	Manager	Attendance
					Mon. Expos		
					East Division		
1969	6th	52	110	.321	48.0	Gene Mauch	1,212,608
1970	6th	73	89	.451	16.0	Gene Mauch	1,424,683
1971	5th	71	90	.441	25.5	Gene Mauch	1,290,963
1972	5th	70	86	.449	26.5	Gene Mauch	1,142,145
1973	4th	79	83	.488	3.5	Gene Mauch	1,246,863
1974	4th	79	82	.491	8.5	Gene Mauch	1,019,134
1975	5th (Tie)	75	87	.463	17.5	Gene Mauch	908,292
1976	6th	55	107	.340	46.0	Karl Kuehl, Charlie Fox	646,704
1977	5th	75	87	.463	26.0	Dick Williams	1,433,757
1978	4th	76	86	.469	14.0	Dick Williams	1,427,007
1979	2nd	95	65	.594	2.0	Dick Williams	2,102,173
1980	2nd	90	72	.556	1.0	Dick Williams	2,208,175
1981*	3rd/1st	60	48	.556	4.0/+0.5	Dick Williams, Jim Fanning	1,534,564
1982	3rd	86	76	.531	6.0	Jim Fanning	2,318,292
1983	3rd	82	80	.506	8.0	Bill Virdon	2,320,651
1984	5th	78	83	.484	18.0	Bill Virdon, Jim Fanning	1,606,531
1985	3rd	84	77	.522	16.5	Buck Rodgers	1,502,494
1986	4th	78	83	.484	29.5	Buck Rodgers	1,128,981
1987	3rd	91	71	.562	4.0	Buck Rodgers	1,850,324
1988	3rd	81	81	.500	20.0	Buck Rodgers	1,478,659
1989	4th	81	81	.500	12.0	Buck Rodgers	1,783,533
1990	3rd	85	77	.525	10.0	Buck Rodgers	1,373,087
1991	6th	71	90	.441	26.5	Buck Rodgers, Tom Runnells	934,742
1992	2nd	87	75	.537	9.0	Tom Runnells, Felipe Alou	1,669,077
1993	2nd	94	68	.580	3.0	Felipe Alou	1,641,437
1994	1st	74	40	.649	+6.0	Felipe Alou	1,276,250
1995	5th	66	78	.458	24.0	Felipe Alou	1,309,618
1996	2nd	88	74	.543	8.0	Felipe Alou	1,616,709
1997	4th	78	84	.481	23.0	Felipe Alou	1,497,609
1998	4th	65	97	.401	41.0	Felipe Alou	914,717
1999	4th	68	94	.420	35.0	Felipe Alou	773,277
2000	4th	67	95	.414	28.0	Felipe Alou	926,263
2001	5th	68	94	.420	20.0	Felipe Alou, Jeff Torborg	609,473
2002	2nd	83	79	.512	19.0	Frank Robinson	732,901
2003	4th	83	79	.512	18.0	Frank Robinson	1,025,639
2004	5th	67	95	.414	29.0	Frank Robinson	748,550
					Was. Nationals		
2005	5th	81	81	.500	9.0	Frank Robinson	2,731,993
2006	5th	71	91	.438	26.0	Frank Robinson	2,153,058
2007	4th	73	89	.451	16.0	Manny Acta	1,961,606

Year	Finish	Wins	Losses	Percentage	Games Behind	Manager	Attendance
2008	5th	59	102	.366	32.5	Manny Acta	2,320,400
2009	5th	59	103	.364	34.0	Manny Acta, Jim Riggleman	1,817,226
2010	5th	69	93	.425	28.0	Jim Riggleman	1,828,065
2011	3rd	80	81	.497	21.5	Jim Riggleman, Davey Johnson	1,940,478
2012	1st	98	64	.605	0.0	Davey Johnson	2,370,794
2013	2nd	86	76	.531	10.0	Davey Johnson	2,652,422
2014	1st	96	66	.597	+17.0	Matt Williams	2,579,389
2015	2nd	83	79	.512	7.0	Matt Williams	2,619,843
2016	1st	95	67	.586	+8.0	Dusty Baker	2,481,938
2017	1st	97	65	.599	+20.0	Dusty Baker	2,524,980
2018	2nd	82	80	.506	8.0	Dave Martinez	2,529,604
2019	2nd	93	69	.574	4.0	Dave Martinez	2,259,781
2020	5th	26	34	.433	9.0	Dave Martinez	0
2021	5th	65	97	.401	23.5	Dave Martinez	1,465,543
2022	5th	55	107	.340	46.0	Dave Martinez	2,026,401

* Split season.

Awards

Most Valuable Player
Bryce Harper, outfield, 2015

Rookie of the Year
Carl Morton, pitcher, 1970 (Mon.)
Andre Dawson, outfield, 1977 (Mon.)
Bryce Harper, outfield, 2012

Cy Young
Pedro Martinez, 1997 (Mon.)
Max Scherzer, 2016
Max Scherzer, 2017

Manager of the Year (Since 1983)
Buck Rodgers, 1987 (Mon.)
Felipe Alou, 1994 (Mon.)
Davey Johnson, 2012
Matt Williams, 2014

Hall of Famers Who Played for the Expos
Gary Carter, catcher, 1974–84 and 1992
Andre Dawson, outfield, 1976–86
Vladimir Guerrero, outfield, 1996–2003
Randy Johnson, pitcher, 1988–89
Pedro Martinez, pitcher, 1994–97
Tony Perez, first base, 1977–79
Tim Raines, outfield, 1979–90, 2001
Lee Smith, pitcher, 1997
Larry Walker, outfield, 1989–94

Hall of Famers Who Played for the Nationals
Ivan Rodriguez, catcher, 2010–11

Retired Numbers (Mon.)
CB .... Charles Bronfman
8 .... Gary Carter
10 .... Rusty Staub
10 .... Andre Dawson
11 .... Ryan Zimmerman
30 .... Tim Raines

League Leaders, Batting

Batting Average, Season
Al Oliver, 1982 (Mon.) .... .331
Tim Raines, 1986 (Mon.)........... .334
Juan Soto, 2020 .... .351
Trea Turner*, 2021 .... .328

* 322 with Was. Nationals and .338 with L.A. Dodgers.

Home Runs, Season
Bryce Harper, 2015.................. 42 (Tie)

RBIs, Season
Al Oliver, 1982 (Mon.) .... 109 (Tie)
Gary Carter, 1984 (Mon.).... 106 (Tie)

Stolen Bases, Season
Ron LeFlore, 1980 (Mon.).............. 97
Tim Raines, 1981 (Mon.)............... 71
Tim Raines, 1982 (Mon.)............... 78
Tim Raines, 1983 (Mon.)............... 90
Tim Raines, 1984 (Mon.)............... 75
Marquis Grissom, 1991 (Mon.) 76
Marquis Grissom, 1992 (Mon.) 78
Trea Turner, 2018 43
Trea Turner*, 2021 32

* 21 with Was. Nationals and 11 with L.A. Dodgers.

Total Bases, Season
Al Oliver, 1982 (Mon.) 317
Andre Dawson, 1983 (Mon.) 341
Andres Galarraga, 1988 (Mon.) .. 329
Vladimir Guerrero, 2002 (Mon.) .. 364
Trea Turner*, 2021 319

* 202 with Was. Nationals and 117 with L.A. Dodgers.

Most Hits, Season
Al Oliver, 1982 (Mon.) 204
Andre Dawson, 1983 (Mon.)] 189 (Tie)
Andres Galarraga, 1988 (Mon.) .. 184
Vladimir Guerrero, 2002 (Mon.) .. 206
Denard Span, 2014 .... 184 (Tie)
Trea Turner*, 2021 195

* 125 with Was. Nationals and 70 with L.A. Dodgers.

Most Runs, Season
Tim Raines, 1983 (Mon.)............. 133
Tim Raines, 1987 (Mon.)............. 123
Anthony Rendon, 2014............... 111
Bryce Harper, 2015 118

Batting Feats

Triple Crown Winners
[No player]

Hitting for the Cycle
Tim Foli, Apr. 22, 1976 (Mon.)
Chris Speier, Jul. 20, 1978 (Mon.)
Tim Raines, Aug. 16, 1987 (Mon.)
Rondell White, Jun. 11, 1995 (Mon.)
Brad Wilkerson, Jun. 24, 2003 (Mon.)
Vladimir Guerrero, Sep. 14, 2003 (Mon.)
Trea Turner, Apr. 25, 2017

Trea Turner, Jul. 23, 2019
Trea Turner, Jun. 30, 2021

Six Hits in a Game
Rondell White, Jun. 11, 1995*
   (Mon.)
Brad Wilkerson, Apr. 6, 2005
Cristian Guzman, Aug. 28, 2008
Anthony Rendon, Apr. 30, 2017
* Extra-inning game.

40 or More Home Runs, Season
46 .... Alfonso Soriano, 2006
44 .... Vladimir Guerrero, 2000 (Mon.)
42 .... Vladimir Guerrero, 1999 (Mon.)
         Bryce Harper, 2015

League Leaders, Pitching

Most Wins, Season
Ken Hill, 1994 (Mon.) .... 16 (Tie)
Gio Gonzalez, 2012 21
Jordan Zimmerman, 2013 ...... 19 (Tie)
Max Scherzer, 2016 20
Max Scherzer, 2018 .... 18 (Tie)
Stephen Strasburg, 2019 18

Most Strikeouts, Season
Stephen Strasburg, 2014 ..... 242 (Tie)
Max Scherzer, 2016 284
Max Scherzer, 2017 268
Max Scherzer, 2018 300

Lowest ERA, Season
Steve Rogers, 1982 (Mon.) 2.40
Dennis Martinez, 1991 (Mon.) 2.39
Pedro Martinez, 1997 (Mon.) 1.90

Most Saves, Season
Mike Marshall, 1973 (Mon.) 31
Jeff Reardon, 1985 (Mon.) 41
Ugueth Urbina, 1999 (Mon.) 41
Chad Cordero, 2005 47

Best Won–Lost Percentage, Season
[No player]

Pitching Feats

20 Wins, Season
Ross Grimsley, 1978 (Mon.) 20–11
Bartolo Colon*, 2002 (Mon.) 20–8
Gio Gonzalez, 2012 21–8
Max Scherzer, 2016 20–7
* 10–4 with Cle. Indians (AL) and 10–4 with Mon. Expos.

No-Hitters
Bill Stoneman (vs. Phi. Phillies), Apr.
   17, 1969 (final: 7–0) (Mon.)
Bill Stoneman (vs. N.Y. Mets), Oct. 2,
   1972 (final: 7–0) (Mon.)
Charlie Lea (vs. S.F. Giants), May 10,
   1981 (final: 4–0) (Mon.)
Dennis Martinez (Mon.) (vs. L.A.
   Dodgers), Jul. 28, 1991 (final: 2–0)
   (perfect game) (Mon.)
Jordan Zimmermann (vs. Mia. Marlins),
   Sep. 28, 2014 (final: 1–0)
Max Scherzer (vs. Pit. Pirates), Jun. 20,
   2015 (final: 6–0)
Max Scherzer (vs. N.Y. Mets), Oct. 3,
   2015 (final: 2–0)
No-Hitters Pitched Against
Larry Dierker, Hou. Astros, Jul. 9,
   1976 (final: 6–0) (Mon.)

Bob Forsch, St.L. Cardinals, Sep. 26,
   1983 (final: 3–0) (Mon.)
Tommy Greene, Phi. Phillies, May 23,
   1991 (final: 2–0) (Mon.)
David Cone, N.Y. Yankees (AL), Jul.
   18, 1999 (final: 6–0) (perfect game)
   (Mon.)

Postseason Play

1981   Second-Half Division Playoff
         Series vs. Phi. Phillies, won 3
         games to 2 (Mon.)
         League Championship Series vs.
         L.A. Dodgers, lost 3 games
         to 2 (Mon.)
2012   Division Series vs. St.L. Cardinals,
         lost 3 games to 2
2014   Division Series vs. S.F. Giants,
         lost 3 games to 1
2016   Division Series vs. L.A. Dodgers,
         lost 3 games to 2
2017   Division Series vs. Chi. Cubs, lost
         3 games to 2
2019   NL Wild Card Playoff Game vs.
         Mil. Brewers, won
         Division Series vs. L.A. Dodgers,
         won 3 games to 2
         League Championship Series vs.
         St.L. Cardinals, won 4 games
         to 0
         World Series vs. Hou. Astros
         (AL), won 4 games to 3

Baltimore Orioles

Dates of Operation: 1901–02
Overall Record: 118 wins, 153 losses (.435)
Stadiums: Oriole Park IV

Year-by-Year Finishes

Year	Finish	Wins	Losses	Percentage	Games Behind	Manager	Attendance
1901	5th	68	65	.511	13.5	John McGraw	141,952
1902	8th	50	88	.362	34.0	John McGraw, Wilbert Robinson	174,606

Awards

Most Valuable Player
[No player]

Rookie of the Year
[No player]

Cy Young
[No player]

**Hall of Famers Who Played
for the Baltimore Orioles**
Roger Bresnahan, catcher, third base,
and outfield, 1901–02
Joe Kelley, outfield, 1902
Joe McGinnity, pitcher, 1901–02
John McGraw, third base, 1901–02
Wilbert Robinson, catcher, 1901–02

League Leaders, Batting

Batting Average, Season
[No player]

Home Runs, Season
[No player]

RBIs, Season
[No player]

Stolen Bases, Season
[No player]

Total Bases, Season
[No player]

Most Hits, Season
[No player]

Most Runs, Season
[No player]

Batting Feats

Triple Crown Winners
[No player]

Hitting for the Cycle
[No player]

Six Hits in a Game
Mike Donlin, Jun. 24, 1901
Jimmy Williams, Aug. 25, 1902

40 or More Home Runs, Season
[No player]

League Leaders,
Pitching (Post-1900)

Most Wins, Season
[No player]

Most Strikeouts, Season
[No player]

Lowest ERA, Season
[No player]

Most Saves, Season
[No player]

Pitching Feats

Triple Crown Winner
[No player]

20 Wins, Season
Joe McGinnity, 1901 26–20

No-Hitters
[No player]

No-Hitters Pitched Against
[No player]

Postseason Play

[None]

Boston Braves

Dates of Operation: 1876–1952 (77 years)
Overall Record: 5118 wins, 5598 losses (.478)
Stadiums: South End Grounds, 1876–93 and 1895–1914; Congress Street Grounds, 1894; Fenway Park, 1914–15 and 1946; Braves Field, 1915–52 (capacity: 44,500)
Other Names: Red Stockings, Red Caps, Beaneaters, Nationals, Doves, Rustlers, Bees

Year-by-Year Finishes

Year	Finish	Wins	Losses	Percentage	Games Behind	Manager	Attendance
1876	4th	39	31	.557	15.0	Harry Wright	not available
1877	1st	42	18	.700	+7.0	Harry Wright	not available
1878	1st	41	19	.683	+4.0	Harry Wright	not available
1879	2nd	49	29	.628	6.0	Harry Wright	not available
1880	6th	40	44	.476	27.0	Harry Wright	not available
1881	6th	38	45	.458	17.5	Harry Wright	not available
1882	3rd (Tie)	45	39	.536	10.0	John Morrill	not available
1883	1st	63	35	.643	+4.0	Jack Burdock, John Morrill	not available
1884	2nd	73	38	.658	10.5	John Morrill	not available
1885	5th	48	66	.410	31.0	John Morrill	not available
1886	5th	56	61	.478	30.5	John Morrill	not available
1887	5th	61	60	.504	16.5	John Morrill	not available
1888	4th	70	64	.522	15.5	John Morrill	not available
1889	2nd	83	45	.648	1.0	Jim Hart	not available
1890	5th	76	57	.571	12.0	Frank Selee	not available
1891	1st	87	51	.630	+3.5	Frank Selee	not available
1892	1st	102	48	.680	+9.5	Frank Selee	not available
1893	1st	86	44	.662	+4.5	Frank Selee	not available
1894	3rd	83	49	.629	8.0	Frank Selee	not available
1895	5th (Tie)	71	60	.542	16.5	Frank Selee	not available
1896	4th	74	57	.565	17.0	Frank Selee	not available
1897	1st	93	39	.705	+2.0	Frank Selee	not available
1898	1st	102	47	.685	+6.0	Frank Selee	not available
1899	2nd	95	57	.625	4.0	Frank Selee	not available
1900	4th	66	72	.478	17.0	Frank Selee	not available
1901	5th	69	69	.500	20.5	Frank Selee	146,502
1902	3rd	73	64	.533	29.0	Al Buckenberger	116,960
1903	6th	58	80	.420	32.0	Al Buckenberger	143,155
1904	7th	55	98	.359	51.0	Al Buckenberger	140,694
1905	7th	51	103	.331	54.5	Fred Tenney	150,003
1906	8th	49	102	.325	66.5	Fred Tenney	143,280
1907	7th	58	90	.392	47.0	Fred Tenney	203,221
1908	6th	63	91	.409	36.0	Joe Kelley	253,750
1909	8th	45	108	.294	65.5	Fred Bowerman, Harry Smith	195,188
1910	8th	53	100	.346	50.5	Fred Lake	149,027
1911	8th	44	107	.291	54.0	Fred Tenney	96,000
1912	8th	52	101	.340	52.0	Johnny Kling	121,000

Year	Finish	Wins	Losses	Percentage	Games Behind	Manager	Attendance
1913	5th	69	82	.457	31.5	George Stallings	208,000
1914	1st	94	59	.614	+10.5	George Stallings	382,913
1915	2nd	83	69	.546	7.0	George Stallings	376,283
1916	3rd	89	63	.586	4.0	George Stallings	313,495
1917	6th	72	81	.471	25.5	George Stallings	174,253
1918	7th	53	71	.427	28.5	George Stallings	84,938
1919	6th	57	82	.410	38.5	George Stallings	167,401
1920	7th	62	90	.408	30.0	George Stallings	162,483
1921	4th	79	74	.516	15.0	Fred Mitchell	318,627
1922	8th	53	100	.346	39.5	Fred Mitchell	167,965
1923	7th	54	100	.351	41.5	Fred Mitchell	227,802
1924	8th	53	100	.346	40.0	Dave Bancroft	177,478
1925	5th	70	83	.458	25.0	Dave Bancroft	313,528
1926	7th	66	86	.434	22.0	Dave Bancroft	303,598
1927	7th	60	94	.390	34.0	Dave Bancroft	288,685
1928	7th	50	103	.327	44.5	Jack Slattery, Rogers Hornsby	227,001
1929	8th	56	98	.364	43.0	Judge Emil Fuchs	372,351
1930	6th	70	84	.455	22.0	Bill McKechnie	464,835
1931	7th	64	90	.416	37.0	Bill McKechnie	515,005
1932	5th	77	77	.500	13.0	Bill McKechnie	507,606
1933	4th	83	71	.539	9.0	Bill McKechnie	517,803
1934	4th	78	73	.517	16.0	Bill McKechnie	303,205
1935	8th	38	115	.248	61.5	Bill McKechnie	232,754
1936	6th	71	83	.461	21.0	Bill McKechnie	340,585
1937	5th	79	73	.520	16.0	Bill McKechnie	385,339
1938	5th	77	75	.507	12.0	Casey Stengel	341,149
1939	7th	63	88	.417	32.5	Casey Stengel	285,994
1940	7th	65	87	.428	34.5	Casey Stengel	241,616
1941	7th	62	92	.403	38.0	Casey Stengel	263,680
1942	7th	59	89	.399	44.0	Casey Stengel	285,322
1943	6th	68	85	.444	36.5	Casey Stengel	271,289
1944	6th	65	89	.422	40.0	Bob Coleman	208,691
1945	6th	67	85	.441	30.0	Bob Coleman, Del Bissonette	374,178
1946	4th	81	72	.529	15.5	Billy Southworth	969,673
1947	3rd	86	68	.558	8.0	Billy Southworth	1,277,361
1948	1st	91	62	.595	+6.5	Billy Southworth	1,455,439
1949	4th	75	79	.487	22.0	Billy Southworth	1,081,795
1950	4th	83	71	.539	8.0	Billy Southworth	944,391
1951	4th	76	78	.494	20.5	Billy Southworth, Tommy Holmes	487,475
1952	7th	64	89	.418	32.0	Tommy Holmes, Charlie Grimm	281,278

Awards

Most Valuable Player
Johnny Evers, second base, 1914
Bob Elliott, third base, 1947

Rookie of the Year
Alvin Dark, shortstop, 1948
Sam Jethroe, outfield, 1950

Cy Young
[No player]

Hall of Famers Who Played for the Boston Braves
Earl Averill, outfield, 1941
Dave Bancroft, shortstop, 1924–27
Dan Brouthers, first base, 1889
John Clarkson, pitcher, 1888–92
Hugh Duffy, outfield, 1892–1900
Johnny Evers, second base, 1914–17
Burleigh Grimes, pitcher, 1930
Billy Hamilton, outfield, 1896–1901
Billy Herman, second base, 1946
Rogers Hornsby, second base, 1928
Joe Kelley, outfield, 1891 and 1908
King Kelly, outfield and catcher, 1887–90
Ernie Lombardi, catcher, 1942
Al Lopez, catcher, 1936–40
Rabbit Maranville, shortstop, 1912–20 and 1929–35
Rube Marquard, pitcher, 1922–25
Eddie Mathews, third base, 1952
Tommy McCarthy, outfield and infield, 1885 and 1892–95
Bill McKechnie, infield, 1913
Joe Medwick, outfield, 1945
Kid Nichols, pitcher, 1890–1901
Jim O'Rourke, outfield and infield, 1876–78
Old Hoss Radbourn, pitcher, 1886–89
Babe Ruth, outfield, 1935
Al Simmons, outfield, 1939
George Sisler, first base, 1928–30
Billy Southworth, outfield, 1921–23
Warren Spahn, pitcher, 1942 and 1946–52
Casey Stengel, outfield, 1924–25
Ed Walsh, pitcher, 1917
Lloyd Waner, outfield, 1941
Paul Waner, outfield, 1941–42
Vic Willis, pitcher, 1898–1905
Cy Young, pitcher, 1911

League Leaders, Batting (Post-1900)

Batting Average, Season
Rogers Hornsby, 1928 .... .387
Ernie Lombardi, 1942 .... .330

Home Runs, Season
Herman Long, 1900 12
Dave Brain, 1907 10
Fred Beck, 1910 .... 10 (Tie)
Wally Berger, 1935 34
Tommy Holmes, 1945 28

RBIs, Season
Wally Berger, 1935 130

Stolen Bases, Season
Sam Jethroe, 1950 35
Sam Jethroe, 1951 35

Total Bases, Season
Tommy Holmes, 1945 367

Most Hits, Season
Ginger Beaumont, 1907 187
Doc Miller, 1911 192
Eddie Brown, 1926 201
Tommy Holmes, 1945 224
Tommy Holmes, 1947 191

Most Runs, Season
Earl Torgeson, 1950 120

Batting Feats

Triple Crown Winners
[No player]

Hitting for the Cycle
Herman Long, May 9, 1896
Duff Colley, Jun. 20, 1904
John Bates, Apr. 26, 1907
Bill Collins, Oct. 6, 1910

Six Hits in a Game
Sam Wise, Jun. 20, 1883
King Kelly, Aug. 27, 1887
Bobby Lowe, Jun. 11, 1891
Fred Tenney, May 31, 1897
Chick Stahl, May 31, 1899

40 or More Home Runs, Season
[No player]

League Leaders, Pitching (Post-1900)

Most Wins, Season
Dick Rudolph, 1914 .... 27 (Tie)
Johnny Sain, 1948 24
Warren Spahn, 1949 21
Warren Spahn, 1950 21
Warren Spahn, 1953 .... 23 (Tie)

Most Strikeouts, Season
Vic Willis, 1902 226
Warren Spahn, 1949 151
Warren Spahn, 1950 191
Warren Spahn, 1951 .... 164 (Tie)
Warren Spahn, 1952 183

Lowest ERA, Season
Jim Turner, 1937 .... 2.38
Warren Spahn, 1947 .... 2.33
Chet Nichols, 1951 .... 2.88

Most Saves, Season
[No player]

Best Won–Lost Percentage, Season
Bill James, 1914 .... 26–7 ... .788
Tom Hughes, 1916 .... 16–3 ... .842
Ben Cantwell, 1933 ... 20–10 ... .667

Pitching Feats

Triple Crown Winner
Tommy Bond, 1877 (40–17, 2.11 ERA, 170 SO)
John Clarkson, 1889 (49–19, 2.73 ERA, 284 SO)

20 Wins, Season (1900–52)
Bill Dinneen, 1900 21–15
Vic Willis, 1901 20–17
Togie Pittinger, 1902 27–16
Vic Willis, 1902 27–20
Irv Young, 1905 20–21
Bill James, 1914 26–7
Dick Rudolph, 1914 26–10
Dick Rudolph, 1915 22–19
Joe Oeschger, 1921 20–14
Ben Cantwell, 1933 20–10
Lou Fette, 1937 20–10
Jim Turner, 1937 20–11
Johnny Sain, 1946 20–14
Warren Spahn, 1947 21–10
Johnny Sain, 1947 21–12
Johnny Sain, 1948 24–15
Warren Spahn, 1948 20–7
Warren Spahn, 1949 21–14
Warren Spahn, 1950 21–17

Johnny Sain, 1950 20–13

Warren Spahn, 1951 22–14

No-Hitters

Fred Pfeffer (vs. Cin. Reds), May 8, 1907 (final: 6–0)

George Davis (vs. Phi. Phillies), Sep. 9, 1914 (final: 7–0)

Tom Hughes (vs. Pit. Pirates), Jun. 16, 1916 (final: 2–0)

Jim Tobin (vs. Brk. Dodgers), Apr. 27, 1944 (final: 2–0)

Vern Bickford (vs. Brk. Dodgers), Aug. 11, 1950 (final: 7–0)

No-Hitters Pitched Against

Nap Rucker, Brk. Dodgers, Sep. 5, 1908 (final: 6–0)

Jesse Haines, St.L. Cardinals, Jul. 17, 1924 (final: 5–0)

Johnny Vander Meer, Cin. Reds, Jun. 11, 1938 (final: 3–0)

Clyde Shoun, Cin. Reds, May 15, 1944 (final: 1–0)

Ed Head, Brk. Dodgers, Apr. 23, 1946 (final: 5–0)

Ewell Blackwell, Cin. Reds, Jun. 18, 1947 (final: 6–0)

Cliff Chambers, Pit. Pirates, May 6, 1951 (final: 3–0)

Postseason Play

1914 World Series vs. Phi. A's (AL), won 4 games to 0

1948 World Series vs. Cle. Indians (AL), lost 4 games to 2

Brooklyn Dodgers

Dates of Operation: 1890–1957 (68 years)

Overall Record: 5214 wins, 4926 losses (.514)

Stadiums: Washington Park II, 1890; Eastern Park, 1891–97; West N.Y. Field Club Grounds, 1898; Washington Park III, 1898–1912; Ebbets Field, 1913–57; Roosevelt Stadium (Jersey City, NJ) 1956–57 (capacity: 31,903)

Other Names: Bridegrooms, Superbas, Trolley Dodgers, Robins

Year-by-Year Finishes

Year	Finish	Wins	Losses	Percentage	Games Behind	Manager	Attendance
1890	1st	86	43	.667	+6.5	Bill McGunnigle	not available
1891	6th	61	76	.445	25.5	Monte Ward	not available
1892	3rd	95	59	.617	9.0	Monte Ward	not available
1893	6th	65	63	.508	20.0	Dave Foutz	not available
1894	5th	70	61	.534	25.5	Dave Foutz	not available
1895	5th	71	60	.542	16.5	Dave Foutz	not available
1896	9th	57	73	.443	33.0	Dave Foutz	not available
1897	6th	61	71	.462	32.0	Billy Barnie	not available
1898	10th	54	91	.372	46.0	Billy Barnie, Mike Griffin, Charlie Ebbets	not available
1899	1st	88	42	.677	+4.0	Ned Hanlon	not available
1900	1st	82	54	.603	+4.5	Ned Hanlon	not available
1901	3rd	79	57	.581	9.5	Ned Hanlon	198,200
1902	2nd	75	63	.543	27.5	Ned Hanlon	199,868
1903	5th	70	66	.515	19.0	Ned Hanlon	224,670
1904	6th	56	97	.366	50.0	Ned Hanlon	214,600
1905	8th	48	104	.316	56.5	Ned Hanlon	227,924
1906	5th	66	86	.434	50.0	Patsy Donovan	277,400
1907	5th	65	83	.439	40.0	Patsy Donovan	312,500
1908	7th	53	101	.344	46.0	Patsy Donovan	275,600
1909	6th	55	98	.359	55.5	Harry Lumley	321,300
1910	6th	64	90	.416	40.0	Bill Dahlen	279,321
1911	7th	64	86	.427	33.5	Bill Dahlen	269,000
1912	7th	58	95	.379	46.0	Bill Dahlen	243,000
1913	6th	65	84	.436	34.5	Bill Dahlen	347,000
1914	5th	75	79	.487	19.5	Wilbert Robinson	122,671
1915	3rd	80	72	.526	10.0	Wilbert Robinson	279,766
1916	1st	94	60	.610	+2.5	Wilbert Robinson	447,747
1917	7th	70	81	.464	26.5	Wilbert Robinson	221,619
1918	5th	57	69	.452	25.5	Wilbert Robinson	83,831
1919	5th	69	71	.493	27.0	Wilbert Robinson	360,721
1920	1st	93	61	.604	+7.0	Wilbert Robinson	808,722
1921	5th	77	75	.507	16.5	Wilbert Robinson	613,245
1922	6th	76	78	.494	17.0	Wilbert Robinson	498,865
1923	6th	76	78	.494	19.5	Wilbert Robinson	564,666
1924	2nd	92	62	.597	1.5	Wilbert Robinson	818,883
1925	6th (Tie)	68	85	.444	27.0	Wilbert Robinson	659,435
1926	6th	71	82	.464	17.5	Wilbert Robinson	650,819
1927	6th	65	88	.425	28.5	Wilbert Robinson	637,230
1928	6th	77	76	.503	17.5	Wilbert Robinson	664,863

Year	Finish	Wins	Losses	Percentage	Games Behind	Manager	Attendance
1929	6th	70	83	.458	28.5	Wilbert Robinson	731,886
1930	4th	86	68	.558	6.0	Wilbert Robinson	1,097,339
1931	4th	79	73	.520	21.0	Wilbert Robinson	753,133
1932	3rd	81	73	.526	9.0	Max Carey	681,827
1933	6th	65	88	.425	26.5	Max Carey	526,815
1934	6th	71	81	.467	23.5	Casey Stengel	434,188
1935	5th	70	83	.458	29.5	Casey Stengel	470,517
1936	7th	67	87	.435	25.0	Casey Stengel	489,618
1937	6th	62	91	.405	33.5	Burleigh Grimes	482,481
1938	7th	69	80	.463	18.5	Burleigh Grimes	663,087
1939	3rd	84	69	.549	12.5	Leo Durocher	955,668
1940	2nd	88	65	.575	12.0	Leo Durocher	975,978
1941	1st	100	54	.649	+2.5	Leo Durocher	1,214,910
1942	2nd	104	50	.675	2.0	Leo Durocher	1,037,765
1943	3rd	81	72	.529	23.5	Leo Durocher	661,739
1944	7th	63	91	.409	42.0	Leo Durocher	605,905
1945	3rd	87	67	.565	11.0	Leo Durocher	1,059,220
1946	2nd	96	60	.616	2.0	Leo Durocher	1,796,824
1947	1st	94	60	.610	+5.0	Burt Shotton	1,807,526
1948	3rd	84	70	.545	7.5	Leo Durocher, Burt Shotton	1,398,967
1949	1st	97	57	.630	+1.0	Burt Shotton	1,633,747
1950	2nd	89	65	.578	2.0	Burt Shotton	1,185,896
1951	2nd	97	60	.618	1.0	Chuck Dressen	1,282,628
1952	1st	96	57	.627	+4.5	Chuck Dressen	1,088,704
1953	1st	105	49	.682	+13.0	Chuck Dressen	1,163,419
1954	2nd	92	62	.597	5.0	Walter Alston	1,020,531
1955	1st	98	55	.641	+13.5	Walter Alston	1,033,589
1956	1st	93	61	.604	+1.0	Walter Alston	1,213,562
1957	3rd	84	70	.545	11.0	Walter Alston	1,028,258

Awards

Most Valuable Player

Jake Daubert, first base, 1913

Dazzy Vance, pitcher, 1924

Dolph Camilli, first base, 1941

Jackie Robinson, second base, 1949

Roy Campanella, catcher, 1951

Roy Campanella, catcher, 1953

Roy Campanella, catcher, 1955

Don Newcombe, pitcher, 1956

Rookie of the Year

Jackie Robinson, first base, 1947

Don Newcombe, pitcher, 1949

Joe Black, pitcher, 1952

Junior Gilliam, second base, 1953

Cy Young

Don Newcombe, 1956

Hall of Famers Who Played for the Brooklyn Dodgers

Dave Bancroft, shortstop, 1928–29

Dan Brouthers, first base, 1892–93

Roy Campanella, catcher, 1948–57

Max Carey, outfield, 1926–29

Kiki Cuyler, outfield, 1938

Don Drysdale, pitcher, 1956–57

Leo Durocher, shortstop, 1938–41, 1943, and 1945

Burleigh Grimes, pitcher, 1918–26

Billy Herman, second base, 1941–43 and 1946

Waite Hoyt, pitcher, 1932 and 1937–38

Hughie Jennings, infield, 1899–1900

Willie Keeler, outfield, 1893 and 1899–1902

Joe Kelley, outfield, 1899–1901

George Kelly, first base, 1932

Sandy Koufax, pitcher, 1955–57

Tony Lazzeri, second base, 1939

Fred Lindstrom, third base, 1936

Ernie Lombardi, catcher, 1931

Al Lopez, catcher, 1928 and 1930–35

Heinie Manush, outfield, 1937–38

Rabbit Maranville, shortstop, 1926

Rube Marquard, pitcher, 1915–20

Tommy McCarthy, outfield and infield, 1896

Joe McGinnity, pitcher, 1900

Joe Medwick, outfield, 1940–43 and 1946

Pee Wee Reese, shortstop, 1940–42 and 1946–57

Jackie Robinson, infield, 1947–56

Duke Snider, outfield, 1947–57
Casey Stengel, outfield, 1912–17
Dazzy Vance, pitcher, 1922–32 and 1935
Arky Vaughan, infield, 1942–43 and 1947–48
Paul Waner, outfield, 1941 and 1943–44
John Montgomery Ward, infield and pitcher, 1890–92
Zack Wheat, outfield, 1909–26
Hack Wilson, outfield, 1932–34

League Leaders, Batting (Post-1900)

Batting Average, Season

Jake Daubert, 1913 .... .350
Jake Daubert, 1914 .... .329
Zack Wheat, 1918 .... .335
Lefty O'Doul, 1932 .... .368
Pete Reiser, 1941 .... .343
Dixie Walker, 1944 .... .357
Jackie Robinson, 1949 .... .342
Carl Furillo, 1953 .... .344

Home Runs, Season

Jimmy Sheckard, 1903 9
Harry Lumley, 1904 9
Tim Jordan, 1906 12
Tim Jordan, 1908 12
Jack Fournier, 1924 27
Dolph Camilli, 1941 34
Duke Snider, 1956 43

RBIs, Season

Hy Myers, 1919 72
Dolph Camilli, 1941 120
Dixie Walker, 1945 124
Roy Campanella, 1953 142
Duke Snider, 1955 136

Stolen Bases, Season

Jimmy Sheckard, 1903 67
Pete Reiser, 1942 20
Arky Vaughan, 1943 20
Pete Reiser, 1946 34
Jackie Robinson, 1947 29
Jackie Robinson, 1949 37
Pee Wee Reese, 1952 30

Total Bases, Season

Zack Wheat, 1916 262
Hy Myers, 1919 223
Pete Reiser, 1941 299
Duke Snider, 1950 343
Duke Snider, 1953 370
Duke Snider, 1954 378

Most Hits, Season

Willie Keeler, 1900 208
Ivy Olson, 1919 164
Duke Snider, 1950 199

Most Runs, Season

Pete Reiser, 1941 117
Arky Vaughan, 1943 112
Eddie Stanky, 1945 128
Pee Wee Reese, 1949 132
Duke Snider, 1953 132
Duke Snider, 1954 .... 120 (Tie)
Duke Snider, 1955 126

Batting Feats

Triple Crown Winners

[No player]

Hitting for the Cycle

Tom Burns, Aug. 1, 1890
Jimmy Johnston, May 25, 1922
Babe Herman, May 18, 1931
Babe Herman, Jul. 24, 1931
Dixie Walker, Sep. 2, 1944
Jackie Robinson, Aug. 29, 1948
Gil Hodges, Jun. 25, 1949

Six Hits in a Game

George Cutshaw, Aug. 9, 1915
Jack Fournier, Jun. 29, 1923
Hank DeBerry, Jun. 23, 1929*
Wally Gilbert, May 30, 1931
Cookie Lavagetto, Sep. 23, 1939
* Extra-inning game.

40 or More Home Runs, Season

43 .... Duke Snider, 1956
42 .... Duke Snider, 1953
                              Gil Hodges, 1954
                              Duke Snider, 1955
41 .... Roy Campanella, 1953
40 .... Gil Hodges, 1951
                              Duke Snider, 1954
                              Duke Snider, 1957

League Leaders, Pitching (Post-1900)

Most Wins, Season

Bill Donovan, 1901 25
Burleigh Grimes, 1921 .... 22 (Tie)
Dazzy Vance, 1924 28
Dazzy Vance, 1925 22
Kirby Higbe, 1941 .... 22 (Tie)
Whit Wyatt, 1941 .... 22 (Tie)
Don Newcombe, 1956 27

Most Strikeouts, Season

Burleigh Grimes, 1921 136
Dazzy Vance, 1922 134
Dazzy Vance, 1923 197
Dazzy Vance, 1924 262
Dazzy Vance, 1925 221
Dazzy Vance, 1926 140
Dazzy Vance, 1927 184
Dazzy Vance, 1928 200
Van Lingle Mungo, 1936 238
Don Newcombe, 1951 .... 164 (Tie)

Lowest ERA, Season

Dazzy Vance, 1924 .... 2.16
Dazzy Vance, 1928 .... 2.09
Dazzy Vance, 1930 .... 2.61
Johnny Podres, 1957 .... 2.66

Most Saves, Season

[No player]

Best Won–Lost Percentage, Season

Joe McGinnity, 1900 ...... 29–9 . .763
Burleigh Grimes, 1920 ... 23–11 . .676
Freddie Fitzsimmons, 1940.16–2 . .889
Larry French, 1942 .... 15–4 . .789
Preacher Roe, 1949 .... 15–6 . .714
Preacher Roe, 1951 .... 22–3 . .880
Carl Erskine, 1953 .... 20–6 . .769
Don Newcombe, 1955 ... 20–5 . .800
Don Newcombe, 1956 ... 27–7 . .794

Pitching Feats

Triple Crown Winner

Dazzy Vance, 1924 (28–6, 2.16 ERA, 262 SO)

20 Wins, Season (1900–57)

Joe McGinnity, 1900 29–9
William Kennedy, 1900 22–15
Bill Dinneen, 1901 25–15
Henry Schmidt, 1903 22–13

Nap Rucker, 1911 22–18
Jeff Pfeffer, 1914 23–12
Jeff Pfeffer, 1916 25–11
Burleigh Grimes, 1920 23–11
Burleigh Grimes, 1921 22–13
Dutch Ruether, 1922 21–12
Burleigh Grimes, 1923 21–18
Dazzy Vance, 1924 28–6
Burleigh Grimes, 1924 22–13
Dazzy Vance, 1925 22–9
Dazzy Vance, 1928 22–10
Watty Clark, 1932 20–12
Luke Hamlin, 1939 20–13
Kirby Higbe, 1941 22–9
Whit Wyatt, 1941 22–10
Ralph Branca, 1947 21–12
Preacher Roe, 1951 22–3
Don Newcombe, 1951 20–9
Carl Erskine, 1953 20–6
Don Newcombe, 1955 20–5
Don Newcombe, 1956 27–7

No-Hitters

Mal Eason (vs. St.L. Cardinals), Jul. 20, 1906 (final: 2–0)
Nap Rucker (vs. Bos. Doves), Sep. 5, 1908 (final: 6–0)
Dazzy Vance (vs. Phi. Phillies), Sep. 13, 925 (final: 10–1)

Tex Carleton (vs. Cin. Reds), Apr. 30, 1940 (final: 3–0)
Ed Head (vs. Bos. Braves), Apr. 23, 1946 (final: 5–0)
Rex Barney (vs. N.Y. Giants), Sep. 9, 1948 (final: 2–0)
Carl Erskine (vs. Chi. Cubs), Jun. 19, 1952 (final: 5–0)
Carl Erskine (vs. N.Y. Giants), May 12, 1956 (final: 3–0)
Sal Maglie (vs. Phi. Phillies), Sep. 25, 1956 (final: 5–0)

No-Hitters Pitched Against

John Lush, Phi. Phillies, May 1, 1906 (final: 1–0)
Nick Maddox, Pit. Pirates, Sep. 29, 1907 (final: 2–1)
Rube Marquard, N.Y. Giants, Apr. 15, 1915 (final: 2–0)
Paul Dean, St.L. Cardinals, Sep. 21, 1934 (final: 3–0)
Johnny Vander Meer, Cin. Reds, Jun. 15, 1938 (final: 6–0)
Jim Tobin, Bos. Braves, Apr. 27, 1944 (final: 2–0)
Vern Bickford, Bos. Braves, Aug. 11, 1950 (final: 7–0)

Don Larsen, N.Y. Yankees, Oct. 8, 1956 (final: 2–0) (World Series) (perfect game)

Postseason Play

1916 World Series vs. Bos. Red Sox (AL), lost 4 games to 1
1920 World Series vs. Cle. Indians (AL), lost 5 games to 2
1941 World Series vs. N.Y. Yankees (AL), lost 4 games to 1
1946 Pennant Playoff Series vs. St.L. Cardinals, lost 2 games to 0
1947 World Series vs. N.Y. Yankees (AL), lost 4 games to 3
1949 World Series vs. N.Y. Yankees (AL), lost 4 games to 1
1951 Pennant Playoff Series vs. N.Y. Giants, lost 2 games to 1
1952 World Series vs. N.Y. Yankees (AL), lost 4 games to 3
1953 World Series vs. N.Y. Yankees (AL), lost 4 games to 2
1955 World Series vs. N.Y. Yankees (AL), won 4 games to 3
1956 World Series vs. N.Y. Yankees (AL), lost 4 games to 3

New York Giants

Dates of Operation: 1876, 1883–1957 (76 years)

Overall Record: 6088 wins, 4933 losses (.552)

Stadiums: Polo Grounds I, 1876, 1883–88; Oakland Park, 1889; St. George Cricket Grounds, 1889; Polo Grounds III, 1889–90; Harrison Field, 1890–99 and 1918 (Sundays only); Polo Grounds IV, 1891–1911; Hilltop Park, 1911; Polo Grounds V, 1911–57 (capacity: 55,137)

Other Names: Maroons, Gothams

Year-by-Year Finishes

Year	Finish	Wins	Losses	Percentage	Games Behind	Manager	Attendance
1883	6th	46	50	.479	16.0	John Clapp	not available
1884	4th (Tie)	62	50	.544	22.0	James Price, Monte Ward	not available
1885	2nd	85	27	.758	2.0	Jim Mutrie	not available
1886	3rd	75	44	.630	12.5	Jim Mutrie	not available
1887	4th	68	55	.553	10.5	Jim Mutrie	not available
1888	1st	84	47	.641	+9.0	Jim Mutrie	not available
1889	1st	83	43	.659	+1.0	Jim Mutrie	not available
1890	6th	63	68	.481	24.0	Jim Mutrie	not available
1891	3rd	71	61	.538	13.0	Jim Mutrie	not available
1892	8th	71	80	.470	31.5	Pat Powers	not available
1893	5th	68	64	.515	19.0	Monte Ward	not available
1894	2nd	88	44	.667	3.0	Monte Ward	not available
1895	9th	66	65	.504	21.5	George Davis, Jack Doyle, Harvey Watkins	not available
1896	7th	64	67	.489	37.0	Arthur Irwin, Bill Joyce	not available
1897	3rd	83	48	.634	9.5	Bill Joyce	not available
1898	7th	77	73	.513	25.5	Bill Joyce, Cap Anson	not available
1899	10th	60	86	.411	26.0	John Day, Fred Hoey	not available
1900	8th	60	78	.435	23.0	Buck Ewing, George Davis	not available
1901	7th	52	85	.380	37.0	George Davis	297,650
1902	8th	48	88	.353	53.5	Horace Fogel, Heinie Smith, John McGraw	302,875
1903	2nd	84	55	.604	6.5	John McGraw	579,530
1904	1st	106	47	.693	+13.0	John McGraw	609,826
1905	1st	105	48	.686	+9.0	John McGraw	552,700
1906	2nd	96	56	.632	20.0	John McGraw	402,850
1907	4th	82	71	.536	25.5	John McGraw	538,350
1908	2nd (Tie)	98	56	.636	1.0	John McGraw	910,000
1909	3rd	92	61	.601	18.5	John McGraw	783,700
1910	2nd	91	63	.591	13.0	John McGraw	511,785
1911	1st	99	54	.647	+7.5	John McGraw	675,000
1912	1st	103	48	.682	+10.0	John McGraw	638,000
1913	1st	101	51	.664	+12.5	John McGraw	630,000
1914	2nd	84	70	.545	10.5	John McGraw	364,313
1915	8th	69	83	.454	21.0	John McGraw	391,850
1916	4th	86	66	.566	7.0	John McGraw	552,056
1917	1st	98	56	.636	+10.0	John McGraw	500,264
1918	2nd	71	53	.573	10.5	John McGraw	256,618
1919	2nd	87	53	.621	9.0	John McGraw	708,857

Year	Finish	Wins	Losses	Percentage	Games Behind	Manager	Attendance
1920	2nd	86	68	.558	7.0	John McGraw	929,609
1921	1st	94	59	.614	+4.0	John McGraw	773,477
1922	1st	93	61	.604	+7.0	John McGraw	945,809
1923	1st	95	58	.621	+4.5	John McGraw	820,780
1924	1st	93	60	.608	+1.5	John McGraw	844,068
1925	2nd	86	66	.566	8.5	John McGraw	778,993
1926	5th	74	77	.490	13.5	John McGraw	700,362
1927	3rd	92	62	.597	2.0	John McGraw	858,190
1928	2nd	93	61	.604	2.0	John McGraw	916,191
1929	3rd	84	67	.556	13.5	John McGraw	868,806
1930	3rd	87	67	.565	5.0	John McGraw	868,714
1931	2nd	87	65	.572	13.0	John McGraw	812,163
1932	6th (Tie)	72	82	.468	18.0	John McGraw, Bill Terry	484,868
1933	1st	91	61	.599	+5.0	Bill Terry	604,471
1934	2nd	93	60	.608	2.0	Bill Terry	730,851
1935	3rd	91	62	.595	8.5	Bill Terry	748,748
1936	1st	92	62	.597	+5.0	Bill Terry	837,952
1937	1st	95	57	.625	+3.0	Bill Terry	926,887
1938	3rd	83	67	.553	5.0	Bill Terry	799,633
1939	5th	77	74	.510	18.5	Bill Terry	702,457
1940	6th (Tie)	72	80	.474	27.5	Bill Terry	747,852
1941	5th	74	79	.484	25.5	Bill Terry	763,098
1942	3rd	85	67	.559	20.0	Mel Ott	779,621
1943	8th	55	98	.359	49.5	Mel Ott	466,095
1944	5th	67	87	.435	38.0	Mel Ott	674,083
1945	5th	78	74	.513	19.0	Mel Ott	1,016,468
1946	8th	61	93	.396	36.0	Mel Ott	1,219,873
1947	4th	81	73	.526	13.0	Mel Ott	1,600,793
1948	5th	78	76	.506	13.5	Mel Ott, Leo Durocher	1,459,269
1949	5th	73	81	.474	24.0	Leo Durocher	1,218,446
1950	3rd	86	68	.558	5.0	Leo Durocher	1,008,876
1951	1st	98	59	.624	+1.0	Leo Durocher	1,059,539
1952	2nd	92	62	.597	4.5	Leo Durocher	984,940
1953	5th	70	84	.455	35.0	Leo Durocher	811,518
1954	1st	97	57	.630	+5.0	Leo Durocher	1,155,067
1955	3rd	80	74	.519	18.5	Leo Durocher	824,112
1956	6th	67	87	.435	26.0	Bill Rigney	629,179
1957	6th	69	85	.448	26.0	Bill Rigney	653,923

Awards

Most Valuable Player

Larry Doyle, second base, 1912
Carl Hubbell, pitcher, 1933
Carl Hubbell, pitcher, 1936
Willie Mays, outfield, 1954

Rookie of the Year

Willie Mays, outfield, 1951

Cy Young

[No player]

Hall of Famers Who Played for the New York Giants

Dave Bancroft, shortstop, 1920–23 and 1930
Jake Beckley, first base, 1896–97
Roger Bresnahan, catcher, 1902–08
Dan Brouthers, first base, 1904
Jesse Burkett, outfield, 1890

Roger Connor, first base, 1883–89, 1891, and 1893–94
George Davis, outfield and infield, 1893–1901 and 1903
Buck Ewing, catcher and infield, 1883–89 and 1891–92
Frankie Frisch, second base, 1919–26
Burleigh Grimes, pitcher, 1927
Gabby Hartnett, catcher, 1941
Waite Hoyt, pitcher, 1918 and 1932
Monte Irvin, outfield, 1949–55

Travis Jackson, shortstop, 1922–36
Tim Keefe, pitcher, 1885–91
Willie Keeler, outfield, 1892–93 and 1910
George Kelly, first base, 1915–17 and 1919–26
King Kelly, catcher and infield, 1893
Tony Lazzeri, second base, 1939
Fred Lindstrom, third base, 1924–32
Ernie Lombardi, catcher, 1943–47
Rube Marquard, pitcher, 1908–15
Christy Mathewson, pitcher, 1900–16
Willie Mays, outfield, 1951–52 and 1954–57
Joe McGinnity, pitcher, 1902–08
John McGraw, infield, 1902–06
Bill McKechnie, third base, 1916
Joe Medwick, outfield, 1943–45
Johnny Mize, first base, 1942 and 1946–49
Jim O'Rourke, catcher, outfield, and infield, 1885–89, 1904
Mel Ott, outfield, 1926–47
Edd Roush, outfield, 1916 and 1927–29
Amos Rusie, pitcher, 1890–95 and 1897–98
Ray Schalk, catcher, 1929
Red Schoendienst, second base, 1956–57
Billy Southworth, outfield, 1924–26
Casey Stengel, outfield, 1921–23
Bill Terry, first base, 1923–36
Monte Ward, infield and pitcher, 1883–89
Mickey Welch, pitcher, 1883–92
Hoyt Wilhelm, pitcher, 1952–56
Hack Wilson, outfield, 1923–25
Ross Youngs, outfield, 1917–26

League Leaders, Batting (Post-1900)

Batting Average, Season
Larry Doyle, 1915 .... .320
Bill Terry, 1930 .... .401
Willie Mays, 1954 .... .345

Home Runs, Season
Red Murray, 1909 7
Dave Robertson, 1916 .... 12 (Tie)
Dave Robertson, 1917 .... 12 (Tie)
George Kelly, 1921 23
Mel Ott, 1932 .... 38 (Tie)

Mel Ott, 1934 .... 35 (Tie)
Mel Ott, 1936 33
Mel Ott, 1937 .... 31 (Tie)
Mel Ott, 1938 .... 36 (Tie)
Mel Ott, 1942 30
Johnny Mize, 1947 .... 51 (Tie)
Johnny Mize, 1948 .... 40 (Tie)
Willie Mays, 1955 51

RBIs, Season
Heinie Zimmerman*, 1916 83
Heinie Zimmerman, 1917 102
George Kelly, 1920 .... 94 (Tie)
Irish Meusel, 1923 125
George Kelly, 1924 136
Mel Ott, 1934 135
Johnny Mize, 1942 110
Johnny Mize, 1947 138
Monte Irvin, 1951 121
* 64 with Chi. Cubs and 19 with N.Y. Giants.

Stolen Bases, Season
Art Devlin, 1905 .... 59 (Tie)
George J. Burns, 1914 62
George J. Burns, 1919 40
Frankie Frisch, 1921 49
Willie Mays, 1956 40
Willie Mays, 1957 38

Total Bases, Season
Frankie Frisch, 1923 311
Willie Mays, 1955 382

Most Hits, Season
Larry Doyle, 1909 172
Larry Doyle, 1915 189
Frankie Frisch, 1923 223
Fred Lindstrom, 1928 231
Bill Terry, 1930 254
Don Mueller, 1954 212

Most Runs, Season
George Browne, 1904 99
Mike Donlin, 1905 124
Spike Shannon, 1907 104
Fred Tenney, 1908 101
George J. Burns, 1914 100
George J. Burns, 1916 105
George J. Burns, 1917 103
George J. Burns, 1919 86
George J. Burns, 1920 115
Ross Youngs, 1923 121

Frankie Frisch, 1924 .... 121 (Tie)
Rogers Hornsby, 1927 .... 133 (Tie)
Bill Terry, 1931 .... 121 (Tie)
Mel Ott, 1938 116
Mel Ott, 1942 118
Johnny Mize, 1947 137

Batting Feats

Triple Crown Winners
[No player]

Hitting for the Cycle
Dave Orr, Jun. 12, 1885
Dave Orr, Aug. 10, 1887
Mike Tiernan, Aug. 25, 1888
Mike Tiernan, Aug. 28, 1890
Sam Mertes, Oct. 4, 1904
Chief Meyers, Jun. 10, 1912
George J. Burns, Sep. 17, 1920
Dave Bancroft, Jun. 1, 1921
Ross Youngs, Apr. 29, 1922
Bill Terry, May 29, 1928
Mel Ott, May 16, 1929
Fred Lindstrom, May 8, 1930
Sam Leslie, May 24, 1936
Harry Danning, Jun. 15, 1940
Don Mueller, Jul. 11, 1954

Six Hits in a Game
Kip Selbach, Jun. 9, 1901
Dave Bancroft, Jun. 28, 1920
Frankie Frisch, Sep. 10, 1924

40 or More Home Runs, Season
51 .... Johnny Mize, 1947
                               Willie Mays, 1955
42 .... Mel Ott, 1929
41 .... Willie Mays, 1954
40 .... Johnny Mize, 1948

League Leaders, Pitching (Post-1900)

Most Wins, Season
Joe McGinnity, 1900 29
Joe McGinnity, 1903 31
Joe McGinnity, 1904 35
Christy Mathewson, 1905 31
Joe McGinnity, 1906 27
Christy Mathewson, 1907 24
Christy Mathewson, 1908 37
Christy Mathewson, 1910 27
Rube Marquard, 1912 .... 26 (Tie)

Jesse Barnes, 1919 25
Larry Benton, 1928 .... 25 (Tie)
Carl Hubbell, 1933 23
Carl Hubbell, 1936 26
Carl Hubbell, 1937 22
Larry Jansen, 1951 .... 23 (Tie)
Sal Maglie, 1951 .... 23 (Tie)

Most Strikeouts, Season

Christy Mathewson, 1903 267
Christy Mathewson, 1904 212
Christy Mathewson, 1905 206
Christy Mathewson, 1907 178
Christy Mathewson, 1908 259
Christy Mathewson, 1910 190
Rube Marquard, 1911 237
Carl Hubbell, 1937 159
Bill Voiselle, 1944 161

Lowest ERA, Season

Jeff Tesreau, 1912 .... 1.96
Christy Mathewson, 1913 .... 2.06
Rosy Ryan, 1922 .... 3.00
Bill Walker, 1929 .... 3.08
Bill Walker, 1931 .... 2.26
Carl Hubbell, 1933 .... 1.66
Carl Hubbell, 1934 .... 2.30
Carl Hubbell, 1936 .... 2.31
Dave Koslo, 1949 .... 2.50
Jim Hearn*, 1950 .... 2.49
Hoyt Wilhelm, 1952 .... 2.43
Johnny Antonelli, 1954 .... 2.29
* 10.00 with St.L. Cardinals and 1.94 with N.Y. Giants.

Most Saves, Season

[No player]

Best Won–Lost Percentage, Season

Joe McGinnity, 1904 .... 35–8 ... .814
Christy Mathewson,
  1909 .... 25–6 ..... .806 (Tie)
Rube Marquard, 1911 .. 24–7 ... .774
Ferdie Schupp, 1917 ... 21–7 ... .750
Larry Benton*, 1927 ... 17–7 ... .708
Larry Benton, 1928 ...... 25–9 ... .735
Freddie Fitzsimmons,
  1930 .... 19–7 ... .731
Carl Hubbell, 1936 ...... 26–6 ... .813
Carl Hubbell, 1937 .... 22–8 ... .733
Larry Jansen, 1947 ... 21–5 ... .808
Sal Maglie, 1950 .... 18–4 ... .818
Hoyt Wilhelm, 1952 ..... 15–3 ... .833

Johnny Antonelli, 1954 .21–7 ... .750
* .667 with Bos. Braves and .722 with N.Y. Giants.

Pitching Feats

Triple Crown Winner

Tim Keefe, 1888 (35–12, 1.74 ERA, 335 SO)
Amos Rusie, 1894 (36–13, 2.78 ERA, 195 SO)
Christy Mathewson, 1905 (31–9, 1.28 ERA, 206 SO)
Christy Mathewson, 1908 (37–11, 1.43 ERA, 259 SO)

20 Wins, Season (1900–57)

Christy Mathewson, 1901 20–17
Joe McGinnity*, 1902 21–18
Joe McGinnity, 1903 31–20
Christy Mathewson, 1903 30–13
Joe McGinnity, 1904 35–8
Christy Mathewson, 1904 33–12
Dummy Taylor, 1904 21–15
Christy Mathewson, 1905 31–9
Red Ames, 1905 22–8
Joe McGinnity, 1905 21–15
Joe McGinnity, 1906 27–12
Christy Mathewson, 1906 22–12
Christy Mathewson, 1907 24–12
Christy Mathewson, 1908 37–11
Hooks Wiltse, 1908 23–14
Christy Mathewson, 1909 25–6
Hooks Wiltse, 1909 20–11
Christy Mathewson, 1910 27–9
Christy Mathewson, 1911 26–13
Rube Marquard, 1911 24–7
Rube Marquard, 1912 26–11
Christy Mathewson, 1912 23–12
Christy Mathewson, 1913 25–11
Rube Marquard, 1913 23–10
Jeff Tesreau, 1913 22–13
Jeff Tesreau, 1914 26–10
Christy Mathewson, 1914 24–13
Ferdie Schupp, 1917 21–7
Jesse Barnes, 1919 25–9
Fred Toney, 1920 21–11
Art Nehf, 1920 21–12
Jesse Barnes, 1920 20–15
Art Nehf, 1921 20–10
Larry Benton, 1928 25–9
Freddie Fitzsimmons, 1928 20–9
Carl Hubbell, 1933 23–12
Hal Schumacher, 1934 23–10

Carl Hubbell, 1934 21–12
Carl Hubbell, 1935 23–12
Carl Hubbell, 1936 26–6
Carl Hubbell, 1937 22–8
Cliff Melton, 1937 20–9
Bill Voiselle, 1944 21–16
Larry Jansen, 1947 21–5
Sal Maglie, 1951 23–6
Larry Jansen, 1951 23–11
Johnny Antonelli, 1954 21–7
Johnny Antonelli, 1956 20–13
* 13–10 with Bal. Orioles (AL) and 8–8 with N.Y. Giants.

No-Hitters

Christy Mathewson (vs. St.L. Cardinals), Jul. 15, 1901 (final: 4–0)
Christy Mathewson (vs. Chi. Cubs), Jun. 13, 1905 (final: 1–0)
Hooks Wiltse (vs. Phi. Phillies), Sep. 5, 1908 (final: 1–0) (10 innings)
Jeff Tesreau (vs. Phi. Phillies), Sep. 6, 1912 (final: 3–0)
Rube Marquard (vs. Brk. Dodgers), Apr. 15, 1915 (final: 2–0)
Jesse Barnes (vs. Phi. Phillies), May 7, 1922 (final: 6–0)
Carl Hubbell (vs. Pit. Pirates), May 8, 1929 (final: 11–0)

No-Hitters Pitched Against

Bob Wicker, Chi. Cubs, Jun. 11, 1904 (final: 1–0) (allowed hit in 10th and won in 12th)
Jimmy Lavender, Chi. Cubs, Aug. 31, 1915 (final: 2–0)
Rex Barney, Brk. Dodgers, Sep. 9, 1948 (final: 2–0)
Carl Erskine, Brk. Dodgers, May 12, 1956 (final: 3–0)

Postseason Play

1905 World Series vs. Phi. A's (AL), won 4 games to 1
1908 Pennant Playoff Game vs. Chi. Cubs (NL), lost
1911 World Series vs. Phi. A's (AL), lost 4 games to 2
1912 World Series vs. Bos. Red Sox (AL), lost 4 games to 3
1913 World Series vs. Phi. A's (AL), lost 4 games to 1

1917 World Series vs. Chi. White Sox
      (AL), lost 4 games to 2
1921 World Series vs. N.Y. Yankees
      (AL), won 5 games to 3
1922 World Series vs. N.Y. Yankees
      (AL), won 4 games to 0
1923 World Series vs. N.Y. Yankees
      (AL), lost 4 games to 2

1924 World Series vs. Was. Senators
      (AL), lost 4 games to 3
1933 World Series vs. Was. Senators
      (AL), won 4 games to 1
1936 World Series vs. N.Y. Yankees
      (AL), lost 4 games to 2
1937 World Series vs. N.Y. Yankees
      (AL), lost 4 games to 1

1951 Pennant Playoff Series vs. Brk.
      Dodgers (NL), won 2 games
      to 1
      World Series vs. N.Y. Yankees
      (AL), lost 4 games to 2
1954 World Series vs. Cle. Indians (AL),
      won 4 games to 0

Philadelphia Athletics

Dates of Operation: 1901–54 (54 years)
Overall Record: 3886 wins, 4248 losses (.478)
Stadiums: Columbia Park, 1901–08; Shibe Park (also known as Connie Mack Stadium), 1909–54
(capacity: 33,000)
Other Name: A's

Year-by-Year Finishes

Year	Finish	Wins	Losses	Percentage	Games Behind	Manager	Attendance
1901	4th	74	62	.544	9.0	Connie Mack	206,329
1902	1st	83	53	.610	+5.0	Connie Mack	442,473
1903	2nd	75	60	.556	14.5	Connie Mack	420,078
1904	5th	81	70	.536	12.5	Connie Mack	512,294
1905	1st	92	56	.622	+2.0	Connie Mack	554,576
1906	4th	78	67	.538	12.0	Connie Mack	489,129
1907	2nd	88	57	.607	1.5	Connie Mack	625,581
1908	6th	68	85	.444	22.0	Connie Mack	455,062
1909	2nd	95	58	.621	3.5	Connie Mack	674,915
1910	1st	102	48	.680	+14.5	Connie Mack	588,905
1911	1st	101	50	.669	+13.5	Connie Mack	605,749
1912	3rd	90	62	.592	15.0	Connie Mack	517,653
1913	1st	96	57	.627	+6.5	Connie Mack	571,896
1914	1st	99	53	.651	+8.5	Connie Mack	346,641
1915	8th	43	109	.283	58.5	Connie Mack	146,223
1916	8th	36	117	.235	54.5	Connie Mack	184,471
1917	8th	55	98	.359	44.5	Connie Mack	221,432
1918	8th	52	76	.406	24.0	Connie Mack	177,926
1919	8th	36	104	.257	52.0	Connie Mack	225,209
1920	8th	48	106	.312	50.0	Connie Mack	287,888
1921	8th	53	100	.346	45.0	Connie Mack	344,430
1922	7th	65	89	.422	29.0	Connie Mack	425,356
1923	6th	69	83	.454	29.0	Connie Mack	534,122
1924	5th	71	81	.467	20.0	Connie Mack	531,992
1925	2nd	88	64	.579	8.5	Connie Mack	869,703
1926	3rd	83	67	.553	6.0	Connie Mack	714,308
1927	2nd	91	63	.591	19.0	Connie Mack	605,529
1928	2nd	98	55	.641	2.5	Connie Mack	689,756
1929	1st	104	46	.693	+18.0	Connie Mack	839,176
1930	1st	102	52	.662	+8.0	Connie Mack	721,663
1931	1st	107	45	.704	+13.5	Connie Mack	627,464
1932	2nd	94	60	.610	13.0	Connie Mack	405,500
1933	3rd	79	72	.523	19.5	Connie Mack	297,138
1934	5th	68	82	.453	31.0	Connie Mack	305,847
1935	8th	58	91	.389	34.0	Connie Mack	233,173
1936	8th	53	100	.346	49.0	Connie Mack	285,173
1937	7th	54	97	.358	46.5	Connie Mack	430,733
1938	8th	53	99	.349	46.0	Connie Mack	385,357
1939	7th	55	97	.362	51.5	Connie Mack	395,022
1940	8th	54	100	.351	36.0	Connie Mack	432,145
1941	8th	64	90	.416	37.0	Connie Mack	528,894

Year	Finish	Wins	Losses	Percentage	Games Behind	Manager	Attendance
1942	8th	55	99	.357	48.0	Connie Mack	423,487
1943	8th	49	105	.318	49.0	Connie Mack	376,735
1944	5th (Tie)	72	82	.468	17.0	Connie Mack	505,322
1945	8th	52	98	.347	34.5	Connie Mack	462,631
1946	8th	49	105	.318	55.0	Connie Mack	621,793
1947	5th	78	76	.506	19.0	Connie Mack	911,566
1948	4th	84	70	.545	12.5	Connie Mack	945,076
1949	5th	81	73	.526	16.0	Connie Mack	816,514
1950	8th	52	102	.338	46.0	Connie Mack	309,805
1951	6th	70	84	.455	28.0	Jimmy Dykes	465,469
1952	4th	79	75	.513	16.0	Jimmy Dykes	627,100
1953	7th	59	95	.383	41.5	Jimmy Dykes	362,113
1954	8th	51	103	.331	60.0	Eddie Joost	304,666

Awards

Most Valuable Player
Eddie Collins, second base, 1914
Mickey Cochrane, catcher, 1928
Lefty Grove, pitcher, 1931
Jimmie Foxx, first base, 1932
Jimmie Foxx, first base, 1933
Bobby Shantz, pitcher, 1952

Rookie of the Year
Harry Byrd, pitcher, 1952

Cy Young
[No player]

Hall of Famers Who Played for the Philadelphia Athletics
Home Run Baker, third base, 1908–14
Chief Bender, pitcher, 1903–14
Ty Cobb, outfield, 1927–28
Mickey Cochrane, catcher, 1925–33
Eddie Collins, second base, 1906–14 and 1927–30
Jimmy Collins, third base, 1907–08
Stan Coveleski, pitcher, 1912
Jimmie Foxx, catcher, third base, and first base, 1925–35
Waite Hoyt, pitcher, 1931
George Kell, third base, 1943–46
Nap Lajoie, second base, 1901–02, 1915–16
Herb Pennock, pitcher, 1912–15
Eddie Plank, pitcher, 1901–14
Al Simmons, outfield, 1924–32, 1940–41, and 1944

Tris Speaker, outfield, 1928
Rube Waddell, pitcher, 1902–07
Zack Wheat, outfield, 1927

League Leaders, Batting

Batting Average, Season
Nap Lajoie, 1901 .... .426
Al Simmons, 1930 .... .381
Al Simmons, 1931 .... .390
Jimmie Foxx, 1933 .... .356
Ferris Fain, 1951 .... .344
Ferris Fain, 1952 .... .327

Home Runs, Season
Nap Lajoie, 1901 14
Socks Seybold, 1902.................... 16
Harry Davis, 1904 10
Harry Davis, 1905 8
Harry Davis, 1906 12
Harry Davis, 1907 8
Home Run Baker, 1911 11
Home Run Baker, 1912.......... 10 (Tie)
Home Run Baker, 1913 12
Home Run Baker, 1914 9
Tilly Walker, 1918 .... 11 (Tie)
Jimmie Foxx, 1932 58
Jimmie Foxx, 1933 48
Jimmie Foxx, 1935 .... 36 (Tie)
Gus Zernial*, 1951...................... 33
* 0 with Chi. White Sox and 33 with Phi. A's.

RBIs, Season
Home Run Baker, 1912 133
Home Run Baker, 1913 126

George H. Burns, 1918 .... 74 (Tie)
Al Simmons, 1929 157
Jimmie Foxx, 1932................... 169
Jimmie Foxx, 1933 163
Gus Zernial*, 1951................... 129
* 4 with Chi. White Sox and 125 with Phi. A's.

Stolen Bases, Season
Topsy Hartsel, 1902 54
Danny Hoffman, 1905 46
Eddie Collins, 1910 81
Billy Werber, 1937............... 35 (Tie)

Total Bases, Season
Nap Lajoie, 1901 345
George H. Burns, 1918 236
Al Simmons, 1925 392
Al Simmons, 1929 373
Jimmie Foxx, 1932.................... 438
Jimmie Foxx, 1933 403

Most Hits, Season
Nap Lajoie, 1901 229
George H. Burns, 1918 178
Al Simmons, 1925 253
Al Simmons, 1932 216

Most Runs, Season
Nap Lajoie, 1901 145
Dave Fultz, 1902 110
Harry Davis, 1905 92
Eddie Collins, 1912 137
Eddie Collins, 1913 125
Eddie Collins, 1914 122

Al Simmons, 1930 152

Jimmie Foxx, 1932 151

Batting Feats

Triple Crown Winners

Nap Lajoie, 1901 (.426 BA, 14 HRs, 125 RBIs)

Hitting for the Cycle

Harry Davis, Jul. 10, 1901

Nap Lajoie, Jul. 30, 1901

Danny Murphy, Aug. 25, 1910

Home Run Baker, Jul. 3, 1911

Mickey Cochrane, Jul. 22, 1932

Mickey Cochrane, Aug. 2, 1933

Pinky Higgins, Aug. 6, 1933

Jimmie Foxx, Aug. 14, 1933

Doc Cramer, Jun. 10, 1934

Sam Chapman, May 5, 1939

Elmer Valo, Aug. 2, 1950

Six Hits in a Game

Danny Murphy, Jul. 8, 1902

Jimmie Foxx, May 30, 1930*

Doc Cramer, Jun. 20, 1932

Jimmie Foxx, Jul. 10, 1932*

Bob Johnson, Jun. 16, 1934*

Doc Cramer, Jul. 13, 1935

* Extra-inning game.

40 or More Home Runs, Season

58 .... Jimmie Foxx, 1932

48 .... Jimmie Foxx, 1933

44 .... Jimmie Foxx, 1934

42 .... Gus Zernial, 1953

League Leaders, Pitching

Most Wins, Season

Rube Waddell, 1905 27

Jack Coombs, 1910 31

Jack Coombs, 1911 28

Ed Rommel, 1922 27

Ed Rommel, 1925 .... 21 (Tie)

Lefty Grove, 1928 .... 24 (Tie)

George Earnshaw, 1929 24

Lefty Grove, 1930 28

Lefty Grove, 1931 31

Lefty Grove, 1933 .... 24 (Tie)

Bobby Shantz, 1952 24

Most Strikeouts, Season

Rube Waddell, 1902 210

Rube Waddell, 1903 301

Rube Waddell, 1904 349

Rube Waddell, 1905 286

Rube Waddell, 1906 203

Rube Waddell, 1907 226

Lefty Grove, 1925 116

Lefty Grove, 1926 194

Lefty Grove, 1927 174

Lefty Grove, 1928 183

Lefty Grove, 1929 170

Lefty Grove, 1930 209

Lefty Grove, 1931 175

Lowest ERA, Season

Lefty Grove, 1926 .... 2.51

Lefty Grove, 1929 .... 2.81

Lefty Grove, 1930 .... 2.54

Lefty Grove, 1931 .... 2.06

Lefty Grove, 1932 .... 2.84

Most Saves, Season

[No player]

Best Won–Lost Percentage, Season

Eddie Plank, 1906 .... 19–8 ... .760

Chief Bender, 1910 ...... 23–5 ... .821

Chief Bender, 1911 ...... 17–9 ... .773

Chief Bender, 1914 ...... 17–3 ... .850

Lefty Grove, 1929 .... 20–6 ... .769

Lefty Grove, 1930 .... 28–5 ... .848

Lefty Grove, 1931 .... 31–4 ... .886

Lefty Grove, 1933 .... 24–8 ... .750

Bobby Shantz, 1952 .... 24–7 ... .774

Pitching Feats

Triple Crown Winner

Rube Waddell, 1905 (27–10, 1.48 ERA, 287 SO)

Lefty Grove, 1930 (28–5, 2.54 ERA, 209 SO)

Lefty Grove, 1931 (31–4, 2.06 ERA, 175 SO)

20 Wins, Season

Chick Fraser, 1901 22–16

Rube Waddell, 1902 23–7

Eddie Plank, 1902 20–15

Eddie Plank, 1903 23–16

Rube Waddell, 1903 21–16

Eddie Plank, 1904 26–17

Rube Waddell, 1904 25–19

Rube Waddell, 1905 26–11

Eddie Plank, 1905 25–12

Eddie Plank, 1907 24–16

Jimmy Dygert, 1907 20–9

Jack Coombs, 1910 31–9

Chief Bender, 1910 23–5

Jack Coombs, 1911 28–12

Eddie Plank, 1911 22–8

Eddie Plank, 1912 26–6

Jack Coombs, 1912 21–10

Chief Bender, 1913 21–10

Scott Perry, 1918 21–19

Eddie Rommel, 1922 27–13

Eddie Rommel, 1925 21–10

Lefty Grove, 1927 20–13

Lefty Grove, 1928 24–8

George Earnshaw, 1929 24–8

Lefty Grove, 1929 20–6

Lefty Grove, 1930 28–5

George Earnshaw, 1930 22–13

Lefty Grove, 1931 31–4

George Earnshaw, 1931 21–7

Rube Walberg, 1931 20–12

Lefty Grove, 1932 25–10

Lefty Grove, 1933 24–8

Alex Kellner, 1949 20–12

Bobby Shantz, 1952 24–7

No-Hitters

Weldon Henley (vs. St.L. Browns), Jul. 22, 1905 (final: 6–0)

Chief Bender (vs. Cle. Indians), May 12, 1910 (final: 4–0)

Joe Bush (vs. Cle. Indians), Aug. 26, 1916 (final: 5–0)

Dick Fowler (vs. St.L. Browns), Sep. 9, 1945 (final: 1–0)

Bill McCahan (vs. Was. Senators), Sep. 3, 1947 (final: 3–0)

No-Hitters Pitched Against

Cy Young, Bos. Red Sox, May 5, 1904 (final: 3–0) (perfect game)

Frank Smith, Chi. White Sox, Sep. 20, 1908 (final: 1–0)

Sam Jones, N.Y. Yankees, Sep. 4, 1923 (final: 4–0)

Howard Ehmke, Bos. Red Sox, Sep. 7, 1923 (final: 4–0)

Don Black, Cle. Indians, Jul. 10, 1947 (final: 3–0)

Bobo Holloman, St.L. Browns, May 6, 1953 (final: 6–0)

Postseason Play

1905 World Series vs. N.Y. Giants
 (NL), lost 4 games to 1

1910 World Series vs. Chi. Cubs (NL),
 won 4 games to 1

1911 World Series vs. N.Y. Giants
 (NL), won 4 games to 2

1913 World Series vs. N.Y. Giants (NL),
 won 4 games to 1

1914 World Series vs. Bos. Braves (NL),
 lost 4 games to 0

1929 World Series vs. Chi. Cubs (NL),
 won 4 games to 1

1930 World Series vs. St.L. Cardinals
 (NL), won 4 games to 3

1931 World Series vs. St.L. Cardinals
 (NL), lost 4 games to 2

St. Louis Browns (formerly the Milwaukee Brewers)

Date of Operation: (as the Milwaukee Brewers) 1901 (1 year)
Overall Record: 48 wins, 89 losses (.350)
Stadium: Lloyd Street Park, 1901

Dates of Operation: (as the St. Louis Browns) 1902–53 (52 years)
Overall Record: 3414 wins, 4465 losses (.433)
Stadiums: Sportsman's Park IV, 1902–08; Sportsman's Park V, 1909–53 (capacity: 30,500)

Year-by-Year Finishes

Year	Finish	Wins	Losses	Percentage	Games Behind	Manager	Attendance
					Mil. Brewers		
1901	8th	48	89	.350	35.5	Hugh Duffy	139,034
					St.L. Browns		
1902	2nd	78	58	.574	5.0	Jimmy McAleer	272,283
1903	6th	65	74	.468	26.5	Jimmy McAleer	380,405
1904	6th	65	87	.428	29.0	Jimmy McAleer	318,108
1905	8th	54	99	.353	40.5	Jimmy McAleer	339,112
1906	5th	76	73	.510	16.0	Jimmy McAleer	389,157
1907	6th	69	83	.454	24.0	Jimmy McAleer	419,025
1908	4th	83	69	.546	6.5	Jimmy McAleer	618,947
1909	7th	61	89	.407	36.0	Jimmy McAleer	366,274
1910	8th	47	107	.305	57.0	Jack O'Connor	249,889
1911	8th	45	107	.296	56.5	Bobby Wallace	207,984
1912	7th	53	101	.344	53.0	Bobby Wallace, George Stovall	214,070
1913	8th	57	96	.373	39.0	George Stovall, Branch Rickey	250,330
1914	5th	71	82	.464	28.5	Branch Rickey	244,714
1915	6th	63	91	.409	39.5	Branch Rickey	150,358
1916	5th	79	75	.513	12.0	Fielder Jones	335,740
1917	7th	57	97	.370	43.0	Fielder Jones	210,486
1918	5th	58	64	.475	15.0	Fielder Jones, Jimmy Austin, Jimmy Burke	122,076
1919	5th	67	72	.482	20.5	Jimmy Burke	349,350
1920	4th	76	77	.497	21.5	Jimmy Burke	419,311
1921	3rd	81	73	.526	17.5	Lee Fohl	355,978
1922	2nd	93	61	.604	1.0	Lee Fohl	712,918
1923	5th	74	78	.487	24.0	Lee Fohl, Jimmy Austin	430,296
1924	4th	74	78	.487	17.0	George Sisler	533,349
1925	3rd	82	71	.536	15.0	George Sisler	462,898
1926	7th	62	92	.403	29.0	George Sisler	283,986
1927	7th	59	94	.386	50.5	Dan Howley	247,879
1928	3rd	82	72	.532	19.0	Dan Howley	339,497
1929	4th	79	73	.520	26.0	Dan Howley	280,697
1930	6th	64	90	.416	38.0	Bill Killefer	152,088
1931	5th	63	91	.409	45.0	Bill Killefer	179,126
1932	6th	63	91	.409	44.0	Bill Killefer	112,558
1933	8th	55	96	.364	43.5	Bill Killefer, Allen Sothoron, Rogers Hornsby	88,113

Year	Finish	Wins	Losses	Percentage	Games Behind	Manager	Attendance
1934	6th	67	85	.441	33.0	Rogers Hornsby	115,305
1935	7th	65	87	.428	28.5	Rogers Hornsby	80,922
1936	7th	57	95	.375	44.5	Rogers Hornsby	93,267
1937	8th	46	108	.299	56.0	Rogers Hornsby, Jim Bottomley	123,121
1938	7th	55	97	.362	44.0	Gabby Street	130,417
1939	8th	43	111	.279	64.5	Fred Haney	109,159
1940	6th	67	87	.435	23.0	Fred Haney	239,591
1941	6th (Tie)	70	84	.455	31.0	Fred Haney, Luke Sewell	176,240
1942	3rd	82	69	.543	19.5	Luke Sewell	255,617
1943	6th	72	80	.474	25.0	Luke Sewell	214,392
1944	1st	89	65	.578	+1.0	Luke Sewell	508,644
1945	3rd	81	70	.536	6.0	Luke Sewell	482,986
1946	7th	66	88	.429	38.0	Luke Sewell, Zack Taylor	526,435
1947	8th	59	95	.383	38.0	Muddy Ruel	320,474
1948	6th	59	94	.386	37.0	Zack Taylor	335,546
1949	7th	53	101	.344	44.0	Zack Taylor	270,936
1950	7th	58	96	.377	40.0	Zack Taylor	247,131
1951	8th	52	102	.338	46.0	Zack Taylor	293,790
1952	7th	64	90	.416	31.0	Rogers Hornsby, Marty Marion	518,796
1953	8th	54	100	.351	46.5	Marty Marion	297,238

Awards

Most Valuable Player
George Sisler, first base, 1922

Rookie of the Year
Roy Sievers, outfield, 1949

Cy Young
[No player]

Hall of Famers Who Played for the St. Louis Browns
Jim Bottomley, first base, 1936–37
Jesse Burkett, outfield, 1902–04
Rick Ferrell, catcher, 1929–33 and
   1941–43
Goose Goslin, outfield, 1930–32
Heinie Manush, outfield, 1928–30
Satchel Paige, pitcher, 1951–53
Eddie Plank, pitcher, 1916–17
Branch Rickey, catcher, 1905–06 and
   1914
George Sisler, first base, 1915–22 and
   1924–27
Rube Waddell, pitcher, 1908–10
Bobby Wallace, shortstop, 1902–16

League Leaders, Batting

Batting Average, Season
George Stone, 1906 .... .358
George Sisler, 1920 .... .407
George Sisler, 1922 .... .420

Home Runs, Season
Ken Williams, 1922 39
Vern Stephens, 1945 24

RBIs, Season
Ken Williams, 1922 155
Vern Stephens, 1944 109

Stolen Bases, Season
George Sisler, 1918 45
George Sisler, 1921 35
George Sisler, 1922 51
George Sisler, 1927 27
Lyn Lary, 1936 37
Bob Dillinger, 1947 34
Bob Dillinger, 1948 28
Bob Dillinger, 1949 20

Total Bases, Season
George Stone, 1905 260
George Stone, 1906 288
George Sisler, 1920 399
Ken Williams, 1922 367

Most Hits, Season
George Stone, 1905 187
George Sisler, 1920 257
George Sisler, 1922 246
Heinie Manush, 1928 241
Beau Bell, 1937 218
Rip Radcliff, 1940 .... 200 (Tie)
Bob Dillinger, 1948 207

Most Runs, Season
George Sisler, 1922 134

Batting Feats

Triple Crown Winners
[No player]

Hitting for the Cycle
George Sisler, Aug. 8, 1920
George Sisler, Aug. 13, 1921
Baby Doll Jacobson, Apr. 17, 1924
Oscar Mellilo, May 23, 1929
George McQuinn, Jul. 19, 1941

Six Hits in a Game
George Sisler, Aug. 9, 1921*
Sammy West, Apr. 13, 1933*
* Extra-inning game.

40 or More Home Runs, Season
[No player]

League Leaders, Pitching

Most Wins, Season
Urban Shocker, 1921 .... 27 (Tie)

Most Strikeouts, Season
Urban Shocker, 1922 149

Lowest ERA, Season
[No player]

Most Saves, Season
[No player]

Best Won–Lost Percentage, Season
General Crowder, 1928..21–5.... .808

Pitching Feats

20 Wins, Season (1901–53)
Frank Donahue, 1902............. 22–11
Jack Powell, 1902.................. 22–17

Willie Sudhoff, 1903 21–15
Allen Sothoron, 1919 21–11
Urban Shocker, 1920 20–10
Urban Shocker, 1921 27–12
Urban Shocker, 1922 24–17
Urban Shocker, 1923 20–12
General Crowder, 1928............ 21–5
Sam Gray, 1928.................... 20–12
Lefty Stewart, 1930 20–12
Bobo Newsom, 1938 20–16
Ned Garver, 1951 20–12

No-Hitters
Earl Hamilton (vs. Det. Tigers), Aug. 30, 1912 (final: 5–1)
Ernie Koob (vs. Chi. White Sox), May 5, 1917 (final: 1–0)
Bob Groom (vs. Chi. White Sox), May 6, 1917 (final: 3–0)
Bobo Newsom (vs. Bos. Red Sox), Sep. 18, 1934 (final: 1–2) (lost in 10th)
Bobo Holloman (vs. Phi. A's), May 6, 1953 (final: 6–0)

No-Hitters Pitched Against
Weldon Henley, Phi. A's, Jul. 22, 1905 (final: 6–0)
Smoky Joe Wood, Bos. Red Sox, Jul. 29, 1911 (final: 5–0)
George Mullin, Det. Tigers, Jul. 4, 1912 (final: 7–0)
Hub Leonard, Bos. Red Sox, Aug. 30, 1916 (final: 4–0)
Eddie Cicotte, Chi. White Sox, Apr. 14, 1917 (final: 11–0)
Wes Ferrell, Cle. Indians, Apr. 29, 1931 (final: 9–0)
Vern Kennedy, Chi. White Sox, Aug. 31, 1935 (final: 5–0)
Bill Dietrich, Chi. White Sox, Jun. 1, 1937 (final: 8–0)
Dick Fowler, Phi. A's, Sep. 9, 1945 (final: 1–0)

Postseason Play

1944 World Series vs. St.L. Cardinals (NL), lost 4 games to 2

Washington Senators

Dates of Operation: (as the Washington Senators) 1901–60 (60 years)
Overall Record: 4223 wins, 4864 losses (.465)
Stadiums: American League Park I, 1901–03; American League Park II, 1904–10; Griffith Stadium
(formerly National Park, 1911–21; Clark Griffith Park, 1922), 1911–60
Other Name: Nationals

Dates of Operation: (as the Washington Senators II) 1961–71 (11 years)
Overall Record: 740 wins, 1032 losses (.418)
Stadiums: Griffith Stadium, 1961; Robert F. Kennedy (RFK) Stadium, 1962–71
Other Name: Nats

Year-by-Year Finishes

Year	Finish	Wins	Losses	Percentage	Games Behind	Manager	Attendance
					Was. Senators		
1901	6th	61	72	.459	20.5	Jimmy Manning	161,661
1902	6th	61	75	.449	22.0	Tom Loftus	188,158
1903	8th	43	94	.314	47.5	Tom Loftus	128,878
1904	8th	38	113	.252	55.5	Patsy Donovan	131,744
1905	7th	64	87	.424	29.5	Jake Stahl	252,027
1906	7th	55	95	.367	37.5	Jake Stahl	129,903
1907	8th	49	102	.325	43.5	Joe Cantillon	221,929
1908	7th	67	85	.441	22.5	Joe Cantillon	264,252
1909	8th	42	110	.276	56.0	Joe Cantillon	205,199
1910	7th	66	85	.437	36.5	Jimmy McAleer	254,591
1911	7th	64	90	.416	38.5	Jimmy McAleer	244,884
1912	2nd	91	61	.599	14.0	Clark Griffith	350,663
1913	2nd	90	64	.584	6.5	Clark Griffith	325,831
1914	3rd	81	73	.526	19.0	Clark Griffith	243,888
1915	4th	85	68	.556	17.0	Clark Griffith	167,332
1916	7th	76	77	.497	14.5	Clark Griffith	177,265
1917	5th	74	79	.484	25.5	Clark Griffith	89,682
1918	3rd	72	56	.563	4.0	Clark Griffith	182,122
1919	7th	56	84	.400	32.0	Clark Griffith	234,096
1920	6th	68	84	.447	29.0	Clark Griffith	359,260
1921	4th	80	73	.523	18.0	George McBride	456,069
1922	6th	69	85	.448	25.0	Clyde Milan	458,552
1923	4th	75	78	.490	23.5	Donie Bush	357,406
1924	1st	92	62	.597	+2.0	Bucky Harris	534,310
1925	1st	96	55	.636	+8.5	Bucky Harris	817,199
1926	4th	81	69	.540	8.0	Bucky Harris	551,580
1927	3rd	85	69	.552	25.0	Bucky Harris	528,976
1928	4th	75	79	.487	26.0	Bucky Harris	378,501
1929	5th	71	81	.467	34.0	Walter Johnson	355,506
1930	2nd	94	60	.610	8.0	Walter Johnson	614,474
1931	3rd	92	62	.597	16.0	Walter Johnson	492,657
1932	3rd	93	61	.604	14.0	Walter Johnson	371,396
1933	1st	99	53	.651	+7.0	Joe Cronin	437,533
1934	7th	66	86	.434	34.0	Joe Cronin	330,374
1935	6th	67	86	.438	27.0	Bucky Harris	255,011

Year	Finish	Wins	Losses	Percentage	Games Behind	Manager	Attendance
1936	4th	82	71	.536	20.0	Bucky Harris	379,525
1937	6th	73	80	.477	28.5	Bucky Harris	397,799
1938	5th	75	76	.497	23.5	Bucky Harris	522,694
1939	6th	65	87	.428	41.5	Bucky Harris	339,257
1940	7th	64	90	.416	26.0	Bucky Harris	381,241
1941	6th (Tie)	70	84	.455	31.0	Bucky Harris	415,663
1942	7th	62	89	.411	39.5	Bucky Harris	403,493
1943	2nd	84	69	.549	13.5	Ossie Bluege	574,694
1944	8th	64	90	.416	25.0	Ossie Bluege	525,235
1945	2nd	87	67	.565	1.5	Ossie Bluege	652,660
1946	4th	76	78	.494	28.0	Ossie Bluege	1,027,216
1947	7th	64	90	.416	33.0	Ossie Bluege	850,758
1948	7th	56	97	.366	40.0	Joe Kuhel	795,254
1949	8th	50	104	.325	47.0	Joe Kuhel	770,745
1950	5th	67	87	.435	31.0	Bucky Harris	699,697
1951	7th	62	92	.403	36.0	Bucky Harris	695,167
1952	5th	78	76	.506	17.0	Bucky Harris	699,457
1953	5th	76	76	.500	23.5	Bucky Harris	595,594
1954	6th	66	88	.429	45.0	Bucky Harris	503,542
1955	8th	53	101	.344	43.0	Chuck Dressen	425,238
1956	7th	59	95	.383	38.0	Chuck Dressen	431,647
1957	8th	55	99	.357	43.0	Chuck Dressen, Cookie Lavagetto	457,079
1958	8th	61	93	.396	31.0	Cookie Lavagetto	475,288
1959	8th	63	91	.409	31.0	Cookie Lavagetto	615,372
1960	5th	73	81	.474	24.0	Cookie Lavagetto	743,404

Was. Senators II

Year	Finish	Wins	Losses	Percentage	Games Behind	Manager	Attendance
1961	9th (Tie)	61	100	.379	47.5	Mickey Vernon	597,287
1962	10th	60	101	.373	35.5	Mickey Vernon	729,775
1963	10th	56	106	.346	48.5	Mickey Vernon, Gil Hodges	535,604
1964	9th	62	100	.383	37.0	Gil Hodges	600,106
1965	8th	70	92	.432	32.0	Gil Hodges	560,083
1966	8th	71	88	.447	25.5	Gil Hodges	576,260
1967	6th (Tie)	76	85	.472	15.5	Gil Hodges	770,863
1968	10th	65	96	.404	37.5	Jim Lemon	546,661

East Division

Year	Finish	Wins	Losses	Percentage	Games Behind	Manager	Attendance
1969	4th	86	76	.531	23.0	Ted Williams	918,106
1970	6th	70	92	.432	38.0	Ted Williams	824,789
1971	5th	63	96	.396	38.5	Ted Williams	655,156

Awards

Most Valuable Player

Walter Johnson, pitcher, 1913

Walter Johnson, pitcher, 1924

Roger Peckinpaugh, shortstop, 1925

Rookie of the Year

Albie Pearson, outfield, 1958

Bob Allison, outfield, 1959

Cy Young

[No player]

Hall of Famers Who Played for the Senators

Stan Coveleski, pitcher, 1925–27

Joe Cronin, shortstop, 1928–34

Ed Delahanty, first base and outfield, 1902–03

Rick Ferrell, catcher, 1937–41, 1944–45, and 1947

Lefty Gomez, pitcher, 1943

Goose Goslin, outfield, 1921–30, 1933, and 1938

Bucky Harris, second base, 1919–28

Walter Johnson, pitcher, 1907–27

Jim Kaat, pitcher, 1959–60

Harmon Killebrew, third base and first base, 1956–60

Heinie Manush, outfield, 1930–35
Minnie Minoso, outfield and infield, 1963
Sam Rice, outfield, 1915–33
Al Simmons, outfield, 1937–38
Early Wynn, pitcher, 1939, 1941–44,
    and 1946–48

League Leaders, Batting

Batting Average, Season

Ed Delahanty, 1902 .... .376
Goose Goslin, 1928................... .379
Buddy Myer, 1935 .... .349
Mickey Vernon, 1946 .... .353
Mickey Vernon, 1953 .... .337

Home Runs, Season

Roy Sievers, 1957......................42
Harmon Killebrew, 1959........42 (Tie)
Frank Howard, 1968 (Senators II) ..44
Frank Howard, 1970 (Senators II) ..44

RBIs, Season

Goose Goslin, 1924....................129
Roy Sievers, 1957 114
Frank Howard, 1970 (Senators II) 126

Stolen Bases, Season

John Anderson, 1906 .... 39 (Tie)
Clyde Milan, 1912........................88
Clyde Milan, 1913........................75
Sam Rice, 1920............................63
Ben Chapman*, 1937 .... 35 (Tie)
George Case, 1939 51
George Case, 1940 35
George Case, 1941 33
George Case, 1942 44
George Case, 1943 61
* 27 with Bos. Red Sox and 8 with Was.
    Senators.

Total Bases, Season

Roy Sievers, 1957......................331
Frank Howard, 1968 (Senators II) 330
Frank Howard, 1969 (Senators II) 340

Most Hits, Season

Sam Rice, 1924..........................216
Sam Rice, 1926.................. 216 (Tie)
Heinie Manush, 1933.................221
Cecil Travis, 1941......................218

Most Runs, Season

George Case, 1943 102

Batting Feats

Triple Crown Winners
[No player]

Hitting for the Cycle
Otis Clymer, Oct. 2, 1908
Goose Goslin, Aug. 28, 1924
Joe Cronin, Sep. 2, 1929
Mickey Vernon, May 19, 1946
Jim King, May 26, 1964 (Senators II)

Six Hits in a Game
George Myatt, May 1, 1944
Stan Spence, Jun. 1, 1944

40 or More Home Runs, Season
48 ..Frank Howard, 1969 (Senators II)
44 ..Frank Howard, 1968 (Senators II)
        Frank Howard, 1970 (Senators II)
42 ....Roy Sievers, 1957
        Harmon Killebrew, 1959

League Leaders, Pitching

Most Wins, Season
Walter Johnson, 1913 36
Walter Johnson, 1914 28
Walter Johnson, 1915 27
Walter Johnson, 1916 25
Walter Johnson, 1918 23
Walter Johnson, 1924 23
General Crowder, 1932................26
General Crowder, 1933.........24 (Tie)
Bob Porterfield, 1953 22

Most Strikeouts, Season
Walter Johnson, 1910 313
Walter Johnson, 1912 303
Walter Johnson, 1913 243
Walter Johnson, 1914 225
Walter Johnson, 1915 203
Walter Johnson, 1916 228
Walter Johnson, 1917 188
Walter Johnson, 1918 162
Walter Johnson, 1919 147
Walter Johnson, 1921 143
Walter Johnson, 1923 130
Walter Johnson, 1924 158
Bobo Newsom, 1942 ....113 (Tie)

Lowest ERA, Season
Walter Johnson, 1913 ....1.14
Walter Johnson, 1918 ....1.27

Walter Johnson, 1919 ....1.49
Walter Johnson, 1924 ....2.72
Stan Coveleski, 1925 ....2.84
Garland Braxton, 1928..............2.52
Dick Donovan, 1961 (Senators II) .2.40
Dick Bosman, 1969 (Senators II) .2.19

Most Saves, Season
[No player]

Best Won–Lost Percentage, Season
Walter Johnson, 1913 ..36–7 ... .837
Walter Johnson, 1924 ..23–7 ... .767
Stan Coveleski, 1925 ...20–5 ... .800

Pitching Feats

Triple Crown Winner
Walter Johnson, 1913 (36–7, 1.14
    ERA, 243 SO)
Walter Johnson, 1918 (23–13, 1.27
    ERA, 162 SO)
Walter Johnson, 1924 (23–7, 2.72
    ERA, 158 SO)

20 Wins, Season
Walter Johnson, 1910 25–17
Walter Johnson, 1911 25–13
Walter Johnson, 1912 33–12
Bob Groom, 1912.................. 24–13
Walter Johnson, 1913 36–7
Walter Johnson, 1914 28–18
Walter Johnson, 1915 27–13
Walter Johnson, 1916 25–20
Walter Johnson, 1917 23–16
Walter Johnson, 1918 23–13
Walter Johnson, 1919 20–14
Walter Johnson, 1924 23–7
Stan Coveleski, 1925 20–5
Walter Johnson, 1925 20–7
General Crowder, 1932........... 26–13
Monte Weaver, 1932 22–10
General Crowder, 1933.......... 24–15
Earl Whitehill, 1933................ 22–8
Dutch Leonard, 1939............... 20–8
Roger Wolff, 1945 20–10
Bob Porterfield, 1953 22–10

No-Hitters
Walter Johnson (vs. Bos. Red Sox),
    Jul. 1, 1920 (final: 1–0)
Bob Burke (vs. Bos. Red Sox), Aug.
    8, 1931 (final: 5–0)

No-Hitters Pitched Against

Ernie Shore, Bos. Red Sox, Jun. 23,
   1917 (final: 4–0) (perfect game)
Bill McCahan, Phi. A's, Sep. 3,
   1947 (final: 3–0)
Virgil Trucks, Det. Tigers, May 15,
   1952 (final: 1–0)
Bob Keegan, Chi. White Sox, Aug.
   20, 1957 (final: 6–0)
Sonny Siebert, Cle. Indians, Jun.
   10, 1966 (final: 2–0) (Senators II)

Postseason Play

1924 World Series vs. N.Y. Giants
      (NL), won 4 games to 3
1925 World Series vs. Pit. Pirates
      (NL), lost 4 games to 3
1933 World Series vs. N.Y. Giants
      (NL), lost 4 games to 1

Federal League

Baltimore Terrapins

Dates of Operation: 1914–15 (2 seasons)
Overall Record: 131–177–6 (.417)
Stadiums: Terrapin Park

Year-by-Year Finishes

Year	Finish	Wins	Losses	Ties	Percentage	Games Behind	Manager
1914	3rd	84	70	6	.525	4.5	Otto Knabe
1915	8th	47	107	0	.305	40.0	Otto Knabe

Hall of Famers Who Played for the Terrapins
Charles Bender, pitcher, 1915

League Leaders, Batting

Batting Average, Season
[No player]

Home Runs, Seasons
[No player]

RBIs, Season
[No player]

Stolen Bases, Season
[No player]

Total Bases, Season
[No player]

Most Hits, Season
[No player]

Most Runs, Season
[No player]

Batting Feats

Hitting for the Cycle
[No player]

League Leaders, Pitching

Most Wins, Season
[No player]

Most Strikeouts, Season
[No player]

Lowest ERA, Season
[No player]

Most Saves, Season
[No player]

Best Won-Lost Percentage, Season
[No player]

Pitching Feats

20 Wins, Season
Jack Quinn, 1914..................... 26–14
George Suggs, 1914 24–14

No-Hitters
[No player]

No-Hitters Pitched Against
[No player]

Brooklyn Tip-Tops

Dates of Operation: 1914–15 (2 seasons)
Overall Record: 147–159–4 (.474)
Stadiums: Washington Park IV

Year-by-Year Finishes

Year	Finish	Wins	Losses	Ties	Percentage	Games Behind	Manager
1914	5th	77	77	3	.490	11.5	Bill Bradley
1915	7th	70	82	1	.458	16.0	Lee Magee, John Ganzel

Hall of Famers Who Played for the Tip-Tops
Mordecai Brown, pitcher, 1914

League Leaders, Batting

Batting Average, Season
Benny Kauff, 1915 .... .342

Home Runs, Seasons
[No player]

RBIs, Season
[No player]

Stolen Bases, Season
Benny Kauff, 1915 55

Total Bases, Season
[No player]

Most Hits, Season
[No player]

Most Runs, Season
[No player]

Batting Feats

Hitting for the Cycle
[No player]

League Leaders, Pitching

Most Wins, Season
[No player]

Most Strikeouts, Season
[No player]

Lowest ERA, Season
[No player]

Most Saves, Season
[No player]

Best Won-Lost Percentage, Season
[No player]

Pitching Feats

20 Wins, Season
Tom Seaton, 1914 25–14

No-Hitters
Ed Lafitte (vs. K.C. Packers), Sep. 19, 1914 (final: 6–2)

No-Hitters Pitched Against
[No player]

Buffalo Blues

Dates of Operation: 1914–15 (2 seasons)
Overall Record: 154–149–5 (.500)
Stadiums: Federal League Park
Other Names: Buffalo Buffeds (1914)

Year-by-Year Finishes

Year	Finish	Wins	Losses	Ties	Percentage	Games Behind	Manager
			Buf. Buffeds				
1914	4th	80	71	4	.516	7.0	Larry Schlafly
			Buf. Blues				
1915	6th	74	78	1	.484	12.0	Larry Schlafly, Walter Blair, Harry Lord

Hall of Famers Who Played for the Buffeds/Blues
[No player]

League Leaders, Batting

Batting Average, Season
[No player]

Home Runs, Seasons
Hal Chase, 1915 17

RBIs, Season
[No player]

Stolen Bases, Season
[No player]

Total Bases, Season
[No player]

Most Hits, Season
[No player]

Most Runs, Season
[No player]

Batting Feats

Hitting for the Cycle
[No player]

League Leaders, Pitching

Most Wins, Season
[No player]

Most Strikeouts, Season
[No player]

Lowest ERA, Season
[No player]

Most Saves, Season
[No player]

Best Won-Lost Percentage, Season
[No player]

Pitching Feats

20 Wins, Season
Russ Ford, 1914 .... 21–6 (Buffeds)
Al Schultz, 1915 21–14

No-Hitters
[No player]

No-Hitters Pitched Against
Alex Main, K.C. Packers, Sep. 7, 1915
(final: 5–0) (perfect game)

Chicago Whales

Dates of Operation: 1914–15 (2 seasons)
Overall Record: 173–133–6 (.554)
Stadiums: Weeghman Park
Other Names: Chicago Chi-Feds (1914)

Year-by-Year Finishes

Year	Finish	Wins	Losses	Ties	Percentage	Games Behind	Manager
				Chi. Chi-Feds			
1914	2nd	87	67	3	.554	1.5	Joe Tinker
				Chi. Whales			
1915	1st (Tie)	86	66	3	.555	—	Joe Tinker

Hall of Famers Who Played for the Whales/Chi-Feds
Mordecai Brown, pitcher, 1915
Joe Tinker, shortstop, 1914–15

League Leaders, Batting

Batting Average, Season
[No player]

Home Runs, Seasons
Dutch Zwilling, 1914 ....16 (Chi-Feds)

RBIs, Season
Dutch Zwilling, 1915 94

Stolen Bases, Season
[No player]

Total Bases, Season
[No player]

Most Hits, Season
[No player]

Most Runs, Season
[No player]

Batting Feats

Hitting for the Cycle
[No player]

League Leaders, Pitching

Most Wins, Season
Claude Hendrix, 1914 ......29 (Chi.Feds)
George McConnell, 1915.................25

Most Strikeouts, Season
[No player]

Lowest ERA, Season
Claude Hendrix, 1914 ..1.69 (Chi-Feds)

Most Saves, Season
Russ Ford, 1914................6 (Chi-Feds)

Best Won-Lost Percentage, Season
Russ Ford, 1914... 21–6 (.778) (Chi-Feds)
George McConnell, 1915...25–10 (.714)

Pitching Feats

20 Wins, Season
Claude Hendrix, 1914... 29–10 (Chi-Feds)
George McConnell, 1915.......... 25–10

No-Hitters
Claude Hendrix (vs. Pit. Rebels), May 15, 1915 (final: 10–0) (perfect game)

No-Hitters Pitched Against
Dave Davenport, St.L. Terriers, Sep. 7, 1915 (final: 3–0) (perfect game)

Newark Pepper

Dates of Operation: 1914–15 (2 seasons)
Overall Record: 168–137–7 (.538)
Stadiums: Federal League Park
Other Names: Indianapolis Hoosiers (1914)

Year-by-Year Finishes

Year	Finish	Wins	Losses	Ties	Percentage	Games Behind	Manager
				Ind. Hoosiers			
1914	1st	88	65	4	.561	1.5	Bill Phillips
				New. Pepper			
1915	5th	80	72	3	.516	6.0	Bill Phillips, Bill McKechnie

Hall of Famers Who Played for the Pepper/Hoosiers
Bill McKechnie, infield, 1914–15
Ed Roush, outfield, 1914–15

League Leaders, Batting

Batting Average, Season
Benny Kauff, 1914 ....370 (Ind.)

Home Runs, Seasons
[No player]

RBIs, Season
Frank LaPorte, 1914 ....107 (Ind.)

Stolen Bases, Season
Benny Kauff, 1914 ....75 (Ind.)

Total Bases, Season
Benny Kauff, 1914 ....305 (Ind.)

Most Hits, Season
Benny Kauff, 1914 ....211 (Ind.)

Most Runs, Season
Benny Kauff, 1914 ....120 (Ind.)

Batting Feats

Hitting for the Cycle
[No player]

League Leaders, Pitching

Most Wins, Season
[No player]

Most Strikeouts, Season
Cy Falkenberg, 1914 ....236 (Ind.)

Lowest ERA, Season
Earl Moseley, 1915.......................1.91

Most Saves, Season
[No player]

Best Won-Lost Percentage, Season
[No player]

Pitching Feats

20 Wins, Season
Cy Falkenberg, 1914 ....25–16 (Ind.)
Ed Reulbach, 1915 21–10

No-Hitters
[No player]

No-Hitters Pitched Against
[No player]

Kansas City Packers

Dates of Operation: 1914–15 (2 seasons)
Overall Record: 148–156–3 (.482)
Stadiums: Gordon and Koppel Field

Year-by-Year Finishes

Year	Finish	Wins	Losses	Ties	Percentage	Games Behind	Manager
1914	6th	67	84	3	.435	20.0	George Stovall
1915	4th	81	72	0	.529	5.5	George Stovall

Hall of Famers Who Played for the Packers
[No player]

League Leaders, Batting

Batting Average, Season
[No player]

Home Runs, Seasons
[No player]

RBIs, Season
[No player]

Stolen Bases, Season
[No player]

Total Bases, Season
[No player]

Most Hits, Season
[No player]

Most Runs, Season
[No player]

Batting Feats

Hitting for the Cycle
[No player]

League Leaders, Pitching

Most Wins, Season
[No player]

Most Strikeouts, Season
[No player]

Lowest ERA, Season
[No player]

Most Saves, Season
[No player]

Best Won-Lost Percentage, Season
[No player]

Pitching Feats

20 Wins, Season
Gene Packard, 1914 20–14
Nick Cullop, 1915 22–11
Gene Packard, 1915 20–12

No-Hitters
Alex Main (vs. Buf. Blues), Sep. 7, 1915 (final: 5–0) (perfect game)

No-Hitters Pitched Against
Ed Lafitte, Bklyn. Tip-Tops, Sep. 19, 1914 (final: 6–2)

Pittsburgh Rebels

Dates of Operation: 1914–15 (2 seasons)
Overall Record: 150–153–7 (.484)
Stadiums: Exposition Park III

Year-by-Year Finishes

Year	Finish	Wins	Losses	Ties	Percentage	Games Behind	Manager
1914	7th	64	86	4	.416	22.5	Doc Gessler, Rebel Oakes
1915	3rd	86	67	3	.551	0.5	Rebel Oakes

Hall of Famers Who Played for the Rebels
[No player]

League Leaders, Batting

Batting Average, Season
[No player]

Home Runs, Seasons
[No player]

RBIs, Season
[No player]

Stolen Bases, Season
[No player]

Total Bases, Season
Ed Konetchy, 1915 278

Most Hits, Season
[No player]

Most Runs, Season
[No player]

Batting Feats

Hitting for the Cycle
Ed Lennox, May 6, 1914

League Leaders, Pitching

Most Wins, Season
[No player]

Most Strikeouts, Season
[No player]

Lowest ERA, Season
[No player]

Most Saves, Season
[No player]

Best Won-Lost Percentage, Season
[No player]

Pitching Feats

20 Wins, Season

Elmer Knetzer, 1914 20–12
Frank Allen, 1915 23–13

No-Hitters
Frank Allen (vs. St.L. Terriers), Apr. 24, 1915 (final: 2–0) (perfect game)

No-Hitters Pitched Against
Claude Hendrix, Chi. Whales, May 15, 1915 (final: 10–0) (perfect game)

St. Louis Terriers

Dates of Operation: 1914–15 (2 seasons)
Overall Record: 149–156–8 (.476)
Stadiums: Handlan's Park

Year-by-Year Finishes

Year	Finish	Wins	Losses	Ties	Percentage	Games Behind	Manager
1914	8th	62	89	3	.403	25.0	Mordecai Brown, Fielder Jones
1915	1st (Tie)	87	67	5	.547	—	Fielder Jones

Hall of Famers Who Played for the Terriers
Mordecai Brown, pitcher, 1914
Eddie Plank, pitcher, 1915

League Leaders, Batting

Batting Average, Season
[No player]

Home Runs, Seasons
[No player]

RBIs, Season
[No player]

Stolen Bases, Season
[No player]

Total Bases, Season
[No player]

Most Hits, Season
Jack Tobin, 1915..........................184

Most Runs, Season
Babe Borton, 1915.........................97

Batting Feats

Hitting for the Cycle
[No player]

League Leaders, Pitching

Most Wins, Season
[No player]

Most Strikeouts, Season
[No player]

Lowest ERA, Season
[No player]

Most Saves, Season
[No player]

Best Won-Lost Percentage, Season
[No player]

Pitching Feats

20 Wins, Season
Dave Davenport, 1915.............. 22–18
Doc Crandall, 1915.................. 21–15
Eddie Plank, 1915.................... 21–11

No-Hitters
Dave Davenport (vs. Chi. Whales), Sep. 7, 1915 (final: 3–0) (perfect game)

No-Hitters Pitched Against
Frank Allen, Pit. Rebels, Apr. 24, 1915 (final: 2–0) (perfect game)

OTHER GREAT BASEBALL BOOKS FROM SPORTS PUBLISHING

The New Book of Baseball Trivia
More than 500 Questions for Avid Fans
by Wayne Stewart

The New Book of Baseball Trivia includes 500 fun and engaging questions and answers on everyone's favorite former and active players and coaches. Readers are awarded a single, double, triple, or homer based on the difficulty level of the question, with the goal to score as many runs as possible by the end of the book. They are kept on their toes by answers head-scratchers such as:

- Which team became the first one ever to have three of its players hit 40+ homers in a season?
- Who was the shortest man ever to appear in a big-league game?
- Which two brothers combined for more lifetime home runs than any other brother act?
- When Shane Bieber won the 2020 Cy Young Award, he became the fifth Cleveland Indian to capture that honor. Name three of the other four men to accomplish this.
- Which two men bashed more home runs while teammates than any other teammate combo?
- And many more!

This book makes the perfect gift for the baseball-loving fan!

$17.99 Paperback • ISBN 978-1-68358-434-6

**The New Baseball Bible
Notes, Nuggets, Lists, and
Legends from Our National
Pastime**
By Dan Schlossberg; Preface by
Al Clark and Foreword by John
Thorn

For fans of baseball trivia, this
updated version of *The New
Baseball Bible*, first published as
The Baseball Catalog in 1980,
is sure to provide something for
everyone, regardless of team alle-
giance. Veteran sportswriter Dan
Schlossberg weaves in facts, figures, and famous quotes, discuss-
es strategy, and provides stats and images—many of them never previ-
ously published elsewhere, including:

- beginnings of baseball
- rules and records
- the language of baseball
- superstitiions and traditions
- and so much more!

The New Baseball Bible serves as the perfect gift for fans of America's
pastime.

$17.99 Paperback • ISBN 978-1-68358-346-2

Dingers
The 101 Most Memorable Home Runs
in Baseball History
by Joshua Shifrin and Tommy Shea

From splitters to spitters; from a frozen rope to the suicide squeeze; from extra innings to no hitters, baseball is truly a great game. But nothing hypes up a crowd like a home run, a round tripper, a big bomb . . . the long ball! Hitting the ball out of the park is one of the greatest feats in baseball, and doing so in the clutch can make an average player a hero overnight.

In *Dingers*, authors Joshua Shifrin and Tom Shea break down the 101 most memorable home runs in baseball history, telling their stories and how they affected the game of baseball. Whether it's "The Shot Heard 'Round the World" or Hank Aaron's 715th blast, readers will get an inside scoop on some of the most famous moments that now live in baseball lore.

$19.99 Paperback • ISBN 978-1-68358-453-7

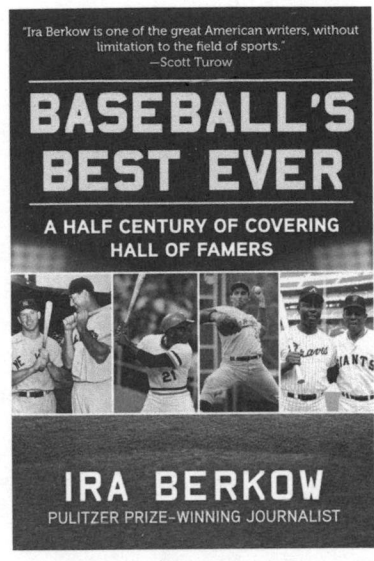

Baseball's Best Ever
A Half Century of Covering Hall of Famers
by Ira Berkow

Encompassing a selection of some one hundred columns and featured stories written over 50-plus years, Pulitzer Prize–winning journalist Ira Berkow share stories on some of the greatest baseball players to ever grace the diamond. But rather than snippets and information known to anyone following the game, Berkow, shares insights on these men: men dealing with tragedy, struggle, highs and lows—showing that while they we at the top of the game, at the end of the day they are mere mortals.

With stories from Satchel Paige throwing his "bow tie pitch" close to a batter's brow, the humorous side of Phil Rizzuto and Casey Stengel, a rookie Carl Yastrzemski battling through a slump, and Ted Williams talking about is *favorite* subject—no, not hitting: fishing.

Offering an inside view as to who these men truly are, readers will be able to better understand their favorite ballplayers. While they have accomplished things we only do in our dreams, you will see that these men, under the surface, are no different than any of us.

$40.00 Hardcover • ISBN 978-1-68358-445-2